For Reference

Not to be taken from this room

DATE			

© THE BAKER & TAYLOR CO

OHIO MARRIAGES

Extracted from
The Old Northwest Genealogical Quarterly

OHIO MARRIAGES

Extracted from
The Old Northwest Genealogical Quarterly

Edited By
MARJORIE SMITH

Baltimore
GENEALOGICAL PUBLISHING CO., INC.
1980

Reprinted by arrangement with Heritage House
(an imprint of Ye Olde Genealogie Shoppe), by
Genealogical Publishing Co., Inc.
Baltimore, 1980
Library of Congress Catalogue Card Number 80-67935
International Standard Book Number 0-8063-0902-4
Made in the United States of America

INTRODUCTION

Fifteen volumes of *The "Old Northwest" Genealogical Quarterly* were
published from 1898 through 1912 by The "Old Northwest" Genealogical
Society. The contents of these volumes included genealogies, cemetery
inscriptions, church records, court records and other information mostly
for the state of Ohio.

The Ohio marriages from these fifteen volumes have been extracted
and reprinted in this book. Each bride and groom has two entries, one
for the groom's surname and the other for the bride's maiden name. All
the marriages are in one alphabetical sequence. Duplications in the
original volumes were discarded with any varying information so noted.

Portions of the introductory remarks to the original articles are
repeated below since they give some background to the record and tell
the location of the record at that time. Also given is the name of the
person who contributed the copied records, the years covered by the
record and the reference citation in the original publication of the
first appearance of the record. Most of the records were continued
through several numbers.

<u>Marriage Record, Franklin County, Ohio</u> (1803-1830), p. 36, vol. 1, 1898.
    By Miss May Mermod Scott, of Columbus, Ohio.

<u>Marriage Records, Jackson County, Ohio</u> (1816-1826), p. 174, vol. 7, 1904.
    Copied by Frank T. Cole.

<u>Marriage Records, Licking County, Ohio</u> (1808-1820), p. 206, vol. 12, 1909.
    Copied by Mrs. L. Bancroft Fant.

*Licking County was organized in 1808. In 1875 the old Courthouse was
burned, in 1879 fire destroyed the upper story of the new structure, hence
the universal belief that all the marriage records had been destroyed.
Three volumes escaped the flames, but the first is really the most inter-
esting, in that it shows conclusively that the matrimonial bureau was not
deemed the most important of the legal departments. Vol. I is a think
little book containing 109 entries written in a perplexing variety of
"hand" and whenever the officiating party "happened in town." After turning
many empty pages one comes to the dates when a few J. P.'s took the oath of
office and all seemingly written by the Hon. Stephan McDougal.*

Marriage Records, Marion County, Ohio (1824-1825), p. 176, vol. 7, 1904.
    Contributed by D. E. Phillips.

Record of Marriage Licenses Issued in Pickaway County (1810-1815),
    p. 116, vol. 7, 1904. Contributed by G. A. Teegardin, Circleville,
    Ohio.

Record of Marriages in Ross County, Ohio (1803-1806), p. 95, vol. 6, 1903.

*Ross County was established August 20, 1798, having been part of
Adams County from July 10, 1797, and before that, part of Hamilton county.
The entries are nearly all in the handwriting of the different Justices,
and it was evidently their custom to make the entries whenever they
happened to be at the county seat. No records can be found previous to
April, 1803. Where the previous marriages were recorded is not known.
Copied from the original deerskin-bound folio "Book A," May 21, 1903.*

Early New Connecticut Marriages (Trumbull County, Ohio) (1800-03),
    p. 64, vol. 2, 1899. By Harley Barnes of Painesville, Ohio.

*On July 10, 1800, the county of Trumbull was erected by the government
of the Northwest Territory. It included the entire Western Reserve, with
the county seat at Warren. Previous to this date the New Connecticut land
had been at different times nominally included in Washington and Jefferson
counties, and a part of it in Wayne county, and, perhaps, at an earlier
date, in Augusta county, Virginia, but the jurisdiction of the United States
was disputed by the few inhabitants, and no organized government existed
until August 25, 1800. On this date the first "Court of Quarter Sessions
of the Peace" was "begun and holden at Warren."*

*John Stark Edwards, of Mesopotamia, was the first Recorder, and with
him were recorded the marriages solemnized under Territorial jurisdiction.
Other marriages were known to have taken place prior to the organization
of Trumbull county, but we have found no record of them. The following
are from Vol. A of Trumbull County Records of Deeds, pages 225, 226, 227
and 228, and are believed to include all of the Territorial Marriage Records
on the Western Reserve.*

Marriage Record, Washington County, Ohio (1790-1822), p. 130, vol. 3, 1900.
    By William H. Jennings, Esq. of Columbus, Ohio.

Friends' Marriage Records - Miami Monthly Meeting (1804-1828), p. 52, vol. 8,
    1905. Contributed by W. R. Kersey.

*The Miami Monthly Meeting of Friends was established at Waynesville,
Ohio, October 13, 1803. The list of marriages includes all that were
allowed by the Monthly meeting and solemnized under its auspices, up to the
time of the unfortunate division of the Society of Friends into two branches
popularly known as "Orthodox" and "Hicksite." Through the courtesy of Clark-
son Betterworth, the custodian of the records, who kindly furnished every
facility for their examination, this copy was made. "Book Eight" of the
records bears upon its title page in the old-fashioned cursive of the first
Recorder of Marriages this designation: "The Book of Record of Marriage
Sertificates for Miamie Monthly Meeting of Friends." In the division of*

*property incident to the Separation above referred to, the records prior
to 1828 fell to the "Hicksites," they being at that time the most numerous
branch.*

Register of Marriages, Putnam Presbyterian Church (1841-1897), p. 52,
    vol. 4, 1901. By Miss M. Josephine Tilton, of Columbus, Ohio.

    *This church was established, about 1840, at Putnam, which is now a
part of the city of Zanesville, Ohio.*

The Parish Register of St. John's Church, Worthington, Ohio (1833-1875),
    p. 125, vol. 1, 1898. By Horace W. Whayman.

    *This book, "The Property of St. John's Church, Worthington, Ohio,
Presented by I. N. Whiting," and now in the custody of the Rev. Norman N.
Badger, Rector of the Parish, is a well preserved fiolio of 156 pages,
bound in paper boards with leather back. On the first page is the
following: "Note, this Register was commenced on Easter Monday, April
8th, A.D. 1833, by the Rev. Erastus Burr, then in Deacon's orders, at
which time he became minister of the Parish. Previous to the above
mentioned time no public register (so far as can be ascertained) has
been kept," and in a later hand is written, "The Records, beginning
with the Rectorship of the Rev. C. H. Young (March 1st, 1875), are
contained in the New Register."*

The Parish Register of St. Luke's Church, Marietta, Ohio (1821-1883),
    p. 28, vol. 2, 1899. By Miss M. Josephine Tilton, of Columbus, Ohio.

The Parish Register of St. Paul's Parish, Marion, Ohio (1849-1870),
    p. 207, vol. 8, 1905. By Horace W. Whayman.

    *This, the earliest record belonging to the Parish, is in the possession
of the Rev. A. R. Taylor, and is one of the few registers preserved in the
Parish to which they belong, within the Diocese of Ohio. The book was presented to the Parish by its first rector, the Rev. George Thompson, and con-
tains on the second page the following note:*

    *"Rev. I. B. Britton received a call from St. Paul's, Marion, on June
3rd, 1868; preached his first sermon July 5th, 1868; accepted the call
July 17th, and began regular services July 26th, 1868. Thirty-seven names
were then registered as those of communicants reported to the last conven-
tion of the Diocese, and there was a congregation of from 50 to 80 persons
and a Sunday School of 50 children. The first member, Communicant Miss
Ella Hardy, was added on the 1st Sunday in October, 1868, and no baptism
had taken place up to that time. The congregation, although small, is
highly respectable in character and the services are maintained with
spirity. The Vestry pledged the rector $1,100 for the first year, to be
paid as nearly as possible quarterly in advance, and up to October 4th
have paid on the first quarter $215.42. The offertory at communion this
4th of October, 1868, amount to $7.05."*

1810 Oct 26   -----, Amelia (belonging to Isaac Williams) and Josephus Stephens
               by John Brough, JP, Washington Co.

1806 --- --   -----, Catherine and Wm. Burgon by John Robins, Ross Co.

1808 Sep 8   -----, Doratha, a Black woman, who was liberated by David Nelson,
               and Tom, a Black man, formerly raised by Jno. Dill, by Arthur
               O'Harra, Franklin Co.

1807 Aug 4   -----, Dyner, a free black girl, and Samuel Robenson, a black man,
               by Arthur O'Harra, Franklin Co.

1844 Apr 19   -----, Harvey and Elizabeth Greer by Rev. R.S. Elder, St. John's
               Church, Worthington, Franklin Co.

1813 Mar 14   -----, Lucy and Matthew Matthews by E. Griswold, Franklin Co.

1805 May 5   -----, Mary and Phineas Blazier by Samuel Edwards, Ross Co.

1817 Dec 17   -----, Nancy and James Guthrie by Robert G. Hanna, JP, Jackson Co.

1805 Mar 28   -----, Susanna and Benjamin Rasor by John Greene, Washington Co.

1808 Sep 8   -----, Tom, a Black man, formerly raised by Jno. Dill, and Doratha,
               a Black woman, who was liberated by David Nelson by Arthur
               O'Harra, Franklin Co.

1873 Jun 10   Abbot, Charles H. and Ella S. Brown by Rev. A. Kingsbury, Putnam
               Presbyterian Church, Muskingum Co.

1813 Nov 4   Abbot, Joel and Melina McDowell by Jon. B. Johnston, Franklin Co.

1825 Sep 21   Abbot, Mary Ann and Philo Burr by Ebn'r Washburn,VDM, Franklin Co.

1810 Feb 1   Abbot, Philip and Polly Sandburn by Rev. S.P. Robbins, Washington
               Co.

1819 Jun 22   Abbott, Erastus and Polly Bills by Samuel Bancroft,JP, recorded
               June 25, Licking Co.

1897 May 18   Abbott, James H. and Lillian Maharry, both of Zanesville, by Rev.
               George F. Moore, Putnam Presbyterian Church, Muskingum Co.

1803 Feb 8   Abbott, John and Sarah Biggastaff by Wm. Harper,JP, Washington Co.

1822 Nov 16   Abbott, Loice and Zedina Purse by Eli C. King,JP, Franklin Co.

1816 Feb 15   Abbott, Lydia and Henry Williams by Obadiah Scott, Washington Co.

1804 Feb 13   Abel, Nancy and Thomas Sull by Samuel Smith, Ross Co.

1887 Nov 7   Abele, Mary B. and James A. Bowers, both of Zanesville by Rev.
               George F. Moore, Putnam Presbyterian Church, Muskingum Co.

1895 Mar 14   Abell, Ella A. and Alex. C. Richards, both of Zanesville, by Rev.
               George F. Moore, Putnam Presbyterian Church, Muskingum Co.

1882 Sep 24   Abell, Kate L. of Putnam, and George L. Blake, of Zanesville, by
               Rev. George F. Moore, Putnam Presbyterian Church, Muskingum
               Co.

1814 Jun 28   Abrahams, James and Catherine West by J. Crow,JP, Licking Co.

1813 Sep 29   Abrahams, John and Mary Kelso, Licking Co.

1816 Sep 2   Abrams, John and Abigail Cook by Geo. Hoover,JP, Licking Co.

1891 Sep 29   Acheson, Ada A. of Zanesville and Wilber J. McCaid of Colorado
              by Rev. George F. Moore, Putnam Presbyterian Church, Mus-
              kingum Co.

1821 Aug 30   Ackley, Clarissa and John Atherton by Noah Fidler, recorded
              Nov. 19, Licking Co.

1822 Apr 25   Ackley, Clarissa and Isaac Humphrey by Jacob Young,MMEC, Wash-
              ington Co.

1813 Aug 13   Ackley, Lydia and David Goss by Rev. Stephen Lindsley, Washing-
              ton Co.

1825 Sep 1   Acord, Volantine and Elizabeth Oliver by John Anglin,JP, Jack-
              son Co.

1855 Jun 20   Adams, Betsy and Albert Hendricks by T. Corlett, St. Luke's
              Church, Granville, Licking Co.

1818 Sep 27   Adams, Demas and Susan Barns by Rev. Philander Chase, Franklin
              Co.

1818 Apr 1   Adams, Elizabeth and Esack Inman by Joseph Gorton, Franklin Co.

1820 Jun 23   Adams, Elizabeth and Ashael Atherton by Nath'l W. Anderson, JP,
              Jackson Co.

1822 Apr 17   Adams, George and Elizabeth Hutchinson by John Curtiss, JP,
              Washington Co.

1813 Oct 5   Adams, James and Harriet Bailey by N. Hamilton, JP, Washington
              Co.

1820 Nov 14   Adams, John and Susan Webb by Sanford Converse, JP, Licking Co.

1821 Apr 29   Adams, John and Hannah Smothers by Russel Bigelow, Franklin Co.

1838 Sep 25   Adams, Magdalen and Lewis Swan, St. Luke's Church, Granville,
              Licking Co.

1821 Jan 4   Adams, Margaret and Daniel Avery by A. Allen, Franklin Co.

1814 Jan 9   Adams, Patty and Levi Waterman by Isaac Baker, Washington Co.

1866 Apr 25   Adams, Miss Sophro and Rev. Thos. Burrows by N.C.N. Dudley,
              St. Paul's Church, Marion, Marion Co.

1850 Sep 15   Adams, Susan and Marcus W. Wilner by E.A. Strong, St. Luke's
              Church, Granville, Licking Co.

1819 Feb 25   Adams, Thomas and Margaret Breckenridge by Percival Adams,
              Franklin Co.

1811 Mar 31   Adi, Susanah and David Stump by Z. Carlisle, JPHT, Licking Co.

1813 Mar 28   Adkins, Jacob and Polly Phoebus (license date), Pickaway Co.

1821 Dec 27   Afflick, William and Phebe Mitchell by Sam'l' Dye,JP, Washing-
              ton Co.

1825 Jul 19   Agler, Sarah and Henry Zinn by C. Henkel, Franklin Co.

1814 Mar 3   Agney, Abraham and Jane Slane by Noah Fidler, Licking Co.

1818 Dec 10   Aikens, Robert Jr. and Elizabeth Nash by Rev. Tho. A. Morris,
              Washington Co.

1817 Oct 9   Akins, Elizabeth and Lancelot Oliver by Pelatiah White, JP, Washington Co.

1816 Feb 18   Akins, James and Catharine Ballinger by Joseph Gorton, Franklin Co.

1810 Sep --   Albany, Ann and Peter Orr by Wm. Taylor, JP, recorded Nov. 11, Licking Co.

1820 Feb 19   Albery, Anthony and Rebecca Jones, by M. Black, JP, Licking Co.

1821 Jan 18   Albery, Elizabeth and Joseph Giger by M. Black, JP, Licking Co.

1820 Jan 29   Albery, James and Anna Jenkins by Josias Ewing, JP, recorded Mar. 18, Licking Co.

1806 Nov 20   Alcock, Richard and Eliza Case by Seth Washburn, Washington Co.

1813 Dec 30   Alcock, Richard and Wealthy Buell by Rev. S.P. Robbins, Washington Co.

1812 Nov 1   Alcock, Sally and James M. Booth by Stephen Lindsly, Washington Co.

1813 May 1   Alcock, Thomas and Sally Wells by Rev. Stephen Lindsley, Washington Co.

1811 Mar 24   Alcock, William and Frances Posey by Stephen Lindsly, Washington Co.

1820 Jan 26   Alcock, William and Sally Posey by Danl H. Buell, JP, Washington Co.

1809 Jan 13   Alcorn, Robert and Polly Jordan by Wm. Gray, Washington Co.

1821 Mar 29   Alden, Margaret and John Gorman by Ami Lawrence, JP, Washington Co.

1820 Mar 23   Alden, Mary and Thomas Phelps by Thomas White, JP, Washington Co.

1819 Oct 16   Alden, Phebe and Ambrose Allen by Elihu Bigelow, Licking Co.

1821 Sep 13   Alden, Sarah and James Baker by Thomas White, JP, Washington Co.

1824 Mar 30   Alderfer, Polly, widow, and Leonard Sahl, widower, by C. Henkel, Franklin Co.

1819 Jan 28   Aldridge, Anna and Wm. Rambaugh by Jacob Delay, MG, Jackson Co.

1824 Jan 10   Alebrion, Sarah and John Peterbook by Robert W. Riley, Franklin Co.

1811 Apr 21   Alexander, David and Pency Rector (license date), Pickaway Co.

1806 Feb 1   Alexander, James and Polly Hatton by J. Gardner, JP, Ross Co.

1819 May 16   Alexander, James and Lucinda Howe by John Russell, JP, Washington Co.

1803 Aug 22   Alexander, Jane and John McKee by J. Gardner, JP, Ross Co.

1818 Jan 29   Alexander, William M. and Catherine Huckins by J.W. Patterson, MG, Licking Co.

1817 Nov 25   Alison, Alexander and Nancy Cyphert by John Russell, Washington Co.

1813 Dec 29   Alkire, Dolly and Samuel Alkire (license date), Pickaway Co.

1813 May 14   Alkire, Lydia and John Graham (license date), Pickaway Co.

1814 Dec 18   Alkire, Michael and Polly Barton by David Henderson, JP, Picka-
               way Co.

1809 Jun 20   Alkire, Robert and Elizabeth an Lip (date recorded), by John
               Smith, JP, Franklin Co.

1813 Dec 29   Alkire, Samuel and Dolly Alkire (license date), Pickaway Co.

1818 Dec 13   Allard, Martha and Nathaniel Place by Stephen Guthrie, Wash-
               ington Co.

1818 Dec 13   Allard, Reuben and Polly Allen by Stephen Guthrie, Washington
               Co.

1819 May 31   Allard, Samuel and Laurana Maxson by Dan'l G. Stanley, JP,
               Washington Co.

1828 Mar 13   Allberry, Francis and Hanner Kinner by A. Allison, Franklin Co.

1818 Oct 8   Allbery, Margaret and John Beem by Rev. Noah Fidler, Licking Co.

1816 Sep 26   Allbery, Thomas and Elizabeth Rhoads by Noah Fidler, Licking Co.

1819 Oct 16   Allen, Ambrose and Phebe Alden by Elihu Bigelow, Licking Co.

1821 May 1   Allen, Cyrus and Mina Coe by James Hoge, Franklin Co.

1824 May 25   Allen, David and Polelly Harelett by John Kirby,JP, Marion Co.

1808 Oct 6   Allen, Elisha and Elizabeth Perkins by Stephen Lindsly, Wash-
               ington Co.

1801 Jun 13   Allen, Elizabeth and Peter Galer by Robt. Oliver, JP, Washing-
               ton Co.

1856 Mar 18   Allen, Fidelia A. and Wm. H. McWherton by Rev. Geo. B. Sturges,
               St. Paul's Church, Marion, Marion Co.

1815 Dec 19   Allen, James and Mary McBridge by Joseph Chapman, JP, Washing-
               ton Co.

1814 Dec 28   Allen, John and Sally Misner by Stephen Guthrie, JP, Washing-
               ton Co.

1791 Jun 23   Allen, Justus and Polly Devol, Washington Co.

1808 Oct 5   Allen, Martha and Hezekiah Chapman by Stephen Lindsly, Wash-
               ington Co.

1826 Jul 16   Allen, Minus and G.W. Glaspill by Henry Mathes, ME Minister,
               Franklin Co.

1794 Nov 11   Allen, Polly and Andrew McCluer by Robert Oliver, JP, Washing-
               ton Co.

1818 Dec 13   Allen, Polly and Reuben Allard by Stephen Guthrie, Washington
               Co.

1858 Oct 14   Allen, Rosetta and John H. Drake by Rev. A. Kingsbury, Putnam
               Presbyterian Church, Muskingum Co.

1800 Dec 17   Allen, Ruth and Andrew Galen by Wm. Burnham, JP, Washington Co.

1818 Jan 24   Allen, Samuel and Lydia Glidden by Danl. G. Stanley, JP, Washington Co.

1824 May 30   Allen, Seth and Ease Cline by Amos Neely, JP, Marion Co.

1817 Apr 3   Allen, Simeon and Sophia Baldwin by Thomas Spellman, JP, Licking Co.

1808 Nov 10   Aller, James and Catharine Hess by James Hoge, Franklin Co.

1826 Aug 3   Allin, Asaph and Cara Williard by Samuel Abbott, JP, Franklin Co.

1816 Apr 30   Allington, Phebe and James Baley by James Sharp, JP, Washington Co.

1816 Feb 22   Allison, Andrew and Sarah Blackburn by T.D. Baird, UDM, Licking Co.

1822 Apr 4   Allison, Andrew and Nancy Sinclair by John Green, JP, Washington Co.

1812 Jun 24   Allison, Charles and Hester Stubbs by John Greene, JP, Washington Co.

1816 Mar 11   Allison, Charles and Sally Allison by Sardine Stone, JP, Washington Co.

1804 Apr 10   Allison, Hannah and Daniel Ovens by Jacob Lindly, Washington Co.

1813 Dec 30   Allison, Henrietta and Josiah Wittits (license date) Pickaway Co.

1809 Aug 27   Allison, Hugh and Patience Niel by N. Davis, Minister, Washington Co.

1805 Jan 17   Allison, Nancy and Elisha Davis by Jacob Lindly, Washington Co.

1827 Jul 12   Allison, Nancy and Charles Scott by H. Mathews, MMEC, Franklin Co.

1811 May 9   Allison, Polly and Frederick Davis by Dudley Davis, JP, Washington Co.

1816 Mar 11   Allison, Sally and Charles Allison by Sardine Stone, JP, Washington Co.

1819 Feb 4   Allison, Sophia and Chester Johnson by Amos Wilson, Washington Co.

1820 May 18   Allison, Stephen and Abigail Kinney by Amos Wilson, JP, Washington Co.

1814 May 29   Allison, William and Elizabeth Finney by Simeon Deming, JP, Washington Co.

1810 Jan 15   Allkire, Elizabeth and Samuel Powell by John Smith (another entry on 27 Feb. 1810), Franklin Co.

1825 Nov 26   Alspach, Michael and Molly Himrode by Conrad Roth, JP, Marion Co.

1825 Apr 5   Altman, Salome and Sephen Berryhill by C. Henkel, Franklin Co.

1818 Jun 17   Amas (or Amos), George and Rachael Dix by Eli C. King, Franklin Co.

1853 May 11   Amberg, Lizzie and Peleg Bunker by Rev. Geo. B. Sturges, St.
               Paul's Church, Marion, Marion Co.

1815 Oct 1   Ames, Anna and Samuel Null by Artemas Knapp, JP, Washington Co.

1801 May 3   Ames, Cyrus and Azuba More by I. Peine, Washington Co.

1815 Oct 23   Ames, Joseph and Ida Tison by Jno. Russell, JP, Washington Co.

1799 Oct 22   Amlen, John Jr. and Jean Campbell by Thos. Stanley, Washington
               Co.

1808 Mar 16   Amlin, Elizabeth and Ephm. True by Thos. Stanley, Washington Co.

1798 Jan 2   Amlin, James and Nancy Campbell by Josiah Munro, Washington Co.

1822 Jan 31   Amlin, Martha and Wm. Hill, Jr. by Rev. S.P. Robbins, Washing-
               ton Co.

1818 Jan 18   Amlin, Sally D. and Patrick Campbell by Solomon Goss, MMEC,
               Washington Co.

1806 Nov 26   Amlin, Samuel and Betsy Mitchel by Stephen Lindsly, Washington
               Co.

1818 Jun 17   Amos (or Amas), George and Rachel Dix by Eli C. King, Franklin
               Co.

1814 Mar 27   Amsbury, Otis and Mary Carver by Rev. S. Lindsley, Washington
               Co.

1819 Dec 16   Anders, Timothy and Ruth B. Fisher by Isaac Fisher, Franklin Co.

1810 Jul 26   Anderson, Abraham and Mary Reley (license date), Pickaway Co.

1806 Jan 30   Anderson, Annabelea and Jeremiah Crabb by Peter Jackson, JP,
               Ross Co.

1824 Dec 14   Anderson, David and Jane Scott by Samuel McDowell, JP, Jackson
               Co.

1821 Sep 3   Anderson, David B. and Eunice Hall by Rev. Saml. P. Robbins,
               Washington Co.

1804 Jul 24   Anderson, Edward and Sally Calvin by Asahel Cooley, Washington
               Co.

1817 Apr 10   Anderson, Ephraim and Sarah Glaze by James Quism Elder, MEC,
               Licking Co.

1860 Jun 21   Anderson, Eunice and Austin B. Regnier of Harmar by Rev. John
               Boyd, St. Luke's Church, Marietta, Washington Co.

1824 Sep 25   Anderson, George H. and Mariah Wiles by Isaac Fisher, Franklin
               Co.

1804 Feb 27   Anderson, Hannah and William Green by Thomas Scott, JP Scioto
               Tp., Ross Co.

1823 Oct 27   Anderson, Jane and George Feasle by Isaac Painter, Franklin Co.

1811 Nov 24   Anderson, Joseph and Prescilla Morrison (license date), Pick-
               away Co.

1886 Sep 24   Anderson, Julia D. and George Brady by Rev. George F. Moore,
               Putnam Presbyterian Church, Muskingum Co.

1804 Feb 11   Anderson, Lewis and Elenor Fulton by John Brough, JP, Washington
              Co.

1808 Mar 5   Anderson, Lewis and Martha Hickman by S. Lindsly, Washington Co.

1863 Jun 10   Anderson, Martin and Louise Meison by Rev. John Boyd, St. Luke's
              Church, Marietta, Washington Co.

1855 Sep 10   Anderson, Mary L. and John D. Barker by Rev. John Boyd, St.
              Luke's Church, Marietta, Washington Co.

1817 Oct 15   Anderson, Nancy and Elihu Webster by Eli C. King, Franklin Co.

1823 Nov 16   Anderson, Polly and Nathaniel Painter by Joseph Smith, JP,
              Franklin Co.

1805 Jun 20   Anderson, Wm. and Lidia Hopkins by David Shelby, JP, Ross Co.

1827 Dec 23   Andress, Mahala and L.C. Strong, by H. Hubbert, PC, Franklin Co.

1822 Dec 5   Andrews, Adam and Nancy Sharp by Wm. C. Duff, JP, Franklin Co.

1825 Jul 17   Andrews, Amanda and David Weaver by Aristarchus Walker, Frank-
              lin Co.

1817 Apr 17   Andrews, Betsy and John Wallace by Ezra Griswold, Franklin Co.

1821 Oct 24   Andrews, Betsey and Harvey Skeels by Nathl. Little, Franklin Co.

1818 Nov 29   Andrews, Clarisa and John Goodrich by Stephen Maynard, JP,
              Franklin Co.

1813 Apr 15   Andrews, Cynthia and Eliphalet Barker by Ezra Griswold, Frank-
              lin Co.

1817 Jan 5   Andrews, David and Betsey McMullin by Simon Merwin, Washington
              Co.

1818 Apr 2   Andrews, Elizabeth and William Rardin by Salmon N. Cook, Wash-
              ington Co.

1815 Jun 15   Andrews, John and Sally Jarrett by Joseph Palmer, JP, Washing-
              ton Co.

1818 Sep 14   Andrews, John and Margaret Dutton by Salmon N. Cook, JP, Wash-
              ington Co.

1827 Dec 18   Andrews, John and Phoebe Lord by Philander Chase, Bishop PEC,
              Franklin Co.

1834 Jul 27   Andrews, Juliet and Burr Kellogg by Rev. E. Burr, St. John's
              Church, Worthington, Franklin Co.

1825 Mar 12   Andrews, Laura and Horrace I. Bull by Joseph Carper, Franklin
              Co.

1818 Dec 6   Andrews, Lyman and Persy M. Vining by Vinol Stewart, Franklin
              Co.

1891 Apr 8   Andrews, Mary C. of Zanesville and James T. Beckwith of Malta,
              O., by Rev. George F. Moore, Putnam Presbyterian Church,
              Muskingum Co.

1812 Mar 29   Andrews, Mira and Orier Case by Ezra Griswold, Franklin Co.

1807 Feb 22   Andrews, Noah and Ruth Griswold by James Kilbourne, JP, Frank-
              lin Co.

1812 Dec 3   Andrews, Samuel and Elizabeth Morris by Rev. Stephen Lindley,
               Washington Co.

1827 Jun 27   Andrews, Samuel and Mary Clark by Henry Matthews, Franklin Co.

1812 Nov 29   Andrews, Thomas and Ruth Rose by Jacob Tharp, Franklin Co.

1864 May 12   Andrews, William C. and Jennie Dunlap by Rev. A. Kingsbury,
               Putnam Presbyterian Church, Muskingum Co.

1840 Aug --   Andros, William C. and Eunice G. Toppin by Rev. A. Helfenstine,
               St. John's Church, Worthington, Franklin Co.

1801 Mar 20   Anerum, Elizabeth and Daniel Wills by Philip Witten, JP, Wash-
               ington Co.

1800 Aug 14   Anerum, Nancy and Francis Thomas by Philip Witten, JP, Washing-
               ton Co.

1813 Apr 1   Angles, Priscilla and Abraham Moyer (license date), Pickaway Co.

1816 Aug 22   Ankrom, Linsey and Margaret Franks by Simon Merwin, Washington
               Co.

1893 Jan 8   Ansel, Burgers C. of Buckingham, O., and Sarah Davis of Redfield,
               O., by Rev. George F. Moore,. Putnam Presbyterian Church,
               Muskingum Co.

1826 Mar 16   Anthony, David and Nancy McGrady by Solomon Goodenagh, JP,
               Jackson Co.

1816 Sep 26   Anthony, George and Margaret Bailey by James Hoge (another entry
               on 27 Mar 1817), Franklin Co.

1823 Oct 21   Anthony, George and Clariss Parish by Charles Waddell, Franklin
               Co.

1826 May 25   Anthony, Geo. Jr. and Jane Everton by Solomon Goodenough, JP,
               Jackson Co.

1825 5 mo 5   Anthony, Henrietta P. and Abram Nordyke, Miami Monthly Meeting,
               Warren Co.

1825 Jan 23   Anthony, Mary and Paul Timberman by Robert Ward, JP, Jackson Co.

1825 Jul 28   Anthony, Phillip and Hannah Timberman by Rob't Ward, JP, Jack-
               son Co.

1814 7 mo 7   Anthony, Rachel and Lot Pugh, Miami Monthly Meeting, Warren Co.

1861 Nov 5   Applegate, Robert M. of Zanesville and Julia M. Russell by Rev.
               John Boyd, St. Luke's Church, Marietta, Washington Co.

1801 Sep 8   Archer, Joseph and Sarah Wells by Philip Witten, Washington Co.

1810 Jun 7   Archer, Michael and Rhoda Granden by Amos Porter, JP, Washing-
               ton Co.

1814 Mar 13   Archer, Patrick and Lydia Petty by Dan'l H. Buell, JP, Wash-
               ington Co.

1821 Jun 3   Archer, Sarah (alias Sarah Smith) and Daniel Triplet by John
               Davis, JP, Franklin Co.

1828 Jul 24   Armintage, James and Eliza Jameson by Jacob Grubb, JP, Franklin
               Co.

1810 Aug 11   Armistead, Wm. and Lucy Wait by Benjamin Lakin, GM, Franklin Co.

1807 Jun 9   Armitage, Joshua and Harriet Thornelly by Saml P. Robbins, Washington Co.

1820 Sep 8   Armitage, Rebecah and Jorge Ragart by Robert Elliott, JP, Franklin Co.

1825 Jun 2   Armstead, Wm. and Mary Gorton by Jos. Carper, Franklin Co.

1799 Oct 3   Armstrong, Elizabeth and Mathew Lasley Kilgor by Robert Safford, Washington Co.

1816 Aug 8   Armstrong, George and Alice Vance by Alex Holden, Licking Co.

1817 Aug 7   Armstrong, Henry and Patty Barrett by David Mitchell, JP, Jackson Co.

1807 Apr 12   Armstrong, Jeremiah and Polly Minter by James Marshall, JP, Franklin Co.

1838 Nov --   Armstrong, Jeremiah and Lucy Phelps by Rev. A. Helfenstine, St. John's Church, Worthington, Franklin Co.

1819 Jun 15   Armstrong, John and Ruhema Thompson by James Hoge, Franklin Co.

1861 Dec 4   Armstrong, John, M.D., of Ravenswood, Va., Catherine S. Devine, by Rev. John Boyd, St. Luke's Church, Marietta, Washington Co.

1816 Mar 3   Armstrong, Margaret and James Glover by Rev. Stephen Lindsley, Washington Co.

1813 Apr 10   Armstrong, Polly and John Tootle (license date), Pickaway Co.

1818 Dec 21   Armstrong, Robert and Sarah Thompson by James Hoge, Franklin Co.

1816 Dec 19   Armstrong, Sarah and Hanson Thomas by J.W. Patterson, JP, Licking Co.

1822 Nov 7   Armstrong, William and Jane Delano by James Hoge, Franklin Co.

1827 Sep 15   Arnald, Randall R. and Mary Baldwin by G.W. Hart, JP, Franklin Co.

1810 Jun 12   Arnhart, William and Jane Patterson (license date), Pickaway Co.

1814 Dec 14   Arnold, Ira and Lena Ingram by Recompense Stansbery, JP, Franklin Co.

1818 Jan 1   Arnold, Nathan and Betsy Cutler by Venal Stewart, Preacher, Franklin Co.

1803 Nov 25   Arnold, Noah and Nancy Chadwick by John Brough, Esq., Washington Co.

1804 Jun 18   Arrahood, Eva and Martin Boots by J. Gardner, JP, Ross Co.

1813 Jan 26   Arrowhood, Job and Rebecca Micael (license date), Pickaway Co.

1804 Nov 27   ArrowSmith, Samuel and Elizabeth Thiller by Abraham Miller, Ross Co.

1820 Oct 10   Arthur, Amos and Anna A. Elliot by John Shumate, JP, Jackson Co.

1817 Feb 14   Arthur, Benjamin and Catherine Radebaugh by John Horton, JP, Jackson Co.

1799 Aug 29   Arwin, Jean and William Dawson Atkinson by Robert Safford, JP,
               Washington Co.

1841 Nov 16   Ascher, Mary and James Brown, St. Luke's Church, Granville,
               Licking Co.

1806 Jul 31   Ashbaugh, John and Suffiah Sells by James Marshall, JP, Franklin
               Co.

1802 Oct 4   Ashcraft, Ruth and James Stone by Wm. Burnham, JP, Washington Co.

1805 Jul 4   Ashcroft, Ann and Mathew Corner by Jacob Lindly, Washington Co.

1815 Sep 6   Ashcroft, Margaret and Peter Taylor by Stephen Lindsley, MG,
               Washington Co.

1810 Jan 14   Ashcroft, Mary and James Stone by Wm. Nixon, JP, Washington Co.

1800 Apr 24   Atchinson, John and Elizabeth Fulton by Thos. Stanley, Washing-
               ton Co.

1811 Nov 3   Atchinson, John and Ruth Corwin (license date), Pickaway Co.

1801 Jan 20   Atchinson, Reuben and Polly Seaman by Josiah Munro, Washington
               Co.

1814 Dec 25   Atchison, William and Nancy Gratton by Chas. Cade, JP, Pickaway
               Co.

1805 Mar 21   Ater, Isaac and Betsey Smith by Peter Jackson, JP, Ross Co.

1896 Feb 29   Ater, Willard F. of Zanesville and Cora B. Rosser of McLuney, O.,
               by Rev. George F. Moore, Putnam Presbyterian Church, Mus-
               kingum Co.

1814 Dec 20   Ater, William and Margaret Coldson by Chas. Cade, JP, Pickaway
               Co.

1820 Jun 23   Atherton, Ashael and Elizabeth Adams by Nath'l W. Andrews, JP,
               Jackson Co.

1821 Aug 30   Atherton, John and Clarissa Ackley by Noah Fidler, Licking Co.

1870 Oct 1   Athey, Alice and Joseph C. Schofield by Rev. John Boyd, St.
               Luke's Church, Marietta, Washington Co.

1820 Nov 23   Athey, Elijah and Darens Bagley by Reuben Golliday, Franklin Co.

1885 Jun 18   Atkinson, Carrie E. and Thomas E. Roberts both of Zanesville by
               Rev. George F. Moore, Putnam Presbyterian Church, Muskingum
               Co.

1799 Aug 29   Atkinson, William Dawson and Jean Arwin by Robert Safford, JP,
               Washington Co.

1801 Nov 21   Atwater, Amzi and Mrs. Huldah Sheldon of Hudson by Ebenezer
               Sheldon, JP, Trumbull Co.

1803 Apr 3   Atwater, Jotham and Laura Kellogg both of Hudson by David
               Hudson, JP, Trumbull Co.

1819 Nov 29   Atwood, Rosanna and Alexander Thrall by George Evans, MG,
               Licking Co.

1819 --- --   Aubent(?), Catherine and John Nichels by -----, Licking Co.

1806 Sep 25 Aulcram, Jacob and Nancy Porter by Stephen Lindsly, Washington
             Co.

1818 Aug 15 Ausburn, Samuel and Hannah Meeker by Rev. Geo. Callanhan,
             Licking Co.

1819 Oct 13 Austin, Silas and Emily Buckland by Levan Randall, JP, recorded
             Nov. 24, Licking Co.

1821 Jul 21 Auten, John T. and Betsey Tevenderf by Robert W. Riley, JP,
             Franklin Co.

1872 Dec 31 Averbeck, Carrie A. and Charles T. Fisher by Rev. John Boyd,
             St. Luke's Church, Marietta, Washington Co.

1826 Sep 19 Avery, Betsy and Tree Butterfield by Amaziah Hutchinson, JP,
             Franklin Co.

1821 Jan 4 Avery, Daniel and Margaret Adams by A. Allen, Franklin Co.

1816 Oct 30 Avery, George and Eliza Page by Rev. T. Harris, Licking Co.

1820 Mar 26 Avery, Sally and George Quick by Osgood McFarland, JP, Washing-
             ton Co.

1828 Feb 25 Avery, William and Margaret Pickle by Lyndes L. Latimer, JP,
             Franklin Co.

1818 Apr 2 Avey, Polly and Amasiah Hutchisan, Jr. by Robert Elliott, JP,
             Franklin Co.

1820 Jan 24 Avory, Amanda and Alexander Britton by Osgood McFarland, JP,
             Washington Co.

1824 Apr 15 Avry, Anne and Benjamin West by Uriah Clark, Franklin Co.

1824 Jun 12 Aye, Nancy and Barnet Falthery (license date), Marion Co.

1888(?)   Ayers, Edward and Clara E. Kappes both of Zanesville by Rev.
             George F. Moore, Putnam Presbyterian Church, Muskingum Co.

1820 Oct 19 Ayers, Lavinna and Selvester Searls by T. Lee, Franklin Co.

1825 Mar 31 Ayers, Samuel and Eliza Canfield by Jacob Smith, Franklin Co.

1825 Jun 30 Ayle, John, widower, and Elizabeth Kenaday, widow, by Jacob
             Gundy, JP, Franklin Co.

1811 Nov 16 Ayle, Mary and Thomas Lawson by Moses Varnum, JP, Washington Co.

1814 Apr 20 Ayles, Elias and Mary Walker by William Miller, JP, Washington
             Co.

1817 Jul 20 Ayles, Hannah and John Lowe by John True, Washington Co.

1818 May 5 Ayles, Louisa and John Hall by Ira Hill, JP, Washington Co.

1810 Mar 17 Aymes, Cyrus and Polly Rice by Daniel Goodno, Washington Co.

1819 Mar 21 B----(?), Abraham and Barbara Stover by Noah Fidler, Licking Co.

1824(?)Mar 30 Babbet, Sanford, widower, and Phebe Norris, widow, by Aristar-
             chus Walker, Franklin Co.

1803 Feb 20   Babcock, Hannah and David Chandler by Jesse Phelps, JP, Trumbull
               Co.

1822 Mar 5   Babcock, Martha and John Crawford by Rev. Cornelius Springer,
               Washington Co.

1819 Dec 4   Babcock, Patience and Truman Wells by Elijah Dunlap, Licking Co.

1818 Jan 24   Bacchus, Hannah and William George by James Hoge, Franklin Co.

1811 Nov 25   Bacchus, Thomas and Temperance Williams by James Marshall,
               Franklin Co.

1819 Sep 30   Backar, Henry and Margret Lee by Richard Courtright, Franklin
               Co.

1817 May 11   Backer, Joseph Jr. and Melissa W. Stone by Rev. S.P. Robbins,
               Washington Co.

1826 Apr 27   Backus, Matilda and Wm. Barton by Thomas Vaughn, JP, Jackson Co.

1828 Mar 27   Bacon, Anna and Stephen Tripp by Jason Bull, Franklin Co.

1841 Nov 21   Bacon, Balsara L. and John T. Otstott by Rev. R.S. Elder, St.
               John's Church, Worthington, Franklin Co.

1816 Nov 7   Bacon, Sarah and Isaac Worthington by P. White, Washington Co.

1817 Mar 9   Bacon, William and Eleanor Mellor by P. White, JP, Washington
               Co.

1824 Nov 18   Badger, Archibald and Kesia Park by Joseph Badger, JP, Franklin
               Co.

1818 May 21   Badger, Archibald and Mary Seeds by Wm. Brown, JP, Franklin Co.

1819 Apr 15   Badger, Martha and Moses Foley by Joseph Gorton, Franklin Co.

1820 Mar 22   Badger, Robert and Nancy Park by James Hoge, Franklin Co.

1814 Jun 16   Badger, Wm. and Margaret Breckenridge by James Hoge, Franklin
               Co.

1803 Apr 7   Baeggs, Mary and Stephen Reves by Henry Smith, JP, Washington
               Co.

1824 Nov 2   Baety, Susanna and William Grifus by Jacob Gundy, JP, (recorded
               date), Franklin Co.

1893 Aug 2   Bagley, Annetta P. of Zanesville and Charles E. Baker of Colum-
               bus by Rev. George F. Moore, Putnam Presbyterian Church,
               Muskingum Co.

1820 Nov 23   Bagley, Darens and Elijah Athey by Reuben Golliday, Franklin Co.

1791 Jul 24   Bailey, Caleb and Anne James by Benj. Tupper, Washington Co.

1811 Jan 7   Bailey, Elizabeth and James Nicholls by James Sharp, Washington
               Co.

1827 Apr 3   Bailey, Elizabeth and W.A. Tully by Samuel Hamilton, Elder in
               the MEC, Franklin Co.

1854 Jan 3   Bailey, Erastus and Martha A. Hatch by Rev. A. Kingsbury,
               Putnam Presbyterian Church, Muskingum Co.

1815 Oct 1   Bailey, Esther and Ridgway Craft by James Sharp, JP, Washington
              Co.

1864 Jun 22   Bailey, H.P. [groom] and R.R. Beckwith by Rev. John Boyd, St.
              Luke's Church, Marietta, Washington Co.

1813 Oct 5   Bailey, Harriet and James Adams by N. Hamilton, JP, Washington
              Co.

1820 12 mo 7 Bailey, Hiram and Rachel Thomas, Miami Monthly Meeting, Warren
              Co.

1815 Oct 3   Bailey, James Willard and Rachel Cannon by Cyrus Ames, Washing-
              ton Co.

1816 Sep 26   Bailey, Margaret and George Anthony by James Hoge (another entry
              27 Mar 1817), Franklin Co.

1854 Oct 17   Bailey, Margaret A. of Putnam and Norton S. Townsend of Elyria
              by Rev. A. Kingsbury, Putnam Presbyterian Church, Muskingum
              Co.

1820 Feb 14   Bailey, Mariah and William M. James by Elihu Bigelow, JP,
              Licking Co.

1809 Apr 24   Bailey, Martin and Betsey Clark by E.B. Dana, Washington Co.

1816 Sep 5   Bailey, Matthew and Anna Harrison by William Brown, JP, Frank-
              lin Co.

1810 Mar 21   Bailey, Nancy and Wm. Sinclair by John Brough, JP, Washington Co.

1817 Jan 26   Bailey, Sally and James Dutton by Stephen Guthrie, Washington Co.

1816 Apr 1   Bailey, Stewart and Martha Overdear by James Hoge, Franklin Co.

1820 Sep 10   Bailey, Washington and Eliza Buck by James M. Booth, JP, Wash-
              ington Co.

1821 Dec 20   Bailey, Wealthy and Bazel A. Cross by Joel Tuttle, Jr., Wash-
              ington Co.

1828 Jan 26   Baily, Jane and Andrew Fry by William Long, JP, Franklin Co.

1800 Jan 29   Baily, John Jr. and Sarah Farmer by Alvin Bingham, JP, Washing-
              ton Co.

1823 Feb 27   Baily, Rhoda and Charles Harrison by Jacob Grubb, Franklin Co.

1825 Nov 17   Bair, Susanna and Abraham Sims by Benj. Davis, JP, Marion Co.

1810 Nov 25   Baird, Rob't Jr. and Leah Grigsby by Stephen Lindsly, Washing-
              ton Co.

1813 Oct 21   Baird (Beard), Sarah and Andrew Hoskinson (Hoskins) by J.W.
              Patterson, Licking Co.

1828 Feb 17   Baker, Ann and Oliver Still by William Dalzell, Franklin Co.

1819 Nov 11   Baker, Anna and Veloris Graves by Samuel Bancroft, JP, Licking
              Co.

1820 Jan 13   Baker, Anna and Jacob Johnson by John D. Chamberlain, Washing-
              ton Co.

1791 Sep 1   Baker, Benjamin and Sarah Newton by Benj. Tupper ICCCP, Wash-
              ington Co.

1799 Oct 3   Baker, Catherine and John Beaver by Henry Smith, Washington Co.

1893 Aug 2   Baker, Charles E. of Columbus and Annetta P. Bagley of Zanes-
               ville by Rev. George F. Moore, Putnam Presbyterian Church,
               Muskingum Co.

1820 Dec 21   Baker, Clarisa and Jeremiah Jewett by Samuel Bancroft, JP,
               Licking Co.

1816 Jan 21   Baker, Clarissa and Mishael Gard by J. Russell, Washington Co.

1821 Apr 5   Baker, Clarissa and Thomas Ingham by Samuel Bancroft, JP,
               Licking Co.

1817 Jul 8   Baker, Cyrene and Asa Brown by Rev. T. Harris, Licking Co.

1823 Jun 20   Baker, Cyrus and Rachel Washington by William Gilmer, JP,
               Franklin Co.

1825 Apr 10   Baker, Dexter and Sarah Kimble by Conrad Roth, JP, Marion Co.

1827 Apr 11   Baker, Eliza and William Hunter by C. Henkel, Franklin Co.

1825 Jan 6   Baker, Geo. W. and Louisa Davis by Isaac Blayck, JP, Marion Co.

1825 Feb 10   Baker, Hannah and Isaac Woods by Rob't Hopkins, JP, Marion Co.

1804 Apr 19   Baker, Isaac and Susanna M. Dodge by Simeon Deming, Washington
               Co.

1822 Dec 24   Baker, Isaac and Rebecca Schoonover by C. Waddell, LM, Franklin
               Co.

1817 Jun 20   Baker, James and Sophia White by Titan Kimball, JP, Washington
               Co.

1821 Sep 13   Baker, James and Sarah Alden by Thomas White, JP, Washington Co.

1820 Dec 18   Baker, Jerusha and Daniel Beem by G. Callanhan, EMEC, Licking Co.

1806 Feb 18   Baker, John and Mary Johnston by James Quinn, Ross Co.

1820 Mar 1   Baker, John and Pricilla Combs by T.D. Bierd, Licking Co.

1817 Apr 22   Baker, John P. and Catherine Wilkins by J.W. Patterson, JP,
               Licking Co.

1806 Jan 28   Baker, Joseph and Martha Jackson by Peter Jackson, JP, Ross Co.

1816 Mar 24   Baker, Joseph and Rachel Hutchison by W. O'Bannon, JP, Licking
               Co.

1822 May 21   Baker, Margret and Abraham Schonover by Richard Courtright, JP,
               Franklin Co.

1813 Jun 12   Baker, Nancy and Thomas Ross (license date), Pickaway Co.

1799 Jan 24   Baker, Rhoda and Asa Coburn by Robert Oliver, Washington Co.

1828 Jun 8   Baker, Samuel and Rebecca Bridges by Aristarchus Walker, JP,
               Franklin Co.

---- Dec 16   Baker, Sam'l Jr. and Margaret Kelly by Robert Oliver, Washington
               Co.

1819 Feb 4   Baker, Sarah and Michael Trout by Thomas Scott, JP, Licking Co.

1810 Oct 14   Baker, Seth and Phebe Vanvaley by Wm. Gray, JP, Washington Co.

1826 Oct 22   Baker, Stacy and Frederick Spake by C. Henkel, Franklin Co.

1808 Apr 7   Baker, Thomas and Elizabeth Williams by J. Brough, Washington
               Co.

1801 Feb 19   Baker, Wm. and Jane Bieber by Lewis Hubner, Washington Co.

1825 Sep 13   Baker, Wm. M. and Elizabeth B. Tompkins by Wm. Cochran, JP,
               Marion Co.

1827 May 10   Baldwin, Deborah and Gabriel Bishop by Nathan Emery, MG,
               Franklin Co.

1823 May 13   Baldwin, Elias and Jane Powers by Nathan Emery, JP, Franklin Co.

1804 11m 18   Baldwin, Enos and Sarah Hunt, Miami Monthly Meeting, Warren Co.

1805 May 23   Baldwin, Francis and Margaret Meachouse by Thomas Scott, JP,
               Ross Co.

1821 Feb 17   Baldwin, Hannah and Riley Meacham by Reuben Carpenter, JP,
               Franklin Co.

1817 Jan 2   Baldwin, Hozanna and Wm. Thompson by Jos. S. Hughes, JP, Frank-
               lin Co.

1817 Dec 4   Baldwin, Isaac L. and Mary Blackmer by Thomas White, JP, Wash-
               ington Co.

1805 Jan 1   Baldwin, Jesse and Mary Hill by Dudley Davis, Washington Co.

1824 Nov 28   Baldwin, Levi and Salenda Bigalo by Nathan Emery, Elder in the
               ME Church, Franklin Co.

1828 Nov 27   Baldwin, Mariah and Jonah Stagg by Wm. Long, JP, Franklin Co.

1827 Sep 15   Baldwin, Mary and Randall R. Arnald by G.W. Hart, JP, Franklin
               Co.

1821 Jun 3   Baldwin, Sarah and Lyman B. House by Nathl. Little, JP, Frank-
               lin Co.

1817 Apr 3   Baldwin, Sophia and Simeon Allen by Thomas Spellman, JP,
               Licking Co.

1800 Nov 3   Baldwin, Stephen and Rebecca Rush both of Youngstown, by
               William Wick, VDM, Trumbull Co.

---- --- --   Baley, Elioner and Saml. Macky by John Tevis, Franklin Co.

1816 Apr 30   Baley, James and Phebe Allington by James Sharp, JP, Washington
               Co.

1814 Dec 1   Baley, Luzen and Absolom Petty by Henry Davis, JP, Pickaway Co.

1824 Jun 24   Baley, Mary and Daniel Bigalow by C. Waddell, Franklin Co.

1818 Aug 16   Ball, Abraham and Sally Fletcher by Cyrus Ames, Washington Co.

1811 Feb 7   Ball, Andrew and Nancy Ball by James Hoge, Franklin Co.

1823 Dec 9   Ball, Mary and Lewis Risley by Charles Waddle, LM, Franklin Co.

1811 Feb 7   Ball, Nancy and Andrew Ball by James Hoge, Franklin Co.

1807 Jan 21   Ball, Polly and Henry Leaf by Arthur O'Harra, Franklin Co.

1819 --- --   Ball, Polly and Jacob Keller by Joseph Grate, Franklin Co.

1812 Jul 30   Ball, Rachel and John Glaze (license date), Pickaway Co.

1806 May 7   Ball, Sally and Edward Penace by James Marshall, JP, Franklin Co.

1812 Dec 19   Ballah, James and Caty Hitler (license date), Pickaway Co.

1815 Jan 18   Ballard, Barbara and John Stevenson by Wm. Florence, JP, Pickaway Co.

1816 Feb 18   Ballinger, Catharine and James Akins by Joseph Gorton, Franklin Co.

1816 Jun 11   Ballinger, Joseph and Mary Bryant by Saml. Dyer, JP, Franklin Co.

1812 Jul 7   Ballinger, Nancy and Samuel White by James Hoge, Franklin Co.

1814 Jul 31   Ballinger, Peggy and Benjamin Ford by Nicholas Goitschies, Franklin Co.

1819 May 16   Ballinger, Samuel and Rody Thomston by Samuel Dyer, JP, Franklin Co.

1862 Jan 8   Ballinger, Solomon F., M.D., and Marietta Farquhar by Rev. A. Kingsbury, Putnam Presbyterian Church, Muskingum Co.

1823 Jan 16   Baly, Stewart and Lucinda Goldson by Robert W. Riley, JP, Franklin Co.

1817 Feb 5   Bancroft, Lucretia and Pindoles Lannel by Rev. T. Harris, Licking Co.

1817 Jul 13   Bancroft, Mrs. Lucy and William Smedley by Samuel Bancroft, JP, Licking Co.

1819 Apr 20   Bancroft, Matilda and Lester Case by Geo. Evans, JP, Licking Co.

1791 Sep 9   Bandeau, Francis and Jeannette Demier by J.G. Petitt, JCCCP, Washington Co.

1815 Feb 15   Banham, Elisha and Catherine Dustemme by Isaiah Wilkinson, Licking Co.

1815 Jul 5   Banick, John and Nancy Boucher by Wm. O'Bannon, Licking Co.

1802 Jun 24   Bantham, Nancy and Isaac Butler by Seth Cashart, JP, Washington Co.

1828 Feb 21   Barbee, David and Mary Haughn by P. Adams, Franklin Co.

1822 Mar 12   Barbee, Mary and Eli Spangler by James Hoge, Franklin Co.

1804 Jul 5   Barbee, Nancy and Wm. Comer both of Jefferson Tp., by J. Gardner, Ross Co.

1814 Feb 3   Barber, Elam and Violet Willcox by Ezra Griswold, Franklin Co.

1835 Sep 23   Barber, Eliza and Felix Regnirs by Rev. J.T. Wheat, St. Luke's Church, Marietta, Washington Co.

1803 Feb 15   Barber, Levi and Betsey Roun by Daniel Story, Clerk, Washington Co.

1803 Dec 22   Barber, Sarah and John Comer by John Odle, JP, Ross Co.

1851 Nov 27   Barbour, Goodrich H. of Madison, Ind., and Harriet C. Ward, by
               Rev. John Boyd, St. Luke's Church, Marietta, Washington Co.

1811 Dec 26   Barbour, Huldy and Samuel Loyd by James Marshall, Franklin Co.

1819 Mar 20   Barden, Elizabeth and Denis Karson by Elihu Bigelow, JP,
               Licking Co.

1820 Nov 2   Bardmass, John and Margaret Snodgrass by David Davis, Washing-
               ton Co.

1874 Aug 2   Barger, Benjamin F. and Sally Pearce Boyd at Hillsboro, by Rev.
               John Boyd, St. Luke's Church, Marietta, Washington Co.

1817 Mar 23   Bariet (or Barut), James and Moriah Christman by Townsend
               Nichols, JP, Franklin Co.

1797 Oct 5   Barker, Almy and Benjamin Smith by Peregrine Foster, JCCCP,
               Washington Co.

1871 Dec 6   Barker, Arthur W. and Josephine Maxwell by Rev. John Boyd, St.
               Luke's Church, Marietta, Washington Co.

1825 Apr --   Barker, Cintha and Chester Pinney by P. Chase, Franklin Co.

1807 Nov 18   Barker, Chauncy and Philamela Sage by James Kilbourn, Franklin
               Co.

1813 Aug 22   Barker, Daniel and Mary Varnum by Sardine Stone, JP, Washington
               Co.

1827 Jan 31   Barker, David B. and Almeda Park by J.W. Ladd, JP, Franklin Co.

1813 Apr 15   Barker, Eliphalet and Cynthia Andrews by Ezra Griswold, Frank-
               lin Co.

1814 Jan 2   Barker, Eliza and Rufus P. Stone, by Peter Howe, JP, Washington
               Co.

1820 Jan 25   Barker, Elizabeth and Samuel Dearduff by Joseph Gorton, Frank-
               lin Co.

1880 Sep 14   Barker, Eva A. and James A. Carroll by Rev. John Boyd, St.
               Luke's Church, Marietta, Washington Co.

1818 Jun 11   Barker, Gracy and Voluntine Hart by Joseph Grate, Franklin Co.

1804 Apr 10   Barker, Isaac and Christina Harper by James Graham, Washington
               Co.

1855 Sep 10   Barker, John D. and Mary L. Anderson by Rev. John Boyd, St.
               Luke's Church, Marietta

1825 Jul 20   Barker, Joseph and Isabella Stranahan by W.C. Duff, JP,
               Franklin Co.

1821 Mar 6   Barker, Luther D. and Maria Devol by Rev. Saml. P. Robbins,
               Washington Co.

1801 Apr 1   Barker, Michael and Isabella Harper by Wm. Harper, Washington
               Co.

1806 Jun 9   Barker, Orlando and Elizebeth Slack by Ezekiel Brown, JP,
               Franklin Co.

1813 Apr 15   Barker, Peter and Zelpha Taylor by Ezra Griswold, Franklin Co.

1800 Apr 2   Barker, Rhoda and Israel Ward by Alvin Bingham, Washington Co,

1813 Mar 21   Barker, Rhoda E. and Nathan Nye by S. Stone, JP, Washington Co.

1818 Sep 13   Barker, Samuel and Nancy Vance by Rev. Philander Chase, Franklin
               Co.

1803 Jul 4   Barker, Sarah and Ebenezer Ryan by Henry Smith, JP, Washington
               Co.

1821 Dec 25   Barker, Simeon and Rhoda Goodrich by A. Buttles, JP, Franklin Co.

1819 Oct 27   Barker, Sophia and Wm. Rufus Browning by Rev. Saml. P. Robbins,
               Washington Co.

1817 Aug 10   Barkley, Elizabeth and William Burroughs by Cyrus Ames, JP,
               Washington Co.

1822 Apr 22   Barkly, Darcus and John Marcy and C. Henkel, Franklin Co.

1816 Jan 28   Barlow, Betsey and David Jewit by Ezra Griswold, Franklin Co.

1815 Dec 9   Barnald, Anthony and Peggy Burnet by Percival Adams, Franklin Co.

1827 Jan 9   Barnehart, Elizabeth and Abraham H. Clymer by Abram Williams, JP,
               Franklin Co.

1819 Sep 3   Barner, John and Polly Colter by Rev. Noah Fidler, Licking Co.

1825 Feb 16   Barnes, Benj. and Abigail Felly by Joseph Clara, JP, Marion Co.

1806 Feb 20   Barnes, James and Elizabeth Sergent by William Talbott, Ross Co.

1818 Jan 7   Barnes, John and Ann Giffin by L.D. Baird, VDM, Licking Co.

1815 Oct 10   Barnes, Mary and William Cockran by T.D. Baird, Licking Co.

1829 Jun 11   Barnes, Peter and Mary E. Davis by I.N. Walter, ECC, Franklin Co.

1815 Feb 19   Barnes, Polly and Charles Brady by Anth'y Sheets, Washington Co.

1820 Mar 5   Barnes, Polly and Jacob Fulk by Alexander Holden, JPCC, Licking
               Co.

1813 Mar 10   Barnes, Rebecca and Daniel Wilkins by J.W. Patterson, Licking Co.

1793 Aug 22   Barnes, Samuel and Cynthia Goodale by D. Loring, CCCP, Washing-
               ton Co.

1813 Dec 2   Barnes, Susana and David Marsh (license date), Pickaway Co.

1813 Sep 2   Barnes, William and Sarah Marguiss (license date), Pickaway Co.

1823 Sep 25   Barnett, Elizabeth and Nicholas E. Laning by Nathan Emery, Elder
               in ME Church, Franklin Co.

1825 May 12   Barnett, Margret and Wm. Thrall by Henry Mathews, Franklin Co.

1824 Mar 16   Barnhart, Elizabeth and Andrew L. Burk by Charles Waddell,
               Franklin Co.

1819 Oct 13   Barnhart, Michael and Elizabeth Parks by John McMahan, Licking
               Co.

1808 Jun 5   Barns, Cynthia and James Kilbourn by Alexander Morrison, Jr.,
               Franklin Co.

1819 Aug 1   Barns, Mira and Cyrus Fay by Rev. Philander Chase, Franklin Co.

1818 Sep 27   Barns, Susan and Demas Adams by Rev. Philander Chase, Franklin
               Co.

1821 Dec 1   Barnwell, Matthew and Lois Wait by Danl. H. Buell, JP, Washing-
               ton Co.

1819 Mar 28   Barr, Isabella and Luke Reynolds by Cyrus Ames, JP, Washington
               Co.

1817 Aug 3   Barr, James and Polly Smith by Cyrus Ames, JP, Washington Co.

1811 Aug 24   Barr, John and Nancy Nelson by James Hoge, Franklin Co.

1817 Mar 27   Barr, Mary and James Lindsey by James Hoge, Franklin Co.

1824 Dec 23   Barr, Rhoda and John James by John Green, JP, Marion Co.

1813 Jun 22   Barr, Samuel and Sarah Pennell by Nath. Cushing, JP, Washington
               Co.

1814 Mar 29   Barr, Samuel and Rachel Jamison by Joseph S. Hughs, Franklin Co.

1816 Feb 22   Barr, Samuel and Mary Terey by Cornelius Hougland, Esq., Wash-
               ington Co.

1826 Jul 5   Barr, Samuel and Catharine Bull by Rev. James Hoge, Franklin Co.

1817 Aug 7   Barrett, Patty and Henry Armstrong by David Mitchell, JP, Jack-
               son Co.

1824 Dec 31   Barrett, Zachariah and Hannah Darling by Zachariah Welch, JP,
               Marion Co.

1820 Feb 7   Barrey, Sarah and John McClain by Joseph Dickerson, Washington
               Co.

1880 Oct 4   Barron, Alice of Putnam and Frank R. Johnson of Zanesville, by
               Rev. George F. Moore, Putnam Presbyterian Church, Muskingum
               Co.

1799 Jul 28   Barrows, Henry and Bethial Hewitt by J. Munro, Washington Co.

1802 Apr 18   Barrowy, Johanna and Abraham Roring by Lewis Hubener, Washing-
               ton Co.

1801 Nov 8   Barrowy, Maria Catharine and Michael Rimel by Lewis Hubener,
               Minister, Washington Co.

1800 Dec 22   Barrrch, Margaret and Elijah Harvey by Seth Cashart, JP, Wash-
               ington Co.

1812 Jun 25   Barry, Joshua and Mary Pen by John Green, JP, Licking Co.

1816 Oct 22   Barslow, Maria and Eli Thompson by Stephen Guthrie, Washington
               Co.

1814 Oct 15   Barstow, Sylvina and Major Reed by Rev. Marcus Lindsey, Wash-
               ington Co.

1803 Sep 24   Barth, Katharine and Elizar Carver by Enoch Shepard, Washington
               Co.

1799 Jan 23   Barthelot, Florence and Anthony Claudius Vincent by Josiah
               Munro, Washington Co.

1806 May 22   Barthley, Jacob and Sarah West by Wm. Bennett, JP, Franklin Co.

1813 Feb 18   Bartholomew, Cynthia and George Kreiger by J.W. Patterson,
               Licking Co.

1819 Jun 21   Bartholemew, Elizabeth and Robert Patton by J.W. Patterson, MG,
               Licking Co.

1817 Jun 12   Bartlet, Jemima and Oliver Clark by Isaac Griswold, Franklin Co.

1821 Feb 3   Bartlet, John and Mary Blakesley by A. Allen, Franklin Co.

1806 Sep 16   Bartlett, Amos and Mary Rardon by Rob't Oliver, Washington Co.

1822 Feb 8   Bartlett, Cynthia and Pearson Burpee by John D. Chamberlain, JP,
               Washington Co.

1810 May 17   Bartlett, Isaac and Jemima Bunning by Ezra Griswold, JP, Frank-
               lin Co.

1821 Feb 7   Bartlett, Keziah and Rasellus Wood by John D. Chamberlain, JP,
               Washington Co.

1817 Jan 30   Bartlett, Levy and Robert Gibson by James Sharp, JP, Washington
               Co.

1824 Apr 22   Bartlett, Thrssy and Charles Hunter by C. Henkel, Franklin Co.

1819 Feb 3   Bartlett, Wirum and Sally D. Kinney by John Green, JP, Washing-
               ton Co.

1806 Jul 10   Bartley, David and Rachel Canor by J. Brough, JP, Washington Co.

1816 Jul 21   Bartley, Judith and James Mason by John Green, JP, Washington Co.

1815 Nov 9   Barton, Nancy and William Cook by Solomon Goss, Washington Co.

1814 Dec 18   Barton, Polly and Michael Alkire by David Henderson, JP,
               Pickaway Co.

1815 Apr 6   Barton, Robert C. and Rachel B. Vanduyn by Rev. Stephen Lindsley,
               Washington Co.

1826 Apr 27   Barton, Wm. and Matilda Backus by Thomas Vaughn, JP, Jackson Co.

1817 Mar 23   Barut (or Bariet), James and Moriah Christman by Townsend
               Nichols, JP, Franklin Co.

1821 Apr 15   Bassett, Lyda and Simon Prouty by Spencer Wright, JPGT, Licking
               Co.

1855 Jan 25   Bate, Henry and Martha Stitt by Rev. John Boyd, St. Luke's
               Church, Marietta, Washington Co.

1817 1 mo 2   Bateman, Ann and Joel Wright, Miami Monthly Meeting, Warren Co.

1815 11 mo 1   Bateman, Rachel and Isaac E. Jones, Miami Monthly Meeting,
               Warren Co.

1813 Feb 21   Bateman, Sarah and Forest Belknap by Eli Cogswell, Washington Co.

1805 Oct 3   Bates, Daniel and Jane Hankins by Thos. Hicks, Ross Co.

1815 Jan 13   Bates, Dolly and Solomon Myers by Wm. Taylor, Licking Co.

1804 Apr 12   Bates, Emer and Mary Greentree by Noble Crawford, Ross Co.

1874 May 6   Bates, James, M.D., and Sarah J. Farquhar by Rev. A. Kingsbury,
               Putnam Presbyterian Church, Muskingum Co.

1801 May 21   Battle, Francis and Abigail Welch by Rufus Putnam, JP, Washing-
               ton Co.

1824 May 6   Bats, Catharin and James Williams by Andrew Allison, JP, Frank-
               lin Co.

1815 Jan 1   Bauch, Michael and Nancy Owens by Wm. Jones, JP, Pickaway Co.

1810 Nov 12   Bauder, Anthony and Christian Strouser (license date), Pickaway
               Co.

1813 Jul 24   Baugh, Caty and Daniel Justice (license date), Pickaway Co.

1815 Jan 12   Baugh, Eve and James Driver by Henry Davis, JP, Pickaway Co.

1813 Jan 14   Baugh, Margaret and Van B. Delishmot (license date), Pickaway
               Co.

1813 Mar 24   Baugh, Polly and James Caldwell (license date), Pickaway Co.

1824 Nov 2   Baughman, David and Elizabeth Neal by Alex Kinnear, MG, Marion
               Co.

1827 Nov 12   Baughman, Elizabeth and John Swickard by A. Allison, JP, Frank-
               lin Co.

1825 May 26   Baughman, Jesse and Catherine Terney by C. Henkel, Franklin Co.

1828 Jan 24   Baughman, L. and Thomas Havens by A. Allison, Franklin Co.

1824 Jan 1   Baughman, Sally and Jonathan Swickard by C. Henkel, Franklin Co.

1813 Jun 10   Baughman, Susan and John Eagler by Simeon Moore, Franklin Co.

1825 Apr 28   Baugman, David and Maria Canfield by Jacob Smith, JP, Franklin
               Co.

1884 Dec 31   Baum, Charles and Maggie Ryan both of Zanesville by Rev. George
               F. Moore, Putnam Presbyterian Church, Muskingum Co.

1813 Jun 28   Baum, Elizabeth and John Huston (license date), Pickaway Co.

1813 Jan 12   Baum, Kitty and Thomas Leeper (license date), Pickaway Co.

1815 Feb 23   Baum, Mary and Peter Baum by John Scott, JP, Pickaway Co.

1815 Feb 23   Baum, Peter and Mary Baum by John Scott, JP, Pickaway Co.

1813 Nov 14   Baum, Sally and Phillip Grable (license date), Pickaway Co.

1815 Feb 24   Baum, Sarah and Wm. Bilsland by John Scott, JP, Pickaway Co.

1811 Jan 6   Bayley, Mary and Cornelius Michall (license date), Pickaway Co.

1825 Dec 1   Baylor, Elizabeth and Joshua (or Joseph) Meeker by C. Hinkel,
               Franklin Co.

1804 Feb 8   Beach, Chalotte and Levi Pinny by Zachariah Stephen, JP, Frank-
               lin Co.

1872 Sep 15   Beach, D. Payson and C. Isabelle Johnson by Wm. Bower, St.
               Luke's Church, Granville, Licking Co.

1816 Sep 15   Beach, Jere. and Hannah Gorham by Tracy Wilcox, JP, (another
               entry on 16 Sep 1816), Franklin Co.

1824 Dec 11   Beach, Lorenzo and Edith Bull by Aristarchus Walker, Franklin
               Co.

1815 Aug 1   Beach, Nancy and Adam Strause by Michael Patton, JP, Franklin
               Co.

1799 Feb 21   Beach, Sabina and Alexander McCoy by Robert Oliver, JP, Wash-
               ington Co.

1805 Jan 24   Beacher, Frederick and Christian Larkings by John C. McCan,
               Ross Co.

1825 Apr 14   Beadle, Clarinda and Joseph Whitherd by Conrad Roth, JP, Marion
               Co.

1823 Feb 13   Beal, Electa and Alexander Westover by Joseph Badger, JP, Frank-
               lin Co.

1825 Apr 25   Beal, Sally and Alanson Perry by Thomas Barcus, JP, Franklin Co.

1805 Dec 26   Beal, William and Mary Jones by Stephen Linsly, Washington Co.

1807 9 mo 16   Beals, Jacob and Mary Thornburgh, Miami Monthly Meeting, Warren
               Co.

1827 12 mo 5   Beals, Jesse and Dinah Moon, Miami Monthly Meeting, Warren Co.

1800 Aug 4   Beals, Sarah and Jesse Hiet by Robert Safford, Washington Co.

1816 Feb 1   Beam, Benjamin and Sarah Hufman by George Callahan, EMEC,
               Licking Co.

1827 Nov 15   Beam, Jacob and Phebe Reose by J. Davis, JP, Franklin Co.

1828 Jan 13   Beam, John and Sarah Swisher by Abraham Williams, JP, Franklin
               Co.

1816 Jan 4   Beam, Pheby and William Ward by Geo. Callanhan, EMEC, Licking
               Co.

1818 Jul 23   Beam, William and Catherine Rhoads by Geo. Callahan, MG,
               Licking Co.

1821 Dec 27   Beard, Catharine and Isaac Dearduff by A. Allen, Franklin Co.

1824 Nov 18   Beard, Joel and Catharine Potter by W.T. Martin, JP, Franklin Co.

1809 --- --   Beard, John and Elizabeth Hoskins by ----- Holden, JP, Licking
               Co.

1821 Dec 27   Beard, John and Sally Hellen by A. Allen, Franklin Co.

1823 Dec 16   Beard, John and Martha Swan by Charles Waddle, Franklin Co.

1816 Feb 27   Beard, John S. and Jane Browning by Joseph Gorton, Franklin Co.

1815 Dec 31   Beard, Margaret and John Brown by J. Greenman, Washington Co.

1810 Jun 28   Beard, Mary and John Scott by Thomas Seely, JP, Washington Co.

1813 Oct 21   Beard (Baird), Sarah and Andrew Hoskinson (Hoskins) by J.W.
               Patterson, Licking Co.

1825 Nov 24   Beardslee, Bennett and Evalina Meeker by Vincent Southard, JP, Jackson Co.

1864 May 2   Beardslee, George W. and Jane D. Curtis by Rev. A. Kingsbury, Putnam Presbyterian Church, Muskingum Co.

1820 Apr 8   Beardsley, Barna and Polly Boylen by J. Johnston, JPHT, Licking Co.

1820 Feb 26   Beardsley, Phinehas and Mary Ann Rosan Gurez by Judah M. Chamberlain, JP, Washington Co.

1825 Feb 16   Bears, Louise and Israel Smith Jr. by Alex Kinnear, MG, Marion Co.

1824 May 24   Bearss, Joshua and Susannah Wade by J.B. Packard, JP, Marion Co.

1826 Aug 31   Beatty, Elizabeth and Nathan Woten by John Horton, JP, Jackson Co.

1812 Aug 11   Beatty, Samuel and Polly Duncan by John B. Johnson, JP, Franklin Co.

1825 Mar 22   Beatty, Sarah and Joel Martin by J.B. Gilliland, JP, Jackson Co.

1808 Nov 22   Beaty, Elisybeth and Cornelias Rose by Wm. Shaw, Franklin Co.

1822 Jan 19   Beaty, Isabella and Thomas Benscoder by B. Bull, JP, Franklin Co.

1820 Nov 9   Beaty, James and Milcha Reynols by Reuben Golliday, JP, Franklin Co.

1815 Nov 11   Beaty, Jonathan and Eliz. Helphrey by J. Green, Licking Co.

1820 Aug --   Beaty, Polly and James Sewel by Reuben Golliday, JP, Franklin Co.

1815 Sep 7   Beaty, Susanna and Peter Peters by John Turner, Franklin Co.

1794 Mar 4   Beaudot, Jean and Margarette Margaret by J.G. Petitt, Washington Co.

1818 Aug 13   Beaver, Jamima and John Brown by Rev. Geo. Callanhan, Licking Co.

1799 Oct 3   Beaver, John and Catherine Baker by Henry Smith, Washington Co.

1820 Jun 20   Beaver, Susan and Philip Pratt by Benjamin Cloves, Baptist minister, Licking Co.

1815 Dec 14   Beaver, Susanna and Samuel Holmes by Geo. Callanhan, Licking Co.

1804 Nov 28   Beck, Alexander and Mary McKinney by John G. McCan, Ross Co.

1809 Jun 20   Beck, Barbra and Aron Chery by John Smith (date recorded), Franklin Co.

1821 Feb 7   Becket, Benjamin and Mariah Kerr by Reuben Golliday, Franklin Co.

1813 May 31   Beckett, Elizabeth and James Beckett (license date), Pickaway Co.

1813 May 31   Beckett, James and Elizabeth Beckett (license date), Pickaway Co.

1891 Apr 8   Beckwith, James T. of Malta, O., and Mary C. Andrews of Zanesville, by Rev. George F. Moore, Putnam Presbyterian Church, Muskingum Co.

1864 Jun 22   Beckwith, R.R. and H.P. Bailey by Rev. John Boyd, St. Luke's Church, Marietta, Washington Co.

1819 Mar 25   Bee, Martha and George Freemyer by Moses Williamson, JP, Washington Co.

1818 Oct 18   Beebe, Cynthia and Levi Goodanow by Rev. Philander Chase, Franklin Co.

1803 Dec --   Beebe, Elizabeth and William Ford by Daniel Story, Washington Co.

1803 Jul 3   Beebe, Eunice and John Keating by Daniel Story, clerk, Washington Co.

1810 Nov 25   Beebe, Polly and Joseph T. Bennett by Wm. Browning, JP, Washington Co.

1818 Oct 18   Beebe, Sally and Daniel Freeman by Rev. Philander Chase, Franklin Co.

1826 Jan 19   Beebe, Shedden and Temperance Denman by R.W. Cowles, Franklin Co.

1876 Dec 28   Beebe, W. Loring and Maria Trevor Harte by Rev. John Boyd, St. Luke's Church, Marietta, Washington Co.

1817 Feb 17   Beebe, William and Mary Loring by Cyrus Ames, JP, Washington Co.

1817 Oct 31   Beech, Lucy and John Shepard by Danl. H. Buell, Washington Co.

1808 Feb 14   Beech, Samuel Jr. and Violet C. Case by Alex'r. Morrison, Jr., Franklin Co.

1815 Mar 15   Beecher, Sarah and Van Simmons by J. Green, Licking Co.

1823 Jan --   Beed, Susan S. and Jason Ellis by James Hoge, Franklin Co.

1818 Dec 29   Beedle, Benjamin and Bethsheba Cushing by Wm. Rand, Washington Co.

1800 Jun 12   Beel, Mary and James Smith by Philip Whitten, Washington Co.

1820 Dec 18   Beem, Daniel and Jerusha Baker by G. Callanhan, EMEC, Licking Co.

1818 Oct 8   Beem, John and Margaret Allbery by Rev. Noah Fidler, Licking Co.

1820 Apr 22   Beem, Michael and Rachel Rhoads by Rev. Geo. Callanhan, Licking Co.

1826 Feb 2   Been, Adam and Keziah Clymer by J. Gander, Franklin Co.

1818 May 7   Beers, David and Margaret Rowe by John Smith, JP, Franklin Co.

1828 Jan 3   Belford, Morjalin and Cassander Giles by John F. Solomon, Franklin Co.

1854 Jun 6   Belknap, Amelia and Hezekiah Sturges by Rev. A. Kingsbury, Putnam Presbyterian Church, Muskingum Co.

1868 May 27   Belknap, Caroline M. and William H. Howard of Boston, Mass., by Rev. A. Kingsbury, Putnam Presbyterian Church, Muskingum Co.

1813 Feb 21   Belknap, Forest and Sarah Bateman by Eli Cogswell, Washington Co.

1872 Oct 2   Belknap, Margaret M. of Putnam and Henry B. Heston of Philadelphia, Pa., by Rev. A. Kingsbury, Putnam Presbyterian Church, Muskingum Co.

1813 Mar 26   Bell, Abner and Mersy Smith (license date), Pickaway Co.

1878 Nov 28   Bell, Alice Morton and Livy Blair Boyd at Hillsboro by Rev. John
               Boyd, St. Luke's Church, Marietta, Washington Co.

1824 Oct 9   Bell, Benjamin and Mirandor Taylor by T. Lee, JP, Franklin Co.

1821 Aug 27   Bell, David and Eliza Ann Owens by Noah Fidler, Licking Co.

1817 Mar 4   Bell, Elizabeth and Enoch Bodwell by Cornelius Houghland, JP,
               Washington Co.

1821 Jan 6   Bell, Isabelle and John Morfet by John True, Washington Co.

1821 Jun 19   Bell, James and Margaret Cunning by W.T. Martin, JP, Franklin Co.

1804 Jul 20   Bell, John and Nancy Pool by John Brough, JP, Washington Co.

1820 Feb 3   Bell, John and Elizabeth Rice by Eli C. King, JP, Franklin Co.

1804 Apr 15   Bell, Johnson and Susanna Frances by John Brough, JP, Washing-
               ton Co.

1814 Mar 22   Bell, Josiah and Phoebe Bowman by Jesse Morral, JP, Pickaway Co.

1820 Dec 21   Bell, Margaret and David Jackson, Jr., by Dudley Davis, JP,
               Washington Co.

1813 Dec 14   Bell, Thomas and Ruth Forsman by Jas. Robinson, Pickaway Co.

1875 Sep 23   Bell, William S. and Isabel Munch by Rev. A. Kingsbury, Putnam
               Presbyterian Church, Muskingum Co.

1808 Sep 25   Bellows, Anna and Wm. Humphry by D. Loring, JP, Washington Co.

1804 Dec 6   Bellows, Benjamin and Elizabeth Littleton by D. Loring, Wash-
               ington Co.

1814 Jun 28   Bellows, Elias and Martha Ellenwood by Rev. Isaac Quinn, Wash-
               ington Co.

1809 Jan 23   Belt, Benedick and Elizabeth Fraize by Wm. Haines, JP, Licking
               Co.

1813 Nov 9   Belt, Dorsey and Margaret McCroskey by S. Donnavan, JP, Licking
               Co.

1812 Feb 15   Belt, Elisa and Esais Methen by Wm. Haines, Licking Co.

1817 Jan 30   Belt, Polly and John Jackson by Noah Fidler, Licking Co.

1816 Jan 4   Beman, Peter and Mary Steward by Noah Fidler, Licking Co.

1825 Apr 20   Benard, John B. and Harriet Wilcox by Aristarchus Walker,
               Franklin Co.

1799 Jul 9   Benbebber, Jesse and Rachel Greenlee by Robert Safford, Wash-
               ington Co.

1819 11 mo 4   Benbow, Evan and Mariah Venable, Miami Monthly Meeting, Warren
               Co.

1825 Oct 26   Benedict, Asahel and Ebelina More by Aristarchus Walker,
               Franklin Co.

1825 Mar 10   Benedict, Catharine S., daughter of Obediah Benedict, and Jacob
               H. Lewis by Aristarcrus Walker, Franklin Co.

1823 Dec 31   Benedict, Eley and Robert Justice, Jr., by Aristochus Walker,
               Franklin Co.

1818 Nov 26   Benedict, Hannah and Jacob Fairfield, Jr., by R. Stansbery,
               Franklin Co.

1816 Mar 24   Benedict, Hezekiah and Elizabeth Lewis by Ezra Griswold, Frank-
               lin Co.

1825 Oct 5   Benedict, Obadiah and Hetty Little by R.W. Cowles, Franklin Co.

1817 Dec 9   Benedict, Obadiah, Jr. and Caty McClean by Wm. Swaze, Minister,
               (marriage return filed Dec. 13), Franklin Co.

1825 Mar 3   Benedict, Saphrona and Moses Granger by Aristarcrus Walker,
               Franklin Co.

1816 May 30   Benfield, Archibald and Rebecka Stewart by Joseph L. Hughs,
               Franklin Co.

1798 Apr 5   Benjamin, Mary and Phineas Ford by Josiah Munro, Washington Co.

1818 Feb 15   Benjamin, Mary and John Vankirk by James Holmes, JP, Licking Co.

1818 Sep 29   Benjamin, Rebecca and Peter Gaich by James Holmes, JP, Licking
               Co.

1819 Dec 2   Benjamin, William and Rhoda Nott by John D. Chamberlain, JP,
               Washington Co.

1810 Mar 8   Benjiman, Jane and Isaac Ingman by -----, Licking Co.

1820 Dec 4   Benner, Christian and Sally Frank by John Cunningham, JP,
               Licking Co.

1819 Feb 11   Benner, Danie and Catherine Roberts by John Spencer, JP, Lick-
               ing Co.

1821 Apr 15   Benner, Henry and Ann Hizer by Andrew Henkel, Minister, Licking
               Co.

1821 Aug 3   Bennet, Darias and Phebe Nickleson by Richard Courtright, Frank-
               lin Co.

1816 Dec 20   Bennet, Elijay and Mabel Smothers by Thomas B. Patterson, JP,
               Franklin Co.

1817 May 4   Bennet, Elizabeth and Robert Blakesly by Emmor Cox, Franklin Co.

1818 Mar 12   Bennet, Elizabeth and Robert McEntire by Thos. B. Patterson, JP,
               Franklin Co.

1818 Feb 10   Bennet, Iray and Cathrin Rose by Tho. B. Patterson, Franklin Co.

1822 Feb 28   Bennet, Polly and John Pancake by Nicholas Goetschius, JP,
               Franklin Co.

1816 Aug 29   Bennett, Anny and Martin Borer by William Badger, JP, Franklin
               Co.

1812 Sep 7   Bennett, Hiram and Peggy Scott by Jacob Tharp, Franklin Co.

1803 Oct 27   Bennett, Jane and Stephen Short by Wm. Bennett, JP, Franklin Co.

1816 Jan 17   Bennett, John and Anne Stockham by D. Mitchell, JP, Lick Tp.,
               Jackson Co.

1810 Nov 25   Bennett, Joseph T. and Polly Beebe by Wm. Browning, JP, Wash-
               ington Co.

1878 Sep 5   Bennett, Lucy A. and John T. Nelson by Rev. John Boyd, St. Luke's
              Church, Marietta, Washington Co.

1822 Mar 18   Bennett, Patsey and Daniel Straw by Reuben Carpenter, Franklin
              Co.

1818 May 17   Bennit, Myers and Solome Slusser by Michael J. Steck, MG, Frank-
              lin Co.

1805 Nov 14   Benny, James and Nancy Smith by Thomas Hicks, Ross Co.

1822 Jan 19   Benscoder, Thomas and Isabella Beaty by B. Bull, JP, Franklin Co.

1816 Oct 11   Bensley, James and Catharine Pope by P. White, Washington Co.

1818 Aug 6   Benson, Christianna and James Nichols by William Dana, JP, Wash-
              ington Co.

1804 Mar 8   Benson, Rojin and Jane Joab by Thos. Scott, JP, Ross Co.

1802 Jan 18   Bent, Abner and Eliza Williams by Daniel Story, Clerk, Washing-
              ton Co.

1817 Jan 25   Bent, Abner and Betsey Dilley by Cyrus Ames, JP, Washington Co.

1816 Feb 4   Bent, Dorcas and William Dana by Cyrus Ames, JP, Washington Co.

1810 Mar 16   Bent, Nathan and Susan Ditty by Wm. Browning, JP, Washington Co.

1818 Feb 2   Bentan, Edward W. and Reuby Seeley by Stephen Maynard, JP,
              Franklin Co.

1803 Mar 17   Bentley, Elenor and David Stevens by Wm. Burnham, JP, Washing-
              ton Co.

1804 Feb 8   Bentley, Jane and Thomas Nott by Jacob Lindly, Washington Co.

1815 Aug 29   Benton, Nathan and Isabel Nurce by Recompence Stansbery, Frank-
              lin Co.

1792 Jun 6   Benzelin, Elizabeth and Jules Lemane Dwellers by J.G. Petitt,
              Washington Co.

1811 May 5   Berans, William and Sarah Headley by Wm. Haines, JP, Licking Co.

1811 May 30   Berbrige, James and Elizabeth Reeves (license date), Pickaway
              Co.

1815 Jun 8   Berely (or Birdy), Elizabeth and Thomas John by John Stipp, JP,
              Franklin Co.

1815 Apr 17   Berely (or Beverly), George and Lidia D. Vaux by John Stipp,
              Franklin Co.

1824 Apr 13   Berkstresser, Phillip and Eliza Myers by N. Goetschius, Frank-
              lin Co.

1815 Aug 22   Berman, Susan and William Foley (or Faley) by James Marshall,
              Franklin Co.

1797 May 20   Bernard, Michel and Marie Magdelaine Chandevert by J. Gilman,
              Washington Co.

1818 Dec 12   Berrington, Sarah and Aaron Huff by Thomas B. Patterson,
              Franklin Co.

1820 Dec 16   Berry, Betsey and Willis White by Wm. Hull, JP, Licking Co.

1824 Nov 19   Berry, Elizabeth and Henry Milizer (license date), Marion Co.

1813 Feb 28   Berry, John and Hannah Harbert by J.W. Patterson, Licking Co.

1816 Feb 20   Berry, John and Hannah Hull by Uriah Hull, JP, Licking Co.

1814 May 29   Berry, Nancy and Samuel Harbert by Levi Shinn, Licking Co.

1821 Mar 1   Berry, Ruth and Evan Evans by Wm. Hull, JP, Licking Co.

1825 Sep 29   Berry, Sophia and Thomas Bounce (license date), Marion Co.

1825 Apr 5   Berryhill, Sephen and Salome Altman by C. Henkel, Franklin Co.

1815 Jan 25   Bers, Pamela and Jeremiah Hanley by O. Scott, JP, Washington Co.

1821 Mar 10   Bessey, Elizabeth and John M. Strain by James Hoge, Franklin Co.

1821 May 19   Best, Nicholas and Polly Sparks by Nicholas Goetschius, Frank-
               lin Co.

1859 Nov 7   Bestwick, Sarah E. and Samuel G. Williams by Rev. John Boyd,
               St. Luke's Church, Marietta, Washington Co.

1802 Nov 11   Bethel, Edward and Pamelia Swank by Robert Oliver, JP, Wash-
               ington Co.

1803 Jul 19   Betz, Elizabeth and David Shepherd by John G. McCan, Ross Co.

1818 Apr 9   Beuher, Eneas and Hannah Nichols by Rev. T. Harris, Licking Co.

1814 Nov 19   Bevans, Polly and David Layton by Wm. King, JP, Pickaway Co.

1826 Aug 15   Bevelhymer, Jacob and Amelia Steadman by Absm. Williams, JP,
               Franklin Co.

1822 Jul 4   Bevelhymer, Susan and Daniel Tague by John Davis, Franklin Co.

1822 Aug --   Bevens, Thomas and Anny Gundy by Reuben Golliday, Franklin Co.

1815 Apr 17   Beverly (or Berely), George and Lidia D. Vaux by John Stipp,
               Franklin Co.

1810 May 31   Beward, Hannah and James Seward by Robert Clark, MMC, Licking
               Co.

1883 Mar 17   Bibee, Wornick and Savannah Stallman by Rev. John Boyd, St.
               Luke's Church, Marietta, Washington Co.

1820 Jun 24   Bickford, Joshua, Jr. and Abigail Springer by Cyrus Ames, JP,
               Washington Co.

1824 Mar 17   Bickle, Henry and Clarissa Merrille by Gershom Stillman, MG,
               Jackson Co.

1817 Jun 8   Bickmore, Eliza and John James by Simon Merwin, Washington Co.

1791 Sep 26   Biddle, Ben and Abigail Convis by Benj. Tupper, Washington Co.

1808 Aug 14   Biddle, Samuel and Elizabeth Dickenson by Philip Whitten, JP,
               Washington Co.

1878 Feb 26   Biddle, Samuel and Mary M. Hall by Rev. John Boyd, St. Luke's
               Church, Marietta, Washington Co.

1809 Dec 31   Bidlack, Elenor and John Gilbert by Wm. D. Hendren, JP, Franklin
                Co.

1825 Feb 23   Bidwell, Polly and Carmi Tuller by Aristarcrus Walker, JP,
                Franklin Co.

1824 Feb 5   Bidwell, Russell and Sally Blout by Peter Clover, Franklin Co.

1801 Feb 19   Bieber, Jane and Wm. Baker by Lewis Hubner, Washington Co.

1816 Nov 17   Bierce, Columbus and Mary Curtis by Stephen Guthrie, JP,
                Washington Co.

1821 Jan 18   Bierd, Daniel and Susan Dearduff by A. Allen, JP, Franklin Co.

1813 Dec 23   Bierly, Darick and Mary Cole by Matth. Mitchell, JP, Pickaway Co.

1800 Jul 8   Biers, Sally and James Burford by Robert Safford, JP, Washington
                Co.

1824 Nov 28   Bigalo, Salenda and Levi Baldwin by Nathan Emery, Elder in the
                ME Church, Franklin Co.

1824 Jun 24   Bigalow, Daniel and Mary Baley by C. Waddell, Franklin Co.

1826 Oct 22   Bigalow, Polly and Worthy P. Micham by Nathan Emery, MG, Frank-
                lin Co.

1838 Jan 1   Bigelow, Adalina E. and Orville Case, St. Luke's Church,
                Granville, Licking Co.

1814 Jan 16   Bigelow, Alpeas and Ursula Case by Isaac Fisher, Franklin Co.

1818 May 11   Bigelow, Elihu and Hannah Karson(?) by Geo. Hoover, JP, Licking
                Co.

1818 Dec 6   Bigelow, Nabby and John Rumford by Noah Fidler, MG, Licking Co.

1827 Jun 10   Bigelow, Sarah and J.H. Lewis by William Long, Franklin Co.

1801 Jan 22   Bigerstaff, Nancy and Frederick Fonty by Alvan Bingham, Washing-
                ton Co.

1816 Jul 20   Bigford, James and Catherine Levistone by Wm. O'Gannon, JP,
                Licking Co.

1818 Dec 8   Bigford, John and Mary Haight by Rev. Saml. Hamilton, Washington
                Co.

1803 Feb 8   Biggastaff, Sarah and John Abbott by Wm. Harper, JP, Washington
                Co.

1824 Feb 10   Biggert, Mary and Thomas Forgerson by James Hoge, Franklin Co.

1804 Jan 7   Biggins, John and Sarah Orison by Jacob Lindly, Washington Co.

1865 Jul 4   Biggins, Samuel of Palmer and Hannah Guy by Rev. John Boyd,
                St. Luke's Church, Marietta, Washington Co.

1802 Nov 9   Biggirstaff, John and Mary Leivis by A. Bingham, Washington Co.

1817 Feb 27   Biglaw, Selinda and James White by Isaac Griswold, JP, Franklin
                Co.

1806 Oct 22   Biles, Elizabeth and Benjamin Springer by Nehemiah Gates,
                Franklin Co.

1817 Nov 13   Billard, Sarah Ann and Isaac Jones Hatch by Amos Wilson, PJ,
              Washington Co.

1816 Jul 18   Billingsley, Margaret and William Thompson by Wm. O'Bannon, JP,
              Licking Co.

1815 May 8   Billingsly, Peme and Benjamin Dun by Jacob Hahn, JP, Licking Co.

1808 Jan 18   Billington, Seth and Miley Slack by Jos. Eaton, Franklin Co.

1817 Aug 28   Bills, Levi and Maria Wheeler by Rev. Saml. P. Robbins, Washing-
              ton Co.

1819 Jun 22   Bills, Polly and Erastus Abbott by Samuel Bancroft, JP, Licking
              Co.

1829 Jan 25   Bills, William M. and Sarah Ann Weaks by Isaac Fisher, Elder CC,
              Franklin Co.

1815 Feb 9   Bilsland, Margaret and Joshua Reed by Jno. Scott, JP, Pickaway
              Co.

1815 Feb 24   Bilsland, Wm. and Sarah Baum by John Scott, JP, Pickaway Co.

1801 Feb 19   Bingham, Elizabeth and John Harris by Alvan Bingham, Washington
              Co.

1803 Apr 15   Binhard, Rebecca and Wm. Gorrel by Sam'l. Williamson, Washing-
              ton Co.

1817 Mar 4   Bird, Catharine and Thomas Usher by Danl. G. Stanley, JP, Wash-
              ington Co.

1813 Jan 14   Bird, Nancy and James Walker by Wm. Miller, Washington Co.

1844 Oct 26   Bird, Thomas of Covington, Ky., and Ellen Blakeway by Rev.
              Edward Winthrop, St. Luke's Church, Marietta, Washington Co.

1815 Jun 8   Birdy (or Berely), Elizabeth and Thomas John by John Stipp, JP,
              Franklin Co.

1824 Mar 24   Birge, David and Mariah Ingham by Aristarchus Walker, Franklin
              Co.

1812 Mar 3   Birnett, Anthony and Hannah Rose by Jacob Tharp, JP, Franklin
              Co.

1822 Jan 3   Biser, Polly and Hugh H. Giles by C. Henkel, Franklin Co.

1825 Jan 13   Bishop, Angeline Catharine and Elias Camel by Nathan Emery,
              Franklin Co.

1829 Feb 15   Bishop, Elizabeth and David Pancake by Leroy Swornstead,
              Franklin Co.

1827 May 10   Bishop, Gabriel and Deborah Baldwin by Nathan Emery, MG,
              Franklin Co.

1828 Nov 16   Bishop, John and Sally Whitzel by J. Gander, JP, Franklin Co.

1814 Jun 13   Bishop, Katy and Isaac Decker by Shadrach Cole, JP, Pickaway Co.

1819 Dec 21   Bishop, Margaret and Jacob Bogart by Emmor Cox, Franklin Co.

1816 Jul 7   Bishop, Mary and Frederick Frutchey by Elisha Decker, JP, Frank-
              lin Co.

1814 Oct 23   Bishop, Nathaniel and Elizabeth Giles by John Brough, Esq., Washington Co.

1815 Nov 24   Bishop, Rebeca and Danl. Hawkins by Elisha Decker, JP, Franklin Co.

1801 Nov 5   Bishop, Mrs. Ruth and Stephen Perking, both of Hudson, by David Hudson, JP, Trumbull Co.

1806 May 27   Bishop, Samuel and Mary Wolf by Wm. Bennett, JP, Franklin Co.

1806 Dec 28   Bishop, Sarah and Andrew Sawyer by Asa Shinn, MG, Franklin Co.

1810 Sep 14   Bishop, Susan and Elisha Deckir by Massey Clymer, Franklin Co.

1820 Feb 25   Bitzer, Anthony and Elizabeth Purdy by Semuel Lain, Franklin Co.

1826 Mar 30   Bivans, Elizabeth and Abraham Ingham (or Ingram) by Jacob Gundy, Franklin Co.

1826 Feb 23   Bivans, Nancy and William Kimmons by Jacob Gundy, Franklin Co.

1880 Jan 22   Black, Jennie and John K. Wendell, both of Putnam, by Rev. George F. Moore, Putnam Presbyterian Church, Muskingum Co.

1810 Feb 22   Black, Margaret and James Taylor by Rev. Geo. Vanaman, Licking Co.

1809 Nov 15   Black, Matthew and Nancy Taylor by Rev. Timothy Harris, Licking Co.

1827 Apr 5   Black, Samuel and J. Sells by Samuel S. Davis, JP, Franklin Co.

1815 Jan 8   Black, Thomas and Elizabeth Johnson by James Sharp, JP, Washington Co.

1817 Mar 25   Blackburn, Elizabeth and Mathew Findley by T.D. Baird, HDMB, Licking Co.

1801 Aug 13   Blackburn, John and Nancy Trindle, at Youngstown, by Turhand Kirtland, Judge of Court of Common Pleas, Trumbull Co.

1809 Nov 28   Blackburn, Mange and Moses Moore by Rev. George Vanaman, Licking Co.

1816 Feb 22   Blackburn, Sarah and Andrew Allison by T.B. Baird, UDM, Licking Co.

1818 Jun 23   Blackman, Nathaniel and Hannah Smith by John Vance, JP, Licking Co.

1817 Dec 4   Blackmer, Mary and Isaac L. Baldwin by Thomas White, JP, Washington Co.

1804 Aug 15   Blackmer, Polly and Jesse Davis by Jacob Lindly, Washington Co.

1825 Dec 1   Blackmore, Rachel and Jesse Foos (license date), Marion Co.

1821 Aug 27   Blackmore, Rufus and Rachel James by J. Green, JP, Licking Co.

1813 Feb 25   Blackmorx, Samany and John Nixon by Thomas White, JP, Washington Co.

1810 Jan 11   Blackstone, Ebenezer and Sophia White by Stephen Lindsly, Washington Co.

1818 Jul 5   Blackwell, Samuel and Elizabeth McCown by Rev. Geo. Callanhan, Licking Co.

1826 Jan 22   Blagg, Samuel W. and Mary Donnally by J.P. Gilliland, JP, Jackson Co.

1828 Aug 28   Blain, James and Abigail Eder by Geo. Jefferies, Franklin Co.

1821 Jun 7   **Blair, Jesse and Mary Vandimark by Nicholas Goetschius, Franklin Co.**

1806 Oct 14   **Blair, Mary and Frederick Ritter by James Marshall, JP, Franklin Co.**

1805 Aug 8   **Blair, Samuel and Francis McNut by Zachariah Stephen, JP, Franklin Co.**

1813 Apr 4   **Blake, Benjamin and Lucy Stanley by Rev. James Cunningham, Washington Co.**

1815 May 25   **Blake, Fanny and Francis Thierry by D.H. Buell, JP, Washington Co.**

1882 Sep 24   **Blake, George L. of Zanesville and Kate L. Abell of Putnam by Rev. George F. Moore, Putnam Presbyterian Church, Muskingum Co.**

1811 Nov 5   **Blake, Hannah D. and Alexander Campbell by Nehemiah Davis, Washington Co.**

1824 Feb 5   Blake, Jennie and John Lone by John Horton, JP, Jackson Co.

1816 Nov 18   Blake, Ladotia and Jesse Wood by Rev. Jacob Young, Washington Co.

1815 Sep 2   Blake, Martha and Philo Trobridge by John Russell, JP, Washington Co.

1806 Aug 23   Blake, Sarah and John Phelps by Edwin Putnam, Washington Co.

1797 Dec 14   Blake, Simeon and Lavina Peck by Josiah Munro, JP, Washington Co.

1828 Jan 15   **Blakely, Elizabeth and Joseph Myers by I. Gander, JP, Franklin Co.**

1828 May 15   **Blakely, Elizabeth and John Fairchild by I. Gander, Franklin Co.**

1823 Mar 2   **Blakely, Jane and Isaac Crown by N. Goetschieus, JP, Franklin Co.**

1828 Nov 24   **Blakely, Margaret and Daniel Decker by Wm. Patterson, Franklin Co.**

1821 Feb 3   **Blakesley, Mary and John Bartlet by A. Allen, Franklin Co.**

1819 May 9   **Blakesley, Samuel and Polly Decker by Billingslea Bull, Franklin Co.**

1817 May 4   **Blakesly, Robert and Elizabeth Bennet by Emmor Cox, Franklin Co.**

1844 Oct 26   **Blakeway, Ellen and Thomas Bird of Covington, Ky., by Rev. Edward Winthrop, St. Luke's Church, Marietta, Washington Co.**

1884 Jun 4   **Blanchard, John S. of Concord, N.H., and Sarah E. Guthrie of Putnam, by Rev. George F. Moore, Putnam Presbyterian Church, Muskingum Co.**

1805 May 5   **Blazier, Phineas and Mary ------ by Samuel Edwards, Ross Co.**

1819 Oct 14 Blennis, Henry O. and Letty McKibben by Samuel Dye, JP, Washington Co.

1818 Nov 12 Blennis, Rachel O. and James Mitchell by Rev. Saml. P. Robbins, Washington Co.

1795 Nov 8 Blin, Francis and Francis Davons by J.G. Petit, JP, Washington Co.

1802 Apr 13 Blin, Richard H. and Sally Doan both of Cleveland, by Amos Spafford, JP, Trumbull Co.

1811 Aug 9 Bliss, James and Anna Prouds by Thomas Morris, Franklin Co.

1811 Jun 11 Blizzard, Reuben and Sophia Hickerson by ------, Licking Co.

1828 Jan 27 Blodgett, Nancy and Moses Strickland by William Dalzell, JP, Franklin Co.

1824 Feb 13 Bloget, Juliann and Elijah Olmstead by Nathan Emery, Elder in ME Church, Franklin Co.

1824 Feb 13 Bloget, Harvey and Sarah Cutler by Nathan Emery, Franklin Co.

1825 Feb 3 Blont, Allen and Elithe Boyd by John McCan, JP, Franklin Co.

1824 Feb 5 Blont, Sally and Russell Bidwell by Peter Clover, Franklin Co.

1812 Jan 9 Bloxom, Jeremiah and Susana Justice (license date), Pickaway Co.

1814 Apr 25 Blue, Frederick and Elizabeth Reddin by Rev. Geo. Alkire, Pickaway Co.

1805 Dec 22 Blue, James and Elizabeth West by Wm. Bennett, JP, Franklin Co.

1813 Feb 11 Blue, Martha and George Bogart (license date), Pickaway Co.

1827 Mar 1 Blue, Polly and Richard Dukes by P. Adams, Franklin Co.

1815 Dec 31 Blue, Sarah and Jacob Eby by Geo. C. Bogart, JP, Franklin Co.

1805 Feb 14 Blumar, Benjamin and Sarah Oaverman by Samuel Evans, JP, Ross Co.

1820 Aug 31 Boalt, Eben and Hannah Comstock by Wm. Rand, JP, Washington Co.

1821 Nov 4 Boardman, Emily and Sylvester Spelman by Samuel Bancroft, JP, Licking Co.

1808 Sep 27 Boardman, Jeremiah and Jemimah Church by Alex'r Morrison, Franklin Co.

1816 Nov 12 Boardman, Mary and Joseph Fasset by Rev. T. Harris, Licking Co.

1826 Apr 10 Boblit, Michael and Jane Douglass by Timothy Ratcliffe, JP, Jackson Co.

1799 Feb 19 Bobo, Betsey and Israel Huct by Alvan Bingham, JP, Washington Co.

1801 Apr 2 Bobo, Israel and Margaret Graham by Wm. Harper, Washington Co.

1803 Jun 21 Bobo, Letty and Jacob Shidler by Wm. Harper, JP, Washington Co.

1804 Aug 2 Bobo, Martin and Sarah Ross by J. Graham, JP, Washington Co.

1811 Jan 24 Bodkin, Mary and William Johnson by Daniel Goodno, Washington Co.

1818 Apr 5 Bodkin, Nancy and Nathaniel Richardson by John Russell, Washington Co.

1813 Sep 19   Bodkin, Richard and Betsy Withington by S.P. Robbins, Washington
              Co.

1803 Oct 6   Bodkin, Sarah and Loyd Howard by J. Gardner, JP, Ross Co.

1815 Apr 27   Bodle, Polly and John Davis by S. Dunnavan, Licking Co.

1815 Feb 15   Bodle, Susannah and John Brown by Samuel Dunnavan, Licking Co.

1817 Nov 20   Bodwell, Edith and Elijah Davis by Saml. Dye, JP, Washington Co.

1814 Oct 16   Bodwell, Elizabeth and David Davis by John H. White, JP, Wash-
              ington Co.

1817 Mar 4   Bodwell, Enoch and Elizabeth Bell by Cornelius Hougland, JP,
              Washington Co.

1814 Jun 12   Bodwell, Priscilla and William Watrous by Dan'l H. Buell, JP,
              Washington Co.

1820 Mar 26   Bodwell, Rhoda and Charles Sylvester by James M. Booth, JP,
              Washington Co.

1813 Feb 11   Bogart, George and Martha Blue (license date), Pickaway Co.

1819 Dec 21   Bogart, Jacob and Margaret Bishop by Emmor Cox, Franklin Co.

1827 Sep 3   Bogart, John and Mary Featheringale by I. Gander, Franklin Co.

1806 Feb 18   Bogart, Joseph and Janny Rollings by Wm. Bennet, JP, Franklin Co.

1806 Feb 4   Bogart, Joshua and Janey Cambel by Wm. Bennett, JP, Franklin Co.

1820 Jul 27   Boger, Mary and William Tyhurst by J. Cunningham, JP, Licking Co.

1816 Sep 17   Boggs, Anthony and Mary Friend by Gabriel McNiel, MG, Jackson Co.

1820 Nov 19   Boggs, Elsa and James Lang by Rob't G. Hanna, JP, Jackson Co.

1818 Jan 29   Boggs, Jane and Joel Lang by Robert G. Hanna, JP, Jackson Co.

1819 Mar 3   Boggs, Martha E. and Nathan Sheward by Adriel Hussey, Elder in
              the Christian Church, Jackson Co.

1804 Nov 1   Boggs, Nancy and Benjamin McMachlan by David Shelby, Ross Co.

1836 --- --   Bohl, Elizabeth and Ollef Nielssen by Rev. J. T. Wheat, St.
              Luke's Church, Marietta, Washington Co.

1822 Jul 28   Boid, Luther and Esther English by A. Buttles, Franklin Co.

1816 Sep 24   Boid, Nathan and Hannah Dowing by Geo. Hoover, JP, Licking Co.

1846 Jan 1   Boies, David E. and Esther E. Gillespie by Rev. A. Kingsbury,
              Putnam Presbyterian Church, Muskingum Co.

1803 Jun 23   Bolton, James and Nancy Cox by E. Langham, JP, Ross Co.

1821 Jun 7   Bolton, Thomas and Mary White by Nathl. Little, Franklin Co.

1826 Apr 30   Boman, Daniel and Mary Turner by MEC John F. Solomon, Franklin
              Co.

1826 Jan 17   Boman, Elizabeth and William Ramsey by Percivel Adams, Franklin
              Co.

1815 Mar 23   Bomngardner, Magalen and James Cunningham by Joseph Gorton,
              Franklin Co.

1824 Feb 26   Bond, Elizabeth and Joseph Heath by Jacob Grubb, Franklin Co.

1854 Jun 5   Bond, John H. and Amanda B. Sturges by Rev. A. Kingsbury, Putnam Presbyterian Church, Muskingum Co.

1816 Jan 4   Bond, Sophiah and John R.(?) Smith by James Marshall, Franklin Co.

1816 Feb 14   Bondinct, Sarah R. and John S. White by Rev. Stephen Lindsley, Washington Co.

1820 Sep 9   Boner, David and Hester Deweese by Wm. O'Bannon, JP, Licking Co.

1826 Jan 13   Boner, Philander and Esther Edger by A. Allison, Franklin Co.

1820 Jan 22   Bonham, Johnson and Polly Keaton by John Johnson, JP, Licking Co.

1894 Jan 10   Bonifield, David of Pleasant Valley, O., and Sadie McCaid of Duncan's Falls, O., by Rev. George F. Moore, Putnam Presbyterian Church, Muskingum Co.

1817 Jan 25   Boocher, Thankful and Thomas Castle by Samuel Carpenter, JP, Licking Co.

1822 Aug 27   Booker, Mary and John Updegraft by Jacob Sharp, Franklin Co.

1819 Dec 16   Booker, Rebecca and Charles Roberts by -----, Licking Co.

1891 Dec 29   Bootes, Samuel B. and Mrs. Clara G. Clark both of Zanesville, by Rev. George F. Moore, Putnam Presbyterian Church, Muskingum Co.

1812 Mar 1   Booth, James M. and Sally Alcock by Stephen Lindsly, Washington Co.

1894 Dec 24   Booth, Robert E. of Indiana and Bertha A. Leader of Zanesville by Rev. George F. Moore, Putnam Presbyterian Church, Muskingum Co.

1796 Jul 3   Boothby, Sally and John Denny by J. Gilman, Washington Co.

1804 Jun 18   Boots, Martin and Eva Arrahood by J. Gardner, JP, Ross Co.

1805 Sep 1   Boots, Martin and Mary Odle by J. Gardner, JP, Ross Co.

1848 Aug 15   Borden, Hon. James W. and Jane Conkling by W.C. French, St. Luke's Church, Granville, Licking Co.

1817 Oct 14   Bordinot, John and Margaret Williams by John Patterson, Washington Co.

1815 Jul 19   Bordon, William and Susanna Harris by Isaac Humphreys, JP, Washington Co.

1807 Nov 24   Boreaff, Polly and David Hays by Wm. Irwin, Franklin Co.

1817 Mar 27   Boreland, Wm. and Jane Flanigan by James Hoge (date of return), Franklin Co.

1825 Apr 29   Boreman, Lorane, spinster, and Henry G. Jewatt, batcholor, by Wm. Long, JP

1816 Aug 29   Borer, Martin and Anny Bennett by William Badger, JP, Franklin Co.

1820 Dec 20   Borer, Meomea and Samuel Brunk by Benjamin Britton, Franklin Co.

1818 Mar 15   Borer, Peter and Pheabe Vanskay by Daniel Harrel, JP, Jackson Co.

1825 Apr 28   Borman, Philip and Catherine Ridenauer by C. Hinkle, Franklin Co.

1814 Jul 5   Borrer, Christine and Paterson Morris by Nicholas Gaicthies,
               Franklin Co.

1818 Mar 23   Borrer, Jacob and Catherine Canrod by William Badger, Franklin
               Co.

1823 Aug 27   Borror, Isaac and Elizabeth Fishel by Wolry Conrad, JP, Franklin
               Co.

1827 Dec 6   Borror, Solomon and Delila Miller by Wooley Conrad, Franklin Co.

1825 12 mo 7   Borton, Rebecca and John Brown, Miami Monthly Meeting, Warren Co.

1824 Dec 13   Bosset, Susanna and William Thompson by Uriah Clark, JP, Frank-
               lin Co.

1820 Sep 23   Bosworth, Charles and Betsey Wilson by Rev. Saml. P. Robbins,
               Washington Co.

1866 Jun 20   Bosworth, D. Perkins Jr. and Clara M. Van Zandt by Rev. John
               Boyd, St. Luke's Church, Marietta, Washington Co.

1817 Mar 27   Bosworth, Zepheniah and Lucy Burlingame by Rev. Saml. P. Robbins,
               Washington Co.

1803 Jul 19   Botz, Elizabeth and David Shepherd by John G. Macan, Ross Co.

1815 Jul 5   Boucher, Nancy and John Banick by Wm. O'Bannon, Licking Co.

1811 Nov 26   Boughman, Elizabeth and David Ridenour by Simeon Moore, JP,
               Franklin Co.

1812 Apr 8   Boughman, Henry and Mary Eagler by Simeon Moore, Franklin Co.

1810 Jul 10   Boughman, Polly and George Teague by Wm. Shaw, Franklin Co.

1825 Sep 29   Bounce, Thomas and Sophia Berry (license date), Marion Co.

1824 Apr 6   Bowan, Elizabeth and Jacob Elmer by C. Henkel, Franklin Co.

1805 Mar 28   Bowdle, Anna and John Hubbard by Peter Jackson, JP, Ross Co.

1826 Oct 16   Bowen, Absolum and Electa Ann Gay by Henry Mathus, Franklin Co.

1883 Oct 16   Bowen, Arthur H. and Margaret W. Mathews by Rev. John Boyd,
               St. Luke's Church, Marietta, Washington Co.

1811 Oct 17   Bowen, Daniel and Elizabeth Knight by Philip Witten, Washington
               Co.

1811 May 11   Bowen, David and Sarah Wooley (license date), Pickaway Co.

1817 Oct 30   Bowen, Elizabeth and John McDowell by Samuel McDowell, JP,
               Jackson Co.

1818 Aug --   Bowen, Elizabeth and Joseph Stephenson by D. Mitchell, JP,
               Jackson Co.

1818 Sep 23   Bowen, James and Betsey Cushing by Wm. Rand, JP, Washington Co.

1811 Jul 28   Bowen, John and Eleanor Scott by Philip Whitten, JP, Washington
               Co.

1807 Jan 20   Bowen, Rachel and Peter Whitten by James Riggs, Washington Co.

1809 Apr 20   Bowen, Sarah and William Scripton by Philip Witten, JP, Washington Co.

1810 Jun 8   Bowen, Truman and Nancy Lewis (license date), Pickaway Co.

1810 Aug 2   Bowen, William and Peggy Kerr (license date), Pickaway Co.

1825 Feb 6   Bowen, Wm. and Margaret Stinor by J.B. Gilliland, JP, Jackson Co.

1819 Dec 23   Bower, Barbara and William Raver by Charles Bradford, JP of Bowling Green Tp., Licking Co.

1818 Jun 4   Bower, Joseph and Isabell Hull by Mich Ellis, Minister, Licking Co.

1827 May 27   Bowers, Alon and C.N. Pratton by A. Miller, Franklin Co.

1818 --- --   Bowers, Elizabeth and Darius Hartshorn by James M. Booth, Washington Co.

1820 Sep 19   Bowers, Elizabeth and Benjamin Coursen by Charles Bradford, JP, Licking Co.

1820 Jan 17   Bowers, Jacob and Peggy Reed by Achiel Hussey, Minister of the Christian Church, Jackson Co.

1887 Nov 7   Bowers, James A. and Mary B. Abele both of Zanesville, by Rev. George F. Moore, Putnam Presbyterian Church, Muskingum Co.

1827 Mar 1   Bowin, Anna and Julius G. Godman by S. Hamilton, Elder in MEC Church, Franklin Co.

1814 Mar 22   Bowman, Phoebe and Josiah Bell by Jesse Morral, JP, Pickaway Co.

1817 Nov 26   Bowrd, Martha and Benoni Humphry by Danl. H. Buell, JP, Washington Co.

1815 Jan 26   Bowsher, Anthony and Sarah Reeder by Jas. Jackson, JP, Pickaway Co.

1813 Jul 2   Bowsher, Barbara and John Buck by J.B. Johnson, JP, Franklin Co.

1813 Jan 30   Bowsher, Caty and Jesse Justice (license date), Pickaway Co.

1811 Oct 20   Bowsher, Daniel and Polly Freese (license date), Pickaway Co.

1819 Jun 8   Boyce, Elijah and Mary Stacy by Rev. Saml. P. Robbins, Washington Co.

1816 Oct 8   Boyd, Anna and Samuel Hoover by Samuel Bancroft, JP, Licking Co.

1825 Feb 3   Boyd, Elithe and Allen Blont by John McCan, JP, Franklin Co.

1883 May 16   Boyd, Emma A. of Newton Twp., and Obijah W. Carroll of Athens Co., O., by Rev. George F. Moore, Putnam Presbyterian Church, Muskingum Co.

1826 Nov 2   Boyd, Hannah and Thomas T. Kain by R.C. Rabb, MG, Franklin Co.

1826 Mar 16   Boyd, James and Ann Postles by John McCan, JP, Franklin Co.

1803 Jul 7   Boyd, Jonathan and Elizabeth Heart by Wm. Davis, JP, Ross Co.

1825 Jun 12   Boyd, Josiah and Charlotte Butterfield by John Goodrich, JP, Franklin Co.

1878 Nov 28   Boyd, Livy Blair and Alice Morton Bell at Hillsboro by Rev. John
               Boyd, St. Luke's Church, Marietta, Washington Co.

1821 Jan 15   Boyd, Margaret and John Haas, Jr. by John Green, ECC, Licking Co.

1882 Nov 4   Boyd, Mary and Charles C. Hale by Rev. John Boyd, St. Luke's
               Church, Marietta, Washington Co.

1875 Sep 2   Boyd, Mary M. and J.A.O. Yeoman at Hillsboro by Rev. John Boyd,
               St. Luke's Church, Marietta, Washington Co.

1807 Apr 9   Boyd, Robert and Caty Kepler by Josiah McKinney, Franklin Co.

1817 Jan 25   Boyd, Robert and Electy Rice by Daniel Brunk, JP, Franklin Co.

1826 Nov 26   Boyd, Robert and Jane Killpatrick by Amaziah Hutchinson,
               Franklin Co.

1816 Jun 27   Boyd, Sally and John Hamlin by Michael Patton, Franklin Co.

1874 Aug 2   Boyd, Sally Pearce and Benjamin F. Barger at Hillsboro by Rev.
               John Boyd, St. Luke's Church, Marietta, Washington Co.

1819 Sep 5   Boyer, Rachel and Samuel Foggar by Zach Carlisle, JP, Licking Co.

1811 Oct 25   Boyer, Samuel and Elizabeth Hutt (license date), Pickaway Co.

1819 Oct 31   Boyl, Conel and Hannah Collens by Townsand Niccles, JP, Franklin
               Co.

1821 Apr 12   Boyland, Elizabeth and Simon Hill by J. Johnson, JP, Licking Co.

1820 Apr 8   Boylen, Polly and Barna Beardsley by J. Johnston, JPHT, Licking
               Co.

1825 Mar 30   Boyord, Gasper and Rebecca Nichels by Daniel Clark, JP, Jackson
               Co.

1893 Apr 18   Bozman, Beverly W. of Cincinnati and Rosetta A. Drake of Zanes-
               ville by Rev. George F. Moore, Putnam Presbyterian Church,
               Muskingum Co.

1803 Feb 5   Brachbill, Catharine and John Mansfield by Alvan Bingham,
               Washington Co.

1821 Dec 7   Brackenridge, John and Agnes Fleming by Rev. Sam'l. P. Robbins,
               Washington Co.

1816 Apr 1   Brackenrige, Mary and James Ross by James Hoge, Franklin Co.

1819 Feb 17   Brackinridge, John and Peggy Walker by George Hays, Franklin Co.

1827 Mar 20   Brackinridge, Martha and Caleb Davis by Ruben Golliday, Frank-
               lin Co.

1812 Dec 10   Bradford, Robert and Louis Pond by John Green, Minister, Wash-
               ington Co.

1810 Oct 21   Bradford, Sally and Ira W. Peir by Saml. P. Robbins, Washington
               Co.

1818 Jun 4   Bradley, Bun and Esther N. Plummer by Jacob Lindley, VDM, Wash-
               ington Co.

1806 Jan 14   Bradley, Hannah and John Pairl by J. Brough, JP, Washington Co.

1805 Oct 3   Bradley, Isaac and Elenor Scott by Thos. Hicks, Ross Co.

1798 Nov 17   Bradley, Peggy and William Vovers by Josiah Munro, Washington Co.

1806 Sep 26   Bradley, Sally and David G. Smith by Seth Washburn, Washington
               Co.

1809 May 6   Bradley, Susannah and Abraham Johnston by Nehemiah Gates, Frank-
               lin Co.

1816 Sep 26   Bradley, Sylvy and Caleb Turner by Joseph Armstrong, JP, Jackson
               Co.

1815 Feb 19   Brady, Charles and Polly Barnes by Anth'y Sheets, Washington Co.

1886 Sep 24   Brady, George and Julia D. Anderson by Rev. George F. Moore,
               Putnam Presbyterian Church, Muskingum Co.

1820 Dec 14   Bragg, Harvey and Amelia Gavit by Noah Fidler, Licking Co.

1819 Jan 5   Brakebill, Philip and Catherine Johnston by J. Cunningham, JP,
               Licking Co.

1825 Dec 29   Braley, Massee and John Whetzel by Zephaniah Brown, JP, Jackson
               Co.

1805 May 23   Bramble, Nancy and James Gibbs by Thomas Scott, JP, Ross Co.

1805 Jan 27   Bramonburgh, Elizabeth and David W. Davis by David Mitchell, JP,
               Ross Co.

1813 May 18   Bratton, John and Lavina Warren by Percival Adams, JP, Franklin
               Co.

1812 Oct 15   Bray, Amaziah and Rebecca Wilcox by Rev. S.P. Robbins, Washing-
               ton Co.

1836 Nov --   Bray, Betsey E. and Jas. H. Dudley by Rev. E. Burr, St. John's
               Church, Worthington, Franklin Co.

1818 Sep 21   Breck, Anna and John Salmon by Daniel G. Stanley, Washington Co.

1813 Sep 29   Breckenridge, Margaret and James Taylor by Jas. Hauge, Franklin
               Co.

1814 Jun 16   Breckenridge, Margaret and Wm. Badger by James Hoge, Franklin Co.

1819 Feb 25   Breckenridge, Margaret and Thomas Adams by Percival Adams,
               Franklin Co.

1808 Jul 6   Breckinridge, James and Margaret Brotherton by Wm. Irwin, Frank-
               lin Co.

1808 Jan 20   Breckinridge, Margaret and Constantine McMahan by Wm. Irwin,
               Franklin Co.

1827 Apr 12   Brellsford, Almir and Eliza Orr by Amaziah Hutchinson, Franklin
               Co.

1866 Dec 25   Brelsford, J.W. and Mary E. Manly by Rev. A. Kingsbury, Putnam
               Presbyterian Church, Muskingum Co.

1814 Jul 5   Brevoort, Chloe and James Cumstock by W. Droddy, Franklin Co.

1820 Jun 7   Brewer, Mary and Luther Davis by John Stinson, JP, Jackson Co.

1824 Jun 16   Brewer, Willis and Catherine Hoffman by Timothy Ratcliff, JP,
              Jackson Co.

1820 Mar 3   Brewster, Levi and Lydia Waterman by Wm. Woodford, Washington Co.

1817 Jan 10   Brewster, William and Lucretia Fuller by Sam'l. Fairlamb, JP,
              Washington Co.

1810 May 15   Brick, John and Nancy Stanley by Stephen Lindsly, Washington Co.

1804 Apr 5   Brickel, John and Susannah Stokes by James Marshall, JP, Frank-
              lin Co.

1827 Dec 25   Brickell, Elcy and Charles Knoder by W.T. Martin, Franklin Co.

1827 Aug 16   Bricker, George and Sophia King by W.T. Martin, JP, Franklin Co.

1805 6 mo 26 Bridges, Jemima and William Edwards, Miami Monthly Meeting,
              Warren Co.

1828 Jun 8   Bridges, Rebecca and Samuel Baker by Aristarchus Walker, JP,
              Franklin Co.

1822 Apr 25   Brien, Suson O. and Milton Smith by Jacob Young, Washington Co.

1814 Jul 21   Brierly, Jane and Ebenezer Hern Matton by Joseph Gortton,
              Franklin Co.

1818 Dec 24   Briggs, Abigail and John Miller by Thomas White, JP, Washington
              Co.

1809 Jan 22   Briggs, Catharine and David White by Sam'l P. Robbins, Washing-
              ton Co.

1819 Jun 18   Briggs, Hannah and John Wiser by James Whitney, JP, Washington
              Co.

1817 Jul 31   Briggs, Lara and Sally Penny by Sardine Stone, JP, Washington Co.

1820 Aug 10   Briggs, Marcus D. and Highly C. Woodword by Sardine Stone, JP,
              Washington Co.

1876 Jul 26   Brigham, Asa M. of Beverly, O., and Mary F. Richards of Putnam,
              by Rev. A. Kingsbury, Putnam Presbyterian Church, Muskingum
              Co.

1810 Jun 12   Briner, John and Marah Roade (license date), Pickaway Co.

1814 Oct 21   Brink, Hannah and Peter Dearduff by George Bogart, JP, Franklin
              Co.

1829 Mar 12   Brinkerhoof, S. and Elizabeth Clymer by Leroy Swornstead,
              Franklin Co.

1824 Sep 16   Brintlinger, Sarah and Joseph Williams by Robert W. Riley, JP,
              Franklin Co.

1799 Jun 10   Brion, Phebe and Samuel Yates by Robert Safford, JP, Washington
              Co.

1807 Dec 25   Bristol, Adna and Lura Buttles by James Kilbourne, Franklin Co.

1825 Nov 6   Bristol, Leavice and Elijah Denman by Samuel Abbott, JP, Frank-
              lin Co.

1804 Jun 28   Bristol, Lois and Ira Woolcox by James Marshall, JP, Franklin Co.

1825 Mar 3 Britten, Mary and William Chiles by John F. Solomon, Franklin Co.

1826 Mar 16 Brittenham, Sally and Jesse Jerman, Franklin Co.

1804 Feb 9 Brittian, Elinor and James McDougral by Wm. Creighton, Ross Co.

1820 Jan 24 Britton, Alexander and Amanda Avory by Osgood McFarland, JP, Washington Co.

1829 Aug 14 Britton, Asenith and John Seeds by Geo. H. Patterson, ECC, Franklin Co.

1816 Apr 4 Britton, Benjamin and Elizabeth Brunk by Alexander Bassett, Franklin Co.

1824 Feb 5 Britton, Elizabeth and John Grom by John F. Solomon, Franklin Co.

1870 Oct 22 Britton, Emma and Henry H. Burton by Rev. John Boyd, St. Luke's Church, Marietta, Washington Co.

1828 Dec 25 Britton, William and Margaret Temple by Wm. Delzell, Franklin Co.

1820 Nov 6 Broadhurst, Thomas and Mary Sears by Stephen Lindsley, VDM, Washington Co.

1801 Sep 20 Brockway, Titus and Minerva Palmer at Vernon by Martin Smith, JP, Trumbull Co.

1814 Nov 15 Brodrick, Ann and Thomas L. Howkins by James Hoge, Franklin Co.

1819 Nov 26 Brodrick, John C. and Elizabeth P. Delano by Rev. Philander Chase, Franklin Co.

1817 Mar 27 Brodrick, Maril and J.M. Wolcott by James Hoge, Franklin Co.

1813 Sep 29 Brodrick, Mary and Henry Brown by Jas. Hauge, Franklin Co.

1817 Mar 27 Brokbill, Mary and Andrew Burk by James Hoge, Franklin Co.

1816 Sep 26 Brokebill, Betsy and Andrew Burk by James Hoge, Franklin Co.

1822 Dec 18 Brook David and Keziah Hamlin by C. Henkel, Franklin Co.

1869 Sep 30 Brooker, Major N. of Lowell and Mrs. Sarah Jane Richards by Rev. John Boyd, St. Luke's Church, Marietta, Washington Co.

1820 Feb 17 Brooker, Sibyl and John Conway by Amos Wilson, JP, Washington Co.

1821 Feb 27 Brooks, Abijah and Harriet Brooks by Rev. Saml. P. Robbins, Washington Co.

1821 Feb 27 Brooks, Harriet and Abijah Brooks by Rev. Saml. P. Robbins, Washington Co.

1801 Jul 3 Brooks, John and Delany Heancy by Edwin McGinnis, JP, Washington Co.

1810 --- -- Brooks, John and Margret Pogue by -----, Licking Co.

1802 Jun 30 Brooks, Jonathan and Rachel Clark at Burton by Turhand Kirtland, JP, Trumbull Co.

1821 Mar 25 Brooks, Nathan and Polly F. Pratt by S. Bancroft, JP, Licking Co.

1818 Aug 6 Brooks, Sally and David Chadwick by Rev. Noah Fidler, Licking Co.

1815 Jun 17 Brooks, Sarah and Nathan Low by John Green, Licking Co.

1814 Feb 13   Broom, Jemima and Nathaniel Smith by Dan'l H. Buell, JP, Washington Co.

1812 Dec 3   Broom, Peter and Elizabeth Davis by Simon Tuttle, JP, Washington Co.

1815 Apr 19   Brotherton, Adam and Elizabeth Crawford by James Hoge, Franklin Co.

1821 Apr 30   Brotherton, Elizabeth and Henry Kooken by James Hoge, Franklin Co.

1808 Jul 6   Brotherton, Margaret and James Breckinridge by Wm. Irwin, Franklin Co.

1818 Dec 8   Brotherton, Robert and Mary Kooken by James Hoge, Franklin Co.

1808 Mar 17   Brough, John and Jane Garnett by S. Lindsly, Washington Co.

1822 Mar 21   Brough, John and Bridget Cross by Daniel H. Buell, JP, Washington Co.

1825 Mar 17   Brown, Abarham and Fronica Coon by Abner Bent, JP, Marion Co.

1800 Apr 27   Brown, Ajucah and James Owen by Nehemiah Davis, Pastor Baptist Church, Washington Co.

1818 Oct 11   Brown, Alexander and Jane Riley by Simeon Pool, JP, Washington Co.

1804 Feb 22   Brown, Andrew and Jane Gallaspie by John Hoddy, JP, Ross Co.

1817 Jul 8   Brown, Asa and Cyrene Baker by Rev. T. Harris, Licking Co.

1827 5 mo 2   Brown, Asher and Esther Jones, Miami Monthly Meeting, Warren Co.

1828 Dec 7   Brown, Aurilea and John Hutchinson by W.T. Martin, JP, Franklin Co.

1821 11 mo 7   Brown, Benjamin and Sarah Chapman, Miami Monthly Meeting, Warren Co.

1827 10 mo 3   Brown, Benjamin and Mary Ann Craig, Miami Monthly Meeting, Warren Co.

1825 Aug 18   Brown, Catherine and Malachi Vinson by John Brown, MG, Jackson Co.

1802 Nov 14   Brown, Clarissa and Amsa Davis by Wm. Burnham, Washington Co.

1807 Feb 19   Brown, Elizabeth and Asahel Hart by Arthur O'Harra, JP, Franklin Co.

1813 Jun 30   Brown, Elizabeth and David Motes by S. Dunnavan, JP, Licking Co.

1813 12 mo 1   Brown, Elizabeth and James Mills, Miami Monthly Meeting, Warren Co.

1817 Jun 5   Brown, Elizabeth and Solomon Brown by Jeremiah Brown, JP, Jackson Co.

1873 Jun 10   Brown, Ella S. and Charles H. Abbot by Rev. A. Kingsbury, Putnam Presbyterian Church, Muskingum Co.

1819 May 6   Brown, Ephraim and Betsy Deavaun by William Hall, JP, Licking Co.

1819 Oct 19   Brown, Ezekel and Altha Rogers by Stephen Maynard, Franklin Co.

1808 Feb 18   Brown, Fanny and Josiah Kilbourn by James Marshall, Franklin Co.

---- --- --   Brown, Hannah and John Jurdon by Levi Shinn, Licking Co.

1822 2 mo 13 Brown, Hannah and Joseph Lukens, Miami Monthly Meeting, Warren Co.

1813 Sep 29   Brown, Henry and Mary Brodrick by Jas. Hauge, Franklin Co.

1814 Nov 22   Brown, Henry and Jane Gormly by Wm. Jones, JP, Pickaway Co.

1824 Dec 9   Brown, Hyliann and Israel Case by William C. Duff, JP, Franklin Co.

1824 Sep 7   Brown, Israel and Jemima Downing by James Boyd, JP, Franklin Co.

1873 Mar 31   Brown, J. Munro of New York City and Anna L. Price of Putnam by Rev. A. Kingsbury, Putnam Presbyterian Church, Muskingum Co.

1800 Oct 28   Brown, James and Isabella Oliver by Robert Oliver, JP, Washington Co.

1824 Jun 2   Brown, James and Almeda Skeels by A. Walker, JP, Franklin Co.

1841 Nov 16   Brown, James and Mary Ascher, St. Luke's Church, Granville, Licking Co.

1805 Oct 31   Brown, Jane and Enoch Domigan by Zachariah Stephen, JP, Franklin Co.

1815 Mar 7   Brown, Jane and Jesse Gale by Isaac Case, JP, Franklin Co.

1802 Mar 25   Brown, John and Elizabeth Devol by Nehemiah Davis, Washington Co.

1804 'Sep 6 Brown, John and Nicy King by James Marshall, JP, Franklin Co.

1806 Jan 5   Brown, John and Anna Sollars by Peter Jackson, JP, Ross Co.

1810 Aug 27   Brown, John and Mary Philip by Dudley Davis, JP, Washington Co.

1810 Sep 13   Brown, John and Rebecca Fearing by Dudley Davis, JP, Washington Co.

1815 Feb 15   Brown, John and Susannah Bodle by Samuel Dunnavan, Licking Co.

1815 Dec 31   Brown, John and Margaret Beard by J. Greenman, Washington Co.

1818 Aug 13   Brown, John and Jamima Beaver by Rev. Geo. Callanahan, Licking Co.

1820 Jan 18   Brown, John and Nancy Justice by Joseph Grate, Franklin Co.

1825 12 mo 7 Brown, John and Rebecca Borton, Miami Monthly Meeting, Warren Co.

1826 Feb 16   Brown, John and Margaret Teters by Peter Clover, JP, Franklin Co.

1828 Dec 15   Brown, Joseph and Elizabeth Emery by Thomas Wood, Franklin Co.

1811 Jan 3   Brown, Joshua and Actious Hall (license date), Pickaway Co.

1826 Oct 4   Brown, Louisa and Abraham Sells by Charles Sells, JP, Franklin Co.

1820 Jun 1   Brown, Margaret and Abel Sherman by John Patterson, Washington Co.

1819 Dec 23   Brown, Margaret and William Stranahan by James Hoge, Franklin Co.

1822 Aug 8   Brown, Margret and Oliver Codner by Richard Courtright, Franklin
               Co.

1823 Feb 25   Brown, Mariah and Levi Buttles by C. Henkel, Franklin Co.

1803 Aug 15   Brown, Martha and John Overdear by Ezekiel Brown, JP, Franklin Co.

1807 Feb 26   Brown, Mary and John Drown by Stephen Lindsly, Washington Co.

1824 Mar 25   Brown, Mary and John Hall by Jacob Grubb, Franklin Co.

1824 1 mo 7   Brown, Mary C. and James Smith, Miami Monthly Meeting, Warren Co.

1809 3 mo 16   Brown, Mercer and Mary Smith, Miami Monthly Meeting, Warren Co.

1878 Sep 5   Brown, Miles P. and Lucy A. Henderson by Rev. John Boyd, St.
               Luke's Church, Marietta, Washington Co.

1812 Aug 18   Brown, Moses and Margaret Stewart (license date), Pickaway Co.

1822 Jan 27   Brown, Nicy and John Offerall by Jacob Grundy, Franklin Co.

1838 Feb 1   Brown, Oliver T. and Susan Hasbrook, St. Luke's Church, Granville,
               Licking Co.

1817 Jan 2   Brown, Phebe G. and Joshua Sprague by John Green, JP, Washington
               Co.

1798 Apr 30   Brown, Polly and Josiah Sherman by Robert Oliver, Washington Co.

1800 Mar 25   Brown, Polly and William Brown by E. Cutler, JCCCP, Washington Co.

1833 Sep 22   Brown, Polly and C.H. Lynch by Rev. E. Burr, St. John's Church,
               Worthington, Franklin Co.

1814 Jul 24   Brown, Rachel and David Cline by Anth'y Sheets, Esq., Washington
               Co.

1814 9 mo 8   Brown, Rebecca and David Morgan, Miami Monthly Meeting, Warren Co.

1818 Apr 2   Brown, Reuben and Sarah Jones by Jere. Brown, JP, Jackson Co.

1794 Apr 3   Brown, Sally and Andrew Webster by R.J. Meigs, Washington Co.

1810 Dec 6   Brown, Sally and Thompson Mills of Knox Co. by James Scott,
               Licking Co.

1827 Dec 1   Brown, Sally and John S. Runyon by James Hoge, Franklin Co.

1812 5 mo 7   Brown, Samuel and Rebecca Evans, Miami Monthly Meeting, Warren Co.

1815 Oct 14   Brown, Saml. and Anna Duff by James Hoge, Franklin Co.

1818 9 mo 2   Brown, Samuel and Ruth Gause, Miami Monthly Meeting, Warren Co.

1819 Jan 21   Brown, Sarah and Edward Smith by Eli C. King, Franklin Co.

1823 Mar 4   Brown, Sarah and Elijah Glover by D.W. Deshler, JP, Franklin Co.

1828 Nov 16   Brown, Sidney and Ann Hart by Nathan Stern, Franklin Co.

1817 Jun 5   Brown, Solomon and Elizabeth Brown by Jeremiah Brown, JP,
               Jackson Co.

1826 Jan 18   Brown, Susan and James Ramsey by Percival Adams, JP, Franklin Co.

1815 Dec 14   Brown, Susannah and Andrew Cooperider by Alex. Morrison, Licking
               Co.

1816 Sep 13   Brown, Titus and Polly Pangbourn by Simion Overturf, Licking Co.

1800 Mar 25   Brown, William and Polly Brown by E. Cutler, JCCCP, Washington Co.

1817 Mar 27   Brown, Wm. and Hannah Thomas by James Hoge, Franklin Co.

1818 Oct 12   Brown, William and Isabel Wills by William Hull, JP, Licking Co.

1819 Sep 30   Brown, Wm. and Patsey Burris by Rob't G. Hanna, Jackson Co.

1821 Dec 12   Brown, William and Almedia Wilson by Joseph Palmer, JP, Washington Co.

1822 Jul 3   Brown, William and Eliza Cooken by C. Henkel, Franklin Co.

1815 Jan 20   Brown, William P. and Nancy Devol by John Green, JP, Washington Co.

1887 Apr 21   Browne, Warren C. of Cincinnati, O., and Julia E. Drake of Zanes-
               ville, by Rev. George F. Moore, Putnam Presbyterian Church,
               Muskingum Co.

1809 Nov 30   Brownin, Thomas and Sally McKeever by John Porter, Washington Co.

1817 Dec 8   Browning, Anna and Hezekiah Hurndun by Samuel P. Robbins, Wash-
               ington Co.

1818 Dec 3   Browning, Asa and Margaret Foster by Geo. Callanhan, EME Ch.,
               Licking Co.

1814 May 29   Browning, Bazilia and Ann Mead by Rev. Jas. Cunningham, Washing-
               ton Co.

1816 Feb 27   Browning, Jane and John S. Beard by Joseph Gorton, Franklin Co.

1818 Dec 31   Browning, Jeremiah and Dorcas Farmer by Geo. Callanhan, EMEC,
               Licking Co.

1817 Aug 12   Browning, Margaret and Thomas Rynolds by Samuel Dyer, Franklin Co.

1812 Nov 24   Browning, Sarah and Jeptha Ritchee by Rev. S.P. Robbins, Washing-
               ton Co.

1791 Apr 10   Browning, Wm. and Abigail Putnam by Rufus Putnam, Washington Co.

1805 Apr 25   Browning, Wm. and Mary Foster by D. Loring, Washington Co.

1819 Oct 27   Browning, Wm. Rufus and Sophia Barker by Rev. Saml. P. Robbins,
               Washington Co.

1800 Apr 27   Brownwell, Patience and Presburry Devol by E. Cutler, Washington
               Co.

1805 May 9   Bruff, Mary and Zachariah Woods by Thomas Scott, JP, Ross Co.

1796 Feb 15   Brunie, Madalane and Stephen Chandivert by Robert Safford, JP,
               Washington Co.

1816 Apr 4   Brunk, Elizabeth and Benjamin Britton by Alexander Bassett,
               Franklin Co.

1820 Dec 20   Brunk, Samuel and Meomea Borer by Benjamin Britton, Franklin Co.

1824 May 27   Brunk, Susannah and Robert Ellit by Benjamin Britton, Franklin Co.

1821 Apr 5   Bryan, Levina and Nathan Cole by Danl. H. Buell, JP, Washington
               Co.

1875 Jul --   Bryan, Mary and ----- Stedman by Mr. Nash, St. Luke's Church,
               Granville, Licking Co.

1818 Sep 9   Bryant, Hannah and Marton Misavey by John C. Smith, JP, Licking Co.

1816 Jun 11   Bryant, Mary and Joseph Ballinger by Saml. Dyer, JP, Franklin Co.

1826 Jun 22   Bryden, James and Margret Glass by Henry Matthews, Franklin Co.

1827 Jan 7   Bryson, Thomas and Sarah Cutler by Jacob Young, Franklin Co.

1819 Feb 7   Buchanan, Jeffery and Rachel Prouty by John Russell, JP, Washing-
               ton Co.

1808 May 27   Buck, Abigail and Hugh McArty by E.B. Dana, JP, Washington Co.

1820 Sep 10   Buck, Eliza and Washington Bailey by James M. Booth, JP, Washing-
               ton Co.

1810 Dec 25   Buck, Elizabeth and Edward Larkins (license date), Pickaway Co.

1809 Oct 19   Buck, John and Catharine Maythorm by David Mitchell, Franklin Co.

1813 Jul 2   Buck, John and Barbara Bowsher by J.B. Johnson, JP, Franklin Co.

1819 Jul 30   Buck, John and Deaduna Cawls by John Smith, Franklin Co.

1804 Sep 5   Buck, Omy and John Smith by James Marshall, JP, Franklin Co.

1811 Dec 12   Buck, Rose and Mary Evans by Rev. G. Vanaman, Licking Co.

1805 Oct 17   Buck, Rosy and Moses Donalson by Wm. Bennett, JP, Franklin Co.

1805 Jun 27   Buck, Sarah and Jonathan Hankins by Wm. Bennett, JP, Franklin Co.

1799 Jun 2   Buck, Titus and Betsey Hart by J. Munro, JP, Washington Co.

1803 Aug 11   Buck, William and Feby Smith by Wm. Bennett, JP, Franklin Co.

1845 Nov 4   Buckingham, Benjamin H. and Martha E. Potwin by Rev. A. Kings-
               bury, Putnam Presbyterian Church, Muskingum Co.

1809 Aug 15   Buckingham, Bradley and Maria Darlington by Wm. Haines, JP,
               Licking Co.

1805 Nov 27   Buckingham, Ebenezer and Catharine Putnam by Stephen Lindsly,
               Washington Co. (Parents of Gen. Catharinus Putnam Buckingham)

1853 May 5   Buckingham, Ebenezer and Lucy H. Sturges by Rev. A. Kingsbury,
               Putnam Presbyterian Church, Muskingum Co.

1891 Jan 28   Buckingham, Julia and Sherwood Mortley Pinkerton both of Zanes-
               ville by Rev. George F. Moore, Putnam Presbyterian Church,
               Muskingum Co.

1849 Oct 11   Buckingham, Julia Ann of Putnam and Samuel S. Cox of Cincinnati
               by Rev. A. Kingsbury, Putnam Presbyterian Church, Muskingum
               Co.

1846 Jun 4   Buckingham, Martha H. of Putnam and William H. Trimble of Hills-
               boro by Rev. A. Kingsbury, Putnam Presbyterian Church,
               Muskingum Co.

1887 Jan 26   Buckingham, Mary H. of Zanesville and Edward A. Green of Alex-
               andria, Va., by Rev. George F. Moore, Putnam Presbyterian
               Church, Muskingum Co.

1802 Jan 13   Buckingham, Stephen and Easter Cooley by I's.Peine, JP, Washington
               Co.

1819 Oct 13   Buckland, Emily and Silas Austin by Levan Randall, JP, Licking Co.

1824 Sep 4   Buckley, Margrett and Geo. M. Fickele (license date), Marion Co.

1825 Sep 14   Bucklin, Esther and Horace Pratt by Benj. Davis, JP, Marion Co.

1816 Oct 24   Budd, John and Sarah Lee by Frederick Peterson, JP, Franklin Co.

1813 Apr 18   Buell, Dan'l H. and Phoebe Ward by Rev. Stephen Lindley, Washing-
               ton Co.

1817 Apr 30   Buell, Eliza and Salmon D. Buell by Rev. Saml. P. Robbins, Wash-
               ington Co.

1821 Oct 28   Buell, Maria and James H. Hebard by Rev. James McAboy, Washington
               Co.

1814 Mar 17   Buell, Mathew and Lila Hatch by Rev. Stephen Lindsley, Washington
               Co.

1817 Apr 30   Buell, Salmon D. and Eliza Buell by Rev. Saml. P. Robbins, Wash-
               ington Co.

1818 Nov 25   Buell, Silina and Stephen Devol by John Patterson, JP, Washington
               Co.

1812 Feb 5   Buell, Timothy and Clarissa Plummer by Stephen Lindsly, Washing-
               ton Co.

1813 Dec 30   Buell, Wealthy and Richard Alcock by Rev. S.P. Robbins, Washing-
               ton Co.

1818 Jan 4   Buell, Wm. Henry and Savina Rogers by Rev. Saml. P. Robbins,
               Washington Co.

1798 Dec 25   Buffington, William and Sarah Hayes by D. Loring, Washington Co.

1822 May 22   Bull, Allonson and Hannah Lenard by Nathan Emery, Franklin Co.

1822 Sep 19   Bull, Betsey Ann and Walter Bull by William Jones, Franklin Co.

1826 Jul 5   Bull, Catharine and Samuel Barr by Rev. James Hoge, Franklin Co.

1824 Dec 11   Bull, Edith and Lorenzo Beach by Aristarchus Walker, Franklin Co.

1825 Mar 12   Bull, Horrace I. and Laura Andrews by Joseph Carper, Franklin Co.

1815 Jan 3   Bull, Jason and Delia Mattoon by James Cumpstock, Franklin Co.

1825 Jul 28   Bull, John W. and Nancy Rickets by Wm. D. Henders, JP, Franklin Co.

1820 Jan 26   Bull, Thompson and Fidelia Wilson by John Smith, Franklin Co.

1822 Sep 19   Bull, Walter and Betsey Ann Bull by William Jones, Franklin Co.

1825 Sep 28   Bum, Michael and Lucinda Rose by Jacob Smith, JP, Franklin Co.

1820 Apr 6   Bumgardmer, Elizabeth and James Butler by William Badger, JP,
               Franklin Co.

1824 Mar 22   Bumgardner, Leonard and Elizabeth Graham by R.W. Riley, Franklin
               Co.

1823 Nov 2   Bumgardner, Rebecca and George K. Haughn by Robert W. Riley,
               Franklin Co.

1826 Feb 6   Bumgartner, Philip and Hannah Sable by William C. Duff, Franklin Co.

1853 May 11   Bunker, Peleg and Lizzie Amberg by Rev. Geo. B. Sturges, St. Paul's
               Church, Marion, Marion Co.

1824 Mar 22   Bunn, Peter and Tacy How by Vincent Southard, JP, Jackson Co.

1871 Jun 1   Bunn, Romein and Kate R. Rhodes by Rev. John Boyd, St. Luke's
               Church, Marietta, Washington Co.

1819 Jan --   Bunn, Samuel and Elizabeth Nelson by D. Mitchell, JP, Jackson Co.

1810 May 17   Bunning, Jemima and Isaac Bartlett by Ezra Griswold, JP, Franklin
               Co.

1818 Aug 23   Burch, Betsey and Benjamin Chidester by Amos Wilson, JP, Washing-
               ton Co.

1818 Jan 1   Burch, Gratia and Amos Morris by Amos Wilson, JP, Washington Co.

1810 Nov 27   Burch, Louisha and Edmond B. Dana by Sam'l P. Robbins, Washington
               Co.

1811 Feb 10   Burchett, Jemimah and John Ross by Rev. John Green, Washington Co.

1817 May 14   Burchett, Patty and George Riley by Nath'l Hamilton, JP, Washington
               Co.

1866 Oct 23   Burckhart, Leopold and Sarah Prossor by N.C.N. Dudley, St. Paul's
               Church, Marion, Marion Co.

1820 Apr 21   Burden, Jane and John Meeks by John Patterson, Washington Co.

1805 Dec 10   Bureer, Ann and Wm. Caree by Wm. Creighton, Ross Co.

1800 Jul 8   Burford, James and Sally Biers by Robert Safford, JP, Washington Co.

1821 Sep 1   Burge, Anna and Archibald Dixon by John Crow, JP, Licking Co.

1814 Feb 6   Burgett, Huldah and Martin DeWitt by William Florence, JP, Pickaway
               Co.

1806 --- --   Burgon, Wm. and Catharine ----- by John Robins, Ross Co.

1816 Sep 26   Burk, Andrew and Betsy Brokebill by James Hoge, Franklin Co.

1817 Mar 27   Burk, Andrew and Mary Brokbill by James Hoge, Franklin Co.

1824 Mar 16   Burk, Andrew L. and Elizabeth Barnhart by Charles Waddell, Frank-
               lin Co.

1804 Sep 24   Burk, Anna and John England by J. Gardner, JP, Ross Co.

1815 Jan 26   Burkana (or Burkance), Nelly and Wm. Manning by Jos. Gorton, JP,
               Franklin Co.

1815 Jan 26   Burkance (or Burkana), Nelly and Wm. Manning by Jos. Gorton, JP,
               Franklin Co.

1811 Jun 11   Burkey, Johanna and William King by James Marshall, Franklin Co.

1818 Mar 15   Burkley, Samuel and Nancy Burroughs by Rev. John Brown, Washing-
               ton Co.

1821 Apr 9   Burley, George and Sally Mixer by Daniel H. Buell, JP, Washington
               Co.

1817 Mar 27   Burlingame, Lucy and Zepheniah Bosworth by Rev. Saml. P. Robbins, Washington Co.

1810 Sep 5   Burlingame, Patty and Rev. Sam'l P. Robbins by Timothy Harris, Washington Co.

1819 Mar 14   Burlinggame, Edwin and Jane Evans by Rev. Saml. P. Robbins, Washington Co.

1810 Feb 9   Burlinggame, Persis Marie and Benj. Hubbard Miles by Rev. S.P. Robbins, Washington Co.

1807 Nov 29   Burlinggame, Susanna and George Corner by S.P. Robbins, Washington Co.

1817 Oct 1   Burlingen, Nathan and Anne Burnam by John Shields, MG, Franklin Co.

1817 Oct 1   Burnam, Anne and Nathan Burlinger by John Shields, MG, Franklin Co.

1822 2 mo 16   Burnet, John and Elizabeth Hawkins, Miami Monthly Meeting, Warren Co.

1815 Dec 9   Burnet, Peggy and Anthony Barnald by Percival Adams, Franklin Co.

1813 6 mo 2   Burnet, Rachel and David Evans, Miami Monthly Meeting, Warren Co.

1822 Feb 21   Burnham, Abigail H. and Wm. Harris by Rev. Wm. Boris, Washington Co.

1817 Jan 29   Burnham, Dolly and Charles Ross by Simon Merwin, Washington Co.

1789 Aug 27   Burnham, Wm. and Christian Oliver by Ben Tupper, Washington Co.

1817 Dec 7   Burns, Elizabeth and Thomas Jones by Patrick Shearer, JP, Jackson Co.

1890 Oct 14   Burns, Franks S. and Chyde M. Smaill both of Zanesville, by Rev. George F. Moore, Putnam Presbyterian Church, Muskingum Co.

1823 Oct 1   Burns, Hannah and John Fairchild by Robert Boyd, Franklin Co.

1820 Feb 17   Burns, Israel and Polly Keith by John Green, JP, Washington Co.

1806 Jun 30   Burns, John S. and Nancy Moore by L. Barber, JP, Washington Co.

1825 Mar 22   Burnside, Mary and John Shoemaker by J.B. Gilliland, JP, Jackson Co.

1822 Feb 8   Burpee, Pearson and Cynthia Bartlett by John D. Chamberlain, JP, Washington Co.

1825 Sep 21   Burr, Philo and Mary Ann Abbot by Ebn'r Washburn, VDM, Franklin Co.

1802 Jun 24   Burrill, Nancy and Samuel Morrison by Seth Cashart, Washington Co.

1821 Jan 14   Burris, Mary and John L. Webster by John Patterson, JP, Washington Co.

1819 Sep 30   Burris, Patsey and Wm. Brown by Rob't G. Hanna, Jackson Co.

1819 Nov 18   Burris, Wm. and Charlotte Ross by Rob't G. Hanna, Jackson Co.

1821 Sep 2   Burroughs, Jarvis and Susan Stone by Rev. Saml. P. Robbins, Washington Co.

1818 Mar 15   Burroughs, Nancy and Samuel Burkley by Rev. John Brown, Washington Co.

1817 Aug 10   Burroughs, William and Elizabeth Barkley by Cyrus Ames, JP, Washington Co.

1866 Apr 25   Burrows, Rev. Thos. and Sophro Adams by N.C.N. Dudley, St. Paul's
               Church, Marion, Marion Co.

1824 Oct 12   Burthley, Henry and Mary Johnson by William Godman, Franklin Co.

1870 Oct 22   Burton, Henry H. and Emma Britton by Rev. John Boyd, St. Luke's
               Church, Marietta, Washington Co.

1826 Oct 15   Burton, Joseph and Susannah Chiles by I. Gander, Franklin Co.

1827 Sep 3   Burton, Joshua and Susannah Childs by I. Gander, Franklin Co.

1803 Mar 24   Burton, Sarah and Jaremiah White by William Bennett, JP, Franklin
               Co.

1816 Dec 24   Burton, Thomas and Charlotte Haile by Robert G. Hanna, JP,
               Jackson Co.

1811 Mar 21   Burton, William and Polly Cole (license date), Pickaway Co.

1814 Feb 14   Bury, Hulky and Martin Dewett (license date), Pickaway Co.

1811 Mar 28   Bush, Catherine and Lewis Farmer by James McMillen, JP, Licking Co.

1803 Jun 2   Bush, Eva and Abraham Stockey by Jos. Gardner, JP, Ross Co.

1821 Feb 22   Bushnell, Harriet and Noble Root by Rev. T. Harris, Licking Co.

1809 Jun 11   Busic, Benjamin and Elizabeth Healy by John Smith, Franklin Co.

1828 Jan 10   Butcher, C. and Sam'l Willson by Geo. Jefferies, Franklin Co.

1824 Nov 11   Butcher, Celia and George Stanton by Henry Matthews, Franklin Co.

1826 Apr 18   Butcher, Maria and Aaron Henry by Henry Mathews, Franklin Co.

1797 Mar 12   Buthe, Hannah M. and John L. Maldon by Robert Safford, Washington
               Co.

1819 Nov 20   Butler, Ann and Leuman Woodruff by Samuel Bancroft, JP, Licking Co.

1849 Sep 5   Butler, Harriet M. and M.P. Wells by Rev. D.W. Tolford, St. Luke's
               Church, Marietta, Washington Co.

1802 Jun 24   Butler, Isaac and Nancy Bantham by Seth Cashart, JP, Washington Co.

1820 Apr 6   Butler, James and Elizabeth Bumgardmer by Wm. Badger, JP, Franklin
               Co.

1857 Nov 30   Butler, John R. and Mrs. Hannah Van Allen by Rev. John Boyd, St.
               Luke's Church, Marietta

1817 Jan 30   Butt, Hazle and Susanna Stackhouse by Elihu Bigelow, Licking Co.

1825 Feb 29   Butt, Jacob and Mary Mutchler by Abner Bent, JP, Marion Co.

1824 May 26   Butterfield, Brittavia and Hezekiah Gillett by R.W. Cowles, JP,
               Franklin Co.

1821 Sep 23   Butterfield, Bula and Peter Hoffman by Nathl. Little, Franklin Co.

1825 Jun 12   Butterfield, Charlotte and Josiah Boyd by John Goodrich, JP,
               Franklin Co.

1818 Mar 26   Butterfield, Nancy and William J. Powers by Ezra Griswold, JP,
               Franklin Co.

1826 Sep 19   Butterfield, Tree and Betsy Avery by Amaziah Hutchinson, JP,
               Franklin Co.

1825 9 mo 7   Butterworth, Moorman and Fanny Smith, Miami Monthly Meeting,
               Warren Co.

1817 Mar 13   Buttle, Eli and Lydia Philbrook by Rev. Timothy Harris, Licking Co.

1821 Apr 12   Buttles, Arora and Harriet Case by Phier Chase, Franklin Co.

1815 Feb 6   Buttles, Julia and Job W. Case by Recompence Stansbery, Franklin Co.

1823 Feb 25   Buttles, Levi and Mariah Brown by C. Henkel, Franklin Co.

1807 Dec 25   Buttles, Lura and Adna Bristol by James Kilbourne, Franklin Co.

1823 Jul 3   Buttles, Mary and Peleg Scisson by C. Henkel, Franklin Co.

1806 Jul 4   Buttles, Sally and Alexander Morrison, Jr. by James Kilbourn, JP,
               Franklin Co.

1874 Jun 15   Butts, George C. and Ida M. Slocum by Rev. John Boyd, St. Luke's
               Church, Marietta, Washington Co.

1801 Jan 3   Buzelin, Elizabeth and James Laurent by Robert Safford, JP,
               Washington Co.

1817 Jul 31   Byard, Samuel and Hannah Freemire by Anthony Sheets, JP,
               Washington Co.

1805 Jul 14   Byers, Elizabeth and John Dise by Wm. Creighton, Ross Co.

1826 Apr 11   Byers, John and Matilda Hunter by James Hoge, Franklin Co.

1838 Jul 23   Bynner, Emma and James Knowles Linnel, St. Luke's Church,
               Granville, Licking Co.

1812 May 28   Bysor, Sally and Joseph Runnells by Dudley Davis, JP, Washington Co.

1819 Feb 11   Byshop, Catherine and Jacob Weedman by Charles Waddell, Minister,
               Licking Co.

1816 Oct 26   Cabb (or Cobb), Catharine and John Cramer by James Taylor, JP,
               Franklin Co.

1818 Aug 27   Cable, Apphia and Washington Olney by John Green, JP, Washington Co.

1814 Apr 6   Cable (or Coble), Mary and Daniel Cremar by James Taylor (another
               entry 9 Apr. 1817), Franklin Co.

1796 Dec 9   Caddot, Jean and Charles F. Duthe by Robert Safford, JP, Washing-
               ton Co.

1810 Aug 2   Cade, Elizabeth and James Frazier (license date), Pickaway Co.

1825 Apr 5   Cadey, Elias and Elizabeth Hughs by Samuel Carrick, JP, Jackson Co.

1817 12 mo 4   Cadwalader, Esther and James Hollingsworth, Miami Monthly Meeting,
               Warren Co.

1813 12 mo 1   Cadwalader, Jonah and Priscilla Whitacre, Miami Monthly Meeting,
               Warren Co.

1817 12 mo 4   Cadwalader, Naomi and Elijah Thomas, Miami Monthly Meeting,
               Warren Co.

1818 6 mo 4   Cadwalader, Thomas and Vashti Thomas, Miami Monthly Meeting,
               Warren Co.

1865 Nov 7   Cadwallader, Augusta and Alpheus B. Quackenbush by Rev. John Boyd,
               St. Luke's Church, Marietta, Washington Co.

1870 Jun 15   Cadwallader, Ellen and Johnson M. Welch of Athens, O., by Rev.
               John Boyd, St. Luke's Church, Marietta, Washington Co.

1861 Oct 8   Cadwallader, Emma M. and Edward C. Guild of Canton, Mass., by
               Rev. John Boyd, St. Luke's Church, Marietta, Washington Co.

1872 Dec 25   Cadwallader, J. Dallas and Julia Wheeler by Rev. John Boyd, St.
               Luke's Church, Marietta, Washington Co.

1816 Apr 11   Cady, Easther and John Hamilton by James Marshall, Franklin Co.

1827 Apr 26   Cady, Elnnora and Joseph Miller by D.W. Deshler, Franklin Co.

1813 Oct 22   Cady, Fanny and William Kelley by Dan'l H. Buell, JP, Washington Co.

1816 Aug 8   Cady, Hannah and Abraham Wagoner (Waggoner) by Emmor Cady (or Cox),
               JP, Franklin Co.

1827 Nov 2   Cady, Keziah and Joseph Seals by William Long, Franklin Co.

1817 Apr 23   Cady (or Cody), Samuel and Sarah Nicosan by Emmor Cox, Franklin Co.

1816 Feb 12   Cady, William and Elizabeth Harris by Benj. Talbot, JP, Washington
               Co.

1815 Jun 8   Caffee, Amos H. and Hannah Henderson by J.W. Patterson, Minister,
               Licking Co.

1818 Oct 19   Cafrey, Rebecca and Jonathan Whitebery by Alex Holden, JP,
               Licking Co.

1818 Nov --   Cahill, John and Elizabeth Wils by David Mitchell, JP, Jackson Co.

1806 --- --   Cahoon, Nancy and Mathew Kelly by John Robins, Ross Co.

1804 Aug 24   Cailer, Betsy and John Miller by Abm. Miller, Ross Co.

1820 Dec 27   Cain, Matilda and Joseph Leiley by James Hoge, Franklin Co.

1806 Aug 27   Calahan, Anna and Abel Gates by Rob't Oliver, JP, Washington Co.

1818 Jun 29   Calahan, George and Elizabeth Whitehead by James Holmes, JP,
               Licking Co.

1819 Mar 11   Calb, John and Anna Morison by Jno. Trois, Franklin Co.

1814 Nov 24   Calbermsten (or Culbertson or Calhunteen), John and Patsey
               Forguson by John Turner, JP, Franklin Co.

1811 Jan 31   Caldwell, Ann and Christopher L. White by James Marshall, Franklin
               Co.

1824 Dec 30   Caldwell, Eliza Ann and Rob't Price by Mathias Markley, JP,
               Marion Co.

1813 Mar 24   Caldwell, James and Polly Baugh (license date), Pickaway Co.

1801 Mar 5   Caldwell, James Irving and Rossana Moore at Youngstown, by
               William Wick, VDM, Trumbull Co.

1826 Oct 3   Caldwell, Nancy and Joseph K. Johnson by P. Adams, Franklin Co.

1869 Oct 28   Caldwell, Robert W. and Maggie Irwin by Rev. A. Kingsbury,
Putnam Presbyterian Church, Muskingum Co.

1847 Jun 22   Calhoun, Henry and Jane Metcalf by Rev. A. Kingsbury, Putnam
Presbyterian Church, Muskingum Co.

1814 Nov 24   Calhunteen (or Culbertson or Calbermsten), John and Patsey
Forguson by John Turner, JP, Franklin Co.

1808 Sep 4   Calkings, Elezer and Paty Westgate by Daniel Dunfee, Washington Co.

1820 Oct 26   Calkins, Chloe and Josiah Sabin by Rev. Philander Chase, Franklin
Co.

1826 Feb 2   Callagan, Benj. and Nancy McClure by John Stephenson, JP,
Jackson Co.

1820 Aug 18   Callahan, Priscilla and Abraham Hooper by Joseph Thrap, MG,
Licking Co.

1814 Nov 20   Callahan, Rachael and Abel Oxford by Wm. Florence, JP, Pickaway Co.

1818 Jan 11   Callahan, William and Mariah Coffman by Titan Kimball, JP, Washington Co.

1821 Apr 15   Callanhan, Sarah and Benjamin Pitzer by A. Goff, MG, Licking Co.

1816 Apr 26   Calvin, Charles and Elizabeth Goff by Simeon Overturf, JP,
Licking Co.

1804 Jul 24   Calvin, Sally and Edward Anderson by Asahel Cooley, Washington Co.

1806 Feb 4   Cambel, Janey and Joshua Bogart by Wm. Bennett, JP, Franklin Co.

1818 Feb 4   Cambelin, Frigit and Daniel Etinger by Joseph Grate, Franklin Co.

1810 Sep 16   Camble, Ishabelle and Drucilla Williamson (license date), Pickaway
Co.

1811 Aug 10   Camble, Jane and John Hornbeck (license date), Pickaway Co.

1825 Nov 24   Camble, William and Lucinda Reed by A. Allison, Franklin Co.

1804 Aug 14   Cambridge, James and Sally Nickins by J. Gardner, JP, Ross Co.

1825 Jan 13   Camel, Elias and Angeline Catharine Bishop by Nathan Emery,
Franklin Co.

1801 Jul 15   Cameron, Catherine and Robt. Safford by E. Cutler, Washington Co.

1812 4 mo 1   Cammack, John and Jane Hollingsworth, Miami Monthly Meeting,
Warren Co.

1819 7 mo 8   Cammack, Samuel and Hannah Hollingsworth, Miami Monthly Meeting,
Warren Co.

1819 Nov 18   Cammel, Eliza and William Young by Jacob Keller, Franklin Co.

1871 Sep 5   Cammel, Homer and Carrie C. Smith by Rev. John Boyd, St. Luke's
Church, Marietta, Washington Co.

1800 Dec 27   Camp, Aaron and Mary Mustard by John Struthers, JP, Trumbull Co.

1820 Apr 15   Camp, David and Julia Comstack by Ezra Griswold, JP, Franklin Co.

1864 Aug 11   Camp, Rosila and Timothy Carpenter by Wm. Bower, St. Luke's
Church, Granville, Licking Co.

1811 Nov 5   Campbell, Alexander and Hannah D. Blake by Nehemiah Davis, Wash-
               ington Co.

1895 Dec 25   Campbell, Annie and John A. Spalding both of Marietta, O., by
               Rev. George F. Moore, Putnam Presbyterian Church, Muskingum Co.

1869 Oct 28   Campbell, Bessie A. and Emmor C. Farquhar, M.D., by Rev. A. Kings-
               bury, Putnam Presbyterian Church, Muskingum Co.

1817 May 3   Campbell, Catherine and Nathaniel Toothaker by -----, Licking Co.

1818 Oct 8   Campbell, Elizabeth and James Rankins by Rev. Noah Fidler, Licking
               Co.

1811 Jan 15   Campbell, Fanny and Solomon Crose by Rev. Simon Cokrane, Franklin
               Co.

1822 Dec 13   Campbell, George and Susan Amanda Farber by John Davis, JP, Frank-
               lin Co.

1865 Aug 10   Campbell, Harry J. and Margaret Stone by Rev. John Boyd, St.
               Luke's Church, Marietta, Washington Co.

1799 Oct 22   Campbell, Jean and John Amlen, Jr. by Thos. Stanley, Washington Co.

1800 Nov 7   Campbell, John and Sally Ely both of Warren, by Calvin Austin, JP,
               Trumbull Co.

1819 Jun 22   Campt, Julia and Jesse Saunder by R. Stansberry, Franklin Co.

1798 Jan 2   Campbell, Nancy and James Amlin by Josiah Munro, Washington Co.

1818 Jan 18   Campbell, Patrick and Sally D. Amlin by Solomon Goss, MMEC,
               Washington Co.

1815 Jul 30   Campbell, Oren and Mary Glidden by Artemas Knapp, JP, Washington Co.

1804 Aug 28   Campbell, Rebecca and James Mountain of New Market Tp., by John
               Davidson, Ross Co.

1808 1 mo 20   Canby, Joseph and Lydia Pedrick, Miami Monthly Meeting, Warren Co.

1870 Jun 15   Canby, William M. of Wilmington, Del., and Edith D. Mathews of
               Putnam by Rev. A. Kingsbury, Putnam Presbyterian Church,
               Muskingum Co.

1825 Mar 31   Canfield, Eliza and Samuel Ayers by Jacob Smith, Franklin Co.

1826 May 4   Canfield, James and Sally Ogden by D.W. Deshler, Acting JP,
               Franklin Co.

1825 Apr 28   Canfield, Maria and David Baugman by Jacob Smith, JP, Franklin Co.

1820 Jul 6   Canidy, James and Elizabeth Griffeth by Samuel Dyer, Franklin Co.

1814 Apr 10   Cann (or Carns), Elizabeth and Elexander Patton by Daniel Hess,
               Franklin Co.

1811 Apr 15   Cann, Maryan and John Dalby (license date), Pickaway Co.

1818 Aug 15   Cannon, John and Hannah Parker by Dan'l H. Buell, JP, Washington Co.

1815 Oct 3   Cannon, Rachel and James Willard Bailey by Cyrus Ames, Washington
               Co.

1818 Nov 5   Cannon, Susanna and David Starks by Cyrus Ames, Washington Co.

1815 Apr 27   Canon (or Carson), Robert and Sophia Shind by Joseph Gorton,
               Franklin Co.

1806 Jul 10   Canor, Rachel and David Bartley by J. Brough, JP, Washington Co.

1818 Mar 23   Canrod, Catherine and Jacob Borrer by William Badges, Franklin Co.

1825 Dec 29   Canter, Henry and Rebecca Canter by John Horton, JP, Jackson Co.

1825 Dec 29   Canter, Rebecca and Henry Canter by John Horton, JP, Jackson Co.

1815 Mar 28   Caom (or Coon), Rebecca and George Miller by Elijah Austin, JP,
               Franklin Co.

1789 Jul 9   Capron, Marianne and John Rogers by Ben Tupper, Washington Co.

1805 Feb 19   Carder, George and Jenny Ross by John Hoddy, Ross Co.

1805 Dec 10   Caree, Wm. and Ann Bureer by Wm. Creighton, Ross Co.

1808 Feb 25   Carey, David and Elizabeth Ewing and David Mitchell, Franklin Co.

1808 May 31   Carey, Elizabeth and James Ewing by David Mitchell, Franklin Co.

1819 Jul 14   Carga, Polly and William Shannon by Josias Ewing, JP, Licking Co.

1818 Dec 24   Carl, Peggy and Mathias Newel by Samuel Stewart, Licking Co.

1851 Sep 25   Carl, Phebe Ann and Zebedee Trot by Rev. Geo. B. Sturges, St.
               Paul's Church, Marion, Marion Co.

1818 Dec 22   Carl, William and Margaret Goodwin by Wm. Rand, Washington Co.

1805 Mar 25   Carlisle, Nancy and John Pickens by Wm. Creighton, Ross Co.

1820 Dec 21   Carmical, Isaac and Mary Lauhrey by John Waggonner, JP, Licking Co.

1811 Oct 31   Carnahan, Eleanor and Enos Davis (license date), Pickaway Co.

1821 Nov 4   Carnahan, Nancy and Thomas Reynols by Reuben Golliday, JP, Franklin
               Co.

1806 May 15   Carnock, John and Susanna Greene by J. Brough, JP, Washington Co.

1814 Apr 10   Carns (or Cann), Elizabeth and Elexander Patton by Daniel Hess,
               Franklin Co.

1816 Jan 16   Carns, John and Betsey Johnston by Joseph Gorton, Franklin Co.

1824 Aug 24   Carothers, Isabella and George Ford by Wm. C. Duff, JP, Franklin Co.

1820 Oct 22   Carow, Mary F. and James Peterson by Alex Anderson, JP, Jackson Co.

1810 Feb 27   Carpenter, Amos and Susannah Rose by Rev. T. Harris, Licking Co.

1820 Dec 7   Carpenter, Benjamin and Sophia Searl by Sanford Converse, JP,
               Licking Co.

1822 Oct 10   Carpenter, Benjamin O. and Matilda Silvester by Jacob Smith,
               Franklin Co.

1824 Feb 22   Carpenter, Cyrus T. and Eliza S. Hunt, by Reuben Carpenter, JP,
               Franklin Co.

1806 Feb 5   Carpenter, Elisha and Elizabeth Odle by John Odle, JP, Ross Co.

1814 Nov 3   Carpenter, Emanuel and Sally Hess by Joseph Gorton, Franklin Co.

1812 Jul 6   Carpenter, James and Lydia Williams by Rev. T. Harris, Licking Co.

1821 Jan 8   Carpenter, James and Helpa Case by Timothy Harris, Licking Co.

1811 Dec 25   Carpenter, Jane and Justus Stephens by Rev. T. Harris, Licking Co.

1819 Feb 8   Carpenter, John W. and Huldah Tinkham by Reuben Carpenter, JP,
               Franklin Co.

1821 Feb 3   Carpenter, Joseph and Polly Searl by Sanford Converse, JP,
               Licking Co.

1810 Jun 18   Carpenter, L. Nathan and Naomi Cornell by Rev. T. Harris, Licking
               Co.

1840 Aug 20   Carpenter, Louisa and Sabin Hough, St. Luke's Church, Granville,
               Licking Co.

1821 Feb 25   Carpenter, Lovine and Jeremiah Williams by Reuben Carpenter,
               Franklin Co.

1806 Jul 31   Carpenter, Lucinda and James Swinerton by Josiah McKinnie,
               Franklin Co.

1813 May 8   Carpenter, Lucy and Thomas Fallon by Reuben Carpenter, Franklin Co.

1803 Jul 2   Carpenter, Rebecca and James Franklin by J. Gardner, JP, Ross Co.

1819 Dec 16   Carpenter, Royal and Rosey Thompson (license date), by Samuel
               Lain, Franklin Co.

1810 Jun 6   Carpenter, Sally and Sylvanus Cornell by Rev. T. Harris, Licking Co.

1810 Dec 21   Carpenter, Samuel and Meney Cornell by Rev. T. Harris, Licking Co.

1864 Aug 11   Carpenter, Timothy and Rosila Camp by Wm. Bower, St. Luke's
               Church, Granville, Licking Co.

1820 Jan 17   Carpenter, William and Margaret Pence by Simeon Overturf, JP,
               Licking Co.

1825? Feb 10   Carper, Thomas and Sarah Ransburgh by James Hoge, Franklin Co.

1791 Apr 19   Carr, Abigail and Andrew Doude by J. Gilman, JCCCP, Washington Co.

1807 4 mo 15   Carr, Elizabeth and Daniel Mills, Miami Monthly Meeting, Warren Co.

1827 Dec 18   Carr, Iona and W.B. Sylvester by Hugh Liams, Franklin Co.

1806 9 mo 17   Carr, Job and Ruth Mason, Miami Monthly Meeting, Warren Co.

1814 Oct 20   Carr, John and Mary Scothorn by Jesse Morral, JP, Pickaway Co.

1880 Sep 14   Carroll, James A. and Eva A. Barker by Rev. John Boyd, St. Luke's
               Church, Marietta, Washington Co.

1883 May 16   Carroll, Obijah W. of Athens Co., O., and Emma A. Boyd of Newton
               Twp., by Rev. George F. Moore, Putnam Presbyterian Church,
               Muskingum Co.

1821 Mar 13   Carroll, Sarah and Mathew Porter by John Spencer, JP, Licking Co.

1820 Mar 16   Carson, Elizabeth and Parker Crawford by John W. Patterson, MG,
               Licking Co.

1826 Jan 10   Carson, James and Calista Stephen by John F. Solomon, Franklin Co.

1815 Apr 27   Carson (or Canon), Robert and Sophia Shind by Joseph Gorton,
               Franklin Co.

1827 Oct 27   Carson, Robert R. and Eliza Meredeth by James Hoge, Franklin Co.

1821 May 31   Carter, Catherine and Benjamin Dean by John W. Patterson, MG,
               Licking Co.

1838 Feb 24   Carter, Ephraim and Rebecca Green, St. Luke's Church, Granville,
               Licking Co.

1818 Aug 2   Carter, Lyman and Anna Griswold by Rev. Philander Chase, Franklin
               Co.

1854 Dec 4   Carter, Margaret Jane and Edward Postlethwayte Page by Rev. John
               Boyd, St. Luke's Church, Marietta, Washington Co.

1816 Jul 14   Carter, Mary and Asa Willcox by Robert Elliott, JP, Franklin Co.

1822 Jan 31   Carter, Rufus and Sally Chidester by Samuel Beach, JP, Washington
               Co.

1806 Jan 14   Carter, Thomas and Barbary Given by Wm. Creighton, Ross Co.

1793 May 30   Carteron, Sophia and Charles Nicholas Visinier by J.G. Petitt,
               Washington Co.

1813 Feb 21   Cartwright, Hannah and Benjamin F. Stone by Rev. S.P. Robbins,
               Washington Co.

1814 Oct 30   Cartwright, Reuben and Catharine Protsman by Dan'l H. Buell, Esq.,
               Washington Co.

1807 Mar 19   Carvel, Andrew and Letitia Gorman by Robert Oliver, JP, Washington
               Co.

1803 Aug 18   Carvel, George and Mima Ward by Robert Oliver, JP, Washington Co.

1803 Aug 7   Carver, Caleb and Mary (or Polly) Flagg by Daniel Story, Clerk,
               Washington Co.

1803 Sep 24   Carver, Elizar and Katharine Barth by Enoch Shepard, Washington Co.

1809 Nov 4   Carver, Elizur and Polly Walker by J. Dare, JP, Washington Co.

1827 Oct 16   Carver, Hannah and William Thrailkill by G.W. Hart, Franklin Co.

1820 May 14   Carver, John and Hannah Chaney by T. Lee, Franklin Co.

1814 Mar 27   Carver, Mary and Otis Amsbury by Rev. S. Lindsley, Washington Co.

1805 Mar 28   Cary, Abijah and Catharine Johnson by Joshua Ewing, Franklin Co.

1876 Oct 17   Cary, Edward R. and Minnie W. Jewell by Rev. A. Kingsbury, Putnam
               Presbyterian Church, Muskingum Co.

1817 Jan 9   Cary, John and Dorcus Wilcox by R. Stansbury, Franklin Co.

1825 Jan 16   Cary, Mary and Joseph Prince by Conrad Roth, JP, Marion Co.

1805 Jun 14   Cary, Phebe and Alexander Reed by Hiram Merick Curry, Franklin Co.

1871 May 4   Cary, S. Augusta and Morgan Lansom by Rev. A. Kingsbury, Putnam
               Presbyterian Church, Muskingum Co.

1825 Jan 10   Cary, Susan and Charles Merrim by David Dudley, MG, Marion Co.

1814 May 31   Case, Augustus and Lucinda Curtis by Rev. Sam'l. P. Robbins,
               Washington Co.

1824 Oct 7   Case, Chloe and Waters Cummins by John Goodrich, JP, Franklin Co.

1806 Nov 20   Case, Eliza and Richard Alcock by Seth Washburn, Washington Co.

1815 Jun 7   Case, Emily and William Webster, Jr. by Ezra Griswold, Franklin Co.

1808 Apr 14   Case, George Jr. and Mira Sage by James Kilbourn, Franklin Co.

1818 Dec 12   Case, George W. and Amarilla Lampson by Rev. T. Harris, Licking Co.

1814 Dec 22   Case, Hannah and Robert Wells by Rev. S.P. Robbins, Washington Co.

1821 Apr 12   Case, Harriet and Arora Buttles by Phier Chase, Franklin Co.

1872 Mar 7   Case, Helen and Thos. O. Ward by Wm. Bower, St. Luke's Church,
              Granville, Licking Co.

1821 Jan 8   Case, Helpa and James Carpenter by Timothy Harris, Licking Co.

1815 Feb 6   Case, Job W. and Julia Buttles by Recompence Stansbery, Franklin Co.

1824 Dec 9   Case, Israel and Hyliann Brown by William C. Duff, JP, Franklin Co.

1819 Apr 20   Case, Lester and Matilda Bancroft by Geo. Evans, JP, Licking Co.

1812 Nov 11   Case, Luther and Susannah Taylor by E. Griswold, Franklin Co.

1828 Nov 6   Case, Newton and Azubah Gay by Aristarches Walker, JP, Franklin Co.

1812 Mar 29   Case, Orier and Mira Andrews by Ezra Griswold, Franklin Co.

1815 Dec 14   Case, Orland and Sally Crippen by Tracey Williams, JP, Franklin Co.

1838 Jan 1   Case, Orville and Adalina E. Bigelow, St. Luke's Church, Granville,
              Licking Co.

1805 Nov 13   Case, Polly and Joseph Cole by John Brough, JP, Washington Co.

1811 Feb 5   Case, Polly and Chester Wells by Rev. T. Harris, Licking Co.

1818 Nov 19   Case, Pyrine and Onessimas Whitehead by R. Stansbery, Franklin Co.

1810 Jun 26   Case, Sabra and Samuel Soo by Rev. T. Harris, Licking Co.

1813 Feb 11   Case, Timothy and Elizabeth Spelman by Rev. Timothy Harris, Licking
              Co.

1806 Jul 16   Case, Truman and Azenith Wilcox by Arthur O'Harra, JP, Franklin Co.

1814 Jan 16   Case, Ursula and Alpeas Bigelow by Isaac Fisher, Franklin Co.

1808 Feb 14   Case, Violet C. and Samuel Beech, Jr. and Alex'r Morrison, Jr.,
              Franklin Co.

1809 Nov 2   Case, Wm. M. and Marian Posey by Stephen Lindsly, Washington Co.

1819 Feb 8   Casel, Henry and Polly Wiles by D. Mitchell, JP, Jackson Co.

1825 Jul 21   Casey, Betsey and Samuel Smith by J. Gander, JP, Franklin Co.

1807 Apr 23   Casey, Jemima and Jacob Johnston by Nehemiah Gates, JP, Franklin Co.

1807 Sep 3   Casey, Salley and Peter Sells by James Marshall, Franklin Co.

1812 Mar 1   Casey, Thomas and Margarey McDowell by Wm. D. Hendren, Franklin Co.

1789 Oct 25   Casey, Wanton and Elizabeth Goodale by Ben Tupper, Washington Co.

1827 Feb 1   Cashman, George and Betsey Mahan by C. Henkel, Franklin Co.

1813 Jun 25   Casler, James and Mary Whiteside (license date), Pickaway Co.

1824 Oct 5   Casner, Elizabeth and Joseph Kesler by Wm. Godman, JP, Franklin Co.

1802 Feb 3   Cass, Deborah W. and Willis Silliman by Seth Coshart, JP, Wash-
               ington Co.

1809 May 18   Cass, George W. and Sophia Lord by Sam'l P. Robbins, Washington Co.

1811 Mar 26   Cassady, Elizabeth and Andrew Douglas (license date), Pickaway Co.

1882 Sep 6   Cassell, William R. and Mrs. Addie Severance by Rev. John Boyd,
               St. Luke's Church, Marietta, Washington Co.

1824 Aug 26   Cassill, Susanna and Solomon Waldren by Geo. Claypoole, JP,
               Jackson Co.

1814 Apr 12   Cassner, Martin and Betsey Witmer by Jacob Leist, JP, Pickaway Co.

1819 Nov 7   Casteel, William and Mary Downing by Reuben Golliday, Franklin Co.

1818 Feb 5   Caster, Elizabeth and John Henthorn by J. Ewing, Licking Co.

1818 Dec 28   Castler, Amanda and Cornelius Lake by Stephen Guthrie, Washington
               Co.

1806 Dec 26   Castler, George and Abie Newton by L. Barber, Washington Co.

1803 Mar 29   Castler, Henry and Rachael Shepard by J. Graham, JP, Washington Co.

1817 Jan 25   Castler, Thomas and Thankful Boocher by Samuel Carpenter, JP,
               Licking Co.

1809 Jan 12   Casto, Eliza and William Taylor by David Mitchell, Franklin Co.

1804 Mar 22   Cating, Ann and Andrew Kelly by John Odle, JP, Ross Co.

1805 Apr 25   Cating, Elizabeth and William Jolly by J. Gardner, JP, Ross Co.

1820 Feb 17   Cating, Orlinda and Joseph McCune by Thos Cox, JP, Jackson Co.

1806 Jan 23   Cating, Susannah and James Taylor by John Odle, JP, Ross Co.

1833 Dec 11   Catley, Richard and Lois Pinney by Rev. E. Burr, St. John's Church,
               Worthington, Franklin Co.

1819 May 13   Cats, Philip and Mary Mason by J. Cunningham, Licking Co.

1818 Oct 1   Caughelan, Elizabeth and Philip Ford by Rev. Noah Fidler, Licking
               Co.

1822 Sep 12   Caulkins, Clarinda and Ira Metcalf by A. Buttles, Franklin Co.

1826 Oct 25   Caulkins, Delia and Edwin H. Topping by John W. Ladd, JP, Franklin
               Co.

1811 Aug 8   Caunden, Ester and Samuel Higenbotham by J.W. Patterson, Licking Co.

1851 Sep 7   Cave, Sarah and Timothy Richards by Rev. John Boyd, St. Luke's
               Church, Marietta, Washington Co.

1803 Jan 13   Caven, Jane and Robert Flack by Daniel Story, Clerk, Washington Co.

1804 Nov 16   Cavender, Sarah and George Williams by Samuel Edwards, Ross Co.

1819 Jul 30   Cawls, Deaduna and John Buck by John Smith, Franklin Co.

1812 May 10   Cawood, Fanny and Jona. Dye by Samuel Dye, JP, Washington Co.

1825 Dec 1   Cazad, Mercy and Mathew Miller by William C. Duff, Franklin Co.

1819 Aug 4   Ceask, Fanny and Samuel M. White by Jacob Keller, Franklin Co.

1825 Jun 16   Ceasy, Mary and George Waggoner by John F. Solomon, Franklin Co.

1814 Mar 27   Center, Betsey and Robert Stanley by Wm. Creighton, JP, Pickaway Co.

1803 Jul 20   Chad, Margaret and David Watkins by Griffin Greene, JP, Washington
               Co.

1818 Jan 1   Chadwick, Betsy and Enos Grant by Noah Fidler, Licking Co.

1818 Aug 6   Chadwick, David and Sally Brooks by Rev. Noah Fidler, Licking Co.

1803 Nov 25   Chadwick, Nancy and Noah Arnold by John Brough, Esq., Washington Co.

1818 Jan 8   Chadwick, Samuel and Catherine Jackson by Noah Fidler, Licking Co.

1805 Jan 31   Chadwick, Susanna and Uriah Tippy by Wm. Harper, Washington Co.

1820 May 7   Chamberlain, Anna B. and Nicholas Chapman by Titan Kimble, JP,
               Washington Co.

1818 Feb 12   Chamberlain, Judah M. and Rhoda Ann McIntosh by Danl. H. Buell, JP,
               Washington Co.

1817 Sep 24   Chambers, Elizabeth and Thomas Goldsmith by Jacob Keller, Franklin
               Co.

1854 Mar 9   Chambers, Jane and John C. Dickson by Rev. A. Kingsbury, Putnam
               Presbyterian Church, Muskingum Co.

1827 Mar 29   Chambers, Margaret and Isaac Morris by W. T. Martin, Franklin Co.

1814 Mar 10   Champ, Abraham and Rose Walston by Rev. Geo. Alkire, Pickaway Co.

1892 Sep 21   Champ, Florence and W.V. Freeborn by Rev. George F. Moore, Putnam
               Presbyterian Church, Muskingum Co.

1805 Aug 8   Champ, Nancy and Jacob Crabb by Peter Jackson, JP, Ross Co.

1814 Mar 3   Champ, Polly and John Downing by Rev. Geo. Alkire, Pickaway Co.

1814 Jul 28   Champlin, Nancy and Alpha Devol by Obadiah Scott, JP, Washington Co.

1797 May 20   Chandevert, Marie Magdelaine and Michel Bernard by J. Gilman,
               Washington Co.

1796 Feb 15   Chandivert, Stephen and Madalane Brunie by Robert Safford, JP,
               Washington Co.

1816 Apr 1   Chandler, Benjamin and Sarah McGown by James Hoge, Franklin Co.

1803 Feb 20   Chandler, David and Hannah Babcock by Jesse Phelps, JP, Trumbull Co.

1821 May 19   Chandler, Henry and Sally Humiston by John Green, JP, Washington Co.

1820 Sep 7   Chandler, Sally and Faulkner Simons by Amos Wilson, Washington Co.

1820 May 14   Chaney, Hannah and John Carver by T. Lee, Franklin Co.

1825 Nov 24   Chaney, Sarah and Jacob Ruse by W.T. Martin, JP, Franklin Co.

1820 Feb 9   Channel, Jeremiah and Eliz. Stone by Rev. Noah Fidler, Licking Co.

1819 Apr 22   Channel, Jesse and Margaret Edwards by Thomas Carr, Licking Co.

1821 May 1   Channel, Prudence and George Stone by Noah Fidler, Licking Co.

1811 Jan 25   Channell, Joseph and Melley Channell by Wm. Haines, JP, Licking Co.

1815 Apr 9   Channell, Lavina and Phillip Siler by Noah Fidler, Licking Co.

1811 Jan 25   Channell, Melley and Joseph Channell by Wm. Haines, JP, Licking Co.

1812 Apr 9   Channell, Prady and John Montgomery by Noah Fidler, Licking Co.

1813 Nov 14   Chapin, Milly and Hezekiah Lewis by Rev. S.P. Robbins, Washington Co.

1804 Jul 19   Chaply, Susan and David Wilfong by Abm. Miller, Ross Co.

1800 Oct 21   Chapman, Betsey and Asael Griffin by Daniel Story, Clerk,Washington
               Co.

1861 Nov 10   Chapman, Carrie E. of Putnam and John A. Forsythe by Rev. A.
               Kingsbury, Putnam Presbyterian Church, Muskingum Co.

1799 Feb 28   Chapman, David and Peggy McCall by Peregrine Foster, JCCCP,
               Washington Co.

1810 Mar 30   Chapman, Elisha and Nancy Magee by Stephen Lindsly, Washington Co.

1879 Jan 1   Chapman, Erwin C. of Zanesville and Ella E. Ottinger of Putnam by
               Rev. George F. Moore, Putnam Presbyterian Church, Muskingum Co.

1799 Nov 13   Chapman, Ezra and Betsey Jones by Thos. Stanley, Washington Co.

1814 Dec 15   Chapman, Ezra and Mary Corner by Rev. S.P. Robbins, Washington Co.

1807 Nov 5   Chapman, Harvey and Ruth Hill by S.P. Robbins, Washington Co.

1808 Oct 5   Chapman, Hezekiah and Martha Allen by Stephen Lindsly, Washington Co.

1805 May 7   Chapman, Isaac and Sally Perkins by Stephen Lindly, Washington Co.

1818 Jul 21   Chapman, Levi and Eliza Sutherd by John Johnston, JP, Licking Co.

1874 Dec 24   Chapman, Maggie and Erastus A. Jennings, M.D., by Rev. A. Kings-
               bury, Putnam Presbyterian Church, Muskingum Co.

1860 Dec 31   Chapman, Milton H. and Josephine Sims by Rev. A. Kingsbury, Putnam
               Presbyterian Church, Muskingum Co.

1808 Apr 14   Chapman, Nathaniel and Amirila Stephens by Thos. Stanley, JP,
               Washington Co.

1820 May 7   Chapman, Nicholas P. and Anna B. Chamberlain by Titan Kimble, JP,
               Washington Co.

1821 Jun 21   Chapman, Norman and Sarah Parker by Samuel Bancroft, JP, Licking Co.

1808 Sep 22   Chapman, Parley and Polly Ogle by Amos Porter, JP, Washington Co.

1816 Jan 25   Chapman, R.R. and Phebe Stanbery by Recompence Stanbery, Franklin Co.

1820 May 4   Chapman, Ruth and Lyman Laflin by John D. Chamberlin, JP, Washington
               Co.

1816 Dec 1   Chapman, Samuel and Catharine Clark by Nath'l Hamilton, JP, Washing-
               ton Co.

1821 Mar 1   Chapman, Sarah and John Whitney by Saml. Beach, JP, Washington Co.

1821 11 mo 7   Chapman, Sarah and Benjamin Brown, Miami Monthly Meeting, Warren Co.

1820 Dec 28   Cahpman, Seldon and Elizabeth Stanley by Joel Tuttle, Jr., JP,
               Washington Co.

1816 Feb 27   Charles, Polly and John H. Evans by Geo. Callanhan, EMEC, Licking Co.

1821 Dec 7   Chase, Benjamin and Elvira Gloyd by Samuel Abbott, Franklin Co.

1818 Oct 22   Chase, Christeeny and Samuel Hedley by George Hells, JP, Franklin Co.

1822 Feb 6   Chase, John and Lydia Dennis by James M. Booth, JP, Washington Co.

1817 Feb 24   Chatick, Richard and Mary Drown by David Smithers, Washington Co.

1802 Jan 20   Cheadle, Asa and Nancy Hersey by Nehemiah Davis, Pastor, Washing-
               ton Co.

1816 Aug 22   Cheadle, Asa and Sally Divens by E. Townsend, JP, Washington Co.

1808 Feb 14   Cheadle, Cyrus and Abigail Van Clief by Asa Cheadle, JP, Washing-
               ton Co.

1809 Nov 16   Cheadle, Jesse and Henretta Morris by Stephen Lindlsy, Washington Co.

1810 Jan 27   Cheadle, John and Sarah Sills by Asa Cheadle, JP, Washington Co.

1809 Dec 25   Cheadle, Joseph and Sarah Hand by Asa Cheadle, JP, Washington Co.

1815 Dec 28   Cheadle, Lecty and James Davis by Richard Cheadle, JP, Washington Co.

1812 Jan 19   Cheadle, Patty and John Craft by Thomas White, JP, Washington Co.

1809 Nov 29   Cheadle, Sally and Elisha Harris by Asa Cheadle, JP, Washington Co.

1817 Mar 21   Cheadle, Tryphena and Oran Olney by Asa Cheadle, JP, Washington Co.

1818 Aug 13   Cheadle, Tryphena and Sylvanus Olney by Wm. Davis, Washington Co.

1817 Mar 12   Chenoweth, Benjamin and Fanny McKinsey by Samuel Dyer (another
               entry 16 Mar 1817), Franklin Co.

1811 Mar 10   Chenoweth, John and Margaret Ferguson by Rev. Simon Cokrane,
               Franklin Co.

1827 Oct 4   Chenoweth, Rachel and Jesse Wood by John Rathbone, JP, Franklin Co.

1814 Dec 29   Chenoweth, Ruth and Ira Wingfield Parish by John Turner, Franklin Co.

1828 Apr 3   Chenoweth, Ruth and James Davidson by Samuel P. Shaw, Franklin Co.

1804 Dec 6   Chenoweth, Sally and John Kerr by Arthur Chenoweth, JP, Ross Co.

1814 Jan 27   Chenoweth, Sarah and Moses Sutton by J.W. Patterson, JP, Licking Co.

1813 Jan 29   Chenworth, Mary and John Hains by Simon Cochran, JP, Franklin Co.

1855 Jul 3   Cherry, Catherine E. and Henry Evitt by Rev. A. Kingsbury, Putnam
               Presbyterian Church, Muskingum Co.

1897 Sep 22   Cherry, Edgar V. and Elizabeth Wilson both of White Cottage, O., by
               Rev. George F. Moore, Putnam Presbyterian Church, Muskingum Co.

1865 May 2   Cherry, Robert M. and Lucy T. McCarty by Rev. A. Kingsbury, Putnam
               Presbyterian Church, Muskingum Co.

1809 Jun 20   Chery, Aron and Barbra Beck by John Smith (date recorded), Franklin
               Co.

1817 Aug 18   Chesebra, Amos and Lydia Maxson by James Whitney, JP, Washington Co.

1811 Feb 14   Cheser, John and Sarah Enises by Thomas Morris, Franklin Co.

1827? --- -   Chester, Elias, Jr. and Ann M. Smith by George Jefferies, MG,
               Franklin Co.

1829 Jul 12   Chester, Franklin B. and Nancy Porter by Geo. Jefferies, Franklin Co.

1819 Apr 25   Chesters, Margaret and Danl. Wright by Jeremiah Converse, MG,
               Franklin Co.

1794 Mar 27   Chezeau, Auguste and Jeanne Francois Duraille by J.G. Petitt,
               Washington Co.

1818 Aug 23   Chidester, Benjamin and Betsey Burch by Amos Wilson, JP, Washington
               Co.

1822 Jan 31   Chidester, Sally and Rufus Carter by Samuel Beach, JP, Washington Co.

1814 Dec 8   Chidwick, Mary and Chancy Phillips by Rev. T. Harris, Licking Co.

1821 Feb 25   Childs, Isaac and Elizabeth Pope by Rev. Elnathan Raymond, Wash-
               ington Co.

1825 Aug 25   Childs, Sarah and John Giberson by Wm. Godman, JP, Franklin Co.

1827 Sep 3   Childs, Susannah and Joshua Burton by I. Gander, Franklin Co.

1826 Oct 15   Chiles, Susannah and Joseph Burton by I. Gander, Franklin Co.

1825 Mar 3   Chiles, William and Mary Britten by John F. Solomon, Franklin Co.

1819 Jun 28   Chilson, Harvy and Rachael Crown by Stephen Maynard, Franklin Co.

1816 Mar 14   Chilson, Jessie and Matilda Oden by Michael Patton, Franklin Co.

1806 Apr 6   Chinenton, John and Rebekah Patten by L. Barber, Washington Co.

1825 Jan 27   Chinoweth, Thomas and Rachel Perrin by Robert W. Riley, JP,
               Franklin Co.

1816 Dec 12   Chinowith, Joseph and Margaret Heth (or Heath) by Joseph Gorton,
               JP, Franklin Co.

1819 Nov 10   Chissman, Lillian and Solomon Wheeler by Noah Fidler, Licking Co.

1809 Aug 22   Chivington, John and Martha Dickey by Edwin Putnam, Washington Co.

1803 Sep 12   Choney, Andrew and Elizabeth Redding by John Hoddy, JP, Ross Co.

1866 Sep 12   Christian, Dr. J.M. and Josephine Norris by N.C.N. Dudley, St.
               Paul's Church, Marion, Marion Co.

1817 Mar 23   Christman, Moriah and James Barut (or Bariet) by Townsend Nichols,
               JP, Franklin Co.

1870 Nov 17   Christy, Charles T. and Sarah Meyer by I.B. Britton, St. Paul's
               Church, Marion, Marion Co.

1857 Oct --   Church, Aron and Ellen Dennis by C.S. Doolittle, St. Luke's Church,
               Granville, Licking Co.

1808 Sep 27   Church, Jemimah and Jeremiah Boardman by Alex'r Morrison, Franklin
               Co.

1811 Aug 27   Churchan, Margaret and Thomas Perkins by -----, Licking Co.

1818 Mar 15   Churchill, Solomon and Mary Pritchard by Sardine Stone, JP,
               Washington Co.

1826 Dec 19   Cinnett, Hannah and Livey Rettinhouse by James Hoge, Franklin Co.

1819 Nov 12   Ciscow, Charlot and Charles Dohaty by Jacob Smith (another entry
               21 Nov 1819), Franklin Co.

1853 Mar 3   Cisler, Catherine and Conrad Miller by Rev. John Boyd, St. Luke's
               Church, Marietta, Washington Co.

1849 Dec 2   Cisler, Elizabeth and Frederick Grohs by Rev. D.W. Tolford, St.
               Luke's Church, Marietta, Washington Co.

1853 Jan 3   Cisler, Joshua and Caroline Danker by Rev. John Boyd, St. Luke's
               Church, Marietta, Washington Co.

1820 Dec 30   Clapp, Jonathan T. and Addah Hillier by Samuel Bancroft, JP,
               (mar. Mar 31), Licking Co.

1805 Feb 3   Clarage, William and Mary Cox by Samuel Smith, Ross Co.

1805 May 8   Clark, Abraham and Sarah Jamison by Wm. Robinson, Ross Co.

1820 Dec 14   Clark, Almira S. and Hugh Cochrun by Rev. Saml. P. Robbins,
               Washington Co.

1818 May 16   Clark, Alsey and Isaac Griffeth by Jacob Keller, Franklin Co.

1813 Jan 6   Clark, Anna and William Clark (license date), Pickaway Co.

1809 Apr 24   Clark, Betsey and Martin Bailey by E.B. Dana, Washington Co.

1816 Dec 1   Clark, Catharine and Samuel Chapman by Nath'l. Hamilton, JP,
               Washington Co.

1891 Dec 29   Clark, Mrs. Clara G. and Samuel B. Bootes both of Zanesville by
               Rev. George F. Moore, Putnam Presbyterian Church, Muskingum Co.

1817 Sep 17   Clark, Dally and Samuel Gilson by R. Stansberry, JP, (another
               entry 17 Sep 1819), Franklin Co.

1818 Oct 8   Clark, Elizabeth and John White by Wm. How, JP, Jackson Co.

1825 May 4   Clark, Esther and Joseph Harris by Henry Mathews, Minister of the
               ME Church, Franklin Co.

1821 Aug 20   Clark, Fanny and Alexander McClure by Ami Lawrence, Washington Co.

1872 Feb 28   Clark, Fannie E. and Hiram B. Iams by Rev. John Boyd, St. Luke's
               Church, Marietta, Washington Co.

1809 Dec 7   Clark, Hannah and Oliver Reckord by E.B. Dana, Washington Co.

1816 Feb 24   Clark, Hannah and Lenard Goodrich by John Cunningham, JP, Licking
               Co.

1819 Mar 11   Clark, Hannah and Jeremiah Jones by Danl. G. Stanley, JP, Wash-
               ington Co.

1816 Jul 21   Clark, Henry and Patty Henington by Dan'l H. Buell, JP, Washing-
               ton Co.

1816 Aug 13   Clark, Hester and David Kyrk by Isaac Case, Franklin Co.

1826 Nov 9   Clark, Jeremiah and Jane Morris by James Hoge, Franklin Co.

1818 May 28   Clark, Jerusha Matilda and Harvey Clemons by Samuel Bancroft, JP,
               Licking Co.

1870 Jun 1   Clark, Joanna R. of Putnam and William W. Wiley of Orange,NJ., by
               Rev. A. Kingsbury, Putnam Presbyterian Church, Muskingum Co.

1798 Oct 19   Clark, John and Lorena Shepard by Josiah Munro, JP, Washington Co.

1803 Apr 21   Clark, John and Prudence Hody by Wm. Robinson, JP, Ross Co.

1825 Dec 9   Clark, John and Caslina Fisher by Benja. Britton, Franklin Co.

1811 Jun 19   Clark, John S. and Eliza Peese by Stephen Lindsly, Washington Co.

1816 Nov 12   Clark, Lucy and Enoch Traves by Rev. T. Harris, Licking Co.

1818 Dec 10   Clark, Lydia and Abel Dircon by Stephen Maynard, Franklin Co.

1810 Feb 27   Clark, M. and Thomas Spelman by Rev. T. Harris, Licking Co.

1827 Jun 27   Clark, Mary and Samuel Andrews by Henry Matthews, Franklin Co.

1821 Aug 30   Clark, Mindwell and Enoch Graves by Rev. T. Harris, Granville,
               Licking Co.

1818 Apr 16   Clark, Nancy and Lemuel Jones by John Green, MG, Licking Co.

1804 Jul 17   Clark, Obadiah and Sally Erving by D. Loring, Washington Co.

1817 Jun 12   Clark, Oliver and Jemima Bartlet by Isaac Griswold, Franklin Co.

1801 Oct 28   Clark, Polly and Joseph Moss at Burton by Turhand Kirtland,
               Justice of Court of Common Pleas, Trumbull Co.

1814 Nov 3   Clark, Polly and Jason R. Curtis by Dan'l H. Buell, Washington Co.

1818 Sep 18   Clark, Polly and Andrew Fouts by B.W. Talbot, JP, Washington Co.

1804 Aug 29   Clark, Priscilla and Robert McGuire by J. Gardner, JP, Ross Co.

1802 Jun 30   Clark, Rachel and Jonathan Brooks at Burton by Turhand Kirtland,
               JP, Trumbull Co.

1815 Mar 13   Clark, Rachel and Erasmas Jones by John Green, Preacher, Licking Co.

1813 Jun 9   Clark, Richard and Drusella Wood by John Turner, Franklin Co.

1805 Jan 30   Clark, Ruth and James Manwell by Enoch Shepard, Washington Co.

1813 May 12   Clark, Sally and Benajah Curtis by Rev. Stephen Lindsley, Wash-
               ington Co.

1804 Apr 3   Clark, Sarah and Jacob Foster by Wm. Davis, Ross Co.

1820 May 18   Clark, Seneca and Catharine Stull by John Patterson, Washington Co.

1804 Jan 25   Clark, Sidney and Wm. Niblack by Wm. Creighton, Ross Co.

1814 Dec 8   Clark, Strong and Rhoda Grewes by Rev. Timothy Harris, Licking Co.

1816 Jul 28   Clark, Uriah and Nancy Piper by Alexander Bassett, JP, Franklin Co.

1808 Aug 13   Clark, Wm. and Nancy Green by Arthur O'Harra, Franklin Co.

1813 Jan 6   Clark, William and Anna Clark (license date), Pickaway Co.

1840 Sep 10   Clark, William B. and Elizabeth A. Putnam, both of Union, by Rev.
               James Bonnar, St. Luke's Church, Marietta, Washington Co.

1877 Jun 10   Clark, William H. and Clara D. Guthrie by Rev. A. Kingsbury,
               Putnam Presbyterian Church, Muskingum Co.

1819 May 6   Clarke, Adelia and Daniel Howe by Geo. Evans, JP, Licking Co.

1873 Oct 1   Clarke, Cambridge C. and Alice L. Rolston by Rev. John Boyd, St.
               Luke's Church, Marietta, Washington Co.

1810 Apr 1   Clarke, Carley and James Johnston by Rev. Simon Cokrane, Franklin Co.

1806 Jul 31   Clarke, Charles and Deborah Monroe by Josiah McKinnie, Franklin Co.

1814 Oct 27   Clarke, George and Mary Sutton by Wm. Taylor, Licking Co.

1825 Dec 8   Clarke, Polly and William Patrick by William Godman, Franklin Co.

1817 Nov 24   Claton, John and Hannah Hennesy by John Green, Licking Co.

1816 Dec 1   Clause (or Clouse), Jacob and Elizabeth Dage (or Dague) by Jacob
              Smith, JP, Franklin Co.

1804 Apr 5   Clawson, Betsy and Wm. Staggs by Wm. Robinson, Ross Co.

1819 Mar 21   Clay, Daniel Jr. and Martha Davis by Dudley Davis, Washington Co.

1820 Apr 19   Clay, Deborah and William Wharf by Dudley Davis, JP, Washington Co.

1818 Oct 1   Claybaugh, Isaac and Margaret Houser by John P. Patterson, MG,
              Licking Co.

1828 Apr 15   Claybaugh, May Ann and Nicholas Watts by Sam'l Hamilton, Franklin Co.

1816 May 28   Claybaugh, Rachel and John Hinton by Mich Alis, Licking Co.

1819 May 4   Claypool, Leah and Aaron Lantz by Joseph Lockard, JP, Jackson Co.

1818 Sep 3   Clayton, Jonathan and Nancy Malone by Mich. Trout, JP, Licking Co.

1816 4 mo 3   Cleaver, Abigal and Josiah Rogers, Miami Monthly Meeting, Warren Co.

1824 4 mo 8   Cleaver, Ezekiel L. and Mary Taylor, Miami Monthly Meeting,
              Warren Co.

1820 5 mo 3   Cleaver, Lydia and Nathan Davis, Miami Monthly Meeting, Warren Co.

1806 7 mo 16 Cleaver, Martha and John Dutton, Miami Monthly Meeting, Warren Co.

1808 12 mo 14 Cleaver, Mary and William Gray, Miami Monthly Meeting, Warren Co.

1819 5 mo 5   Cleaver, Peter and Sarah Crew, Miami Monthly Meeting, Warren Co.

1814 Nov 11   Clemmaus, William and Lydia Rose by Rev. T. Harris, Licking Co.

1820 Aug 10   Clemmons, John Jr. and Ruth Peterson by Sam'l. W. McDowell, JP,
              Jackson Co.

1818 May 28   Clemons, Harvey and Jerusha Matilda Clark by Samuel Bancroft, JP,
              Licking Co.

1815 Apr 18   Clepper, Fany and Nicholas Tusing by Frederick Peterson, Franklin Co.

1829 Jan 25   Clevenger, Jacob and Sarah Rimer by John F. Solomon, Franklin Co.

1804 Mar 24   Clevenger, Polly and Reuben Crabb by Isaac Cook, JP, Ross Co.

1822 May 23   Clevenger, William and Elizabeth Henry by Richard Courtright,
              Franklin Co.

1817 Jul 27   Clevinger, Benjamin and Sarah Flemming by John Hite, MG, Franklin Co.

1814 Nov 20   Clifton, M. and J. Fettsworth by Jos. Hays, JP, Pickaway Co.

1826 Feb 2   Climer, Keziah and Adam Read by J. Gander, Franklin Co.

1816 Aug 17   Climons, Sarah and James Craigo by David Mitchell, JP, Jackson Co.

1880 Feb 17   Cline, Adeline and Robert Lynch by Rev. John Boyd, St. Luke's
              Church, Marietta, Washington Co.

1808 Nov 21   Cline, Catharine and John Frie by James Riggs, JP, Washington Co.

1807 Feb 18   Cline, Christina and Obediah Paden by Philip Witten, Washington Co.

1813 Jun 29   Cline, David and Sarah Mills by Anthony Sheets, JP, Washington Co.

1814 Jul 24   Cline, David and Rachel Brown by Anth'y Sheets,Esq., Washington Co.

1824 May 30   Cline, Ease and Seth Allen by Amos Neely, JP, Marion Co.

1796 Dec 29   Cline, Elisabeth and Robert Sutton by J. Munro, Washington Co.

1807 Feb 23   Cline, George and Christina Linn by James Riggs, JP, Washington Co.

1809 May 16   Cline, Rosannah and Solomon Tice by James Riggs, JP, Washington Co.

1808 Oct 13   Cline, Susanna and Anthony Evens by James Riggs, JP, Washington Co.

1803 Aug 9   Cline, Wm. and Mary Linn by Sam'l Williamson, JP, Washington Co.

1816 Sep 30   Cliver, Henry and Mary Humphrey by Zach. Carlisle, JP, Licking Co.

1818 Jul 30   Clock?, David and Margaret Gance by John Green, JP, Licking Co.

1816 Dec 15   Cloton, Jane and Adam Ile by John Green, Licking Co.

1816 Jan 25   Cloud, Fanny and Levin Fisher by John Cunningham, Licking Co.

1806 10 mo 15 Cloud, Joseph and Jane Mecoy, Miami Monthly Meeting, Warren Co.

1817 May 1   Cloud, Mary and Samuel Kinneman by John Spencer, JP, Licking Co.

1804 Apr 29   Clough, Aaron and Sarah Delano by D. Loring, Washington Co.

1816 Dec 1   Clouse (or Clause), Jacob and Elizabeth Dage (or Dague), by Jacob
               Smith, JP, Franklin Co.

1814 Aug 2   Clouse, Sally and Wm. Coheirt by Simeon Moore, Franklin Co.

1823 Sep 18   Clover, Henry Jr. and Maryann McKendree by Peter Clover, JP,
               Franklin Co.

1820 Jun 19   Clover, Jacob and Experience Hazle by Vinal Stewart, MG in
               Methodist Episcopal Church, Franklin Co.

1828 Oct 12   Clover, Margaret and Joshua Cole by Rev. H. Crabb, Franklin Co.

1824 Dec 23   Clover, Samuel and Sidney Walker by Henderson Crabb, Deacon MEC,
               Franklin Co.

1814 Sep 28   Clute, Sarah and Evan Pugh by Peter Pence, JP, Licking Co.

1827 Jan 9   Clymer, Abraham H. and Elizabeth Barnehart by Abram Williams, JP,
               Franklin Co.

1829 Mar 12   Clymer, Elizabeth and O. Brinkerhoof by Leroy Swornstead,
               Franklin Co.

1826 Feb 2   Clymer, Keziah and Adam Been by J. Gander, Franklin Co.

1825 May 26   Clymer, Massie and Mary Krist by John Davis, JP, Franklin Co.

1815 10 mo 4   Coate, Henry and Rebekah Wilson, Miami Monthly Meeting, Warren Co.

1816 Oct 26   Cobb (or Cabb), Catharine and John Cramer by James Taylor, JP,
               Franklin Co.

1818 Jun 18   Cobborly, Eliza and Harvey Richmond by L. Randall, JP, Licking Co.

1790 Mar 25   Cobern, Mary and Gilbert Devol by Benj. Tupper, Washington Co.

1796 Jul 18   Cobern, Phinehas and Patience Olney by Robert Oliver, JP, Wash-
               ington Co.

1790 Jul 14   Cobern, Susanna and William Mason by Benj. Tupper, Washington Co.

1819 Sep 19   Coble, Margaret and Joseph Nickison by Richard Courtright, JP,
               Franklin Co.

1814 Apr 6   Coble (or Cable), Mary and Daniel Cremar by James Taylor (another
               entry 9 Apr 1817), Franklin Co.

1828 Oct 16   Coble, Sally and James Piercy by Wm. Long, JP, Franklin Co.

1804 Sep 4   Cobler, David and Ann Freeman by Wm. Davis, JP, Ross Co.

1799 Jan 24   Coburn, Asa and Rhoda Baker by Robert Oliver, Washington Co.

1819 Mar 28   Coburn, Barzillia and Anna Cuddington by Thomas White, Washington Co.

1814 Nov 17   Coburn, Mary and Adelphia Webster by Thos. White, JP, Washington Co.

1817 May 1   Coburn, Phineas and Polly Spencer by John Patterson, JP, Washington
               Co.

1814 Oct 27   Cochran, Catharine and George Wright by Jos. Gorton, Franklin Co.

1804 Aug 30   Cochran, James and Rachel Kerr by W. Robinson, Ross Co.

1815 Oct 10   Cochran, William and Mary Barnes by T.D. Baird, Licking Co.

1818 Nov 18   Cochrane, Hester R. and James B. Gibson by Isaac Baker, JP, Jackson
               Co.

1867 Jan 10   Cockrell, Mattie E. and Romulus S.T. Russell by Rev. A. Kingsbury,
               Putnam Presbyterian Church, Muskingum Co.

1820 Dec 14   Cochrun, Hugh and Almira S. Clark by Rev. Saml. P. Robbins, Wash-
               ington Co.

1819 Dec 11   Cochrun, Susannah, dau of Simon, and Oliver Ellsworth (license
               date), Franklin Co.

1823 Feb 13   Codner, Hannah and John Hury (or Huey or Henry) by Richard Court-
               right, Franklin Co.

1822 Aug 8   Codner, Oliver and Margaret Brown by Richard Courtright, Franklin
               Co.

1814 Mar 17   Cody, Jeremiah and Dolly Martin by Rev. Geo. Alkire, Pickaway Co.

1818 Nov 25   Cody, Sally and Gilman Lincoln by Michael Patton, Franklin Co.

1817 Apr 23   Cody (or Cady), Samuel and Sarah Nicosan by Emmor Cox, Franklin Co.

1818 May 17   Coe, Betsy and Jonithan Sherman by Ezra Griswold, Franklin Co.

1815 Aug 29   Coe, Electe and James Kirk by Michael Patton, Franklin Co.

1824 May 13   Coe, Martha and Moses R. Spurgeon by Henry Matthews, Franklin Co.

1821 May 1   Coe, Mina and Cyrus Allen by James Hoge, Franklin Co.

1821 Aug 7   Coffman, Deborah and William Winchell by Seth Baker, JP, Washington
               Co.

1808 May 18   Coffman, Henry and Margaret Sells by Arthur O'Harra, Franklin Co.

1817 Sep 5   Coffman, Jacob M. and Polly Dolin by John Patterson, Washington Co.

1818 Jan 11   Coffman, Mariah and William Callahan by Titan Kimball, JP, Wash-
               ington Co.

1826 Feb 19   Coffman, Mattilda and Moses Davis by Charles Sells, JP, Franklin Co.

1812 Feb 15   Coffman, Polly and William Young by -----, Licking Co.

1821 Apr 5   Coffman, Rebecca and George Howard by John Green, JP, Licking Co.

1816 Aug 8   Coffman, Sarah and Joseph Graham by Noah Fidler, Licking Co.

1814 Nov 9   Coggshall, Job and Lydia Weatherby by Stephen Guthrie, Washington Co.

1817 Aug 25   Coit, Edwin Washington and Hulda Woodruff by John Cunningham, JP,
               Licking Co.

1823 Jun 27   Colb, George W. and Rebecca Stevenson by Richard Courtright,
               Franklin Co.

1817 Nov 2   Colburn, Ebenezer and Julia Ann Smith by Danl. H. Buell, JP,
               Washington Co.

1815 Jan 3   Coldson, Henry and Elizabeth Mitchell by Chas. Cade, JP, Pickaway Co.

1814 Dec 20   Coldson, Margaret and William Ater by Chas. Cade, JP, Pickaway Co.

1807 12 mo 10 Coldwell, James and Martha Townsend, Miami Monthly Meeting, Warren
               Co.

1801 May 2   Coldwell, Jane and Samuel S. Stevart by Philip Witten, Washington Co.

1820 Jul 30   Cole, Andrew and Mary Olney by John Green, JP, Washington Co.

1819 May 30   Cole, Ashia and Lewis Finch by Philip Cole, JP, Washington Co.

1821 Jan 25   Cole, Clara and William Hardy by Philip Cole, JP, Washington Co.

1812 May 24   Cole, Cynthia and Amos Delanl by Dan'l Goodno, Washington Co.

1822 Jul 20   Cole, David and Catharine Shofe by John F. Solomon, Franklin Co.

1811 May 15   Cole, Deborah and James Withee by Philip Cole, Washington Co.

1825 Apr 7   Cole, Demit and Martha Jermon by John F. Solomon, Franklin Co.

1821 Jul 8   Cole, Dolly and Henry Thompson by Walter Curtis, JP, Washington Co.

1819 Oct 16   Cole, Elias and Sibel Matilda Hollister by Bial Stedman, JP,
               Washington Co.

1822 Feb 24   Cole, Harty and Melvin Lowry by Philip Cole, JP, Washington Co.

1818 Apr 18   Cole, Hezekiah and Cathrin Hagar (or Hagan) by Thos. B. Patterson,
               Franklin Co.

1807 Jun 23   Cole, John and Nancy Harden by Levi Barber, Washington Co.

1815 Mar 16   Cole, John and Milla Lewis by Alex Rowen, JP, Pickaway Co.

1805 Nov 13   Cole, Joseph and Polly Case by John Brough, JP, Washington Co.

1811 Feb 7   Cole, Joshua and Susana Rynear (license date), Pickaway Co.

1828 Oct 12   Cole, Joshua and Margaret Clover by Rev. H. Crabb, Franklin Co.

1814 Mar 27   Cole, Levi and Sally Duncan by Rev. S. Lindsley, Washington Co.

1819 Feb 7   Cole, Lydia and Horace Curtis by Stephen Guthrie, JP, Washington Co.

1816 Jan 21   Cole, Malachi and Romantha Harris by James Sharp, JP, Washington Co.

1813 Dec 23   Cole, Mary and Darick Bierly by Matth. Mitchell, JP, Pickaway Co.

1816 Jun 15   Cole, Mary and Owens Jett by Isaac Humphreys, JP, Washington Co.

1814 Jul 13   Cole, Nancy and Thomas Pattin by Isaac Humphrys, Washington Co.

1821 Apr 5   Cole, Nathan and Levina Bryan by Danl. H. Buell, JP, Washington Co.

1811 Mar 21   Cole, Polly and William Burton (license date), Pickaway Co.

1814 Apr 14   Cole, Polly and Michael W. Rogers by J.W. Patterson, Licking Co.

1821 Aug 23   Cole, Rachel and John Hornbaker by John F. Solomon, Franklin Co.

1812 Jan 28   Cole, Sampson and Polly Duncan by Stephen Lindsly, Washington Co.

1845 May 18   Cole, Sarah E. and George Howe by Rev. Edward Winthrop, St. Luke's
              Church, Marietta, Washington Co.

1882 Aug 1   Cole, Thomas H. and Rhoda Mowery by Rev. John Boyd, St. Luke's
              Church, Marietta, Washington Co.

1817 Apr 13   Coleman, Asa and Julian Avalina Griffin by Daniel Baker, JP,
              Licking Co.

1802 Aug 2   Coleman, Daniel and Mary Nott by Robert Oliver, JP, Washington Co.

1818 Aug 5   Coleman, Elijah and Nancy Jennings by Pelatiah White, Washington Co.

1799 Feb 14   Coleman, Elizabeth and Hezekiel Davis by Robert Oliver, Washington
              Co.

1797 Nov 19   Coleman, Peggy and John Niswanger by Josiah Munro, Washington Co.

1800 Aug 18   Coleman, Thomas and Jane Raridin by D. Loring, JCCCP, Washington Co.

1818 May 20   Colemans, Deborah and John Praither by David Mitchell, JP, Jackson
              Co.

1813 Mar 26   Coleston, Nancy and John Muskings (license date), Pickaway Co.

1812 Apr 5   Coley, William H. and Mary Vincent by Edwin Putnam, JP, Washington
              Co.

1814 Aug 2   Colheirt, Wm. and Sally Clouse by Simeon Moore, Franklin Co.

1803 Nov 1   Collans, Sarah and Martin Sheets by Samuel Williamson, JP, Wash-
              ington Co.

1819 Feb 19   Collar, Abraham and Rebecca Donaldson by James Holmes, JP, Licking
              Co.

1819 Oct 31   Collens, Hannah and Conel Boyl by Townsend Niccles, JP, Franklin Co.

1870 Jun 26   Collins, Eliza and Clarence Stanley by Wm. Bower, St. Luke's Church,
              Granville, Licking Co.

1821 Jul 10   Collins, Eunice and David Halsey by Ami Lawrence, JP, Washington Co.

1816 Oct 6   Collins, Joanna and John Sparling by Cyrus Ames, Washington Co.

1807 Feb 3   Collins, John and Rachel Edwards by Philip Witten, Washington Co.

1816 Nov 21   Collins, John and Charlotte Williams by Ezra Griswold, JP,
              Franklin Co.

1813 Nov 7   Collins, Margaret and William Starten by N. Hamilton, Washington Co.

1821 Apr 10   Collins, Mary and William Needles by Richard Courtright, JP, Franklin
              Co.

1810 Oct 1   Collins, Nancy and Stephen Page by William Brundridge, Franklin Co.

1812 Aug 16   Collins, Nelly and Jesse Fleming by Henry Jolly, JP, Washington Co.

1884 Jun 30   Collis, George B. of Corning, O., and Isabel Cunningham of Putnam,
              by Rev. George F. Moore, Putnam Presbyterian Church, Muskingum
              Co.

1814 Jan 10   Colly, Lucy and Isaac Munkton by Isaac Baker, Esq., Washington Co.

1820 Nov 7   Colmon, Elizabeth and Peter Hins by Jacob Antime, Franklin Co.

1803 Apr 25   Colon, Ruth and Joseph Holdron by Sam'l Williamson, Washington Co.

1819 Sep 3   Colter, Polly and John Barner by Rev. Noah Fidler, Licking Co.

1824? Mar 25 Colvin, David and Mary Soule by Aristarchus Walker, Franklin Co.

1815 Oct 31   Colvin, Rachael and Simons Shepherd by Recompence Stanbery,
              Franklin Co.

1828 Dec 4   Colwell, Eleanor and Phillip Rhoades by Geo. Beals, JP, Franklin Co.

1797 May 10   Colvin, Sam'l and Sarah Daly by J. Pierce, JCCCP, Washington Co.

1814 Sep 4   Comb, Jacob and Catherine Stotts by Wm. Taylor, Licking Co.

1809 Oct 20   Combs, Ann and Grandison Norman by John Brough, JP, Washington Co.

1820 Mar 1   Combs, Pricilla and John Baker by T.D. Bierd, Licking Co.

1803 Dec 22   Comer, John and Sarah Barber by John Odle, JP, Ross Co.

1803 Jun 2   Comer, Mary and Samuel Richardson by Jos. Gardner, JP, Ross Co.

1803 Nov 28   Comer, Rebecca and Elexander Graves by John Odle, JP, Ross Co.

1804 Jul 5   Comer, Wm. and Nancy Barbee both of Jefferson Tp. by J. Gardner,
              Ross Co.

1811 Aug 6   Comes, James and Polly Miller by John Greene, Washington Co.

1825 Mar 9   Comines, Anthony and Rachel Rodgers by Joseph Clara, JP, Marion Co.

1826 May 29   Commans, Plina and Elizabeth Morrow by Joseph Baker, MG, Jackson Co.

1826 Jan 6   Compona, Joseph and Burinde Walter by Eigah Smurgan, Franklin Co.

1820 Apr 15   Comstack, Julia and David Camp by Ezra Comstack, JP, Franklin Co.

1837 Oct 25   Comstock, Cicero and S.C. Stiles by Rev. E. Burr, St. John's
              Church, Worthington, Franklin Co.

1844 Feb 8   Comstock, Cicero and Caroline Griswold by Rev. R.S. Elder, St.
              John's Church, Worthington, Franklin Co.

1820 Aug 31   Comstock, Hannah and Eben Boalt by Wm. Rand, JP, Washington Co.

1806 5 mo 15 Comton, Elizabeth and John Horner, Miami Monthly Meeting, Warren Co.

1807 3 mo 18 Comton, John and Ann Peddrick, Miami Monthly Meeting, Warren Co.

1805 11 mo 27 Comton, Joseph and Christiana Steddom, Miami Monthly Meeting,
              Warren Co.

1806 12 mo 18 Comton, Rebekah and Willis Whitson, Miami Monthly Meeting,
              Warren Co.

1817 Dec 25   Conard, Hannah and Frederick Iles by John Green, Licking Co.

1819 Jan 20   Conard, Jane and James Russel by John Green, MG, Licking Co.

1813 Dec 12   Conbre, Ebenezer and Mary Fetters by John B. Johnston, Franklin Co.

1820 Nov 9   Condran, James and Peggy Haruff by Eli C. King, JP, Franklin Co.

1867 Oct 22   Cone, Joseph S. and Anna Reppert by Rev. John Boyd, St. Luke's Church, Marietta, Washington Co.

1871 May 23   Conger, C.C. and Sarah A. Hall by Rev. John Boyd, St. Luke's Church, Marietta, Washington Co.

1825 Oct 26   Conklin, Eliza and Sam'l Holmes by Robert Hopkins, JP, Marion Co.

1848 Aug 15   Conkling, Jane and Hon. James Borden by W.C. French, St. Luke's Church, Granville, Licking Co.

1817 Jan 1   Conkrite, Richard and Hannah Gardner by David Smithers, Washington Co.

1804 Dec 27   Connal, Abner and Jane Shannon by Wm. Harper, JP, Washington Co.

1818 Jan 20   Connel, Mary and Dennis Hurly by James Holmes, JP, Licking Co.

1814 Sep 1   Connelly, Mary and David Crow by John Scott, JP, Pickaway Co.

1813 Apr 20   Conner, Hannah and Robert Parker by Jacob Hahn, JP, Licking Co.

1814 Dec 17   Conner, Isaac and Rachel Kersey by Z. Carlisle, JP, Licking Co.

1818 Aug 31   Conner, James and Catharine Morison by Robert Elliott, Franklin Co.

1813 Mar 25   Conner, Martha and George Hunter by Rev. James Scott, Licking Co.

1816 Aug 19   Conner, Sally and Nathan Parker by John Johnston, JP, Licking Co.

1800 Apr 3   Converse, Daniel and Sally Munro by D. Loring, Washington Co.

1821 Dec 19   Converse, Daniel and Rachel Cook by -----, Franklin Co.

1818 Sep 24   Conway, Ester and Shubel Little by Zach. Carlisle, JP, Licking Co.

1805 Jan 3   Converse, Hannah and Cook Devol by Jacob Lindly, Washington Co.

1795 Oct 18   Converse, James and Lois Olney by Robert Oliver, Washington Co.

1791 Sep 26   Convis, Abigail and Ben Biddle by Benj. Tupper, Washington Co.

1791 Sep 26   Convis, Easter and David Willson by Benj. Tupper, Washington Co.

1822 Oct 21   Conway, James and Sarah Needles by Richard Courtright, Franklin Co.

1820 Feb 17   Conway, John and Sibyl Brooker by Amos Wilson, JP, Washington Co.

1816 Sep 2   Cook, Abigail and John Abrams by Geo. Hoover, JP, Licking Co.

1814 Nov 3   Cook, Barker and Polly McClintock by Dan'l H. Buell, Washington Co.

1820 May 25   Cook, Frederick and Civilla Reed by Noah Fidler, Licking Co.

1821 Sep 6   Cook Elisa and Samuel English by Noah Fidler, Licking Co.

1807 11 mo 26 Cook, James and Eleanor Maddock, Miami Monthly Meeting, Warren Co.

1817 Apr 13   Cook, Joanna and Thomas Perfect by Geo. Hoover, JP, Licking Co.

1805 Nov 16   Cook, John and Letitia Ross by Samuel Edwards, Ross Co.

1805 11 mo 27 Cook, John and Dinah Spray, Miami Monthly Meeting, Warren Co.

1814 May 19   Cook, Johnson P. and Mary Maxon by Derrick Stone, Esq., Washington Co.

1817 Nov 23   Cook, Joseph and Rhoda Cook by Rev. John Brown, Washington Co.

1812 Nov 29   Cook, Joseph Jr. and Clarissa Devol by Peter Howe, JP, Washington Co.

1819 4 mo 7   Cook, Levi and Ann Hasket, Miami Monthly Meeting, Warren Co.

1820 Nov 13   Cook, Lucy and Wesley Newman by Eli C. King, Franklin Co.

1819 Mar 1   Cook, Pardon and Polly Russell by Sardine Stone, JP, Washington Co.

1806 11 mo 20 Cook, Phebe and Francis Mador, Miami Monthly Meeting, Warren Co.

1814 Apr 4   Cook, Philiela and Ezra Griswold by Ezra Griswold, JP, Franklin Co.

1821 Dec 19   Cook, Rachel and Daniel Converse by -----, Franklin Co.

1817 Apr 27   Cook, Rebecca and Elisha Rose by Samuel Dye, JP, Washington Co.

1807 Aug 19   Cook, Rhoda and Samuel P. Hildreth by D. Loring, Washington Co.

1817 Nov 23   Cook, Rhoda and Joseph Cook by Rev. John Brown, Washington Co.

1818 3 mo 4   Cook, Ruth and Seth Cook, Miami Monthly Meeting, Warren Co.

1799 Oct 10   Cook, Sally and Levi Johnson by D. Loring, Washington Co.

1818 3 mo 4   Cook, Seth and Ruth Cook, Miami Monthly Meeting, Warren Co.

1811 Jan 17   Cook, Silas and Sally Mitchell by Stephen Lindsly, Washington Co.

1812 9 mo 2   Cook, Stephen and Elizabeth Evans, Miami Monthly Meeting, Warren Co.

1820 Jun 9   Cook Tillinghast and Betsey Russell by Sardine Stone, JP, Washington
               Co.

1815 Nov 9   Cook, William and Nancy Barton by Solomon Goss, Washington Co.

1850 Mar 13   Cooke, Jonathan R. and Susan M. Dodge by Rev. D.W. Tolford, St.
               Luke's Church, Marietta, Washington Co.

1797 Oct 10   Cooke, Phebe and Moses Huet by Peregrine Foster, JCCCP, Washington
               Co.

1822 Jul 3   Cooken, Eliza and William Brown by C. Henkel, Franklin Co.

1811 May 15   Cool, Peter and Sophia Harris by W. Haines, JP, Licking Co.

1820 May 20   Cooley, Asa and Chrintina McInturf by Elijah Dorsey, Licking Co.

1802 Jan 13   Cooley, Easter and Stephen Buckingham by I's Peine, JP, Washington
               Co.

1819 Feb 11   Cooley, Elizabeth and Bartemans French by Thomas Soctt, JP,
               Jackson Co.

1820 Mar 11   Cooley, Mathew and Nancy Cuppleberger by Samuel Bancroft, JP,
               Licking Co.

1818 Nov 19   Cooley, William and Sophia Havens by Rev. Wm. Davis, Washington Co.

1818 Feb 12   Cooly, Candia and Samy Parr by Alex Holden, JP, Licking Co.

1825 Mar 17   Coon, Fronica and Aberham Brown by Abner Bent, JP, Marion Co.

1813 Mar 10   Coon, George and Sarah Cutler (license date), Pickaway Co.

1870 Nov 3   Coon, George W. and Clara Koontz by Rev. A. Kingsbury, Putnam
               Presbyterian Church, Muskingum Co.

1805 Apr 13   Coon, Hanah and Michael Delcever by Nathaniel Wyatt, Ross Co.

1811 Aug 16   Coon, Peggy and Jacob Helm (license date), Pickaway Co.

1815 Mar 28   Coon (or Caom), Rebecca and George Miller by Elijah Austin, JP,
               Franklin Co.

1804 Jun 19   Coone, Adam and Hannah Marquis by Geo. Williams, Ross Co.

1826 Mar 16   Cooney (or Coorey), Asa and Nancy McCauly by Henry Matthews,
               Franklin Co.

1822 Aug 23   Coonrad, Margaret and Solomon Kious by Wm. C. Duff, Franklin Co.

1814 Mar 15   Coonrod, Betsey and James McConnel by Wm. Jones, JP, Pickaway Co.

1803 Jan 30   Coonrod, Eve of Cleveland and Daniel Kerker by James Kingsbury, JP,
               Trumbull Co.

1828 Jan 10   Coons, Betsey and Isaac Creighton by John Hanover, Franklin Co.

1827 Jul 29   Coons, Rachel and Jacob Shatts by John Hanover, Franklin Co.

1826 May 18   Cooper, Abitha and Nathan L.L. Latimore by John McCan, Franklin Co.

1813 Aug 26   Cooper, Alexander and Elen Hickman by J. Marshall, Franklin Co.

1826 Oct 6   Cooper, Archibald and Margaret R. Kilgore by James Hoge, Franklin Co.

1815 Jan 12   Cooper, Catherine and Jacob Hines by Chas. Cade, JP, Pickaway Co.

1810 Dec 6   Cooper, Comfort and John Hickman by James Marshall, Franklin Co.

1814 Jun 9   Cooper, Darkey and Ephram Johnston by A. O'Harra, Franklin Co.

1820 Sep 21   Cooper, Jacob and Lydia Oakley by John D. Chamberlain, JP,
               Washington Co.

1806 Mar 5   Cooper, Joel and Jane McMullin by J. Gardner, JP, Ross Co.

1822 Feb 17   Cooper, Lemuel and Lucy Deruse by Rev. James McAboy, Washington Co.

1817 Aug 28   Cooper, Mayry and John Courson by Joseph Grate, Franklin Co.

1800 Dec 16   Cooper, Polly and William Trotter by Robt. Safford, JP, Washington
               Co.

1819 Jan 7   Cooper, Samuel and Polly Postle by Joseph Grate, Franklin Co.

1819 Aug 19   Cooper, Samuel and Caroline Thrall by Spencer Wright, JP, Licking Co.

1812 Feb 6   Cooper, Susan and William Hopper by James Marshall, Franklin Co.

1815 Dec 14   Cooperider, Andrew and Susannah Brown by Alex. Morrison, Licking Co.

1820 Aug 17   Cooperider, William and Susannah Crouse by Andrew Henhel, MG,
               Licking Co.

1825 Apr 15   Copperstone, Mary and Joseph Harper by Conrad Roth, JP, Marion Co.

1826 Mar 16   Coorey (or Cooney), Asa and Nancy McCauly by Henry Matthews,
               Franklin Co.

1826 Apr 13   Corbit, James and Sarah Wright by John Stephenson, JP, Jackson Co.

1826 Apr 11   Corey, James K. and Mariah S. Lampson by James Hoge

1820 Apr 6   Corey, Mary and Richard Ross by Thomas White, JP, Washington Co.

1791 Apr 17   Corey, Polly and David Welles by Benj. Tupper, Washington Co.

1791 Feb 17   Corey, Thomas and Nancy Welles by Benj. Tupper, Washington Co.

1818 Oct 8   Corn, Jesse and Uley Harmon by John Norton, JP, Jackson Co.

1825 Dec 15   Corn, John Jr. and Anna Miller by Vincent Southard, JP, Jackson Co.

1826 Oct 5   Corn, Lucy and Jephthea Mussey by John Shumate, JP, Jackson Co.

1826 Nov 2   Corn, Peter and Rebecca Mussey by John Shumate, JP, Jackson Co.

1824 Dec 28   Corn, Wm. and Mary Massy by John Shumate, JP, Jackson Co.

1810 Dec 21   Cornell, Meney and Samuel Carpenter by Rev. T. Harris, Licking Co.

1814 Dec 4   Cornell, Nancy and Alex Holmes by G. Callanhan, EMEC, Licking Co.

1810 Jun 18   Cornell, Naomi and L. Nathan Carpenter by Rev. T. Harris, Licking Co.

1810 Jun 6   Cornell, Sylvanus and Sally Carpenter by Rev. T. Harris, Licking Co.

1814 Mar 24   Cornell, Wm. and Persilla Inks by John Stevenson, Franklin Co.

1806 Mar 18   Corner, Ann and George Nulton by Robert Oliver, JP, Washington Co.

1810 Feb 22   Corner, Ann Marie and Richard Miner by Stephen Lindsly, Washington
               Co.

1844 Feb 7   Corner, Celinda and John Percival Sanford by Rev. Edward Winthrop,
               St. Luke's Church, Marietta, Washington Co.

1820 Nov 19   Corner, Edwin and Rachel Howe by Stephen Lindsley, Washington Co.

1807 Nov 29   Corner, George and Susanna Burlinggame by S.P. Robbins, Washington
               Co.

1806 Feb 23   Corner, Mary and Whittington McGrath by Stephen Lindley, Washington
               Co.

1796 Aug 20   Corner, Mary and Israel Stone by J. Gilman, Washington Co.

1814 Dec 15   Corner, Mary and Ezra Chapman by Rev. S.P. Robbins, Washington Co.

1805 Jul 4   Corner, Mathew and Ann Ashcroft by Jacob Lindly, Washington Co.

1881 May 4   Corner, Nancy E. and Franklin C. Palmer by Rev. John Boyd, St.
               Luke's Church, Marietta, Washington Co.

1811 Nov 21   Corner, Wm. and Sarah Maxson by Stephen Lindsly, Washington Co.

1803 Dec 4   Cornes, Sarah and James Flagg by Stephen Lindly, Washington Co.

1826 Aug --   Cornett, Elizabeth and William Strickley by I. Gander, Franklin Co.

1826 Apr 20   Cornett, Polly and Abram Miller by J. Gander, Franklin Co.

1811 Oct 10   Cornish, Abraham and Lydia Lawrence by Wm. Gray, JP, Washington Co.

1819 Jan 30   Corns, Henry and Mary Pugh by Salmon N. Cook, JP, Washington Co.

1817 Aug 31   Corns, John and Polly Danley by Salmon N. Cook, JP, Washington Co.

1808 Dec 31   Corp, Benj. and Mary Thornley by Stephen Lindsly, Washington Co.

1816 Aug 27   Corp, John and Elizabeth Dodd by Rev. Saml. P. Robbins, Washington
               Co.

1810 Aug 17   Cornwell, Gideon and Julia Sobdate by J.W. Patterson, Licking Co.

1813 Jan 19   Corwin, Oliver and Polly McConnell (license date), Pickaway Co.

1811 Nov 3   Corwin, Ruth and John Atchinson (license date), Pickaway Co.

1818 Aug 18   Corwin, Susanna and William McNeil by Danl. H. Buell, JP, Washington Co.

1811 Feb 11   Cory, Abija and Anna Martin (license date), Pickaway Co.

1813 Apr 18   Cory, Charles S. and Anna White by Thomas White, JP, Washington Co.

1807 May 2   Coton, Lucy and John Parker by Stephen Lindsly, Washington Co.

1816 Jan 7   Cotter, Margaret and Coleman Holdren by Wm. Dana, JP, Washington Co.

1845 May 8   Cotton, Dr. John T. and Sarah A. Fitzhugh both of Jackson Co., Va., by Rev. Edward Winthrop, St. Luke's Church, Marietta, Washington Co.

1804 Feb 12   Cotton, Polly White and Moses Norton by John Johnston, JP of Pope Twp., Ross Co.

1819 Jan 22   Coulter, Eliza and Wilfred Owings by Noah Fidler, Licking Co.

1880 Sep 30   Coulter, Florence O. of Putnam and Benson L. Gray of Zanesville by Rev. George F. Moore, Putnam Presbyterian Church, Muskingum Co.

1817 Oct 2   Coulter, John and Nancy Hughes by Geo. Callanhan, EMEC, Licking Co.

1801 Jan 26   Coulter, Mary and George De Pu by E. Cutler, JP, Washington Co.

1820 Sep 19   Coulter, Samuel and Margaret Myers by Noah Fidler, MG, Licking Co.

1804 Sep 26   Countriman, Chrislar and Elias William by Wm. Davis, JP, Ross Co.

1803 Jul 20   Countriman, Elizabeth and James Washburn by Wm. Davis, JP, Ross Co.

1820 Sep 19   Coursen, Benjamin and Elizabeth Bowers by Charles Bradford, JP, Licking Co.

1817 Aug 28   Courson, John and Mayry Cooper by Joseph Grate, Franklin Co.

1826 Oct 26   Courson, Poly and William Mitchell by Reuben Golliday, JP, Franklin Co.

1796 Nov 22   Courtney, Neal and Polly McLeane by J. Munro, JP, Washington Co.

1823 Mar 5   Courtright, Julian and Sherman Travis by Robert Boyd, JP, Franklin Co.

1816 Jun 25   Courtright, Nely and Gilbert Smith by Joseph Grate, Franklin Co.

1816 Apr 14   Courtright, Sally and John Smith by Daniel Brunk, Franklin Co.

1826 Aug 10   Courtwright, Jemima and Moses Mitchel (or Michel) by Tracy Willcox, Franklin Co.

1822 Mar 24   Cowan, Simeon P. and Mary Ann Worstell by Dan'l H. Buell, Washington Co.

1818 Nov 9   Cowden, Margaret and Abiathar N. Taylor by James Hoge, Franklin Co.

1817 Nov 12   Cowee, Tabitha and John Crooks by John Patterson, JP, Washington Co.

1820 Jul 25   Cowee, William and Hannah M. Vanvaley by John Patterson, JP, Washington Co.

1806 Jun 9   Cowgill, Axey and Olivel Still by Ezekiel Brown, JP, Franklin Co.

1804 Jan 12   Cowgle, Alexander and Mary Crow by Isaac Dawson, Ross Co.

1842 May 1	Cowles, Cynthia and Henry L. Richards by Rev. R.S. Elder, St. John's Church, Worthington, Franklin Co.
1879 Dec 3	Cowles, Jessie E. and Francis L. Rowlands by Rev. John Boyd, St. Luke's Church, Marietta, Washington Co.
1827 Dec 25	Cowles, Mary H. and Byron Kilbourn by Marcus T.C. Wing, Franklin Co.
1818 Sep 27	Cowles, Renssalaer W. and Laura Kilbourn by Rev. Philander Chase, Franklin Co.
1817 Apr 17	Cox, Ann and John Ramsey by George Hays, Franklin Co.
1806 Mar 31	Cox, Catharine and Cornelius Neff by J. Gardner, JP, Ross Co.
1805 Aug 1	Cox, Charrety and Nathan Moffett by J. Gardner, JP, Ross Co.
1817 2 mo 5	Cox, David and Mary Cox, Miami Monthly Meeting, Warren Co.
1824 Apr 12	Cox, Elizabeth and John Emmerson by W.T. Martin, Franklin Co.
1872 Jan 11	Cox, Emily Jane and Melvin D. Douglass by Rev. John Boyd, St. Luke's Church, Marietta, Washington Co.
1817 Jan 23	Cox, Hannah and William Ramsey by George Hays, JP, Franklin Co.
1813 9 mo 1	Cox, Jonathan and Charity Hollingsworth, Miami Monthly Meeting, Warren Co.
1879 Jan 4	Cox, Lizzie M. of Zanesville and Theodore G. Sullivan of Providence, R.I., by Rev. George F. Moore, Putnam Presbyterian Church, Muskingum Co.
1805 Feb 3	Cox, Mary and William Clarage by Samuel Smith, Ross Co.
1817 2 mo 5	Cox, Mary and David Cox, Miami Monthly Meeting, Warren Co.
1826 Oct 15	Cox, Mary and John Ramsey by John F. Solomon, Franklin Co.
1803 Jun 23	Cox, Nancy and James Bolton by E. Langham, JP, Ross Co.
1803 Apr 7	Cox, Rachel and William Rudie by Felix Renick, Ross Co.
1805 Feb 5	Cox, Rebecah and Solomon Moffett by J. Gardner, JP, Ross Co.
1823 Jun 4	Cox, Rebeckah and Epraim Stephens by W.T. Martin, JP, Franklin Co.
1826 Jan 2	Cox, Samuel and Elizabeth Ellison by Solomon Redfern, JP, Jackson Co.
1849 Oct 11	Cox, Samuel S. of Cincinnati and Julia Ann Buckingham of Putnam by Rev. A. Kingsbury, Putnam Presbyterian Church, Muskingum Co.
1867 Mar 8	Cox, Susan V. and John B. Triplett by Rev. John Boyd, St. Luke's Church, Marietta, Washington Co.
1829 Jan 15	Cox, William and Sarah Ward by George Jefferies, Franklin Co.
1820 Apr 3	Cozad, Abraham and Charity Davis by Joseph Lockland, JP, Jackson Co.
1818 Nov --	Cozad, Elizabeth and Ezekiel W. Roberts by David Mitchell, JP, Jackson Co.
1826 Apr 4	Cozad, William and Martha Wells by Solomon Redfern, JP, Jackson Co.
1806 Mar 20	Crabb, Edward and Nancy Smith by Peter Jackson, JP, Ross Co.
1805 Aug 8	Crabb, Jacob and Nancy Champ by Peter Jackson, JP, Ross Co.
1806 Jan 30	Crabb, Jeremiah and Annabelea Anderson by Peter Jackson, JP, Ross Co.
1804 Mar 24	Crabb, Reuben and Polly Clevenger by Isaac Cook, JP, Ross Co.

1813 Feb 24   Crable, Polly and Samuel Phoebus (license date), Pickaway Co.

1819 Nov 23   Crabtree, James and Alsay Throckmorton by Sam'l McDowell, Jackson Co.

1817 Aug 21   Crabtree, Louis and Anna Dixon by Thomas Holland, JP, Jackson Co.

1825 Apr 1   Crabtree, Samuel and Elizabeth Murphy by David W. Walton, JP,
               Jackson Co.

1826 Apr 23   Crabtree, Sarah and David Traxler by J.B. Gilleland, JP, Jackson Co.

1818 Feb 28   Craford, Isaac and Agnus Frasure by Tho. B. Patterson, Franklin Co.

1812 Jan 19   Craft, John and Patty Cheadle by Thomas White, JP, Washington Co.

1815 Oct 1   Craft, Ridgway and Esther Bailey by James Sharp, JP, Washington Co.

1825 Mar 25   Crag, John and Peggy McIntire by Joseph Clara, JP, Marion Co.

1821 Jun 23   Crage, Rachel and Charles P. Hemsted by Ebenezer Washburn, VDM,
               Franklin Co.

1823 11 mo 6   Craig, Letitia and Thomas Kersey, Miami Monthly Meeting, Warren Co.

1813 Jun 1   Craig, Mary and William Davis (license date), Pickaway Co.

1827 10 mo 3   Craig, Mary Ann and Benjamin Brown, Miami Monthly Meeting, Warren Co.

1801 Feb 17   Craig, Samuel and Fanny Johnson by Robt. Safford, Washington Co.

1819 Jan 28   Craig, Samuel and Elizabeth Jenkins by Samuel McDowell, JP,
               Jackson Co.

1824 Feb 5   Craig, Samuel and Patsy Ann McCray by Samuel Carrick, JP, Jackson
               Co.

1818 Mar 12   Craig, Thomas and Elizabeth Deavon by Isaac Baker, JP, Jackson Co.

1819 Feb 11   Craige, Della and Joseph Eubanks by D. Mitchell, JP, Jackson Co.

1820 Oct 9   Craige, Sarah and Mathias Snook by David Culbertson, DD, Jackson Co.

1797 Dec 7   Craigg, Joel and Betsy Putnam by Peregrine Foster, JCCCP, Washing-
               ton Co.

1816 Aug 17   Craigo, James and Sarah Climons by David Mitchell, JP, Jackson Co.

1801 May 14   Cram, John and Anna Spafford both of Cleveland by James Kingsbury,
               Judge of Court of Common Pleas, Trumbull Co.

1853 Oct 4   Cram, Rebecca N. and James D. Sturgess of Duncan's Falls by Rev.
               John Boyd, St. Luke's Church, Marietta, Washington Co.

1865 Dec 25   Cram, Sarah A. and L. Frank Gilbert by Rev. John Boyd, St. Luke's
               Church, Marietta, Washington Co.

1825 Sep 25   Cramer, Catherine and Levi Rhoads by Abm. Williams, JP, Franklin Co.

1816 Mar 16   Cramer, Isaiah and Mary Reed by Wm. O'Bannon, Licking Co.

1816 Oct 26   Cramer, John and Catharine Cobb (or Cabb) by James Taylor, JP,
               Franklin Co.

1813 Nov 24   Cramer, May and David Johnston by Silas Winchell, JP, Licking Co.

1817 Aug 15   Crampton, Hannah and Timothy James by John Cunningham, JPNAT,
               Licking Co.

1817 3 mo 6   Crampton, Rachel and Andrew Hampton, Miami Monthly Meeting, Warren
               Co.

1816 2 mo 7   Crampton, Samuel and Anna Hampton, Miami Monthly Meeting, Warren Co.

1819 Oct 19   Crandol, Zedekiah and Cynthia Stillson by James M. Booth, JP,
              Washington Co.

1818 Jun 29   Crane, Clarissa Ann and John Gates by Thomas Moore, VDM, Washington
              Co.

1819 Oct 10   Crane, Lydia and William Humphrey by Rev. Saml. P. Robbins, Wash-
              ington Co.

1816 Sep 26   Crane, Nancy and James M. Crune by James Hoge (another entry
              27 Mar 1817), Franklin Co.

1816 Feb 1   Crassen, Rhody and Joseph Morrie (or Morris) by James Marshall,
              Franklin Co.

1814 Jul 28   Crath, Caleb and Mary Shafer by Jno. Scott, Pickaway Co.

1822 May 5   Craun, Abram and Rosanna Miller by N. Goetschius, Franklin Co.

1814 Mar 3   Craun, Catharin and Abram DeLong by Elijah Austin, Franklin Co.

1810 Jul 9   Craun, Elizabeth and Edward Green by Massey Clymer, Franklin Co.

1815 Jul 19   Craun, Jacob and Catherine Miller by Frederick Peterson, Franklin Co.

1823 Jun 26   Craun, Sarrah and Joshua Downing by Nicholas Goetschius, JP,
              Franklin Co.

1825 Mar 13   Crawford, Asa and Polly Garner by Webster Sadley, JP, Marion Co.

1815 Oct 12   Crawford, Catharine and Eli James by Stephen Lindsly, Washington Co.

1821 Dec 4   Crawford, Charles and Sophia Maxson by Amos Wilson, JP, Washington
              Co.

1815 Apr 19   Crawford, Elizabeth and Adam Brotherton by James Hoge, Franklin Co.

1822 Mar 5   Crawford, John and Martha Babcock by Rev. Cornelius Springer,
              Washington Co.

1823 Jun 11   Crawford, Mary and Joseph Graham by Isaac Painter, JP, Franklin Co.

1818 May 12   Crawford, Nancy and James Perry by James Hoge, Franklin Co.

1805 Jun 16   Crawford, Nelly and Ignatius Waterman by James Quinn, Elder,
              Washington Co.

1820 Mar 16   Crawford, Parker and Elizabeth Carson by John W. Patterson, MG,
              Licking Co.

1825 Mar 3   Crawford,Pricella and Andrew Straub by Thos. Rodgers, JP, Marion Co.

1820 Dec 31   Crawford, William and Saphrona Wills by Dudley Davis, Washington Co.

1819 Apr 29   Crawn?, Sarah W. and Bailis Redman by Joseph Thorp, MG, Licking Co.

1815 Jan 24   Creighton, Ann and David Huder by Thos. Mace, JP, Pickaway Co.

1869 Dec 9   Creighton, Elizabeth and Jacob Templeton by Rev. John Boyd, St.
              Luke's Church, Marietta, Washington Co.

1828 Jan 10   Creighton, Isaac and Betsey Coons by John Hanover, Franklin Co.

1814 Apr 6   Cremar, Daniel and Mary Coble (or Cable) by James Taylor (another
              entry 9 Apr 1817), Franklin Co.

1814 Sep 18   Cremer, George and Margaret Whitesel by Emmor C. Cox, JP, Franklin
               Co.

1805 May 22   Crepin, Comfort and Alexander Steadman by Joseph Strickland,
               Washington Co.

1814 Aug 25   Crevisto, John and Polly Mock by John Emmett, JP, Pickaway Co.

1811 Aug 22   Creviston, Peggy and Peter Rush (license date), Pickaway Co.

1804 Mar 20   Creviston, Polly and James Rush by Samuel Smith, Ross Co.

1804 Jan 29   Creviston, Rachel and Henry Rush by Samuel Smith, Ross Co.

1819 5 mo 5   Crew, Sarah and Peter Cleaver, Miami Monthly Meeting, Warren Co.

1823 Jul 3   Crider, Benjamin and Elizabeth Hart by Daniel Brunk, JP, Franklin Co.

1805 Mar 10   Crider, Michael and Elizabeth Smith by Abraham Miller, Ross Co.

1815 Dec 7   Crippen, Henry and Elizabeth Ingles by Cyrus Ames, JP, Washington Co.

1815 Dec 14   Crippen, Sally and Orland Case by Tracey Williams, JP, Franklin Co.

1827 11 mo 7   Crispin, Mary W. and Joseph Hopkins, Miami Monthly Meeting, Warren
               Co.

1813 Mar 15   Critchet, Jonathan and Sally Handy by James McMillen, Licking Co.

1818 May 21   Critten, Amy and Mathias Miller by John McMahon, Licking Co.

1818 Jan 8   Croan (or Crone), Adam and Naomi Wright by Abner Goff, Minister,
               Licking Co.

1819 Nov 16   Croan, John and Mary Eshleman by Simeon Overturf, JP, Licking Co.

1819 Dec 20   Crock, Sarah and Joseph Neiber by M. Trout, JP, Licking Co.

1818 Jan 8   Crone (or Croan), Adam and Naomi Wright by Abner Goff, Minister,
               Licking Co.

1819 Jul 22   Crone, Alexander and Susan Hayse by James Hoge, Franklin Co.

1828 Sep 28   Cronston, Pebe Ann and Thomas Johnston by S. Hamilton, Elder in
               the ME Church, Franklin Co.

1803 Oct 13   Crook, Joseph and Susanna Geblur by Samuel Evans, Ross Co.

1817 Nov 12   Crooks, John and Tabitha Cowee by John Patterson, JP, Washington Co.

1825 Nov 6   Crosby, E.H. and Elizabeth Washburn by Conrad Roth, JP, Marion Co.

1821 Feb 22   Crosby, Harvey and Emely Starr by Jacob Drake, NDM, Franklin Co.

1826 Dec 4   Crosby, Samuel and Margaret McLene by James Hoge, Franklin Co.

1811 Jan 15   Crose, Solomon and Fanny Campbell by Rev. Simon Cokrane, Franklin Co.

1821 Dec 20   Cross, Bazel A. and Wealthy Bailey by Joel Tuttle, Jr., Washington
               Co.

1822 Mar 21   Cross, Bridgett and John Brough by Daniel H. Buell, JP, Washington
               Co.

1855 Apr 12   Cross, George P. and Margaret P. Williams by T. Corlett, St. Luke's
               Church, Granville, Licking Co.

1821 Apr 15   Cross, Lucius and Thirza Stanley by Rev. Saml. P. Robbins, Washing-
               ton Co.

1804 May 27   Cross, Waid and Bridgart Foree by John Brough, JP, Washington Co.

1818 Oct 3   Crosset, Nancy and Hugh M. Ross by Matthew Taylor, Franklin Co.

1820 Jan 15   Crossett, Samuel and Jane Taylor by Matthew Taylor, Franklin Co.

1816 Jul 28   Crossley, William and Sally Pankake by Joseph Grate, Franklin Co.

1820 Apr 10   Crossmock, Michael and Rebecca Ruble by M. Black, JP, Licking Co.

1819 Nov 8   Crouch, Catherine and Christian Holdeman by Simeon Overturf, JP,
              Licking Co.

1804 Jan 31   Crouch, Joseph and Margaret McCall by Abm. Miller, Ross Co.

1804 Jan 17   Crouch, Mary and William Montgomery by Abm. Miller, Ross Co.

1804 Aug 21   Crouch, Rebecca and Arra Smith by Abm. Miller, Ross Co.

1820 Aug 17   Crouse, Susannah and William Cooperider by Andrew Henhel, MG,
              Licking Co.

1820 Jan 24   Crow, Ann and Adam Patterson by John Green, MG, Licking Co.

1814 Sep 1   Crow, David and Mary Connelly by John Scott, JP, Pickaway Co.

1816 Oct 11   Crow, Elizabeth and John Motz by David Mitchell, JP, Jackson Co.

1825 Jan 3   Crow, Isaac and Louisa James by Thomas Daugherty, JP, Jackson Co.

1804 Jan 12   Crow, Mary and Alexander Cowgle by Isaac Dawson, Ross Co.

1823 Mar 2   Crown, Isaac and Jane Blakely by N. Goetschieus, JP, Franklin Co.

1819 Jun 28   Crown, Rachael and Harvy Chilson by Stephen Maynard, Franklin Co.

1828 Dec 14   Croy, David and Sally Wasson by Amaziah Hutchinson, Franklin Co.

1815 Feb 11   Cruch, Reason and Catherine Laid by Noah Fidler, Licking Co.

1815 Jan 12   Crum, Ruth and Enoch Kile by Shadrach Cole, JP, Pickaway Co.

1826 Apr 2   Crum, Sarah Ann and Samuel Thompson by Henry Matthews, Franklin Co.

1818 Jul 30   Crump, Mary and Andrew Faulkner by Gabriel McNeil, JP, Jackson Co.

1816 Sep 26   Crune, James M. and Nancy Crane by James Hoge (another entry
              27 Mar 1817), Franklin Co.

1829 Feb 1   Cryder, Emanuel and Polly McGill by Geo. Black, JP, Franklin Co.

1822 Dec 5   Cubbage, Elizabeth and Alexander Needles by Charles Waddell,
              Franklin Co.

1804 Dec 18   Cubbage, Philip and Betsey Newton by John Brough, JP, Washington
              Co.

1819 Mar 28   Cuddington, Anna and Barzillia Coburn by Thomas White, Washington
              Co.

1818 Aug 29   Cuddington, Jane and David Pritchard by Sardine Stone, JP, Washing-
              ton Co.

1815 Jan 1   Cuddington, Lydia and Curtis Sherman by Thomas Seely, Esq.,
              Washington Co.

1814 Dec 4   Cuddington, Uriah and Theodosia Fuller by Thos. Seely, Washington
              Co.

1806 Jan 30   Culbertson, Elisabeth and Andrew Dill by Zachariah Stephen, JP,
               Franklin Co.

1823 May 15   Culbertson, Isabella and John Emmich by James Hoge, Franklin Co.

1814 Nov 24   Culbertson (or Calhunteen or Calbermsten), John and Patsey
               Forguson by John Turner, JP, Franklin Co.

1817 Dec 22   Culbertson, Mary and William Shannon by James Hoge, Franklin Co.

1819 Dec 21   Culbertson, Rebecca and Nathaniel W. Smith by James Hoge,
               Franklin Co.

1815 Apr 19   Culbertson, Robert and Elizabeth Irwin by James Hoge, Franklin Co.

1817 Mar 27   Culbertson, Robert and Jane Park by James Hoge, Franklin Co.

1815 Jul 11   Cully, Rebecca and James Taylor by Nathan Cunningham, Licking Co.

1822 May 20   Culver, Levin and Sarah Smith by John F. Solomon, Franklin Co.

1813 Jul 25   Cummings, Elizabeth and George Hull by Rev. Levi Shinn, Licking Co.

1824 Oct 7   Cummins, Waters and Chloe Case by John Goodrich, JP, Franklin Co.

1814 Nov 5   Cumpstock, Buckley and Margaret Jane Dixon by Ezra Griswold, JP,
               Franklin Co.

1814 Jul 5   Cumstock, James and Chloe Brevoort by W. Droddy, Franklin Co.

1821 Jan 28   Cune, Susanah and Henry Snook by David Culbertson, DD, Jackson Co.

1853 Apr 23   Cuningham, John and Martha A. Short by Rev. Geo. B. Sturges, St.
               Paul's Church, Marion, Marion Co.

1821 Jun 19   Cunning, Margaret and James Bell by W.T. Martin, JP, Franklin Co.

1818 May 3   Cunningham, Caty and John George by Geo. Callanahn, MEM, Licking Co.

1816 Dec 25   Cunningham, Ebenezer and Sally Mogrudge by John Patterson,
               Washington Co.

1819 Jan 6   Cunningham, Elizabeth and Samuel Moore by T.D. Bierd, Licking Co.

1884 Jun 30   Cunningham, Isabel of Putnam and George B. Collis of Corning, O.,
               by Rev. George F. Moore, Putnam Presbyterian Church,
               Muskingum Co.

1808 Feb 25   Cunningham, James and Margaret Miers by John Hollister, JPHT,
               Licking Co.

1815 Mar 23   Cunningham, James and Magdalen Bomngardner by Joseph Gorton,
               Franklin Co.

1812 Jan 14   Cunningham, Jane and Hira Pettee by Rev. G. Vanaman, Licking Co.

1812 Jun 23   Cunningham, John and Mary Eliot by -----, Licking Co.

1814 Apr 28   Cunningham, Joseph and Margaret Wheeler by -----, Licking Co.

1815 Mar 13   Cunningham, Rebecca and James Watson by Rev. T. Harris, Licking Co.

1826 Mar 26   Cunningham, Ruth and James Stone by Geo. Callanhan, EMEC, Licking
               Co.

1817 Jan 1   Cunningham, Sally and John Morgaridge by Jos. Chapman, JP, Washing-
               ton Co.

1824 Jul 1   Cup, Peter and Sarah M. Green by B. Bull, Franklin Co.

1820 Mar 11   Cuppleberger, Nancy and Mathew Cooley by Samuel Bancroft, JP,
              Licking Co.

1813 Apr 22   Currell, Mary and Peter Dehaven (license date), Pickaway Co.

1810 Dec 23   Currey, William and Atsey Green (license date), Pickaway Co.

1814 Jan 6   Currier, William and Peggy Hill by Rev. S.P. Robbins, Washington Co.

1821 Aug 30   Curry, Hiram M. and Elizabeth Lane by C. Henkel, Franklin Co.

1828 May 20   Curry, John and E.C. Henderson by James Hoge, Franklin Co.

1818 Mar 9   Curry, Nancy and Samuel Henderson by James Hoge, Franklin Co.

1813 May 12   Curtis, Benajah and Sally Clark by Rev. Stephen Lindsley, Washing-
              ton Co.

1815 Mar 19   Curtis, Clarissa and Samuel Knowles by Stephen Guthrie, JP, Wash-
              ington Co.

1812 Jun 24   Curtis, Eleazer Stan and Esther Knowles by Dan'l Goodno, JP,
              Washington Co.

1820 Apr 22   Curtis, Eunacy and Joseph Eaton by James Smith, ECC, Licking Co.

1813 Jan 19   Curtis, Hector and Margaret Pontius (license date), Pickaway Co.

1819 Feb 7   Curtis, Horace and Lydia Cole by Stephen Guthrie, JP, Washington Co.

1813 Nov 24   Curtis, Hosmer, son of Zarah Curtis and a brother of the Hon. Henry
              B. Curtis of Mt. Vernon, O., and Elenor Miclick by Silas
              Winchell, JP, Licking Co.

1864 May 2   Curtis, Jane D. and George W. Beardslee by Rev. A. Kingsbury,
              Putnam Presbyterian Church, Muskingum Co.

1814 Nov 3   Curtis, Jason R. and Polly Clark by Dan'l H. Buell, Washington Co.

1814 May 31   Curtis, Lucinda and Augustus Case by Rev. Sam'l P. Robbins,
              Washington Co.

1816 Nov 17   Curtis, Mary and Columbus Bierce by Stephen Guthrie, JP, Washington
              Co.

1819 Feb 4   Curtis, Walter and Almira Guthrie by Cyrus Ames, JP, Washington Co.

1804 Apr 15   Curtiss, John and Polly Woodruff by Simeon Deming, Washington Co.

1870 Nov 17   Cusac, James and Mary E. Snyder by Rev. A. Kingsbury, Putnam
              Presbyterian Church, Muskingum Co.

1818 Dec 29   Cushing, Bethsheba and Benjamin Beedle by Wm. Rand, Washington Co.

1806 May 4   Cushing, Betsy and Peregrine P. Foster by D. Loring, Washington Co.

1818 Sep 23   Cushing, Betsey and James Bowen by Wm. Rand, JP, Washington Co.

1819 Dec 21   Cushing, Gen'l Nathan G. and Susan Merwin by Rev. Sam'l P. Robbins,
              Washington Co.

1802 Apr --   Cushing, Sally and Daniel Goodno by J. Pierce, JCCCP, Washington Co.

1794 Feb 5   Cushing, Samuel and Bathsheba Devol by Rufus Putnam, Judge TNWRO,
              Washington Co.

1820 Feb 3   Cushing, Samuel and Almira Scott by William Rand, Washington Co.

1812 Oct 4   Cu(s)terline, Benjamin and Elizabeth Waldron by Wm. Moody, JP,
               Licking Co.

1818 Jan 1   Cutler, Betsy and Nathan Arnold by Venal Stewart, Preacher,
               Franklin Co.

1819 Dec 16   Cutler, Irene and Hiram Wakefield by T. Lee, Franklin Co.

1810 Aug 2   Cutler, John and Caty Lee (license date), Pickaway Co.

1825 Jul 14   Cutler, John and Malelda Aann McGown by Rev. Joseph Carper,
               Franklin Co.

1820 Nov 28   Cutler, Mary Ann and Levi L. Waterman by Rev. Saml. P. Robbins,
               Washington Co.

1816 Mar 25   Cutler, Polly and Joseph Welch by Ezra Griswold, Franklin Co.

1813 Mar 10   Cutler, Sarah and George Coon (license date), Pickaway Co.

1824 Feb 13   Cutler, Sarah and Harvey Bloget by Nathan Emery, Franklin Co.

1827 Jan 7   Cutler, Sarah and Thomas Bryson by Jacob Young, Franklin Co.

1805 Nov 22   Cutright, Nancy and James Washburn by Charles Cade, Ross Co.

1817 Jan 1   Cutwright, Nancy and Peleg Potter by Joseph Armstrong, JP, Jackson
               Co.

1867 Sep 30   Cylp, Henry C. and Mary A. Eaton by Rev. John Boyd, St. Luke's
               Church, Marietta, Washington Co.

1817 Nov 25   Cyphert, Nancy and Alexander Alison by John Russell, Washington Co.

1816 Dec 1   Dage (or Dague), Elizabeth and Jacob Clause (or Clouse) by Jacob
               Smith, JP, Franklin Co.

1828 Nov 27   Dage, Lucy and Phillip Hay by Joseph Long, Franklin Co.

1822 Jun 11   Dage, Sally and Andrew Swickerd by John Davis, Franklin Co.

1814 Dec 4   Dagg (or Dague), Matthias Jr. and Mima Rose by Jacob Tharp, JP,
               Franklin Co.

1816 Dec 1   Dague (or Dage), Elizabeth and Jacob Clause (or Clouse) by Jacob
               Smith, JP, Franklin Co.

1812 Apr 30   Dague, John and Mrs. Jemime Strate by Jacob Tharp, Franklin Co.

1814 Dec 4   Dague (or Dagg), Matthias Jr. and Mima Rose by Jacob Tharp, JP,
               Franklin Co.

1806 Jun 5   Daily, Charles and Sally Gates by Robert Oliver, JP, Washington Co.

1804 Dec 2   Daily, Francis and James Shephard by John Hoddy, JP, Ross Co.

1815 Oct 17   Dailey, John and Mary Dewees by Anthony Sheets, JP, Washington Co.

1817 Nov 16   Dailey, Nancy and Stephen Parr by Rev. David Smithers, Washington
               Co.

1811 Apr 14   Dalby, John and Maryan Cann (license date), Pickaway Co.

1871 Sep 14   Dale, Edward R. and Sarah V. Rolston by Rev. John Boyd, St. Luke's Church, Marietta, Washington Co.

1820 May 24   Dale, Jeremiah and Nancy B. Plummer by Rev. Saml. P. Robbins, Washington Co.

1807 Oct 18   Daley, Sally and Joseph Dickerson by James Riggs, JP, Washington Co.

1809 Nov 20   Dallarson, Martha and Benedict Hurst by Luther Dana, JP, Washington Co.

1797 May 10   Daly, Sarah and Sam'l Colvin by J. Pierce, JCCCP, Washington Co.

1822 Nov 28   Dalzell, Catharine and Joseph McElvain by James Hoge, Franklin Co.

1798 Apr 17   Dana, Benjamin and Sally Shaw by Robert Oliver, JP, Washington Co.

1810 Nov 27   Dana, Edmond B. and Louisha Burch by Sam'l P. Robbins, Washington Co.

1811 Nov 12   Dana, Frances and Charles Shipman by Stephen Lindsly, Washington Co.

1816 Sep 22   Dana, George and Deborah Fisher by Rev. Saml. P. Robbins, Washington Co.

1808 Nov 17   Dana, Levi and Sarah Dutten by Nehemiah Davis, MG, Washington Co.

1799 Mar 17   Dana, Luther and Grace Stone by Peregrine Foster, JCCCP, Washington Co.

1810 Jul 29   Dana, Mary and Caleb Emerson by Rev. Sam'l P. Robbins, Washington Co.

1821 Aug 14   Dana, Mary and Benjamin P. Putnam by Jacob Lindley, VDM, Washington Co.

1807 Apr 14   Dana, Stephen and Betsy M. Foster by D. Loring, JP, Washington Co.

1816 Feb 4   Dana, William and Dorcas Bent by Cyrus Ames, JP, Washington Co.

1802 May 2   Dana, Wm. and Polly Foster by J. Pierce, Washington Co.

1808 Aug 20   Danacey, Archabald and Hannah Witighin by Joseph Palmer, JP, Washington Co.

1817 Feb 6   Danford, Philip and Esther Foster by Obadiah Scott, JP, Washington Co.

1886 May 19   Danford, William C. of St. Clairsville, O., and Sarah M. Judkins of Woodsfield, O., by Rev. George F. Moore, Putnam Presbyterian Church, Muskingum Co.

1824 Oct 24   Daniel, Brinkley and Jean Sanborn by George Jefferies, MG, Franklin Co.

1801 Mar 5   Daniel, David M. and Betsy McCarley by Robt. Safford, Washington Co.

1800 Jan 23   Daniel, Jenny and William Reburn by Robert Safford, Washington Co.

1855 Jan 3   Daniel, Mary L. Peter Richards by T. Corlett, St. Luke's Church, Granville, Licking Co.

1813 Apr 25   Danielson, Ilyna and Polly Starlin by Nath Hamilton, JP, Washington Co.

1853 Jan 3   Danker, Caroline and Joshua Cisler by Rev. John Boyd, St. Luke's Church, Marietta, Washington Co.

1817 Aug 31	Danley, Polly and John Corns by Salmon N. Cook, JP, Washington Co.
1882 Jul 1	Danson, Anna J. and Dana N. Hitt by Rev. John Boyd, St. Luke's Church, Marietta, Washington Co.
1812 Dec 6	Dare, Jeremiah and Charlotte Lyons by Rev. Stephen Lindley, Washington Co.
1824 Sep 4	Darland, Hiley and Peter Long (license date), Marion Co.
1824 Aug 18	Darley, Wm. and Margaret Davis by Timothy Ratcliff, JP, Jackson Co.
1824 Dec 31	Darling, Hannah and Zachariah Barrett by Zachariah Welch, JP, Marion Co.
1810 May 2	Darlington, Fedelia and Isaac Wilson by John W. Patterson, JP, Licking Co.
1809 Aug 15	Darlington, Maria and Bradley Buckingham by Wm. Haines, JP, Licking Co.
1806 Apr 10	Darrough, Russell and Catharine Eveland by Robt. Oliver, Washington Co.
1801 Oct 11	Darrow, George and Olive Gaylord both of Hudson by David Hudson, JP, Trumbull Co.
1803 Apr 17	Darrow, Joseph and Sally Prior both of Hudson by David Hudson, JP, Trumbull Co.
1825 Dec 29	Daud, Eunice and James Dorland (license date), Marion Co.
1818 Jan 19	Daugherty, Edward and Hannah Queen by William Brawn, Franklin Co.
1800 Apr 14	Daugherty, Margery and Joseph Saates by Seth Cashart, Washington Co.
1823 Dec 26	Daugherty, Sarah and George McCollum by C. Waddell, LM, Franklin Co.
1819 Oct 28	Dauthet, Harriet and Hickman Powers by John Horton, Jackson Co.
1815 Jan 15	Daval, Harriet and George Statten by Z. Carlisle, Licking Co.
1793 Dec 8	Davenport, Patty and Elijah Warren by R.J. Meigs, JP, Washington Co.
1815 May 14	David, John and Nancy Evans by Samuel Dunnavan, Licking Co.
1814 Feb 10	David, Joseph and Sally Drivier by William King, JP, Pickaway Co.
1829 Feb 17	Davidson, Elizabeth and Isaac Guffy by John Swisher, JP, Franklin Co.
1801 Oct 8	Davidson, Esther and John Gibson at Youngstown by William Wicks, VDM, Trumbull Co.
1828 Apr 3	Davidson, James and Ruth Chenoweth by Samuel P. Shaw, Franklin Co.
1824 Jun 10	Davidson, Joseph and Martha Priscott by Jacob Grubb, Franklin Co.
1817 Jan 5	Davidson, Melly and Jeremiah William Falloway by James Taylor, JP, Franklin Co.
1815 Mar 16	Davidson, Nancy and Wm. Mattocks by Frederick Peterson, Franklin Co.
1821 Apr 12	Davidson, Rachael and John Henry by Richard Courtright, Franklin Co.
1825 Oct 9	Davidson, Sally and Smith Monroe by J. Gander, Franklin Co.
1821 Mar 25	Davidson, William and Rebecca Evans by Rev. Thrap, Licking Co.
1828 Nov 12	Davidson, William and Polly Hellman by Jacob Grubb, Franklin Co.

1820 Jul 20   Davies?, Wm. and Margaret Sproull? by W. O'Bannon, JP, Licking Co.

1816 May 2   Davis, Aaron and Ruth Edwards by Nathan Parr, JP, Washington Co.

1813 Mar 25   Davis, Amelia and Jacob Rush (license date), Pickaway Co.

1802 Nov 14   Davis, Amsa and Clarissa Brown by Wm. Burnham, Washington Co.

1801 Mar 15   Davis, Anna and Joseph Fuller by Nehemiah Davis, Washington Co.

1802 Mar 25   Davis, Asa and Joanna Olney by Nehemiah Davis, Washington Co.

1803 Apr 14   Davis, Benjamin and Patty Reding by Wm. Robinson, JP, Ross Co.

1813 Dec 30   Davis, Benjamin and Elizabeth Steeley (license date), Pickaway Co.

1827 Mar 20   Davis, Caleb and Martha Brackinridge by Ruben Golliday, Franklin Co.

1811 Mar 24   Davis, Catherine and Adam Metz (license date), Pickaway Co.

1820 Apr 3   Davis, Charity and Abraham Cozad by Joseph Lockland, JP, Jackson Co.

1817 Nov 16   Davis, Charles Jr. and Nancy Hutchins by Dudley Davis, Washington Co.

1821 Jan 21   Davis, Charlotte and Oliver Green by John Green, JP, Washington Co.

1795 Jan 7   Davis, Daniel and Drusilla Olney by R.J. Meigs, JP, Washington Co.

1799 Feb 14   Davis, Daniel and Sally Olney by Robert Oliver, Washington Co.

1819 Feb 15   Davis, Daniel and Polly Dutton by Rev. Wm. Davis, Washington Co.

1805 Nov 14   Davis, Daniel Jr. and Olive Foster by Jacob Lindly, Washington Co.

1814 Oct 16   Davis, David and Elizabeth Bodwell by John H. White, JP, Washington
              Co.

1805 Jan 27   Davis, David W. and Elizabeth Bramonburgh by David Mitchell, JP,
              Ross Co.

1819 Nov 4   Davis, Dudley W. and Rebecca Lawrence by Thomas White, JP, Washing-
              ton Co.

1817 Nov 20   Davis, Elijah and Edith Bodwell by Saml. Dye, JP, Washington Co.

1821 Oct 24   Davis, Elijah and Nancy Dutton by Osgood McFarland, JP, Washington
              Co.

1805 Jan 17   Davis, Elisha and Nancy Allison by Jacob Lindly, Washington Co.

1820 Oct 22   Davis, Elisha and Susanna Mason by John Green, JP, Washington Co.

1803 Aug 2   Davis, Elizabeth and William Parker by Wm. Davis, JP, Ross Co.

1812 Dec 3   Davis, Elizabeth and Peter Broom by Simon Tuttle, JP, Washington Co.

1817 Apr 19   Davis, Elizabeth and Nathaniel Hinckley by Peliatiah White, JP,
              Washington Co.

1811 Oct 31   Davis, Enos and Eleanor Carnahan (license date), Pickaway Co.

1811 May 9   Davis, Frederick and Polly Allison by Dudley Davis, JP, Washington
              Co.

1813 Dec 1   Davis, George and Rachel Glaze (license date), Pickaway Co.

1826 Mar 2   Davis, George and Catharine Gordon by J. Carper, Franklin Co.

1809 Apr 12   Davis, Hannah and Curtice Knight by Philip Whitten, Washington Co.

1799 Feb 14   Davis, Hezekiel and Elizabeth Coleman by Robert Oliver, Washington Co.

1825 Mar 27   Davis, Isaac and Susan Toosinge by Wm. Henden, JP, Franklin Co.

1808 Aug 5   Davis, James and Mary G. Greene by Wm. Haines, JP, Licking Co.

1813 Jun 4   Davis, James and Eliza Hartshorne by Wm. Miller, JP, Washington Co.

1814 Mar 20   Davis, James and Nancy Stevens by Simeon Deming, JP, Washington Co.

1815 Dec 28   Davis, James and Lecty Cheadle by Richard Cheadle, JP, Washington Co.

1821 Apr 18   Davis, James and Susan Groves by Noah Fidler, Licking Co.

1804 Aug 15   Davis, Jesse and Polly Blackmer by Jacob Lindly, Washington Co.

1814 Jul 7   Davis, John and Nancy Davis by Rev. Geo. Alkire, Pickaway Co.

1815 Apr 27   Davis, John and Polly Bodle by S. Dunnavan, Licking Co.

1817 Aug 21   Davis, John and Mary Price by Eli C. King, Franklin Co.

1819 Jun 10   Davis, Joseph and Rosanna Hutchins by Dudley Davis, JP, Washington
              Co.

1827 May 13   Davis, Joseph and O.I. Davis by J.N. Walter, Franklin Co.

1825 Jan 6   Davis, Louisa and Geo. W. Baker by Isaac Blayck, JP, Marion Co.

1817 Jun 19   Davis, Lovy and Jonathan Hughes by John Evans, JP, Licking Co.

1799 Feb 14   Davis, Lucena and James Mann by Robert Oliver, JP, Washington Co.

1818 Mar 15   Davis, Lucena and Thomas Devin by Sardine Stone, Washington Co.

1820 Jun 7   Davis, Luther and Mary Brewer by John Stinson, JP, Jackson Co.

1824 Aug 18   Davis, Margaret and Wm. Darley by Timothy Ratcliff, JP, Jackson Co.

1828 Feb 21   Davis, Margaretretta and I.D. Middleton by John F. Solomon,
              Franklin Co.

1819 Mar 21   Davis, Martha and Daniel Clay Jr. by Dudley Davis, Washington Co.

1816 Aug 18   Davis, Marvel and Anna Stull by Obadiah Scott, JP, Washington Co.

1829 Jun 11   Davis, Mary E. and Peter Barnes by I.N. Walter, ECC, Franklin Co.

1826 Feb 19   Davis, Moses and Mattilda Coffman by Charles Sells, JP, Franklin Co.

1809 Oct 26   Davis, Nancy and Henry Young by James Riggs, JP, Washington Co.

1814 Jul 7   Davis, Nancy and John Davis by Rev. Geo. Alkire, Pickaway Co.

1820 5 mo 3   Davis, Nathan and Lydia Cleaver, Miami Monthly Meeting, Warren Co.

1820 May 25   Davis, Nathan Jr. and Eliza Dye by Osgood McFarland, JP, Washington
              Co.

1827 May 13   Davis, O.I. and Joseph Davis by J.N. Walter, Franklin Co.

1815 Apr 13   Davis, Phebe and Ezekiel Dye by Sam'l Dye, JP, Washington Co.

1815 Jul 2   Davis, Russell and Polly Jones by Rev. S.P. Robbins, Washington Co.

1809 Jan 24   Davis, Salley and Robert Perrish by James Marshall, Franklin Co.

1807 1 mo 15 Davis, Samuel and Dorkis Jones, Miami Monthly Meeting, Warren Co.

1809 Apr 4   Davis, Samuel and Sarah Hughes by W. Haines, JP, Licking Co.

1825 Jun 11   Davis, Samuel and Matilda Kilbourn by Charles Sells, JP, Franklin Co.

1805 Nov 7	Davis, Sarah and Narnum G. Wells by N. Davis, Washington Co.
1809 Nov 19	Davis, Sarah and Richard Green by -----, Licking Co.
1820 Dec 6	Davis, Sarah and John Neher by John Waggonner, JP, Licking Co.
1893 Jan 8	Davis, Sarah of Redfield, O., and Burgers C. Ansel of Buckingham, O., by Rev. George F. Moore, Putnam Presbyterian Church, Muskingum Co.
1813 Jun 1	Davis, William and Mary Craig (license date), Pickaway Co.
1825 Mar 31	Davis, Wm. and Nancy Jenkins by J.B. Gilliland, JP, Jackson Co.
1812 Feb 14	Davis, Zachariah and Elizabeth Roberts by James McMillen, JP, Licking Co.
1815 May 12	Davison, Elizabeth and William Woodcock by James Taylor, JP, Franklin Co.
1820 Aug 3	Davison, Mary and Thomas Deacon by Richard Courtright, JP, Franklin Co.
1813 Apr 1	Davison, Nancy and John Lock (license date), Pickaway Co.
1795 Nov 8	Davons, Francis and Francis Blin by J.G. Petit, JP, Washington Co.
1800 Jul 13	Davrange, Constance and John Dazet by Robert Safford, Washington Co.
1825 Aug 17	Dawd, Elihu and Polly Ketcham by John Green, JP, Marion Co.
1804 Jan 24	Dawson, Millia and James Brice Webster by Abm. Miller, Ross Co.
1861 May 30	Day, Anna Jane and Wm. Woodcock by Rev. Henry Payne in presence of Geo. Smith, Mr. Woodcock, Sr., and others, St. Paul's Church, Marion, Marion Co.
1827 Aug 15	Day, Earlis and Sarah Evans by Townsend Nichols, Franklin Co.
1821 Apr 12	Day, Isaac and Elizabeth Gold by James Cunningham, VDM, Licking Co.
1817 Jul --	Day, Mary and Thomas McCallaugh by John Hunter, Franklin Co.
1799 Sep 6	Day, Noah and Bitha Gates by Robert Oliver, JP, Washington Co.
1816 Aug 27	Dayton, Spencer and Eader Ford by Joseph Grate, Franklin Co.
1800 Jul 13	Dazel, John and Constance Davrange by Robert Safford, Washington Co.
1887 Oct 20	Deacon, Anna M. and William A. Weaver both of Zanesville by Rev. George F. Moore, Putnam Presbyterian Church, Muskingum Co.
1820 Aug 3	Deacon, Thomas and Mary Davison by Richard Courtright, JP, Franklin Co.
1825 Feb 22	Deal, Conrad and Elizabeth Rowles by Hugh S. Smith, JP, Marion Co.
1821 May 31	Dean, Benjamin and Catherine Carter by John W. Patterson, MG, Licking Co.
1811 Nov 17	Dean, Eleanor and Alexander Miller by Philip Witten, JP, Washington Co.
1825? Feb 17	Dean, James and Jane Starr by James Hoge, Franklin Co.
1823 Apr 1	Dean, Nancy and Alexander Ross by James Hoge, Franklin Co.
1828 Sep 30	Dean, Sally and Clark Matthews by James Laws, Franklin Co.

1818 May 24   Dearborn, Luther and Julia Sentiff by Asa Cheadle, Washington Co.

1812 Feb 6   Dearborn, Nathan and Sarah Seely by Jer. Greenman, JP, Washington Co.

1816 Jun 25   Dearduff, Anney and James Kent by Alexander Bassett, Franklin Co.

1812 May 5   Dearduff, Daniel and Jane Ferguson by John Turner, JP, Franklin Co.

1824 Apr 1   Dearduff, David and Rachel Stiarwalt by Jacob Grubb, Franklin Co.

1821 Dec 27   Dearduff, Isaac and Catharine Beard by A. Allen, Franklin Co.

1816 Apr 13   Dearduff, John and Sally Johnston by Joseph Grate, Franklin Co.

1814 Oct 21   Dearduff, Peter and Hannah Brink by George Bogart, JP, Franklin Co.

1820 Jan 25   Dearduff, Samuel and Elizabeth Barker by Joseph Gorton, Franklin Co.

1821 Jan 18   Dearduff, Susan and Daniel Bierd by A. Allen, JP, Franklin Co.

1819 May 6   Deavaun, Betsy and Ephraim Brown by William Hall, JP, Licking Co.

1815 May 30   Deaver, Eleanor and Joseph Mason by Sardine Stone, Washington Co.

1817 Mar 15   Deaver, Hannah and William Martin by Francis Holland, JP Scioto Tp.,
               Jackson Co.

1818 Mar 12   Deavon, Elizabeth and Thomas Craig by Isaac Baker, JP, Jackson Co.

1859 Oct 27   DeBeck, William Loomis of Cincinnati and Isabelle C. Soyez by Rev.
               John Boyd, St. Luke's Church, Marietta, Washington Co.

1815 Feb 2   Debolt, Rachel and John Parr by J.W. Patterson, JP, Licking Co.

1821 Jan 17   Debott, Elizabeth and John Pitzer by J.W. Patterson, MG, Licking Co.

1819 Feb 27   Deckar, Rebeccah and Adam Miller by James Hoge, Franklin Co.

1814 Dec 28   Deckcon, Azubah and Rena Knight by Dan Case, JP, Franklin Co.

1824 Dec 7   Decker, Andrew and Phatima Walters by Wm. Godman, JP, Franklin Co.

1814 Jun 30   Decker, Ann and Charles Leonard by Wm. King, JP, Pickaway Co.

1820 Feb 10   Decker, Betsey and Michael Fritz by T. Lee, JP, Franklin Co.

1819 May 9   Decker, Catherin and Cotten M. Febor by Emmor Cox, Franklin Co.

1810 Aug 19   Decker, Conrad and Elenor Tillbury by Ebenezer Richards, Franklin Co.

1828 Nov 24   Decker, Daniel and Margaret Blakely by Wm. Patterson, Franklin Co.

1824 Mar 22   Decker, Effy and George Tittler by N. Goetschius, Franklin Co.

1820 Nov 23   Decker, Elias and Sarah Dildine by John F. Solomon, Minister of the
               Gospel in the Methodist Episcopal Church, Franklin Co.

1817 Jul 20   Decker, Elizabeth and Thomas Vance by James Hoge, Franklin Co.

1814 Jun 13   Decker, Isaac and Katy Bishop by Shadrach Cole, JP, Pickaway Co.

1817 Feb 18   Decker, James and Clariss Lines by Elisha Decker, Franklin Co.

1816 Oct 29   Decker, John and Catharine Wagener by Jacob Smith, Franklin Co.

1814 Apr 3   Decker, Joseph and Mary Trachey by Shadrach Cole, JP, Pickaway Co.

1826 Mar 23   Decker, Nelly and Robert Johns by J. Gander, Franklin Co.

1819 May 9   Decker, Polly and Samuel Blakesley by Billingslea Bull, Franklin Co.

1816 Apr 23   Decker, Richard and Betsey Thompson by Frederick Peterson,
               Franklin Co.

1821 Oct 2   Decker, Sarah Ann and William Tall by John Shields, MG, Franklin Co.

1810 Sep 14   Deckir, Elisha and Susan Bishop by Massey Clymer, Franklin Co.

1808 Dec 2   Deewese, Jethro and Ann Eddington by W. Haines, JP, Licking Co.

1813 Apr 22   Dehaven, Peter and Mary Currell (license date), Pickaway Co.

1862 Oct 16   Delafield, Mary of Duncan Falls, O., and George Sturges of Chicago,
               Ill., by Rev. A. Kingsbury, Putnam Presbyterian Church,
               Muskingum Co.

1812 May 24   Delanl, Amos and Cynthia Cole by Dan'l Goodno, Washington Co.

1792 Aug 8   Delano, Cornelius and Sarah Goodale by J. Gilman, Washington Co.

1818 Sep 24   Delano, Cynthia and Thomas Delano by Jonathan Dunham, JP,
               Washington Co.

1819 Nov 26   Delano, Elizabeth P. and John C. Brodrick by Rev. Philander Chase,
               Franklin Co.

1804 Apr 29   Delano, Sarah and Aaron Clough by D. Loring, Washington Co.

1822 Nov 7   Delano, Jane and William Armstrong by James Hoge, Franklin Co.

1818 Sep 24   Delano, Thomas and Cynthia Delano by Jonathan Dunham, JP,
               Washington Co.

1805 Jun 4   Delany, Isaac and Patty Jones by J. Gardner, JP, Ross Co.

1796 Jul 10   DeLargiullon, Francis and Hannah Harris by Robert Safford, JP,
               Washington Co.

1881 Sep 28   de la Vergne, Estelle and James R. Hall by Rev. John Boyd, St.
               Luke's Church, Marietta, Washington Co.

1826 Jan 19   Delay, Betsy and John Wilcox by Zeph Brown, JP, Jackson Co.

1825 Mar 31   Delay, James and Farney (or Hoover) by J.B. Gilliland, JP,
               Jackson Co.

1804 Jun 5   Delay, Jonathan and Deborah Hollinshead by Isaac Dawson, Ross Co.

1805 Apr 13   Delcever, Michael and Hanah Coon by Nathaniel Wyatt, Ross Co.

1813 Jan 14   Delishmot, Van B. and Margaret Baugh (license date), Pickaway Co.

1824 Oct 18   Delly, Polly and George Sidner by Alex Perry, JP, Marion Co.

1814 Mar 3   DeLong, Abram and Catharin Craun by Elijah Austin, Franklin Co.

1795 May 15   Delong, Hannah and Samuel Sprague by Robert Oliver, Washington Co.

1806 Sep 23   Delong, Henry and Sally Heit by Jacob Lindly, Washington Co.

1815 Jan 2   Delong, Isaac and Nancy Hill by James Sharp, JP, Washington Co.

1815 Jan 12   Delong, Lydia and Edward Hartshorn by John True, JP, Washington Co.

1806 Jan 1   Delong, Polly and Charles Harwood by Jacob Lindly, Washington Co.

1816 Aug 15   Delong, Rachel and John McKee by D. Stephens, JP, Washington Co.

1810 Jul 30   Delong, Rebeckah and William Sheoman by Thomas Seely, Washington Co.

1809 Apr 14 Delong, Sally and Thos. Gilkison by Amos Porter, Washington Co.

1817 Dec 17 Delzal, James and Cynthia Rathborn by -----, Licking Co.

1820 Dec 14 Demerest, Daniel and Phebe Smith by Nicholas Goetschius, Franklin Co.

1791 Sep 9 Demier, Jeannette and Francis Bandeau by J.G. Petitt, JCCCP, Washington Co.

1811 Jun 28 Deming, Betsey and Judah Ford by John Greene, Washington Co.

1816 Aug 27 Deming, David and Ann Henry by Nathaniel Hamilton, JP, Washington Co.

1820 Jul 25 Deming, Ezekiel and Abigail Stanley by Danl H. Buell, JP, Washington Co.

1805 Jul 28 Deming, Honor and Benjamin Hart by Jacob Lindly, Washington Co.

1812 Oct 9 Deming, John P. and Deborah Starlin by Nath'l Hamilton, JP, Washington Co.

1819 Jul 1 Demorest, Nicholas and Sally Smith by Joseph Gorton, Franklin Co.

1828 Dec 25 Demorest, Sarah and George Goldsmith by W.T. Martin, Franklin Co.

1824 Jul 8 Denison, John and Jain Moorhead by Robert W. Riley, Franklin Co.

1838 Jun 22 Denker, Bessy and John George Schwartz by Rev. C.L.F. Haensel, St. Luke's Church, Marietta, Washington Co.

1819 Jan 15 Denman, Abagail and Tobias Livingston by Zach Carlisle, Licking Co.

1825 Nov 6 Denman, Elijah and Leavice Bristol by Samuel Abbott, JP, Franklin Co.

1818 Jan 22 Denman, Hulda and John M. Neighbarger by John Johnston, JP, Licking Co.

1809 May 6 Denman, Philip and Amelia Foos by John Hollister, JPHT, Licking Co.

1826 Jan 19 Denman, Temperance and Shedden Beebe by R.W. Cowles, Franklin Co.

1816 Dec 5 Denman, William and Polly Neighbarger by Wm. O'Bannon, JP, Licking Co.

1815 Apr 16 Dennis, Daniel and Amy Eveland by Thomas White, JP, Washington Co.

1819 Feb 14 Dennis, Daniel and Cassandra Stump by Thos. White, Washington Co.

1857 Oct -- Dennis, Ellen and Aron Church by C.S. Doolittle, St. Luke's Church, Granville, Licking Co.

1814 Aug 4 Dennis, Henry and Marry Grove by J.W. Patterson, JP, Licking Co.

1822 Feb 6 Dennis, Lydia and John Chase by James M. Booth, JP, Washington Co.

1821 Oct 18 Dennis, Samuel and Mary Ann Russell by Rev. Wm. Davis, Washington Co.

1813 Dec 30 Dennis, Thomas and Susanna Nulton by George Meller, JP, Washington Co.

1796 Jul 3 Denny, John and Sally Boothby by J. Gilman, Washington Co.

1806 Dec -- Denny, John and Letticia Rawlings by Wm. Bennett, JP, Franklin Co.

1813 Feb 9 Denny, Lettice and Phillip Gattwood (license date), Pickaway Co.

1825 Dec 1 Denoon, Catharine and John Kissinger by C. Hinkel, Franklin Co.

1825 Jan 13   Denoon, John and Nancy Smith by George Jefferies, ordained and
               licensed Minister, Franklin Co.

1801 Jan 26   DePu, George and Mary Coulter by E. Cutler, JP, Washington Co.

1820 Jan 6   Derby, Nancy and Jacob Dixon by Thos. Cox, JP, Jackson Co.

1814 Sep 25   Dereau, Catherine and John Martin by Henry Davis, JP, Pickaway Co.

1819 Nov 7   Derick, Richard and Jamima Dunick by Richard Courtright, Franklin Co.

1812 Mar 7   Derickson, John S. and Sarah Hamblin by James Hoge, Franklin Co.

1822 Mar 19   Derrick, Maryan and John Taylor by B. Bull, Franklin Co.

1822 Feb 17   Deruse, Lucy and Lemuel Cooper by Rev. James McAboy, Washington Co.

1890 Dec 18   Deselm, Maggie S. and John J. Russi both of Zanesville by Rev.
               George F. Moore, Putnam Presbyterian Church, Muskingum Co.

1817 Feb 20   Detty, Elsy and Robert Flora by Samuel L. Donnelly, JP, Jackson Co.

1821 Jun 14   Devees, Sally and Jesse Philips by Richard Taylor, JP, Washington Co.

1827 May 21   Devenport, Lewis and Susan Wagganer by A. Allison, Franklin Co.

1826 Dec 21   Devenport, Melvina and Charles Smith by Abraham Williams, Franklin
               Co.

1826 Mar 29   Devenport, Samuel and Margret Sisco by Abms. Williams, JP, Franklin
               Co.

1822 Feb 21   Devenport, Sarah and Ambresy C. Straight by Jacob Smith, Franklin Co.

1819 Jan 7   Dever, Polly and Benjamin Flack by Isaac Baker, JP, Jackson Co.

1818 Mar 15   Devin, Thomas and Lucena Davis by Sardine Stone, Washington Co.

1814 Sep 26   Devin, Catharine and Luke Emerson by Thomas White, JP, Washington Co.

1861 Dec 4   Devine, Catherine S. and John M.D. Armstrong of Ravenswood, Va., by
               Rev. John Boyd, St. Luke's Church, Marietta, Washington Co.

1814 Jul 28   Devol, Alpha and Nancy Champlin by Obadiah Scott, JP, Washington Co.

1808 Sep 20   Devol, Arphaxan and Mary Dye by Jacob Lindsly, Washington Co.

1794 Feb 5   Devol, Bathsheba and Samuel Cushing by Rufus Putnam, Judge TNWRO,
               Washington Co.

1802 May 24   Devol, Charlotte and Hanford Powers by Wm. Burnham, JP, Washington
               Co.

1812 Sep 8   Devol, Clarissa and Charles Sullivan by Jeremiah Greenman, JP,
               Washington Co.

1812 Nov 29   Devol, Clarissa and Joseph Cook Jr. by Peter Howe, JP, Washington Co.

1805 Jan 3   Devol, Cook and Hannah Converse by Jacob Lindly, Washington Co.

1819 Aug 3   Devol, Cook and Mary Thomas by William Rand, JP, Washington Co.

1816 Nov 3   Devol, Cynthia and Daniel Phillips by Sardine Stone, JP, Washington
               Co.

1802 Mar 25   Devol, Elizabeth and John Brown by Nehemiah Davis, Washington Co.

1818 Apr 12   Devol, Francis and Nancy Dunbar by John Russell, Washington Co.

1790 Mar 25   Devol, Gilbert and Mary Cobern by Benj. Tupper, Washington Co.

1803 Jul 14   Devol, Gilbert and Rachael Peck by Nehemiah Davis, Pastor, Washing-
               ton Co.

1811 Apr 4   Devol, Gilbert and Anna Hatch by Nathaniel Hamilton, Washington Co.

1855 Jun 6   Devol, Grace of Dowell and Robert Williams of Beverly by Rev. John
               Boyd, St. Luke's Church, Marietta, Washington Co.

1812 Jul 8   Devol, Harriet and George Dunlevy by Rev. Stephen Lindley, Washing-
               ton Co.

1794 Nov 11   Devol, Jonathan and Clarissa Sherman by Robert Oliver, Washington Co.

1815 Dec 4   Devol, Lucinda and Wayne Sprague by John Green, JP, Washington Co.

1816 Dec 25   Devol, Lucy and Isaac Rice by D.H. Buell, JP, Washington Co.

1821 Mar 6   Devol, Maria and Luther D. Barker by Rev. Saml. P. Robbins,
               Washington Co.

1794 May 29   Devol, Nancy and John Drown by R.J. Meigs, Washington Co.

1815 Jan 20   Devol, Nancy and William P. Brown by John Green, JP, Washington Co.

1817 Aug 21   Devol, Nancy and John Seavers by Simon Merwin, Washington Co.

1813 Dec 25   Devol, Philip and Hannah P. Hatch by J. Greenman, JP, Washington Co.

1791 Jun 23   Devol, Polly and Justus Allen by -----, Washington Co.

1812 Nov 19   Devol, Polly and Solomon Goss, Jr. by Rev. David Young, Washington
               Co.

1800 Apr 27   Devol, Presburry and Patience Brownwell by E. Cutler, Washington Co.

1821 Oct 6   Devol, Rachel and Oliver Sheets by Rev. John McMahon, Washington Co.

1810 Mar 1   Devol, Rosanna and Benj. J. Stone by Stephen Lindsly, Washington Co.

1822 Jan 10   Devol, Simeon and Ruby Sprague by John Green, JP, Washington Co.

1815 Mar 11   Devol, Stephen and Rebecca Wilson by Rev. Thomas Moore, Washington
               Co.

1818 Nov 25   Devol, Stephen and Silina Buell by John Patterson, JP, Washington
               Co.

1820 Feb 24   Devol, William and Sarah Silvey by John Patterson, JP, Washington
               Co.

1800 Oct 16   Devol, Wing and Clara Hart by J. Munro, JP, Washington Co.

1808 Nov 20   Devoll, Elizabeth and John Green by Nehemiah Davis, Washington Co.

1789 Oct 11   Devoll, Presilla and John White by Ben Tupper, JCCCP, Washington Co.

1817 Feb 1   Devon, Walter and Pricilla Reading by T.D. Baird, Licking Co.

1803 May 17   Devore, Josias and Catherine Whetstone by Jos. Gardner, JP, Ross Co.

1825 Mar 20   Devore, Peggy and Hugh Riley by J.B. Gilliland, JP, Jackson Co.

1810 Feb 5   Dewalt, Enes and Christean Woolcutt by James Marsahll, Franklin Co.

1815 Oct 17   Dewees, Mary and John Dailey by Anthony Sheets, JP, Washington Co.

1815 Oct 21   Deweese, Catherine and Thomas Doogan by J. Cunningham, Licking Co.

1820 Sep 9   Deweese, Hester and David Boner by Wm. O'Bannon, JP, Licking Co.

1815 Aug 31   Dewese, Samuel and Mary Doogan by J. Cunningham, Licking Co.

1814 Feb 14   Dewett, Martin and Hulky Bury (license date), Pickaway Co.

1810 Jan 22   DeWitt, Margaret and David Rardon by Joseph Palmer, JP, Washington Co.

1814 Feb 6   DeWitt, Martin and Huldah Burgett by Wm. Florence, JP, Pickaway Co.

1811 Sep 10   DeWitt, Peggy and Joseph Morris (license date), Pickaway Co.

1824 Dec 23   Dickens, Martin and Elizabeth Staley by John Stealy, JP, Marion Co.

1808 Aug 14   Dickenson, Elizabeth and Samuel Biddle by Philip Whitten, JP,
               Washington Co.

1812 Nov 27   Dickenson, Oliver C. and Louise Rose by -----, Licking Co.

1800 Jun 10   Dickerson, Deborah and Samuel Williamson by Philip Whitten, JP,
               Washington Co.

1817 Mar 6   Dickerson, Elizabeth and Jolly Kenze by David Smithers, Washington Co.

1807 Oct 18   Dickerson, Joseph and Sally Daley by James Riggs, JP, Washington Co.

1817 Jan 16   Dickerson, Nelly and Silas Ellis by David Smithers, MMEC, Washington
               Co.

1819 Jul 2   Dickerson, Oliver and Lydia Rose by Rev. Timothy Harris, Licking Co.

1816 Apr 11   Dickerson, Vachel and Liddy Jolly by Anth'y Sheets, JP, Washington Co.

1817 Feb 13   Dickerson, Zadoh and Mary Thorn by Dan'l H. Buell, JP, Washington Co.

1816 Aug 22   Dickey, Catherine and Tilman Simmon by John Green, MG, Licking Co.

1809 Aug 22   Dickey, Martha and John Chivington by Edwin Putnam, Washington Co.

1805 Feb 7   Dickey, Solomon and Sally Welch by J. Brough, JP, Washington Co.

1804 Apr 5   Dickinson, Isaac and Peggy Martin by Peter Jackson, JP, Ross Co.

1815 Aug 27   Dickinson, Susannah and John Harbert by Uriah Hull, Licking Co.

1811 Mar 2   Dickison, William and Eleanor Fitzgerald (license date), Pickaway Co.

1806 May 8   Dickson, Agness and John Lee by Zachariah Stephen, JP, Franklin Co.

1805 Feb 15   Dickson, Anna and Josiah Scott by John Brough, JP, Washington Co.

1812 May 21   Dickson, Betsey and Isaac Miller by Alexander Commins, Franklin Co.

1800 Nov 5   Dickson, Christopher and Francis Lewis by Philip Witten, JP,
               Washington Co.

1820 Sep 21   Dickson, James and Matilda McMillen by Robert W. Riley, JP, Franklin
               Co.

1820 Jun 1   Dickson, John and Elizabeth Silva by Amos Wilson, Washington Co.

1854 Mar 9   Dickson, John C. and Jane Chambers by Rev. A. Kingsbury, Putnam
               Presbyterian Church, Muskingum Co.

1880 Sep 8   Dickson, John C. and Sarah J. MacDonald both of Putnam by Rev.
               George F. Moore, Putnam Presbyterian Church, Muskingum Co.

1887 Mar 23   Dickson, John C. and Carrie E. Scott both of Zanesville by Rev.
               George F. Moore, Putnam Presbyterian Church, Muskingum Co.

1812 Nov 23   Dickson, Robert and Hannah Miller (license date), Pickaway Co.

1816 Jan 13   Dier, John and Polly Sandusky by Jacob Keller, JP, Franklin Co.

1826 Sep 21   Diexson, Hiram and Betsey Howard by Gideon W. Hart, Franklin Co.

1797 Jun 19   Diggans, Betsy and Joseph Miller by Robert Safford, JP, Washington
               Co.

1811 Feb 7   Dilaha, Polly and Joseph Gifford (license date), Pickaway Co.

1829 Jan 29   Dildin, Catherine and Solomon Woodring by JFS, Franklin Co.

1820 Dec 14   Dildine, Andrew and Jane Seymore by William Jones, Franklin Co.

1806 Apr 3   Dildine, Catharine and John Right by Wm. Bennett, JP, Franklin Co.

1828 May 22   Dildine, Elisha and Eleanor Kraner by Charles Rarrey, ME Church,
               Franklin Co.

1825 Sep 4   Dildine, Elezabeth and William Seymour by Wm. Godman, Franklin Co.

1821 Apr 12   Dildine, Mary and William Seymore by John F. Solomon, Franklin Co.

1820 Nov 23   Dildine, Sarah and Elias Decker by John F. Solomon, Minister of the
               Gospel in the Methodist Episcopal Church, Franklin Co.

1818 Aug 9   Dilino, Philip and Ester Linkham by Venal Steward, MG, Franklin Co.

1806 Jan 30   Dill, Andrew and Elisabeth Culbertson by Zachariah Stephen, JP,
               Franklin Co.

1897 Jul 18   Dilles, Mrs. Solo. O. of Zanesville and James Straley ob Lancaster,
               O., by Rev. George F. More, Putnam Presbyterian Church,
               Muskingum Co.

1817 Jan 25   Dilley, Betsey and Abner Bent by Cyrus Ames, JP, Washington Co.

1810 Feb 15   Dilly, John and Nancy Plow by E.B. Dana, Washington Co.

1812 Sep 13   Dilman, Elizabeth and Robert Kuder (license date), Pickaway Co.

1804 Jan 2   Dines, James and Leah Littleton by Samuel Smith, Ross Co.

1818 Dec 10   Dircon, Abel and Lydia Clark by Stephen Maynard, Franklin Co.

1805 Jul 14   Dise, John and Elizabeth Byers by Wm. Creighton, Ross Co.

1811 Apr 14   Dison, Zepheniah and Deborah Williamson by Philip Witten, JP,
               Washington Co.

1816 Apr 23   Dispennet, Barbara and George Neff by Isaiah Hoskinson, JP,
               Licking Co.

1817 Dec 14   Dispennet, Catherine and John Smith by John W. Petterson, MG.
               Licking Co.

1818 Mar 4   Dispennett, Margaret and John Harter by Isaiah Hopkinson, JP,
               Licking Co.

1884 Oct 2   Districk, Thomas J. and Clara A. Jenkins both of Brush Creek Twp.,
               by Rev. George F. Moore, Putnam Presbyterian Church, Muskingum
               Co.

1810 Mar 16   Ditty, Susan and Nathan Bent by Wm. Browning, JP, Washington Co.

1812 Nov 14   Ditzel, Ann and Gideon Rathbone by Wm. Moody, JP, Licking Co.

1816 Aug 22   Divens, Sally and Asa Cheadle by E. Townsend, JP, Washington Co.

1813 Jul 22   Dix, Charles and Sally Hill by Saml. White, Franklin Co.

1818 Jun 17   Dix, Rachel and George Amos (or Amas) by Eli C. King, Franklin Co.

1821 Dec 30   Dix, Sally and Charles Hatton by W.T. Martin, JP, Franklin Co.

1815 Feb 5   Dixen, Sophia and James Johnson by Jas. Jackson, JP, Pickaway Co.

1817 Aug 21   Dixon, Anna and Louis Crabtree by Thomas Holland, JP, Jackson Co.

1821 Sep 1   Dixon, Archibald and Anna Burge by John Crow, JP, Licking Co.

1822 Jan 24   Dixon, Archibald and Louis Ingham by Aristarchus Walker, JP,
               Franklin Co.

1824 Jun 13   Dixon, Dinah and John Ray by Geo. Claypoole, JP, Jackson Co.

1820 Jan 6   Dixon, Jacob and Nancy Derby by Thos. Cox, JP, Jackson Co.

1817 Mar 20   Dixon, Jane and James Ogle by John True, JP, Washington Co.

1807 Jul 21   Dixon, John and Elizabeth Lambert by Wm. Irwin, JP, Franklin Co.

1820 Apr 13   Dixon, John and Frances Ray by Thos. Cox, JP, Jackson Co.

1819 Feb 4   Dixon, Joseph and Rachel Wilkinson by Jesse Rudrick, JP, Jackson Co.

1826 Jul 28   Dixon, Juliana and Benjamin Nicholson by Joseph Baker, MG, Jackson
               Co.

1825 Mar 2   Dixon, Lemuel and Rosanna Graves by Timothy Ratcliff, JP, Jackson
               Co.

1814 Nov 5   Dixon, Margaret Jane and Buckley Cumpstock by Ezra Griswold, JP,
               Franklin Co.

1815 Dec 13   Dixon, Mary and Jacob More by J. Green, Licking Co.

1823 Sep 16   Dixon, Mary and Henry Halterman by Samuel McDowell, JP, Jackson Co.

1825 Apr 7   Dixon, Mary and William Turner by Timothy Ratcliff, JP, Jackson Co.

1817 Mar 20   Dixon, Nathan and Rachel Graham by Francis Holland, JP Scioto Tp.,
               Jackson Co.

1807 Dec 20   Dixon, Sarah and Richard Tibbott by David Marks, JP, Franklin Co.

1801 Dec 25   Dixon, Thomas and Roesey Myers by Henry Smith, JP, Washington Co.

1816 Aug 9   Dixson, Henry Jr. and Elizabeth Rickabaugh by Francis Holland, JP
               Scioto Tp., Jackson Co.

1809 Oct 3   DLashmutt (or Lashmutt), Elias N. and Elizabeth O'Harra by James
               Marshall, Franklin Co.

1822 7 mo 4   Doan, Jacob and Hannah Stubbs, Miami Monthly Meeting, Warren Co.

1802 Apr 13   Doan, Sally and Richard H. Blin both of Cleveland by Amos Spafford,
               JP, Trumbull Co.

1819 Jul 8   Dockum, James Sr. and Phebe Jones by J.C. Smith, JP, Licking Co.

1816 Aug 27   Dodd, Elizabeth and John Corp by Rev. Saml. P. Robbins, Washington
               Co.

1820 Apr 6   Dodge, Anna and Ezra Green by John Green, JP, Washington Co.

1825 Apr 3   Dodge, Dr. Benjamin Stewart Pitt and Mrs. Lydia Tuller by
               Aristarcrus Walker, Franklin Co.

1816 Jul 20   Dodge, Joel and Sylina Greene by J. Humphreys, JP, Washington Co.

1799 Jul 10   Dodge, John and Katharine Galand by Daniel Story, Washington Co.

1808 Mar 24   Dodge, Katharine and Dickinson Jordin by Rob't Oliver, JP,
               Washington Co.

1821 Apr 3   Dodge, Mary and John Irwin by Noah Fidler, Licking Co.

1800 Jul 24   Dodge, Oliver and Anna Manchester by Daniel Story, Clerk, Washing-
               ton Co.

1813 Apr 22   Dodge, Oliver Jr. and Docia Wing by Sardine Stone, Washington Co.

1848 Dec 24   Dodge, Richard M. and Sally Ann Jump by Rev. D.W. Tolford, St.
               Luke's Church, Marietta, Washington Co.

1856 Apr 2   Dodge, Mrs. Sally Ann and Thomas B. Norris by Rev. John Boyd, St.
               Luke's Church, Marietta, Washington Co.

1821 May 8   Dodge, Sidney and Mary Hall by Elnathan Raymond, MMEC, Washington Co.

1850 Mar 13   Dodge, Susan M. and Jonathan R. Cooke by Rev. D.W. Tolford, St.
               Luke's Church, Marietta, Washington Co.

1804 Apr 19   Dodge, Susanna M. and Isaac Baker by Simeon Deming, Washington Co.

1840 Apr 29   Dodge, Wallace and Harriet Holeden by Rev. James Bonnar, St. Luke's
               Church, Marietta, Washington Co.

1809 Jun 27   Dodson, Jane and William McDonald by Wm. Haines, JP, Licking Co.

1819 Nov 12   Dohaty, Charles and Charlot Ciscow by Jacob Smith, Franklin Co.

1821 Jul 10   Doherty, William and Eliza McLene by James Hoge, Franklin Co.

1816 Jun 16   Dohn, Betsy and George Willis by Thomas White, JP, Washington Co.

1819 Sep 23   Dolin, John and Sarah Morris by Titan Kimble, JP, Washington Co.

1817 Sep 5   Dolin, Polly and Jacob M. Coffman by John Patterson, Washington Co.

1804 Jan 16   Doll, Mary and Wm. Lockard by J. Gardner, JP, Ross Co.

1805 Oct 31   Domigan, Enoch and Jane Brown by Zachariah Stephen, JP, Franklin Co.

1821 Aug 30   Domigan, William and Mary Sheperd by Eli C. King, Franklin Co.

1819 Feb 19   Donaldson, Rebecca and Abraham Collar by James Holmes, JP, Licking
               Co.

1805 Oct 17   Donalson, Moses and Rosy Buck by Wm. Bennett, JP, Franklin Co.

1818 Apr 7   Doneker, Jacob and Elizabeth Potts by Pelatiah White, Washington Co.

1806 --- --   Donhady, Elinor and John McCartney by John Robins, Ross Co.

1826 Jan 22   Donnally, Mary and Samuel W. Blagg by J.P. Gilliland, JP, Jackson
               Co.

1805 Jun 27   Donough, Robert and Pricilla Stephens by Wm. Creighton

1815 Aug 31   Doogan, Mary and Samuel Dewese by J. Cunningham, Licking Co.

1815 Oct 21   Doogan, Thomas and Catherine Deweese by J. Cunningham, Licking Co.

1825 Dec 29   Dorland, James and Eunice Daud (license date), Marion Co.

1871 Feb 4   Dornan, Ellen and John Nelson by Rev. John Boyd, St. Luke's
               Church, Marietta, Washington Co.

1871 Sep 14   Dornan, Irene and Charles F. Robinson by Rev. John Boyd, St.
               Luke's Church, Marietta, Washington Co.

1799 Feb 7   Dorr, Edmon and Anna Farmen by Alvan Bingham, Washington Co.

1804 Mar 20   Dorr, Rhoda and Christopher Wolf by Samuel Brown, Washington Co.

1810 Aug 25   Dorraned, Ezra and Ann Owings by Rev. T. Harris, Licking Co.

1805 Aug 11   Dorsen, Zadock and Ann Oneal by James Quinn, Elder, Ross Co.

1797 Sep 17   Doubleday, Mary and Thomas Lane by Josiah Munro, Washington Co.

1882 Oct 10   Doubt, Samuel and Elizabeth P. Putnam by Rev. John Boyd, St.
               Luke's Church, Marietta, Washington Co.

1791 Apr 19   Doude, Andrew and Abigail Carr by J. Gilman, JCCCP, Washington Co.

1819 Sep 2   Dougal, Anna and James Neal by J. Cunningham, JP, Licking Co.

1876 May 15   Douglas, Charles L. and Mary B. Loveall by Rev. John Boyd, St. Luke's
               Church, Marietta, Washington Co.

1869 Dec 15   Douglas, James A., M.D., and Anna E. Farquhar by Rev. A. Kingsbury,
               Putnam Presbyterian Church, Muskingum Co.

1811 Mar 26   Douglass, Andrew and Elizabeth Cassady (license date), Pickaway Co.

1826 Apr 10   Douglass, Jane and Michael Boblit by Timothy Ratcliffe, JP, Jackson
               Co.

1804 Jan 15   Douglass, John and Nelly Sheppart by Jacob Earhart, JP, Washington
               Co.

1824 Aug 11   Douglass, Margret and Dayton Topping by R.W. Cowls, Franklin Co.

1872 Jan 11   Douglass, Melvin D. and Emily Jane Cox by Rev. John Boyd, St. Luke's
               Church, Marietta, Washington Co.

1819 Sep 30   Douthitt, John and Phebe Littlefield by Joel Tuttle, Jr., JP,
               Washington Co.

1804 Jun 24   Dowall, Elizabeth and John More by John Brough, JP, Washington Co.

1816 Sep 24   Dowing, Hannah and Nathan Boid by Geo. Hoover, JP, Licking Co.

1820 Jun 27   Downing, Dennis and Amella Marsh by Nicholas Goetschius, JP,
               Franklin Co.

1824 Sep 7   Downing, Jemima and Israel Brown by James Boyd, JP, Franklin Co.

1814 Mar 3   Downing, John and Polly Champ by Rev. Geo. Alkire, Pickaway Co.

1823 Jun 26   Downing, Joshua and Sarrah Craun by Nicholas Goetschius, JP,
               Franklin Co.

1819 Nov 7   Downing, Mary and William Casteel by Reuben Golliday, Franklin Co.

1823 Jul 3   Downing, Nancy and William Henry Howe by Joseph Badger, Franklin Co.

1827 Nov 29   Downing, Timothy and Rachel Hayden by H. Crabb, MEC, Franklin Co.

1805 Oct 17   Downs, David and Sarah Murphy by Wm. Creighton, Ross Co.

1823 Mar 20   Downs, Eleanor and Isaac Goetchieus by Jacob Grubb, Franklin Co.

1823 Oct 9   Downs, James and Olive Wilber by Robert W. Riley, JP, Franklin Co.

1826 Mar 30   Downs, Sarah and George Raredon by Henry Matthews, Franklin Co.

1801 Sep 14   Doyl, Mary and Joseph Rolland by Wm. Harper, JP, Washington Co.

1825 Jun 22   Drake, Ann Marie and James Hughey by John Stealy, JP, Marion Co.

1893 Mar 8   Drake, Clara R. and Frank T. Little both of Zanesville by Rev.
               George F. Moore, Putnam Presbyterian Church, Muskingum Co.

1821 Mar 15   Drake, Fanny and Jesse Patterson by Sanford Converse, JP, Licking Co.

1821 Jul 22   Drake, Huldy and Jacob King by John F. Solomon, Franklin Co.

1858 Oct 14   Drake, John H. and Rosetta Allen by Rev. A. Kingsbury, Putnam
               Presbyterian Church, Muskingum Co.

1887 Apr 21   Drake, Julia E. of Zanesville and Warren C. Browne of Cincinnati,
               by Rev. George F. Moore, Putnam Presbyterian Church, Muskingum
               Co.

1810 Jan 25   Drake, Margret and Thomas Marshall by Geo. Wells, JP, Licking Co.

1818 Jun 25   Drake, Mary and John Reighter by Benj Beem, JP, Licking Co.

1893 Apr 18   Drake, Rosetta A. of Zanesville and Beverly W. Bozman of Cincinnati,
               by Rev. George F. Moore, Putnam Presbyterian Church, Muskingum
               Co.

1817 Feb 20   Drake, Sarah and William Foster by Geo. Callanhan, EMEC, Licking Co.

1872 Mar 25   Draper, Sarah and William Peaker by Rev. John Boyd, St. Luke's
               Church, Marietta, Washington Co.

1816 May 7   Drew, Elijah and Sarah Smith by Nathan Cunningham, Licking Co.

1811 Jun 13   Driesbach, Henry and Mary Hedges (license date), Pickaway Co.

1803 Nov 9   Drigs, Mary and Ethan Hewitt by Jacob Earhart, Washington Co.

1815 Jan 12   Driver, James and Eve Baugh by Henry Davis, JP, Pickaway Co.

1814 Feb 10   Drivier, Sally and Joseph David by William King, JP, Pickaway Co.

1814 Jun 20   Droddy, Aaron and Fanny Eaton by W. Droddy, Franklin Co.

1813 Jun 1   Droddy, Margaret and Mahlon Goodin by D. Hess, Franklin Co.

1816 Sep 28   Droddy, William and Elizabeth Woolcut by Michael Patton, JP,
               another entry 28 Nov 1816, Franklin Co.

1794 May 29   Drown, John and Nancy Devol by R.J. Meigs, Washington Co.

1807 Feb 26   Drown, John and Mary Brown by Stephen Lindsly, Washington Co.

1817 Feb 24   Drown, Mary and Richard Chatick by David Smithers, Washington Co.

1820 Apr 11   Drown, Notley and Polly Hook by Daniel H. Buell, JP, Washington Co.

1821 Nov 21   Drumm, Peter and Sally Pritchett by Edward Hursey, JP, Licking Co.

1836 Nov --   Dudley, Jas. H. and Betsey E. Bray by Rev. E. Burr, St. John's
               Church, Worthington, Franklin Co.

1815 Oct 14   Duff, Anna and Saml. Brown by James Hoge, Franklin Co.

1829 Jul 16   Duff, Nancy and Micajah Parrish by Geo. Jefferies, Franklin Co.

1806 Feb 24   Dugan, Thomas and Nancy Hewitt by Thomas Hicks, Ross Co.

1822 Feb 26   Duggin, Michael and Eleanor Inks by Russel Bigelow, MG, Franklin Co.

1821 Jan 15   Duke, David and Martha Lance? by J. Cunningham, Licking Co.

1818 12 mo 2   Dukeminer, Elizabeth and Gershom Perdue, Miami Monthly Meeting,
               Warren Co.

1815 Dec 6   Dukes, Mary and William Powel by John Stipp, Franklin Co.

1827 Mar 1   Dukes, Richard and Polly Blue by P. Adams, Franklin Co.

1824 Apr 20   Dulin, Ann and Smith Dulin by Woolry Conrad, JP, Franklin Co.

1824 Apr 20   Dulin, Smith and Ann Dulin by Woolry Conrad, JP, Franklin Co.

1815 May 8   Dun, Benjamin and Peme Billingsly by Jacob Hahn, JP, Licking Co.

1815 Nov 2   Dunbar, Anna and Martin Shewey by Jno. Russell, Washington Co.

1821 May 27   Dunbar, Emily and Bertrand Meruben by John Russell, JP, Washington
               Co.

1818 Apr 12   Dunbar, Nancy and Francis Devol by John Russell, Washington Co.

1817 Mar 19   Dunbar, William and Elizabeth English by Ephraim Cutler, JP,
               Washington Co.

1818 Mar 18   Dunbar, William and Martha Elizabeth Gard by Salmon N. Cook, JP,
               Washington Co.

1820 Jan 20   Duncan, Charles and Charity Gard by S.N. Cook, JP, Washington Co.

1810 Oct 23   Duncan, Maria and Alexander McLain (license date), Pickaway Co.

1812 Jan 28   Duncan, Polly and Sampson Cole by Stephen Lindsly, Washington Co.

1812 Aug 11   Duncan, Polly and Samuel Beatty by John B. Johnson, JP, Franklin Co.

1814 Mar 27   Duncan, Sally and Levi Cole by Rev. S. Lindsley, Washington Co.

1804 Dec 27   Dunham, Amos and Laura Matilda Guthrie by Joseph Strickland,
               Washington Co.

1797 Aug 21   Dunham, Bathsheba and Joseph Tilton by J. Pierce, Washington Co.

1797 Mar 23   Dunham, Daniel and Keziah Swett by Josiah Munro, Washington Co.

1871 Feb 27   Dunham, Olive and Moses Hogue by Rev. John Boyd, St. Luke's Church,
               Marietta, Washington Co.

1791 Jul 24   Dunham, Ruth and Simeon Wright by Benj. Tupper, Washington Co.

1810 Nov 8   Dunhoe, Precilla and James Moore (license date), Pickaway Co.

1819 Nov 7   Dunick, Jamima and Richard Derick by Richard Courtright, Franklin Co.

1802 Jan 6   Dunken, John of Youngstown and Elizabeth McClain of Pennsylvania
               by Caleb Baldwin, JP, Trumbull Co.

1819 Apr 9   Dunlap, Elizabeth and Alexander Hopper by Joseph Grate, Franklin Co.

1820 Sep 18   Dunlap, Jane and William Wills by Wm. Hull, JP, Licking Co.

1864 May 12   Dunlap, Jennie and William C. Andrews by Rev. A. Kingsbury, Putnam
               Presbyterian Church, Muskingum Co.

1812 Dec 21   Dunlap, Joseph and Rachel Mathew by Nathan Connard, Licking Co.

1848 Jan 8   Dunalp, Rachel Ellen of Putnam and Stewart A. Lasley of Springfield,
               O., by Rev. A. Kingsbury, Putnam Presbyterian Church, Muskingum
               Co.

1804 Mar 29   Dunlap, Robert and Rebecca Taylor by Noble Crawford, Ross Co.

1841 Mar 4   Dunlap, Robert N. and Martha Ann Gillespie by Rev. A. Kingsbury,
               Putnam Presbyterian Church, Muskingum Co.

1812 Jul 8   Dunlevy, George and Harriet Devol by Rev. Stephen Lindley,
               Washington Co.

1818 Feb 18   Dunn, Mary and William Ramsey by James Hoge, Franklin Co.

1817 Jan 12   Dunn, Susanna and Thomas Healton (or Halston) by James Hoge,
               Franklin Co. (another entry 27 Mar 1817)

1817 Feb 28   Dunnavan, Elizabeth and David Letts by John Spencer, JP, Licking Co.

1819 Jan 14   Dunneick, Joseph and Catharine Wright by Richard Courtright, JP,
               Franklin Co.

1825 Jun 30   Dunnivan, Fanny and John Lathmore by Reuben Golliday, Franklin Co.

1794 Mar 27   Duraille, Jeanne Francois and Auguste Chezeau by J.G. Petitt,
               Washington Co.

1813 Apr 2   Durbin, Anna and James Jones (license date), Pickaway Co.

1821 Dec 6   Durfie, Abigail and Sylvanus Howe by Rev. Sam'l P. Robbins,
               Washington Co.

1802 Jul 26   Durgee, Silas and Eleanor Williams by Daniel Story, Clerk,
               Washington Co.

1804 Mar 7   Durham, Margaret and Martin Mansfield by James Graham, JP,
               Washington Co.

1818 Aug 2   Dursels, John and Susannah Goodwin by George Hays, Franklin Co.

1796 Dec 9   Duthe, Charles F. and Jean Caddot by Robert Safford, JP, Washington
               Co.

1896 Jul 6   Dutro, Anna Grace of Zanesville and Elmer E. Holler by Newark, O.,
               by Rev. George F. Moore, Putnam Presbyterian Church, Muskingum
               Co.

1898 May 17   Dutro, Wheeler S. and Mary E. Harper both of Zanesville by Rev.
               George F. Moore, Putnam Presbyterian Church, Muskingum Co.

1808 Nov 17   Dutten, Sarah and Levi Dana by Nehemiah Davis, MG, Washington Co.

1808 Dec 30   Dutton, Abigail and Jacob Galor by Daniel Dunfee, Washington Co.

1813 Feb 4   Dutton, David and Mary Fearing by Joseph Frye, Washington Co.

1806 Sep 25   Dutton, Hannah and James Haugh by Thomas Stanley, Washington Co.

1806 Jun 26   Dutton, Jain and Wm. Garret Gaylor by Thos. Stanley, Washington Co.

1817 Jan 26   Dutton, James and Sally Bailey by Stephen Guthrie, Washington Co.

1806 7 mo 16   Dutton, John and Martha Cleaver, Miami Monthly Meeting, Warren Co.

1818 Sep 14   Dutton, Margaret and John Andrews by Salmon N. Cook, JP, Washington
               Co.

1821 Oct 24   Dutton, Nancy and Elijah Davis by Osgood McFarland, JP, Washington Co.

1869 Oct 8   Dutton, Phelista and John P. Peker by Rev. John Boyd, St. Luke's
               Church, Marietta, Washington Co.

1819 Feb 15   Dutton, Polly and Daniel Davis by Rev. Wm. Davis, Washington Co.

1806 Feb 25   Duvall, Benjamin and Nancy Reed by Wm. Bennett, JP, Franklin Co.

1865 Jun 28   Duvall, Charles of Baltimore, Md., and Martha A. Rankin of Putnam
               by Rev. A. Kingsbury, Putnam Presbyterian Church, Muskingum Co.

1856 Dec 23   Duvall, George W. of Baltimore, Md., and Margaret M. Rankin of
               Putnam by Rev. A. Kingsbury, Putnam Presbyterian Church,
               Muskingum Co.

1792 Jun 6   Dwellers, Jules Lemane and Elizabeth Benzelin by J.G. Petitt,
               Washington Co.

1864 Oct 24   Dyar, Joseph of Rainbow and Frances M. Kendrick by Rev. John Boyd,
               St. Luke's Church, Marietta, Washington Co.

1814 Dec 13   Dye, A. and P. Harrison by Jos. Hays, JP, Pickaway Co.

1797 Aug 15   Dye, Abigail and Zoeth Hammond by Robert Oliver, JP, Washington Co.

1820 May 25   Dye, Eliza and Nathan Davis, Jr. by Osgood McFarland, JP,
               Washington Co.

1812 Apr 9   Dye, Enoch and Mary Ann Ridgway by Henry Jolly, Washington Co.

1815 Apr 13   Dye, Ezekiel and Phebe Davis by Sam'l Dye, JP, Washington Co.

1811 Dec 8   Dye, John and Priscilla Ridgway by Henry Jolly, JP, Washington Co.

1812 May 10   Dye, Jona and Fanny Cawood by Samuel Dye, JP, Washington Co.

1808 Sep 20   Dye, Mary and Arphaxan Devol by Jacob Lindsly, Washington Co.

1814 Sep 23   Dye, Mary and James Hoff by Samuel Dye, Washington Co.

1818 Oct 6   Dye, Mary and Thomas Jenkins by Sardine Stone, JP, Washington Co.

1815 Sep 25   Dye, Polly and John Faulkner by John True, JP, Washington Co.

1811 Apr 7   Dye, Reuben F. and Polly Tewel by Henry Jolly, JP, Washington Co.

1811 Jul 30   Dye, Sally and Thomas Worthington by Stephen Lindsly, Washington Co.

1819 Dec 2   Dye, Susan and Robert Pierce by Rev. Saml. P. Robbins, Washington Co.

1817 Jun 29   Dye, Thomas and Elizabeth Hill by Elias Conger, Washington Co.

1827 Dec 27   Dyer, Martha and John Roberts by John Tipton, JP, Franklin Co.

1819 Feb 8   Eaging, James and Elizabeth Phelps by J. Evans, JP, Licking Co.

1819 Apr 2   Eagler, Catharine and Archelaus Winson by James Hoge, Franklin Co.

1813 Jun 10   Eagler, John and Susan Baughman by Simeon Moore, Franklin Co.

1812 Apr 8   Eagler, Mary and Henry Boughman by Simeon Moore, Franklin Co.

1816 Apr 1   Eagler, Susan and Peter Putnam by Rev. James Hoge, Franklin Co.

1821 Jan 25   Eairs, Nancy and Wills Spencer by Thos. B. Patterson, Franklin Co.

1814 Sep 24   Eaker, Margaret and Moses Rush by James Emmett, JP, Pickaway Co.

1803 Jun 1   Eakins, Sarah and Hugh McGill by Oliver Ross, Ross Co.

1805 Apr 16   Eamins, John and Nancy Moss by John Davidson, Ross Co.

1805 Aug 8   Earl, Granthem and Margaret Funston by Thomas Hicks, Ross Co.

1814 May 24   Earl, Matthew and Phoebe Tiffin by Charles Cade, JP, Pickaway Co.

1827 Feb 22   Early, Eliza and Jacob Elmore by Rev. James Hoge, Franklin Co.

1817 Dec 26   Early, Elizabeth and Colbert Stewart by Townsend Nichols, JP,
               Franklin Co.

1828 Mar 30   Early, Lydia and Reuben Rice by Samuel Hamilton, Franklin Co.

1817 Oct 12   Earnest, Amelia and Samuel Parr by John W. Patterson, JP, Licking Co.

1814 Oct 16   Eastman, Hannah and William Miles by Stephen Guthrie, Washington Co.

1825 Mar 20   Eastwood, Isaac and Nancy Foley (widow) by C. Henkel, Franklin Co.

1818 Dec 27   Eastman, Sally and Barzillia T. Miles by Rev. Saml. P. Robbins,
               Washington Co.

1825 Sep 8   Eaton, Amelia and David Kellogg by Conrad Roth, JP, Marion Co.

1865 Sep 12   Eaton, Eben F. and Maria L. Haskell by Wm. Bower, St. Luke's Church,
               Granville, Licking Co.

1814 Jun 20   Eaton, Fanny and Aaron Droddy by W. Droddy, Franklin Co.

1820 Apr 22   Eaton, Joseph and Eunacy Curtis by James Smith, ECC, Licking Co.

1867 Sep 30   Eaton, Mary A. and Henry C. Cylp by Rev. John Boyd, St. Luke's
               Church, Marietta, Washington Co.

1804 Apr 13   Eator, Jacob and Nancy Sollers by John Hoddy, JP, Ross Co.

1822 Jul 13   Ebey, Susana and Daniel Hutchinson by Jacob Grubb, Franklin Co.

1815 Dec 31   Eby, Jacob and Sarah Blue by Geo. C. Bogart, JP, Franklin Co.

1808 Dec 2   Eddington, Ann and Jethro Deewese by W. Haines, JP, licking Co.

1821 Nov 29   Eddleblute, Elizabeth and Isaac Ellis by Rev. Wm. Davis, Washington
               Co.

1828 Aug 28   Eder, Abigail and James Blain by Geo. Jefferies, Franklin Co.

1870 Oct 27   Edgar, Anna and George H. Green by Rev. A. Kingsbury, Putnam
               Presbyterian Church, Muskingum Co.

1820 Mar 7   Edgar, James and Anne Stagg by James Hoge, Franklin Co.

1814 Jan 30   Edgar, Jane and Lewis Ogden by Jacob Thompson, Franklin Co.

1852 Jul 8   Edgar, John W. and Mary Ann Humphrey by Rev. A. Kingsbury, Putnam
               Presbyterian Church, Muskingum Co.

1874 Jun 23   Edgar, Margaret E. and Alex. McClelland by Rev. A. Kingsbury,
               Putnam Presbyterian Church, Muskingum Co.

1826 Jan 13   Edger, Esther and Philander Boner by A. Allison, Franklin Co.

1821 Mar 27   Edgerton, Giles and Dorcas Ross by Moses Williamson, JP,
               Washington Co.

1874 Jun 3   Edgerton, James Watson and Mary Hildreth Ross by Rev. John Boyd,
               St. Luke's Church, Marietta, Washington Co.

1821 Jan 4   Edger, Joseph and Abegal Ogden by Thos. B. Patterson, JP,
               Franklin Co.

1821 Feb 15   Edgerton, Mary Ann and William H. Shipman by Rev. Saml. P. Robbins,
               Washington Co.

1821 Jan 1   Edgerton, Sarah L. and Samuel A. Westcott by Rev. Saml. P. Robbins,
               Washington Co.

1820 Apr 25   Edington, Jacob and Ruth Parks by Uriah Hull, JP, Licking Co.

1803 Jul 27   Edington, John and Malander Walls by Seth Cashart, JP, Washington Co.

1817 Nov 27   Edman, William and Anna McKinley by Josias Ewing, JP, Licking Co.

1822 Jun 22   Edmiston, John M. and Matilda Gwynne by James Hoge, Franklin Co.

1820 Jul 15   Edmond, Paul and Hannah Harris by Thomas Can, MG, Licking Co.

1815 Jan 12   Edwards, Catherine and John McKinley by Nathan Connard, JP,
               Licking Co.

1817 Oct 13   Edwards, John and Polly Stephens by Abner Goff, MG, Licking Co.

1818 Jan 1   Edwards, Joshua and Margaret Reed by Noah Fidler, Licking Co.

1819 Apr 23   Edwards, Margaret and Jesse Channel by Thomas Carr, Licking Co.

1820 Aug 30   Edwards, Mary and John Larabee by Uriah Hull, JP, Licking Co.

1819 Feb 25   Edwards, Nancy and Hugh Reed by Noah Fidler, Licking Co.

1812 Nov 10   Edwards, Polly and Jacob Gegerform by -----, Licking Co.

1807 Feb 3   Edwards, Rachel and John Collins by Philip Witten, Washington Co.

1821 Jan 11   Edwards, Roberts and Solomon Munsell by Knowles Lennel, JP, Licking
               Co.

1816 May 2   Edwards, Ruth and Aaron Davis by Nathan Parr, JP, Washington Co.

1805 6 mo 26   Edwards, William and Jemima Bridges, Miami Monthly Meeting, Warren
               Co.

1814 Apr 10   Edwards, Wm. and Mary Valentine by Thos Mace, JP, Pickaway Co.

1822 11 mo 6   Edwards, William and Elizabeth Newman, Miami Monthly Meeting,
               Warren Co.

1816 Jun 27   Elder, James and Sarah Rynard by Nathan Tarr, JP, Washington Co.

1821 Aug 30   Elder, Thomas and Amnis Welton by William Jones, Franklin Co.

1826 Feb 9   Elder, Washington and Sarah Rine by J. Gander, Franklin Co.

1826 Jun 3   Elder, William and Elizabeth Whitmore by I. Gander, JP, Franklin Co.

1798 Mar 18   Elenwood, Daniel and Fanny Inglas by J. Pierce, JCCCP, Washington
               Co.

1812 Jun 10   Eliot, Jane and Henry Shirtz by -----, Licking Co.

1812 Jun 23   Eliot, Mary and John Cunningham by -----, Licking Co.

1812 Feb 27   Eliot, Robert and Margaret Roberts by -----, Licking Co.

1818 Oct 18   Ellenwood, Frances and Gideon Norton by Jonathan Dunah, JP,
               Washington Co.

1814 Jun 28   Ellenwood, Martha and Elias Bellows by Rev. Isaac Quinn, Washington
              Co.

1818 Dec 8   Ellinwood, Mary and John Kierns by Rev. Saml. Hamilton, Deacon,
              Washington Co.

1820 Oct 10   Elliot, Anna A. and Amos Arthur by John Shumate, JP, Jackson Co.

1813 Jun 24   Elliott, Alexander and Jane Elliott by John Tulloss, JP, Licking Co.

1820 Mar 28   Elliott, Ann and William Moore by T. D. Baird, VDM, Licking Co.

1819 Jan 11   Elliott, James and Nancy Green by -----, Licking Co.

1820 Dec 14   Elliott, James and Margaret McCray by John Shumate, JP, Jackson Co.

1828 Sep 25   Elliott, James and Chloe Foley by Benj. Britton, ECC, Franklin Co.

1893 Jan 25   Elliott, James R. of Zanesville and Jane Gray of Scotland by Rev.
              George F. Moore, Putnam Presbyterian Church, Muskingum Co.

1809 May 18   Elliott, Jane and Stephen Gill by Wm. Haines, JP, Licking Co.

1813 Jun 24   Elliott, Jane and Alexander Elliott by John Tulloss, JP, Licking Co.

1825 Mar 3   Elliott, Mary and John Radabaugh by Samuel Garrick, JP, Jackson Co.

1811 Aug 11   Elliott, Peggy and Noah Harris by -----, Licking Co.

1821 Oct 18   Ellis, Alfred and Sally Lane by Rev. Wm. Davis, Washington Co.

1876 Sep 6   Ellis, Charles F. of St. Louis, Mo., and Cora Potwin of Putnam by
              Rev. A. Kingsbury, Putnam Presbyterian Church, Muskingum Co.

1827 Apr 17   Ellis, Elijah and Mary Kerr by James Hoge, Franklin Co.

1814 Jan 23   Ellis, Elizabeth and Dennis Poool by Anth'y Sheets, Washington Co.

1878 Oct 3   Ellis, Frank R. and Mary E. Rhodes by Rev. Dudley W. Rhodes, St.
              Luke's Church, Marietta, Washington Co.

1821 Nov 29   Ellis, Isaac and Elizabeth Eddleblute by Rev. Wm. Davis, Washington
              Co.

1823 Jan --   Ellis, Jason and Susan S. Beed by James Hoge, Franklin Co.

1822 Feb 21   Ellis, John and Patty Myers by Asa Cheadle, JP, Washington Co.

1817 Jan 16   Ellis, Silas and Nelly Dickerson by David Smithers, MMEC, Washington
              Co.

1826 Jan 2   Ellison, Elizabeth and Samuel Cox by Solomon Redfern, JP, Jackson Co.

1800 Dec 18   Ellison, Nancy and Stephen Frost by Nehemiah Davis, MG, Washington Co.

1816 May 2   Ellison, Sally and John Morris by Amos Wilson, JP, Washington Co.

1824 May 27   Ellit, Robert and Susannah Brunk by Benj. Britton, Franklin Co.

1819 Dec 11   Ellsworth, Oliver and Susannah Cochrun, dau of Simon (license date)
              Franklin Co.

1824 Apr 6   Elmer, Jacob and Elizabeth Bowan by C. Henkel, Franklin Co.

1827 Feb 22   Elmore, Jacob and Eliza Early by Rev. James Hoge, Franklin Co.

1817 Jul 20   Elsey, Edward M. and Elizabeth M. Taylor by James Hoge, Franklin Co.

1816 Jul 23   Elsey, Elizabeth and John Thompson by James Taylor, Franklin Co.

1803 May 1   Ely, Asher and Lydia Lyman both of Franklin by David Hudson, JP,
              Trumbull Co.

1800 Nov 7   Ely, Sally and John Campbell both of Warren by Calvin Austin, JP,
              Trumbull Co.

1823 Apr 22   Elzey, John and Susannah French by Charles Waddell, LM, Franklin Co.

1811 Mar 5   Emerson, Arta and Wm. Sprague by Dudley Davis, Washington Co.

1809 Jan 26   Emerson, Asa Jr. and Elizabeth Olney by Thos. Seely, Washington Co.

1817 Apr 3   Emerson, Benjamin and Mary Hinkley by Obadiah Scott, JP, Washington
              Co.

1810 Jul 29   Emerson, Caleb and Mary Dana by Rev. Sam'l P. Robbins, Washington Co.

1810 Dec 11   Emerson, David and Nancy Sprague by Thomas Seely, JP, Washington Co.

1818 Jan 24   Emerson, David and Betsey Smith by Thomas White, JP, Washington Co.

1815 Apr 20   Emerson, Lettia and John Fryback by Isaac Quinn, Pickaway Co.

1814 Sep 26   Emerson, Luke and Catharine Devin by Thomas White, JP, Washington Co.

1809 Apr 20   Emerson, Susanna and Samuel Gates by Asa Cheadle, JP, Washington Co.

1817 Jul 3   Emery, B. and Susanna Orr by John W. Patterson, JP, Licking Co.

1894 Jul 4   Emery, Cora A. of Zanesville and Alexander Williamson of Findlay, O.,
              by Rev. George F. Moore, Putnam Presbyterian Church, Muskingum
              Co.

1828 Dec 15   Emery, Elizabeth and Joseph Brown by Thomas Wood, Franklin Co.

1883 Aug 8   Emery, Joseph P. and Alice Young both of Zanesville by Rev. George
              F. Moore, Putnam Presbyterian Church, Muskingum Co.

1868 Feb 4   Emery, Lida and John Mayer by Rev. A. Kingsbury, Putnam Presbyterian
              Church, Muskingum Co.

1873 Apr 10   Emery, Ruth H. and Robert J. Parsons by Rev. A. Kingsbury, Putnam
              Presbyterian Church, Muskingum Co.

1867 Feb 26   Emery, Sarah and Andrew Stewart by Rev. A. Kingsbury, Putnam
              Presbyterian Church, Muskingum Co.

1825 Dec 22   Emery, Selphinia and John Johnston by James Boyd, JP, Franklin Co.

1826 Oct 24   Emley, Sally and Martin Wagoner by Jacob Smith, JP, Franklin Co.

1824 Apr 12   Emmerson, John and Elizabeth Cox by W.T. Martin, Franklin Co.

1806 Feb 7   Emmery, George and Ann Francis by Peter Jackson, JP, Ross Co.

1804 Jul 12   Emmery, Marea and Thomas Whitney by Isaac Cook, JP, Ross Co.

1804 Jul 19   Emmery, Margrett and John Page by Isaac Cook, JP, Ross Co.

1823 May 15   Emmich, John and Isabella Culbertson by James Hoge, Franklin Co.

1821 Feb 8   Emrey, Selinah and David Kingrey by Samuel Dyer, Franklin Co.

1811 Jul 25   England, Elizabeth and William Powlson (license date), Pickaway Co.

1804 Sep 24   England, John and Anna Burk by J. Gardner, JP, Ross Co.

1825 11 mo 2 Engle, Isaac and Mary E. Haines, Miami Monthly Meeting, Warren Co.

1817 Mar 19   English, Elizabeth and William Dunbar by Ephraim Cutler, JP,
              Washington Co.

1822 Jul 28   English, Esther and Luther Boid by A. Buttles, Franklin Co.

1819 Jun 10   English, Joseph and Mary Hupp by Alex Holden, JP, Licking Co.

1821 Sep 6   English, Samuel and Elisa Cook by Noah Fidler, Licking Co.

1811 Feb 14   Enises, Sarah and John Cheser by Thomas Morris, Franklin Co.

1811 Jun 2   Enocks, Jesse and Betsey Forshey by Amos Porter, JP, Washington Co.

1856 Sep 24   Ephland, Mary L. and Sidney Fowle by T. Corlett, St. Luke's Church, Granville, Licking Co.

1804 Jul 17   Erving, Sally and Obadiah Clark by D. Loring, Washington Co.

1817 Jul 20   Erwin, John and Charity Parker by Pelatiah White, JP, Washington Co.

1818 Sep 8   Ery, Barbary and William Roy by Amisiah Hutchinson, JP, Franklin Co.

1819 Nov 16   Eshleman, Mary and John Croan by Simeon Overturf, JP, Licking Co.

1825 Jul 28   Essex, Anne and Rilay German by Persinal Adams, JP, Franklin Co.

1825 Aug 18   Essex, Jesse and Catharine Kendall by Wm. Long, JP, Franklin Co.

1825 May 5   Essex, Margret and John Hornbaker by Persovial Adams, JP, Franklin Co.

1826 Sep 14   Essex, Sarah and Joseph Goodwin by P. Adams, JP, Franklin Co.

1818 Feb 4   Etinger, Daniel and Frigit Cambelin by Joseph Grate, Franklin Co.

1818 Dec 11   Eubanks, Joseph and Catharine Nally by Thomas Scott, JP, Jackson Co.

1819 Feb 11   Eubanks, Joseph and Della Craige by D. Mitchell, JP, Jackson Co.

1820 Oct 22   Eutsler, Geo and Betsy Hollingshead by Patrick Shearer, JP, Jackson Co.

1825 Mar 24   Evans, Catharine and James Smith by Joseph Carper, Franklin Co.

1811 Aug 4   Evans, David and Nancy McCreary by John Crow, JP, Licking Co.

1813 6 mo 2   Evans, David and Rachel Burnet, Miami Monthly Meeting, Warren Co.

1817 Apr 28   Evans, Diana and Joseph McKelvy by Noah Fidler, Licking Co.

1812 9 mo 2   Evans, Elizabeth and Stephen Cook, Miami Monthly Meeting, Warren Co.

1819 Jan 7   Evans, Elizabeth and Philip Vandevender by John Green, JP, Licking Co.

1825 Nov 10   Evans, Enoch and Maria Hartsack by John Davis, JP, Franklin Co.

1821 Mar 1   Evans, Evan and Ruth Berry by Wm. Hull, JP, Licking Co.

1809 Dec 27   Evans, George and Jane McCune by -----, Licking Co.

1822 2 mo 6   Evans, George and Mary Hasket, Miami Monthly Meeting, Warren Co.

1820 6 mo 7   Evans, Hannah Ann and John Ward, Miami Monthly Meeting, Warren Co.

1821 2 mo 7   Evans, Hepsabah and Samuel Stevenson, Miami Monthly Meeting, Warren Co.

1828 Sep 9   Evans, James and Huldah Morris by John F. Solomon, Franklin Co.

1819 Mar 14   Evans, Jane and Edwin Burlinggame by Rev. Saml. P. Robbins, Washington Co.

1810 Jan 25   Evans, John and Lydia McCune by Rev. George Vanaman, Licking Co.

1815 Jul 7   Evans, John and Deborah Radcliff by Z. Carlisle, JP, Licking Co.

1817 Jul 9   Evans, John and Elizabeth Radcliff by Zach Carlisle, JP, Licking Co.

1818 Feb 5   Evans, John and Elizabeth Kile by Emmor Cox, Franklin Co.

1818 Jul 6   Evans, John and Nancy Lucas by Wm. Davis, MBC, Washington Co.

1821 Jan 25 Evans, John and Elizabeth Lewis by Samuel Bancroft, JP, Licking Co.

1816 Feb 27 Evans, John H. and Polly Charles by Geo. Callanhan, EMEC, Licking Co.

1827 Mar 15 Evans, Lovett and Mahala Kyrk by Tracy Willcox, JP, Franklin Co.

1809 8 mo 10 Evans, Mary and Levi Hawkins, Miami Monthly Meeting, Warren Co.

1811 Jun 30 Evans, Mary and Samuel Pontius (license date), Pickaway Co.

1811 Dec 12 Evans, Mary and Rose Buck by Rev. G. Vanaman, Licking Co.

1822 11 mo 6 Evans, Mary and Richard Pedrick, Miami Monthly Meeting, Warren Co.

1826 Mar 30 Evans, Mary and Woodford Miller by Geo. Jefferies, MG, Franklin Co.

1821 Jan 11 Evans, Masey and Benjamin Predmore by Zach Carlisle, JP, Licking Co.

1809 Aug 20 Evans, Nancy and Aaron Ward by Zachariah Carlisle, Esq., Licking Co.

1815 May 14 Evans, Nancy and John David by Samuel Dunnavan, Licking Co.

1812 5 mo 7 Evans, Rebecca and Samuel Brown, Miami Monthly Meeting, Warren Co.

1821 Mar 25 Evans, Rebecca and William Davidson by Rev. Thrap, Licking Co.

1811 Aug 29 Evans, Ruth and Isaac Moore (license date), Pickaway Co.

1822 10 mo 3 Evans, Ruth and Benjamin L. Satterthwaite, Miami Monthly Meeting,
             Warren Co.

1820 Jun 1   Evans, Sally and Wells White by Thomas White, JP, Washington Co.

1827 Aug 15 Evans, Sarah and Earlis Day by Townsend Nichols, Franklin Co.

1799 Jun 16 Evans, Wimeon and Elizabeth Miller by Robert Oliver, JP, Washington
             Co.

1813 10 mo 6 Evans, Thomas and Hannah Pedrick, Miami Monthly Meeting, Warren Co.

1811 Mar 24 Evans, William and Mary Radcliff by Zachariah Carlisle, JP HT,
             Licking Co.

1815 Apr 16 Eveland, Amy and Daniel Dennis by Thomas White, JP, Washington Co.

1806 Apr 10 Eveland, Catharine and Russell Darrough by Robt Oliver, Washington
             Co.

1797 Mar 15 Eveland, Frederick and Nancy Lee by Josiah Munro, JP, Washington Co.

1818 Apr 21 Eveland, John and Harriet Newton by Asa Cheadle, JP, Washington Co.

1806 Apr 10 Eveland, Nathaniel and Cynthia Scott by Robt Oliver, Washington Co.

1860 Nov 3   Eveleigh, Charlotte E. and Thomas M. Sloan of Zanesville by Rev.
             John Boyd, St. Luke's Church, Marietta, Washington Co.

1855 Jan 14 Eveleigh, Elias Jr. and Caroline Palmer by Rev. John Boyd, St.
             Luke's Church, Marietta, Washington Co.

1863 Jun 17 Eveleigh, Harriet M. and Henry M. Langley of Zanesville by Rev.
             John Boyd, St. Luke's Church, Marietta, Washington Co.

1808 Oct 13 Evens, Anthony and Susanna Cline by James Riggs, JP, Washington Co.

1807 Apr 12   Evens, Bazel and Susanna Robenette by James Riggs, JP, Washington Co.

1812 Jan 2   Evens, James and Betsey Sutton by Amos Porter, JP, Washington Co.

1815 May 11   Everet, Jane and Thomas Mickey by Dan'l Brink, JP, Franklin Co.

1818 Mar 18   Everett, Samuel and Elizabeth Nichols by Joseph Grate, Franklin Co.

1826 Jul 16   Everett, Samuel and Hannah Thompson by Amaziah Hutchinson, JP,
               Franklin Co.

1817 Jun 5   Evereitl, Flora and Zibra Jones by Samuel Bancroft, JP, Licking Co.

1817 Mar 20   Everitt, Helpa and Ariel Humphrey by Thomas Spelman, JP, Licking Co.

1817 Aug 1   Everitt, Revel and Sabre Rose by Samuel Bancroft, JP, Licking Co.

1814 Dec 24   Everitt, Samuel H. and Drucy Warner by Rev. T. Harris, Licking Co.

1827 Mar 13   Everret, Kesiah and Joseph Scott by G.W. Hart, Franklin Co.

1827 Mar 15   Evert, Aaron and Elsy E. Miller by Amaziah Hutchinson, Franklin Co.

1826 May 25   Everton, Jane and Geo Anthony Jr. by Solomon Goodenough, JP,
               Jackson Co.

1821 Apr 7   Evertson, Elizabeth and John Mantle by Peter Clover, JP, Franklin Co.

1855 Jul 3   Evitt, Henry and Catherine E. Cherry by Rev. A. Kingsbury, Putnam
               Presbyterian Church, Muskingum Co.

1801 Jan 5   Evritt, Maria and Paul Greer by Lewis Hubner, MG, Washington Co.

1810 Oct 3   Ewing, Betsey and Johnston Woolcutt by James Marshall, Franklin Co.

1860 Jul 4   Ewing, Eliza S. and Thomas Hosler by Rev. A. Kingsbury, Putnam
               Presbyterian Church, Muskingum Co.

1808 Feb 25   Ewing, Elizabeth and David Carey by David Mitchell, Franklin Co.

1808 May 31   Ewing, James and Elizabeth Carey by David Mitchell, Franklin Co.

1813 Aug 12   Ewing, William and Sally Giles (license date), Pickaway Co.

1811 Mar 19   Ewins, Martha and Joseph Johnston by J. McMillen, JP, Licking Co.

1818 Feb 19   Fairchild, Hiram and Emily Stanton by Pelatiah White, JP, Washington
               Co.

1823 Oct 1   Fairchild, John and Hannah Burns by Robert Boyd, Franklin Co.

1828 May 15   Fairchild, John and Elizabeth Blakely by I. Gander, Franklin Co.

1826 Dec 17   Fairchilde, Hannah and George Whitemore by Lysides L. Latimore, JP,
               Franklin Co.

1818 Nov 26   Fairfield, Jacob Jr. and Hannah Benedict by R. Stansbery, Franklin
               Co.

1807 Aug 17   Fairlamb, Sam'l and Esther Scott by S. Lindsly, Washington Co.

1815 Aug 22   Faley (or Foley), William and Susan Berman by James Marshall,
               Franklin Co.

1822 Jun 4   Falkner, Elizabeth and William Henry by C. Henkel, Franklin Co.

---- --- --   Falkner, John and Elizabeth Taylor by James Hoge, Franklin Co.

1817 Feb 2   Fall, Aaron and Charity Rood by Obadiah Scott, Washington Co.

1819 Jun 27   Fall, Amanda and Joseph C. Wells by Amos Wilson, JP, Washington Co.

1817 Mar 20   Fall, Lydia and Ira Rood by Obadiah Scott, Washington Co.

1813 May 8   Fallon, Thomas and Lucy Carpenter by Reuben Carpenter, Franklin Co.

1817 Jan 5   Falloway, Jeremiah William and Melly Davidson by James Taylor, JP,
               Franklin Co.

1824 Jun 12   Falthery, Barnet and Nancy Aye (license date), Marion Co.

1822 Dec 13   Farber, Susan Amanda and George Campbell by John Davis, JP, Franklin
               Co.

1820 Nov 16   Farding, Mary and Geo Thrum by Edw Cating, JP, Jackson Co.

1821 Sep 2   Fargo, Harmenio and John Harris by Eli C. King, Franklin Co.

1819 Jan 7   Farley, William and Alney Owens by Zach Carlisle, JP, Licking Co.

1799 Feb 7   Farmen, Anna and Edmon Dorr by Alvan Bingham, Washington Co.

1814 Nov 10   Farmer, Amelia and Jacob Myers by G. Callanhan, EMEC, Licking Co.

1814 Dec 24   Farmer, Amos and Mary Owens by Rev. T. Harris, Licking Co.

1818 Dec 31   Farmer, Dorcas and Jeremiah Browning by Geo. Callanhan, EMEC,
               Licking Co.

1816 Nov 21   Farmer, Ezekiel and Peggy Holmes by Noah Fidler, Licking Co.

1811 Mar 28   Farmer, Lewis and Catherine Bush by James McMillen, JP, Licking Co.

1815 Aug 10   Farmer, Samuel and Sarah Wills by Z. Carlisle, JP, Licking Co.

1800 Jan 29   Farmer, Sarah and John Baily, Jr., by Alvin Bingham, JP, Washington
               Co.

1815 Mar 28   Farmer, Sarah and Samuel Pogue by Z. Carlisle, JP, Licking Co.

1825 Feb 15   Farnam, Henry and Fanny Hamilton by Joseph Corper, Franklin Co.

1825 Mar 31   Farney (or Hoover) and James Delay by J.B. Gilliland, JP, Jackson Co.

1821 --- --   Farnsworth, James D. and Eliza Knapp by James W. Booth, JP, Washing-
               ton Co.

1869 Dec 15   Farquhar, Annie E. and James A. Douglas, M.D., by Rev. A. Kingsbury,
               Putnam Presbyterian Church, Muskingum Co.

1877 Mar 8   Farquhar, Edward A., M.D., and Mrs. Augusta A. Taylor by Rev. A.
               Kingsbury, Putnam Presbyterian Church, Muskingum Co.

1869 Oct 28   Farquhar, Emmor C., M.D., and Bessie A. Campbell by Rev. A. Kings-
               bury, Putnam Presbyterian Church, Muskingum Co.

1862 Jan 8   Farquhar, Marietta and Solomon F. Ballinger, M.D., by Rev. A.
               Kingsbury, Putnam Presbyterian Church, Muskingum Co.

1874 May 6   Farquhar, Sarah J. and James Bates, M.D., by Rev. A. Kingsbury,
               Putnam Presbyterian Church, Muskingum Co.

1826 Jan 25   Farrir, John and Caroline Mills by James Hoge, Franklin Co.

1816 Nov 12   Fasset, Joseph and Mary Boardman by Rev. T. Harris, Licking Co.

1826 Feb 11   Faught, John and Sarah Radcliffe by J.B. Gilliland, Jackson Co.

1826 Mar 30   Faught, Moses and Catharine Traxler by J.B. Gilliland, JP, Jackson
               Co.

1817 Jan 30   Faulkmer, Ann and Rosell Willcox by R. Stansberry, Franklin Co.

1818 Jul 30   Faulkner, Andrew and Mary Crump by Gabriel McNeil, JP, Jackson Co.

1815 Sep 25   Faulkner, John and Polly Dye by John True, JP, Washington Co.

1819 Aug 1   Fay, Cyrus and Mira Barns by Rev. Philander Chase, Franklin Co.

1848 Apr 25   Fay, Henry Tudor and Margaret Sanford by W.C. French, St. Luke's
               Church, Granville, Licking Co.

1817 Jun 26   Fearing, Franklin and Hannah Coolidge by Obadiah Scott, JP,
               Washington Co.

1816 Aug 15   Fearing, Lucy W. and John P. Mayberry by Sam'l P. Robbins, DD,
               Washington Co.

1813 Feb 4   Fearing, Mary and David Dutton by Joseph Frye, Washington Co.

1795 Nov 28   Fearing, Paul and Cynthia Rouse by J. Gilman, Washington Co.

1817 Jan 26   Fearing, Randolph and Betsey Shaw by John Patterson, Washington Co.

1810 Sep 13   Fearing, Rebecca and John Brown by Dudley Davis, JP, Washington Co.

1818 Jun 1   Pearing, Russell and Sally Reed by John Patterson, JP, Washington
               Co.

1818 Dec 24   Feasel, Henry and Jane Kindle by George Hays, Franklin Co.

1823 Oct 27   Feasle, George and Jane Anderson by Isaac Painter, Franklin Co.

1827 Sep 3   Featheringale, Mary and John Bogart by I. Gander, Franklin Co.

1812 Dec 7   Featheringill, George and Rebecca Malahan by Elijah Austin, Franklin
               Co.

1816 --- --   Featherston, Susanna and Robert Legget by John Patterson, JP,
               Washington Co.

1811 Jun 23   Featherstone, John and Sarah Legget by Wm. Gray, Washington Co.

1816 Oct 18   Featherstone, Sally and Abner Fish by P. White, Washington Co.

1819 May 9   Febor, Cotten M. and Catherin Decker by Emmor Cox, Franklin Co.

1790 Sep 14   Feering, Noah and Rebecca Rhea by Benj Tupper, Washington Co.

1868 Dec 1   Fell, A. Grace and George L. Reppert of Pittsburg by Rev. John Boyd,
               St. Luke's Church, Marietta, Washington Co.

1825 Feb 16   Felly, Abigail and Benj Barnes by Joseph Clara, JP, Marion Co.

1824 Dec 9   Fenniken, Tirzah and James Lane by James Hoge, Franklin Co.

1825 Dec 22   Fergeson (or Forgerson), Malinda and George McDonold by H. Craff,
               Minister of the Gospel of the Methodist Epsicopal Church,
               Franklin Co.

1810 May 10   Ferguson, Flemming and Susana Graham (license date), Pickaway Co.

1812 May 5   Ferguson, Jane and Daniel Dearduff by John Turner, JP, Washington Co.

1811 Mar 10   Ferguson, Margaret and John Chenoweth by Rev. Simon Cokrane,
              Franklin Co.

1824 Jan 4   Ferguson, Sally and Edward Penix by Reuben Golliday, Franklin Co.

1805 Jan 31   Ferguson, Thomas and Grace Holdren by John Greene, Washington Co.

1820 May 16   Feris, Joseph and Sarah Smith by Chandler Rogers, JP, Franklin Co.

1799 Mar 22   Ferrard, Peter and Margeret Violet by Robert Safford, Washington Co.

1820 Jan 13   Fethengale, Rebecca and Rudalphus Taylor by Richard Courtright,
              Franklin Co.

1814 Apr 5   Fetherolf, Daniel and Susana Reichelderfer by Jacob Leist, JP,
              Pickaway Co.

1813 Dec 12   Fetters, Mary and Ebenezer Conbre by John B. Johnston, Franklin Co.

1814 Nov 20   Fettsworth, Jr. and M. Clifton by Jos. Hays, JP, Pickaway Co.

1884 Dec 30   Few, Charles D. of High Hill, O., and Nettie Mason of Taylorsville,
              O., by Rev. George F. Moore, Putnam Presbyterian Church,
              Muskingum Co.

1824 Sep 4   Fickele, Geo M. and Margrett Buckley (license date), Marion Co.

1825 May 1   Fickle, Elizabeth and Phineas Packard by Alex Perry, JP, Marion Co.

1825 Mar 25   Fickle, Isaac and Eliza Tipton (license date), Marion Co.

1825 Dec 1   Fickle, Isaac H. and Nancy Young by Conrad Roth, JP, Marion Co.

1824 Jul 13   Fickle, Nancy and Absalom Packard by J.B. Packard, JP, Marion Co.

1824 May 7   Field, Seldon and Lydia Ketchum (license date), Marion Co.

1864 Aug 16   Field, T.G. and Henrietta Medlicott by Rev. John Boyd, St. Luke's
              Church, Marietta, Washington Co.

1814 Oct 13   Fields, Robert and Susan Willets by Samuel Lybrand, JP, Pickaway Co.

1827 Jun 14   Fields, S.B. and Martha Jewett by Charles Henkle, Franklin Co.

1822 Sep 19   Filbury, Matilda and Daniel Hoy by Nicholas Goetschius, Franklin Co.

1819 May 30   Finch, Lewis and Ashia Cole by Philip Cole, JP, Washington Co.

1810 Sep 21   Finch, Solomon and Rachel Justice (license date), Pickaway Co.

1804 Oct 27   Findlay, Margaret and Eli Sherman by Jacob Lindly, Washington Co.

1817 Aug 30   Findlay, Sarah and John Flora by Wm. How, JP, Jackson Co.

1817 Mar 25   Findley, Mathew and Elizabeth Blackburn by T.D. Baird, NDMB, Licking
              Co.

1803 Apr 7   Finley, Hanna and Joseph Hugg by Samuel Evans, Ross Co.

1805 Feb 7   Finley, John J. and Sarah Strain by John Davidson, Ross Co.

1805 Jan 31   Finley, Martha and Joseph Scott by William Creighton, Ross Co.

1814 May 29   Finney, Elizabeth and William Allison by Simeon Deming, JP,
              Washington Co.

1816 Oct 18   Fish, Abner and Sally Featherstone by P. White, Washington Co.

1823 Aug 27   Fishel, Elizabeth and Isaac Borer by Wolry Conrad, JP, Franklin Co.

1806 Jul 13   Fisher, Andrew and Polly Gray by Robert Oliver, Washington Co.

1825 Dec 9   Fisher, Caslina and John Clark by Benja Britton, Franklin Co.

1872 Dec 31   Fisher, Charles T. and Carrie A. Averbeck by Rev. John Boyd, St.
              Luke's Church, Marietta, Washington Co.

1817 Mar 27   Fisher, Christena and Wm. Millan by James Hoge, Franklin Co.

1816 Sep 22   Fisher, Deborah and George Dana by Rev. Saml P. Robbins, Washington
              Co.

1807 Nov 29   Fisher, Elizabeth and Daniel Weeks, Jr. by James Kilbourne, Franklin
              Co.

1811 Mar 12   Fisher, Elizabeth and William Stewart by James Hoge, Franklin Co.

1823 Oct 9   Fisher, Ephraim and Margaret Pegg by John McCan, JP, Franklin Co.

1807 Oct 18   Fisher, Hannah and Seth Fuller by D. Loring, JP, Washington Co.

1860 Mar 1   Fisher, Henrietta and John McBride by Rev. A. Kingsbury, Putnam
              Presbyterian Church, Muskingum Co.

1878 Apr 17   Fisher, John W. and Catherine O. Jones by Rev. John Boyd, St. Luke's
              Church, Marietta, Washington Co.

1825 Sep 15   Fisher, Joseph and Sarah Lantiss by C. Kinkel, Franklin Co.

1814 Jan 2   Fisher, Josiah and Jane White by Glass Cochran, JP, Franklin Co.

1816 Jan 25   Fisher, Levin and Fanny Cloud by John Cunningham, Licking Co.

1827 May 17   Fisher, Mary and James Wilson by A. Allison, Franklin Co.

1826 Oct 11   Fisher, Maximilion and Arthur O'Harra by James Hoge, Franklin Co.

1819 Dec 16   Fisher, Ruth B. and Timothy Anders by Isaac Fisher, Franklin Co.

1817 Dec 19   Fitzgareld, Thomas and Martha Hottan by Wm. Badger, Franklin Co.

1811 Mar 2   Fitzgerald, Eleanor and William Dickison (license date), Pickaway Co.

1813 Jan 29   Fitzgerald, Nancy and Robert Webb (license date), Pickaway Co.

1814 Mar 6   Fitzgerald, Polly and Adam Miller by Rob't Bradshaw, JP, Pickaway Co.

1845 May 8   Fitzhugh, Sarah A. and Dr. John T. Cotton both of Jackson Co., Va.,
              by Rev. Edward Winthrop, St. Luke's Church, Marietta, Washington
              Co.

1819 Jan 7   Flack, Benjamin and Polly Dever by Isaac Baker, JP, Jackson Co.

1803 Jan 13   Flack, Robert and Jane Caven by Daniel Story, Clerk, Washington Co.

1811 Jan 17   Flagg, Cynthia and Joseph Kelley by Stephen Lindsly, Washington Co.

1796 Jun 20   Flagg, Editha and Anthony Phillipean by J. Gilman, Washington Co.

1803 Dec 4   Flagg, James and Sarah Cornes by Stephen Lindly, Washington Co.

1803 Aug 7   Flagg, Mary (or Polly) and Caleb Carver by Daniel Story, Washington Co.

1821 Mar 6   Flanagan, Andrew and Anna Mahan by James Hoge, Franklin Co.

1819 Nov 1   Flanagan, Isaac C. and Anne Franks by James Hoge, Franklin Co.

1817 Mar 27   Flanigan, Jane and Wm. Boreland by James Hoge, Franklin Co.

1811 Mar 10   Flannaghan, Hugh and Nancy Kelly by Dudley Davis, Washington Co.

1802 Oct 3   Flarnenan, Cintia and Jacob Winson by Sam'l Williamson, JP,
                  Washington Co.

1814 Nov 23   Fleeharty, John and Margaret Reed by Jno Ludwig, JP, Pickaway Co.

1810 Aug 23   Fleharty, Nancy and Joshua Shuttlesworth by Joseph Palmer, JP,
                  Washington Co.

1821 Dec 7   Fleming, Agnes and John Brackenridge by Rev. Sam'l P. Robbins,
                  Washington Co.

1812 Aug 16   Fleming, Jesse and Nelly Collins by Henry Jolly, JP, Washington Co.

1818 Jul 14   Fleming, Margaret and George McLean by James McLish, Franklin Co.

1821 Feb 13   Fleming, Samuel and Sally Henderson by Jacob Keller, Franklin Co.

1818 Dec 10   Fleming, Tilla and John Miller by James McLish, Franklin Co.

1825 Jun 23   Flemming, Mariah and Charles O'Harra by Reuben Golliday, JP,
                  Franklin Co.

1811 Aug 4   Flemming, Robert and Eleanor Morrow (license date), Pickaway Co.

1817 Jul 27   Flemming, Sarah and Benjamin Clevinger by John Hite, MG, Franklin Co.

1823 Nov 20   Flenniken, John and Lucy Merrian by James Hoge (parents of John
                  Flanigan), Franklin Co.

1793 Aug 29   Fletcher, Joseph and Catherine Warth by J. Gilman, Washington Co.

1810 Aug 1   Fletcher, Mary and David Irwin by Edwin Putnam, Washington Co.

1818 Aug 16   Fletcher, Sally and Abraham Ball by Cyrus Ames, Washington Co.

1806 Feb 5   Flint, Joseph and Elizabeth Montgomery by Abraham Miller, Ross Co.

1816 Oct 15   Floos, Polly and Peter Miller by Elisha Decker, Franklin Co.

1817 Aug 30   Flora, John and Sarah Findlay by Wm. How, JP, Jackson Co.

1817 Feb 20   Flora, Robert and Elsy Detty by Samuel L. Donnelly, JP, Jackson Co.

1804 Aug 24   Flouron, Debary and Wm. Murphy by Geo. Vinsanhaler, Ross Co.

1820 Feb 23   Flowers, John and Ellin Taylor by Wm. Woodford, Washington Co.

1821 May 19   Floyd, Mime and Joseph Roberts by James Hoge, Franklin Co.

1824 Dec 27   Floyd, Reuben and Catharene Scott by Wm. T. Martin, Franklin Co.

1818 Jul 23   Floyd, Sally and George Straw by Michael Patton, Franklin Co.

1819 Sep 5   Foggar, Samuel and Rachel Boyer by Zach Carlisle, JP, Licking Co.

1828 Sep 25   Foley, Chloe and James Elliott by Benj. Britton, ECC, Franklin Co.

1826 Nov 17   Foley, Mary and Hughey Megill by Ruben Golliday, Franklin Co.

1819 Apr 15   Foley, Moses and Martha Badger by Joseph Gorton, Franklin Co.

1825 Mar 20   Foley, Nancy (widow) and Isaac Eastwood by C. Henkel, Franklin Co.

1824 Nov 11   Foley, Sally, daughter of John Foley, and Daniel O'Harra by Henry
                  Matthews, Minister of the Methodist E. Church, Franklin Co.

1815 Aug 22   Foley (or Faley) and Susan Berman by James Marshall, Franklin Co.

1802 Nov 27   Folsom, Samuel and Catharine Smith by John Robinson, JP, Washington
                  Co.

1814 Aug 14   Foltz, John and Sophia Valentine by Jacob Leist, JP, Pickaway Co.

1801 Jan 22   Fonty, Frederick and Nancy Bigerstaff by Alvan Bingham, Washington Co.

1809 May 6   Foos, Amelia and Philip Denman by John Hollister, JPHT, Licking Co.

1825 Dec 1   Foos, Jesse and Rachel Blackmore (license date), Marion Co.

1822 Dec 31   Foos, Nicholas and Polly Myers by N. Goetschies, Franklin Co.

1823 Jan 14   Forba, Amos and Mary Ann Medford by Richard Courtright, Franklin Co.

1808 Nov 28   Forby, Amy and Abel Galland by Thos. Seely, JP, Washington Co.

1807 Feb 17   Ford, Augustus and Elizabeth Holt by Arthur O'Harra, JP, Franklin Co.

1812 Apr 14   Ford, Benjn and Nancy Thomas by Arthur O'Harra, Franklin Co.

1814 Jul 31   Ford, Benjamin and Peggy Ballinger by Nicholas Goitschies, Franklin
               Co.

1799 Oct 13   Ford, Dianna and William Woodford by Thos. Stanley, JP, Washington Co.

1816 Aug 27   Ford, Eader and Spencer Dayton by Joseph Grate, Franklin Co.

1812 Dec 8   Ford, Frederick and Elizabeth Robinson by James Marshall, Franklin Co.

1804 Nov 1   Ford, Furman and Hannah McFarland by Jacob Lindly, Washington Co.

1824 Aug 24   Ford, George and Isabella Carothers by Wm. C. Duff, JP, Franklin Co.

1824 Jun 9   Ford, James and Elizabeth McElwene by John Kirby, JP, Marion Co.

1811 Jun 28   Ford, Judah and Betsey Deming by John Greene, Washington Co.

1825 Feb 20   Ford, Margaret and John Miller by Wm. C. Duff, Franklin Co.

1818 Oct 1   Ford, Philip and Elizabeth Caughlehan by Rev. Noah Fidler, Licking Co.

1798 Apr 5   Ford, Phineas and Mary Benjamin by Josiah Munro, Washington Co.

1814 Oct 20   Ford, Rachael and Frederick Stairwalt by James Marshall, Franklin Co.

1798 Nov 26   Ford, Sarah and William Ford by Robert Oliver, JP, Washington Co.

1806 Jan 30   Ford, Sarah and Jones Orders by Zachariah Stephen, JP, Franklin Co.

1798 Nov 26   Ford, William and Sarah Ford by Robert Oliver, JP, Washington Co.

1803 Dec --   Ford, William and Elizabeth Beebe by Daniel Story, Washington Co.

1807 Apr 30   Fordyce, John and Fanny Parker by Stephen Lindsly, Washington Co.

1804 May 27   Foree, Bridgart and Waid Cross by John Brough, JP, Washington Co.

1799 Apr 12   Forenark, Charles and Sarah Recharts by Henry Smith, JP, Washington
               Co.

1825 Dec 22   Forgerson (or Fergeson), Malinda and George McDonold by H. Crabb,
               Minister Methodist Episcopal Church, Franklin Co.

1827 Dec 9   Forgerson, Mary and Origin Harris by Nathan Emery, Elder Methodist
               E. Church, Franklin Co.

1824 Feb 10   Forgerson, Thomas and Mary Biggert by James Hoge, Franklin Co.

1814 Nov 24   Forguson, Patsey and John Calhunteen (or Culbertson or Calbermsten)
               by John Turner, JP, Franklin Co.

1801 Jan 19   Forrest, Joseph and Meribah Hammond by Josiah Munro, Washington Co.

1814 Mar 17   Forseman, Margaret and Wm. Miller by Wm. Jones, JP, Pickaway Co.

1811 Jun 2   Forshey, Betsey and Jesse Enocks by Amos Porter, JP, Washington Co.

1813 Dec 14   Forsman, Ruth and Thomas Bell by Jas. Robinson, Pickaway Co.

1861 Nov 10   Forsythe, John A. and Carrie E. Chapman of Putnam by Rev. A. Kingsbury, Putnam Presbyterian Church, Muskingum Co.

1811 Jan 24   Fortner, Betsey and John Littleton by Daniel Goodno, Washington Co.

1811 May 6   Fortner, Sarah and John Tyson by Jeremiah Dare, JP, Washington Co.

1867 Feb 14   Fosdick, Fanny T. and Alf. M. Nichol by Wm. Bower, St. Luke's Church, Granville, Licking Co.

1807 Apr 14   Foster, Betsy M. and Stephen Dana by D. Loring, JP, Washington Co.

1804 Apr 19   Foster, Elizabeth and Francis Lowning by Wm. Davis, Esq., Ross Co.

1812 Sep 17   Foster, Elizabeth and John Thompson by John Turner, Franklin Co.

1806 Oct 8   Foster, Ephraim and Sarah Olney by Nehemiah Davis, Washington Co.

1817 Feb 6   Foster, Esther and Philip Danford by Obadiah Scott, JP, Washington Co.

1804 Apr 3   Foster, Jacob and Sarah Clark by Wm. Davis, Ross Co.

1810 Feb 27   Foster, Jacob and Polly Purgett by John Smith (recorded date), Franklin Co.

1824 Jan 8   Foster, James and Sarah Lewis by Reuben Golliday (another entry 4 Mar 1824), Franklin Co.

1816 Jan 28   Foster, John and Ann Watts by Joseph Gorton, Franklin Co.

1823 Jan 16   Foster, Joseph and Ann Higgins, Franklin Co.

1818 Dec 3   Foster, Margaret and Asa Browning by Geo. Callanhan, EME Ch, Licking Co.

1805 Apr 25   Foster, Mary and Wm. Browning by D. Loring, Washington Co.

1805 Nov 14   Foster, Olive and Daniel Davis, Jr. by Jacob Lindly, Washington Co.

1806 May 4   Foster, Peregrine P. and Betsy Cushing by D. Loring, Washington Co.

1802 May 2   Foster, Polly and Wm. Dana by J. Pierce, Washington Co.

1804 Jan 22   Foster, Polly and John O'Brian by Wm. Davis, JP, Ross Co.

1802 Dec 30   Foster, Sarah and Alexander Hill by Daniel Story, Washington Co.

1820 Dec 31   Foster, Sarah and Joseph Wiggins by Reuben Golliday, Franklin Co.

1819 Apr 1   Foster, Uz and Mary Riley by James M. Booth, Washington Co.

1817 Feb 20   Foster, William and Sarah Drake by Geo. Callanham, EMEC, Licking Co.

1806 Dec 2   Fouch, John and Esther Tyson by Luther Dana, Washington Co.

1812 Dec 22   Fouglar, Caty and Simon Thudy (license date), Pickaway Co.

1808 6 mo 15   Foulke, Judah and Sarah Richards, Miami Monthly Meeting, Warren Co.

1815 2 mo 9   Foulke, Margaret and George Hatton, Miami Monthly Meeting, Warren Co.

1825 Jan 26   Foust, Jesse and Mary Lowder by Amos Neely, JP, Marion Co.

1818 Sep 18   Fouts, Andrew and Polly Clark by B.W. Talbot, JP, Washington Co.

1856 Sep 24   Fowle, Sidney and Mary L. Ephland by T. Corlett, St. Luke's Church,
               Granville, Licking Co.

1817 Nov 23   Fowler, Betsey and Chester Toleman by Solomon Goss, MMEC, Washington
               Co.

1815 Nov 9   Fowler, John S. and Mahitable Littlefield by John Russell, JP,
               Washington Co.

1821 Oct 2   Fowler, Miriam and John Perkins by John True, JP, Washington Co.

1819 Jul 8   Fowler, Thomas and Asenath Perkins by Dudley Davis, JP, Washington Co.

1819 Oct 21   Fowler, Willey and Cynthia Perkins by Dudley Davis, JP, Washington Co.

1870 May 15   Fracker, Harry of Zanesville, O., and Hellen A. Rankin of White
               Cottage by Rev. A. Kingsbury, Putnam Presbyterian Church,
               Muskingum Co.

1815 Aug 22   Fraiser, Harriet and John Ulen by Rev. S.P. Robbins, Washington Co.

1809 Jan 23   Fraize, Elizabeth and Benedick Belt by Wm. Haines, JP, Licking Co.

1809 Mar 22   Fraize, Elizabeth and George Smith by Wm. Haines, JP, Licking Co.

1809 Oct 26   Frakes (or Trakes), Rachiel and Enoch Hanyman by Michael Dickey,
               Franklin Co.

1827 Jan 31   Fraley, Caroline and Samuel Whitsill by Wm. Patterson, Franklin Co.

1819 Mar 20   Frances, Rebecca and William Shadley by J. Johnston, JP, Licking Co.

1820 Jul 18   Frances, Samuel and Amelia Shadly by J. Johnson, JP, Licking Co.

1804 Apr 15   Frances, Susanna and Johnson Bell by John Brough, JP, Washington Co.

1806 Feb 7   Francis, Ann and George Emmery by Peter Jackson, JP, Ross Co.

1804 Aug 21   Francis, Betsy and Thomas Peerce by J. Gardner, JP, Ross Co.

1827 May 24   Francis, D. and Mary Harris by W.T. Martin, JP, Franklin Co.

1794 Mar 27   Francois-Duraille, Jeanne and Auguste Chezeau by J.G. Petitt,
               Washington Co.

1820 Dec 4   Frank, Sally and Christian Benner by John Cunningham, JP, Licking Co.

1826 Jan 5   Frankelberry (or Frankelbury), Betsy and Wm. Manning by Jacob Grubb,
               (date of license 5 Jan; return filed 21 Jan), Franklin Co.

1803 Jul 2   Franklin, James and Rebecca Carpenter by J. Gardner, JP, Ross Co.

1849 May 3   Franklin, John Hooper and Elizabeth S. Heeley by W.C. French, St.
               Luke's Church, Granville, Licking Co.

1819 Nov 1   Franks, Ann and Isaac C. Flanagan by James Hoge, Franklin Co.

1816 Aug 22   Franks, Margaret and Linsey Ankrom by Simon Merwin, Washington Co.

1818 Feb 28   Frasure, Agnus and Isaac Craford by Tho. P. Patterson, Franklin Co.

1825 Jan 6   Frazee, Augustus and Sarah McCray by J.B. Gilliland, JP, Jackson Co.

1802 Feb 9   Frazee, Leah and Isaac Powers by Jonthan Struthers, JP, Trumbull Co.

1816 Mar 16   Freazel, Lena and Daniel Motherspaw by Uriah Hull, JP, Licking Co.

1814 Jul 28   Frazer, Alexander and Hannah Swisher by Rev. Phillip Clurry, Pickaway
               Co.

1814 Mar 14   Frazer, Annaliza and Newton E. Westfall by Rev. Stephen Lindsley, Washington Co.

1820 Apr 11   Frazer, Betsy and Benja^n Gardiner by Rev. Philander Chase, Franklin Co.

1823 Jun 9   Frazer, Betsey and Benjamin Tappan by James Hoge, Franklin Co.

1807 May 3   Frazer, Margaret and Amos Harvey by Stephen Lindsly, Washington Co.

1809 Nov 28   Frazier, Eliphatel and Betsy Lord by Sam'l P. Robbins, Washington Co.

1810 Aug 2   Frazier, James and Elizabeth Cade. (license date), Pickaway Co.

1817 Dec 9   Frazier, Mary and Charles Little by Rev. Saml P. Robbins, Washington Co.

1805 Feb 14   Frederick, Henry and Catharine Weeder by Isaac Damson, Ross Co.

1817 Jun 12   Frederick, Sally and John Woolard (or Woollard) by Eli C. King, Franklin Co.

1808 Nov 21   Free, John and Catharine Cline by James Riggs, JP, Washington Co.

1892 Sep 21   Freeborn, W.V. and Florence Champ by Rev. George F. Moore, Putnam Presbyterian Church, Muskingum Co.

1804 Feb 29   Freeland, Lake and Ruth Thompson by John Hoddy, JP, Ross Co.

1804 Sep 4   Freeman, Ann and David Cobler by Wm. Davis, JP, Ross Co.

1814 Oct 14   Freeman, Benjamin and Nellie Webb by Rev. Geo. Alkire, Pickaway Co.

1818 Oct 18   Freeman, Daniel and Sally Beebe by Rev. Philander Chase, Franklin Co.

1811 Dec 20   Freeman, Isaac and Nelly Wilson (license date), Pickaway Co.

1826 Nov 6   Freeman, James S. and Mary Wright by Henry Matthews, Franklin Co.

1817 Jul 31   Freemire, Hannah and Samuel Byard by Anthony Sheets, JP, Washington Co.

1815 Feb 10   Freemire, Margaret and John Johnson by Anth'y Sheets, Washington Co.

1819 Mar 25   Freemyer, George and Martha Bee by Moses Williamson, JP, Washington Co.

1811 Oct 12   Freese, Barbara and James Waddle (license date), Pickaway Co.

1811 Oct 20   Freese, Polly and Daniel Bowsher (license date), Pickaway Co.

1819 Feb 11   French, Bartemans and Elizabeth Cooley by Thomas Scott, JP, Jackson Co.

1804 Apr 10   French, Charles and Sarah Robenet by. Sam'l Williamson, JP, Washington Co.

1829 May 28   French, David and Sarah Ingham by Geo. Jefferies, Franklin Co.

1808 Jun 8   French, Isaac and Electa Rathbone by Edmund B. Dana, JP, Washington Co.

1823 Jun 5   French, Jonathan and Jane Graham by Mathew Crawford, JP, Franklin Co.

1825 Mar 14   French, Mary and William Graham by John Long, JP, Franklin Co.

1817 Oct 30   French, Nancy and Richard Hanlen by Nathan Parr, JP, Washington Co.

1823 Apr 22   French, Susannah and John Elzey by Charles Waddell, LM, Franklin Co.

1806 Dec 14   French, William and Phoebe Swearingame by Luther Dana, Washington Co.

1813 Mar 22   Freshwater, Christ^r and Elizabeth Hill by Daniel Brink, Franklin Co.

1800 Dec 18   Frost, Stephen and Nancy Ellison by Nehemiah Davis, MG, Washington
               Co.

1813 May 5   Frickle, Mary and Richard Swank (license date), Pickaway Co.

1816 Sep 17   Friend, Mary and Anthony Boggs by Gabriel McNeil, MG, Jackson Co.

1825 Dec 22   Fritts, John and Betsy Hone by A. Allison, Franklin Co.

1820 Feb 10   Fritz, Michael and Betsey Decker by T. Lee, JP, Franklin Co.

1887 Mar 16   Fritz, Rose K. and Harry E. Hollister both of Zanesville by Rev.
               George F. Moore, Putnam Presbyterian Church, Muskingum Co.

1882 Jul 3   Frost, Lydia A. and Elijah G. Garnett by Rev. John Boyd, St. Luke's
               Church, Marietta, Washington Co.

1821 Jan 21   Frost, Nancy and Joseph Hickerson by Joseph Thrap, MG, Licking Co.

1815 Jun 17   Frost, William and Elizabeth Jones by J.T. Thrap - Stephen McDougal,
               Licking Co.

1827 Sep 3   Fruchey, Frederick and Elizabeth Wilton by I. Gander, Franklin Co.

1816 Jul 7   Frutchey, Frederick and Mary Bishop by Elisha Decker, JP, Franklin Co.

1828 Jan 26   Fry, Andrew and Jane Baily by William Long, JP, Franklin Co.

1812 Jun 25   Fry, Barbary and Henry Spohn by A. Winegarner, JP, Licking Co.

1811 Jan 31   Fry, Catherine and James Imberson (license date), Pickaway Co.

1814 Jun 26   Fry, Jones and Catherine C. Powers by Wm. Taylor, Licking Co.

1813 Jul 16   Fry, Susan and David Waggoner by S. Pogeu, JP, Licking Co.

1813 Apr 10   Fryback, Anna and John Jackson (license date), Pickaway Co.

1815 Apr 20   Fryback, John and Lettia Emerson by Isaac Quinn, Pickaway Co.

1816 Feb 29   Fulk, Betsey and John Justice (or Gustice) by Michael Patton,
               Franklin Co.

1820 Mar 1   Fulk, Christopher and Susanna Myers by Thomas Cunningham, JP,
               Licking Co.

1815 Feb 28   Fulk, Henry and Catherine Green by Thos. Mace, JP, Pickaway Co.

1820 Mar 5   Fulk, Jacob and Polly Barnes by Alexander Holden, JPCC, Licking Co.

1817 Jul 10   Fulk, John and Sally Harter by I. Hoskinson, JP, Licking Co.

1838 Sep --   Fuller, Aleen and Alvira Maynard by Rev. A. Helfenstine, St. John's
               Church, Worthington, Franklin Co.

1810 Mar 13   Fuller, Almira and Oren Newton by Thos Stanley, JP, Washington Co.

1827 Jun 30   Fuller, Alvin and Betsey Willson by Hiland Hulberd, PC, Franklin Co.

1819 May 26   Fuller, Ezekel and Mary Tinkham by Reuben Carpenter, Franklin Co.

1817 Nov 27   Fuller, Irdediah and Nancy Nesmith by Rev. Saml. P. Robbins,
               Washington Co.

1796 Apr 13   Fuller, Joseph and Susanna Stacy by Josiah Munro, Washington Co.

1801 Mar 15   Fuller, Joseph and Anna Davis by Nehemiah Davis, Washington Co.

1817 Jan 10   Fuller, Lucretia and William Brewster by Sam'l Fairlamb, JP,
               Washington Co.

1826 Jul 13   Fuller, Lyia and James Ely Woodbridge by Samuel Abbott, Franklin Co.

1817 Aug 3   Fuller, Nathaniel and Celestina Scott by Pelatiah White, Washington
               Co.

1819 Nov 14   Fuller, Orlands and Frances Taylor by James Hoge, Franklin Co.

1806 Apr 3   Fuller, Resolved and Elizabeth Nash by Thos. Stanley, JP, Washington
               Co.

1820 Apr 2   Fuller, Roswell and Sally Harrington by Rev. Philander Chase,
               Franklin Co.

1813 Oct 13   Fuller, Samuel and Huldah Record by John H. White, JP, Washington Co.

1807 Oct 18   Fuller, Seth and Hannah Fisher by D. Loring, JP, Washington Co.

1809 Feb 9   Fuller, Stephen and Mary Record by Thos. Stanley, Washington Co.

1814 Dec 4   Fuller, Theodosia and Uriah Cuddington by Thos. Seely, Washington Co.

1820 Oct 28   Fuller, Wm. and Rachel Wisham by Alex. Anderson, JP, Jackson Co.

1811 Mar 12   Fuller, Zeppora and Elisha Rose by Stephen Lindsly, Washington Co.

1819 Dec 30   Fullerton, Jane and Wm. Hale by Elisha Lang, JP, Jackson Co.

1818 Feb 8   Pulsome, John and Temperance Schonover by Stephen Guthrie,
               Washington Co.

1804 Feb 11   Fulton, Elenor and Lewis Anderson by John Brough, JP, Washington Co.

1800 Apr 24   Fulton, Elizabeth and John Atchinson by Thos. Stanley, Washington Co.

1806 Aug 19   Fulton, Hugh and Margaret Henderson by James Marshall, JP, Franklin
               Co.

1807 Mar 26   Fulton, James and Lydia Leonard by Stephen Lindsly, Washington Co.

1858 Nov 10   Fulton, James and Mary S. Guthrie by Rev. A. Kingsbury, Putnam
               Presbyterian Church, Muskingum Co.

1811 Sep 17   Fulton, Lydia and Charles McKewne by Jeremiah Dare, JP, Washington
               Co.

1816 Aug 8   Fulton, Mary and Caleb Price (or Rice) by John Hunter, JP, Franklin
               Co.

1808 Feb 16   Fulton, Samuel and Ruhanna Jackson by Thos. Stanley, JP, Washington
               Co.

1820 Nov 30   Fulton, Thomas and Agnes King by Rob't Wallace, MG, Licking Co.

1817 Apr 1   Fulton, William and Patsey Mitchell by John Hunter, JP, Franklin Co.

1820 Aug 20   Funston, Elizabeth and Jenkin Phillips by David Culbertson, DD,
               Jackson Co.

1805 Aug 8   Funston, Margaret and Granthem Earl by Thomas Hicks, Ross Co.

1820 Jun 14   Funston, Rosanna and Isaac Horton by John Wyman, JP, Jackson Co.

1813 Mar 12   Funston, William and Priscilla Lapirry (license date), Pickaway Co.

1818 Jun 18   Furby, Caleb and Anna Simons by Joseph Grate, Franklin Co.

1805 Jun 28   Furman, Margarett and Thomas Hinton by Nathaniel Wyatt, Ross Co.

1826 3 mo 2   Furnas, Joseph and Patience N. Mills, Miami Monthly Meeting,
              Warren Co.

1849 --- --   Gabandan, Catherine W. and D. Ross Sims of Greenupsburg, Ky., by
              Rev. D.W. Tolford, St. Luke's Church, Marietta, Washington Co.

1817 Feb 27   Gable, Anna and Thomas McKinley by John Russell, JP, Washington Co.

1819 Oct 25   Gaffield, John and Harriet Munsel by Knowls Linnel, JP, Licking Co.

1818 Sep 29   Gaich, Peter and Rebecca Benjamin by James Holmes, JP, Licking Co.

1818 Oct 15   Gaimin, Kaziah and Joseph Junes by Percival Adams, Franklin Co.

1799 Jul 10   Galand, Katharine and John Dodge by Daniel Story, Washington Co.

1801 Apr 12   Galbraith, John and Sally Prior by Robt Safford, Washington Co.

1886?Feb --   Galbraith, Mrs. Mary R. and David Potts both of Zanesville by Rev.
              George F. Moore, Putnam Presbyterian Church, Muskingum Co.

1814 Dec 22   Galbreath, Sarah and Meredith Parish by Wm. Jones, JP, Pickaway Co.

1805 Jan 1   Galbreth, Betsey and William Richee by David Shelby, Ross Co.

1821 Jul 26   Gale, Abigal and Salmon Wallace by Chandler Rogers, JP, Franklin Co.

1821 Jan 15   Gale, Christena and James Tunis? by Shadrick Ruard?, MG, Licking Co.

1815 Mar 7   Gale, Jesse and Jane Brown by Isaac Case, JP, Franklin Co.

1819 Aug 12   Gale, William and Chloe Howel by Chandler Rogers, Franklin Co.

1800 Dec 17   Galen, Andrew and Ruth Allen by Wm. Burnham, JP, Washington Co.

1801 Jun 13   Galer, Peter and Elizabeth Allen by Robt Oliver, JP, Washington Co.

1821 Oct 28   Gales, Israel and Polly Mattocks by Nicholas Goetschius, Franklin Co.

1877 Apr 4   Gallaher, John A. and Laura H. Woodbridge by Rev. John Boyd, St.
              Luke's Church, Marietta, Washington Co.

1808 Nov 28   Galland, Abel and Amy Forby by Thos. Seely, JP, Washington Co.

1804 Feb 22   Gallaspie, Jane and Andrew Brown by John Hoddy, JP, Ross Co.

1875 Feb --   Gallaway, ----- and Georgia Grover by Mr. Dudley, St. Luke's
              Church, Granville, Licking Co.

1807 Jun 15   Gallison, Hannah and Jasper Gates by S. Lindsly, Washington Co.

1808 Dec 30   Galor, Jacob and Abigail Dutton by Daniel Dunfee, Washington Co.

1809 Jan 15   Gamble, Samuel and Welthy Knight by Edwin Putnam, Washington Co.

1884 Oct 15   Gammel, Mary Ann of Putnam and Jeremiah Terrell of Roney Point,
              W.Va., by Rev. George F. Moore, Putnam Presbyterian Church,
              Muskingum Co.

1851 Aug 19   Gammel, Templeton and William Weaver by Rev. A. Kingsbury, Putnam
              Presbyterian Church

1818 Jul 30   Gance, Margaret and David Clock? by John Green, JP, Licking Co.

1813 May 16   Ganda, Daniel and Rosannah Ruly by Peter Pence, Licking Co.

1868 Oct 15	Gane, Philip and Emily Haskell by Wm. Bower, St. Luke's Church, Granville, Licking Co.	
1816 Jul 11	Gantz, Elizabeth and Titan Henderson by T.D. Baird, JP, Licking Co.	
1820 Jan 20	Gard, Charity and Charles Duncan by S.N. Cook, JP, Washington Co.	
1818 Feb 12	Gard, Lucy and George Hutchinson by Cornelius Hougland, JP, Washington Co.	
1818 Mar 18	Gard, Martha Elizabeth and William Dunbar by Salmon N. Cook, JP, Washington Co.	
1816 Jan 21	Gard, Mishael and Clarissa Baker by J. Russell, Washington Co.	
1816 May 8	Gard, Rebecca and William Lothery by David Stevens, JP, Washington Co.	
1820 Apr 11	Gardiner, Benja^{n} and Betsy Frazer by Rev. Philander Chase, Franklin Co.	
1826 Dec 14	Gardiner, Elizabeth and Joseph Milvin by John Tipton, JP, Franklin Co.	
1810 Oct 5	Gardiner, James B. and Polly Pool by Jeremiah Dare, JP, Washington Co.	
1794 Feb 14	Gardiner, John and Margaret Letite Robinson by J.G. Petitt, Washington Co.	
1797 Oct 3	Gardiner, Sally and Jacob Larrow by Josiah Munro, Washington Co.	
1817 Jan 1	Gardner, Hannah and Richard Conkrite by David Smithers, Washington Co.	
1818 May 28	Gardner, Levine? and Ishu Sinnet by Rev. T. Harris, Licking Co.	
1818 Jan 8	Gardner, Lucinda and Samuel Reynolds by John Russell, JP, Washington Co.	
1808 Dec 20	Gardner, Lydia and George Nye by J. Wright, Washington Co.	
1802 Nov 21	Gardner, Silence and Ebenezer Nye by Nehemiah Davis, Pastor, Washington Co.	
1813 Apr 8	Gardy, Anne and Elisha Vance (license date), Pickaway Co.	
1881 Dec 28	Garges, Gertrude of Putnam and Roscoe E. Thomas of Darke Co., O., by Rev. George F. Moore, Putnam Presbyterian Church, Muskingum Co.	
1825 Mar 13	Garner, Polly and Asa Crawford by Webster Sadley, JP, Marion Co.	
1882 Jul 3	Garnett, Elijah G. and Lydia A. Frost by Rev. John Boyd, St. Luke's Church, Marietta, Washington Co.	
1808 Mar 17	Garnett, Jane and John Brough by S. Lindsly, Washington Co.	
1857 Aug 3	Garnett, Thomas and Mary M. Geren by Rev. John Boyd, St. Luke's Church, Marietta, Washington Co.	
1828 Sep 22	Garretson, John J. and Mary Goodson by John Tipton, JP, Franklin Co.	
1825 Mar 3	Garrett, George and Nancy Walker by J.B. Finley, MG, Marion Co.	
1825 May 7	Garrison, Sally and Nathaniel Tower (Towers) by George Jefferies, Ordained Minister of the Gospel, Franklin Co.	
1807 Dec 16	Garton, David and Martha Harris by David Mitchell, Franklin Co.	
1806 Jun 21	Garwood, Daniel and Habsebas Stokes by David Mitchell, Franklin Co.	
1823 May 29	Gary, Roland and Hesther Vansciver by Wm. C. Duff, JP, Franklin Co.	

1803 Sep 22   Gaskins, James and Mary McCallum by Wm. Davis, JP, Ross Co.

1806 Aug 27   Gates, Abel and Anna Calahan by Robt Oliver, JP, Washington Co.

1816 Jun 4   Gates, Betsey and Samuel Loper by Thomas White, Washington Co.

1799 Sep 6   Gates, Bitha and Noah Day by Robert Oliver, JP, Washington Co.

1811 Sep 19   Gates, James and Mary B. Taylor by Jeremiah Dare, Washington Co.

1821 Dec 25   Gates, Jared and Rebecca Ann Lobdille by Asa Morey, Washington Co.

1807 Jun 15   Gates, Jasper and Hannah Gallison by S. Lindsly, Washington Co.

1818 Jun 29   Gates, John and Clarissa Ann Crane by Thomas Moore, VDM, Washington
               Co.

1815 Sep 7   Gates, Mary and Wilson Lee Gates by Thomas White, Washington Co.

1807 Mar 17   Gates, Nathaniel and Anne Hally by Stephen Lindsly, Washington Co.

1822 Feb 7   Gates, Pamela and Romes Lawrance by Seth Baker, JP, Washington Co.

1806 Jun 5   Gates, Sally and Charles Daily by Robert Oliver, JP, Washington Co.

1809 Apr 20   Gates, Samuel and Susanna Emerson by Asa Cheadle, JP, Washington Co.

1814 Jul 10   Gates, Stephen and Jane Mills by John Brough, Esq., Washington Co.

1807 Aug 25   Gates, Susanna and Timothy Gates by Wm. Gray, JP, Washington Co.

1818 May 23   Gates, Thompson and Sarah Gold by D.H. Buell, JP, Washington Co.

1800 May 14   Gates, Timothy and Margaret Hughs by Wm. Burnham, JP, Washington Co.

1807 Aug 25   Gates, Timothy and Susanna Gates by Wm. Gray, JP, Washington Co.

1815 Sep 7   Gates, Wilson Lee and Mary Gates by Thomas White, Washington Co.

1813 Feb 9   Gattwood, Phillip and Lettice Denny (license date), Pickaway Co.

1818 9 mo 2   Gause, Ruth and Samuel Brown, Miami Monthly Meeting, Warren Co.

1820 Dec 14   Gavit, Amelia and Harvey Bragg by Noah Fidler, Licking Co.

1815 Jul 13   Gavit, John and Alla Smith by J. Cunningham, Licking Co.

1816 Oct 10   Gavit, Sally and Robert Moore by J. Cunningham, JPNAT, Licking Co.

1828 Nov 6   Gay, Azubah and Newton Case by Aristarches Walker, JP, Franklin Co.

1826 Oct 16   Gay, Electa Ann and Absolum Bowen by Henry Mathus, Franklin Co.

1819 Mar 5   Gay, Laura and William Masse by Edward Hursey, JP, Licking Co.

1811 May 2   Gay, Mollie and William Vandoran (license date), Pickaway Co.

1807 Oct 23   Gaylor, Elizabeth and Henry Maxson by Thos. Stanley, Washington Co.

1806 Jun 26   Gaylor, Wm. Garret and Jain Dutton by Thos, Stanley, Washington Co.

1797 Aug 22   Gaylord, Mary and Charles Honeywood Martin by Josiah Munro,
               Washington Co.

1801 Oct 11   Gaylord, Olive and George Darrow both of Hudson by David Hudson, JP,
               Trumbull Co.

1817 Mar 13   Gearman, William and Fanny Gray by Percival Adams, Franklin Co.

1803 Oct 13   Geblur, Susanna and Joseph Crook by Samuel Evans, Ross Co.

1819 Jun 11   Geer, Lawra and Mathew Seley by Rev. Philander Chase, Franklin Co.

1812 Jun 15   Geering, Hannah and John Hill by Jeremiah Dare, JP, Washington Co.

1817 Jul 30   Geering, Joseph and Nancy Hill by Danl H. Buell, Washington Co.

1811 Aug 1   Geering, Sam'l Jr. and Jane Hill by Edwin Putnam, JP, Washington Co.

1812 Nov 10   Gegerform, Jacob and Polly Edwards by -----, Licking Co.

1814 Mar 3   Genn, Malinda and George Powell by John Stevenson, Franklin Co.

1818 May 3   George, John and Caty Cunningham by Geo. Callanhan, MEM, Licking Co.

1823 Apr 18   George, Matthew and Nancy Leonard by Reuben Golliday, JP, Franklin
               Co.

1814 Nov 24   George, Rebecca and James McKenzie by Wm. Florence, JP, Pickaway Co.

1818 Jan 24   George, William and Hannah Bacchus by James Hoge, Franklin Co.

1864 Mar 24   Geren, Lottie and Thomas Wiseman by Rev. John Boyd, St. Luke's
               Church, Marietta, Washington Co.

1857 Aug 3   Geren, Mary M. and Thomas Garnett by Rev. John Boyd, St. Luke's
               Church, Marietta, Washington Co.

1817 Dec 25   German, Metilda and Jack Milton by George Hays, Franklin Co.

1810 Jun 7   German, Polly and Alexander McDole by David Spangler, Franklin Co.

1825 Jul 28   German, Rilay and Anne Essex by Persinal Adams, JP, Franklin Co.

1816 Feb 20   Gibbons, Mary and John Hull by Uriah Hull, Licking Co.

1895 Sep 14   Gibbons, Mrs. Sarah E. of Zanesville and David M. Wilson of
               Lancaster, O., by Rev. George F. Moore, Putnam Presbyterian
               Church, Muskingum Co.

1826 Mar 24   Gibbs, Daniel and Margaret Sorden (or Sordon) by Percival Adams,
               Franklin Co.

1816 Feb 25   Gibbs, Elizabeth and James Taylor by David Stevens, Washington Co.

1805 May 23   Gibbs, James and Nancy Bramble by Thomas Scott, JP, Ross Co.

1806 Jan 31   Gibbs, Melinda and Balace Nichols by James Quinn, Ross Co.

1825 Aug 25   Giberson, John and Sarah Childs by William Godman, JP, Franklin Co.

1818 Nov 18   Gibson, James B. and Hester R. Cochrane by Isaac Baker, JP,
               Jackson Co.

1815 May 4   Gibson, Jane and Joseph Hill by Dan'l H. Buell, JP, Washington Co.

1819 Mar 7   Gibson, John and Anna Pearsons by James M. Booth, JP, Washington Co.

1801 Oct 8   Gibson, John and Esther Davidson at Youngstown, by William Wicks,
               VDM, Trumbull Co.

1809 May 6   Gibson, Lorin (Levin) and Rachael Lane by Jonathan Minshall,
               Franklin Co.

1810 Aug 9   Gibson, Robert and Amelia Reid (license date), Pickaway Co.

1817 Jan 30   Gibson, Robert and Levy Bartlett by James Sharp, JP, Washington Co.

1896 Dec 9   Gibson, Rosa E. and Arthur O. Williams both of Roseville, O., by
               Rev. George F. Moore, Putnam Presbyterian Church, Muskingum Co.

1805 Feb 3   Gibson, William and Sarah Samard by William Creighton, Ross Co.

1828 Jul 17   Gibson, William and Uri Ann Godown by Geo. Black, JP, Franklin Co.

1874 Mar 23   Giffens, Susan and Sebastin Wertsberger by Rev. John Boyd, St.
               Luke's Church, Marietta

1818 Jan 7   Giffin, Ann and John Barnes by L.D. Baird, VDM, Licking Co.

1816 Mar 21   Giffin, Stephan and Margaret Stadden by T.D. Baird, UDM, Licking Co.

1811 Feb 7   Gifford, Joseph and Polly Dilaha (license date), Pickaway Co.

1817 Jan 22   Gifford, Roxana and Robert Henry by Nath'l Hamilton, Washington Co.

1805 Dec 25   Gibbord, Timothy and Elizabeth McDonald by Wm. Creighton, Ross Co.

1821 Jan 18   Giger, Joseph and Elizabeth Albery by M. Black, JP, Licking Co.

1810 Apr 22   Gilbert, Amos and Sally Magruder by Wm. Browning, Washington Co.

1809 Dec 31   Gilbert, John and Elenor Bidlack by Wm. D. Hendren, JP, Franklin Co.

1865 Dec 25   Gilbert, L. Frank and Sarah A. Cram by Rev. John Boyd, St. Luke's
               Church, Marietta, Washington Co.

1825 Jul 6   Gilem, Michal and James Wilson by David W. Walton, JP, Jackson Co.

1828 Jan 3   Giles, Cassander and Morjalin Belford by John F. Solomon, Franklin
               Co.

1814 Oct 23   Giles, Elizabeth and Nathaniel Bishop by John Brough, Esq., Washing-
               ton Co.

1822 Jan 3   Giles, Hugh H. and Polly Biser by C. Henkel, Franklin Co.

1813 Aug 12   Giles, Sally and William Ewing (license date), Pickaway Co.

1809 Apr 14   Gilkison, Thos. and Sally Delong by Amos Porter, Washington Co.

1873 Nov 17   Gill, Elias and Mrs. Mary Angeline Parlow by Rev. John Boyd, St.
               Luke's Church, Marietta, Washington Co.

1817 Nov 13   Gill, James and Cynthia Taylor by Noah Fidler, Licking Co.

1807 May 7   Gill, John and Lucy Holburt by Thos. Stanley, Washington Co.

1809 May 18   Gill, Stephen and Jane Elliott by Wm. Haines, JP, Licking Co.

1817 Nov 1   Gillaspie, Moses and Chloe Phelps by Ebenezer Washburn, Franklin Co.

1824 Mar 16   Gillespy, Martha and Jos. Richards by Thos. Daugherty, JP, Jackson
               Co.

1824 May 26   Gillett, Hezekiah and Brittavia Butterfield by R.W. Cowles, JP,
               Franklin Co.

1811 Jun 10   Gilliland, John and Elizabeth Thomas by Rev. Simon Cokrane,
               Franklin Co.

1822 Mar 21   Gilliland, John and Betsey McAtee by John Russell, JP, Washington Co.

1820 Jun 25   Gilliland, John B. and Sarah Johnston by Nath'l W. Andrews, JP,
               Jackson Co.

1846 Jan 1   Gillespie, Esther E. and David E. Boies by Rev. A. Kingsbury,
               Putnam Presbyterian Church, Muskingum Co.

1841 Mar 4   Gillespie, Martha Ann and Robert N. Dunlap by Rev. A. Kingsbury,
               Putnam Presbyterian Church, Muskingum Co.

1826 Oct 1   Gillmore, Sally and William L. Moore by P. Adams, Franklin Co.

1823 Aug 6   Gillunon, Zebide and Mary Philips by John F. Solomon, MG, Franklin Co.

1820 Aug 2   Gilman, Elisha and Sophronia D. Taylor by Rev. T. Harris, Licking Co.

1819 Sep 20   Gilman, Fhidelia and A.H. Prichard by Samuel Bancroft, JP, Licking Co.

1807 Nov 28   Gilman, Jane Robbins and Dudley Woodbridge by S.P. Robbins, Washington Co.

1806 Aug 3   Gilman, Nathaniel C. and Sarah Goodwin by Edwin Putnam, Washington Co.

1808 Aug 11   Gilman, Ruth and Spencer Spelman by Rev. Timothy Harris, Licking Co.

1808 Dec 22   Gilmore, David and Sally Mixer by Sam'l P. Robbins, Washington Co.

1817 Nov 27   Gilmore, Jane and Nash L. Pitzer by James Hoge, Franklin Co.

1827 Dec 14   Gilmore, John S. and Mary Nicholes by S. Hamilton, Franklin Co.

1820 Feb 28   Gilmore, Robert and Mariah Pilgrim by James Hoge, Franklin Co.

1853 Dec 19   Gilson, May M. and C.F. Rachly by Rev. Geo. B. Sturges, St. Paul's Church, Marion, Marion Co.

1817 Sep 17   Gilson, Samuel and Dally Clark by R. Stansberry, JP, (another entry 17 Sep 1819), Franklin Co.

1807 Apr 16   Gitteau, Benjamin and Maria Taylor by Samuel P. Robbins, Washington Co.

1802 Feb 7   Gitteau, Jerusha and William R. Putnam by Daniel Story, Washington Co.

1806 Jan 14   Given, Barbary and Thomas Carter by Wm. Creighton, Ross Co.

1809 Oct 19   Glack, Maria and Stephan McDougal by Wm. Haines, JP, Licking Co.

1819 Jan 5   Gladden, Nancy and Joshua Plummer by Samuel Stover, JP, Licking Co.

1826 Jul 16   Glaspill, G.W. and Minus Allen by Henry Mathes, Minister of the ME Church, Franklin Co.

1810 Oct 31   Glaspy, Enos and Fanny White by Isaac Case, JP, Franklin Co.

1810 Sep 13   Glass, Ida and Joseph Glass (license date), Pickaway Co.

1810 Sep 13   Glass, Joseph and Ida Glass (license date), Pickaway Co.

1826 Jun 22   Glass, Margret and James Bryden by Henry Matthews, Franklin Co.

1811 Aug 21   Glaze, Eliza and Richard Stage (license date), Pickaway Co.

1810 Aug 30   Glaze, Henry and Sarah Green by Ralph Lotspeitch, Licking Co.

1812 Jul 30   Glaze, John and Rachel Ball (license date), Pickaway Co.

1811 Feb 28   Glaze, Mary E. and Tunis Peters (license date), Pickaway Co.

1812 Jul 27   Glaze, Polly and Zachariah Stevenson (license date), Pickaway Co.

1813 Dec 1   Glaze, Rachel and George Davis (license date), Pickaway Co.

1804 Sep 27   Glaze, Richard, and Nancy Vansickle by Geo. Williams, JP, Ross Co.

1815 Mar 23   Glaze, Sarah and Thomas Loofborough by Henry Davis, JP, Pickaway Co.

1817 Apr 10   Glaze, Sarah and Ephraim Anderson by James Quism Elder, MEC,
               Licking Co.

1825 Jun 9   Gleason, Laura and George Tiper by J.B. Finley, MG, Marion Co.

1825 Jan --   Gleason, Louis and Samuel Smith by Thomas Rodgers, JP, Marion Co.

1814 Aug 6   Glick, Solomon and Polly Spangler by Jacob Leist, JP, Pickaway Co.

1818 Jan 24   Glidden, Lydia and Samuel Allen by Danl. G. Stanley, JP, Washington
               Co.

1815 Jul 30   Glidden, Mary and Oren Campbell by Artemas Knapp, JP, Washington Co.

1806 Jan 15   Glines, Joseph and Polly Hill by Thos. Stanley, Washington Co.

1805 Aug 4   Glove, Jane and George Kinser by David Shelby, JP, Ross Co.

1823 Mar 4   Glover, Elijah and Sarah Brown by D.W. Deshler, JP, Franklin Co.

1816 Mar 3   Glover, James and Margaret Armstrong by Rev. Stephen Lindsley,
               Washington Co.

1821 Dec 7   Gloyd, Corrintha and Wallace McCloud by Samuel Abbott, JP, Franklin
               Co.

1821 Dec 7   Gloyd, Elvira and Benjamin Chase by Samuel Abbott, Franklin Co.

1814 Jul 27   Gluhard, Polly and Wm. Knight by Abm. Christ, JP, Pickaway Co.

1815 Aug 7   Gobin, Samuel and Peggy Sneas by Thomas White, JP, Washington Co.

1818 Jul 6   Godfrey, Rachel and Jacob Vance by James Campbell, JP, Licking Co.

1827 Mar 1   Godman, Julius G. and Anna Bowin by S. Hamilton, Elder in MEC Church,
               Franklin Co.

1828 Dec 4   Godman, Otho and Maria Watts by Leory Swornstead, Franklin Co.

1823 Feb 21   Godman, Richard G. and Martha McCrea by Wm. Godman, JP, Franklin Co.

1823 Mar 7   Godner, Samuel and Lidia Peters by Richard Courtright, JP, Franklin.
               Co.

1828 Jul 17   Godown, Uri Ann and William Gibson by Geo. Black, JP, Franklin Co.

1814 Oct 13   Goetcheus, John and Nancy Wait by James Marshall, Franklin Co.

1823 Mar 20   Goetchieus, Isaac and Eleanor Downs by Jacob Grubb, Franklin Co.

1816 Apr 26   Goff, Elizabeth and Charles Calvin by Simeon Overturf, JP, Licking
               Co.

1824 Mar 30   Gohagan, Silas S. and Margaret Rice by Charles Waddell, Franklin Co.

1819 Mar 29   Gold, Edmund C. and Jane Norwood by Jacob Smith, JP, Franklin Co.

1821 Apr 12   Gold, Elizabeth and Isaac Day by James Cunningham, VDM, Licking Co.

1818 May 23   Gold, Sarah and Thompson Gates by D.H. Buell, JP, Washington Co.

1810 Mar 1   Goldsbrough, Polly and John Waldo by D. Loring, JP, Washington Co.

1816 Oct 31   Goldsmith, Angelania and Thomas Stanley by R.S.P. Robbins,
               Washington Co.

1816 Jun 16   Goldsmith, Burfot and Charlotte Smith by Simon Merwin, JP,
               Washington Co.

1816 Apr 25   Goldsmith, Elizabeth and Isaac Keller by Simon Merwin, Washington Co.

1828 Dec 25   Goldsmith, George and Sarah Demorest by W.T. Martin, Franklin Co.

1817 Sep 24   Goldsmith, Thomas and Elizabeth Chambers by Jacob Keller, Franklin
               Co.

1814 Feb 10   Goldsmith, William and Eleanor Walker by Rev. S.P. Robbins,
               Washington Co.

1823 Jan 16   Goldson, Lucinda and Stewart Baly by Robert W. Riley, JP, Franklin Co.

1826 Dec 26   Golliday, John and Nancy Johnson by D.W. Deshler, JP, Franklin Co.

1823 Jan 2   Golliday, Patsy and William Scott by Jacob Gundy, JP, Franklin Co.

1793 Aug 22   Goodale, Cynthia and Samuel Barnes by D. Loring, CCCP, Washington Co.

1789 Oct 25   Goodale, Elizabeth and Wanton Casey by Ben Tupper, Washington Co.

1792 Aug 8   Goodale, Sarah and Cornelius Delano by J. Gilman, Washington Co.

1802 Jun 7   Goodale, Susan and Hezekiah Smith by J. Pierce, Washington Co.

1818 Oct 18   Goodanow, Levi and Cynthia Beebe by Rev. Philander Chase, Franklin Co.

1826 Oct 29   Gooderich, Ezekiel and Mary Raney by John Davis, JP, Franklin Co.

1813 Jun 1   Goodin, Mahlon and Margaret Droddy by D. Hess, Franklin Co.

1828 Jul 8   Gooding, Susanna and John McElhany by Eb'r Washburn, VDM, Franklin Co.

1824 Jun 8   Gooding, Sylvester R. and Eliza Love by Samuel Fish, JP, Marion Co.

1879 Sep 17   Goodloe, William M. and Mary Stephens by Rev. John Boyd, St. Luke's
               Church, Marietta, Washington Co.

1869 Nov 4   Goodman, Jane E. and William H. Goodman by Rev. John Boyd, St.
               Luke's Church, Marietta, Washington Co.

1813 May 5   Goodman, John and Eve Stapleton (license date), Pickaway Co.

1846 Apr 13   Goodman, Mary Ann and Henry J. Lynch of Pittsburg, Pa., by Rev.
               Edward Winthrop, St. Luke's Church, Marietta, Washington Co.

1869 Nov 4   Goodman, William H. and Jane E. Goodman by Rev. John Boyd, St.
               Luke's Church, Marietta, Washington Co.

1802 Apr --   Goodno, Daniel and Sally Cushing by J. Pierce, JCCCP, Washington Co.

1820 Feb 21   Goodno, Thaddeus and Betsey Woodruff by Rev. I. Hooper, Washington Co.

1819 Oct 6   Goodrich, Henry and Eleanor Jones by Joseph Thrap, MG, Licking Co.

1809 Sep 14   Goodrich, Jacob and Sally Thrall by Rev. Timothy Harris, Licking Co.

1818 Nov 29   Goodrich, John and Clarisa Andrews by Stephen Maynard, JP, Franklin
               Co.

1816 Feb 24   Goodrich, Lenard and Hannah Clark by John Cunningham, JP, Licking Co.

1822 Jan 22   Goodrich, Lucy and David Patterson by A. Buttles, Franklin Co.

1816 Apr 2   Goodrich, Nancy and Legget Gray by J.W. Patterson, JP, Licking Co.

1821 Dec 25   Goodrich, Rhoda and Simeon Barker by A. Buttles, JP, Franklin Co.

1812 Apr 16   Goodrich, Salinda and Job Hughes by Rev. G. Vanaman, Licking Co.

1815 Jul 6   Goodrich, Timothy and Minerva Howe by John Russell, JP, Washington Co.

1828 Sep 22   Goodson, Mary and John J. Garretson by John Tipton, JP, Franklin Co.

1810 Aug 13   Goodwin, Asa and Hannah Williams by Stephen Lindsly, Washington Co.

1826 Sep 14   Goodwin, Joseph and Sarah Essex by P. Adams, JP, Franklin Co.

1818 Dec 22   Goodwin, Margaret and William Carl by Wm. Rand, Washington Co.

1806 Aug 3   Goodwin, Sarah and Nathaniel C. Gilman by Edwin Putnam, Washington Co

1819 May 13   Goodwin, Sarah and Josiah Heard by Samuel H. Buell, JP, Washington Co

1818 Aug 2   Goodwin, Susannah and John Dursels by George Hays, Franklin Co.

1809 Jan 9   Goold, Elizabeth and Andrew Hains by Dan'l Dunfee, Washington Co.

1824 Sep 9   Gorden, Wm. and Mary Keller by David W. Walter, JP, Jackson Co.

1823 Feb 20   Gordner, Azed and Jane Willson by St M. Cott, JP, Franklin Co.

1812 Sep 17   Gordon, Ann and David Hedelston by Henry Jolly, JP, Washington Co.

1826 Mar 2   Gordon, Catharine and George Davis by J. Carper, Franklin Co.

1825 Oct 6   Gordon, Mary and Joseph Shrom by Jacob Grubb, JP, Franklin Co.

1813 Apr 19   Gordy, Polly and Jacob Trullinger (license date), Pickaway Co.

1814 Feb 23   Gordy, Sally and Daniel Wilson by John Ludwig, JP, Pickaway Co.

1810 Dec 13   Goremly, Maria and Martin B. Randaver by Isaac Case, Franklin Co.

1816 Sep 15   Gorham, Hannah and Jere Beach by Tracy Wilcox, JP, (another entry
               16 Sep 1816), Franklin Co.

1815 Nov 12   Gorman, Jane and Andrew Grubb by J. Greenman, JP, Washington Co.

1821 Mar 29   Gorman, John and Margaret Alden by Ami Lawrence, JP, Washington Co.

1807 Mar 19   Gorman, Letitia and Andrew Carvel by Robert Oliver, JP, Washington Co

1814 Nov 22   Gormly, Jane and Henry Brown by Wm. Jones, JP, Pickaway Co.

1803 Apr 15   Gorrel, Wm. and Rebecca Binhard by Sam'l Williamson, Washington Co.

1825 Jun 2   Gorton, Mary and Wm. Armstead by Jos. Carper, Franklin Co.

1827 Apr 3   Gorton, Rosanna and Enos Henry by Rheuben Golliday, JP, Franklin Co.

1819 Apr 20   Gorton, Sally and Daniel Hess by Jacob Keller, Franklin Co.

1816 Nov 6   Gosnel, Sarah and Moses Thrap by John Spencer, JP, Licking Co.

1818 Nov 28   Gosnell, Joshua and Mary Myers by M. Tharp, JP, Licking Co.

1813 Aug 13   Goss, David and Lydia Ackley by Rev. Stephen Lindsley, Washington Co.

1798 May 17   Goss, Elizabeth and Andrew Lake by Josiah Munro, Washington Co.

1819 Jul 9   Goss, Lydia and John Spranklin by Rev. A. Robinson, Washington Co.

1812 Nov 19   Goss, Solomon Jr. and Polly Devol by Rev. David Young, Washington Co.

1817 Sep 10   Gossett, Daniel and Susan Riley by Danl H. Buell, JP, Washington Co.

1812 Feb 9   Gossett, Jacob and Mary Orison by Nathaniel Hamilton, JP, Washington
               Co.

1865 Apr 29   Gossett, Lucinda and Martin Wilson by Rev. John Boyd, St. Luke's
               Church, Marietta, Washington Co.

1813 Jul 15   Gossett, Margaret and William Riley by Nath. Hamilton, Washington Co.

1821 Oct 18   Gossett, Matilda and Zachariah Peck by Wm. Woodford, JP, Washington
               Co.

1818 May 5   Gossett, Sarah and William Liffingwell by Salmon N. Cook, JP,
               Washington Co.

1803 Jul 15   Gowens, Catharine and Robert Long by Thos. Scott, JP of Scioto Tp.,
               Ross Co.

1817 Apr 19   Gowns, Maria and William Seber by -----, Licking Co.

1813 Nov 14   Grable, Phillip and Sally Baum (license date), Pickaway Co.

1810 Apr 12   Grace, Isaac and McMahan Nelly by Michael Fisher, Franklin Co.

1828 Apr 24   Grace, Loger and Sarah Jones by Charles Sells, JP, Franklin Co.

1824 Oct 20   Grace, Stephen and Catharine Sells by Benjamin Briton, Franklin Co.

1821 Dec 20   Graham, Agnis and David Graham by John Long, JP, Franklin Co.

1821 Dec 20   Graham, David and Agnis Graham by John Long, JP, Franklin Co.

1824 Mar 22   Graham, Elizabeth and Leonard Bumgardner by R.W. Riley, Franklin Co.

1828 Feb 5   Graham, Geo. and Sarah Graham by Sam'l McLean, Franklin Co.

1867 Oct 11   Graham, James A. and Nancy E. Melrose by Rev. John Boyd, St. Luke's
               Church, Marietta, Washington Co.

1823 Jun 5   Graham, Jane and Jonathan French by Mathew Crawford, JP, Franklin Co.

1804 Feb 21   Graham, John and Clernda Norman by James Graham, JP, Washington Co.

1813 May 14   Graham, John and Lydia Alkire (license date), Pickaway Co.

1824 Nov 4   Graham, John and Elenor Leach by Robert Ward, JP, Jackson Co.

1816 Aug 8   Graham, Joseph and Sarah Coffman by Noah Fidler, Licking Co.

1823 Jun 11   Graham, Joseph and Mary Crawford by Isaac Painter, JP, Franklin Co.

1801 Apr 2   Graham, Margaret and Israel Bobo by Wm. Harper, Washington Co.

1811 Sep 24   Graham, Margaret and Jacob Veil (license date), Pickaway Co.

1824 Apr 29   Graham, Martha and James W. Taylor by John Donaldson, Franklin Co.

1853 Feb 21   Graham, Martha and James W. Williams by Rev. Geo. B. Sturges, St.
               Paul's Church, Marion, Marion Co.

1819 Jan 14   Graham, Mary and John Livingston by John Jenks, JP, Franklin Co.

1806 Nov 22   Graham, Patsy and Alexander Oliver by S. Lindsly, Washington Co.

1817 Mar 20   Graham, Rachel and Nathan Dixon by Francis Holland, JP Scioto Tp.,
               Jackson Co.

1823 Aug 14   Graham, Samuel and Nancy Thomas by Wm. Duff, Franklin Co.

1828 Feb 5   Graham, Sarah and Geo. Graham by Sam'l McLean, Franklin Co.

1810 May 10   Graham, Susana and Flemming Ferguson (license date), Pickaway Co.

1825 Mar 14   Graham, William and Mary French by John Long, JP, Franklin Co.

1804 Jan 1   Grambel, Daniel and Sally Jones by Samuel Smith, Ross Co.

1815 Mar 30   Gramer, Christopher and Sarah Taylor by Rederick Peterson, JP,
               Franklin Co.

1810 Jun 7   Granden, Rhoda and Michael Archer by Amos Porter, JP, Washington Co.

1817 Sep 18   Grandstaff, Moses and Catharine Waller by John Patterson, Washington
               Co.

1819 Jan 31   Granger, Anna and Aaron Pratt by Rev. Timothy Harris, Licking Co.

1825 Mar 3   Granger, Moses and Saphrona Benedict by Aristarcrus Walker, Franklin
               Co.

1813 Jul 4   Granger, Ralph and Hannah Spelman by J. Tulloss, JP, Licking Co.

1821 Dec 23   Grant, Elexander and Lucy Parrish by Jacob Grundy, JP, Franklin Co.

1818 Jan 1   Grant, Enos and Betsy Chadwick by Noah Fidler, Licking Co.

1887 Apr 6   Grant, Frederick J. of Seattle, Wash., and Bessie D. Hoge of Zanes-
               ville by Rev. George F. Moore, Putnam Presbyterian Church,
               Muskingum Co.

1825 Jul 6   Grant, Geo. and Anna Stancliff by Robert Ward, JP, Jackson Co.

1820 Dec 26   Grant, Isabella and Benjamin Wood by Reuben Golliday, JP, Franklin Co.

1819 Dec 31   Grant, Leafy and George McDaniel by James M. Booth, JP, Washington Co.

1812 Jun 6   Grant, Peter and Casey Martin (license date), Pickaway Co.

1825 Sep 13   Grant, Polly and Gabriel Postles by Wm. C. Duff, Franklin Co.

1814 Dec 25   Gratton, Nancy and William Atchison by Chas. Cade, JP, Pickaway Co.

1825 Mar 3   Graves, Alice and Henry Graves by Timothy Ratcliff, JP, Jackson Co.

1820 Apr 4   Graves, Benjamin Jr. and Martha W. Webb by A. Buttles, JP, Franklin Co

1812 Nov 7   Graves, C. and E. Rose by Rev. T. Harris, Licking Co.

1811 Nov 7   Graves, Cladious and Electa Rose by Rev. T. Harris, Licking Co.

1803 Nov 28   Graves, Elexander and Rebecca Comer by John Odle, JP, Ross Co.

1821 Aug 30   Graves, Enoch and Mindwell Clark by Rev. T. Harris, Granville,
               Licking Co.

1825 Mar 3   Graves, Henry and Alice Graves by Timothy Ratcliff, JP, Jackson Co.

1804 Jan 24   Graves, Nelly and William Rush by Samuel Smith, Ross Co.

1809 Jun 11   Graves, Orpah and Joshua Linnell by Silas Winchell, JP, Licking Co.

1825 Mar 2   Graves, Rosanna and Lemuel Dixon by Timothy Ratcliff, JP, Jackson Co.

1818 Jan 15   Graves, Roswell and Sally Ridley by T. Harris, Licking Co.

1819 Nov 11   Graves, Veloris and Anna Baker by Samuel Bancroft, JP, Licking Co.

1805 Jan 8   Graves, William and Elizabeth Stinson by Robert Adams, Ross Co.

1824 Mar 25   Graves, William and Elizabeth Waldren by Geo. Claypoole, JP,
               Jackson Co.

1813 Dec 23   Gravis, Louis and Elizabeth Wilson (license date), Pickaway Co.

1880 Sep 30   Gray, Benson L. of Zanesville and Florence O. Coulter of Putnam by
               Rev. George F. Moore, Putnam Presbyterian Church, Muskingum Co.

1819 Dec 8   Gray, Catherine and Thomas Smith by T.D. Bierd, Licking Co.

1821 Nov 17   Gray, Deborah and Jesse Loring by Rev. William Boris, Washington Co.

1828 Apr 2   Gray, Edey and William Spooner by Adam Miller, Franklin Co.

1826 Mar 30   Gray, Elisha and Jacob Shoaf by P. Adams, Franklin Co.

1817 Mar 13   Gray, Fanny and William Gearman by Percival Adams, Franklin Co.

1893 Jan 25   Gray, Jane of Scotland and James R. Elliott of Zanesville by Rev.
               George F. Moore, Putnam Presbyterian Church, Muskingum Co.

1826 Aug 10   Gray, Joseph and Polly Lewis by P. Adams, Franklin Co.

1816 Apr 2   Gray, Legget and Nancy Goodrich by J.W. Patterson, JP, Licking Co.

1828 Jul 15   Gray, Littleton and Anna Needles by Nathan Emery, Elder in the
               Methodist E. Church, Franklin Co.

1806 Jul 13   Gray, Polly and Andrew Fisher by Robert Oliver, Washington Co.

1888 Dec 6   Gray, Sarah of Zanesville and Clarence F. Shilling of Morgan Co. by
               Rev. George F. Moore, Putnam Presbyterian Church, Muskingum Co.

1810 Dec 27   Gray, Thomas and Dosha Huff by Thomas Morris, JP, Franklin Co.

1827 Aug 2   Gray, Thomas and Harriet Hughes by Wm. Patterson, JP, Franklin Co.

1808 12 mo 14 Gray, William and Mary Cleaver, Miami Monthly Meeting, Warren Co.

1826 Dec 14   Grayham, James and Issabel S. Marshall by Wm. Sterewalt, Franklin Co.

1827 May 4   Grayham, John and May Grayham by John Long, Franklin Co.

1827 May 4   Grayham, May and John Grayham by John Long, Franklin Co.

1820 Apr 20   Greaves, Joseph and Jane McVey by Joseph Lockard, JP, Jackson Co.

1810 Dec 23   Green, Atsey and William Currey (license date), Pickaway Co.

1802 Mar 24   Green, Catharine and Eliphaz Perkins by Griffin Green, JP, Washington
               Co.

1815 Feb 28   Green, Catherine and Henry Fulk by Thos. Mace, JP, Pickaway Co.

1850 Sep 25   Green, Christopher and Mary F. Wood both of Newport, Ky., by Rev.
               D.W. Tolford, St. Luke's Church, Marietta, Washington Co.

1816 Mar 30   Green, Daniel and Elizabeth Pitzer by Noah Fidler, Licking Co.

1826 12 mo 6   Green, David and Mary Jessup, Miami Monthly Meeting, Warren Co.

1810 Jul 9   Green, Edward and Elizabeth Craun by Massey Clymer, Franklin Co.

1883 Feb 11   Green, Edward of Zanesville and Kate Hemphill of Putnam by Rev.
               George F. Moore, Putnam Presbyterian Church, Muskingum Co.

1887 Jan 26   Green, Edward A. of Alexandria, Va., and Mary H. Buckingham of
               Zanesville by Rev. George F. Moore, Putnam Presbyterian
               Church, Muskingum Co.

1801 Jan 5   Green, Elizabeth and John Staden by Henry Smith, JP, Washington Co.

1812 Aug --   Green, Eliz. and Edward Laughry by A. Holden, JP, Licking Co.

1819 Jan 19   Green, Elizabeth and John Green by Geo. Hoover, JP, Licking Co.

1810 Mar 18   Green, Elizabeth Wells and James Holmes by -----, Licking Co.

1820 Apr 6   Green, Ezra and Anna Dodge by John Green, JP, Washington Co.

1870 Oct 27   Green, George H. and Anna Edgar by Rev. A. Kingsbury, Putnam
               Presbyterian Church, Muskingum Co.

1827 May 24   Green, Hoapy and John Inks, Jr. by A. Allison, Franklin Co.

1808 Nov 20   Green, John and Elizabeth Devoll by Nehemiah Davis, Washington Co.

1813 Mar 28   Green, John and Barbara Grove by A. Holden, JP, Licking Co.

1819 Jan 19   Green, John and Elizabeth Green by Geo. Hoover, JP, Licking Co.

1827 May 30   Green, Luther and May Jenks by Hugh Liams, JP, Franklin Co.

1811 Jan 13   Green, Margaret and Isaac Woodrough by John Green, MG, Washington Co.

1819 Mar 7   Green, Mary and Ira Mollery by Noah Fidler, Licking Co.

1808 Aug 13   Green, Nancy and Wm. Clark by Arthur O'Harra, Franklin Co.

1816 Jun 6   Green, Nancy and Alexander Patton by James Marshall, Franklin Co.

1819 Jan 11   Green, Nancy and James Elliott by -----, Licking Co.

1814 Apr 29   Green, Naomi and Thomas Hinton by John Cunningham, Licking Co.

1808 Dec 7   Green, Nathaniel and Sophia (Harris) Hider by Wm. Haines, JP,
               Licking Co.

1821 Jan 21   Green, Oliver and Charlotte Davis by John Green, JP, Washington Co.

1819 Apr 23   Green, Palmela and Samuel H. Reynolds by Rev. Abel Robinson,
               Washington Co.

1792 Apr 8   Green, Phebe and Jonathan Haskel by J. Gilman, Washington Co.

1812 Jun 14   Green, Polly and Samuel Haden by -----, Licking Co.

1815 Nov 16   Green, Rebecca and Jesse Hill by Elihu Bigelow, JP, Licking Co.

1838 Feb 24   Green, Rebecca and Ephraim Carter, St. Luke's Church, Granville,
               Licking Co.

1809 Nov 19   Green, Richard and Sarah Davis by -----, Licking Co.

1813 Dec 13   Green, Richard and Rebecca Lawton by Rev. David Young, Washington Co.

1810 Aug 30   Green, Sarah and Henry Glaze by Ralph Lotspeitch, Licking Co.

1824 Jul 1   Green, Sarah M. and Peter Cup by B. Bull, Franklin Co.

1813 Nov 21   Green, Smith and Sally Mellor by N. Hamilton, JP, Washington Co.

1813 Mar 21   Green, Thomas and Sally Marsh by Rev. Stephen Lindley, Washington Co.

1820 Oct 26   Green, Thomas and Polly Willison by Clement D. Wolf, JP, Licking Co.

1804 Feb 27   Green, William and Hannah Anderson by Thomas Scott, JP Scioto Tp.,
               Ross Co.

1821 Mar 8   Green, William and Sarah Pitzer by Geo. Callanhan, EMEC, Licking Co.

1811 Jun 6   Greene, Benjamin and Susanna Perry by Thomas Stanley, JP, Washington
               Co.

1812 Dec 17   Greene, Caleb and Catharine McMasters by Rev. Stephen Lindley,
               Washington Co.

1814 Mar 31   Greene, Caleb and Jerusha Palmer by Cornelius Horyland, JP,
              Washington Co.

1846 Apr 27   Greene, Caroline S. and Charles B. Hall by Rev. Edward Winthrop,
              St. Luke's Church, Marietta, Washington Co.

1811 Apr 18   Greene, Duty Jr. and Polly Henry by Rev. John Greene, Washington Co.

1805 Oct 21   Greene, Ezra and Sally Proctor by Jacob Lindly, Washington Co.

1840 Sep 30   Greene, Isabella and William Holden by Rev. James Bonnar, St. Luke's
              Church, Marietta, Washington Co.

1841 Oct 6   Greene, James H. and Eunice McFarland by Rev. James Bonnar, St.
              Luke's Church, Marietta, Washington Co.

1808 Jun 22   Greene, John and Polly Hill by Stephen Lindsly, Washington Co.

1808 Aug 5   Greene, Mary G. and James Davis by Wm. Haines, JP, Licking Co.

1806 Nov 18   Greene, Nancy and David James by S. Lindsly, Washington Co.

1807 Nov 14   Greene, Ruth and James Whitney by S.P. Robbins, Washington Co.

1806 May 15   Greene, Susanna and John Carnock by J. Brough, JP, Washington Co.

1816 Jul 20   Greene, Sylvina and Joel Dodge by J. Humphreys, JP, Washington Co.

1817 May 18   Greenleaf, Lucy and William Holyoke by Rev. S.P. Robbins, Washington
              Co.

1805 Dec 4   Greenlee, Elizabeth and James Tuttle by Noble Crawford, JP, Ross Co.

1799 Jul 9   Greenlee, Rachel and Jesse Benbebber by Robert Safford, Washington Co.

1818 Nov 26   Greenman, Jeremiah Jr. and Latitia McCoy by Titan Kimble, JP,
              Washington Co.

1804 Apr 12   Greentree, Mary and Emer Bates by Noble Crawford, Ross Co.

1804 --- --   Greenwood, Eliz. and Titus Hubbard by Wm. Robinson, Ross Co.

1822 Oct 1   Greenwood, Hannah and Samuel Russell by Samuel Gillet, JP, Franklin
              Co.

1844 Apr 19   Greer, Elizabeth and Harvey ----- by Rev. R. S. Elder, St. John's
              Church, Worthington, Franklin Co.

1836 May 12   Greer, Isabella and Dr. T.V. Morrow by Rev. E. Burr, St. John's
              Church, Worthington, Franklin Co.

1813 Aug 2   Greer, James and Mary Hays (license date), Pickaway Co.

1841 Dec 21   Greer, Joanna and Benjamin L. Hill by Rev. R.S. Elder, St. John's
              Church, Worthington, Franklin Co.

1822 Dec 5   Greer, John and Sufey Keesner by Percival Adams, Franklin Co.

1839 Mar --   Greer, Laura K. and L.A. Pierce by Rev. A. Helfenstine, St. John's
              Church, Worthington, Franklin Co.

1801 Jan 5   Greer, Paul and Maria Evritt by Lewis Hubner, MG, Washington Co.

1820 Sep 21   Gregg, Jane and Charles Pain by Wm. Woodford, JP, Washington Co.

1822 Apr 2   Gregory, David and Parmelia Platt by James Hoge, Franklin Co.

1820 May 2   Gregory, Wm. and Frances Long by Jeremiah Brown, JP, Jackson Co.

1814 Dec 8   Grewes, Rhoda and Strong Clark by Rev. Timothy Harris, Licking Co.

1821 Aug 26   Gridley, Catharine and James C. Wilson by James Hoge, Franklin Co.

1826 Dec 10   Gridley, Livinia and Cyrus Parker by James Hoge, Franklin Co.

1890 Jul 30   Griems, Harry E. and Julia M. Rayse both of Zanesville by Rev.
               George F. Moore, Putnam Presbyterian Church, Muskingum Co.

1820 Jul 6   Griffeth, Elizabeth and James Canidy by Samuel Dyer, Franklin Co.

1818 May 16   Griffeth, Isaac and Alsey Clark by Jacob Keller, Franklin Co.

1800 Oct 21   Griffin, Asael and Betsey Chapman by Daniel Story, Clerk, Washington
               Co.

1827 Nov 22   Griffin, Betsy and Ebenezer Randol by Jacob Gundy, Franklin Co.

1827 Dec --   Griffin, Betsy and Moses Nickens by Geo. Jefferies, Franklin Co.

1817 Apr 13   Griffin, Julian Avalina and Asa Coleman by Daniel Baker, JP,
               Licking Co.

1797 Jun 19   Griffing, Ebenezar and Grace Roberts by D. Loring, Jus. Com. Pleas,
               Washington Co.

1818 Nov 3   Griffith, G. and Peggy Woolard by Noah Fidler, Licking Co.

1814 Mar 8   Griffith, Hester and Edward James by John H. Phillips, Licking Co.

1824 May 13   Griffith, Lutisha and Benjamin Noris by Jacob Gundy, Franklin Co.

1883 Aug 6   Griffith, Mollie L. of Putnam and Robert B. Seymour of Alliance, O.,
               by Rev. George F. Moore, Putnam Presbyterian Church, Muskingum
               Co.

1842 Oct 25   Griffith, Timothy and Lydia Ann Weaver by Rev. R.S. Elder, St. John's
               Church, Worthington, Franklin Co.

1823 Apr 22   Griffy, Easter and Joseph McCollester by Joseph Badger, Franklin Co.

1822 May 23   Grifith, Margann and James Roberts by Jacob Gundy, Franklin Co.

1824 Nov 2   Grifus, Wm. and Susanna Baety by Jacob Gundy, JP (date recorded),
               Franklin Co.

1810 Nov 25   Grigsby, Leah and Rob't Baird, Jr. by Stephen Lindsly, Washington Co.

1811 May 23   Grim, David and Susana Wanamacher (license date), Pickaway Co.

1804 Jul 19   Grimes, Thomas and Elornor Mount both of Pe Pe Tp. by John Johnson,
               Ross Co.

1818 Dec 23   Grist, Isaac and Mariah Wilson by James Holmes, Licking Co.

1818 Aug 2   Griswold, Anna and Lyman Carter by Rev. Philander Chase, Franklin Co.

1844 Feb 8   Griswold, Caroline and Cicero Comstock by Rev. R.S. Elder, St. John's
               Church, Worthington, Franklin Co.

1840 Mar 16   Griswold, Emily and Franklin Johnson by Rev. A. Helfenstine, St.
               John's Church, Worthington, Franklin Co.

1814 Apr 4   Griswold, Ezra and Philiela Cook by Ezra Griswold, JP, Franklin Co.

1820 May 21   Griswold, George Harlow and Mila Thompson by Rev. Philander Chase,
               Franklin Co.

1817 Sep 11   Griswold, Melissa and Caleb Howard by Rev. Philander Chase,
               Franklin Co.

1807 Feb 22   Griswold, Ruth and Noah Andrews by James Kilbourne, JP, Franklin Co.

1823 Mar 30   Griswold, Sylvia and Deloss Warren by A. Buttles, JP, Franklin Co.

1849 Dec 2   Grohs, Frederick and Elizabeth Cisler by Rev. D.W. Tolford, St.
               Luke's Church, Marietta, Washington Co.

1824 Feb 5   Grom, John and Elizabeth Britton by John F. Solomon, Franklin Co.

1828 Sep 11   Groom, Annah and William Suttle by Wm. Stirewalt, JP, Franklin Co.

1814 Mar 17   Groom, Job and Polly Groom by Shadrack Cole, JP, Pickaway Co.

1814 Mar 17   Groom, Polly and Job Groom by Shadrack Cole, JP, Pickaway Co.

1813 Dec 26   Groom, William and Nancy Moore (license date), Pickaway Co.

1821 Feb 11   Grooms, Elin and Martin Miller by Robert Elliott, JP, Franklin Co.

1811 Jan 17   Grooms, Sally and Ebenezer Stevens by Massey Clymer, Franklin Co.

1820 Nov 9   Gross, Francis G.R. and Susan Haruff by Eli C. King, Franklin Co.

1813 Mar 28   Grove, Barbara and John Green by A. Holden, JP, Licking Co.

1820 Jul 19   Grove, Catherine and James Kinney by Iesias Ewing, JP, Licking Co.

1818 Sep 10   Grove, George and Margaret Vanderbarck by A. Goff, Licking Co.

1820 Jul 29   Grove, Joseph and Polly Stover by Noah Fidler, Licking Co.

1814 Aug 4   Grove, Marry and Henry Dennis by J.W. Patterson, JP, Licking Co.

1811 Aug 8   Grove, Nancy and David Sha(r)er by J.W. Patterson, Licking Co.

1875 Feb --   Grover, Georgia and ----- Gallaway by Mr. Dudley, St. Luke's Church,
               Granville, Licking Co.

1819 Dec 7   Groves, John and Sarah Shaver by John W. Patterson, MG, Licking Co.

1818 Mar 5   Groves, Rebecca and Mathias Trumbo by Alex Holden, JP, Licking Co.

1828 Dec 25   Groves, Solomon and Elizabeth Johnston by P. Adams, Franklin Co.

1821 Apr 18   Groves, Susan and James Davis by Noah Fidler, Licking Co.

1812 Apr 16   Groves, Susanna and Simeon Rose by Philip Cole, JP, Washington Co.

1819 May 13   Groves, Thomas and Elizabeth Summers by Andrew Dill, JP, Franklin Co.

1813 Nov 29   Grown, Sally and Benjamin Mathews by John Green, JP, Licking Co.

1815 Nov 12   Grubb, Andrew and Jane Gorman by J. Greenman, JP, Washington Co.

1803 Dec 13   Grubb, Daniel and Barbery Streng by John G. McCan, Ross Co.

1822 Mar 10   Grubb, Eliza and Daniel Starling by Eli C. King, JP, Franklin Co.

1818 Dec 31   Grubb, Elizabeth and Wm. Lawrence by Pelatiah White, JP, Washington
               Co.

1815 Feb 19   Grubb, James and Cynthia White by Isaac Baker, Esq., Washington Co.

1820 Jul 5   Grubb, John and Elizabeth Wilson by John D. Chamberlain, JP,
               Washington Co.

1821 Mar 15   Grubb, Peter and Betsey Townsend by John D. Chamberlain, JP,
               Washington Co.

1806 Sep 11   Grubb, Susan and Jacob Overdear by James Marshall, JP, Franklin Co.

1813 Sep 2   Grun, Deborea and Phillip Strouse (license date), Pickaway Co.

1813 Mar 10   Grun, Mary and George Hays (license date), Pickaway Co.

1829 Feb 17   Guffy, Isaac and Elizabeth Davidson by John Swisher, JP, Franklin Co.

1810 Nov 27   Guffy, John and Nancy Pennington by Billingslea Bull, JP, Franklin
               Co.

1807 Mar 10   Guffy, Margaret and James Lafferty by Wm. Bennett, JP, Franklin Co.

1861 Oct 8   Guild, Edward C. of Canton, Mass., and Emma M. Cadwallader by Rev.
               John Boyd, St. Luke's Church, Marietta, Washington Co.

1879 May 15   Guille, Amelia of Putnam and James B. Milligan of Lancaster, O., by
               Rev. George F. Moore, Putnam Presbyterian Church, Muskingum Co.

1809 May 18   Guitteau, Jonathan and Polly Lord by Samuel P. Robbins, Washington Co.

1813 Sep 12   Guitteau, Jonathan and Sally Mills by Rev. S.P. Robbins, Washington
               Co.

1813 Mar 14   Guitteau, Patience and Jonas Moore by Rev.S.P. Robbins, Washington Co.

1814 Dec 22   Gumford, Mary and James Lyle by Geo. Bogart, Franklin Co.

1805 May 14   Gunday, Catharine and John Kite by Wm. Robinson, Ross Co.

1822 Aug --   Gundy, Anny and Thomas Bevens by Reuben Golliday, Franklin Co.

1828 Nov 20   Gundy, Elizabeth and Abraham Wood by John Tipton, Franklin Co.

1828 Dec 18   Gundy, William and Keziah Johnston by John Tipton, Franklin Co.

1820 Feb 26   Gurez, Mary Ann Rosan and Phinehas Beardsley by Judah M. Chamberlain,
               Jp, Washington Co.

1860 Dec 27   Gussinger, Amelia and Lewellen Scarvell by Rev. A. Kingsbury,
               Putnam Presbyterian Church, Muskingum Co.

1816 Feb 29   Gustice (or Justice), John and Betsy Fulk by Michael Patton,
               Franklin Co.

1821 Jan 2   Guthridge, William and Joanna Nicholls by Thomas Cummins, JP,
               Licking Co.

1819 Feb 4   Guthrie, Almira and Walter Curtis by Cyrus Ames, JP, Washington Co.

1862 Jul 24   Guthrie, Amelia of Putnam and John S. King of Orange, NJ., by Rev.
               A. Kingsbury, Putnam Presbyterian Church, Muskingum Co.

1877 Jun 10   Guthrie, Clara D. and William H. Clark by Rev. A. Kingsbury,
               Putnam Presbyterian Church, Muskingum Co.

1821 Jul 3   Guthrie, Erastus and Achsah Palmer by James Whitney, JP, Washington
               Co.

1853 Apr 7   Guthrie, Esther S. of Putnam and James Silvey of Chillocothe by
               Rev. A. Kingsbury, Putnam Presbyterian Church, Muskingum Co.

1796 Jul 21   Guthrie, Freeman and Elizabeth Stone by J. Gilman, Washington Co.

1817 Dec 17   Guthrie, James and Nancy ----- by Robert G. Hanna, JP, Jackson Co.

1804 Dec 27   Guthrie, Laura Matilda and Amos Dunham by Joseph Strickland,
               Washington Co.

1868 Oct 12   Guthrie, Lillian P. and Christopher C. Waite of Toledo by Rev. A.
               Kingsbury, Putnam Presbyterian Church, Muskingum Co.

1865 Sep 13   Guthrie, Mary C. and Edward P. Strong by Rev. A. Kingsbury, Putnam
               Presbyterian Church, Muskingum Co.

1858 Nov 10   Guthrie, Mary S. and James Fulton by Rev. A. Kingsbury, Putnam
               Presbyterian Church, Muskingum Co.

1847 Jan 7   Guthrie, Sarah E. of Putnam and Chancey R. Kelley of New York City
               by Rev. A. Kingsbury, Putnam Presbyterian Church, Muskingum Co.

1884 Jun 4   Guthrie, Sarah E. of Putnam and John S. Blanchard of Concord, NH.,
               by Rev. George F. Moore, Putnam Presbyterian Church, Muskingum
               Co.

1865 Jul 4   Guy, Hannah and Samuel Biggins of Palmer by Rev. John Boyd, St.
               Luke's Church, Marietta, Washington Co.

1819 Dec 11   Guy, Mary and Joseph C. Thompson by Rev. Philander Chase, Franklin Co.

1822 Jun 22   Gwynne, Matilda and John M. Edmiston by James Hoge, Franklin Co.

1818 May 5   Guy, Polly and Samuel Hunter by James Cunningham, Licking Co.

1821 Jan 15   Maas, John Jr. and Margaret Boyd by John Green, ECC, Licking Co.

1819 Mar 17   Hackett, Sally and Walker Logan by Eli C. King, JP, Franklin Co.

1812 Jun 14   Haden, Samuel and Polly Green by -----, Licking Co.

1818 Apr 18   Hagan (or Hagar), Cathrin and Hezekiah Cole by Thos. B. Patterson,
               Franklin Co.

1821 Jul 27   Hagans, Betsey and Andrew Wilson by Dudley Davis, JP, Washington Co.

1818 Apr 18   Hagar (or Hagan), Cathrin and Hezekiah Cole by Thos B. Patterson,
               Franklin Co.

1819 Jan 7   Haguman, James and Phoebe Robinson by John Patterson, Washington Co.

1818 Dec 8   Haight, Mary and John Bigford by Rev. Saml. Hamilton, Washington Co.

1816 Dec 24   Haile, Charlotte and Thomas Burton by Robert G. Hanna, JP, Jackson Co.

1812 Apr 23   Haines, Elizabeth and Henry Miers by Z. Carlisle, JP, Licking Co.

1825 11 mo 2   Haines, Mary E. and Isaac Engle, Miami Monthly Meeting, Warren Co.

1809 Jan 9   Hains, Andrew and Elizabeth Goold by Dan'l Dunfee, Washington Co.

1813 Jan 29   Hains, John and Mary Chenworth by Simon Cochran, JP, Franklin Co.

1808 6 mo 22   Hains, Noah and Anna Silver, Miami Monthly Meeting, Warren Co.

1819 Jul 2   Halcamb, Oliver H. and Lucinda Webster by Ezra Griswold, Franklin Co.

1854 Jan 24   Hale, Caroline E. of Putnam and David B. Sexton of Cleveland by Rev.
               A. Kingsbury, Putnam Presbyterian Church, Muskingum Co.

1882 Nov 4   Hale, Charles C. and Mary Boyd by Rev. John Boyd, St. Luke's Church,
               Marietta, Washington Co.

1809 Mar 24   Hale, Christian and Margaret Jackson by Amos Porter, JP, Washington
               Co.

1825 Feb 8   Hale, Milley and Wm. Stephenson by Jacob Miller, JP, Jackson Co.

1819 Apr 13   Hale, Rhoda and Alex. Stephenson by James Stephenson, JP, Jackson Co.

1821 Aug 10   Hale, Susan and James Shaw by -----, Licking Co.

1819 Dec 30   Hale, Wm. and Jane Fullerton by Elisha Lang, JP, Jackson Co.

1806 Nov 19   Haley, Thomas and Elizabeth Keating by S. Lindsly, Washington Co.

1811 Jan 3   Hall, Actious and Joshua Brown (license date), Pickaway Co.

1846 Apr 27   Hall, Charles B. and Caroline S. Greene by Rev. Edward Winthrop,
               St. Luke's Church, Marietta, Washington Co.

1817 Mar 30   Hall, Elizabeth and John Leonard by Sardine Stone, JP, Washington Co.

1821 Sep 3   Hall, Eunice and David B. Anderson by Rev. Saml. P. Robbins, Washing-
               ton Co.

1858 Apr 5   Hall, Eunice F. and John W. Snodgrass of Parkersburg, Va., by Rev.
               John Boyd, St. Luke's Church, Marietta, Washington Co.

1867 Dec 3   Hall, Frank B. [sic, bride's name] and George W. Smitley of White
               Cottage by Rev. A. Kingsbury, Putnam Presbyterian Church,
               Muskingum Co.

1798 Aug 30   Hall, George and Mary Jackson by D. Loring, Washington Co.

1816 Jan 4   Hall, Ira and Wealthy Little by Rev. Saml. P. Robbins, Washington Co.

1824 Jun 6   Hall, Isaac and Gatright Slusher by Michael J. Stick, MG, Franklin Co.

1804 Oct 11   Hall, James and Abey Stacker by John G. McCan, Ross Co.

1817 Feb 11   Hall, James and Ruth Metts by Nathan Cunningham, Licking Co.

1820 Sep 14   Hall, James and Sarah Wilkins by Alex. Anderson, JP, Jackson Co.

1881 Sep 28   Hall, James R. and Estelle de la Vergne by Rev. John Boyd, St. Luke's
               Church, Marietta, Washington Co.

1818 May 5   Hall, John and Louisa Ayles by Ira Hill, JP, Washington Co.

1824 Mar 25   Hall, John and Mary Brown by Jacob Grubb, Franklin Co.

1860 Mar 8   Hall, Joseph E. Jr. and Eliza H. Trevor by Rev. John Boyd, St. Luke's
               Church, Marietta, Washington Co.

1834 Nov 20   Hall, Joseph Ely and Rosanna Roe by Rev. J.T. Wheat, St. Luke's
               Church, Marietta, Washington Co.

1817 May 18   Hall, Martha and Ebenezer Rathburn by Cyrus Ames, Washington Co.

1821 May 8   Hall, Mary and Sidney Dodge by Elnathan Raymond, MMEC, Washington Co.

1823 Jun 5   Hall, Mary and Benjamin F. Loofborough by Geo. Jefferies, MG, Frank-
               lin Co.

1868 Feb 17   Hall, Mrs. Mary E. and William L. Howard by Rev. John Boyd, St.
               Luke's Church, Marietta, Washington Co.

1878 Feb 26   Hall, Mary M. and Samuel Biddle by Rev. John Boyd, St. Luke's Church,
               Marietta, Washington Co.

1805 Dec 30   Hall, Sally and Henry Toops by Wm. Creighton, Ross Co.

1817 Aug 10   Hall, Sarah and Shadreck Ruark by Joseph Thrap, MG, Licking Co.

1871 May 23   Hall, Sarah A. and C.C. Conger by Rev. John Boyd, St. Luke's
              Church, Marietta, Washington Co.

1821 Apr 15   Hall, Sophia and Caius M. Wood by Sardine Stone, JP, Washington Co.

1817 Mar 27   Halston, Thomas and Susannah Dunn by James Hoge, Franklin Co.

1818 Dec 5   Hall, Walter and Esther Patterson by Amos Wilson, JP, Washington Co.

1814 Jul 3   Hall, William and Barbara West by Wm. Florence, JP, Pickaway Co.

1837 Sep 14   Hall, Wm. and Mary Hunt by Rev. E. Burr, St. John's Church,
              Worthington, Franklin Co.

1840 Jul 23   Hall, Wyllys and Emma Sullivan by Rev. James Bonnar, St. Luke's
              Church, Marietta, Washington Co.

1882 Jun 12   Hallsman, Florence M. and Henry M. Parsons both of Zanesville by Rev.
              George F. Moore, Putnam Presbyterian Church, Muskingum Co.

1807 Mar 17   Hally, Anne and Nathaniel Gates by Stephen Lindsly, Washington Co.

1805 Jun 6   Halsay, Cassandra and Obadiah Walker by D. Loring, Washington Co.

1821 Jul 10   Halsey, David and Eunice Collins by Ami Lawrence, JP, Washington Co.

1823 Sep 16   Halterman, Henry and Mary Dixon by Samuel McDowell, JP, Jackson Co.

1805 Apr 16   Hambleton, William and Catharine Longwith by Wm. Bennett, JP,
              Franklin Co.

1812 Mar 7   Hamblin, Sarah and John S. Derickson by James Hoge, Franklin Co.

1811 Jan 10   Hamilton, Anna and Peter Hoover by Saml. White, JP, Franklin Co.

1814 Sep 11   Hamilton, Dan'l H. and Wealthy Humiston by Isaac Baker, Esq.,
              Washington Co.

1819 Nov 18   Hamlin, Eliza and Boylston Shan by Wm. Rand, Washington Co.

1809 Apr 9   Hamilton, Elizabeth and Stewart White by James Marshall, Franklin Co.

1825 Feb 15   Hamilton, Fanny and Henry Farnam by Joseph Corper, Franklin Co.

1816 Apr 11   Hamilton, John and Easther Cady by James Marshall, Franklin Co.

1816 Apr 12   Hamilton, Saml. and Sally Kinner by James Marshall, Franklin Co.

1816 Feb 16   Hamilton, Theoron and Mary McCune by James Taylor, Licking Co.

1824 Dec 2   Hamilton, Thomas and Catharine Read by James Hoge, Franklin Co.

1816 Jan 12   Hamlin, Jacob and Betsey Hornbaker by Emmor Cox, Franklin Co.

1816 Jun 27   Hamlin, John and Sally Boyd by Michael Patton, Franklin Co.

1822 Dec 18   Hamlin, Keziah and David Brook by C. Henkel, Franklin Co.

1797 May 18   Hammon, Anna and Gilbert Seamans by Robert Oliver, JP, Washington Co.

1824 Dec 13   Hammon, Leek and Ann Jones by David A. Tanner, JP, Marion Co.

1803 Jan 13   Hammond, Hannah and Richard McBride by Enoch Wing, JP, Washington Co.

1804 Feb 7   Hammond, Joath and Mary Shekley by Enoch Wing, JP, Washington Co.

1801 Jan 19   Hammond, Meribah and Joseph Forrest by Josiah Munro, Washington Co.

1798 Dec 19   Hammond, Michael and Nancy McDonald by Josiah Munro, Washington Co.

1816 Apr 23   Hammond, Phila and Jared Loveland by Obadiah Scott, JP, Washington Co.

1797 Aug 15   Hammond, Joeth and Abigail Dye by Robert Oliver, JP, Washington Co.

1817 3 mo 6   Hampton, Andrew and Rachel Crampton, Miami Monthly Meeting, Warren Co.

1816 2 mo 7   Hampton, Anna and Samuel Crampton, Miami Monthly Meeting, Warren Co.

1818 4 mo 2   Hampton, David D. and Jane Moon, Miami Monthly Meeting, Warren Co.

1817 1 mo 2   Hampton, Elizabeth and Jonathan Votaw, Miami Monthly Meeting, Warren Co.

1812 1 mo 1   Hamton, Andrew and Sarah Mills, Miami Monthly Meeting, Warren Co.

1809 Dec 25   Hand, Sarah and Joseph Cheadle by Asa Cheadle, JP, Washington Co.

1806 Feb 23   Handycock, Rohdy and Robert Mitchel by Wm. Davis, JP, Ross Co.

1813 Mar 15   Handy, Sally and Jonathan Critchet by James McMillen, Licking Co.

1801 May 14   Hanes, Mary and Thomas Jones by Philip Witten, Washington Co.

1805 Oct 3   Hankins, Jane and Daniel Bates by Thos. Hicks, Ross Co.

1805 Jun 27   Hankins, Jonathan and Sarah Buck by Wm. Bennett, JP, Franklin Co.

1826 Jan 1   Hanks, Crissa and Moses Maynard, Jr. by Nathan Emery, Franklin Co.

1817 Oct 30   Hanlen, Richard and Nancy French by Nathan Parr, JP, Washington Co.

1815 Jan 25   Hanley, Jeremiah and Pamela Bers by O. Scott, JP, Washington Co.

1818 Sep --   Hanna, Christopher and Sarah Poor by Nath'l W. Andrews, JP, Jackson Co.

1825 May 26   Hanna, Elizabeth and Geo. Scurlock by John Stephenson, JP, Jackson Co.

1820 Feb 10   Hanna, Jane and Joseph Wilson by Geo. Burris, MG, Jackson Co.

1819 Apr 16   Hannah, Samuel and Rachel Payne by John Spencer, JP, Licking Co.

1808 Jan 9   Hannaman, Elizabeth and Wm. Wyatt by Wm. Brundridge, Franklin Co.

1812 Apr 7   Hannan, Thomas and Elizabeth Reary by Massey Clymer, Franklin Co.

1810 May 15   Hanold, Mary and Jesse Morrell (license date), Pickaway Co.

1814 Jul 25   Hanshaw, Rachael and Henry Stultz by Abm. Christ, JP, Pickaway Co.

1812 Oct 5   Hanson, Abel and Nancy Kindall by John B. Johnson, Franklin Co.

1817 Sep 18   Hanson, Ephraim and Eleanor Waller by John Patterson, Washington Co.

1805 Feb 7   Hanson, Nancy and James Kelly by Stephen Lindly, Washington Co.

1801 Apr 13   Hanson, Peggy and Moyes Stone by Daniel Story, Washington Co.

1813 Oct 24   Hanson, Susanna and Sam'l Parker by Sardine Stone, JP, Washington Co.

1807 Jul 8   Hanway, Eliza and Joseph Holden by S. Lindsly, Washington Co.

1809 Oct 26   Hanyman, Enoch and Rachiel Trakes (or Frakes) by Michael Dickey, Franklin Co.

1813 Feb 28   Harbert, Hannah and John Berry by J.W. Patterson, Licking Co.

1815 Aug 27   Harbert, John and Susannah Dickinson by Uriah Hull, Licking Co.

1804 Jan 5   Harbert, Richard and Calrew? Vandurn by Sam'l Edwards, JP, Ross Co.

1814 May 29   Harbert, Samuel and Nancy Berry by Levi Shinn, Licking Co.

1800 Jun 7   Harden, Mary and Wm. Patten by J. Munro, Washington Co.

1800 Nov 7   Harden, Nancy and Wm. Kazy by J. Munro, Washington Co.

1807 Jun 23   Harden, Nancy and John Cole by Levi Barber, Washington Co.

1802 Apr 17   Harding, James and Sarah Prizel by Griffin Greene, JCCCP, Washington
               Co.

1821 Jan 25   Hardy, William and Clara Cole by Philip Cole, JP, Washington Co.

1824 May 25   Harelett, Polelly and David Allen by John Kirby, JP, Marion Co.

1865 Feb 4   Harlem, Emma and Thomas McCoy by Rev. John Boyd, St. Luke's Church,
               Marietta, Washington Co.

1824 Jan 22   Harlow, Jonas and Nancy Hutcheson by Robert Boyd, Franklin Co.

1826 Feb 9   Harmon, Lewis and Polly White by John White, Jackson Co.

1818 Oct 8   Harmon, Uley and Jesse Corn by John Norton, JP, Jackson Co.

1810 Aug 28   Harnden, Isaac and Catherine Spangler (license date), Pickaway Co.

1804 Apr 10   Harper, Christina and Isaac Barker by James Graham, Washington Co.

1801 Apr 1   Harper, Isabella and Michael Barker by Wm. Harper, Washington Co.

1806 --- --   Harper, Jane and Robert Tate by John Robins, Ross Co.

1825 Apr 15   Harper, Joseph and Mary Copperstone by Conrad Roth, JP, Marion Co.

1806 --- --   Harper, Mary and Daniel Robins by John Robins, Ross Co.

1898 May 17   Harper, Mary E. and Wheeler S. Dutro both of Zanesville by Rev.
               George F. Moore, Putnam Presbyterian Church, Muskingum Co.

1805 Mar 22   Harr, David and Nancy Sheagley by Thomas Scott, JP, Ross Co.

1803 Nov 17   Harr, Mary and James Philips by Thomas Scott, JP Scioto Tp., Ross Co.

1817 May 21   Harrington, Charity and Samuel Raredon by S.N. Cook, JP, Washington
               Co.

1820 Nov 12   Harrington, Gilis C. and Mary Spencer by Rev. T. Harris, Licking Co.

1820 Apr 2   Harrington, Sally and Roswell Fuller by Rev. Philander Chase,
               Franklin Co.

1821 Jun 9   Harris, Averill and Laura Ann Terrill by Philip Cole, JP, Washington
               Co.

1828 Mar 2   Harris, Barnabus and Sara Ann Turner by George Jefferies, Franklin Co.

1820 Apr 16   Harris, Caleb R. and Candace Wells by Joel Tuttle, Jr., JP, Washington
               Co.

1818 Mar 17   Harris, Chloe and Hiram P. Rose by Samuel Bancroft, JP, Licking Co.

1815 Nov 5   Harris, Cynthia and William Mead by Solomon Goss, Washington Co.

1828 Oct 19   Harris, Daniel and Susannah Hawkey by Wm. Long, JP, Franklin Co.

1812 Sep 22   Harris, David and Betsy Spelman by Rev. G. Vanaman, Licking Co.

1815 Apr 8   Harris, David and Anna Hill by Rev. S.P. Robbins, Washington Co.

1827 May 6   Harris, Elenor and Thomas O'Hail by Geo. Jefferies, Franklin Co.

1809 Nov 29   Harris, Elisha and Sally Cheadle by Asa Cheadle, JP, Washington Co.

1805 Oct 10   Harris, Elizabeth and Dennis Lane by Thos. Hicks, Ross Co.

1815 Mar 28   Harris, Elizabeth and Samuel Parr by Wm. Taylor (return date,
               "m. Oct. 1 last"), Licking Co.

1816 Feb 12   Harris, Elizabeth and William Cady by Benj. Talobt, JP, Washington
               Co.

1817 Jan 25   Harris (or Morris), Elizabeth and Daniel Melphrey by John Green,
               Licking Co.

1796 Jul 10   Harris, Hannah and Francis De Larguillon by Robert Safford, JP,
               Washington Co.

1820 Jul 15   Harris, Hannah and Paul Edmond by Thomas Can, MG, Licking Co.

1816 Aug 15   Harris, Jane and Nathaniel Williams by Simion Overturf, Licking Co.

1808 Apr 28   Harris, Jesse and Elizabeth B. Robin by John Emmet, Licking Co.

1801 Feb 19   Harris, John and Elizabeth Bingham by Alvan Bingham, Washington Co.

1817 Mar 6   Harris, John and Casander Hughes by Geo. Callanhan, EMEC, Licking Co.

1821 Sep 2   Harris, John and Harmenio Fargo by Eli C. King, Franklin Co.

1821 Oct 16   Harris, John and Sally Sheets by Jacob Keller, Franklin Co.

1817 Feb 13   Harris, Joseph and Elizabeth Silars by T.D. Baird, Licking Co.

1820 Oct 12   Harris, Joseph and Nancy Price by David Davis, JP, Washington Co.

1825 May 4   Harris, Joseph and Esther Clark by Henry Mathews, Minister of the
               ME Church, Franklin Co.

1820 Nov 18   Harris, Joseph G. and Irene McAllister by James M. Booth, JP,
               Washington Co.

1818 Feb 5   Harris, Margaret and Joshua Leigh by James Holmes, JP, Licking Co.

1818 Oct 20   Harris, Margaret and Daniel Jolly by M. Thorp, JP, Licking Co.

1807 Dec 16   Harris, Martha and David Garton by David Mitchell, Franklin Co.

1827 May 24   Harris, Mary and D. Francis by W.T. Martin, JP, Franklin Co.

1811 Aug 11   Harris, Noah and Peggy Elliott by -----, Licking Co.

1827 Dec 9   Harris, Origin and Mary Forgerson by Nathan Emery, Elder in the
               Methedist E. Church, Franklin Co.

1796 Apr 11   Harris, Peggie and William Lucas by Josiah Munro, JP, Washington Co.

1827 Dec 23   Harris, Rhoda and Sullivant Sweet by Sam'l Hamilton, Elder in the
               M.E. Church, Franklin Co.

1816 Jan 21   Harris, Romantha and Malachi Cole by James Sharp, JP, Washington Co.

1811 May 15   Harris, Sophia and Peter Cool by W. Haines, JP, Licking Co.

1815 Jul 19   Harris, Susanna and William Bordon by Isaac Humphreys, JP, Washington
               Co.

1811 Feb 11   Harris, Thomas and Rachel Sutton by Wm. Taylor, JP, Licking Co.

1819 Nov 25   Harris, Warren and Elizabeth Sennit by A. Goff, MG, Licking Co.

1815 Feb 15   Harris, William and Mary Miers by Wm. Taylor (return date, "m. Oct. 1 last"), Licking Co.

1822 Feb 21   Harris, Wm. and Abigail H. Burnham by Wm. Boris, MG, Washington Co.

1877 Jan 11   Harris, William W. and Harriet D. Rhodes by Rev. John Boyd, St. Luke's Church, Marietta, Washington Co.

1816 Sep 5   Harrison, Anna and Matthew Bailey by Wm. Brown, JP, Franklin Co.

1823 Feb 27   Harrison, Charles and Rhoda Baily by Jacob Grubb, Franklin Co.

1806 May 10   Harrison, Mary and John Taylor by J. Brough, JP, Washington Co.

1814 Dec 13   Harrison, P. and A. Dye by Jos. Hays, JP, Pickaway Co.

1808 Apr 21   Harrison, Robert and Rebekah Wheeler by J. Brough, JP, Washington Co.

1813 Nov 17   Harrison, Robert and Shabariah Henry by Thos. Ferguson, JP, Washington Co.

1819 Jan 5   Harriss, John and Betsey Hill by Eli C. King, Franklin Co.

1808 Aug 29   Harruff, Catharine by John Winset by Wm. Shaw, Franklin Co.

1813 May 7   Harruff, William and Elizabeth Hess by Daniel Hess, JP, Franklin Co.

1853 Dec 29   Harshberger, Jacob R. and Margaret E. Short by Rev. Geo. B. Sturges, St. Paul's Church, Marion, Marion Co.

1858 Dec 16   Harshberger, Jacob R. and Jane Tharp by Rev. H. Hollis, St. Paul's Church, Marion (in presence of F.P. Seffner and others), Marion Co.

1828 Nov 16   Hart, Ann and Sidney Brown by Nathan Stern, Franklin Co.

1807 Feb 19   Hart, Asahel and Elizabeth Brown by Arthur O'Harra, JP, Franklin Co.

1805 Jul 28   Hart, Benjamin and Honor Deming by Jacob Lindly, Washington Co.

1799 Jun 2   Hart, Betsey and Titus Buck by J. Munro, JP, Washington Co.

1800 Oct 16   Hart, Clara and Wing Devol by J. Munro, JP, Washington Co.

1805 Oct 3   Hart, Cyntha and Joseph Vance by Zachariah Stephen, JP, Franklin Co.

1823 Jul 3   Hart, Elizabeth and Benjamin Crider by Daniel Brunk, JP, Franklin Co.

1878 Mar 26   Hart, Josephine M. and George H. Nicholas by Rev. John Boyd, St. Luke's Church, Marietta, Washington Co.

1797 Dec 28   Hart, Josiah and Anna Moulton by Josiah Munro, Washington Co.

1809 Sep 10   Hart, Margaret and Justice Morse by Wm. Gray, JP, Washington Co.

1881 Dec 14   Hart, Olive N. and Hiram V. Reese by Rev. John Boyd, St. Luke's Church, Marietta, Washington Co.

1821 Mar 8   Hart, Thos. J.Y. and Amanda M. Taylor by T. Lee, Franklin Co.

1818 Jun 11   Hart, Voluntine and Gracy Barker by Joseph Grate, Franklin Co.

1818 May 31   Hart, Walter and Hannah Potts by Pelatiah White, JP, Washington Co.

1876 Dec 28   Harte, Maria Trevor and W. Loring Beebe by Rev. John Boyd, St. Luke's Church, Marietta, Washington Co.

1825 Nov 6   Hartel, Sam'l and Zilla Spurgeon by J.B. Finley, JP, Marion Co.

1817 Nov 27   Harter, Catherine and Richard Holtsbury by Geo. Callanhan, EMEC,
               Licking Co.

1818 Jul 13   Harter, Isaac and Sally Hottsbury by Alex Holden, JP, Licking Co.

1818 Mar 4   Harter, John and Margaret Dispennett by Isaiah Hopkinson, JP,
               Licking Co.

1817 Jul 10   Harter, Sally and John Fulk by I. Hoskinson, JP, Licking Co.

1811 Aug 10   Hartle, Jacob and Caty Spade, (license date), Pickaway Co.

1817 Feb 6   Hartley, Thomas and Prudence Newell by Daniel Harrel, JP, Jackson Co.

1825 Nov 10   Hartsack, Maria and Enoch Evans by John Davis, JP, Franklin Co.

1818 --- --   Hartshorn, Darius and Elizabeth Bowers by James M. Booth, Washington
               Co.

1815 Jan 12   Hartshorn, Edward and Lydia Delong by John True, JP, Washington Co.

1818 Nov 26   Hartshorn, Statua and William Sutton by Dudley Davis, Washington Co.

1813 Jun 4   Hartshorne, Eliza and James Davis by Wm. Miller, JP, Washington Co.

1821 Apr 5   Hartwell, Nathan and Naomi McCalla by Noah Fidler, Licking Co.

1820 Nov 9   Haruff, Peggy and James Condran by Eli C. King, JP, Franklin Co.

1820 Nov 9   Haruff, Susan and Francis G.R. Gross by Eli C. King, Franklin Co.

1797 Sep 28   Harvey, Amos and Rebecca Jones by Josiah Munro, Washington Co.

1807 May 3   Harvey, Amos and Margaret Frazer by Stephen Lindsly, Washington Co.

1814 Sep 22   Harvey, Delilah and John Reed by Thomas Mace, JP, Pickaway Co.

1800 Dec 22   Harvey, Elijah and Margaret Barrrck by Seth Cashart, JP, Washington
               Co.

1814 Mar 14   Harvey, James and Nancy Oxford by Rev. Jas. McHenry, Pickaway Co.

1821 Dec 27   Harvie, Mary and Daniel Shaw by Rev. Sam'l P. Robbins, Washington Co.

1810 8 mo 1   Harvey, Samuel and Rebekah Kindley, Miami Monthly Meeting, Warren Co.

1807 11 mo 18 Harvey, William and Rachel Townsend, Miami Monthly Meeting, Warren
               Co.

1806 Jan 1   Harwood, Charles and Polly Delong by Jacob Lindly, Washington Co.

1838 Feb 1   Hasbrook, Susan and Oliver T. Brown, St. Luke's Church, Granville,
               Licking Co.

1822 Mar 14   Hase, Elizabeth and David Kinzey by Moses.Williamson, JP, Washington
               Co.

1812 Apr 29   Hasght, Elizabeth and Francis Satha by Wm. Haines, JP, Licking Co.

1811 Apr 25   Hashman, Mark and Mary Smith by Thomas Morris, Franklin Co.

1792 Apr 8   Haskel, Jonathan and Phebe Green by J. Gilman, Washington Co.

1868 Oct 15   Haskell, Emily and Philip Gane by Wm. Bower, St. Luke's Church,
               Granville, Licking Co.

1821 Nov 6   Haskell, Maria and Jesse Lawton by Rev. Cornelius Springer, Washing-
               ton Co.

1865 Sep 12   Haskell, Maria L. and Eben F. Eaton by Wm. Bower, St. Luke's Church,
              Granville, Licking Co.

1817 Jul 2   Haskell, Rebecca and Isaac Monckton by Danl. H. Buell, JP, Washington
              Co.

1819 4 mo 7   Hasket, Ann and Levi Cook, Miami Monthly Meeting, Warren Co.

1822 2 mo 6   Hasket, Mary and George Evans, Miami Monthly Meeting, Warren Co.

1819 2 mo 3   Haskett, Lydia and Hugh Mills, Miami Monthly Meeting, Warren Co.

1816 Mar 10   Haskins, Walt and Abigail Mead by Simon Merwin, JP, Washington Co.

1803 Mar 14   Haskinson, Sarah and Abner Martin by Philip Witten, JP, Washington Co.

1819 Jul 8   Hass, Adam and Sidney Robinson by T.S. Beard, VDM, Licking Co.

1816 Dec 2   Hass, Christina and Martin Robinson by John Green, Licking Co.

1818 Dec 21   Haswell, Philip and Jane McGown by James Hoge, Franklin Co.

1811 Apr 4   Hatch, Anna and Gilbert Devol by Nathaniel Hamilton, Washington Co.

1813 Dec 25   Hatch, Hannah P. and Philip Devol by J. Greenman, JP, Washington Co.

1817 Nov 13   Hatch, Isaac Jones and Sarah Ann Billard by Amos Wilson, JP, Washing-
              ton Co.

1814 Mar 17   Hatch, Lila and Mathew Buell by Rev. Stephen Lindsley, Washington Co.

1854 Jan 3   Hatch, Martha A. and Erastus Bailey by Rev. A. Kingsbury, Putnam
              Presbyterian Church, Muskingum Co.

1853 Oct 17   Hatch, Mary Jane and John Knox by Rev. A. Kingsbury, Putnam
              Presbyterian Church, Muskingum Co.

1820 Dec 23   Hatfield, Amos and Nancy Holler by Noah Fidler, Licking Co.

1811 Apr 15   Hatfield, Edward and Nelly Stimets by W. Haines, JP, Licking Co.

1809 Apr 1   Hatfield, Nancy and Christopher Price by W. Haines, JP, Licking Co.

1813 Feb 9   Hatfield, Sarah and John Perkins by Wm. Moody, JP, Licking Co.

1812 Jul 5   Hatfield, Thomas and Elizabeth Price by James McMillen, JP, Licking
              Co.

1821 Dec 30   Hatton, Charles and Sally Dix by W.T. Martin, JP, Franklin Co.

1817 3 mo 5   Hatton, Edward and Rachel Lukens, Miami Monthly Meeting, Warren Co.

1815 2 mo 9   Hatton, George and Margeret Foulke, Miami Monthly Meeting, Warren Co.

1806 Feb 1   Hatton, Polly and James Alexander by J. Gardner, JP, Ross Co.

1825 Jan 19   Hatton, Rebecca and Andrew Ridgely (license date), Marion Co.

1806 Sep 25   Haugh, James and Hannah Dutton by Thomas Stanley, Washington Co.

1823 Nov 2   Haughn, George K. and Rebecca Bumgardner by Robert W. Riley, Franklin
              Co.

1828 Feb 21   Haughn, Mary and David Barbee by P. Adams, Franklin Co.

1820 Mar 1   Haughton, John and Maria Williams by James Whitney, JP, Washington Co.

1820 Sep 28   Hauser, Salrah and Mora McKeel by J. B. Gilliland, JP, Jackson Co.

1817 Sep 16   Haven, Abigail and Henry Hildreth by Danl.H. Buell, Washington Co.

1886 Dec 28   Havens, Callie and John Lingle by Rev. George F. Moore, Putnam
              Presbyterian Church, Muskingum Co.

1823 May 4   Havens, Eliza and Thomas Lord by Jacob Grubb, Franklin Co.

1824 Dec 30   Havens, Elizabeth and Martin Waggoner by A. Allison, Franklin Co

1814 May 19   Havens, Henry and Lydia Hinkley by Thomas White, Esq., Washington Co.

1816 Feb 4   Havens, Lidia and John McElvin by Joseph Grate, Franklin Co.

1814 Jul 14   Havens, Lucinea (or Lucinda) and Ezekiel Rice by Joseph Grate, JP,
              Franklin Co.

1820 Mar 15   Havens, Mary and Jacob Mullen by George Smith, JP, Washington Co.

1818 Nov 19   Havens, Sophia and William Cooley by Rev. Wm. Davis, Washington Co.

1828 Jan 24   Havens, Thomas and L. Baughman by A. Allison, Franklin Co.

1861 Jul 11   Haver, Caroline of Putnam and Edward Worthington of Sterling, Ill.,
              by Rev. A. Kingsbury, Putnam Presbyterian Church, Muskingum Co.

1876 May 11   Haver, George of Putnam and Irene Stickney of Cincinnati by Rev.
              A. Kingsbury, Putnam Presbyterian Church, Muskingum Co.

1878 Nov 5   Haver, Lillian of Putnam and George Ogden of Abilene, Kan., by Rev.
              George F. Moore, Putnam Presbyterian Church, Muskingum Co.

1862 Sep 11   Haver, Mary E. and Harlan P. Kingsbury by Rev. A. Kingsbury, Putnam
              Presbyterian Church, Muskingum Co.

1819 Sep 13   Havins, Polly and William Headley by Asa Whitehead, JP, Franklin Co.

1820 Apr 22   Havins, Susan and Jacob Smith by Thos. B. Patterson, Franklin Co.

1825 Oct 20   Haward, James and Margret Wiley by John F. Solomon, Franklin Co.

1817 Aug 10   Haward, Nancy and Samuel Marshall by Percival Adams, Franklin Co.

1825 May 26   Hawken, Mary and Aaron Ogden by John Hawken, JP, Franklin Co.

1828 Oct 19   Hawkey, Susannah and Daniel Harris by Wm. Long, JP, Franklin Co.

1807 11 mo 19 Hawkins, Amos and Rachel Jones, Miami Monthly Meeting, Warren Co.

1815 Nov 24   Hawkins, Danl. and Rebeca Bishop by Elisha Decker, JP, Franklin Co.

1822 2 mo 16 Hawkins, Elizabeth and John Burnet, Miami Monthly Meeting, Warren Co.

1821 9 mo 8   Hawkins, John and Margery Horner, Miami Monthly Meeting, Warren Co.

1809 8 mo 10 Hawkins, Levi and Mary Evans, Miami Monthly Meeting, Warren Co.

1807 11 mo 26 Hawkins, Nathan and Rebekah Robarts, Miami Monthly Meeting, Warren Co.

1814 Jul 3   Hayes, Adam and Elizabeth Pool by Anth'y Sheets, Esq., Washington Co.

1819 Dec 7   Hayes, Hannah and Hezekiah Kilbourn by George Evans, MG, Licking Co.

1798 Dec 25   Hayes, Sarah and William Buffington by D. Loring, Washington Co.

1828 Nov 27   Hay, Phillip and Lucy Dage by Joseph Long, Franklin Co.

1827 Nov 29   Hayden, Rachel and Timothy Downing by H. Crabb, MEC, Franklin Co.

1821 Jan 25   Hayens, Benjamin and Elanor Young by Wm. Richardson, JP, Franklin Co.

1814 Apr 7   Hayes, Luther and Susanna Landis by Wm. D. Hendren, Franklin Co.

1807 Nov 24   Hays, David and Polly Boreaff by Wm. Irwin, Franklin Co.

1824 Oct 5   Hays, Elisha, widower, and Chloe Pool, widower of Pool deacest, by
               Brice Hays, JP, (license date, return filed 10 Dec.), Franklin
               Co.

1813 Mar 10   Hays, George and Mary Grun (license date), Pickaway Co.

1883 Apr 17   Hays, Hervey and Mahala Jones by Rev. John Boyd, St. Luke's Church,
               Marietta, Washington Co.

1825 Sep 4   Hays, Hiram and Lucy Ann Robinson by C. Hinkel, Franklin Co.

1812 Jun 11   Hays, John and Peggy Philips by Henry Jolly, JP, Washington Co.

1823 Aug 24   Hays, John and Matilda Newhouse by Uriah Clark, JP, Franklin Co.

1813 Aug 2   Hays, Mary and James Greer (license date), Pickaway Co.

1821 Jul 26   Hays, Polly and Ezekiel Pegg by Jacob Keller, Franklin Co.

1824 Mar 23   Hays, Sally and Jonson F. Henry by Uriah Clark, Franklin Co.

1824 Feb 26   Hays, William and Anne Piper by Uriah Clark, Franklin Co.

1819 Jul 22   Hayse, Susan and Alexander Crone by James Hoge, Franklin Co.

1808 Dec 15   Haywood, Anna and William Kidd by Thos. Seely, JP, Washington Co.

1807 Jan 29   Haywood, Rothens and Panthea Nye by Sam'l P. Robbins, Washington Co.

1820 Jun 19   Hazle, Experience and Jacob Clover by Vinal Stewart, Minister of the
               Gospel in the Methodist Episcopal Church, Franklin Co.

1810 Feb 15   Hazlerigg, John and Abigail Jimason by John Brough, JP, Washington Co.

1811 May 5   Headley, Sarah and William Berans by Wm. Haines, JP, Licking Co.

1819 Sep 13   Headley, William and Polly Havins by Asa Whitehead, JP, Franklin Co.

1824 Jan 29   Headly, Martha and William Inks by Jacob Smith, JP, Franklin Co.

1826 Sep 26   Headly, Richard and Betsy McCormick by A. Allison, JP, Franklin Co.

1817 Jan 12   Healton, Thomas and Susanna Dunn by James Hoge, Franklin Co.

1809 Jun 11   Healy, Elizabeth and Benjamin Busic by John Smith, Franklin Co.

1801 Jul 3   Heancy, Delany and John Brooks by Edwin McGinnis, JP, Washington Co.

1819 May 13   Heard, Josiah and Sarah Goodwin by Samuel H. Buell, JP, Washington Co.

1818 Oct 18   Hearsey, Samuel and Patty Henin by James M. Booth, JP, Washington Co.

1823 Sep 16   Heath, Christian and Martha Wilson by Joseph Baker, Minister of the
               Christian Church, Jackson Co.

1803 Jul 7   Heart, Elizabeth and Jonathan Boyd by Wm. Davis, JP, Ross Co.

1793 Oct 30   Heart, Selah and Sally Waters by R.J. Meigs, Washington Co.

1804 Aug 7   Heath, John and Nancy Tomlin by Wm. Davis, JP, Ross Co.

1824 Feb 26   Heath, Joseph and Elizabeth Bond by Jacob Grubb, Franklin Co.

1816 Dec 12   Heath (or Heth), Margaret and Joseph Chinowith by Joseph Gorton, JP,
               Franklin Co.

1810 Jun 26   Heath, Rebecca and George Whitman (license date), Pickaway Co.

1842 Oct 30   Heaton, Mary Anne and Israel Neas by Rev. R.S. Elder, St. John's
               Church, Worthington, Franklin Co.

1821 Oct 28   Hebard, James H. and Maria Buell by Rev. James McAboy, Washington Co.

1811 Jan 3   Heckerthorn, Mary and George Word (license date), Pickaway Co.

1812 Sep 17   Hedelston, David and Ann Gordon by Henry Jolly, JP, Washington Co.

1828 May 27   Hedges, Daniel and Ann Ross by James Hoge, Franklin Co.

1813 Jul 27   Hedges, John and Susana Miller (license date), Pickaway Co.

1810 Sep 3   Hedges, Joseph and Mary Nevill (license date), Pickaway Co.

1811 Jun 13   Hedges, Mary and Henry Driesbach (license date), Pickaway Co.

1815 Jan 11   Hedges, Obed and Susana Petty by Henry Coonrod, JP, Pickaway Co.

1814 Feb 24   Hedges, Rhoda and Jeremiah Smith by Hugh Creighton, JP, Pickaway Co.

1818 Oct 22   Hedley, Samuel and Christeeny Chase by George Hells, JP, Franklin Co.

1818 Oct 15   Hedrick, Wm. and Sarah Thomas by Percival Adams, JP, Franklin Co.

1849 May 3   Heeley, Elizabeth S. and John Hooper Franklin by W.C. French, St.
               Luke's Church, Granville, Licking Co.

1821 Jul 8   Heindel, Elizabeth and Abel Tompkins by Charles Henkel, Franklin Co.

1806 Sep 23   Heit, Sally and Henry Delong by Jacob Lindly, Washington Co.

1821 Dec 27   Hellen, Sally and John Beard by A. Allen, Franklin Co.

1828 Nov 12   Hellman, Polly and William Davidson by Jacob Grubb, Franklin Co.

1814 Jun 3   Hellzel, Sarry and Wm. Weatherington by Percival Adams, Franklin Co.

1811 Aug 16   Helm, Jacob and Peggy Coon (license date), Pickaway Co.

1815 Nov 11   Helphrey, Eliz. and Jonathan Beaty by J. Green, Licking Co.

1807 Jul 30   Helpinstine, Mary and David Watson by Nehemiah Gates, JP, Franklin Co.

1827 Sep 3   Helsel, John and Nancy Rine by I. Gander, Franklin Co.

1827 Jul 31   Heltsel, Philip and Magdalena Hiendall by P. Adams, JP, Franklin Co.

1815 Aug 20   Heltzel, Daniel and Mary Hinald by Percival Adams, Franklin Co.

1813 Dec 16   Helwig, John and Rachel Koonce (license date), Pickaway Co.

1883 Feb 11   Hemphill, Kate of Putnam and Edward Green of Zanesville by Rev.
               George F. Moore, Putnam Presbyterian Church, Muskingum Co.

1806 Mar 27   Hempstead, Esther and William McClary by Stephen Lindley, Washington
               Co.

1821 Jun 23   Hemsted, Charles P. and Rachel Crage by Ebenezer Washburn, VDM,
               Franklin Co.

1805 Oct 23   Henderson, Catharine and John McFadgin by Daniel W. Suemey, Ross Co.

1828 May 20   Henderson, E.C. and John Curry by James Hoge, Franklin Co.

1791 May 5   Henderson, Edward and Sally Lovekin by Benj. Tupper, Washington Co.

1815 Jun 8   Henderson, Hannah and Amos H. Caffee by J.W. Patterson, Minister,
               Licking Co.

1822 Aug 27   Henderson, Ira B. and Margret Wilson by James Hoge, Franklin Co.

1811 May 25   Henderson, James and Rachel Henderson (license date), Pickaway Co.

1814 Jun 2   Henderson, James and Rebecca Hyles by Henry Coonrod, JP, Pickaway Co.

1816 Apr 1   Henderson, Jane and Alex^r Rees by James Hoge, Franklin Co.

1821 Jul 12   Henderson, Jane and James Morgan by Robert W. Riley, Franklin Co.

1818 Oct 8   Henderson, Louisa and Serman Johnson by Cyrus Ames, JP, Washington Co.

1815 Jan 23   Henderson, Lucy and Chester Nash by Stephen Guthrie, Washington Co.

1878 Sep 5   Henderson, Lucy A. and Miles P. Brown by Rev. John Boyd, St. Luke's Church, Marietta, Washington Co.

1806 Aug 19   Henderson, Margaret and Hugh Fulton by James.Marshall, JP, Franklin Co.

1811 May 25   Henderson, Rachel and James Henderson (license date), Pickaway Co.

1806 Jan 30   Henderson, Rebecca and Robert Wilson by Zachariah Stephen, JP, Franklin Co.

1819 Apr 21   Henderson, Robert C. and Mary Stewart by James Hoge, Franklin Co.

1821 Feb 13   Henderson, Sally and Samuel Fleming by Jacob Keller, Franklin Co.

1818 Mar 9   Henderson, Samuel and Nancy Curry by James Hoge, Franklin Co.

1855 Jun 29   Henderson, Thomas of Guernsey Co., and Urith Martin by Rev. John Boyd, St. Luke's Church, Marietta, Washington Co.

1816 Jul 11   Henderson, Titan and Elizabeth Gantz by T.D. Baird, JP, Licking Co.

1828 Nov 20   Hendren, Louisa and Abraham Sarber by Geo. Jefferies, Franklin Co.

1863 Sep 22   Hendrick, Mary A. and Don Vincent by Rev. John Boyd, St. Luke's Church, Marietta, Washington Co.

1855 Sep 20   Hendricks, Albert and Betsy Adams by T. Corlett, St. Luke's Church, Granville, Licking Co.

1822 May 9   Hendrixson, William and Sally McClain by Wm. Godman, Franklin Co.

1818 Oct 18   Henin, Patty and Samuel Hearsey by James M. Booth, JP, Washington Co.

1816 Jul 21   Henington, Patty and Henry Clark by Dan'l H. Buell, JP, Washington Co.

1816 Nov 3   Hennan, Eunice and Jonas Main by Sam'l Dye, JP, Washington Co.

1817 Nov 24   Hennesy, Hannah and John Claton by John Green, Licking Co.

1826 Apr 18   Henry, Aaron and Maria Butcher by Henry Mathews, Franklin Co.

1816 Aug 27   Henry, Ann and David Deming by Nathaniel Hamilton, JP, Washington Co.

1804 Sep 11   Henry, Betsy and Robert Henry by Jacob'Lindly, Washington Co.

1822 May 23   Henry, Elizabeth and William Clevenger by Richard Courtright, Franklin Co.

1807 Jul 2   Henry, Enoch and Polly Lewin by Nathan Rawlings, Franklin Co.

1813? --- -   Henry, Enoch and Maria Purce (license date), Pickaway Co.

1827 Apr 3   Henry, Enos and Rosanna Gorton by Rheuben Golliday, JP, Franklin Co.

1879 Nov 12   Henry, George and Maggie Martin by Rev. John Boyd, St. Luke's
               Church, Marietta, Washington Co.

1811 Mar 2   Henry, John and Elizabeth Tanner by Z. Carlisle, JPHT, Licking Co.

1811 Nov 12   Henry, John and Margaret McNitt by Stephen Lindsly, Washington Co.

1815 Jun 13   Henry, John and Nancy Posey by Sam'l Dye, JP, Washington Co.

1818 Jan 8   Henry, John and Phoebe Procter by Cornelius Hougland, JP, Washington
               Co.

1821 Apr 12   Henry, John and Rachael Davidson by Richard Courtright, Franklin Co.

1823 Feb 13   Henry (or Hury or Huey), John and Hannah Codner by Richard Court-
               right, Franklin Co.

1824 Mar 23   Henry, Jonson F. and Sally Hays by Uriah Clark, Franklin Co.

1817 Aug 28   Henry, Mathew and Levina Procter by Cornelius Hougland, JP, Washing-
               ton Co.

1811 Apr 18   Henry, Polly and Duty Greene, Jr. by John Greene, MG, Washington Co.

1821 Aug 4   Henry, Richard and July Wagener by Jacob Smith, Franklin Co.

1804 Sep 11   Henry, Robert and Betsy Henry by Jacob Lindly, Washington Co.

1817 Jan 22   Henry, Robert and Roxana Gifford by Nath'l Hamilton, Washington Co.

1813 Nov 17   Henry, Shabariah and Robert Harrison by Thos. Ferguson, JP, Washing-
               ton Co.

1822 Jun 4   Henry, William and Elizabeth Falkner by C. Henkel, Franklin Co.

1820 Aug 9   Hensly, Samuel and Betsey Pritchard by Wm. Hull, JP, Licking Co.

1825 Jul 28   Henson, Lydia and Henry Radabaugh by John Horton, JP, Jackson Co.

1814 Feb 17   Henst, Dickson and Mallisa Scott by Anth'y Sheets, JP, Washington Co.

1818 Feb 5   Henthorn, John and Elizabeth Caster by J. Ewing, Licking Co.

1809 Dec 17   Henthorn, Sarah and Jacob Moots by Nathan Conrad, JP, Licking Co.

1810 Aug 16   Herder, Simeon and Barbara Wash (license date), Pickaway Co.

1827 Jul 3   Herdman, Elis and Sally Howard by D.W. Deshler, JP, Franklin Co.

1819 Jul 29   Heriff, Polly and Moore Justice by Joseph Grate, Franklin Co.

1814 Jun 22   Herr, Gideon and Elizabeth Peck by Rob't Bradshaw, JP, Pickaway Co.

1811 May 19   Herrington, Daniel and Catharine Young by James Marshall, Franklin Co.

1817 Sep 4   Herrington, Mary and Moses Woodruff by Salmon N. Cook, Washington Co.

1804 Jun 14   Herrod, Mary and Wm. Patterson by Enoch Wing, Washington Co.

1802 Jan 20   Hersey, Nancy and Asa Cheadle by Nehemiah Davis, Pastor, Washington
               Co.

1812 May 7   Hess, Betsey and Isaac Keys by James Hoge, Franklin Co.

1808 Nov 10   Hess, Catharine and John Aller by James Hoge, Franklin Co.

1819 Apr 20   Hess, Daniel and Sally Gorton by Jacob Keller, Franklin Co.

1813 May 7   Hess, Elizabeth and William Harruff by Daniel Hess, JP, Franklin Co.

1814 Nov 3   Hess, Sally and Emanuel Carpenter by Joseph Gorton, Franklin Co.

1872 Oct 2   Heston, Henry B. of Philadelphia, Pa., and Margaret M. Belknap of
              Putnam by Rev. A. Kingsbury, Putnam Presbyterian Church,
              Muskingum Co.

1811 Oct 29   Heter, David and Polly Reeder (license date), Pickaway Co.

1817 Feb --   Heth, Richard and Sarah Tipton by Ruben Goliday, JP, Franklin Co.

1816 Dec 12   Heth (or Heath), Margaret and Joseph Chinowith by Joseph Gorton,
              JP, Franklin Co.

1790 Jun 3   Hewet, Moses and Sally Hewet by Benj. Tupper, Washington Co.

1790 Jun 3   Hewet, Sally and Moses Hewet by Benj. Tupper, Washington Co.

1799 Jul 28   Hewitt, Bethial and Henry Barrows by J. Munro, Washington Co.

1803 Nov 9   Hewitt, Ethan and Mary Drigs by Jacob Earhart, Washington Co.

1818 Oct 22   Hewitt, Moses and Sylvia Robinson by Jonathan Dunham, JP, Washington
              Co.

1806 Feb 24   Hewitt, Nancy and Thomas Dugan by Thomas Hicks, Ross Co.

1829 Jul 9   Hews, Polly and Frederick Whitsell by Abram Shoemaker, JP, Franklin
              Co.

1818 Oct 22   Heyatt, Allen and Catherine Martin by George Hoover, JP, Licking Co.

1811 Feb 17   Hibbs, John and Polly Phebus (license date), Pickaway Co.

1821 Jan 21   Hickerson, Joseph and Nancy Frost by Joseph Thrap, MG, Licking Co.

1811 Jun 11   Hickerson, Sophia and Reuben Blizzard by -----, Licking Co.

1808 May 11   Hickman, Effy and John Rairy by Arthur O'Harra, Franklin Co.

1813 Aug 26   Hickman, Elen and Alexander Cooper by J. Marshall, Franklin Co.

1810 Dec 6   Hickman, John and Comfort Cooper by James Marshall, Franklin Co.

1826 Nov 30   Hickman, Joseph S. and Elenor Higgins by Wm. Sterewalt, JP, Franklin
              Co.

1808 Mar 5   Hickman, Martha and Lewis Anderson by S. Lindsly, Washington Co.

1812 Apr 3   Hickman, Susan and William Stewalt by James Marshall, Franklin Co.

1808 Aug 8   Hickmon, Townsen and Jane Young by James Marshall, Franklin Co.

1819 Jan 15   Hickox, Giles and Matilda Rose by Rev. T. Harris, Licking Co.

1867 Jun 8   Hicks, Mrs. Cornelia J. and Alex. C. Powers by Rev. A. Kingsbury,
              Putnam Presbyterian Church, Muskingum Co.

1867 Dec 10   Hicks, Nellie K. and Mircian McBee by Rev. A. Kingsbury, Putnam
              Presbyterian Church, Muskingum Co.

1819 Aug 26   Hide, Rebecca and Solomon Westbrook by Elihu Bigelow, Licking Co.

1808 Dec 7   Hider, Sophia (Harris) and Nathaniel Green by Wm. Haines, JP,
              Licking Co.

1827 Jul 31   Hiendall, Magdalena and Philip Heltsel by P. Adams, JP, Franklin Co.

1800 Aug 4   Hiet, Jesse and Sarah Beals by Robert Safford, Washington Co.

1811 Aug 8   Higenbotham, Samuel and Ester Caunden by J.W. Patterson, Licking Co.

1818 May 13   Higganbotham, John and Nancy Pemitton by David Mitchell, JP, Jackson
              Co.

1823 Jan 16   Higgins, Ann and Joseph Foster by -----, Franklin Co.

1826 Nov 30   Higgins, Elenor and Joseph S. Hickman by Wm. Sterewalt, JP, Franklin
               Co.

1801 May 16   Higgins, Elizabeth and Enos Thompson by Wm. Harper, Washington Co.

1809 Feb 20   Higgins, Joseph and Elizabeth Thompson by Stephen Lindsly,
               Washington Co.

1814 May 18   Higgins, Josiah Sr. and Moriah Pool by Ezra Griswold, Franklin Co.

1810 May 15   Higgins, Mary and John Magee by Wm. Nixon, Washington Co.

1821 Aug 16   Higgins, Mrs. Mary and Henry Sligh by Robert W. Riley, Franklin Co.

1826 Jan 12   Higgins, Samuel and Permilia Patricke by James Boyd, Franklin Co.

1824 Mar 25   High, Hosea and Mary Ann McCormick by Charles Waddell, LM, Franklin
               Co.

1816 Apr 11   Highbargen, George and Hannah Lane by Thos. White, Washington Co.

1815 Mar 20   Hilands, John and Kiziah Thompson by Abner Christ, JP, Pickaway Co.

1816 Feb 15   Hilbrant, Henry and Hannah Park by Geo. Callanhan, EMEC, Licking Co.

1821 Jan 10   Hilbrant, John and Rebecca Parks by Noah Fidler, Licking Co.

1820 Mar 6   Hilderbrand, Mary and Daniel Viall by Rev. Saml. P. Robbins,
               Washington Co.

1817 Sep 16   Hildreth, Henry and Abigail Haven by Danl. H. Buell, Washington Co.

1807 Aug 19   Hildreth, Samuel P. and Rhoda Cook by D. Loring, Washington Co.

1803 Dec 22   Hile, Henry and Eva Nickins by J. Gardner, Ross Co.

1809 Mar 30   Hile (or Kile), Polly and Wm. Sennett by Arthur O'Harra, Franklin Co.

1802 Dec 30   Hill, Alexander and Sarah Foster by Daniel Story, Washington Co.

1815 Apr 8   Hill, Anna and David Harris by Rev. S.P. Robbins, Washington Co.

1841 Dec 21   Hill, Benjamin L. and Joanna Greer by Rev. R.S. Elder, St. John's
               Church, Worthington, Franklin Co.

1819 Jan 5   Hill, Betsey and John Harriss by Eli C. King, Franklin Co.

1885 Sep 23   Hill, Edson J. of Concord, N.H., and Cora M. Hubbell, Zanesville,
               by Rev. George F. Moore, Putnam Presbyterian Church, Muskingum
               Co.

1805 Jun 6   Hill, Elizabeth and William Hill by J. Brough, JP, Washington Co.

1813 Mar 22   Hill, Elizabeth and Christ^r Freshwater by Daniel Brink, Franklin Co.

1813 Jun 1   Hill, Elizabeth and Jasper Taylor by Rev. Stephen Lindsley,
               Washington Co.

1817 Jun 29   Hill, Elizabeth and Thomas Dye by Elias Conger, Washington Co.

1813 Mar 22   Hill, George and Caroline M. Millington by Daniel Brink, JP,
               Franklin Co.

1811 Nov 14   Hill, Henry and Elizabeth Nicholls by Thos. Ferguson, JP, Washington
               Co.

1807 Oct 15   Hill, Isaac and Polly Huff by Thos. Stanley, JP, Washington Co.

1818 Aug 13	Hill, James and Phoebe Hussey by Daniel G. Stanley, JP, Washington Co.
1810 Feb 8	Hill, Jane and Jacob Ploucher by Jonathan Mintchell, Franklin Co.
1810 Aug 2	Hill, Jane and Edward Mitchell by Stephen Lindsly, Washington Co.
1811 Aug 1	Hill, Jane and Sam'l Geering, Jr. by Edwin Putnam, JP, Washington Co.
1819 Aug 19	Hill, Jemima and Richard Pemelton by Vincent Southard, JP, Jackson Co.
1815 Nov 16	Hill, Jesse and Rebecca Green by Elihu Bigelow, JP, Licking Co.
1807 Nov 18	Hill, John and Patty Ritchey by Stephen Lindsly, Washington Co.
1812 Jun 15	Hill, John and Hannah Geering by Jeremiah Dare, JP, Washington Co.
1815 May 4	Hill, Joseph and Jane Gibson by Dan'l H. Buell, JP, Washington Co.
1813 Aug 6	Hill, Margarett and Reuben McVay by Anthony Sheets, Washington Co.
1813 Feb 4	Hill, Martha and Thomas Kidd by Rev. Jas. Cunningham, Washington Co.
1805 Jan 1	Hill, Mary and Jesse Baldwin by Dudley Davis, Washington Co.
1815 Jan 2	Hill, Nancy and Isaac Delong by James Sharp, JP, Washington Co.
1817 Jul 30	Hill, Nancy and Joseph Geering by Danl. H. Buell, Washington Co.
1814 Jan 6	Hill, Peggy and William Currier by Rev. S.P. Robbins, Washington Co.
1806 Jan 15	Hill, Polly and Joseph Glines by Thos. Sanley, Washington Co.
1808 Jun 22	Hill, Polly and John Greene by Stephen Lindsly, Washington Co.
1816 Mar 31	Hill, Richard and Sally Straight by Saml. P. Robbins, MG, Washington Co.
1807 Nov 5	Hill, Ruth and Harvey Chapman by S.P. Robbins, Washington Co.
1804 Jan 12	Hill, Sally and James Hiss by John Johnson, JP Pope Tp., Ross Co.
1813 Jul 22	Hill, Sally and Charles Dix by Saml. White, Franklin Co.
1808 Jan 28	Hill, Sarah and Jacob Miller by Thos. Stanley, JP, Washington Co.
1821 Apr 12	Hill, Simon and Elizabeth Boylan by J. Johnson, JP, Licking Co.
1813 Mar 25	Hill, Urania and James Stanley by Rev. Jas. Cunningham, Washington Co.
1801 Apr 1	Hill, William and Rachael Rankins by Robt Safford, Washington Co.
1805 Jun 6	Hill, William and Elizabeth Hill by J. Brough, JP, Washington Co.
1809 Feb 23	Hill, William and Sarah Twiggs by Thos. Stanley, JP, Washington Co.
1822 Jan 31	Hill, Wm. Jr. and Martha Amlin by Rev. S.P. Robbins, Washington Co.
1822 Mar 14	Hillary, Luther and Lydia Jewett by Aristarchus Walker, Franklin Co.
1820 Dec 30	Hillier, Addah and Jonathan T. Clapp by Samuel Bancroft, JP, (license date?, "mar. Mar 31"), Licking Co.
1841 Sep 20	Hills, Emily and Lysander Jinks, St. Luke's Church, Granville, Licking Co.
1821 Oct 18	Hills, John A. and Hester Marsh by A. Allen, Franklin Co.
1816 Jan 25	Hilphrey, John and Ann Jinkins by J. Green, Licking Co.
1825 Nov 26	Himrode, Molly and Michael Alspach by Conrad Roth, JP, Marion Co.

1815 Nov 5   Hinald, Elizabeth and George Wightman by Percival Adams, Franklin Co.

1815 Aug 20   Hinald, Mary and Daniel Heltzel by Percival Adams, Franklin Co.

1813 Sep 29   Hinckle, Elias and Peggy Thompson by Jas. Hauge, Franklin Co.

1796 Oct 30   Hinckley, Nath'l and Sally Torry by Robert Oliver, Washington Co.

1817 Apr 19   Hinckley, Nathaniel and Elizabeth Davis by Pelatiah White, JP, Washington Co.

1828 Jan 10   Hindle, Jacob and Margared Worthington by Geo. Jefferies, Franklin Co

1820 May 4   Hines, Elizabeth and Patrick McDonale by Amasiah Hutchison, JP, Franklin Co.

1815 Jan 12   Hines, Jacob and Catherine Cooper by Chas. Cade, JP, Pickaway Co.

1805 Jan 1   Hines, John and Caty Jones by Samuel Smith, Ross Co.

1824 Dec 6   Hinkle, Henry and Susanna Wine by John Stealy, JP, Marion Co.

1805 Sep 24   Hinkle, Jacob and Nancy Kennedy by Wm. Creighton, Ross Co.

1820 Sep 14   Hinkley, Daniel and Lucy Walker by Thomas White, JP, Washington Co.

1814 May 19   Hinkley, Lydia and Henry Havens by Thomas White, Esq., Washington Co.

1817 Apr 3   Hinkley, Mary and Benjamin Emerson by Obadiah Scott, JP, Washington Co.

1819 Jan 30   Hinkley, Ruth and Stephen Hinkley by Thos White, Washington Co.

1819 Jan 30   Hinkley, Stephen and Ruth Hinkley by Thos. White, Washington Co.

1811 Jul 4   Hinkley, Thomas and Rachel Prewitt by Joseph Palmer, JP, Washington Co.

1820 Nov 7   Hins, Peter and Elizabeth Colmon by Jacob Antime, Franklin Co.

1804 Sep 20   Hinson, Benjamin and Anna Tharp by Wm. Bennett, JP, Franklin Co.

1816 May 28   Hinton, John and Rachel Claybaugh by Mich. Alis, Licking Co.

1813 Apr 12   Hinton, Polly and Charles White (license date), Pickaway Co.

1804 Mar 16   Hinton, Rebecca and Daniel Roberts by Abm. Miller, Ross Co.

1805 Jun 28   Hinton, Thomas and Margarett Furman by Nathaniel Wyatt, Ross Co.

1814 Apr 29   Hinton, Thomas and Naomi Green by John Cunningham, Licking Co.

1819 Nov 18   Hisem, Catharine and William McVay by Moses Williamson, Washington Co

1804 Jan 12   Hiss, James and Sally Hill by John Johnson, JP Pope Tp., Ross Co.

1815 Jul 27   Hite, Andrew and Sarah Neighbarger by Wm. O'Bannon, Licking Co.

1820 Aug 28   Hite, David and Elizabeth Stickley by Noah Fidler, Licking Co.

1812 Dec 19   Hitler, Caty and James Ballah (license date), Pickaway Co.

1814 Apr 10   Hitler, Kitty and John Horn by Thos. Mace, Jp, Pickaway Co.

1882 Jul 1   Hitt, Dana N. and Anna J. Danson by Rev. John Boyd, St. Luke's Church, Marietta, Washington Co.

1821 Apr 15   Hizer, Ann and Henry Benner by Andrew Henkel, MG, Licking Co.

1813 Jun 12   Hobbs, Richard and Rachel Ross (license date), Pickaway Co.

1805 Aug 29   Hodges, Daniel and Hannah Miller by J. Gardner, JP, Ross Co.

1824 Jun 15   Hodgskins, Mary Ann and John Young by C. Waddell, Franklin Co.

1880 Jun 15   Hodkinson, Mrs. Nannie C. and William B. Loomis by Rev. John Boyd,
              St. Luke's Church, Marietta, Washington Co.

1866 Nov 26   Hodkinson, Sadie and John Magee by Rev. John Boyd, St. Luke's
              Church, Marietta, Washington Co.

1803 Apr 21   Hody, Prudence and John Clark by Wm. Robinson, JP, Ross Co.

1814 Sep 23   Hoff, James and Mary Dye by Samuel Dye, Washington Co.

1824 Jun 16   Hoffman, Catherine and Willis Brewer by Timothy Ratcliff, JP,
              Jackson Co.

1818 Aug 28   Hoffman, Daniel and July James by D. Mitchell, JP, Jackson Co.

1819 Jun 15   Hoffman, Jacob and Isabella Reeves by John Smith, Franklin Co.

1819 Nov 24   Hoffman, Jacob and Rebecca White by Jacob Keller, Franklin Co.

1825 Jan 19   Hoffman, Margaret and Thomas Seemors by Samuel Reed, JP, Jackson Co.

1821 Sep 23   Hoffman, Peter and Bula Butterfield by Nathl. Little, Franklin Co.

1818 Apr 22   Hoffman, Polly and Abraham Stotts by Joseph Grate, Franklin Co.

1814 May 19   Hoffman, Rachael and Daniel Liggitt by Rob't Bradshaw, JP, Pickaway
              Co.

1822 Jan 18   Hoffman, Rebecca and William McCrackin by Jacob Keller, Franklin Co.

1887 Apr 6   Hoge, Bessie D. of Zanesville and Frederick J. Grant of Seattle, Wash.,
              by Rev. George F. Moore,Putnam Presbyterian Church,Muskingum Co.

1817 May 20   Hogg, Dorothy and Alexander Wilson by J.W. Patterson, JP, Licking Co.

1871 Feb 27   Hogue, Moses and Olive Dunham by Rev. John Boyd, St. Luke's Church,
              Marietta, Washington Co.

1821 Mar 11   Hoit, Sally and Benajah Howe by S.N. Cook, JP, Washington Co.

1807 May 7   Holburt, Lucy and John Gill by Thos. Stanley, Washington Co.

1819 Nov 8   Holdeman, Christian and Catherine Crouch by Simeon Overturf, JP,
              Licking Co.

1819 Oct 24   Holden, Grace and Samuel Parr by Moses.Williamson, JP, Washington Co.

1807 Jul 8   Holden, Joseph and Eliza Hanway by S. Lindsly, Washington Co.

1817 Jul 17   Holden, Lewis and Judith Parr by J.W. Patterson, JP, Licking Co.

1819 Sep 19   Holden, Maria and William Vance by John Patterson, MG, Licking Co.

1835 Dec 24   Holden, Maria and Hugh Trevor by Rev. J.T. Wheat, St. Luke's Church,
              Marietta, Washington Co.

1802 Jan 28   Holden, Mary and Dennis Rasor by Sam'l Williamson, JP, Washington Co.

1840 Sep 30   Holden, William and Isabella Greene by Rev. James Bonnar, St. Luke's
              Church, Marietta, Washington Co.

1808 Jul 18   Holdren, Betsey and Liba McCay by L. Dana, JP, Washington Co.

1816 Jan 7   Holdren, Coleman and Margaret Cotter by Wm. Dana, JP, Washington Co.

1808 Sep 8   Holdren, Ruth and Daniel Knowlton by L. Dana, Washington Co.

1803 Apr 25   Holdron, Joseph and Ruth Colon by Sam'l Williamson, Washington Co.

1805 Jan 31   Holdrun, Grace and Thomas Ferguson by John Greene, Washington Co.

1840 Apr 29   Holeden, Harriet and Wallace Dodge by Rev. James Bonnar, St. Luke's
              Church, Marietta, Washington Co.

1828 Apr 13   Hollam, Edy and Elijah Holloway by Purcival Adams, Franklin Co.

1808 Jul 14   Holleburt, Lydia and Thomas J. Jones by E. Putnam, JP, Washington Co.

1801 Jun 2   Hollenbuk, Casper and Lucy Shermon by Nehemiah Davis, Pastor,
              Washington Co.

1896 Jul 6   Holler, Elmer E. of Newark, O., and Anna Grace Dutro of Zanesville,
              by Rev. George F. Moore, Putnam Presbyterian Church, Muskingum
              Co.

1820 Dec 23   Holler, Nancy and Amos Hatfield by Noah Fidler, Licking Co.

1796 Aug 18   Holleraff, Gratry and Wilber Sprague by Robert Oliver, Washington Co.

1820 Oct 22   Hollingshead, Betsy and Geo. Eutsler by Patrick Shearer, JP, Jackson
              Co.

1817 8 mo 14 Hollingsworth, Abraham and Sarah Pidgeon, Miami Monthly Meeting,
              Warren Co.

1813 9 mo 1   Hollingsworth, Charity and Jonathan Cox, Miami Monthly Meeting,
              Warren Co.

1819 7 mo 8   Hollingsworth, Hannah and Samuel Cammack, Miami Monthly Meeting,
              Warren Co.

1817 12 mo 4 Hollingsworth, James and Esther Cadwalader, Miami Monthly Meeting,
              Warren Co.

1812 4 mo 1   Hollingsworth, Jane and John Cammack, Miami Monthly Meeting, Warren
              Co.

1820 12 mo 7 Hollingsworth, Joseph and Rhoda Whitacre, Miami Monthly Meeting,
              Warren Co.

1807 1 mo 13 Hollingsworth, Susana and Jonathan Mote, Miami Monthly Meeting,
              Warren Co.

1806 5 mo 15 Hollingsworth, Susania and Elisha Jones, Miami Monthly Meeting,
              Warren Co.

1804 Jun 5   Hollinshead, Deborah and Jonathan Delay by Isaac Dawson, Ross Co.

1887 Mar 16   Hollister, Harry E. and Rose K. Fritz both of Zanesville by Rev.
              George F. Moore, Putnam Presbyterian Church, Muskingum Co.

1809 Sep 14   Hollister, John and Ann Philine Hubbard by Rev. Timothy Harris,
              Licking Co.

1819 Oct 16   Hollister, Sibel Matilda and Elias Cole by Bial Stedman, JP,
              Washington Co.

1828 Apr 13   Holloway, Elijah and Edy Hollam by Purcival Adams, Franklin Co.

1825 Apr 19   Holloway, William E., widower, and Eleanor Wilson by John F. Solomon,
              MG, Franklin Co.

1806 Feb 25   Hollyday, Susannah and Maxwell Lamb by Robert B. Dobbins, VDM, Ross
              Co.

1820 Mar 13   Holmes, Agnes and Thomas Simpson by Joseph Thrap, MG, Licking Co.

1814 Dec 4   Holmes, Alex and Nancy Cornell by G. Callanhan, EMEC, Licking Co.

1827 Sep 7   Holmes, Isaac and Maria Moorehead by James Hoge, Franklin Co.

1810 Mar 18   Holmes, James and Elizabeth Wells Green by -----, Licking Co.

1873 Sep 25   Holmes, John R. of St. Louis, Mo., and Julia M. Potwin of Putnam by
               Rev. A. Kingsbury, Putnam Presbyterian Church, Muskingum Co.

1816 Dec 24   Holmes, Joseph and Margaret Lobdil by Geo. Callanhan, EMEC, Licking
               Co.

1816 Nov 21   Holmes, Peggy and Ezekiel Farmer by Noah Fidler, Licking Co.

1815 Dec 14   Holmes, Samuel and Susanna Beaver by Geo. Callanhan, Licking Co.

1825 Oct 26   Holmes, Sam'l. and Eliza Conklin by Robert Hopkins, JP, Marion Co.

1819 Dec 23   Holstead, Sayrs and Pheby Nicholson by Joseph Gorton, Franklin Co.

1812 Jul 27   Holt, Christiana and Daniel Van Wickel (license date), Pickaway Co.

1807 Feb 17   Holt, Elizabeth and Augustus Ford by Arthur O'Harra, JP, Franklin Co.

1817 Dec 19   Holtan, Martha and Thomas Fitzgareld by Wm. Badger, Franklin Co.

1804 Apr 15   Holton, Anna and James Kilgore by Noble Crawford, Ross Co.

1826 Aug 3   Holton, Polly and William Notin by Wooley Conrad, JP, Franklin Co.

1817 Nov 27   Holtsbury, Richard and Catherine Harter by Geo. Callanhan, EMEC,
               Licking Co.

1817 May 18   Holyoke, William and Lucy Greenleaf by Rev. S.P. Robbins, Washington
               Co.

1825 Dec 22   Hone, Betsy and John Fritts by A. Allison, Franklin Co.

1827 Mar 27   Hone, Christeanna and Joseph Saul by A. Allison, Franklin Co.

1801 Dec 14   Hook, John and Esbel McClimans by Daniel Story, Clerk, Washington Co.

1820 Apr 11   Hook, Polly and Notley Drown by Daniel H. Buell, JP, Washington Co.

1820 Aug 18   Hooper, Abraham and Priscilla Callahan by Joseph Thrap, MG, Licking
               Co.

1813 Feb 4   Hooper, Philip and Rachel Stephenson by John Stephenson, JP,
               Franklin Co.

1826 Nov 20   Hooper, Rebecca and Joshua Stevenson by Wm. Patterson, Franklin Co.

1826 Oct 24   Hooper, Samuel and Mary Kolb by Wm. Patterson, JP, Franklin Co.

1817 Sep 18   Hootan, James and Abigail Walker by Wm. Badger, Franklin Co.

1812 Feb 13   Hoover, Abraham and Nancy Robison by James Marshall, Franklin Co.

1818 Oct 13   Hoover, Ann and John Swisgood by Jacob Keller, Franklin Co.

1816 Dec 19   Hoover, Charles and Rachel Ann Strong by J.W. Patterson, JW, Licking
               Co.

1825 Mar 31   Hoover (or Farney) and James Delay by J.B. Gilliland, JP, Jackson Co.

1820 --- --   Hoover, George and Katharine Kiass by Joseph Grate, Franklin Co.

1828 Jun 5   Hoover, Jacob and Catherine Reeder by J. Davis, JP, Franklin Co.

1811 Jan 10   Hoover, Peter and Anna Hamilton by Saml. White, JP, Franklin Co.

1816 Oct 8   Hoover, Samuel and Anna Boyd by Samuel Bancroft, JP, Licking Co.

1806 5 mo 14 Hoover, Susannah and Elijah Wright, Miami Monthly Meeting,
              Warren Co.

1829 Jan 15   Hopkins, Mrs. Ann and Johua Stevenson by Leroy Swornstead, Franklin
              Co.

1805 Jun 20   Hopkins, Lidia and Wm. Anderson by David Shelby, JP, Ross Co.

1827 11 mo 7 Hopkins, Joseph and Mary W. Crispin, Miami Monthly Meeting, Warren Co.

1821 Feb 1   Hopkins, Mathew and Polly Mead by Thos. Scott, JP, Licking Co.

1821 Apr 1   Hopkins, Mercy and Silas Mott by Thos. Scott, JP, Licking Co.

1827 12 mo 5 Hopkins, Richard and Hannah Wharton, Miami Monthly Meeting, Warren Co.

1819 Apr 9   Hopper, Alexander and Elizabeth Dunlap by Joseph Grate, Franklin Co.

1818 Jan 29   Hopper, Betsy and William Perrin by Joseph Grate, Franklin Co.

1807 May 26   Hopper, Mary and John Skidmore by James Marshall, JP, Franklin Co.

1810 Aug 30   Hopper, Nelly and Joshua Skidmore by James Marshall, Franklin Co.

1824 May 27   Hopper, Mary and Thomas Wilcox by Joseph Badger, Franklin Co.

1827 Mar 28   Hopper, Sarah and John Perrin by Rheuben Golliday, Franklin Co.

1823 Feb 6   Hopper, Susan ahd Henry Sly by Joseph Badger, JP, Franklin Co.

1812 Feb 6   Hopper, William and Susan Cooper by James Marshall, Franklin Co.

1824 Sep 12   Horlocker, Christian and Sally Maire by John Davis, JP, (Rev. Daniel
              Horlocker of Columbus, states that his step-mother's name was
              Sally Myers), Franklin Co.

1814 Apr 10   Horn, John and Kitty Hitler by Thos. Mace, JP, Pickaway Co.

1813 May 6   Horn, William and Elizabeth Wilkins by -----, Licking Co.

1815 Feb 16   Hornback, John and M.A. Thomas by Joseph Hays, JP, Pickaway Co.

1812 Apr 13   Hornbacon, Polly and John Whitmore by Thomas Morris, Franklin Co.

1816 Jan 12   Hornbaker, Betsey and Jacob Hamlin by Emmor Cox, Franklin Co.

1811 Sep 4   Hornbacker, Catharine and Robert Seeds by David Spangler, Franklin Co.

1821 Aug 23   Hornbaker, John and Rachel Cole by John F. Solomon, Franklin Co.

1825 May 5   Hornbaker, John and Margret Essex by Persovial Adams, JP, Franklin Co.

1811 Aug 10   Hornbeck, John and Jane Camble (license date), Pickaway Co.

1807 3 mo 18 Horner, David and Sarah Parnell, Miami Monthly Meeting, Warren Co.

1806 5 mo 15 Horner, John and Elizabeth Comton, Miami Monthly Meeting, Warren Co.

1821 9 mo 8   Horner, Margery and John Hawkins, Miami Monthly Meeting, Warren Co.

1817 8 mo 7   Horner, Sarah and Henry Milhous, Miami Monthly Meeting, Warren Co.

1820 Jun 14   Horton, Isaac and Rosanna Funston by John Wyman, JP, Jackson Co.

1805 Dec 13   Hosack, Adam and Eunice Sloper by Ezekiel Brown, JP, Franklin Co.

1811 Aug 9   Hoselton, Joseph and Betsey Long (license date), Pickaway Co.

1813 Oct 21   Hoskins (Hoskinson), Andrew and Sarah Beard (Baird) by J.W. Patterson,
              Licking Co.

1809 --- --   Hoskins, Elizabeth and John Beard by -- Holden, JP, Licking Co.

1813 Oct 21   Hoskinson (Hoskins), Andrew and Sarah Beard (Baird) by J.W. Patterson,
              Licking Co.

1818 Jan 29   Hoskinson, John and Lydia Patterson by John W. Patterson, Licking Co.

1860 Jul 4   Hosler, Thomas and Eliza S. Ewing by Rev. A. Kingsbury, Putnam
              Presbyterian Church, Muskingum Co.

1818 Mar 26   Hottsbury, Polly and John Woollard by Alex Holden, Licking Co.

1818 Jul 13   Hottsbury, Sally and Isaac Harter by Alex Holden, JP, Licking Co.

1840 Aug 20   Hough, Sabin and Louisa Carpenter, St. Luke's Church, Granville,
              Licking Co.

1822 Feb 19   Hougland, Eleanor and Vincent Smith by Rev. Cornelius Springer,
              Washington Co.

1817 Nov 27   Hougland, Margaret and Benjamin F. Palmer by Salmon N. Cook, JP,
              Washington Co.

1821 Jun 9   Hougland, Polly and Edmond McGuines by Abel Robinson, M M Ch,
              Washington Co.

1829 Aug 6   House, Ann W. and James Vanderburgh by Leroy Swormstead, MG,
              Franklin Co.

1820 Mar 1   House, Farlana and Abraham Shafer by Bial Stedman, JP, Washington Co.

1821 Jun 3   House, Lyman B. and Sarah Baldwin by Nathl. Little, JP, Franklin Co.

1818 Oct 1   Houser, Margaret and Isaac Claybaugh by John P. Patterson, MG,
              Licking Co.

1824 Mar 22   How, Tacy and Peter Bunn by Vincent Southard, JP, Jackson Co.

1823 Jul 3   How, William Henry and Nancy Downing by Joseph Badger, Franklin Co.

1826 Sep 21   Howard, Betsey and Hiram Diexson by Gideon W. Hart, Franklin Co.

1817 Sep 11   Howard, Caleb and Melissa Griswold by Rev. Philander Chase, Franklin
              Co.

1815 Dec 20   Howard, Charles and Martha Wilk by Z. Carlisle, Licking Co.

1821 Apr 5   Howard, George and Rebecca Coffman by John Green, JP, Licking Co.

1803 Dec 29   Howard, Lewis and Marian Burns McGalaughlin by Geo. Williams, JP,
              Ross Co.

1803 Oct 6   Howard, Loyd and Sarah Bodkin by J. Gardner, JP, Ross Co.

1827 Sep 21   Howard, Mary and Harvey D. Little by W.T. Martin, Franklin Co.

1813 Jan 16   Howard, Phoebe and Samuel Reason (license date), Pickaway Co.

1827 Jul 3   Howard, Sally and Elis Herdman by D.W. Deshler, JP, Franklin Co.

1813 Apr 26   Howard, Vetchel and Rachel Swank (license date), Pickaway Co.

1819 Dec 16   Howard, Wm. and Margary Whetzel by Jacob Delay, MG, Jackson Co.

1868 May 27   Howard, William H. of Boston, Mass., and Caroline M. Belknap by Rev.
               A. Kingsbury, Putnam Presbyterian Church, Muskingum Co.

1868 Feb 17   Howard, William L. and Mrs. Mary E. Hall by Rev. John Boyd, St.
               Luke's Church, Marietta, Washington Co.

1815 Mar 1   Howe, Adah and Lemuel Rose by Rev. T. Harris, Licking Co.

1821 Mar 11   Howe, Benajah and Sally Hoit by S.N. Cook, JP, Washington Co.

1819 May 6   Howe, Daniel and Adelia Clarke by Geo. Evans, JP, Licking Co.

1802 Sep 7   Howe, George and Mary Whitehouse by Griffin Greene, JP, Washington Co.

1845 May 18   Howe, George and Sarah E. Cole by Rev. Edward Winthrop, St. Luke's
               Church, Marietta, Washington Co.

1819 May 16   Howe, Lucinda and James Alexander by John Russell, JP, Washington Co.

1815 Jul 6   Howe, Minerva and Timothy Goodrich by John Russell, JP, Washington Co.

1822 Jan 1   Howe, Nehemiah and Sally Hutchinson by S.N. Cook, JP, Washington Co.

1798 May 2   Howe, Pearly and Persis Putnam by Josiah Munro, Washington Co.

1820 Nov 19   Howe, Rachel and Edwin Corner by Stephen Lindsley, Washington Co.

1813 Mar 7   Howe, Sophronia and David Trowbridge by Peter Howe, JP, Washington Co.

1821 Dec 6   Howe, Sylvanus and Abigail Durfie by Rev. Sam'l P. Robbins,
               Washington Co.

1819 Aug 12   Howel, Chloe and William Gale by Chandler Rogers, Franklin Co.

1815 Jul 10   Howel, David and Sally Sherr by Josiah Hoskinson, JP, Licking Co.

1807 Mar 10   Howell, Maria and Robert Magee by Stephen Lindsly, Washington Co.

1814 Nov 15   Howkins, Thomas L. and Ann Brodrick by James Hoge, Franklin Co.

1815 Aug 31   Howlet, Charlotte and Rowland Hubbard by Jeremiah Greenman, JP,
               Washington Co.

1822 Sep 19   Hoy, Daniel and Matilda Filbury by Nicholas Goetschius, Franklin Co.

1804 May 22   Hoyt, Anna and Nathaniel Williams by Asahel Cooley, Washington Co.

1814 Mar 1   Hoyt, Cynthia and George Nott by Thomas Seely, Washington Co.

1803 Dec 4   Hoyt, Ezra and Lydia Stone by Stephen Lindley, Washington Co.

1817 May 1   Hoyt, Select and Peggy Statler by John Johnson, JP, Licking Co.

1809 Sep 14   Hubbard, Ann Philine and John Hollister by Rev. Timothy Harris,
               Licking Co.

1802 Apr 10   Hubbard, Hila and Reuben Tupper by Caleb Baldwin, JP, Trumbull Co.

1804 Sep 8   Hubbard, Jacob and Elizabeth Stackhouse by Thos. Scott, Ross Co.

1828 Aug 28   Hudson, James and Elizabeth Stults by John Long, JP, Franklin Co.

1805 Mar 28   Hubbard, John and Anna Bowdle by Peter Jackson, JP, Ross Co.

1805 Jul 18   Hubbard, Phielden and Betsey Stuthard by Thos. Hicks, Ross Co.

1815 Aug 31   Hubbard, Rowland and Charlotte Howlet by Jeremiah Greenman, JP,
               Washington Co.

1804 --- --   Hubbard, Titus and Eliz. Greenwood by Wm. Robinson, Ross Co.

1885 Sep 23   Hubbell, Cora M. of Zanesville and Edson J. Hill of Concord, N.H., by
               Rev. George F. Moore, Putnam Presbyterian Church, Muskingum Co.

1824 Nov 7   Hubel, Ruthy and Tandy Meeker by Samuel McDowell, JP, Jackson Co.

1818 Jan 29   Huckins, Catherine and William M. Alexander by J.W. Patterson, MG,
               Licking Co.

1799 Feb 19   Huct, Israel and Betsey Bobo by Alvan Bingham, JP, Washington Co.

1815 Jan 24   Huder, David and Ann Creighton by Thos. Mace, JP, Pickaway Co.

1868 Jul 30   Hudson, John and Julia A. Stone by I.B. Britton, St. Paul's Church,
               Marion, Marion Co.

1816 Jan 7   Hudson, Whiting and Lucy Springer by J. Greenman, Washington Co.

1797 Oct 10   Huet, Moses and Phebe Cooke by Peregrine Foster, JCCCP, Washington Co.

1823 Feb 13   Huey (or Hury or Henry), John and Hannah Codner by Richard Courtright,
               Franklin Co.

1818 Dec 12   Huff, Aaron and Sarah Berrington by Thomas B. Patterson, Franklin Co.

1810 Jan 4   Huff, Benjamin and Catharine Landes by David Spangler, JP, Franklin
               Co.

1810 Dec 27   Huff, Dosha and Thomas Gray by Thomas Morris, JP, Franklin Co.

1822 Apr 20   Huff, Isaac and Matilda Puntney by Thos. B. Patterson, Franklin Co.

1803 Apr 7   Huff, Joseph and Hanna Finley by Samuel Evans, Ross Co.

1807 Oct 15   Huff, Polly and Isaac Hill by Thos. Stanley, JP, Washington Co.

1813 Jan 21   Huffman, Catharine and Peter Roth by Jas. Marshall, Franklin Co.

1809 1 mo 16   Hufman, Lidia and Isaac Thomas, Miami Monthly Meeting, Warren Co.

1816 Feb 1   Hufman, Sarah and Benjamin Beam by George Callahan, EMEC, Licking Co.

1848 Jul 3   Huggins, Mary L. and Solomon N. Sanford by W.C. French, St. Luke's
               Church, Granville, Licking Co.

1818 Feb 11   Hughbanks, Franky and Francis Oray by Thomas Scott, JP, Jackson Co.

1817 Mar 6   Hughes, Casander and John Harris by Geo. Callanhan, EMEC, Licking Co.

1814 Jul 7   Hughes, David and Sarah Penee by John Cunningham, Licking Co.

1817 Oct 19   Hughes, Drusilla and Amaniah Sutton by Amos Wilson, Washington Co.

1827 Aug 2   Hughes, Harriet and Thomas Gray by William Patterson, JP, Franklin Co.

1820 Oct 18   Hughes, Hathander and Samuel Wooder by J.B. Gilliland, JP, Jackson Co.

1819 Jan 14   Hughes, James and James Wheeler by Geo. Callanhan, EMEC, Licking Co.

1812 Jun 4   Hughes, Jane and Abraham Wright by Peter Pence, Licking Co.

1812 Apr 16   Hughes, Job and Salinda Goodrich by Rev. G. Vanaman, Licking Co.

1817 Jun 19   Hughes, Jonathan and Lovy Davis by John Evans, JP, Licking Co.

1823 Feb 26   Hughes, Margaret L. and Joseph Scooner by Charles Waddell, LM,
               Franklin Co.

1817 Oct 2   Hughes, Nancy and John Coulter by Geo. Callanhan, EMEC, Licking Co.

1815 Jan 10   Hughes, Phebe and Lewis Walker by Thomas Seely, Washington Co.

1809 Apr 4   Hughes, Sarah and Samuel Davis by W. Haines, JP, Licking Co.

1821 Sep 30   Hughes, Sarah and David McCracken by Isaac Painter, JP, Franklin Co.

1825 Jun 22   Hughey, James and Ann Marie Drake by John Stealy, JP, Marion Co.

1798 Dec 23   Hughs, Elizabeth and Abraham Staats by D. Loring, JCCCP, Washington Co.

1825 Apr 5   Hughs, Elizabeth and Elias Cadey by Samuel Carrick, JP, Jackson Co.

1817 Aug 28   Hughs, John and Rebecca Woods by John Spencer, JP, Licking Co.

1800 May 14   Hughs, Margaret and Timothy Gates by Wm. Burnham, JP, Washington Co.

1826 Sep 17   Hughs, Thomas and Elizabeth McCracken by Wm. Long, JP, Franklin Co.

1800 Mar 23   Hughs, Wm. and Elizabeth Lucas by Robt. Oliver, JP, Washington Co.

1799 Jul 3   Hulbert, Abigal and David Stokely by Robert Oliver, Washington Co.

1851 Jul 29   Hull, Edward T. and Martha P. Stout by Rev. Geo. B. Sturges, St. Paul's Church, Marion, Marion Co.

1813 Jul 25   Hull, George and Elizabeth Cummins by Rev. Levi Shinn, Licking Co.

1816 Feb 20   Hull, Hannah and John Berry and Uriah Hull, JP, Licking Co.

1818 Sep 29   Hull, Hannah and Joseph Smith by Wm. Hull, JP, Licking Co.

1818 Jun 4   Hull, Isabel and Joseph Bower by Mich. Ellis, MG, Licking Co.

1816 Apr 22   Hull, James and Rebecky Hull by Edward Hursey, JP, Licking Co.

1816 Feb 20   Hull, John and Mary Gibbons by Uriah Hull, JP, Licking Co.

1815 May 28   Hull, Mary and Jacob Hummel by Uriah Hull, Licking Co.

1817 Nov 5   Hull, Mary and Thomas Johnston by Stephen Guthrie, Washington Co.

1820 Dec 25   Hull, Philip and Sarah McCracken by Martin Hale, MG, Licking Co.

1818 Jun 10   Hull, Prudence and Joseph Taylor by Alex. Holden, JP, Licking Co.

1816 Apr 22   Hull, Rebecky and James Hull by Edward Hursey, JP, Licking Co.

1813 May 17   Hulse, James and Rebecca Van Metre (license date), Pickaway Co.

1820 Oct 26   Humiston, Jason and Margaret Shaw by James Whitney, JP, Washington Co.

1820 Apr 13   Humiston, Lynde and Betsey Starlin by Rev. Abraham Lippet, Washington Co.

1821 May 19   Humiston, Sally and Henry Chandler by John Green, JP, Washington Co.

1814 Sep 11   Humiston, Wealthy and Dan'l.H. Hamilton by Isaac Baker, Esq., Washington Co.

1815 May 28   Hummel, Jacob and Mary Hull by Uriah Hull, Licking Co.

1822 Dec 10   Humphrey, Aaron C. and Betsey Starr by James Hoge, Franklin Co.

1817 Mar 20   Humphrey, Ariel and Helpa Everitt by Thomas Spelman, JP, Licking Co.

1817 Nov 26   Humphrey, Benoni and Danl. H. Buell, JP, Washington Co.

1819 Jul 15   Humphrey, Daniel and Alcey C. Rose by Saml. Bancroft, JP, Licking Co.

1852 Sep 2   Humphrey, Emma and John S. Ross by Rev. A. Kingsbury, Putnam Presbyterian Church, Muskingum Co.

1825 May 3   Humphrey, Harriett and William D. Parcel by Alex. Perry, JP, Marion
              Co.

1822 Apr 25   Humphrey, Isaac and Clarissa Ackley by Jacob Young, MMEC, Washington
              Co.

1816 Sep 30   Humphrey, Mary and Henry Cliver by Zach Carlisle, JP, Licking Co.

1852 Jul 8   Humphrey, Mary Ann and John W. Edgar by Rev. A. Kingsbury, Putnam
              Presbyterian Church, Muskingum Co.

1806 Mar 20   Humphrey, Thomas and Ruth Patten by John Brough, JP, Washington Co.

1819 Oct 10   Humphrey, William and Lydia Crane by Rev. Saml. P. Robbins, Washing-
              ton Co.

1805 Aug 9   Humphreys, Elizabeth and John Russele by J. Gardner, JP, Ross Co.

1809 May 8   Humphreys, Jacob and Ann Ward by Wm. Haines, JP, Licking Co.

1805 Apr 4   Humphry, Jacob and Polly Spacht by D. Loring, Washington Co.

1808 Sep 25   Humphry, Wm. and Anna Bellows by D. Loring, JP, Washington Co.

1876 May 30   Humston, Dr. Chas. M. and Jessie F. McIntosh at Beverly by Rev.
              John Boyd, St. Luke's Church, Marietta, Washington Co.

1803 Dec 1   Hundberry, Mary and William Lowrey by J. Graham, Washington Co.

1805 Oct 18   Hungerford, Mathew and Nancy Walker by John Brough, JP, Washington Co.

1815 Nov 9   Hungerford, Nancy and Adam Smith by D.H. Buell, JP, Washington Co.

1824 Feb 22   Hunt, Eliza S. and Cyrus T. Carpenter by Reuben Carpenter, JP,
              Franklin Co.

1837 Sep 14   Hunt, Mary and Wm. Hall by Rev. E. Burr, St. John's Church,
              Worthington, Franklin Co.

1804 11 mo 18 Hunt, Sarah and Enos Baldwin, Miami Monthly Meeting, Warren Co.

1810 Feb 5   Hunter, Abe. and Wm. Shaw by James Hoge, Franklin Co.

1827 Apr 29   Hunter, Avis and Jacob Miller by J.N. Walter, MG, Franklin Co.

1824 Apr 22   Hunter, Charles and Thrssy Bartlett by C. Henkel, Franklin Co.

1813 Jul 9   Hunter, Elizabeth and Jacob Stotts by W. Taylor, Licking Co.

1813 Mar 25   Hunter, George and Martha Conner by Rev. James Scott, Licking Co.

1823 Apr 22   Hunter, Jane and Andrew McElvaine by James Hoge, Franklin Co.

1813 Jan 28   Hunter, Joseph and Martha McGowin by Wm. Shaw, Franklin Co.

1814 Aug 18   Hunter, Joseph and Unice Starr by James Hoge, Franklin Co.

1817 Jul 20   Hunter, Joseph and Mary Mitchel by James Hoge, Franklin Co.

1814 Apr 12   Hunter, Mary and Daniel Stotts by Wm. Taylor, Licking Co.

1826 Apr 11   Hunter, Matilda and John Byers by James Hoge, Franklin Co.

1806 Jun 26   Hunter, Matty and Samuel Robinson by Zachariah Stephen, JP, Franklin
              Co.

1817 Apr 1   Hunter, Nancy and David Mitchell by Michael Potter, JP, Franklin Co.

1814 Jun 16   Hunter, Patsy and Andrew McElvain by James Hoge, Franklin Co.

1804 Feb 8   Hunter, Robert and Nancy Riddle by Zachariah Stephen, JP, Franklin Co.

1807 Jan 22   Hunter, Robert and Deborah McGowen by Arthur O'Harra, JP, Franklin Co.

1817 May 22   Hunter, Samuel and Anna Rogers by Joseph Grate, Franklin Co.

1818 May 5   Hunter, Samuel and Polly Guy by James Cunningham, Licking Co.

1808 Dec 13   Hunter, Sarah and Francis Jones by James Marshall, Franklin Co.

1817 Nov 17   Hunter, William and Margaret McElvaine by Eli C. King, Acting JP,
               Franklin Co.

1827 Apr 11   Hunter, William and Eliza Baker by C. Henkel, Franklin Co.

1823 Oct 22   Hunterman, Maryann and John Warner by D.W. Deshler, JP, Franklin Co.

1820 Aug 1   Hupp, John and Margaret Ogle by Dudley Davis, JP, Washington Co.

1819 Jun 10   Hupp, Mary and Joseph English by Alex. Holden, JP, Licking Co.

1880 Oct 28   Hurlbut, David S. of Hazelhurst, Mich., and Ella E. Richards of
               Putnam by Rev. George F. Moore, Putnam Presbyterian Church,
               Muskingum Co.

1806 May 13   Hurlbut, John and Betsy Miller by R. Oliver, Washington Co.

1818 Jan 20   Hurly, Dennis and Mary Connel by James Holmes, JP, Licking Co.

1817 Dec 8   Hurndun, Hezekiah and Anna Browning by Rev. Saml. P. Robbins,
               Washington Co.

1814 Sep 8   Hursey, Sarah and John Kergan by J.W. Patterson, JP, Licking Co.

1809 Nov 20   Hurst, Benedict and Martha Dallarson by Luther Dana, JP, Washington
               Co.

1818 Dec 9   Hurst, Hooper and Elizabeth James by Jacob Delay, MG, Jackson Co.

1823 Feb 13   Hury (or Huey or Henry), John and Hannah Codner by Richard Court-
               right, Franklin Co.

1816 Jan 25   Husher, Elizabeth and William J. Jordan by Uriah Hull, JP, Licking Co.

1818 Jul 2   Hussey, Adna and Lydia McFarlin by John Greene, JP, Washington Co.

1818 Sep 10   Hussey, Asa and Sally McFarland by John Green, JP, Washington Co.

1818 Aug 13   Hussey, Lydia and Norman Payne by Daniel G. Stanley, Washington Co.

1818 Aug 13   Hussey, Phebe and James Hill by Daniel M. Stanley, JP, Washington Co.

1828 Jan 24   Huston, I.A. and John Lawyer by I. Grubb, JP, Franklin Co.

1813 Jun 28   Huston, John and Elizabeth Baum (license date), Pickaway Co.

1805 Apr 16   Hustone, Nancy and Thomas Reed by Wm. Creighton, Ross Co.

1824 Jan 22   Hutcheson, Nancy and Jonas Harlow by Robert Boyd, Franklin Co.

1819 Oct 31   Hutcheson, Thomas and Nancy Warren by Orgillous Doan, JP, Washington
               Co.

1822 Mar 7   Hutchesson, Amanda and Charles Sells by Alex. Bassett, JP, Franklin
               Co.

1817 Nov 16   Hutchins, Nancy and Charles Davis, Jr. by Dudley Davis, Washington Co.

1819 Jun 10   Hutchins, Rosanna and Joseph Davis by Dudley Davis, JP, Washington Co.

1822 Jul 13   Hutchinson, Daniel and Susana Ebey by Jacob Grubb, Franklin Co.

1824 Aug 8   Hutchinson, Elisa and Silas Hutson by Benj. Britton, E1NS (license date, return filed 28 Sept.), Franklin Co.

1822 Apr 17   Hutchinson, Elizabeth and George Adams by John Curtiss, JP, Washington Co.

1818 Feb 12   Hutchinson, George and Lucy Gard by Cornelius Hougland, JP, Washington Co.

1822 Mar 31   Hutchinson, George and Catharine Keirns by Bial Stedman, JP, Washington Co.

1848 Jul 9   Hutchinson, George C. and Elizabeth H. Perry by Rev. D.W. Tolford, St. Luke's Church, Marietta, Washington Co.

1812 May 10   Hutchinson, James and Charlotte Pool by Henry Jolly, Washington Co.

1828 Dec 7   Hutchinson, John and Aurilea Brown by W.T. Martin, JP, Franklin Co.

1821 Jun 12   Hutchinson, Lucinda and Matthias Paine by John Curtis, JP, Washington Co.

1823 Jan 12   Hutchinson, Meremia and John Sells, Jr. by Wm. Kilbourn, JP, Franklin Co.

1815 Jun 1   Hutchinson, Nancy and Jacob Siler by Uriah Hull, Licking Co.

1822 Jan 1   Hutchinson, Sally and Nehemiah Howe by S.N. Cook, JP, Washington Co.

1792 Dec 25   Hutchinson, Thomas and Sally Welch by Robert Oliver, Judge, Washington Co.

1821 Sep 13   Hutchinson, Thomas and Lydia Mash by Bial Stedman, JP, Washington Co.

1820 Jan 20   Hutchinson, William and Harriet Kent by Joseph Palmer, JP, Washington Co.

1818 Apr 2   Hutchisan, Amasiah Jr. and Polly Auey by Robert Elliott, JP, Franklin Co.

1816 Mar 24   Hutchison, Rachel and Joseph Baker by W. O'Bannon, JP, Licking Co.

1829 Mar 10   Hutson, Jesse and Mary Needles by John F. Solomon, Franklin Co.

1824 Aug 8   Hutson, Silas and Elisa Hutchinson by Benj. Britton, E1NS, (license date, return filed 28 Sept.), Franklin Co.

1811 Oct 25   Hutt, Elizabeth and Samuel Boyer (license date), Pickaway Co.

1853 Sep 6   Hyar, Lewis and Elizabeth Smith by Rev. John Boyd, St. Luke's Church, Marietta, Washington Co.

1811 Aug 19   Hyatt, Polly and George Potter (license date), Pickaway Co.

1814 Jun 2   Hyles, Rebecca and James Henderson by Henry Coonrod, JP, Pickaway Co.

1872 Feb 28   Iams, Hiram B. and Fannie E. Clark by Rev. John Boyd, St. Luke's Church, Marietta, Washington Co.

1816 Dec 15   Ile, Adam and Jane Cloton by John Green, Licking Co.

1817 Dec 25   Iles, Frederick and Hannah Conard by John Green, Licking Co.

1811 Jan 31   Imberson, James and Catherine Fry (license date), Pickaway Co.

1890 May 14   Ingalls, Lula Cassel and Harvey Alfred Sharpe both of Zanesville by
               Rev. George F. Moore, Putnam Presbyterian Church, Muskingum Co.

1798 Mar 18   Ingals, Fanny and Daniel Elenwood by J. Pierce, JCCCP, Washington Co.

1826 Mar 30   Ingham (or Ingram), Abraham and Elizabeth Bivans by Jacob Gundy,
               Franklin Co.

1822 Jul 4   Ingham, Asahel and Elizabeth Maynard by A. Buttles, Franklin Co.

1822 Jan 24   Ingham, Louis and Archibald Dixon by Aristarchus Walker, JP,
               Franklin Co.

1824 Mar 24   Ingham, Mariah and David Birge by Aristarchus Walker, Franklin Co.

1818 Mar 22   Ingham, Mila and Joel Wells by Samuel Bancroft, JP, Licking Co.

1829 May 28   Ingham, Sarah and David French by Geo. Jefferies, Franklin Co.

1821 Apr 5   Ingham, Thomas and Clarissa Baker by Samuel Bancroft, JP, Licking Co.

1826 Jan 11   Inglaw, Abraham C. and Chloe Inglaw by R.W. Cowles, JP, Franklin Co.

1826 Jan 11   Inglaw, Chloe and Abraham C. Inglaw by R.W. Cowles, JP, Franklin Co.

1815 Dec 7   Ingles, Elizabeth and Henry Crippen by Cyrus Ames, JP, Washington Co.

1819 Dec 9   Ingles, John and Mercy Rathbun by Cyrus Ames, Washington Co.

1810 Mar 8   Ingman, Isaac and Jane Benjiman by -----, Licking Co.

1827 Feb 13   Ingraham, Francis G. and William Sparrow by Amos G. Baldwin, Minister
               of the Pr. Ep. Ch'h., Franklin Co.

1808 Mar 28   Ingram, the widow and Luther Winget by Nehemiah Gates, Franklin Co.

1826 Mar 30   Ingram (or Ingham), Abraham and Elizabeth Bivans by Jacob Gundy,
               Franklin Co.

1814 Dec 14   Ingram, Lena and Ira Arnold by Recompense Stansbery, JP, Franklin Co.

1822 Feb 26   Inks, Eleanor and Michael Duggin by Russel Bigelow, MG, Franklin Co.

1827 May 24   Inks, John Jr. and Hoapy Green by A. Allison, Franklin Co.

1814 Mar 24   Inks, Persilla and Wm. Cornell by John Stevenson, Franklin Co.

1824 Jan 29   Inks, William and Martha Headly by Jacob Smith, JP, Franklin Co.

1818 Apr 1   Inman, Esack and Elizabeth Adams by Joseph Gorton, Franklin Co.

1885 May 13   Inskeep, Campsiadell H. and John A. Sutphen both of Zanesville by
               Rev. George F. Moore, Putnam Presbyterian Church, Muskingum Co.

1827 Nov 11   Ireland, Moses and Sally Laws by A. Walker, JP, Franklin Co.

1866 Jun 28   Irvin, Jane and Everett Messenger by N.C.N. Dudley, St. Paul's
               Church, Marion, Marion Co.

1810 Aug 1   Irwin, David and Mary Fletcher by Edwin Putnam, Washington Co.

1815 Apr 19   Irwin, Elizabeth and Robert Culbertson by James Hoge, Franklin Co.

1820 Nov 20   Irwin, James and Betsey Ann Ships by Abner Goff, MEC, Licking Co.

1821 Apr 3   Irwin, John and Mary Dodge by Noah Fidler, Licking Co.

1869 Oct 28   Irwin, Maggie and Robert W. Caldwell by Rev. A. Kingsbury, Putnam
              Presbyterian Church, Muskingum Co.

1814 Jan 6   Irwin, Nancy and Virgill McCrackin by Percival Adams, Franklin Co.

1797 Jan 2   Isham, Russell and Elisabeth Nott by -----, Washington Co.

1818 Jan 8   Jackson, Catherine and Samuel Chadwick by Noah Fidler, Licking Co.

1825 Nov 20   Jackson, Catharine, widow, and John Vanvorst, widower, by Joseph
              Carper, Franklin Co.

1821 Jul 10   Jackson, Caty and Archabald Nickins by W.T. Martin, Franklin Co.

1820 Dec 21   Jackson, David Jr. and Margaret Bell by Dudley Davis, JP, Washington
              Co.

1816 Feb 6   Jackson, Hugh and Harriet Putnam by Joseph Chapman, JP, Washington Co.

1869 Nov 25   Jackson, James and Anna Mitchell by Rev. John Boyd, St. Luke's Church,
              Marietta, Washington Co.

1818 Jul 2   Jackson, Jane and Joseph Reed by Dudley Davis, Washington Co.

1813 Apr 10   Jackson, John and Anna Fryback (license date), Pickaway Co.

1817 Jan 30   Jackson, John and Polly Belt by Noah Fidler, Licking Co.

1810 Jul 19   Jackson, John G. and Mary Sophia Meigs by Stephen Lindsly,
              Washington Co.

1818 Mar 19   Jackson, John J. and Isabel Peddicord by Noah Fidler, Licking Co.

1809 Mar 24   Jackson, Margaret and Christian Hale by Amos Porter, JP, Washington
              Co.

1806 Jan 28   Jackson, Martha and Joseph Baker by Peter Jackson, JP, Ross Co.

1798 Aug 30   Jackson, Mary and George Hall by D. Loring, Washington Co.

1816 May 31   Jackson, Mary and Charles Root by Noah Fidler, Licking Co.

1815 Oct 27   Jackson, Nancy and Thomas Taylor by John True, Washington Co.

1821 Jan 7   Jackson, Phebe and Nathaniel Mitchell by Dudley Davis, JP, Washington
              Co.

1808 Feb 16   Jackson, Ruhanna and Samuel Fulton by Thos. Stanley, JP, Washington
              Co.

1814 Mar 22   Jackson, Sally and Charles McDaniel by J. Hickey, Licking Co.

1806 Oct 25   Jadding, Nancy and Samuel Mellor by Rob't Oliver, Washington Co.

1822 Jul 4   Jague, Daniel and Susan Bevelhymer by John Davis, Franklin Co.

1812 Nov 30   James, Ann and Samuel Thompson by Jeremiah Dare, JP, Washington Co.

1791 Jul 24   James, Anne and Caleb Bailey by Benj. Tupper, Washington Co.

1815 Jan 1   James, Benjamin and Michel Talbot by Anth'y Sheets, JP, Washington Co.

1806 Nov 18   James, David and Nancy Greene by S. Lindsly, Washington Co.

1814 Mar 8   James, Edward and Hester Griffith by John H. Phillips, Licking Co.

1815 Oct 12   James, Eli and Catharine Crawford by Rev. Stephen Lindsly, Washington Co.

1818 Dec 9   James, Elizabeth and Hooper Hurst by Jacob Delay, JP, Jackson Co.

1797 Oct 29   James, Hannah and Benjamin Johnson by Josiah Munro, Washington Co.

1817 Jun 8   James, John and Eliza Bickmore by Simon Merwin, Washington Co.

1824 Dec 23   James, John and Rhoda Barr by John Green, JP, Marion Co.

1825 May 22   James, Jonathan and Elizabeth Lust by Benj. Bell, JP, Marion Co.

1818 Aug 28   James, July and Daniel Hoffman by D. Mitchell, JP, Jackson Co.

1825 Jan 3   James, Louisa and Isaac Crow by Thos. Daugherty, JP, Jackson Co.

1828 Mar 23   James, Mahala and Samuel King by A. Allison, Franklin Co.

1825 Aug 21   James, Marmoen and Alex. Miller by Rob't Ward, JP, Jackson Co.

1820 Mar 1   James, Phebe and Owen Owens by John C. Smith, JP, Licking Co.

1821 Aug 27   James, Rachel and Rufus Blackmore by J. Green, JP, Licking Co.

1821 Jul 24   James, Roanna and John W. Rathburn by Jacob Delay, MG, Jackson Co.

1814 Sep 15   James, Samuel and Betsey McCollum by James Marshall, Franklin Co.

1806 Jan 1   James, Thomas and Charlotte Massie by Robert B. Dobbins, VDM, Ross Co.

1817 Aug 15   James, Timothy and Hannah Crampton by John Cunningham, JPNAT, Licking Co.

1820 Feb 14   James, William M. and Mariah Bailey by Elihu Bigelow, JP, Licking Co.

1828 Jul 24   Jameson, Eliza and James Armintage by Jacob Grubb, JP, Franklin Co.

1814 Aug 1   Jameson, Margaret and Solomon Jarvis by John Brough, Esq., Washington Co.

1817 Jun 26   Jamisan, Betsy and Edward Phelps by Ebenezer Washburn, VDM, Franklin Co.

1824 Feb 26   Jamison, Andrew and Eleanor Pancake by Jacob Grubb, Franklin Co.

1804 May 10   Jamison, George and Jean Lavezby by W. Robinson, JP, Ross Co.

1805 Feb 19   Jamison, Henrietta and Arthur O'Harra by Zachariah Stephen, JP, Franklin Co.

1816 Jul 6   Jamison, Jane and James Rowland by Samuel Rogue, JP, Licking Co.

---- --- --   Jamison, John and Sally Ann Lawson by Nathan Emery, EMEC (for the date, "Sometime or other he does not say when"), Franklin Co.

1815 Oct 14   Jamison, Joseph and Lydia Stewart by James Hoge, LDM, Franklin Co.

1814 Mar 29   Jamison, Rachel and Samuel Barr by Joseph S. Hughs, Franklin Co.

1822 Oct 29   Jamison, Robert and Betsy Smith by E. Washburn, VDM, Franklin Co.

1817 Dec 4   Jamison, Samuel and Eliza Scott by Rev. James Scott, Licking Co.

1805 May 8   Jamison, Sarah and Abraham Clark by Wm. Robinson, Ross Co.

1815 Jun 15   Jarrett, Sally and John Andrews by Joseph Palmer, JP, Washington Co.

1814 Aug 1   Jarvis, Solomon and Margaret Jameson by John Brough, Esq., Washington Co.

1807 12 mo 3   Jay, John and Mary Steddom, Miami Monthly Meeting, Warren Co.

1806 1 mo 15   Jay, Samuel and Bathsheba Pugh, Miami Monthly Meeting, Warren Co.

1821 10 mo 3   Jeffers, Catharine and Evan Ward, Miami Monthly Meeting, Warren Co.

1826 Jan 15   Jeffords, Sally and William K. Lampson by P. Chase, Franklin Co.

1819 Jul 13   Jeffreys, Sophia and Wm. Keyton by Rob't G. Hanna, JP, Jackson Co.

1822 May 22   Jenkins, Amon and Elizabeth Rathbone by Russell Bigelow, Franklin Co.

1820 Jan 29   Jenkins, Anna and James Albery by Josias Ewing, JP, Licking Co.

1884 Oct 2   Jenkins, Clara A. and Thomas J. Districk both of Brush Creek Twp.,
               by Rev. George F. Moore, Putnam Presbyterian Church, Muskingum
               Co.

1819 Jan 28   Jenkins, Elizabeth and Samuel Craig by Samuel McDowell, JP, Jackson
               Co.

1823 Nov 27   Jenkins, James and Margaret Radabaugh by John Horton, JP, Jackson Co.

1803 Mar 14   Jenkins, James H. and Elizabeth Lyons by Sam'l Williamson, Washington
               Co.

1819 Jan 28   Jenkins, Margaret and James Scurlock by Robt. G. Hanna, JP, Jackson
               Co.

1818 Jul 26   Jenkins, Nancy and Alexander Stephenson by Isaac Baker, JP, Jackson
               Co.

1825 Mar 31   Jenkins, Nancy and Wm. Davis by J.B. Gilliland, JP, Jackson Co.

1818 Oct 6   Jenkins, Thomas and Mary Dye by Sardine Stone, JP, Washington Co.

1809 May 16   Jenkins, William and Elizabeth Napier by Sam'l. P. Robbins, MG,
               Washington Co.

1827 May 30   Jenks, May and Luther Green by Hugh Liams, JP, Franklin Co.

1816 Mar 1   Jennings, Delilah and Joseph Record by Rev. Stephen Lindsley,
               Washington Co.

1810 Dec 23   Jennings, Eliza and William Nixon by Stephen Lindsly, Washington Co.

1874 Dec 24   Jennings, Erastus A., M.D., and Maggie Chapman by Rev. A. Kingsbury,
               Putnam Presbyterian Church, Muskingum Co.

1820 Aug 6   Jennings, Jeniah and Hannah McCabe by Danl. H. Buell, Washington Co.

1811 Dec 25   Jennings, Margaret and George Nixson by Stephen Lindsly, Washington
               Co.

1818 Aug 5   Jennings, Nancy and Elijah Coleman by Pelatiah White, Washington Co.

1870 Jun 1   Jenvey, Anna M. and Jonathan T. McDowell of Franklin, Pa., by Rev.
               John Boyd, St. Luke's Church, Marietta, Washington Co.

1824 Jun 27   Jercockes (or Jergcocks), Abraham and Halan Lawson by C. Waddell,
               LM, (These were parents of James Jaycox who married Femino
               McDonald, dau of William and Catharine Altman McDonald.)
               Franklin Co.

1824 Jun 27   Jergcocks - see Jercockes.

1826 Mar 16   Jerman, Jesse and Sally Brittenham, Franklin Co.

1821 Mar 8   Jermon, Joshua and Catherine Thomas by John F. Solomon, Franklin Co.

1825 Apr 7   Jermon, Martha and Demit Cole by John F. Solomon, Franklin Co.

1826 12 mo 6   Jessup, Mary and David Green, Miami Monthly Meeting, Warren Co.

1821 Nov 25   Jett, Eliza B. and Adam Rice by Rev. James McAboy (Elder),
               Washington Co.

1816 Jun 15   Jett, Owens and Mary Cole by Isaac Humphreys, JP, Washington Co.

1825 Apr 29   Jewatt, Henry G.,Batcholor and Lorane Boreman, spinster, by Wm. Long,
               JP, Franklin Co.

1819 Aug 8   Jewell, John T. and Mary Ann Smithson by Rev. Levi Jewell,
               Washington Co.

1819 Nov 7   Jewell, Joseph and Betsey Lewis by Rev. Levi Jewell, Washington Co.

1876 Oct 17   Jewell, Minnie W. and Edward R. Cary by Rev. A. Kingsbury, Putnam
               Presbyterian Church, Muskingum Co.

1828 Mar 27   Jewett, Caleb R. and Darias Pinney by Aristarchus Walker, Franklin Co.

1820 Dec 21   Jewett, Jeremiah and Clarisa Baker by Samuel Bancroft, JP, Licking Co.

1828 Mar 30   Jewett, Lucy and Benjamin Platt by Jason Bull, Franklin Co.

1822 Mar 14   Jewett, Lydia and Luther Hillary by Aristarchus Walker, Franklin Co.

1827 Jun 14   Jewett, Martha and S.B. Fields by Charles Henkle, Franklin Co.

1816 Jan 28   Jewit, David and Betsey Barlow by Ezra Griswold, Franklin Co.

1810 Feb 15   Jimason, Abigail and John Hazlerigg by John Brough, JP, Washington Co.

1841 Sep 20   Jinks, Lysander and Emily Hills, St. Luke's Church, Granville,
               Licking Co.

1816 Jan 25   Jinkins, Ann and John Hilphrey by J. Green, Licking Co.

1807 2 mo 26   Jinkins, Ely and Ruth Mendinghall, Miami Monthly Meeting, Warren Co.

1804 Mar 8   Joab, Jane and Rojin Benson by Thos. Scott, JP, Ross Co.

1813 Aug 29   John, John and Matilda Rodgers by J. Marshall, Franklin Co.

1815 Jun 8   John, Thomas and Elizabeth Berely (or Birdy) by John Stipp, JP,
               Franklin Co.

1826 Mar 23   Johns, Robert and Nally Decker by J. Gander, Franklin Co.

1819 Mar 9   Johnson, Alderman and Polly Low by Samuel Dye, JP, Washington Co.

1797 Oct 29   Johnson, Benjamin and Hannah James by Josiah Munro, Washington Co.

1872 Sep 15   Johnson, C. Isabelle and D. Payson Beach by Wm. Bower, St. Luke's
               Church, Granville, Licking Co.

1874 Sep 1   Johnson, C. Louise and Edward P. Linnell by Wm. Bower, St. Luke's
               Church, Granville, Licking Co.

1805 Mar 28   Johnson, Catharine and Abijah Cary by Joshua Ewing, Franklin Co.

1819 Feb 4   Johnson, Chester and Sophia Allison by Amos Wilson, Washington Co.

1820 Dec 7   Johnson, Comfort and John Prevolt by Peter Clover, JP, Franklin Co.

1827 Oct 17   Johnson, Eliza A. and Martin L. Lewis by Geo. Jefferies, MBC, Franklin Co.

1815 Jan 8   Johnson, Elizabeth and Thomas Black by James Sharp, JP, Washington Co.

1801 Feb 17   Johnson, Fanny and Samuel Craig by Robt. Safford, Washington Co.

1880 Oct 4   Johnson, Frank R. of Zanesville and Alice Barron of Putnam by Rev. George F. Moore, Putnam Presbyterian Church, Muskingum Co.

1840 Mar 16   Johnson, Franklin and Emily Griswold by Rev. A. Helfenstine, St. John's Church, Worthington, Franklin Co.

1811 Sep 21   Johnson, Hannah and John Williams (license date), Pickaway Co.

1812 Dec 31   Johnson, Hannah and Uzziah Nicholson by Wm. D. Hendren, Franklin Co.

1820 Feb 10   Johnson, Hannah and Sylvester Scott by Wm. Rand, Washington Co.

1827 Jul 5   Johnson, Hanson and Mariah King by S. Hamilton, Elder in the MEC, Franklin Co.

1816 Feb 29   Johnson, Huldah and Thurston Northup by Sam'l Dye, Washington Co.

1804 Oct 11   Johnson, Isaac and Nancy Thomas by John Sharp, Washington Co.

1820 Jan 13   Johnson, Jacob and Anna Baker by John D. Chamberlain, Washington Co.

1815 Feb 5   Johnson, James and Sophia Dixen by Jas. Jackson, JP, Pickaway Co.

1817 Dec 22   Johnson, James and Sally Miller by Joseph Thrap, Licking Co.

1825 Sep 1   Johnson, James and Mary Mills by A. Allison, JP, Franklin Co.

1820 12 mo 6 Johnson, James B. and Rhoda O'Neall, Miami Monthly Meeting, Warren Co.

1813 Feb 14   Johnson, John and Hannah Robertson by John Green, Washington Co.

1815 Feb 10   Johnson, John and Margaret Freemire by Anth'y Sheets, Washington Co.

1799 May 9   Johnson, Joseph and Sarah Wells by Daniel Story, Clerk, Washington Co.

1818 Feb 13   Johnson, Joseph and Matilda Sobditt by Stephen Guthrie, JP, Washington Co.

1826 Oct 3   Johnson, Joseph K. and Nancy Caldwell by P. Adams, Franklin Co.

1799 Oct 10   Johnson, Levi and Sally Cook by D. Loring, Washington Co.

1820 Apr 2   Johnson, Lewis and Lucretia Warren by John Russell, JP, Washington Co.

1803 Jul 28   Johnson, Margrate and Hartley Malone by J. Gardner, JP, Ross Co.

1824 Oct 12   Johnson, Mary and Henry Burthley by Wm. Godman, Franklin Co.

1813 8 mo 4   Johnson, Micajah and Rebecca O'Neall, Miami Monthly Meeting, Warren Co.

1895 May 8   Johnson, Myrta and Richard S. Mercer both of South Zanesville by Rev. George F. Moore, Putnam Presbyterian Church, Muskingum Co.

1820 Jan 23   Johnson, Nancy and John Wyman by Adriel Hussey, MG, Jackson Co.

1826 Dec 26   Johnson, Nancy and John Golliday by D.W. Deshler, JP, Franklin Co.

1801 Jan 27   Johnson, Nancy Taylor and James Kemly by Robt. Safford, Washington Co.

1807 8 mo 19   Johnson, Penelope and John Sears, Miami Monthly Meeting, Warren Co.

1813 May 25   Johnson, Samuel and Elizabeth Kerr (license date), Pickaway Co.

1825 Jan 13   Johnson, Samuel R. and Susan Ward by J.B. Gilliland, JP, Jackson Co.

1818 Oct 8   Johnson, Serman and Louisa Henderson by Cyrus Ames, JP, Washington Co.

1811 Jan 24   Johnson, William and Mary Bodkin by Daniel Goodno, Washington Co.

1876 Sep 13   Johnson, Willis H. and Mary P. Whiffing by Rev. John Boyd, St. Luke's Church, Marietta, Washington Co.

1826 Feb 9   Johnson, Wyatt and Cinthia Richey by Joseph Carper, Franklin Co.

1809 May 6   Johnston, Abraham and Susannah Bradley by Nehemiah Gates, Franklin Co.

1809 Sep 5   Johnston, Abraham and Polly Rosebury by M. Dickey, JP, Franklin Co.

1816 Jan 16   Johnston, Betsey and John Carns by Joseph Gorton, Franklin Co.

1819 Jan 5   Johnston, Catherine and Philip Brakebill by J. Cunningham, JP, Licking Co.

1813 Sep 21   Johnston, Daniel and Rachel Scott by Rev. James Scott, Licking Co.

1811 Jun 20   Johnston, David and Peggy Martin by Thomas Morris, Franklin Co.

1813 Nov 24   Johnston, David and May Cramer by Silas Winchell, JP, Licking Co.

1815 Mar 3   Johnston, Eleanor and Cummings Porter by Stephen Guthrie, JP, Washington Co.

1800 Aug 28   Johnston, Elizabeth and John Montgomery by Josiah Munro, Washington Co.

1819 Jan 14   Johnston, Elizabeth and Moses Monroe by N.W. Andrews, JP, Jackson Co.

1828 Dec 25   Johnston, Elizabeth and Solomon Groves by P. Adams, Franklin Co.

1814 Jun 9   Johnston, Ephram and Darkey Cooper by A. O'Harra, Franklin Co.

1813 Aug 30   Johnston, Henry and Prisilla Pinkring by W. Taylor, Licking Co.

1822 Nov 7   Johnston, Henry and Lucy Locket by Joseph Badger, Franklin Co.

1819 Mar 4   Johnston, Isaac and Nancy Tucker by Eli C. King, Franklin Co.

1807 Apr 23   Johnston, Jacob and Jemima Casey by Nehemiah Gates, JP, Franklin Co.

1804 Sep 20   Johnston, James and Elinor Timmons by Abraham Miller, Ross Co.

1810 Apr 1   Johnston, James and Carley Clarke by Rev. Simon Cokrane, Franklin Co.

1813 Feb 15   Johnston, James and Mary Parker by ----- Phillips, JP, Licking Co.

1825 Dec 22   Johnston, John and Selphenia Emery by James Boyd, JP, Franklin Co.

1811 Mar 19   Johnston, Joseph and Martha Ewins by J. McMillen, JP, Licking Co.

1828 Dec 18   Johnston, Keziah and William Gundy by John Tipton, Franklin Co.

1818 Nov 29   Johnston, Lewis and Elizabeth Strader by James Hoge, Franklin Co.

1819 Dec 28   Johnston, Mrs. Margaret and David Rawles by Jeremiah Brown, JP, Jackson Co.

1806 Feb 18   Johnston, Mary and John Baker by James Quinn, Ross Co.

1807 Aug 25   Johnston, Molly and James Robinson by Rob't Oliver, JP, Washington
               Co.

1826 Jan 29   Johnston, Olive and John M. Laughlin by E. Richman, Deacon ME Church,
               Franklin Co.

1811 Feb 4   Johnston, Otho and Margaret Turner by James Hoge, Franklin Co.

1815 Aug 31   Johnston, Orrange and Acksa Maynard by Recompence Stansbery,
               Franklin Co.

1823 Jun 24   Johnston, Paul and Margart Roads by Isaac Painter, Franklin Co.

1805 Apr 4   Johnston, Rachel and Thomas McCafferty by Robert Adams, Ross Co.

1827 Mar 18   Johnston, S.V. and Nancy Read by P. Adams, Franklin Co.

1816 Apr 13   Johnston, Sally and John Dearduff by Joseph Grate, Franklin Co.

1820 Jun 25   Johnston, Sarah and John B. Gilliland by Nath'l W. Andrews, JP,
               Jackson Co.

1817 Nov 5   Johnston, Thomas and Mary Hull by Stephen Guthrie, Washington Co.

1828 Sep 28   Johnston, Thomas and Pebe Ann Cronston by S. Hamilton, Elder in the
               ME Church, Franklin Co.

1805 May 9   Johnston, Wm. and Peggy McClilman by Peter Jackson, JP, Ross Co.

1818 Oct 20   Jolly, Daniel and Margaret Harris by M. Thorp, JP, Licking Co.

1806 May 31   Jolly, Henry and Christina Williamson by P. Whitten, Washington Co.

1873 Oct 7   Jolly, John M. of Mansfield, O., and Fanny S. Nye of Putnam by Rev.
               A. Kingsbury, Putnam Presbyterian Church, Muskingum Co.

1817 Mar 6   Jolly, Kenze and Elizabeth Dickerson by David Smithers, Washington
               Co.

1816 Apr 11   Jolly, Liddy and Vachel Dickerson by Anth'y Sheets, JP, Washington
               Co.

1800 May 8   Jolly, Mary and Daniel Mulford by Alvin Bingham, Washington Co.

1805 Apr 25   Jolly, William and Elizabeth Cating by J. Gardner, JP, Ross Co.

1817 Dec 4   Jolly, William and Cynthia Martin by Rev. David Smithers, Washington
               Co.

1813 May 6   Jones, Abram and Matilda Newell by Simon Cochran, JP, Franklin Co.

1838 Jul 26   Jones, Alvina and Samuel Swan, St. Luke's Church, Granville,
               Licking Co.

1824 Dec 13   Jones, Ann and Luk Hammon by David A. Tanner, JP, Marion Co.

1799 Nov 13   Jones, Betsey and Ezra Chapman by Thos. Stanley, Washington Co.

1878 Apr 17   Jones, Catherine O. and John W. Fischer by Rev. John Boyd, St.
               Luke's Church, Marietta, Washington Co.

1805 Jan 1   Jones, Caty and John Hines by Samuel Smith, Ross Co.

1805 Dec 19   Jones, David and Mary McDowel by James Marshall, JP, Franklin Co.

1806 Sep 18   Jones, David and Mary Simmons by James Marshall, JP, Franklin Co.

1807 1 mo 15   Jones, Dorkis and Samuel Davis, Miami Monthly Meeting, Warren Co.

1819 Oct 6   Jones, Eleanor and Henry Goodrich by Joseph Thrap, MG, Licking Co.

1806 5 mo 15   Jones, Elisha and Susania Hollingsworth, Miami Monthly Meeting,
               Warren Co.

1804 Jun 7   Jones, Elizabeth and John Jones by James Marshall, JP, Franklin Co.

1815 Jun 17   Jones, Elizabeth and William Frost by J.T. Thrap - Stephan McDougal,
               Licking Co.

1828 Sep 27   Jones, Elizabeth and Daniel Piper by I.N. Walter, ECC, Franklin Co.

1864 Nov 3   Jones, Ellen Rush and John J. Williams by Rt. Rev. G.T. Bedell,
               St. Paul's Church, Marion, Marion Co.

1807 Jan 29   Jones, Ellis and Jane McDowell by Asa Shinn, MG, Franklin Co.

1815 Mar 13   Jones, Erasmas and Rachel Clark by John Green, Preacher, Licking Co.

1827 5 mo 2   Jones, Esther and Asher Brown, Miami Monthly Meeting, Warren Co.

1808 Dec 13   Jones, Francis and Sarah Hunter by James Marshall, Franklin Co.

1821 Apr 19   Jones, Harvey and Phebe Pierson by James Cunningham, Licking Co.

1815 11 mo 1   Jones, Isaac E. and Rachel Bateman, Miami Monthly Meeting, Warren Co.

1833 Jun 6   Jones, J.G. and Cinthia Kilbourn by Rev. E. Burr, St. John's Church,
               Worthington, Franklin Co.

1804 Jul 1   Jones, Jacob (or Joab) and Polly Kelly by Enoch Shepard, Washington
               Co.

1813 Apr 2   Jones, James and Anna Durbin (license date), Pickaway Co.

1819 Mar 11   Jones, Jeremiah and Hannah Clark by Danl. G. Stanley, JP, Washington
               Co.

1804 Jul 1   Jones, Joab (or Jacob) and Polly Kelly by Enoch Shepard, Washington
               Co.

1815? -- --   Jones, Joab and Lydia White by Jeremiah Greenman, JP, Washington Co.

1804 Jun 7   Jones, John and Elizabeth Jones by James Marshall, JP, Franklin Co.

1818 Sep 9   Jones, John and Harriet Meswey by John C. Smith, JP, Licking Co.

1819 Jul 11   Jones, John and Mehitable Weid by J. Thrap, Licking Co.

1826 Oct 15   Jones, John and Dolly Powers by Henry Matthew, Minister of the ME
               Church, Franklin Co.

1868 Jun 11   Jones, John Paul and Catherine H. Medlicott by Rev. John Boyd,
               St. Luke's Church, Marietta, Washington Co.

1880 Jun 9   Jones, Julia Maria and Gideon White by Rev. John Boyd, St. Luke's
               Church, Marietta, Washington Co.

1818 Apr 16   Jones, Lemuel and Nancy Clark by John Green, MG, Licking Co.

1883 Apr 17   Jones, Mahala and Hervey Hays by Rev. John Boyd, St. Luke's Church,
               Marietta, Washington Co.

1879 Aug 21   Jones, Mrs. Martha and William Quimby by Rev. John Boyd, St. Luke's
               Church, Marietta, Washington Co.

1803 Sep 15   Jones, Mary and Abel Miller by J. Graham, Esq., Washington Co.

1805 Dec 26   Jones, Mary and William Beal by Stephen Linsly, Washington Co.

1825 Aug 25   Jones, Mary and John Sharp by Robert Ward, JP, Jackson Co.

1805 Jun 4   Jones, Patty and Isaac Delany by J. Gardner, JP, Ross Co.

1819 Jul 8   Jones, Phebe and James Dockum, Sr. by J.C. Smith, JP, Licking Co.

1815 Jul 2   Jones, Polly and Russell Davis by Rev. S.P. Robbins, Washington Co.

1816 Jun 27   Jones, Polly and Townley Taylor by Cyrus Ames, JP, Washington Co.

1817 May 15   Jones, Polly and Silas Smith by Wm. Brown, Franklin Co.

1807 11 mo 19 Jones, Rachel and Amos Hawkins, Miami Monthly Meeting, Warren Co.

1797 Sep 28   Jones, Rebecca and Amos Harvey by Josiah Munro, Washington Co.

1805 Mar 1   Jones, Rebecca and William Stonerock by Samuel Smith, Ross Co.

1820 Feb 19   Jones, Rebecca and Anthony Albery by M. Black, JP, Licking Co.

1810 Sep 13   Jones, Robert and Agnes ----- (license date), Pickaway Co.

1818 --- --   Jones, Ruth and Eli Westfall by Jacob Delay, MG, Jackson Co.

1804 Jan 1   Jones, Sally and Daniel Grambel by Samuel Smith, Ross Co.

1816 Aug 2   Jones, Sally and Cotton Mather Thrall by Samuel Bancroft, JP,
               Licking Co.

1819 Apr 15   Jones, Samuel B. and Desdemonia Slaughter by Daniel H. Buell, JP,
               Washington Co.

1818 Apr 2   Jones, Sarah and Reuben Brown by Jere. Brown, JP, Jackson Co.

1828 Apr 24   Jones, Sarah and Loger Grace by Charles Sells, JP, Franklin Co.

1801 May 14   Jones, Thomas and Mary Hanes by Philip Witten, Washington Co.

1812 Jun 11   Jones, Thomas and Doratha Pancake by Arthur O'Harra, Franklin Co.

1817 Dec 7   Jones, Thomas and Elizabeth Burns by Patrick Shearer, JP, Jackson Co.

1820 Dec 20   Jones, Thomas and Elizabeth Thomas by Geo. Evans, MG, Licking Co.

1828 Jan 3   Jones, Thomas and Betsey Whitsell by S. Hamilton, Franklin Co.

1808 Jul 14   Jones, Thomas J. and Lydia Holleburt by E. Putnam, JP, Washington Co.

1828 Apr 10   Jones, Uriah and Mary Ward by Wooley Conrad, Franklin Co.

1817 Jun 5   Jones, Zibra and Flora Everitt by Samuel Bancroft, JP, Licking Co.

1827 Oct 25   Jordan, Elenor and Henry Kious by Wooley Conrad, JP, Franklin Co.

1828 Dec 25   Jordan, Nancy and Benjamin Lee by Hiland Hulburd, Franklin Co.

1809 Jan 13   Jordan, Polly and Robert Alcorn by Wm. Gray, Washington Co.

1808 Mar 24   Jordin, Dickinson and Katharine Dodge by Rob't Oliver, JP,
               Washington Co.

1816 Jan 25   Jordon, William J. and Elizabeth Husher by Uriah Hull, JP, Licking Co.

1884 May 8   Josselyn, Mattie A. of Putnam and John N. Palmer, Jr., of Zanesville,
               by Rev. George F. Moore, Putnam Presbyterian Church, Muskingum
               Co.

1887 Oct 25   Josselyn, Nannie B. of Zanesville and Robert L. Lotz of Watertown,
               Dak., by Rev. George F. Moore, Putnam Presbyterian Church,
               Muskingum Co.

1820 Mar 22   Judd, Milly and William Ockerman by John Russell, Washington Co.

1886 May 19   Judkins, Sarah M. of Woodsfield, O., and William C. Danford of
               St. Clairsville, O., by Rev. George F. Moore, Putnam
               Presbyterian Church, Muskingum Co.

1848 Dec 24   Jump, Sally Ann and Richard M. Dodge by Rev. D.W. Tolford, St.
               Luke's Church, Marietta, Washington Co.

1818 Oct 15   Junes, Joseph and Kaziah Gaimin by Percival Adams, Franklin Co.

1814 Feb 3   Jurdon, John and Hannah Brown by Levi Shinn, Licking Co.

1803 May 5   Jurdon, Peggy and Clark Parker by Jesse Phelps, JP, Trumbull Co.

1825 Jul 21   Jurey, Rachel and Moses E. Messenger by John Green, JP, Marion Co.

1813 Apr 22   Justice, Daniel and Nancy Young by Arthur O'Harra, Franklin Co.

1813 Jul 24   Justice, Daniel and Caty Baugh (license date), Pickaway Co.

1827 Jul 12   Justice, Jane and Marcus Millington by Tracy Willcox, JP, Franklin
               Co.

1812 Jul 30   Justice, Jesse and Sarah Teeters (license date), Pickaway Co.

1813 Jan 30   Justice, Jesse and Caty Bowsher (license date), Pickaway Co.

1816 Feb 29   Justice (or Gustice), John and Betsy Fulk by Michael Patton,
               Franklin Co.

1819 Jul 29   Justice, Moor and Polly Heriff by Joseph Grate, Franklin Co.

1820 Jan 18   Justice, Nancy and John Brown by Joseph Grate, Franklin Co.

1827 Jun 24   Justice, Polly and Thomas West by Geo. Jefferies, MG, Franklin Co.

1810 Sep 21   Justice, Rachel and Solomon Finch (license date), Pickaway Co.

1823 Dec 31   Justice, Robert Jr. and Eley Benedict by Aristochus Walker, Franklin
               Co.

1812 Jan 9   Justice, Susana and Jeremiah Bloxon (license date), Pickaway Co.

1826 Mar 16   Justice, Thomas and Lucy Maynard by Tracy Willcox, JP, Franklin Co.

1810 Jan 16   Kain, Polly and Robert Rupell by James Hoge, Franklin Co.

1826 Jan 19   Kain, Rebecca and George Wilcox by Henry Matthews, Franklin Co.

1826 Nov 2   Kain, Thomas T. and Hannah Boyd by R.C. Rabb, MG, Franklin Co.

1828 Mar 15   Kalb, Margaret and Jonathan Rose by I. Gander, Franklin Co.

1888? -- --   Kappes, Clara E. and Edward Ayers both of Zanesville by Rev. George
               F. Moore, Putnam Presbyterian Church, Muskingum Co.

1819 Mar 20   Karson, Denis and Elizabeth Barden by Elihu Bigelow, JP, Licking Co.

1818 May 11   Karson, Hannah and Elihu Bigelow by Geo. Hoover, JP, Licking Co.

1800 Nov 7   Kazy, Wm. and Nancy Harden by J. Munro, Washington Co.

1853 Oct 9   Kearns, Samuel F. of Harrison Co., Va., and Julia A. McIntosh by Rev.
              John Boyd, St. Luke's Church, Marietta, Washington Co.

1814 Aug 30   Keath, Catharine and Nathan Newton by Thos. Seely, Esq., Washington
              Co.

1814 Dec 6   Keath, Elizabeth and Joseph Shirley by Thomas Seely, Washington Co.

1806 Nov 19   Keating, Elizabeth and Thomas Haley by S. Lindsly, Washington Co.

1803 Jul 3   Keating, John and Eunice Beebe by Daniel Story, Clerk, Washington Co.

1820 Jan 22   Keaton, Polly and Johnson Bonham by John Johnson, JP, Licking Co.

1822 Dec 5   Keesner, Sufey and John Greer by Percival Adams, Franklin Co.

1822 Mar 31   Keirns, Catharine and George Hutchinson by Bial Stedman, JP,
              Washington Co.

1815 Aug 8   Keith, Adam and Elizabeth Shirley by Obadiah Scott, JP, Washington Co.

1818 Jul 2   Keith, Peter and Betsey Shockley by Wm. Rand, Washington Co.

1820 Feb 17   Keith, Polly and Israel Burns by John Green, JP, Washington Co.

1799 Sep 24   Keller, Betsey and Thomas Scott by J. Munro, Washington Co.

1826 Jul 27   Keller, Eliza and Thomas Manning by C. Henkel, Franklin Co.

1823 Dec 31   Keller, Elizabeth and Jesse Pancake by Jacob Grubb, Franklin Co.

1803 Oct 26   Keller, George and Betsey Lettell by John G. McCan, Ross Co.

1816 Apr 25   Keller, Isaac and Elizabeth Goldsmith by Simon Merwin, Washington Co.

1819 --- --   Keller, Jacob and Polly Ball by Joseph Grate, Franklin Co.

1822 Oct 1   Keller, Margret and William Read by Jacob Grubb, Franklin Co.

1824 Sep 9   Keller, Mary and Wm. Gorden by David W. Walter, JP, Jackson Co.

1800 Feb 13   Keller, Rachel and Jeremiah Riggs by Josiah Munro, JP, Washington Co.

1825 Aug 18   Keller, Zenas and Mary McDowell by Samuel McDowell, JP, Jackson Co.

1847 Jan 7   Kelley, Chancey R. of New York City and Sarah E. Guthrie of Putnam by
              Rev. A. Kingsbury, Putnam Presbyterian Church, Muskingum Co.

1813 Apr 20   Kelley, Hannah and James Reed (license date), Pickaway Co.

1826 Oct 1   Kelley, James and Elizabeth Manning by Reuben Golliday, Franklin Co.

1811 Jan 17   Kelley, Joseph and Cynthia Flagg by Stephen Lindsly, Washington Co.

1813 Oct 22   Kelley, William and Fanny Cady by Dan'l H. Buell, JP, Washington Co.

1834 Jul 27   Kellogg, Burr and Juliet Andrews by Rev. E. Burr, St. John's Church,
              Worthington, Franklin Co.

1825 Sep 8   Kellogg, David and Amelia Eaton by Conrad Roth, JP, Marion Co.

1803 Apr 3   Kellogg, Laura and Jotham Atwater both of Hudson by David Hudson,
              JP, Trumbull Co.

1804 Mar 22   Kelly, Andrew and Ann Cating by John Odle, JP, Ross Co.

1801 Feb 17   Kelly, George and Nancy Williams by Robert Safford, Washington Co.

1805 Feb 7   Kelly, James and Nancy Hanson by Stephen Lindly, Washington Co.

1805 Feb 24   Kelly, John and Nelly Kelly by Enoch Shepard, Washington Co.

---- Dec 16   Kelly, Margaret and Sam'l Baker, Jr. by Robert Oliver, Washington Co.

1814 6 mo 1   Kelly, Mary and Andrew Whitacre, Miami Monthly Meeting, Warren Co.

1806 --- --   Kelly, Mathew and Nancy Cahoon by John Robins, Ross Co.

1824 11 mo 3   Kelly, Moses and Abigail Satterthwaite, Miami Monthly Meeting,
               Warren Co.

1811 Mar 10   Kelly, Nancy and Hugh Flannaghan by Dudley Davis, Washington Co.

1805 Feb 24   Kelly, Nelly and John Kelly by Enoch Shepard, Washington Co.

1804 Jul 1   Kelly, Polly and Jacob (or Joab) Jones by Enoch Shepard, Washington
               Co.

1826 Jul 13   Kelsel (or Kelzel), Philip and Barbary Kissinger by C. Henkel,
               Franklin Co.

1819 May 27   Kelso, Ann and Irandus Saunders by Simeon Overturf, JP, Licking Co.

1812 Sep 12   Kelso, Eleanor and William Paine by Peter Pence, JP, Licking Co.

1813 Sep 8   Kelso, Ellen and William Payne by P. Pence, JP, Licking Co.

1813 Apr 7   Kelso, Henry and Sarah Payne by P. Pence, JP, Licking Co.

1813 Sep 29   Kelso, Mary and John Abrahams by -----, Licking Co.

1826 Dec 28   Kelso, Robert S. and Ann Rose by A. Allison, JP, Franklin Co.

1818 Nov 16   Kelso, Thomas and Lucinda Kindal by Wm. Hall, JP, Licking Co.

1826 Jul 13   Kelzel (or Kelsel), Philip and Barbary Kissinger by C. Henkel,
               Franklin Co.

1801 Jan 27   Kemly, James and Nancy Taylor Johnson by Robt. Safford, Washington
               Co.

1825 Jun 30   Kenaday, Elizabeth, widow, and John Ayle, widower, by Jacob Gundy,
               JP, Franklin Co.

1825 Aug 18   Kendall, Catharine and Jesse Essex by Wm. Long, JP, Franklin Co.

1824 Feb 5   Kendall, Lucinda and David King by B. Bull, Franklin Co.

1864 Oct 24   Kendrick, Frances M. and Joseph Dyar of Rainbow by Rev. John Boyd,
               St. Luke's Church, Marietta, Washington Co.

1805 Aug 1   Kenedy, Rachel and Jacob Little by Peter Jackson, JP, Ross Co.

1806 May 3   Kenion, Robert and Betsy Rily by L. Barber, Washington Co.

1814 Jun 19   Kenion, Sally, alias Sally Richardson, and Amariah Treat by Jos.
               Gordon, JP, Franklin Co.

1791 Sep 26   Kenne, Nathan and Mary Willson by Benj. Tupper, Washington Co.

1866 Oct 3   Kennedy, Boyd and Ellen D. Prince by Rev. John Boyd, St. Luke's
               Church, Marietta, Washington Co.

1805 Sep 24   Kennedy, Nancy and Jacob Hinkle by Wm. Creighton, Ross Co.

1825 Jan 25   Kensler, John and Sarah Longwell by Wm. T. Martin, JP, Franklin Co.

1826 Oct 10   Kensel, Mathias and Sarah Watkins by C. Henkel, Franklin Co.

1820 Jan 20   Kent, Harriet and William Hutchinson by Joseph Palmer, JP, Washington
               Co.

1816 Jun 25   Kent, James and Anney Dearduff by Alex. Bassett, Franklin Co.

1821 May 31   Kent, Sally and Simeon P. Nott by Thomas White, JP, Washington Co.

1825 Nov 29   Kent, Sally and David Tipton, Marion Co.

1815 Jan 12   Kepler, Abram and Sally Woolcut, Franklin Co.

1807 Apr 9   Kepler, Caty and Robert Boyd by Josiah McKinney, Franklin Co.

1814 Sep 8   Kergan, John and Sarah Hursey by J.W. Patterson, JP, Licking Co.

1803 Jan 30   Kerker, Daniel and Eve Coonrod of Cleveland by James Kingsbury, JP,
               Trumbull Co.

1806 Feb 26   Kerr, Catharine and James Mahon by John McDonald, JP, Ross Co.

1813 May 25   Kerr, Elizabeth and Samuel Johnson (license date), Pickaway Co.

1793 Jan 10   Kerr, Hamilton and Suekey Nyghswonger by J. Gilman, Washington Co.

1823 Apr 17   Kerr, Jane and Thomas Lewis by Reuben Golliday, Franklin Co.

1804 Dec 6   Kerr, John and Sally Chenoweth by Arthur Chenoweth, JP, Ross Co.

1821 Feb 7   Kerr, Mariah and Benjamin Becket by Reuben Golliday, Franklin Co.

1827 Apr 17   Kerr, Mary and Elijah Ellis by James Hoge, Franklin Co.

1810 Aug 2   Kerr, Peggy and William Bowen (license date), Pickaway Co.

1826 Oct 29   Kerr, Polly and Stephen Robinson by H. Matthews, Franklin Co.

1804 Aug 30   Kerr, Rachel and James Cochran by W. Robinson, Ross Co.

1822 Feb 10   Kerr, Robert and Susanna McMullan by N. Little, Franklin Co.

1814 Dec 17   Kersey, Rachel and Isaac Conner by Z. Carlisle, JP, Licking Co.

1823 11 mo 6   Kersey, Thomas and Letitia Craig, Miami Monthly Meeting, Warren Co.

1824 Oct 5   Kesler, Joseph and Elezabeth Casner by Wm. Godman, JP, Franklin Co.

1825 Oct 20   Kesller, James and Christiana Thomas by Percival Adams, JP, Franklin
               Co.

1824 May 10   Kesnor, Naome, dau. of Michael Kesnor, and Moses Meeker by Wm. C.
               Duff, JP, Franklin Co.

1825 Aug 17   Ketcham, Polly and Elihu Dawd by John Green, JP, Marion Co.

1824 May 7   Ketchum, Lydia and Seldon Field (license date), Marion Co.

1813 Dec 16   Keys, Horatio and Francis Maupen (license date), Pickaway Co.

1812 May 7   Keys, Isaac and Betsey Hess by James Hoge, Franklin Co.

1819 Jul 13   Keyton, Wm. and Sophia Jeffreys by Rob't G. Hanna, JP, Jackson Co.

1820 --- --   Kiass, Katharine and George Hoover by Joseph Grate, Franklin Co.

1817 Aug 28   Kidd, Isaac and Kaziah Roberts by Simon Merwin, Washington Co.

1813 Feb 4   Kidd, Thomas and Martha Hill by Rev. Jas. Cunningham, Washington Co.

1808 Dec 15   Kidd, William and Anna Haywood by Thos. Seely, JP, Washington Co.

1819 Jan 26   Kidder, Gideon and Susanna Spears by Dudley Davis, JP, Washington Co.

1818 Dec 8   Kierns, John and Mary Ellinwood by Rev. Saml. Hamilton, Deacon,
               Washington Co.

1827 Dec 25   Kilbourn, Byron and Mary H. Cowles by Marcus T.C. Wing, Franklin Co.

1833 Jun 6   Kilbourn, Cinthia and J.G. Jones by Rev. E. Burr, St. John's Church,
               Worthington, Franklin Co.

1819 Dec 7   Kilbourn, Hezekiah and Hannah Hayes by George Evans, MG, Licking Co.

1808 Jun 5   Kilbourn, James and Cynthia Barns by Alex. Morrison, Jr., Franklin
               Co.

1808 Feb 18   Kilbourn, Josiah and Fanny Brown by James Marshall, Franklin Co.

1818 Sep 27   Kilbourn, Lawra and Renssalaer Cowles by Rev. Philander Chase,
               Franklin Co.

1825 Jun 11   Kilbourn, Matilda and Samuel Davis by Charles Sells, JP, Franklin Co.

1822 Oct 31   Kilbourn, Wm. and Matilda Sells by Nathan Emery, Franklin Co.

1818 Feb 5   Kile, Elizabeth and John Evans by Emmor Cox, Franklin Co.

1815 Jan 12   Kile, Enoch and Ruth Crum by Shadrach Cole, JP, Pickaway Co.

1807 Sep 10   Kile, Hannah and Stephen Thomas by Arthur O'Harra, Franklin Co.

1827 Jul 30   Kile, I.A. and S.A. Winterstein by John Long, Franklin Co.

1823 Apr 20   Kile, Nancy and Archibald C. Needles by Richard Courtright, Franklin
               Co.

1809 Mar 30   Kile (or Hile), Polly and Wm. Sennett by Arthur O'Harra, Franklin Co.

1823 Aug 10   Kile, Sarah and Jacob McLene by Richard Courtright, Franklin Co.

1799 Oct 3   Kilgor, Mathew Lasley and Elizabeth Armstrong by Robert Safford,
               Washington Co.

1822 Dec 19   Kilgore, Betsey and Charles Pettet by James Hoge, Franklin Co.

1804 Apr 15   Kilgore, James and Anna Holton by Noble Crawford, Ross Co.

1809 Oct 26   Kilgore, Jenny and Thomas Patterson by Michael Dickey, Franklin Co.

1809 --- 19   Kilgore, Margaret and Silas Springer by Michael Dickey (signed by
               justice 1 Nov. 1809, recorded 27 Feb. 1810), Franklin Co.

1826 Oct 6   Kilgore, Margaret R. and Archibald Cooper by James Hoge, Franklin Co.

1821 Feb 6   Kilgore, Mary and George White by James Hoge, Franklin Co.

1826 Nov 26   Killpatrick, Jane and Robert Boyd by Amaziah Hutchinson, Franklin Co.

1822 Sep 16   Kilpatrick, Eliza and James Orr by Reuben Golliday, Franklin Co.

1815 Feb 23   Kilpatrick, James and Jane Porter by Alex. Rowen, JP, Pickaway Co.

1811 May 17   Kimble, John and Nancy Riler (license date), Pickaway Co.

1825 Apr 14   Kimble, Rebbecca and Joseph McComb by Conrad Roth, JP, Marion Co.

1825 Apr 10   Kimble, Sarah and Dexter Baker by Conrad Roth, JP, Marion Co.

1804 Aug 16   Kimble, Susannah and David Martin by Wm. Bennett, JP, Franklin Co.

1827 Sep 5   Kimmons, Hansod and Lucy Laws by Jason Bull, Franklin Co.

1827 Sep 20   Kimmons, Nancy and Henry Knight by Jacob Gundy, JP, Franklin Co.

1826 Jan 5   Kimmons, Polly and John Winser by Jacob Gundy, JP, Franklin Co.

1826 Feb 23   Kimmons, William and Nancy Bivans by Jacob Gundy, Franklin Co.

1820 Dec 22   Kindal, Jermiah and Polly White by Wm. Hull, JP, Licking Co.

1818 Nov 16   Kindal, Lucinda and Thomas Kelso by Wm. Hall, JP, Licking Co.

1812 Oct 5   Kindall, Nancy and Abel Johnson by John G. Johnson, Franklin Co.

1818 Dec 24   Kindle, Jane and Henry Feasel by George Hays, Franklin Co.

1826 11 mo 1   Kindley, Dinah and Seth Thomas, Miami Monthly Meeting, Warren Co.

1822 6 mo 12   Kindley, Mary and Cornelius Ratliff, Miami Monthly Meeting, Warren Co.

1810 8 mo 1   Kindley, Rebekah and Samuel Harvey, Miami Monthly Meeting, Warren Co.

1820 Nov 30   King, Agnes and Thomas Fulton by Rob't Wallace, Minister, Licking Co.

1800 Mar 20   King, Anne and Patrick McGarvey by Robert Safford, JP, Washington Co.

1824 Feb 5   King, David and Lucinda Kendall by B. Bull, Franklin Co.

1820 May 17   King, Elizabeth and William Moore, by J. Cunningham, VDM, Licking Co.

1806 Feb 9   King, Freeman and Easten Smith by Peter Jackson, JP, Ross Co.

1821 Jul 22   King, Jacob and Huldy Drake by John F. Solomon, Franklin Co.

1862 Jul 24   King, John S. of Orange, N.J., and Amelia Guthrie of Putnam by Rev.
               A. Kingsbury, Putnam Presbyterian Church, Muskingum Co.

1827 Jul 5   King, Mariah and Hanson Johnson by S. Hamilton, Elder in the MEC,
               Franklin Co.

1826 Apr 6   King, Mary and Gorge P. Truil by John F. Solomon, Franklin Co.

1804 Sep 6   King, Nicy and John Brown by James Marshall, JP, Franklin Co.

1815 Sep 23   King, Pompey and Sally Stonemia by J. Cunningham, Licking Co.

1828 Mar 23   King, Samuel and Mahala James by A. Allison, Franklin Co.

1827 Aug 16   King, Sophia and George Bricker by W.T. Martin, JP, Franklin Co.

1811 Jun 11   King, William and Johanna Burkey by James Marshall, Franklin Co.

1805 Apr 29   Kingam, Grace and John Momson by Arthur Chinworth, JP, Ross Co.

1821 Feb 8   Kingrey, David and Selinah Emrey by Samuel Dyer, Franklin Co.

1862 Sep 11   Kingsbury, Harlan P. and Mary E. Haver by Rev. A. Kingsbury,
               Putnam Presbyterian Church, Muskingum Co.

1866 Jan 18   Kingsbury, J. Addison and Sarah E. Shipman by Rev. A. Kingsbury,
               Putnam Presbyterian Church, Muskingum Co.

1805 May 23   Kinkead, Elizabeth and Jno. Stewart by Wm. Davis, JP, Ross Co.

1817 May 1   Kinneman, Samuel and Mary Cloud by John Spencer, JP, Licking Co.

1821 Jan 25   Kinner, Eliza and Joseph Prosser by Eli C. King, Franklin Co.

1828 Mar 13   Kinner, Hanner and Francis Allberry by A. Allison, Franklin Co.

1816 Apr 12   Kinner, Sally and Saml. Hamilton by James Marshall, Franklin Co.

1820 May 18   Kinney, Abigail and Stephen Allison by Amos Wilson, JP, Washington Co.

1820 Jul 19   Kinney, James and Catherine Grove by Iesias Ewing, JP, Licking Co.

1814 Sep 1   Kinney, John and Betsey Southard by Chas. Cade, JP, Pickaway Co.

1819 Feb 3   Kinney, Sally D. and Wirum Bartlett by John Gree, JP, Washington Co.

1816 Jul 25   Kinnison, Elizabeth and Elisha Vernam by John Brown, JP, Jackson Co.

1816 Jun 4   Kinsal (or Kinsale or Kinsel), John and Polly Pear by Percival Adams,
               Franklin Co.

1816 Jun 4   Kinsale (or Kinsal or Kinsel), John and Polly Pear by Percival Adams,
               Franklin Co.

1816 Jun 4   Kinsel (or Kinsale or Kinsal), John and Polly Pear by Percival Adams,
               Franklin Co.

1805 Aug 4   Kinser, George and Jane Glove by David Shelby, JP, Ross Co.

1810 Apr 26   Kinser, George and Dullene Turness, Pickaway Co.

1822 Mar 14   Kinzey, David and Elizabeth Hase by Moses Williamson, JP, Washington
               Co.

1827 Oct 25   Kious, Henry and Elenor Jordan by Wooley Conrad, JP, Franklin Co.

1822 Aug 23   Kious, Solomon and Margaret Coonrad by Wm. C. Duff, Franklin Co.

1819 Mar 25   Kipple, Mary and John Taylor by Dudley Davis, Washington Co.

1815 Aug 29   Kirk, James and Electe Coe by Michael Patton, Franklin Co.

1804 Mar 22   Kirk, Mary of Scioto Tp. and Wm. Vance of Scioto Tp. by Wm. Creigh-
               ton, Ross Co.

1819 Nov 4   Kirkpatrick, Hannah and David Moore by James Cunningham, MD, Licking
               Co.

1801 Feb 9   Kirkpatrick, James and Susanna Munro by Josiah Munro, Washington Co.

1820 Mar 20   Kirkpatrick, Mary and James McCredy by James Cunningham, VDM,
               Licking Co.

1820 Feb 14   Kirkpatrick, Peter and Margaret McCune by James Cunningham, Licking
               Co.

1826 Sep 7   Kisner, Nocholas and Malinda Stotts by C. Hinkel, Franklin Co.

1818 Oct 15   Kisow, Catherine and John Rusel by Michael Trout, JP, Licking Co.

1826 Jul 13   Kissinger, Barbary and Philip Kelsel (or Kelzel) by C. Henkel,
               Franklin Co.

1816 Dec 19   Kissingar, Catherine and Reuben Statz by Percival Adams, JP, Franklin
               Co.

1825 Dec 1   Kissinger, John and Catharine Denoon by C. Hinkel, Franklin Co.

1816 Sep 26   Kiswell, Betsey and James Unckles (or Uncles) by James Hoge,
               Franklin Co.

1805 May 14   Kite, John and Catharine Gunday by Wm. Robinson, Ross Co.

1824 Feb 26   Kizler, John and Susannah Robbins by Abraham Williams, JP, Franklin
               Co.

1817 Jan 30   Kleiver, Mathias and Elizabeth Neibarger by J.D. Baird, Licking Co.

1811 Sep 24   Kler (Klir?), John and ----- by Z. Carlisle, JP, Licking Co.

1813 Oct 24   Kline, Jacob and Catherine Ludwig (license date), Pickaway Co.

1825 May 31   Kline, John and Sally Thorn (license date), Marion Co.

1811 Sep 24   Klir (Kler?), John and ----- by Z. Carlisle, JP, Licking Co.

1814 Feb 4   Knapp, Artemas and Frances Tucker by John Green, JP, Washington Co.

1821 --- --   Knapp, Eliza and James D. Farnsworth by James W. Booth, JP, Washington Co.

1809 Apr 12   Knight, Curtice and Hannah Davis by Philip Whitten, Washington Co.

1811 Oct 17   Knight, Elizabeth and Daniel Bowen by Philip Witten, Washington Co.

1827 Sep 20   Knight, Henry and Nancy Kimmons by Jacob Gundy, JP, Franklin Co.

1815 Feb 2   Knight, James and Polly Stevenson by Henry Coonrod, JP, Pickaway Co.

1814 Dec 28   Knight, Rena and Azubah Deckcon by Dan Case, JP, Franklin Co.

1809 Jan 15   Knight, Welthy and Samuel Gamble by Edwin Putnam, Washington Co.

1814 Jul 27   Knight, Wm. and Polly Gluhard by Abm. Christ, JP, Pickaway Co.

1827 Dec 25   Knoder, Charles and Elcy Brickell by W.T. Martin, Franklin Co.

1811 Nov 16   Knowles, Amos and Mary Porter by Daniel Goodno, JP, Washington Co.

1812 Jun 24   Knowles, Esther and Stan Eleazer Curtis by Dan'l Goodno, JP, Washington Co.

1815 Mar 19   Knowles, Samuel and Clarissa Curtis by Stephen Guthrie, JP, Washington Co.

1808 Sep 8   Knowlton, Daniel and Ruth Holdren by L. Dana, Washington Co.

1853 Oct 17   Knox, John and Mary Jane Hatch by Rev. A. Kingsbury, Putnam Presbyterian Church, Muskingum Co.

1813 Sep 16   Knox, Titus and Peggam Sinnet by Rev. T. Harris, Licking Co.

1826 Oct 24   Kolb, Mary and Sameel Hooper by Wm. Patterson, JP, Franklin Co.

1821 Apr 30   Kooken, Henry and Elizabeth Brotherton by James Hoge, Franklin Co.

1818 Dec 8   Kooken, Mary and Robert Brotherton by James Hoge, Franklin Co.

1813 Dec 16   Koonce, Rachel and John Helwig (license date), Pickaway Co.

1863 Sep 16   Koons, Frances Adelaide and Wm. D. Whips by Rev. H.H. Messenger (in presence of Wm. Koons, father of bride, Mrs. Koons, Mr. and Mrs. Green and others), St. Paul's Church, Marion, Marion Co.

1870 Nov 3   Koontz, Clara and George W. Coon by Rev. A. Kingsbury, Putnam Presbyterian Church, Muskingum Co.

1828 May 22   Kraner, Eleanor and Elisha Dildine by Charles Rarrey, ME Church, Franklin Co.

1813 Feb 18   Kreiger, George and Cynthia Bartholomew by J.W. Patterson, Licking Co.

1819 Feb 28   Krewson, Bunas and Lydia Pain by Wm. Woodford, JP, Washington Co.

1825 May 26   Krist, Mary and Massie Clymer by John Davis, JP, Franklin Co

1812 Sep 13   Kuder, Robert and Elizabeth Dilman (license date), Pickaway Co.

1821 Jun 7   Kyger, John and Mary Sheets by David Smithers, MMEC, Washington Co.

1810 Jul 31   Kyle, John and Susana Van Meter (license date), Pickaway Co.

1816 Aug 13   Kyrk, David and Hester Clark by Isaac Case, Franklin Co.

1827 Mar 15   Kyrk, Mahala and Lovett Evans by Tracy Willcox, JP, Franklin Co.

1871 Oct 11   Lacey, Martin L. of West Auburn, Pa. and Elizabeth Tupper by Rev.
              A. Kingsbury, Putnam Presbyterian Church, Muskingum Co.

1803 Jun 2   Lackey, James and Nancy Speed by J. Graham, Washington Co.

1798 May 16   Lackey, Samuel and Huldah Wright by Josiah Munro, Washington Co.

1805 Oct 24   Lad, Lucy and Frederick Mitchell by Wm. Creighton, Ross Co.

1794 Mar 30   Laferte, Creatus and Lydia McIntire by J.G. Petitt, Washington Co.

1807 Mar 10   Lafferty, James and Margaret Guffy by Wm. Bennett, JP, Franklin Co.

1806 Jan 17   Lafferty, Mary and David Lambert by Wm. Bennett, JP, Franklin Co.

1820 May 4   Laflin, Lyman and Ruth Chapman by John D. Chamberlain, JP, Washing-
              ton Co.

1798 Sep 18   LaForge, Maria Gabriel and Francis Valodin by Robert Safford,
              Washington Co.

1818 Aug 16   Lagor, Peter and Sally Nichols by James M. Booth, JP, Washington Co.

1815 Feb 11   Laid, Catherine and Reason Cruch by Noah Fidler, Licking Co.

1798 May 17   Lake, Andrew and Elizabeth Goss by Josiah Munro, Washington Co.

1818 Dec 28   Lake, Cornelius and Amanda Castle by Stephen Guthrie, Washington Co.

1819 Feb 18   Lake, Elijah and Lucy Laviston by J. Johnston, JPHT, Licking Co.

1805 Jan 23   Lake, John and Betsy Mathews by Enoch Wing, JP, Washington Co.

1820 Apr 27   Lake, Margaret and Samuel Varner by Abraham Lippet, Washington Co.

1820 Jan 18   Lake, Silas and Eliza Schellenger by Vincent Southard, JP, Jackson Co.

1819 Nov 12   Lake, Vincent and Rachel Lott by John W. Patterson, MG, Licking Co.

1794 Jan 31   LaLance, Katherine and Robert Warth by J. Gilman, Washington Co.

1799 Jan 4   Lalance, Peter and Catherine Rouse by Josiah Munro, Washington Co.

1816 Apr 7   Lamb, Benjamin and Mary Tucker by John Russell, JP, Washington Co.

1811 Sep 26   Lamb, John and Margarite Reed (license date), Pickaway Co.

1806 Feb 25   Lamb, Maxwell and Susannah Hollyday by Robert B. Dobbins, VDM,
              Ross Co.

1805 May 6   Lamb, Ruben and Mary Sloper by Ezekiel Brown, JP, Franklin Co.

1807 Sep 13   Lamb, Reuben and Scynthia Sloper by Thomas Brown, JP, Franklin Co.

1806 Jan 17   Lambert, David and Mary Lafferty by Wm. Bennett, JP, Franklin Co.

1807 Jul 21   Lambert, Elizabeth and John Dixon by Wm. Irwin, JP, Franklin Co.

1809 May 2   Lambert, Isaac and Julian Martin by Arthur O'Harra, Franklin Co.

1828 Dec 13   Lambert, Rebeca and Frederick Spangler by John F. Solomon, Franklin
               Co.

1826 Sep 3   Lamphair, Roxann and John Wise by John H. Power, Minister of the
               Gospel in Methodist E. Church, Franklin Co.

1818 Dec 12   Lampson, Amarilla and George W. Case by Rev. T. Harris, Licking Co.

1826 Apr 11   Lampson, Mariah S. and James K. Corey by James Hoge, Franklin Co.

1826 Jan 15   Lampson, William K. and Sally Jeffords by P. Chase, Franklin Co.

1805 Jan 3   Lance, Catharine and Godfry Wilkins by John Davidson, Ross Co.

1821 Jan 15   Lance?, Martha and David Duke by J. Cunningham, Licking Co.

1855 Jul 3   Land, Thomas and Margaret Marshall by T. Corlett, St. Luke's Church,
               Granville, Licking Co.

1810 Jan 4   Landes, Catharine and Benjamin Huff by David Spangler, JP, Franklin
               Co.

1817 Apr 3   Lanids, Elizabeth and Peter Stimmel by Percival Adams, Franklin Co.

1814 Apr 7   Landis, Susanna and Luther Hayes by Wm. D. Hendren, Franklin Co.

1805 Oct 10   Lane, Dennis and Elizabeth Harris by Thos. Hicks, Ross Co.

1821 Aug 30   Lane, Elizabeth and Hiram M. Curry by C. Henkel, Franklin Co.

1816 Apr 11   Lane, Hannah and George Highbargen by Thos. White, Washington Co.

1824 Dec 9   Lane, James and Tirzah Fenniken by James Hoge, Franklin Co.

1814 Mar 5   Lane, Jamima and Archibald McCullum by Thos. White, JP, Washington Co.

1809 May 6   Lane, Rachael and Lorin (Levin?) Gibson by Jonathan Minshall,
               Franklin Co.

1817 Jan 1   Lane, Rhoda and Graven R. Nott by P. White, JP, Washington Co.

1821 Oct 18   Lane, Sally and Alfred Ellis by Rev. Wm. Davis, Washington Co.

1797 Sep 17   Lane, Thomas and Mary Doubleday by Josiah Munro, Washington Co.

1820 Nov 19   Lang, James and Elsa Boggs by Rob't G. Hanna, JP, Jackson Co.

1818 Jan 29   Lang, Joel and Jane Boggs by Robert G. Hanna, JP, Jackson Co.

1819 Jul 29   Lang, Martha and Joshua Scurlock by Rob't G. Hanna, JP, Jackson Co.

1799 Mar 10   Langford, Dudley and Rebecca Staats by D. Loring, Washington Co.

1863 Jun 17   Langley, Henry M. of Zanesville and Harriet M. Eveleigh by Rev. John
               Boyd, St. Luke's Church, Marietta, Washington Co.

1823 Sep 25   Laning, Nicholas E. and Elizabeth Barnett by Nathan Emery, Elder in
               M.E. Ch., Franklin Co.

1817 Feb 5   Lannel, Pindoles and Lucretia Bancroft by Rev. T. Harris, Licking Co.

1824 Feb 19   Lanning, Huldy and Daniel Raimer by Charles Waddell, Franklin Co.

1818 Nov 26   Lansdown, Betsey and James Patterson by Eli C. King, Franklin Co.

1871 May 4   Lansom, Morgan and S. Augusta Cary by Rev. A. Kingsbury, Putnam
               Presbyterian Church, Muskingum Co.

1820 Mar 9   Lanson, Silas and Susanna Skeels by Stephen Maynard, Franklin Co.

1817 Jun 24   Lantis, Mary and Jacob Stimmel by Percival Adams, Franklin Co.

1826 Aug 31   Lantis, Polly and Daniel Stimmel by C. Henkel, Franklin Co.

1826 Sep 14   Lantis, Sarah and David Sloan by C. Henkel, Franklin Co.

1825 Sep 15   Lantiss, Sarah and Joseph Fisher by C. Hinkel, Franklin Co.

1819 May 4   Lantz, Aaron and Leah Claypool by Joseph Lockard, JP, Jackson Co.

1813 Mar 12   Lapirry, Priscilla and William Funston (license date), Pickaway Co.

1820 Aug 30   Larabee, John and Mary Edwards by Uriah Hull, JP, Licking Co.

1845 Oct 8   Large, Hannah A. and John W. Large by Rev. A. Kingsbury, Putnam
               Presbyterian Church, Muskingum Co.

1845 Oct 8   Large, John W. and Hannah A. Large by Rev. A. Kingsbury, Putnam
               Presbyterian Church, Muskingum Co.

1817 Sep 25   Larimore, Thomas and Hannah Young by James Campbell, Licking Co.

1805 Jan 24   Larkings, Christina and Frederick Beacher by John G. McCan, Ross Co.

1810 Dec 25   Larkins, Edward and Elizabeth Buck (license date), Pickaway Co.

1797 Oct 3   Larrow, Jacob and Sally Gardiner by Josiah Munro, Washington Co.

1867 Jan 30   Larzelere, Joseph R., M.D., and Anna E. Palmer by Rev. A. Kingsbury,
               Putnam Presbyterian Church, Muskingum Co.

1809 Oct 3   Lashmutt (DLashmutt), Elias N. and Elizabeth O'Harra by James
               Marshall, Franklin Co.

1848 Jan 8   Lasley, Stewart A. of Springfield, O., and Rachel Ellen Dunlap of
               Putnam by Rev. A. Kingsbury, Putnam Presbyterian Church,
               Muskingum Co.

1821 Aug 14   Latham, William and Keziah Smith by James Hoge, Franklin Co.

1808 May 25   Lathby, John and Dolly Smith by Henry Smith, JP, Licking Co.

1825 Jun 30   Lathmore, John and Fanny Dunnivan by Reuben Golliday, Franklin Co.

1826 May 18   Latimore, Nathan L.L. and Abitha Cooper by John McCan, Franklin Co.

1823 Apr 8   Latta, Martha and Benjamin S. Leach by James Hoge, Franklin Co.

1826 Jan 29   Laughlin, John M. and Olive Johnston by E. Richman, Deacon M.E.
               Church, Franklin Co.

1812 Aug --   Laughry, Edward and Eliz. Green by A. Holden, JP, Licking Co.

1820 Dec 21   Lauhrey, Mary and Isaac Carmical by John Waggonner, JP, Licking Co.

1814 Aug 4   Launes, Margaret and Albert Peppers by Wm. Jones, JP, Pickaway Co.

1801 Jan 3   Laurent, James and Elizabeth Buzelin by Robert Safford, JP,
               Washington Co.

1803 Nov 27   Lavens, Esther and Thomas Sanford by Daniel Story, Clerk, Washington
               Co.

1804 May 10   Lavezby, Jean and George Jamison by W. Robinson, JP, Ross Co.

1819 Feb 18   Laviston, Lucy and Elijah Lake, Licking Co.

1818 Nov 18   Law, May and Joseph Lockard by D. Mitcehll, JP, Jackson Co.

1797 Nov 28   Law, Sarah and Samuel Seamans by Robert Oliver, JP, Washington Co.

1822 Feb 7   Lawrance, Romes and Pamela Gates by Seth Baker, JP, Washington Co.

1821 Feb 15   Lawrence, Dan and Patty Vaughan by Thomas White, JP, Washington Co.

1816 Apr 18   Lawrence, Gideon and Mary Morris by Thomas White, Washington Co.

1811 Jul 7   Lawrence, Hannah and James Legget by Wm. Gray, JP, Washington Co.

1811 Oct 10   Lawrence, Lydia and Abraham Cornish by Wm. Gray, JP, Washington Co.

1821 Apr 14   Lawrence, Lyman and Anna Olney by Thomas White, JP, Washington Co.

1819 Feb 4   Lawrence, Moses Jr. and Elizabeth Walker by Pelatiah White,
               Washington Co.

1813 Jan 14   Lawrence, Olive and Ellery Perry by Joseph Frye, JP, Washington Co.

1819 Nov 4   Lawrence, Rebecca and Dudley W. Davis by Thomas White, JP, Washing-
               ton Co.

1821 Jan 4   Lawrence, Rufus and Rebecca White by John D. Chamberlain, JP,
               Washington Co.

1811 Mar 17   Lawrence, Sarah and John Paine (license date), Pickaway Co.

1818 Dec 31   Lawrence, William and Elizabeth Grubb by Pelatiah White, JP,
               Washington Co.

1827 Sep 5   Laws, Lucy and Hansod Kimmons by Jason Bull, Franklin Co.

1827 Nov 11   Laws, Sally and Moses Ireland by A. Walker, JP, Franklin Co.

1824 Dec 23   Lawson, Eliza and James M. McCutchon by E. Washburn, VDM, Franklin
               Co.

1824 Jun 27   Lawson, Halan and Abraham Jercockes (or Jergcocks) by C. Waddell,
               LM (see note on Jercockes), Franklin Co.

1826 Nov 21   Lawson, James and Elenor G. M'Cutcheon by Gideon W. Hart, JP,
               Franklin Co.

1816 Apr 9   Lawson, John and Mary Stump by Thomas White, JP, Washington Co.

1825 Jan 20   Lawson, Peter and Loramine Loring by Nathan Emery, Elder in the
               M.E. Church, Franklin Co.

---- --- --   Lawson, Sally Ann and John Jamison by Nathan Emery, EMEC (note on
               date, "some time or other, he does not say when"), Franklin Co.

1811 Nov 16   Lawson, Thomas and Mary Ayle by Moses Varnum, JP, Washington Co.

1821 Nov 6   Lawton, Jesse and Maria Haskell by Rev. Cornelius Springer,
               Washington Co.

1813 Dec 13   Lawton, Rebecca and Richard Green by Rev. David Young, Washington Co.

1828 Jan 24   Lawyer, John and I.A. Huston by I. Grubb, JP, Franklin Co.

1814 Nov 19   Layton, David and Polly Bevans by Wm. King, JP, Pickaway Co.

1826 Jan 8   Layton, John and Jane Martin by Wm. Wyatt, JP, Marion Co.

1818 Sep 10   Leach, Ambrose and Tabitha Westfall by Jacob Delay, MG, Jackson Co.

1825 Apr 21   Leach, Archibald and Rosan Wheatley by Robert Ward, JP, Jackson Co.

1823 Apr 8   Leach, Benjamin S. and Martha Latta by James Hoge, Franklin Co.

1824 Nov 4   Leach, Elenor and John Graham by Robert Ward, JP, Jackson Co.

1819 Mar 14   Leach, Thomas W. and Nancy Rose by Jacob Delay, MG, Jackson Co.

1894 Dec 24   Leader, Bertha A. of Zanesville by Robert E. Booth of Indiana by
               Rev. George F. Moore, Putnam Presbyterian Church, Muskingum Co.

1807 Jan 21   Leaf, Henry and Polly Ball by Arthur O'Harra, JP, Franklin Co.

1816 Mar 8   Leaf, Jacob and Nancy Munture by Percival Adams, Franklin Co.

1803 Mar 23   Leavens, Betsey and Increase Mathews by Daniel Story, Clerk,
               Washington Co.

1821 Nov 7   Lebody, Margaret and Wm. Steel by Rev. Cornelius Springer,
               Washington Co.

1797 Feb 18   Lecroix, Andres and Mary Catterine Aveline Sarot by Robert Safford,
               Washington Co.

1814 Oct 23   Lee, Amos and Rachel Park by George Callanhan, EMEC, Licking Co.

1821 Jan 21   Lee, Asa and Sally Meacham by T. Lee, JP, Franklin Co.

1828 Dec 25   Lee, Benjamin and Nancy Jordan by Hiland Hulburd, Franklin Co.

1823 Apr 20   Lee, Catharine and Joseph Todd by B. Bull, JP, Franklin Co.

1810 Aug 2   Lee, Caty and John Cutler (license date), Pickaway Co.

1825 Apr 12   Lee, Joel and Jane Parker (license date), Marion Co.

1806 May 8   Lee, John and Agness Dickson by Zachariah Stephen, JP, Franklin Co.

1828 Sep 7   Lee, Johnathan and Elizabeth Mullen by J. Gander, JP, Franklin Co.

1819 Sep 30   Lee, Margret and Henry Backar by Richard Courtright, Franklin Co.

1796 Mar 15   Lee, Nancy and Frederick Eveland by Josiah Munro, JP, Washington Co.

1816 Oct 24   Lee, Sarah and John Budd by Fraderick Peterson, JP, Franklin Co.

1821 Jun 14   Lee, Solomon and Elizabeth Scoonover by Russel Bigelow, MI, Franklin
               Co.

1811 Jan 30   Lee, Stephan and Nancy Thompson by Rev. G. Vanaman, Licking Co.

1818 Sep 20   Lee, Zebulon and Lesta Micherson by Billingslea Bull, JP, Franklin Co.

1813 Jan 12   Leeper, Thomas and Kitty Baum (license date), Pickaway Co.

1857 Oct 1   Leffner, Frederick P. and Izora M. Priest by Rev. Geo. B. Sturges,
               St. Paul's Church, Marion, Marion Co.

1827 Oct 4   Legg, Elizabeth and Levy Wiley by Geo. Jefferies, MBC, Franklin Co.

1828 Dec 4   Legg, Lucinda and Thomas O'Harra by George Jefferies, MG, Franklin Co.

1811 Jul 7   Legget, James and Hannah Lawrence by Wm. Gray, JP, Washington Co.

1816 --- --   Legget, Robert and Susanna Featherston by John Patterson, JP,
               Washington Co.

1811 Jun 23   Legget, Sarah and John Featherstone by Wm. Gray, Washington Co.

1818 Feb 5	Leigh, Joshua and Margaret Harris by James Holmes, JP, Licking Co.
1820 Dec 27	Leiley, Joseph and Matilda Cain by James Hoge, Franklin Co.
1820 Aug 5	Lemmon, Joseph and Patsey Pence by John Spencer, JP, Licking Co.
1822 May 22	Lenard, Hannah and Allonson Bull by Nathan Emery, Franklin Co.
1816 May 16	Lenard, Jesse and Sally Rhew by James Marshall, Franklin Co.
1804 Dec 20	Lenes, Frederick and Catharine Trusam by Peter Jackson, JP, Ross Co.
1814 Jun 30	Leonard, Charles and Ann Decker by Wm. King, JP, Pickaway Co.
1852 Dec 8	Leonard, Ezra G. of Madison, Ind., and Henrietta D. Ward by Rev. John Body, St. Luke's Church, Marietta, Washington Co.
1817 Mar 30	Leonard, John and Elizabeth Hall by Sardine Stone, JP, Washington Co.
1825 Jan 6	Leonard, Joseph and Nancy Longwell by Abner Bent, JP, Marion Co.
1807 Mar 26	Leonard, Lydia and James Fulton by Stephen Lindsly, Washington Co.
1823 Apr 18	Leonard, Nancy and Matthew George by Reuben Golliday, JP, Franklin Co.
1827? Jan 23	Leonard, Preserved and Nancy Paxton by Lynes L. Lattimore, Franklin Co.
1802 Jul 10	Leonard, Wm. B. and Lydia Molton by Griffin Greene, JCCCP, Washington Co.
1881 Apr 27	Leonhart, John and Jennie E. Maloney by Rev. John Boyd, St. Luke's Church, Marietta, Washington Co.
1802 May 2	Lerne, Jacob and Elizabeth Randols by Sam'l Williamson, Washington Co.
1794 Feb 1	LeRoi, Marie Francois-Charlotte and John Baptiste C. Talliur by J.G. Petitt, Washington Co.
1803 Oct 26	Lettell, Betsey and George Keller by John G. McCan, Ross Co.
1817 Feb 28	Letts, David and Elizabeth Dunnavan by John Spencer, JP, Licking Co.
1816 Jul 20	Levistone, Catherine and James Bigford by Wm. O'Gannon, JP, Licking Co.
1819 Nov 7	Lewis, Betsey and Joseph Jewell by Rev. Levi Jewell, Washington Co.
1821 Nov 27	Lewis, Elias and Martha Wyley by Nathl. Little, Franklin Co.
1821 Nov 29	Lewis, Eliza and Isaac Wyley by Nathl. Little, Franklin Co.
1816 Mar 24	Lewis, Elizabeth and Hezekiah Benedict by Ezra Griswold, Franklin Co.
1821 Jan 25	Lewis, Elizabeth and John Evans by Samuel Bancroft, JP, Licking Co.
1843 Nov 6	Lewis, Eunice and Warren Weters by Rev. R.S. Elder, near Mt. Vernon, St. John's Church, Worthington, Franklin Co.
1790 Nov 14	Levins, Frances and Joseph Lincoln by Benj. Tupper, Washington Co.
1800 Nov 5	Lewis, Francis and Christopher Dickson by Philip Witten, JP, Washington Co.
1813 Nov 14	Lewis, Hezekiah and Milly Chapin by Rev. S.P. Robbins, Washington Co.
1816 Feb 6	Lewis, Hezekiah and Ruth Rose by Sam'l Dye, JP, Washington Co.
1808 Jan 8	Lewis, Isaac and Fodilla Welch by Nathaniel Wyatt, Franklin Co.

1827 Jun 10   Lewis, J.H. and Sarah Bigelow by Wm. Long, Franklin Co.

1825 Mar 10   Lewis, Jacob H. and Catharine S. Benedict, dau of Obediah Benedict, by Aristarcrus Walker, Franklin Co.

1813 Jul 1   Lewis, Julia and Henry Morrison by Ezra Griswold, Franklin Co.

1821 Nov 29   Lewis, Lucy and Charles Wyley by Nathl. Little, Franklin Co.

1813 Jan 14   Lewis, Margaret and George Stonerock (license date), Pickaway Co.

1827 Oct 17   Lewis, Martin L. and Eliza A. Johnson by Geo. Jefferies, MBC, Franklin Co.

1802 Nov 9   Lewis, Mary and John Biggirstaff by A. Bingham, Washington Co.

1815 Mar 16   Lewis, Milla and John Cole by Alex. Rowen, JP, Pickaway Co.

1810 Jun 8   Lewis, Nancy and Truman Bowen (license date), Pickaway Co.

1811 Jun 6   Lewis, Nancy and Elias Vanaman by Rev. G. Vanaman, Licking Co.

1826 Aug 10   Lewis, Polly and Joseph Gray by P. Adams, Franklin Co.

1814 Nov 3   Lewis, Sarah and H. McKenny by Wm. Florence, JP, Pickaway Co.

1824 Jan 8   Lewis, Sarah and James Foster by Reuben Golliday (another entry 4 Mar 1824), Franklin Co.

1823 Apr 17   Lewis, Thomas and Jane Kerr by Reuben Golliday, Franklin Co.

1818 May 5   Liffingwell, William and Sarah Gossett by Salmon N. Cook, JP, Washington Co.

1804 Apr 3   Ligen, Samuel and Elizabeth Sammas by Samuel Stage, Ross Co.

1814 May 19   Liggitt, Daniel and Rachael Hoffman by Rob't Bradshaw, JP, Pickaway Co.

1861 Sep 11   Lightfritz, Samuel and Catherine Wilgus by Rev. John Boyd, St. Luke's Church, Marietta, Washington Co.

1817 Oct 28   Lincoln, Frances and George Turner by Rev. Saml. P. Robbins, Washington Co.

1818 Nov 8   Lincoln, George and Ruby Wales by Rev. T. Harris, Licking Co.

1818 Nov 25   Lincoln, Gilman and Sally Cody by Michael Patton, Franklin Co.

1790 Nov 14   Lincoln, Joseph and Frances Levins by Benj. Tupper, Washington Co.

1797 Apr 12   Lincoln, Obediah and Peggy McCune by Josiah Munro, JP, Washington Co.

1812 Aug 27   Lindausky, Elizabeth and John Linn by John Turner, Franklin Co.

1817 Mar 27   Lindsey, James and Mary Barr by James Hoge, Franklin Co.

1798 Feb 6   Lindsey, Mary and William Stroud by Peregrine Foster, Washington Co.

1806 May 1   Lindsly, Stephen and Nancy Saltonstall by Jacob Lindsly, Washington Co.

1822 Nov 7   Line, Rachel and James Young by Richard Courtright, Franklin Co.

1817 Feb 18   Lines, Clarissa and James Decker by Elisha Decker, Franklin Co.

1886 Dec 28   Lingle, John and Callie Havens by Rev. George F. Moore, Putnam Presbyterian Church, Muskingum Co.

1818 Aug 9   Linkham, Ester and Philip Dilino by Venal Steward, MG, Franklin Co.

1807 Feb 23   Linn, Christina and George Cline by James Riggs, JP, Washington Co.

1801 Mar 31   Linn, Hannah and Moses Williamson by Samuel Williamson, JP,
               Washington Co.

1812 Aug 27   Linn, John and Elizabeth Lindausky by John Turner, Franklin Co.

1803 Aug 9   Linn, Mary and Wm. Cline by Sam'l. Williamson, JP, Washington Co.

1838 Jul 23   Linnel, James Knowles and Emma Bynner, St. Luke's Church, Granville,
               Licking Co.

1846 Apr 6   Linnel, John A. and Hannah Wood by W.C. French, St. Luke's Church,
               Granville, Licking Co.

1874 Sep 1   Linnell, Edward P. and C. Louise Johnson by Wm. Bower, St. Luke's
               Church, Granville, Licking Co.

1809 Nov 15   Linnell, Elkanah and Mariam Rose by Rev. Timothy Harris, Licking Co.

1809 Jun 11   Linnell, Joshua and Orpah Graves by Silas Winchell, JP, Licking Co.

1871 Jul 24   Linnett, Joanna and Thomas Swadley by Rev. John Boyd, St. Luke's
               Church, Marietta, Washington Co.

1807 Dec 27   Linscott, Israel and Nancy Nulton by Robert Oliver, JP, Washington
               Co.

1806 1 mo 2   Linton, David and Lettitia Silver, Miami Monthly Meeting, Warren Co.

1806 12 mo 31 Linton, Nathan and Rachel Smith, Miami Monthly Meeting, Warren Co.

1809 Jun 20   Lip, Elizabeth An and Roburt Alkire by John Smith, JP (date
               recorded), Franklin Co.

1822 Jan 31   Lisle, John and Thankfull Maynard by N. Little, JP, Franklin Co.

1822 Dec 31   Lisle, Rachel and William Sackett by James Hoge, Franklin Co.

1819 Oct 19   Lisle, Rebeccah and Joseph Young by Wm. Long, Franklin Co.

1820 Nov 1   Lisses, Anny and Henry Smith by John Davis, JP, Franklin Co.

1811 Nov 2   List, George and Barbara Moyer (license date), Pickaway Co.

1817 Dec 9   Little, Charles and Mary Frazier by Saml. P. Robbins, Washington Co.

1893 Mar 8   Little, Frank T. and Clara R. Drake both of Zanesville by Rev.
               George F. Moore, Putnam Presbyterian Church, Muskingum Co.

1827 Sep 21   Little, Harvey D. and Mary Howard by W.T. Martin, Franklin Co.

1825 Oct 5   Little, Hetty and Obediah Benedict by R.W. Cowles, Franklin Co.

1805 Aug 1   Little, Jacob and Rachel Kenedy by Peter Jackson, JP, Ross Co.

1811 Feb 19   Little, Jane and Keshe Molen by Thos. Ferguson, JP, Washington Co.

1809 Apr 12   Little, Nathaniel W. and Harriett Thompson by Alex'r. Morrison, Jr.,
               Franklin Co.

1818 Sep 24   Little, Shubel and Ester Conway by Zach. Carlisle, JP, Licking Co.

1816 Jun 2   Little, Sylvia and Daniel Widders by J. Cunningham, JPNAT, Licking
               Co.

1816 Jan 4   Little, Wealthy and Ira Hall by Rev. Saml. P. Robbins, Washington Co.

1815 Nov 9   Littlefield, Mahitable and John S. Fowler by John Russell, JP,
               Washington Co.

1819 Sep 30   Littlefield, Phebe and John Douthitt by Joel Tuttle, Jr., JP,
               Washington Co.

1824 Jun 24   Littlejohn, Joseph and Elizabeth Starne by Jacob Gundy, JP, Franklin
               Co.

1804 Dec 6   Littleton, Elizabeth and Benjamin Bellows by D. Loring, Washington
               Co.

1811 Jan 24   Littleton, John and Betsey Fortner by Daniel Goodno, Washington Co.

1804 Jan 2   Littleton, Leah and James Dines by Samuel Smith, Ross Co.

1807 Mar 17   Livingston, Edward and Martha Nelson by Robert I. Wilson, Min.,
               Franklin Co.

1819 Jan 14   Livingston, John and Mary Graham by John Jenks, JP, Franklin Co.

1819 Jan 15   Livingston, Tobias and Abagail Denman by Zach Carlisle, Licking Co.

1825 Feb 24   Livisay, Jefferson and Elizabeth Varian by John Shumate, JP, Jackson
               Co.

1814 Jan 12   Lloyd, Polly and William Swank by Wm. Florence, JP, Pickaway Co.

1802 Oct 18   Loath, John and Sally McKee by Joseph Buell, JP, Washington Co.

1816 Dec 24   Lobdil, Margaret and Joseph Holmes by Geo. Callanhan, EMEC, Licking
               Co.

1821 Dec 25   Lobdille, Rebecca Ann and Jared Gates by Asa Morey, Washington Co.

1825 Sep 29   Lock, Geo. and Morelands [sic] by Abner Bent, JP, Marion Co.

1813 Apr 1   Lock, John and Nancy Davison (license date), Pickaway Co.

1818 Nov 18   Lockard, Joseph and May Law by D. Mitchell, JP, Jackson Co.

1804 Jan 16   Lockard, Wm. and Mary Doll by J. Gardner, JP, Ross Co.

1819 Sep 9   Locker, John and Sarah Ann Locker by Rev. Saml. P. Robbins, Washing-
               ton Co.

1819 Sep 9   Locker, Sarah Ann and John Locker by Rev. Saml. P. Robbins, Washing-
               ton Co.

1822 Nov 7   Locket, Lucy and Henry Johnston by Joseph Badger, Franklin Co.

1819 Dec 19   Lockwood, Carlton and Hannah Parker by Spencer Wright, JP, Licking
               Co.

1815 Aug 23   Lockwood, Oliver and Lydia Maynard by Ezra Griswold, Franklin Co.

1825 Mar 31   Lockwood, Rebecca and Amase Wiswell, Jr. by Aristarcrus Walker,
               Franklin Co.

1807 Aug 15   Locoe, Rachel and George McClintock by Luther Dana, JP, Washington
               Co.

1827 Aug 4   Loffland, Mary and I.M. Smith by Wm. Long, JP, Franklin Co.

1809 Jun 30   Logan, Betsey and John Ross by Nehemiah Gates, Franklin Co.

1819 Mar 17   Logan, Walker and Sally Hackett by Eli C. King, JP, Franklin Co.

1820 Apr 6   Loge, Maria and Christopher Warner by Osgood McFarland, JP,
                 Washington Co.

1825 Oct 25   Logue, Samuel and Sally Straw by R.W. Cowles, JP, Franklin Co.

1824 Feb 5   Lone, John and Jennie Blake by John Horton, JP, Jackson Co.

1811 Aug 9   Long, Betsey and Joseph Hoselton (license date), Pickaway Co.

1805 Dec 2   Long, Catharine and Wm. Throup by John Guthree, Ross Co.

1826 Mar 1   Long, Christina and Wm. Strand by Zeph Brown, JP, Jackson Co.

1820 May 2   Long, Frances and Wm. Gregory by Jeremiah Brown, JP, Jackson Co.

1805 Dec 21   Long, John and Catharine Raderick by John Guthree, Ross Co.

1820 Oct 11   Long, John and Teney Myers by Nicholas Goetschius, JP, Franklin Co.

1814 Jun 22   Long, Mathew and Margaret Taylor by James Hoge, Franklin Co.

1824 Sep 4   Long, Peter and Hiley Darland (license date), Marion Co.

1803 Jul 15   Long, Robert and Catharine Gowens by Thos. Scott of Scioto Tp.,
                 Ross Co.

1810 Apr 10   Long, Wm. and Margaret Shaw by James Hoge, Franklin Co.

1813 Sep 29   Long, William and Rebecca Seddick by Jas. Hauge, Franklin Co.

1806 Mar 7   Longshore, James and Peggy Martin by John Johnston, JP, Ross Co.

1825 Jul 21   Longwell, Elizabeth and John Winslow (license date), Marion Co.

1824 Dec 29   Longwell, Isaac and Sarah Winslow by Rob't Hopkins, JP, Marion Co.

1825 Jan 6   Longwell, Nancy and Joseph Leonard by Abner Bent, JP, Marion Co.

1825 Jan 25   Longwell, Sarah and John Kensler by Wm. T. Martin, JP, Franklin Co.

1805 Apr 16   Longwith, Catharine and William Hambleton by Wm. Bennett, JP, Frank-
                 lin Co.

1823 Jun 5   Loofborough, Benjamin F. and Mary Hall by Geo. Jefferies, MG, Frank-
                 lin Co.

1815 Mar 23   Loofborough, Thomas and Sarah Glaze by Henry Davis, JP, Pickaway Co.

1838 Dec --   Loofborrough, John and Mary Plumb in Berkshire by Rev. A. Helfen-
                 stine, St. John's Church, Worthington, Franklin Co.

1828 Nov 10   Loomis, Horace and Jennett Wright by Gideon W. Hunt (or Hart), JP,
                 Franklin Co.

1860 Oct 1   Loomis, William B. and Frances Wheeler by Rev. John Boyd, St. Luke's
                 Church, Marietta, Washington Co.

1880 Jun 15   Loomis, William B. and Mrs. Nannie C. Hodkinson by Rev. John Boyd,
                 St. Luke's Church, Marietta, Washington Co.

1816 Jun 4   Loper, Samuel and Betsey Gates by Thomas White, Washington Co.

1809 Nov 28   Lord, Betsy and Eliphatel Frazier by Sam'l P. Robbins, Washington Co.

1817 Dec 11   Lord, Eliza and Abram J. McDowell by James Hoge, Franklin Co.

1827 Dec 18   Lord, Phoebe and John Andrews by Philander Chase, Bishop PEC,
                 Franklin Co.

1809 May 18   Lord, Polly and Jonathan Guitteau by Samuel P. Robbins, Washington
               Co.

1809 May 18   Lord, Sophia and George W. Cass by Sam'l P. Robbins, Washington Co.

1804 Feb 26   Lord, Temperance and Othniel Williams by Daniel Story, Clerk,
               Washington Co.

1817 Apr 10   Lord, Temperance and Truman Ransom by John Green, Washington Co.

1795 Apr 28   Lord, Thomas and Elanor Oliver by Robert Oliver, JP, Washington Co.

1823 May 4   Lord, Thomas and Eliza Havens by Jacob Grubb, Franklin Co.

1815 Sep 5   Loren, John and Nelly McMillin by James Marshall, Franklin Co.

1791 Jun 23   Loring, Charlotte and Aaron Waldo Putnam by Rufus Putnam ITNWRO,
               Washington Co.

1819 Sep 26   Loring, Charlotte P. and John Stone by Cyrus Ames, JP, Washington Co.

1821 Nov 17   Loring, Jesse and Deborah Gray by Rev. Wm. Boris, Washington Co.

1825 Jan 20   Loring, Loramine and Peter Lawson by Nathan Emery, Elder in the M.E.
               Church, Franklin Co.

1817 Feb 17   Loring, Mary and William Beebe by Cyrus Ames, JP, Washington Co.

1820 Dec 24   Loring, Oliver R. and Fanny Warren by Rev. Saml. P. Robbins,
               Washington Co.

1820 Feb 29   Losey, Jacob and Caroline Risley by Philip Cole, JP, Washington Co.

1809 Sep 17   Losh, John and Polly Orpat by Holden, JP, Licking Co.

1816 May 8   Lothery, William and Rebecca Gard by David Stevens, JP, Washington
               Co.

1819 Nov 12   Lott, Rachel and Vincent Lake by John W. Patterson, MG, Licking Co.

1887 Oct 25   Lotz, Robert L. of Watertown, Dak., and Nannie B. Josselyn of Zanes-
               ville by Rev. George F. Moore, Putnam Presbyterian Church,
               Muskingum Co.

1798 Jan 1   Louvat, Daniel and Phebe West by Peregrine Foster, JCCCP, Washington
               Co.

1824 Jun 8   Love, Eliza and Sylvester R. Gooding by Samuel Fish, JP, Marion Co.

1876 May 15   Loveall, Mary B. and Charles L. Douglas by Rev. John Boyd, St. Luke's
               Church, Marietta, Washington Co.

1791 May 5   Lovekin, Sally and Edward Henderson by Benj. Tupper, Washington Co.

1816 Apr 23   Loveland, Jared and Phila Hammond by Obadiah Scott, JP, Washington
               Co.

1825 Mar 4   Loveland, Robert and Abigal Randall by Wm. Long, JP, Franklin Co.

1821 Sep 3   Lovet, John and Anna Price by John Green, JP, Licking Co.

1815 Jun 17   Low, Nathan and Sarah Brooks by John Green, Licking Co.

1819 Mar 9   Low, Polly and Alderman Johnson by Samuel Dye, JP, Washington Co.

1815 Jun 17   Low, Ruth and Samuel Trig by John Green, Licking Co.

1825 Jan 26   Lowder, Mary and Jesse Foust by Amos Neely, JP, Marion Co.

1817 Jul 20   Lowe, John and Hannah Ayles by John True, Washington Co.

1826 Feb 23   Lowery, John and Margaret Stotts by C. Hinkel, Franklin Co.

1804 Apr 19   Lowning, Francis and Elizabeth Foster by Wm. Davis, Esq., Ross Co.

1803 Dec 1   Lowrey, William and Mary Hundberry by J. Graham, Washington Co.

1822 Feb 24   Lowry, Melvin and Harty Cole by Philip Cole, JP, Washington Co.

1828 Jun 19   Loy, Elizabeth and Archabald Roe by Jason Bull, Franklin Co.

1811 Dec 26   Loyd, Samuel and Huldy Barbour by James Marshall, Franklin Co.

1800 Mar 23   Lucas, Elizabeth and Wm. Hughs by Robt. Oliver, JP, Washington Co.

1808 Mar 3   Lucas, Elizabeth and John Topping by Alex'r Morrison, Jr., Franklin Co.

1818 Jul 6   Lucas, Nancy and John Evans by Wm. Davis, MBC, Washington Co.

1798 Apr 19   Lucas, Samuel and Elizabeth Robertson by Josiah Munro, JP, Washington Co.

1796 Apr 11   Lucas, William and Peggie Harris by Josiah Munro, JP, Washington Co.

1821 Oct 4   Lucas, William and Experience Madison by Judah M. Chamberlain, JP, Washington Co.

1813 Oct 31   Lucas, Williby and Caty McCannal (license date), Pickaway Co.

1825 Oct 30   Luce, Erastus and Maria Platt by W.T. Martin, JP, Franklin Co.

1801 Oct 11   Lucens, Polly and Jasper Stone by Nehemiah Davis, Washington Co.

1869 Oct 5   Ludlow, Arthur F. and Jane E.P. Wells both of England by Rev. John Boyd, St. Luke's Church, Marietta, Washington Co.

1813 Oct 24   Ludwig, Catherine and Jacob Kline (license date), Pickaway Co.

1823 3 mo 5   Lukens, Benjamin and Mary Satterthwaite, Miami Monthly Meeting, Warren Co.

1822 2 mo 13   Lukens, Joseph and Hannah Brown, Miami Monthly Meeting, Warren Co.

1817 3 mo 5   Lukens, Rachel and Edward Hatton, Miami Monthly Meeting, Warren Co.

1805 4 mo 17   Lupton, Grace and William Pope, Miami Monthly Meeting, Warren Co.

1807 3 mo 18   Lupton, Lydia and Jonathan Sanders, Miami Monthly Meeting, Warren Co.

1824 Jul 7   Lusk, Mary and Thos. Needly by H. Matthews, Franklin Co.

1825 May 22   Lust, Elizabeth and Jonathan James by Benj. Bell, JP, Marion Co.

1794 Apr 15   Luton, Victoire Charlotte and Auguste Waldmar Mentel by J.G. Petitt, Washington Co.

1811 Feb 5   Lutz, John H. and Mary Sayler (license date), Pickaway Co.

1895 Dec 25   Lybarger, Grace A. of Zanesville and Charles F. Shaffer of Pittsburgh, Pa., by Rev. George F. Moore, Putnam Presbyterian Church, Muskingum Co.

1852 Jan 14   Lyddane, Jas. P. and Abigail B. Whitcomb by Rev. Geo. B. Sturges, St. Paul's Church, Marion, Marion Co.

1814 Dec 22   Lyle, James and Mary Gumford by Geo. Bogart, Franklin Co.

1814 Jan 13   Lyle, Jane and Samuel Maynard by Ezra Griswold, Franklin Co.

1808 Nov 10   Lyle, Margaret and James McIlvaine by James Hoge, Franklin Co.

1819 Jan 10   Lyman, Ann and Charles Hull Picket by Rev. T. Harris, Licking Co.

1803 May 1   Lyman, Lydia and Asher Ely both of Franklin by David Hudson, JP,
               Trumbull Co.

1833 Sep 2   Lynch, C.H. and Polly Brown by Rev. E. Burr, St. John's Church,
               Worthington, Franklin Co.

1826 Oct 23   Lynch, Cornelius and Elanor Robinson by Benj. Britton, Franklin Co.

1846 Apr 13   Lynch, Henry J. of Pittsburgh, Pa., and Mary Ann Goodman by Rev.
               Edward Winthrop, St. Luke's Church, Marietta, Washington Co.

1821 Nov 21   Lynch, John Jr. and Nancy Scott by Isaac Painter, Franklin Co.

1880 Feb 17   Lynch, Robert and Adeline Cline by Rev. John Boyd, St. Luke's
               Church, Marietta, Washington Co.

1807 Dec 3   Lyon, Abraham and Hannah Price by Jos. Eaton, Franklin Co.

1820 Jan 2   Lyon, Lucinda and Austin Payne by Jno. Trois, Franklin Co.

1812 Dec 6   Lyons, Charlotte and Jeremiah Dare by Rev. Stephen Lindley,
               Washington Co.

1803 Mar 14   Lyons, Elizabeth and James H. Jenkins by Sam'l Williamson,
               Washington Co.

1817 Sep 3   Lyons, Hannah and John Sutherds by Townsend Nichols, Franklin Co.

1892 Sep 14   Lyons, James W. of South Zanesville and Electa Ravennaugh of High
               Hill, O., by Rev. George F. Moore, Putnam Presbyterian Church,
               Muskingum Co.

1819 Jun 17   Lyons, Mary and George Spark by Billingslea Bull, Franklin Co.

1811 Jan 31   Lysle, Elizabeth and Luther Power by James Hoge, Franklin Co.

1885 Sep 23   Mace, Annie C. and William W. Sherlock both of Zanesville by Rev.
               George F. Moore, Putnam Presbyterian Church, Muskingum Co.

---- --- --   Macky, Saml and Elioner Baley by John Tevis, Franklin Co.

1812 Jul 19   Madden, Dennis and Catherine Michall (license date), Pickaway Co.

1812 Jun 28   Madden, Sarah and Isaac Swank (license date), Pickaway Co.

1807 11 mo 26 Maddock, Eleanor and James Cook, Miami Monthly Meeting, Warren Co.

1819 May 19   Maddox, Hiram and Mary Whaley by Saml McDowell, JP, Jackson Co.

1814 Mar 3   Maddox, Sarah and John Tiffin (license date), Pickaway Co.

1821 Oct 4   Madison, Experience and William Lucas by Judah M. Chamberlain, JP,
               Washington Co.

1806 11 mo 20 Mador, Francis and Phebe Cook, Miami Monthly Meeting, Warren Co.

1810 May 15   Magee, John and Mary Higgins by Wm. Nixon, Washington Co.

1866 Nov 26   Magee, John and Sadie Hodkinson by Rev. John Boyd, St. Luke's
              Church, Marietta, Washington Co.

1810 Mar 30   Magee, Nancy and Elisha Chapman by Stephen Lindsly, Washington Co.

1807 Mar 10   Magee, Robert and Maria Howell by Stephen Lindsly, Washington Co.

1810 Apr 22   Magruder, Sally and Amos Gilbert by Wm. Browning, Washington Co.

1821 Mar 6   Mahan, Anna and Andrew Flanagan by James Hoge, Franklin Co.

1827 Feb 1   Mahan, Betsey and George Cashman by C. Henkel, Franklin Co.

1840 Apr 8   Mahan, Harriet and John A. Turner, St. Luke's Church, Granville,
              Licking Co.

1897 May 18   Maharry, Lillian and James H. Abbott both of Zanesville by Rev.
              George F. Moore, Putnam Presbyterian Church, Muskingum Co.

1817 Sep 30   Mahollum, James and Mary Taylor by Noah Fidler, Licking Co.

1806 Feb 26   Mahon, James and Catharine Kerr by John McDonald, JP, Ross Co.

1816 Nov 3   Main, Jonas and Eunice Hennan by Sam'l Dye, JP, Washington Co.

1810 Sep 6   Main, Katherine and Wm. McClean by Henry Jolly, JP, Washington Co.

1812 Aug 6   Main, Polly and Daniel Tewel by Henry Jolly, JP, Washington Co.

1824 Sep 12   Maire, Sally and Christian Horlocker by John Davis, JP (Rev. Daniel
              Horlocker of Columbus stated that his step-mother's name was
              Sally Myers), Franklin Co.

1812 Dec 7   Malahan, Rebecca and George Featheringill by Elijah Austin,
              Franklin Co.

1823 Jan 7   Malbone, Prescilla and Tracy Willcox by Aristochus Walker,
              Franklin Co.

1818 Apr 30   Malbone, Sollimon and Prissila Sole by Wm. Swayze, Itenrant Minister
              in the Methodist Episcopal Church, Franklin Co.

1885 Oct 22   Malcolm, Fred. of New York and Kate B. Potwin of Zanesville by Rev.
              George B. Moore, Putnam Presbyterian Church, Muskingum Co.

1800 Nov 24   Malden, Hannah Mior and Nicholas Shevenin by Robert Safford,
              Washington Co.

1797 Mar 12   Maldon, John L. and Hannah M. Buthe by Robert Safford, Washington Co.

1817 Aug 29   Majors, Irene and David McEvans (or McKevans) by Rev. T. Harris,
              Licking Co.

1812 Jun 21   Mallahon, Sally and John Schoonover by Elijah Austin, JP, Franklin
              Co.

1821 Feb 22   Mallory, Luther and Elizabeth Metcalf by Noah Fidler, Licking Co.

1803 Jul 28   Malone, Hartley and Margrate Johnson by J. Gardner, JP, Ross Co.

1818 Sep 3   Malone, Nancy and Jonathan Clayton by Mich. Trout, JP, Licking Co.

1806 Jan 2   Malone, Rebeckah and Isaac Miller by J. Gardner, JP, Ross Co.

1881 Apr 27   Maloney, Jennie E. and John Leonhart by Rev. John Boyd, St. Luke's
              Church, Marietta, Washington Co.

1819 Jun 15   Manby, Samuel and Margaret Tinsley by James M. Booth, JP, Washington
              Co.

1800 Jul 24   Manchester, Anna and Oliver Dodger by Daniel Story, Clerk,
               Washington Co.

1800 Feb 1   Maneer, Betsy and Philip Piper by Samuel Smith, Ross Co.

1824 Jul 13   Manley, Mercey and John Parcle by J.B. Packard, JP, Marion Co.

1879 Oct 9   Manley, Walter J. of Shawnee, O., and Flora E. Rock of Zanesville,
               O., by Rev. George F. Moore, Putnam Presbyterian Church,
               Muskingum Co.

1866 Dec 25   Manly, Mary E. and J.W. Brelsford by Rev. A. Kingsbury, Putnam
               Presbyterian Church, Muskingum Co.

1799 Feb 14   Mann, James and Lucena Davis by Robert Oliver, JP, Washington Co.

1820 May 31   Mannan, Margret and Robert Park by Jacob Keller, Franklin Co.

1826 Oct 1   Manning, Elizabeth and James Kelley by Reuben Golliday, Franklin Co.

1817 May 20   Manning, John and Christina Seymore by Zach Carlisle, JP, Licking Co.

1812 Mar 8   Manning, Lovice and Windsor Willard by Reuben Carpenter, JP,
               Franklin Co.

1824 Aug 29   Manning, Lovisa and Moses H. Strickland by John Hawkens, JP,
               Franklin Co.

1811 Jun 27   Manning, Samuel W. and Nancy Tipton by W. Haines, JP, Licking Co.

1826 Jul 27   Manning, Thomas and Eliza Keller by C. Henkel, Franklin Co.

1826 Jan 5   Manning, William and Betsy Frankelbury (or Frankelberry) by Jacob
               Grubb (license date, 5 Jan; return filed 21 Jan.), Franklin Co.

1815 Jan 26   Manning, Wm. and Nelly Burkance (or Burkana) by Jos. Gorton, JP,
               Franklin Co.

1803 Feb 5   Mansfield, John and Catharine Brachbill by Alvan Bingham, Washington
               Co.

1804 Mar 7   Mansfield, Martin and Margaret Durham by James Graham, JP, Washing-
               ton Co.

1819 Jun 3   Mantanney, Polly and Eliphalet Trowbridge by James Cunningham,
               Licking Co.

1811 Apr 9   Mantel (or Martle), Elizabeth and Isaac Woods by Rev. Simon Cokrane,
               Franklin Co.

1821 Apr 7   Mantle, John and Elizabeth Evertson by Peter Clover, JP, Franklin Co.

1805 Jan 30   Manwell, James and Ruth Clark by Enoch Shepard, Washington Co.

1827 Jun 28   Mapes, Sarah and Isaac Tinkham by Jason Bull, JP, Franklin Co.

1824 Aug 19   Marble, Betsey and Gorge Robinson by Jacob Gundy, JP, Franklin Co.

1822 Apr 22   Marcy, John and Darcus Barkly by C. Henkel, Franklin Co.

1794 Mar 4   Margaret, Margarette and Jean Beaudot by J.G. Petitt, Washington Co.

1794 Feb 18   Marian, Francois and Louise Nime by J.G. Petitt, Washington Co.

1809 Sep 3   Marks, James and Nancy Vinhirk by Arthur O'Harra, Franklin Co.

1810 11 mo 22 Marmon, Dorothy and Peter Marmon, Miami Monthly Meeting, Warren Co.

1810 11 mo 22 Marmon, Peter and Dorothy Marmon, Miami Monthly Meeting, Warren Co.

1804 Jun 19   Marquis, Hannah and Adam Coone by Geo. Williams, Ross Co.

1813 Sep 2   Marquiss, Sarah and William Barnes (license date), Pickaway Co.

1820 Jun 27   Marsh, Amella and Dennis Downing by Nicholas Goetschius, JP,
              Franklin Co.

1813 Dec 2   Marsh, David and Susana Barnes (license date), Pickaway Co.

1821 Oct 18   Marsh, Hester and John A. Hills by A. Allen, Franklin Co.

1822 Jan 9   Marsh, Marthy and John Swain by Uriah Clark, Franklin Co.

1813 Mar 21   Marsh, Sally and Thomas Green by Rev. Stephen Lindley, Washington Co.

1826 Dec 14   Marshall, Issabel S. and James Grayham by Wm. Sterewalt, Franklin Co.

1824 Apr 7   Marshall, Jane and William S. Sullivant by Jacob Grubb, Franklin Co.

1855 Jul 3   Marshall, Margaret and Thomas Land by T. Corlett, St. Luke's Church,
              Granville, Licking Co.

1817 Aug 10   Marshall, Samuel and Nancy Haward by Percival Adams, Franklin Co.

1810 Jan 25   Marshall, Thomas and Margret Drake by Geo. Wells, JP, Licking Co.

1822 Jun 23   Marshell, Rachel and John Mathes by C. Henkel, Franklin Co.

1803 Mar 14   Martin, Abner and Sarah Haskinson by Philip Witten, JP, Washington
              Co.

1803 Nov 15   Martin, Abner and Elizabeth McGee by John Brough, JP, Washington Co.

1811 Jun 3   Martin, Adam and Caty Pontius (license date), Pickaway Co.

1874 Aug 26   Martin, Albert A. and Ellen L. North by Rev. John Boyd, St. Luke's
              Church, Marietta, Washington Co.

1811 Feb 11   Martin, Anna and Abija Cory (license date), Pickaway Co.

1819 Nov 30   Martin, Anna C. and Cyrus Philbrook by Samuel Bancroft, JP, Licking
              Co.

1812 Jun 6   Martin, Casey and Peter Grant (license date), Pickaway Co.

1819 May 17   Martin, Catharine and Michael Patton by Eli C. King, Franklin Co. —

1818 Oct 22   Martin, Catherine and Allen Heyatt by George Hoover, JP, Licking Co.

1797 Aug 22   Martin, Charles Honeywood and Mary Gaylor by Josiah Munro,
              Washington Co.

1817 Dec 4   Martin, Cynthia and William Jolly by Rev. David Smithers, Washington
              Co.

1804 Aug 16   Martin, David and Susannah Kimble by Wm. Bennett, JP, Franklin Co. ⌐

1826 Jun 8   Martin, David and Elizabeth Smith by Geo. Jefferies, Franklin Co. ⌐

1814 Mar 17   Martin, Dolly and Jeremiah Cody by Rev. Geo. Alkire, Pickaway Co.

1810 Sep 11   Martin, Jacob and Manda Roads (license date), Pickaway Co.

1811 Sep 10   Martin, Jane and David Rawlins (license date), Pickaway Co.

1821 Jul 26   Martin, Jane and Wm. Vernon by Jeremiah Brown, JP, Jackson Co.

1826 Jan 8   Martin, Jane and John Layton by Wm. Wyatt, JP, Marion Co.

1825 Mar 22   Martin, Joel and Sarah Beatty by J.B. Gilliland, JP, Jackson Co.

1814 Sep 25   Martin, John and Catherine Dereau by Henry Davis, JP, Pickaway Co.

1815 Sep 28   Martin, John and Hannah Miller by Percival Adams, Franklin Co.

1826 Mar 19   Martin, John and Sarah Painter by Joseph Carper, Franklin Co.

1809 May 2   Martin, Julian and Isaac Lambert by Arthur O'Harra, Franklin Co.

1879 Nov 12   Martin, Maggie and George Henry by Rev. John Boyd, St. Luke's Church,
              Marietta, Washington Co.

1817 Jan 2   Martin, Mary and Reuben Ricaback by Jacob Delay, Licensed Deacon of
              the Methodist Church, Jackson Co.

1804 Apr 5   Martin, Peggy and Isaac Dickinson by Peter Jackson, JP, Ross Co.

1806 Mar 7   Martin, Peggy and James Longshore by John Johnston, JP, Ross Co.

1811 Jun 20   Martin, Peggy and David Johnston by Thomas Morris, Franklin Co.

1812 Sep 9   Martin, Rachel and John Walker (license date), Pickaway Co.

1826 Feb 26   Martin, Rebecca and Joab Morris by Thomas Vaughn, Jackson Co.

1811 Jul 21   Martin, Sarah and Thomas Shoap (license date), Pickaway Co.

1829 Jan 22   Martin, Thomas and Hannah White by Geo. Jefferies, Franklin Co.

1813 Feb 14   Martin, Tulman and Nancy West (license date), Pickaway Co.

1855 Jun 29   Martin, Urith and Thomas Henderson of Guernsey Co., by Rev. John
              Boyd, St. Luke's Church, Marietta, Washington Co.

1817 Mar 15   Martin, William and Hannah Deaver by Francis Holland, JP Scioto Tp.,
              Jackson Co.

1824 Sep 13   Martin, Wm. and Sarah McIntire by Jacob Delay, MG, Jackson Co.

1811 Apr 9   Martle (or Mantel), Elizabeth and Isaac Woods by Rev. Simon Cokrane,
              Franklin Co.

1815 Sep 28   Marton (or Morton), John and Hanna Miller by Percival Adams,
              Franklin Co.

1791 Jul 21   Marvin, Picket and Polly Worth by -----, Washington Co.

1821 Sep 13   Mash, Lydia and Thomas Hutchinson by Bial Stedman, JP, Washington Co.

1819 Apr 7   Mason, Betsey and William Morris by Amos Wilson, JP, Washington Co.

1826 May 7   Mason, Hannah and John Sheehea by Wm. Ayers, JP, Jackson Co.

1816 Jul 21   Mason, James and Judith Bartley by John Green, JP, Washington Co.

1813 Aug 2   Mason, Jane and George Sprague by John Green, JP, Washington Co.

1822 Jan 24   Mason, Jonas and Beulah Stacy by John Green, JP, Washington Co.

1815 May 30   Mason, Joseph and Eleanor Deaver by Sardine Stone, Esq., Washington
              Co.

1816 May 12   Mason, Joseph and Sally Sprague by John Green, JP, Washington Co.

1819 May 13   Mason, Mary and Philip Cats by J. Cunningham, Licking Co.

1820 Aug 10   Mason, Nancy and William McAtee by Amos Wilson, JP, Washington Co.

1884 Dec 30   Mason, Nettie of Taylorsville, O., and Charles Few of High Hill, O.,
              by Rev. George F. Moore,Putnam Presbyterian Church,Muskingum Co.

1813 Oct 10   Mason, Pamela and John Roach by John Green, JP, Washington Co.

1810 Oct 4   Mason, Rachel and John Starlin by Ephraim Matthews, JP, Washington
              Co.

1806 9 mo 17 Mason, Ruth and Job Carr, Miami Monthly Meeting, Warren Co.

1820 Oct 22   Mason, Susanna and Elisha Davis by John Green, JP, Washington Co.

1818 Apr 22   Mason, William and Lucy Sprague by Wm. Rand, Washington Co.

1790 Jul 14   Mason, William and Susanna Cobern by Benj. Tupper, Washington Co.

1819 Jun 7   Mason, William and Sally Shakley by Amos Wilson, JP, Washington Co.

1819 Mar 5   Masse, William and Laura Gay by Edward Hursey, JP, Licking Co.

1806 Jan 1   Massie, Charlotte and Thomas James by Robert B. Dobbins, VDM, Ross Co.

1820 Apr 22   Massie, Eliza and John Waytes by Moses Williamson, JP, Washington Co.

1824 Dec 28   Massy, Mary and Wm. Corn by John Shumate, JP, Jackson Co.

1820 Feb 2   Mast, Edna and Abner Westorn by Emmor Cox, JP, Franklin Co.

1825 Nov 25   Masters, Nancy and James White by Wm. McClintic, JP, Jackson Co.

1809 Sep 6   Mathan (Mathew), Tena and Jacob Taylor by David Mitchell, Franklin Co.

1811 Apr 18   Matheney, Jane and William Tice by Ephraim Matthews, JP, Washington
              Co.

1820 7 mo 5   Mather, George and Mary Rickitt, Miami Monthly Meeting, Warren Co.

1820 May 16   Mather, Nathaniel and Sarah Mills by James Hoge, Franklin Co.

1822 Jun 23   Mathes, John and Rachel Marshell by C. Henkel, Franklin Co.

1812 Dec 31   Mathew, Deborah and Benj. McKrey by N. Connard, Licking Co.

1812 Dec 21   Mathew, Rachel and Joseph Dunlap by Nathan Connard, Licking Co.

1809 Sep 6   Mathew (or Mathan), Tena and Jacob Taylor by David Mitchell, Franklin
              Co.

1806 Jun 18   Mathews, Abel and Molly Woodarde by Ephm. Mathews, Washington Co.

1813 Nov 29   Mathews, Benjamin and Sally Grown by John Green, JP, Licking Co.

1805 Jan 23   Mathews, Betsy and John Lake by Enoch Wing, JP, Washington Co.

1801 Apr 9   Mathews, Catharine and John Oliver by Daniel Story, Washington Co.

1815 Apr 14   Mathews, Christian and Sarah Stump by Joseph Thrap, JP, Licking Co.

1855 May 15   Mathews, D.G. and Eveline A. Sullivan by Rev. John Boyd, St. Luke's
              Church, Marietta, Washington Co.

1870 Jun 15   Mathews, Edith D. of Putnam and William M. Canby of Wilmington, Del.,
              by Rev. A. Kingsbury, Putnam Presbyterian Church, Muskingum Co.

1819 Jan 12   Mathews, Henry and Marinda Wells by Charles Waddle, PE, Licking Co.

1803 Mar 23   Mathews, Increase and Betsey Leavens by Daniel Story, Clerk,
              Washington Co.

1803 May 29   Mathews, John and Sally Woodbridge by Daniel Story, Washington Co.

1804 May 24   Mathews, John and Sarah McKinney by Thos. Scott, JP, Ross Co.

1883 Oct 16   Mathews, Margaret W. and Arthur H. Bowen by Rev. John Boyd, St.
                Luke's Church, Marietta, Washington Co.

1813 Nov 29   Mathews, Sally and Elijah Moore by John Green, JP, Licking Co.

1821 Aug 1   Matoon, Orra and Oliver Stacy by Russel Bigelow, MG, Franklin Co.

1819 Aug 26   Matthes, Lydia and Charles Sloper by Wm. Long, JP, Franklin Co.

1828 Sep 30   Matthews, Clark and Sally Dean by James Laws, Franklin Co.

1813 Mar 14   Matthews, Matthew and Lucy ----- by E. Griswold, Franklin Co.

1816 Jan 21   Matthews, Newman and Maria Witham by J. Russell, JP, Washington Co.

1814 Mar 13   Matthews, Philo and Eleanor Woodward by Sardine Stone, JP,
                Washington Co.

1821 Oct 28   Mattocks, Polly and Israel Gales by Nicholas Goetschius, Franklin Co.

1815 Mar 16   Mattocks, Wm. and Nancy Davidson by Rederick Peterson, Franklin Co.

1814 Jul 21   Matton, Ebenezer Hern and Jane Brierly by Joseph Gortton, Franklin Co.

1815 Jan 3   Mattoon, Delia and Jason Bull by James Cumpstock, Franklin Co.

1813 Dec 16   Maupen, Francis and Horatio Keys (license date), Pickaway Co.

1807 Oct 23   Maxson, Henry and Elizabeth Gaylor by Thos. Stanley, Washington Co.

1819 May 31   Maxson, Laurana and Samuel Allard by Danl. G. Stanley, JP,
                Washington Co.

1819 Aug 18   Maxson, Lydia and Amos Chesebra by James Whitney, JP, Washington Co.

1814 May 19   Maxson, Mary and Johnson P. Cook by Derrick Stone, Esq., Washington
                Co.

1811 Nov 21   Maxson, Sarah and Wm. Corner by Stephen Lindsly, Washington Co.

1821 Dec 4   Maxson, Sophia and Charles Crawford by Amos Wilson, JP, Washington Co.

1871 Dec 6   Maxwell, Josephine and Arthur W. Barker by Rev. John Boyd, St. Luke's
                Church, Marietta, Washington Co.

1819 Jan 19   May, Elizabeth and Thomas Murphey by Michael Patton, Franklin Co.

1814 May 26   May, Henry and Susan McCutchin by Rev. Rob't. G. Wilson, Pickaway Co.

1816 Aug 15   Mayberry, John P. and Lucy W. Fearing by Sam'l P. Robbins, DD,
                Washington Co.

1820 Apr 26   Mayfield, James and Sarah Mayfield by James Avery, MG, Licking Co.

1820 Apr 26   Mayfield, Sarah and James Mayfield by James Avery, MG, Licking Co.

1820 Jul 4   Maymard, Opolos and Emily Wilcox by A. Buttles, Franklin Co.

1815 Aug 31   Maynard, Acksa and Orrange Johnston by Recompence Stansbery, Franklin
                Co.

1814 Mar 17   Maynard, Alois and Hanry Stevens by Daniel Hess, Franklin Co.

1838 Sep --   Maynard, Alvira and Aleen Fuller by Rev. A. Helfenstine, St. John's
                Church, Worthington, Franklin Co.

1822 Jul 4   Maynard, Elizabeth and Asahel Ingham by A. Buttles, Franklin Co.

1819 Jun 6   Maynard, Larra and Potter Wright by R. Stanberry, Franklin Co.

1826 Mar 16   Maynard, Lucy and Thomas Justice by Tracy Willcox, JP, Franklin Co.

1812 Jan 3   Maynard, Lydia and Samuel Sloper by Isaac Fisher, MG, Franklin Co.

1815 Aug 23   Maynard, Lydia and Oliver Lockwood by Ezra Griswold, Franklin Co.

1826 Jan 1   Maynard, Moses Jr. and Crissa Hanks by Nathan Emery, Franklin Co.

1814 Jan 13   Maynard, Samuel and Jane Lyle by Ezra Griswold, Franklin Co.

1814 Nov 25   Maynard, Stephen and Darcey Pinny by Ezra Griswold, Franklin Co.

1816 Dec 12   Maynard, Stephen and Mary Philips by R. Stansbury, Franklin Co.

1822 Jan 31   Maynard, Thankfull and John Lisle by N. Little, JP, Franklin Co.

1798 Oct 21   Mayo, Daniel and Polly Putnam by Peregrine Foster, JCCCP, Washington
              Co.

1813 Jul 9   Mays, Catharine and Salmon Smith by John Brough, JP, Washington Co.

1816 Feb 18   Mays, Milly and Jacob Reab by Joseph Groton, Franklin Co.

1809 Oct 19   Maythorm, Catharine and John Buck by David Mitchell, Franklin Co.

1814 Apr 12   Maythorn, Mary and Abner Trimble by John Turner, Franklin Co.

1817 Apr 12   McAllister, Cammilla and Richard Thorla by Danl H. Buell, JP,
              Washington Co.

1820 Nov 18   McAllister, Irene and Joseph G. Harris by James M. Booth, JP,
              Washington Co.

1821 Mar 21   McAllister, James and Susanna Owens by James M. Booth, JP, Washington
              Co.

1808 May 27   McArty, Hugh and Abigail Buck by E.B. Dana, JP, Washington Co.

1822 Mar 21   McAtee, Betsey and John Gilliland by John Russell, JP, Washington Co.

1820 Aug 10   McAtee, William and Nancy Mason by Amos Wilson, JP, Washington Co.

1803 Oct 20   McBane, Jennie and Amos Thompson by Jacob Earhart, JP, Washington Co.

1867 Dec 10   McBee, Mircian and Nellie K. Hicks by Rev. A. Kingsbury, Putnam
              Presbyterian Church, Muskingum Co.

1860 Mar 1   McBride, John and Henrietta Fisher by Rev. A. Kingsbury, Putnam
              Presbyterian Church, Muskingum Co.

1815 Dec 19   McBride, Mary and James Allen by Joseph Chapman, JP, Washington Co.

1803 Jan 13   McBride, Richard and Hannah Hammond by Enoch Wing, JP, Washington Co.

1820 Aug 6   McCabe, Hannah and Jeniah Jennings by Danl H. Buell, Washington Co.

1805 Apr 7   McCabe, Isaih and Jean McCune by Samuel Edwards, Ross Co.

1804 Jan 25   McCafferty, James and Elizabeth Richardson by Samuel Smith, Ross Co.

1805 Apr 4   McCafferty, Thomas and Rachel Johnston by Robert Adams, Ross Co.

1894 Jan 10   McCaid, Sadie of Duncan's Falls, O., and David Bonifield of Pleasant
              Valley, O., by Rev. George F. Moore, Putnam Presbyterian Church,
              Muskingum Co.

1891 Sep 29   McCaid, Wilber J. of Colorado and Ada A. Acheson of Zanesville by Rev.
              George F. Moore, Putnam Presbyterian Church, Muskingum Co.

1805 Jan 21   McCaig, Margaret and Philander McCardil by Thos. Stanley, Washington Co.

1814 Apr 12   McCalip, Lydia and Moses Rugg by Noah Fidler, Licking Co.

1802 May 27   McCall, James and Jane Northup by Seth Cashart, Washington Co.

1804 Jan 31   McCall, Margaret and Joseph Crouch by Abm. Miller, Ross Co.

1799 Feb 28   McCall, Peggy and David Chapman by Peregrine Foster, JCCCP, Washington Co.

1821 Apr 5   McCalla, Naomi and Nathan Hartwell by Noah Fidler, Licking Co.

1817 Jul --   McCallaugh, Thomas and Mary Day by John Hunter, Franklin Co.

1803 Sep 22   McCallum, Mary and James Gaskins by Wm. Davis, JP, Ross Co.

1807 Jan 4   M'Candles, Sally and Moses Rawlings by Nathan Rawlings, JP, Franklin Co.

1813 Oct 31   McCannall, Caty and Williby Lucas (license date), Pickaway Co.

1805 Jan 21   McCardil, Philander and Margaret McCaig by Thos. Stanley, Washington Co.

1801 Mar 5   McCarley, Betsy and David M. Daniel by Robt Safford, Washington Co.

1823 Jun 16   McCaron, Claressa and Wesley Turner by C. Waddell, JP, Franklin Co.

1806 --- --   McCartney, John and Elinor Donhady by John Robins, Ross Co.

1865 May 2   McCarty, Lucy T. and Robert M. Cherry by Rev. A. Kingsbury, Putnam Presbyterian Church, Muskingum Co.

1805 Feb 19   McCarty, Margaret and Abraham Rhodes by John Hoddy, Ross Co.

1826 Mar 16   McCauly, Nancy and Asa Coorey (or Cooney) by Henry Matthews, Franklin Co.

1808 Jul 18   McCay, Liba and Betsey Holdren by L. Dana, JP, Washington Co.

1808 Aug 16   McClaer, James and Abigail Stacey by N. Davis, MG, Washington Co.

1802 Jan 6   McClain, Elizabeth of Pennsylvania and John Dunken of Youngstown by Caleb Baldwin, JP, Trumbull Co.

1820 Feb 7   McClain, John and Sarah Barrey by Joseph Dickerson, Washington Co.

1822 May 9   McClain, Sally and Wm. Hendrixson by Wm. Godman, Franklin Co.

1814 Jul 31   McClare, Maria Theresie and Stephen Rouse by Obadiah Scott, JP, Washington Co.

1806 Mar 27   McClary, William and Esther Hempstead by Stephen Lindley, Washington Co.

1817 Mar 27   McClealland (or McClellan), Jane and Samuel Persans (or Parsons) by James Hoge [see note on Samuel Persans], Franklin Co.

1817 Dec 9   McClean, Caty and Obadiah Benedict Jr. by Wm. Swaze, MG (license date 9 Dec; return filed 13 Dec.), Franklin Co.

1810 Sep 6   McClean, Wm. and Katherien Main by Henry Jolly, JP, Washington Co.

1817 Mar 27   McClellan (or McClealland), Jane and Samuel Persans (or Parsons) by James Hoge [see note on Samuel Persans], Franklin Co.

1816 Feb 16	McCune, Mary and Theoron Hamilton by James Taylor, Licking Co.
1797 Apr 12	McCune, Peggy and Obediah Lincoln by Josiah Munro, JP, Washington Co.
1818 Nov --	McCune, Susana and Hugh Scott by -----, Jackson Co.
1821 Feb 15	McCurdy, Barney and Polly Roach by Amos Wilson, JP, Washington Co.
1826 Jul 13	McCutchan, William and Jane McKillips by G.W. Hart, JP, Franklin Co.
1826 Nov 21	M'Cutcheon, Elenor G. and James Lawson by Gideon W. Hart, JP, Franklin Co.
1814 May 26	McCutchin, Susan and Henry May by Rev. Rob't G. Wilson, Pickaway Co.
1824 Dec 23	McCutchon, James M. and Eliza Lawson by E. Washburn, VDM, Franklin Co.
1874 Jun 23	McClelland, Alex. and Margaret E. Edgar by Rev. A. Kingsbury, Putnam Presbyterian Church, Muskingum Co.
1805 May 9	McClilman, Peggy and Wm. Johnston by Peter Jackson, JP, Ross Co.
1802 May 17	McClimane, Jean and Jacob Ragon by Henry Smith, JP, Washington Co.
1801 Dec 14	McClimans, Esbel and John Hook by Daniel Story, Clerk, Washington Co.
1819 Aug 23	McClintick, Nancy and Asa Smith by James Whitney, JP, Washington Co.
1807 Aug 15	McClintock, George and Rachel Locoe by Luther Dana, JP, Washington Co.
1814 Nov 3	McClintock, Polly and Barker Cook by Dan'l H. Buell, Washington Co.
1825 May 19	McCloud, Elisa and Joseph P. Phinney by Nathan Emery, MG, Franklin Co.
1829 Mar 5	McCloud, Maria and Simeon Pool by Leroy Swornstead, Franklin Co.
1826 Mar 19	McCloud, Polly and Joseph Spangler by C. Hinckel, Franklin Co.
1824 Dec 30	McCloud, Thomas and Lovina Reams by John Goodrich Jr., JP, Franklin Co.
1821 Dec 7	McCloud, Wallace and Corrintha Gloyd by Samuel Abbott, JP, Franklin Co.
1794 Nov 11	McCluer, Andrew and Polly Allen by Robert Oliver, JP, Washington Co.
1821 Aug 20	McClure, Alexander and Fanny Clark by Ami Lawrence, Washington Co.
1826 Jan 12	McClure, Arthur and Jame Stephenson by John Shumate, JP, Jackson Co.
1819 Mar 25	McClure, Dolly Kimble and Almond Soul, Jr., by Dudley Davis, Washington Co.
1824 Jan 15	McClure, Martha and Samuel Stephenson by John Shumate, JP, Jackson Co.
1826 Feb 2	McClure, Nancy and Benj. Callagan by John Stephenson, JP, Jackson Co.
1826 Dec 30	McCollin, David and Elisabeth Powell by John Long, Franklin Co.
1819 Feb 12	McCollister, John and Feeby McNutt by D. Mitchell, JP, Jackson Co.
1823 Apr 22	McCollister, Joseph and Easter Griffy by Joseph Badger, Franklin Co.
1865 Jul 26	McCollough, Mary Ann and William Robinson by Rev. John Boyd, St. Luke's Church, Marietta, Washington Co.

1814 Sep 15   McCollum, Betsey and Samuel James by James Marshall, Franklin Co.

1823 Dec 26   McCollum, George and Sarah Daugherty by C. Waddell, LM, Franklin Co.

1825 Apr 14   McComb, Joseph and Rebbecca Kimble by Conrad Roth, JP, Marion Co.

1820 Aug 29   McComb, Margaret and John L. Turner by James Hoge, Franklin Co.

1821 Jun 5   McComb, Martha and Adam Turner by James Hoge, Franklin Co.

1826 Apr 11   McComb, Rebeccah and William Terner by Rev. James Hoge, Franklin Co.

1821 Nov 6   McComb, Samuel and Elizabeth Turner by James Hoge, Franklin Co.

1823 Apr 8   McComb, William and Elizabeth Ramsey by James Hoge, Franklin Co.

1815 Apr 16   McConell, Susan and James Quick by Henry Davis, JP, Pickaway Co.

1814 Mar 15   McConnel, James and Betsey Coonrod by Wm. Jones, JP, Pickaway Co.

1813 Jan 19   McConnell, Polly and Oliver Corwin (license date), Pickaway Co.

1804 Mar 22   McConnell, Wm. and Susanna Pancake by Geo. Williams, Ross Co.

1814 Apr 10   McConnelly, Catherine and Matthias Robbins by Thos. Mace, JP,
               Pickaway Co.

1823 Jun 16   McCormac, Clarissa and Wesley Turner by Charles Waddell, LM,
               Franklin Co.

1888 Mar 21   McCormac, Lizzie of Chandlersville, O., and John R. Moorehead of
               Rix Mills, O., by Rev. George F. Moore, Putnam Presbyterian
               Church, Muskingum Co.

1826 Sep 26   McCormick, Betsy and Richard Headly by A. Allison, JP, Franklin Co.

1824 Jun 24   McCormick, Martha and Elijah Sackett by B. Bull, JP, Franklin Co.

1824 Mar 25   McCormick, Mary Ann and Hosea High by Charles Waddell, LM, Franklin
               Co.

1818 Jul 5   McCown, Elizabeth and Samuel Blackwell by Rev. Geo. Callanhan,
               Licking Co.

1806 Jun 12   McCoy, ----- and Thomas Thomas by Zachariah Stephen, JP, Franklin Co.

1799 Feb 21   McCoy, Alexander and Sabina Beach by Robert Oliver, JP, Washington
               Co.

1821 Feb 27   McCoy, Alexander and Elizabeth Morey by Ami Lawrence, Washington Co.

1828 May 15   McCoy, John and Rachael Sells by Sam'l Hamilton, Elder in the M.E.
               Church, Franklin Co.

1818 Nov 26   McCoy, Latitia and Jeremiah Greenman, Jr. by Titan Kimble, JP,
               Washington Co.

1819 May 4   McCoy, Mary and Townsend Nichols by James Hoge, Franklin Co.

1865 Feb 4   McCoy, Thomas and Emma Harlem by Rev. John Boyd, St. Luke's Church,
               Marietta, Washington Co.

1821 Sep 30   McCracken, David and Sarah Hughes by Isaac Painter, JP, Franklin Co.

1827 Aug 27   McCracken, David and Rachel Powell by Wm. Patterson, JP, Franklin Co.

1826 Sep 17   McCracken, Elizabeth and Thomas Hughs by Wm. Long, JP, Franklin Co.

1825 Apr 15   McCracken, Hugh and Martha Moor (license date), Marion Co.

1827 Feb 15   McCracken, John and Elizabeth Perrin by John Long, JP, Franklin Co.

1820 Dec 25   McCracken, Sarah and Philip Hull by Martin Hale, MG, Licking Co.

1814 Jan 6   McCrackin, Virgill and Nancy Irwin by Percival Adams, Franklin Co.

1822 Jan 18   McCrackin, William and Rebecca Hoffman by Jacob Keller, Franklin Co.

1820 Dec 14   McCray, Margaret and James Elliott by John Shumate, JP, Jackson Co.

1824 Feb 5   McCray, Patsy Ann and Samuel Craig by Samuel Carrick, JP, Jackson Co.

1825 Jan 6   McCray, Sarah and Augustus Frazee by J.B. Gilliland, JP, Jackson Co.

1823 Feb 21   McCrea, Martha and Richard Godman by Wm. Godman, JP, Franklin Co.

1811 Aug 4   McCreary, Nancy and David Evans by John Crow, JP, Licking Co.

1820 Mar 20   McCredy, James and Mary Kirkpatrick by James Cunningham, VDM,
              Licking Co.

1813 Nov 9   McCroskey, Margaret and Dorsey Belt by S. Donnavan, JP, Licking Co.

1802 Aug 3   McCullock, George and Catharine Scritchfield by Seth Cashart,
              Washington Co.

1805 Jul 25   McCullough, Elizabeth and John Taylor by David Mitchell, JP,
              Franklin Co.

1804 Oct 11   McCullough, John and Catharine Myers by John G. McCan, Ross Co.

1814 Mar 5   McCullum, Archibald and Jamima Lane by Thos. White, JP, Washington
              Co.

1813 Sep 3   McCullum, Eliza and Joseph Morris by Thomas White, JP, Washington Co.

1804 Aug 30   McCune, Betsay and Andrew Noteman by W. Robinson, Ross Co.

1810 May 4   McCune, James and Mary McCune by Wm. Dixon, Washington Co.

1809 Dec 27   McCune, Jane and George Evans by -----, Licking Co.

1805 Apr 7   McCune, Jean and Isaih McCabe by Samuel Edwards, Ross Co.

1820 Feb 17   McCune, Joseph and Orlinda Cating by Thos. Cox, JP, Jackson Co.

1810 Jan 25   McCune, Lydia and John Evans by Rev. George Vanaman, Licking Co.

1820 Feb 14   McCune, Margaret and Peter Kirkpatrick by James Cunningham, Licking
              Co.

1810 May 4   McCune, Mary and James McCune by Wm. Dixon, Washington Co.

1814 Mar 22   McDaniel Charles and Sally Jackson by J. Hickey, Licking Co.

1816 Oct 6   McDaniel, Daniel and Catharine Penny by Jos. Chapman, JP, Washington
              Co.

1819 Dec 31   McDaniel, George and Leafy Grant by James M. Booth, JP, Washington
              Co.

1819 Feb 25   McDaniel, Polly and Aaron Moot by Samuel McDowell, Jackson Co.

1804 Jul 5   McDaniels, Catharine and Hugh McKartey by J. Graham, Washington Co.

1804 Jul 19   McDaniels, Isabella and Samuel Smith by J. Graham, JP, Washington Co.

1827 Apr 27   McDermot, George and D.A. Sanford by James Hoge, Franklin Co.

1814 Jun 11   McDill, Dolly, widow, and James Wilson, both black persons, by
              Arthur O'Harra, Franklin Co.

1810 Jun 7   McDole, Alexander and Polly German by David Spangler, Franklin Co.

1810 Sep 7   McDole, Jenny and George Moin by A. Winegarner, JP, Licking Co.

1813 Dec 23   McDolle, Rachael and Jacob Roberts by John B. Johnston, Franklin Co.

1805 Dec 25   McDonald, Elizabeth and Timothy Gifford by Wm. Creighton, Ross Co.

1798 Dec 19   McDonald, Nancy and Michael Hammond by Josiah Munro, Washington Co.

1822 Jun 17   McDonald, Rachel and Isaac K. Russell by W.T. Martin, Franklin Co.

1880 Sep 8   MacDonald, Sarah J. and John C. Dickson both of Putnam by Rev.
               George F. Moore, Putnam Presbyterian Church, Muskingum Co.

1809 Jun 27   McDonald, William and Jane Dodson by Wm. Haines, JP, Licking Co.

1820 May 4   McDonale, Patrick and Elizabeth Hiner by Amasiah Hutchison, JP,
               Franklin Co.

1825 Dec 22   McDonold, George and Malinda Forgerson (or Forgeson) by H. Crabb,
               Minister of the Gospel of the Methodist Episcopal Church,
               Franklin Co.

1826 Apr 22   McDougal, Mary and Patrick Murdock by John Potter, JP, Jackson Co.

1815 Nov 23   McDougal, Sarah and William Taylor by T.S. Baird (Wm. T. was son
               of Judge James Taylor and was himself Associate Judge), Licking
               Co.

1809 Oct 19   McDougal, Stephan and Maria Glack by Wm. Haines, JP, Licking Co.

1804 Feb 9   McDougral, James and Elinor Brittian by Wm. Creighton, Ross Co.

1805 Dec 19   McDowel, Mary and David Jones by James Marshall, JP, Franklin Co.

1817 Dec 11   McDowell, Abram J. and Eliza Lord by James Hoge, Franklin Co.

1818 Dec 31   McDowell, Amy and Nath'l Scott by Alex Anderson, JP, Jackson Co.

1807 Jan 29   McDowell, Jane and Ellis Jones by Asa Shinn, MG, Franklin Co.

1817 Oct 30   McDowell, John and Elizabeth Bowen by Samuel McDowell, JP, Jackson
               Co.

1870 Jun 1   McDowell, Jonathan T. of Franklin, Pa. and Anna M. Jenvey by Rev.
               John Boyd, St. Luke's Church, Marietta, Washington Co.

1812 Mar 1   McDowell, Margarey and Thomas Casey by Wm. D. Hendren, Franklin Co.

1825 Aug 18   McDowell, Mary and Zenas Keller by Samuel McDowell, JP, Jackson Co.

1813 Nov 4   McDowell, Melina and Joel Abbot by Jon B. Johnston, Franklin Co.

1819 Mar 12   McDowell, Sarah and Jeremiah A. Minter by James Hoge, Franklin Co.

1825 Apr 5   McElhaney, Hugh and Sarah Williams by James Hoge, FCCC, Franklin Co.

1828 Jul 8   McElhany, John and Susanna Gooding by Eb'r Washburn, VDM, Franklin
               Co.

1814 Jun 16   McElvain, Andrew and Patsy Hunter by James Hoge, Franklin Co.

1822 Nov 28   McElvain, Joseph and Catharine Dalzell by James Hoge, Franklin Co.

1817 Nov 17   McElvain, Margaret and William Hunter by Eli C. King, JP, Franklin
               Co.

1822 Oct 17   McElvain, Matilda and Arthur Charra, Jr. by Eli C. King, Franklin Co.

1820 May 25   McElvain, Purdy and Levonia Risley by Eli C. King, Franklin Co.

1823 Apr 22   McElvaine, Andrew and Jane Hunter by James Hoge, Franklin Co.

1816 Feb 4   McElvin, John and Lidia Havens by Joseph Grate, Franklin Co.

1824 Jun 9   McElwene, Elizabeth and James Ford by John Kirby, JP, Marion Co.

1810 Aug 3   McEnlarf, John and Hannah Parr by A. Holden, JP, Licking Co.

1828 Jul 24   McEntire, Martha and Nathaniel Painter by Hugh Liams, JP, Franklin
              Co.

1818 Mar 12   McEntire, Robert and Elizabeth Bennet by Thos. B. Patterson, JP,
              Franklin Co.

1817 Aug 29   McEvans, David (or McKevans) and Irene Majors by Rev. T. Harris,
              Licking Co.

1805 Oct 23   McFadgin, John and Catharine Henderson by Daniel W. Suemey, Ross Co.

1808 Jul 30   McFain, Daniel and Polly Thompson by Henry Smith, JPHT, Licking Co.

1841 Oct 6   McFarland, Eunice and James H. Greene by Rev. James Bonnar, St.
              Luke's Church, Marietta, Washington Co.

1804 Nov 1   McFarland, Hannah and Furman Ford by Jacob Lindly, Washington Co.

1820 Apr 20   McFarland, Maria and Thomas Weston by Rev. Saml P. Robbins,
              Washington Co.

1818 Sep 10   McFarland, Sally and Asa Hussey by John Green, JP, Washington Co.

1825 Jun 24   McFarland (or McParland), William and Ann Straw by Brice Hays, JP,
              Franklin Co.

1818 Jul 2   McFarlin, Lydia and Adna Hussey by John Greene, JP, Washington Co.

1816 Feb 15   McFarlin, Peggy and Charles Owen by Jno Green, Washington Co.

1816 Oct 11   McGarry, David and Anna Reed by Jos Chapman, Washington Co.

1800 Mar 20   McGarvy, Patrick and Anne King by Robert Safford, JP, Washington Co.

1803 Nov 15   McGee, Elizabeth and Abner Martin by John Brough, JP, Washington Co.

1897 Aug 31   McGee, Florence of Meadow Farm, O., and S. Emerson Wilkins of Mt.
              Perry by Rev. George F. Moore, Putnam Presbyterian Church,
              Muskingum Co.

1803 Apr 27   McGee, James and Elizabeth Phillips by Sam'l Williamson, JP,
              Washington Co.

1803 Jun 1   McGill, Hugh and Sarah Eakins by Oliver Ross, Ross Co.

1829 Feb 1   McGill, Polly and Emanuel Cryder by Geo. Black, JP, Franklin Co.

1807 May 10   McGill, Rhue and Thomas Springer by David Mitchell, JP, Franklin Co.

1803 Dec 29   McGlaughlin, Marian Burns and Lewis Howard by Geo. Williams, JP,
              Ross Co.

1820 Sep 28   McGonnigal, Elzada and David A. Wheeler by Amos Wilson, Washington
              Co.

1820 Feb 7   McGowen, Ann and Hugh McMaster by Samuel Lain, Franklin Co.

1807 Jan 22   McGowen, Deborah and Robert Hunter by Arthur O'Harra, JP, Franklin
              Co.

1820 Feb 7   McGowen, Hannah and Alpheus Toll by Samuel Lain, Franklin Co.

1824 Jul 23   McGowen, John and Susannah Showers by J.B. Packard, JP, Marion Co.

1813 Jan 28   McGowin, Martha and Joseph Hunter by Wm. Shaw, Franklin Co.

1818 Dec 21   McGown, Jane and Philip Haswell by James Hoge, Franklin Co.

1825 Jul 14   McGown, Malelda Aann and John Cutler by Rev. Joseph Carper,
               Franklin Co.

1818 Dec 21   McGown, Mary H. and J. Shead by James Hoge, Franklin Co.

1816 Apr 1   McGown, Sarah and Benjamin Chandler by James Hoge, Franklin Co.

1826 Mar 16   McGrady, Nancy and David Anthony by Solomon Goodenagh, JP, Jackson
               Co.

1816 Aug 25   McGranahan, Kitty and Jacob Runkle by John Hunter, Franklin Co.

1817 Apr --   McGranahan, Patsy and George Runkle by John Hunter, Franklin Co.

1816 Jan 26   McGrath, Mary and Oliver Woodward by Rev. Stephen Lindsley,
               Washington Co.

1806 Feb 23   McGrath, Whittington and Mary Corner by Stephen Lindley, Washington
               Co.

1891 Jul 4   McGregar, David E. and Viola Spratt both of High Hill, O., by Rev.
               George F. Moore, Putnam Presbyterian Church, Muskingum Co.

1821 Jun 9   McGuines, Edmond and Polly Hougland by Abel Robinson M M Ch,
               Washington Co.

1817 Aug 18   McGuire, Eleanor and Elias Woodruff by Jacob Young, MG, Washington
               Co.

1804 Jun 7   McGuire, Nancy and Thomas McGuire by Thos Scott, JP, Ross Co.

1804 Aug 29   McGuire, Robert and Priscilla Clark by J. Gardner, JP, Ross Co.

1804 Jun 7   McGuire, Thomas and Nancy McGuire by Thos Scott, JP, Ross Co.

1808 Nov 10   McIlvaine, James and Margaret Lyle by James Hoge, Franklin Co.

1810 Apr 11   McIlvaine, Wm. and Rebecca Riddle by James Hoge, Franklin Co.

1818 Aug 8   McInson?, John and Catherine McKinley by Rev. Noah Fidler, Licking
               Co.

1864 Sep 28   McIntire, John R. and Almira Reed by Rev. John Boyd, St. Luke's
               Church, Marietta, Washington Co.

1794 Mar 30   McIntire, Lydia and Creatus Laferte by J.G. Petitt, Washington Co.

1825 Oct 23   McIntire, Mary and Sam'l Wilkins by Abner Bent, JP, Marion Co.

1825 Mar 25   McIntire, Peggy and John Crag by Joseph Clara, JP, Marion Co.

1824 Sep 13   McIntire, Sarah and Wm. Martin by Jacob Delay, MG, Jackson Co.

1868 Dec 22   McIntosh, E.S. of Beverly and Mrs. Clarinda Jane Russell by Rev.
               John Boyd, St. Luke's Church, Marietta, Washington Co.

1816 Nov 26   McIntosh, Enoch S. and Elizabeth Seely by John Green, JP,
               Washington Co.

1876 May 30   McIntosh, Jessie F. and Dr. Chas. M. Humston at Beverly by Rev. John
               Boyd, St. Luke's Church, Marietta, Washington Co.

1853 Oct 9   McIntosh, Julia A. and Samuel F. Kearns of Harrison Co., Va. by Rev.
              John Boyd, St. Luke's Church, Marietta, Washington Co.

1792 Jun 21   McIntosh, Nathan and Rhoda Shepard by J. Gilman, Washington Co.

1818 Feb 12   McIntosh, Rhoda Ann and Judah M. Chamberlain by Danl H. Buell, JP,
              Washington Co.

1820 Dec 21   McIntosh, Wm. W. and Hannah Regnier by Judah M. Chamberlain, JP,
              Washington Co.

1820 May 20   McInturf, Chrintina and Asa Cooley by Elijah Dorsey, Licking Co.

1804 Jul 5   McKartey, Hugh and Catharine McDaniels by J. Graham, Washington Co.

1803 Aug 22   McKee, John and Jane Alexander by J. Gardner, JP, Ross Co.

1816 Aug 15   McKee, John and Rachel Delong by D. Stephens, JP, Washington Co.

1813 Nov 24   McKee, Robert and Ruth Thurlo by Joel Tuttle, JP, Washington Co.

1802 Oct 18   McKee, Sally and John Loath by Joseph Buell, JP, Washington Co.

1820 Sep 28   McKeel, Mora and Salrah Hauser by J.B. Gilliland, JP, Jackson Co.

1809 Nov 30   McKeever, Sally and Thomas Brownin by John Porter, Washington Co.

1817 Apr 28   McKelvy, Joseph and Diana Evans by Noah Fidler, Licking Co.

1823 Sep 18   McKendree, Maryann and Henry Clover, Jr. by Peter Clover, JP,
              Franklin Co.

1814 Nov 3   McKenny, H. and Sarah Lewis by Wm. Florence, JP, Pickaway Co.

1814 Nov 24   McKenzie, James and Rebecca George by Wm. Florence, JP, Pickaway Co.

1813 Dec 9   McKenzie, Sarah and David Williams (license date), Pickaway Co.

1817 Aug 29   McKevans (or McEvans), David and Irene Majors by Rev. T. Harris,
              Licking Co.

1811 Sep 17   McKewne, Charles and Lydia Fulton by Jeremiah Dare, JP, Washington
              Co.

1819 Oct 14   McKibben, Letty and Henry O. Blennis by Saml Dye, JP, Washington Co.

1826 Jul 13   McKillips, Jane and William McCutchan by G.W. Hart, JP, Franklin Co.

1821 Feb 1   McKindley, Mary and Jeremiah Willson by Saml. Beach, JP, Washington
              Co.

1821 Jan 6   McKinley, Ann and Steward Ward by Benj. Coves, MG, Licking Co.

1817 Nov 27   McKinley, Anna and William Edman by Josias Ewing, JP, Licking Co.

1818 Aug 8   McKinley, Catherine and John McInson? by Rev. Noah Fidler, Licking
              Co.

1815 Jan 12   McKinley, John and Catherine Edwards by Nathan Connard, JP, Licking
              Co.

1817 Feb 27   McKinley, Thomas and Anna Gable by John Russell, JP, Washington Co.

1804 Nov 28   McKinney, Mary and Alexander Beck by John G. McCan, Ross Co.

1813 Feb 2   McKinney, Polly and Isaac Radcliffe (license date), Pickaway Co.

1804 May 24   McKinney, Sarah and John Mathews by Thos. Scott, JP, Ross Co.

1824 Sep 14   McKinney, Simeon and Abigail Patterson by R.W. Coles, JP, Franklin
               Co.

1824 Dec 2   McKinnis, Joseph and Louisa Shearer by Robert Ward, JP, Jackson Co.

1817 Mar 12   McKinsey, Fanny and Benjamin Chenoweth by Samuel Dyer (another
               entry on 16 Mar. 1817), Franklin Co.

1812 Dec 31   McKrey, Benj and Deborah Mathew by N. Connard, Licking Co.

1810 Oct 23   McLain, Alexander and Maria Duncan (license date), Pickaway Co.

1822 Jan 3   McLane, Washington and Betsey Nicherson by Nicholas Goetschius,
               Franklin Co.

1817 Apr 30   McLaughlin, James and Deborah Weatherbee by Stephen Guthrie, JP,
               Washington Co.

1817 Jan 2   McLaughlin, John and Elizabeth Shannon by John Drips, JP, Licking Co.

1819 Apr 4   McLaughlin, Martha and John B. Seeley by Stephen Maynard, Franklin
               Co.

1818 Jul 14   McLean, George and Margaret Fleming by James McLish, Franklin Co.

1896 Feb 19   McLean, John A. and Annie Wheeler both of Zanesville by Rev. George
               F. Moore, Putnam Presbyterian Church, Muskingum Co.

1796 Nov 22   McLeane, Polly and Neal Courtney by J. Munro, JP, Washington Co.

1321 Jul 10   McLene, Eliza and William Doherty by James Hoge, Franklin Co.

1823 Aug 10   McLene, Jacob and Sarah Kile by Richard Courtright, Franklin Co.

1826 Dec 4   McLene, Margaret and Samuel Crosby by James Hoge, Franklin Co.

1804 Nov 1   McMachlan, Benjamin and Nancy Boggs by David Shelby, Ross Co.

1808 Jan 20   McMahan, Constantine and Margaret Breckinridge by Wm. Irwin,
               Franklin Co.

1810 Apr 12   McMahan, Nelly and Isaac Grace by Nichael Fisher, Franklin Co.

1816 Feb 4   McMahan, William and Jamimah Norris by Alex Basset, JP, Franklin Co.

1811 Aug 29   McMahon, Nancy and Peter Swank (license date), Pickaway Co.

1820 Feb 7   McMaster, Hugh and Ann McGowen by Samuel Lain, Franklin Co.

1812 Dec 17   McMasters, Catharine and Caleb Greene by Rev. Stephen Lindley,
               Washington Co.

1806 Aug 5   McMillan, Jane and Alexander Vaughn by Jacob Lindly, Washington Co.

1814 Dec 15   McMillen, Andrew and Elizabeth Wilson by Nathan Cunningham, Licking
               Co.

1818 Apr 16   McMillen, Jane and Abigail Seely by Wm. Rand, Washington Co.

1820 Sep 21   McMillen, Matilda and James Dickson by Robert W. Riley, JP, Franklin
               Co.

1818 Jan 22   McMillin, Cendian and James Skinner by Joseph Grate, Franklin Co.

1815 Sep 5   McMillin, Nelly and John Loren by James Marshall, Franklin Co.

1822 Feb 10   McMullan, Susanna and Robert Kerr by N. Little, Franklin Co.

1817 Jan 5   McMullin, Betsey and David Andrews by Simon Merwin, Washington Co.

1806 Mar 5   McMullin, Jane and Joel Cooper by J. Gardner, JP, Ross Co.

1859 Jul 25   McMurray, George T. of California and Sarah M. Norton of Harmar by
              Rev. John Boyd, St. Luke's Church, Marietta, Washington Co.

1810 Nov 4   McNamir, Bryan and Anne Moore (license date), Pickaway Co.

1873 Dec 2   McNeal, Ason and Sarah E. Smith by Rev. John Boyd, St. Luke's Church,
              Marietta, Washington Co.

1818 Aug 18   McNeil, William and Susanna Corwin by Danl H. Buell, JP, Washington
              Co.

1811 Nov 12   McNitt, Margaret and John Henry by Stephen Lindsly, Washington Co.

1819 Feb 12   McNutt, Feeby and John McCollister by D. Mitchell, JP, Jackson Co.

1805 Aug 8   McNut, Francis and Samuel Blair by Zachariah Stephen, JP, Franklin Co.

1825 Jun 24   McParland (or McFarland), William and Ann Stråw by Brice Hays, JP,
              Franklin Co.

1816 Jan 1   McQune, Catherine and James Rabourn by James Marshall, JP, Franklin
              Co.

1815 Feb 9   McVay, Jacob and Polly Nicholson by Thos Ferguson, Washington Co.

1805 Jan 5   McVay, John and Betsy Simmons by John Greene, Washington Co.

1813 Aug 6   McVay, Reuben and Margarett Hill by Anthony Sheets, Washington Co.

1819 Nov 18   McVay, William and Catharine Hisem by Moses Williamson, Washington Co.

1820 Apr 20   McVey, Jane and Joseph Greaves by Joseph Lockard, JP, Jackson Co.

1856 Mar 18   McWherton, Wm. H. and Fidelia A. Allen by Rev. Geo. B. Sturges, St.
              Paul's Church, Marion, Marion Co.

1817 Aug 5   Meacham, Mary and Robert Williams by Danl H. Buell, JP, Washington Co.

1821 Feb 17   Meacham, Riley and Hannah Baldwin by Reuben Carpenter, JP, Franklin
              Co.

1821 Jan 21   Meacham, Sally and Asa Lee by T. Lee, JP, Franklin Co.

1805 May 23   Meachouse, Margaret and Francis Baldwin by Thos Scott, JP, Ross Co.

1812 Feb 3   Meachum, Laura and Simeon Moore, Jr. by Simeon Moore, Franklin Co.

1816 Mar 10   Mead, Abigail and Walt Haskins by Simon Merwin, JP, Washington Co.

1814 May 29   Mead, Ann and Bazilia Browning by Rev. Jas. Cunningham, Washington Co.

1816 Nov 9   Mead, Mahala and Samuel Thrall by Rev. T. Harris, Licking Co.

1819 Nov 17   Mead, Matildah and Timothy M. Rose by Samuel Bancroft, JP, Licking Co.

1812 May 28   Mead, Polly and Augustine Munson by Rev. T. Harris, Licking Co.

1821 Feb 1   Mead, Polly and Mathew Hopkins by Thos Scott, JP, Licking Co.

1817 Feb 8   Mead, Silas and Martha Phelps by Rev. Harris, Licking Co.

1815 Nov 5   Mead, William and Cynthia Harris by Solomon Goss, Washington Co.

1819 Nov 9   Meade, James and Elizabeth Rugg by Spencer Wright, JP, Licking Co.

1806 10 mo 15 Mecoy, Jane and Joseph Cloud, Miami Monthly Meeting, Warren Co.

1814 Apr 3   Medford, Chales and Ruth Wiggins by Wm. D. Hendren, Franklin Co.

1823 Jan 14   Medford, Mary Ann and Amos Forba by Richard Courtright, Franklin Co.

1868 Jun 11   Medlicott, Catherine H. and John Paul Jones by Rev. John Boyd, St.
               Luke's Church, Marietta, Washington Co.

1864 Aug 16   Medlicott, Henrietta and T.G. Field by Rev. John Boyd, St. Luke's
               Church, Marietta, Washington Co.

1864 Mar 21   Medlicott, Jane M. and Frank F. Watson of Vincennes, Ind., by Rev.
               John Boyd, St. Luke's Church, Marietta, Washington Co.

1812 Jul 5   Medskel, George and Nancy Morris (license date), Pickaway Co.

1821 Jul 26   Meed, Ann and David Rogers by Chandler Rogers, Franklin Co.

1825 Mar 5   Meeker, Benj and Susan Smith by Alex Kinnear, MG, Marion Co.

1818 Sep 26   Meeker, Catherine and Rymard Osbond? by Benj Beem, JP, Licking Co.

1825 Nov 24   Meeker, Evalina and Bennett Beardslee by Vincent Southard, JP,
               Jackson Co.

1818 Aug 15   Meeker, Hannah and Samuel Ausburn by Rev. Geo. Callanhan, Licking Co.

1825 Dec 1   Meeker, Joshua (or Joseph)and Elizabeth Baylor by C. Hinkel, Franklin
               Co.

1824 May 10   Meeker, Moses and Naome Kesnor, dau of Michael Kesnor, by Wm. C.
               Duff, JP, Franklin Co.

1812 Aug 13   Meeker, Sally and Reuben Reuby by James Marshall, Franklin Co.

1818 Jul 18   Meeker, Susannah and John Osborn by Benj Beem, JP, Licking Co.

1824 Nov 7   Meeker, Tandy and Ruthy Hubel by Samuel McDowell, JP, Jackson Co.

1810 Nov 10   Meeks, Bazel and Jane Williamson by Henry Jolly, JP, Washington Co.

1820 Apr 21   Meeks, John and Jane Burden by John Patterson, Washington Co.

1826 Nov 17   Megill, Hughey and Mary Foley by Ruben Golliday, Franklin Co.

1810 Jul 19   Meigs, Mary Sophia and John B. Jackson by Stephen Lindsly,
               Washington Co.

1863 Jun 10   Meison, Louise and Martin Anderson by Rev. John Boyd, St. Luke's
               Church, Marietta, Washington Co.

1817 Mar 9   Mellor, Eleanor and William Bacon by P. White, JP, Washington Co.

1813 Nov 29   Mellor, Levi Prudence and Edmund Perry by David Young, MG,
               Washington Co.

1813 Nov 21   Mellor, Sally and Smith Green by N. Hamilton, JP, Washington Co.

1806 Oct 25   Mellor, Samuel and Nancy Jadding by Rob't Oliver, Washington Co.

1817 Aug 31   Mellor, Samuel and Margaret Young by John Patterson, JP, Washington
               Co.

1817 Jan 25   Melphrey, Daniel and Elizabeth Morris (or Harris) by John Green,
               Licking Co.

1867 Oct 11   Melrose, Nancy E. and James A. Graham by Rev. John Boyd, St. Luke's
               Church, Marietta, Washington Co.

1865 Sep 28   Mendenhall, James and Hannah M. Ross by Rev. John Boyd, St. Luke's
               Church, Marietta, Washington Co.

1807 2 mo 26 Mendinghall, Ruth and Ely Jinkins, Miami Monthly Meeting, Warren Co.

1802 Jun 29 Menough, Harriet and George Wallace both of Trumbull Co. by Wm. Wick, VDM, Trumbull Co.

1794 Apr 15 Mentel, Auguste Waldmar and Victoire Charlotte-Luton by J.G. Petitt, Washington Co.

1819 Jun 6 Mentzer, David and Mary Messmore by Alex Holden, JP, Licking Co.

1882 Jul 11 Mercer, Lydia and Charles L. Schleiermacher by Rev. John Boyd, St. Luke's Church, Marietta, Washington Co.

1895 May 8 Mercer, Richard S. and Myrta Johnson both of South Zanesville by Rev. George F. Moore, Putnam Presbyterian Church, Muskingum Co.

1821 Jan 29 Merchant, Barnard and Parmina Sherman by Samuel Bancroft, JP, Licking Co.

1827 Oct 27 Meredeth, Eliza and Robert R. Carson by James Hoge, Franklin Co.

1801 Mar 24 Merrel, Unity and Thomas Sharp by Wm. Harper, JP, Washington Co.

1823 Nov 20 Merrian, Lucy and John Flenniken by James Hoge (a son, John Flanigan, resided in Franklin Co.), Franklin Co.

1825? Jan 25 Merrian, Lydia and John Mooberry by James Hoge, Franklin Co.

1809 Feb 11 Merrian, Wm. and Salley Watts by James Hoge, Franklin Co.

1849 Sep 5 Merrill, John and Leah Turney by Rev. Geo. Thompson, St. Paul's Church, Marion, Marion Co.

1824 Mar 17 Merrille, Clarissa and Henry Bickle by Gershom Stillman, MG, Jackson Co.

1825 Jan 10 Merrim, Charles and Susan Cary by David Dudley, MG, Marion Co.

1816 Feb 7 Merris, Sarah and William Mickey by Alex Basset, Franklin Co.

1824 Apr 29 Merriss, Benjamin and Angelina Strain by Uriah Clark, Franklin Co.

1864 Nov 17 Merritt, William M. and Mary M. Snyder by Rev. John Boyd, St. Luke's Church, Marietta, Washington Co.

1820 Apr 9 Merry, Joseph and Nancy Nicholls by Osgood McFarland, JP, Washington Co.

1821 May 27 Meruben, Bertrand and Emily Dunbar by John Russell, JP, Washington Co.

1819 Dec 21 Merwin, Susan and Gen'l Nathan G. Cushing by Rev. Saml P. Robbins, Washington Co.

1819 Nov 10 Mesewey, Benjamin and Mary West by John C. Smith, JP, Licking Co.

1816 --- -- Mesmore, Naomi and John Tedrick by Alex Holden, Licking Co.

1866 Jun 28 Messenger, Everett and Jane Irvin by N.C.N. Dudley, St. Paul's Church, Marion, Marion Co.

1858 Sep 7 Messenger, Rev. H.H. and Gertrude Jane Turney by Rev. Hollis, St. Paul's Church, Marion, Marion Co.

1865 Mar 14 Messenger, Matilda and Chas. C. Thompson by Rev. H.H. Messenger (in the presence of Mr. & Mrs. Turney and others, at Turney's house), St. Paul's Church, Marion, Marion Co.

1825 Jul 21 Messenger, Moses E. and Rachel Jurey by John Green, JP, Marion Co.

1811 Feb 28 Messick, George and Jane Poland (License date), Pickaway Co.

1826 Aug 31 Messinger, Sarah D. and Isreal S. Wilcox by R.W. Cowls, JP,
             Franklin Co.

1819 Jun 6 Messmore, Mary and David Mentzer by Alex Holden, JP, Licking Co.

1818 Sep 9 Meswey, Harriet and John Jones and John C. Smith, JP, Licking Co.

1821 Feb 22 Metcalf, Elizabeth and Luther Mallory by Noah Fidler, Licking Co.

1822 Sep 12 Metcalf, Ira and Clarinda Caulkins by A. Buttles, Franklin Co.

1847 Jun 22 Metcalf, Jane and Henry Calhoun by Rev. A. Kingsbury, Putnam
             Presbyterian Church, Muskingum Co.

1854 Sep 16 Metcalf, Sarah G. of Putnam and E.W. Smith of Mansfield by Rev. A.
             Kingsbury, Putnam Presbyterian Church, Muskingum Co.

1814 Mar 22 Metger, Polly and Daniel Pontious by Jacob Leist, JP, Pickaway Co.

1812 Feb 15 Methen, Esais and Elisa Belt by Wm. Haines, Likcing Co.

1817 Nov -- Mettle, Abraham and Sally Right by John Hunter, Franklin Co.

1817 Feb 11 Metts, Ruth and James Hall by Nathan Cunningham, Licking Co.

1811 Mar 24 Metz, Adam and Catherine Davis (license date), Pickaway Co.

1815 Apr 23 Metzgar, Henry and Catherine Wise by Thomas Mace, JP, Pickaway Co.

1855 Jun 14 Metzgar, John J. and Caroline E. Prichard by T. Corlett, St. Luke's
             Church, Granville, Licking Co.

1870 Nov 17 Meyer, Sarah and Charles T. Christy by I.B. Britton, St. Paul's
             Church, Marion, Marion Co.

1813 Jan 26 Micael, Rebecca and Job Arrowhood (license date), Pickaway Co.

1826 Feb 11 Michael, Sarah and William Rogers by Wm. Godman, Franklin Co.

1812 Jul 19 Michall, Catherine and Dennis Madden (license date), Pickaway Co.

1811 Jan 6 Michall, Cornelius and Mary Bayley (license date), Pickaway Co.

1826 Oct 22 Micham, Worthy P. and Polly Bigalow by Nathan Emery, MG, Franklin Co.

1826 Aug 10 Michel (or Mitchel), Moses and Jemima Courtwright by Tracy Willcox,
             Franklin Co.

1809 Jul 26 Mickey, Polly and John Thomas by Benj'n Sells, JP, Franklin Co.

1815 Sep 24 Mickey, Sally and Thomas Mickey by Daniel Brunk, JP, Franklin Co.

1815 May 11 Mickey, Thomas and Jane Everet by Dan'l Brink, JP, Franklin Co.

1815 Sep 24 Mickey, Thomas and Sally Mickey by Daniel Brunk, JP, Franklin Co.

1816 Feb 7 Mickey, William and Sarah Merris by Alex Basset, Franklin Co.

1813 Nov 24 Miclick, Elenor and Hosmer Curtis (son of Zarah Curtis and a brother
             of the Hon. Henry B. Curtis of Mt. Vernon, O.) by Silas Winchel,
             JP, Licking Co.

1816 Jul 26 Middleswart, Emily and Hugh Thompson by Geo. Templeton, Esq.,
             Washington Co.

1828 Feb 21   Middleton, I.D. and Magaretretta Davis by John F. Solomon, Franklin
               Co.

1814 Jan 25   Mider, Lucy and Joseph T. Smith by Samuel Dye, JP, Washington Co.

1808 Mar 12   Miers, Catherine and Daniel Staltz by John Hollister, JPHT, Licking
               Co.

1812 Apr 23   Miers, Henry and Elizabeth Haines by Z. Carlisle, JP, Licking Co.

1808 Feb 25   Miers, Margaret and James Cunningham by John Hollister, JPHT,
               Licking Co.

1814 Oct 1   Miers, Mary and William Harris by Wm. Taylor, Licking Co.

1818 Dec 27   Miles, Barzillia T. and Sally Eastman by Rev. Saml. P. Robbins,
               Washington Co.

1810 Feb 9   Miles, Benj. Hubbard and Persis Marie Burlinggame by Rev. S.P.
               Robbins, Washington Co.

1808 Jan 4   Miles, Mary Prescot and Bial Steadman by S.P. Robbins, Washington Co.

1814 Oct 16   Miles, William and Hannah Eastman by Stephen Guthrie, Washington Co.

1805 11 mo 21 Milhous, Henry and Anna Strawn, Miami Monthly Meeting, Warren Co.

1817 8 mo 7   Milhous, Henry and Sarah Horner, Miami Monthly Meeting, Warren Co.

1815 Jan 31   Milisen, Barnett and Catherine Miller by Jacob Zellers, Pickaway Co.

1824 Nov 19   Milizer, Henry and Elizabeth Berry (license date), Marion Co.

1817 Mar 27   Millan, Wm. and Christina Fisher by James Hoge, Franklin Co.

1803 Sep 15   Miller, Abel and Mary Jones by J. Graham, Esq., Washington Co.

1826 Apr 20   Miller, Abram and Polly Cornett by J. Gander, Franklin Co.

1814 Mar 6   Miller, Adam and Polly Fitzgerald by Rob't Bradshaw, JP, Pickaway Co.

1819 Feb 27   Miller, Adam and Rebeccah Deckar by James Hoge, Franklin Co.

1811 Nov 17   Miller, Alexander and Eleanor Dean by Philip Witten, JP, Washington
               Co.

1825 Aug 21   Miller, Alex. and Marmoen James by Rob't Ward, JP, Jackson Co.

1806 Oct 16   Miller, Amos and Polly White by Sam'l P. Robbins, Washington Co.

1825 Dec 15   Miller, Anna and John Corn, Jr. by Vincent Southard, JP, Jackson Co.

1806 May 13   Miller, Betsy and John Hurlbut by R. Oliver, Washington Co.

1815 Jan 31   Miller, Catherine and Barnett Milisen by Jacob Zellers, Pickaway Co.

1815 Jul 19   Miller, Catherine and Jacob Craun by Frederick Peterson, Franklin Co.

1853 Mar 3   Miller, Conrad and Cahterine Cisler by Rev. John Boyd, St. Luke's
               Church, Marietta, Washington Co.

1827 Dec 6   Miller, Delila and Solomon Borror by Wooley Conrad, Franklin Co.

1807 Apr 16   Miller, Edward and Katherine Nulton by Robert Oliver, Washington Co.

1799 Jun 16   Miller, Elizabeth and Simeon Evans by Robert Oliver, JP, Washington
               Co.

1800 Apr 1   Miller, Elizabeth and Ezekiel Rice by Robert Safford, Washington Co.

1827 Mar 15   Miller, Elsy E. and Aaron Evert by Amaziah Hutchinson, Franklin Co.

1814 Apr 3   Miller, Fanny and Joseph Wickingham by Rev. Isaac Quinn, Washington
               Co.

1806 Oct 25   Miller, George and Lois Taylor by Rob't Oliver, JP, Washington Co.

1815 Mar 28   Miller, George and Rebecca Caom (or Coon) by Elijah Austin, PP,
               Franklin Co.

1882 Jan 26   Miller, George W. and Emma L. Semon by Rev. John Boyd, St. Luke's
               Church, Marietta, Washington Co.

1805 Aug 29   Miller, Hannah and Daniel Hodges by J. Gardner, JP, Ross Co.

1812 Nov 23   Miller, Hannah and Robert Dickson (license date), Pickaway Co.

1815 Sep 28   Miller, Hannah and John Martin by Percival Adams, Franklin Co.

1822 Jul 11   Miller, Hannah and Henry Tilberry by N. Goetschius, Franklin Co.

1824 Dec 16   Miller, Henry and Magdelina Wolf by John Stealy, JP, Marion Co.

1827 Dec 30   Miller, I.F. and Annah Warson by A. Hutchinson, JP, Franklin Co.

1806 Jan 2   Miller, Isaac and Rebeckah Malone by J. Gardner, JP, Ross Co.

1812 May 21   Miller, Isaac and Betsey Dickson by Alex. Commins, Franklin Co.

1808 Jan 28   Miller, Jacob and Sarah Hill by Thos. Stanley, JP, Washington Co.

1827 Apr 29   Miller, Jacob and Avis Hunter by J.N. Walter, MG, Franklin Co.

1828 Oct 2   Miller, James C. and Rosey Ann Warson by Daniel Beard, Franklin Co.

1804 Aug 24   Miller, John and Betsy Cailer by Abm. Miller, Ross Co.

1806 Oct 19   Miller, John and Betsy Wheeler by Sam'l P. Robbins, Washington Co.

1808 May 12   Miller, John and Jane Taylor by Stephen Lindly, Washington Co.

1818 Dec 10   Miller, John and Tilla Fleming by James McLish, Franklin Co.

1818 Dec 24   Miller, John and Abigail Briggs, by Thomas White, JP, Washington Co.

1821 Feb 4   Miller, John and Rachel Shad by Eli C. King, Franklin Co.

1825 Feb 20   Miller, John and Margaret Ford by Wm. C. Duff, Franklin Co.

1828 Sep 8   Miller, John and Mary Shrum by Adam Miller, Franklin Co.

1797 Jun 19   Miller, Joseph and Betsy Diggans by Robert Safford, JP, Washington Co.

1827 Apr 26   Miller, Joseph and Elnnora Cady by D.W. Deshler, Franklin Co.

1881 Mar 30   Miller, Levi C. and Dora Nicholas by Rev. John Boyd, St. Luke's
               Church, Marietta, Washington Co.

1821 Feb 11   Miller, Martin and Elin Grooms by Robert Elliott, JP, Franklin Co.

1824 Jun 1   Miller, Mary and Robert Robinson by James Hoge, Franklin Co.

1822 Aug 1   Miller, Mary Ann and Aaron Seeds by Woolry Conrad, Franklin Co.

1857 Oct 8   Miller, Mary Jane and Wm. K. Stockton by Rev. Geo. B. Sturges, St.
               Paul's Church, Marion, Marion Co.

1825 Dec 1   Miller, Mathew and Mercy Cazad by Wm. C. Duff, Franklin Co.

1818 May 21   Miller, Mathias and Amy Critten by John McMahon, Licking Co.

1816 Oct 15   Miller, Peter and Polly Floos by Elisha Decker, Franklin Co.

1811 Aug 6   Miller, Polly and James Comes by John Greene, Washington Co.

1817 Jan 5   Miller, Polly and Richard Parr by John Cunningham, JP, Licking Co.

1804 Jun 14   Miller, Robert and Fanny Mooney by Abm. Miller, Ross Co.

1822 May 5   Miller, Rosanna and Abram Craun by N. Goetschius, Franklin Co.

1817 Dec 22   Miller, Sally and James Johnson by Joseph Thrap, Licking Co.

1805 Jul 4   Miller, Samuel and Hanah Pursell by Wm. Robinson, Ross Co.

1813 Jul 27   Miller, Susana and John Hedges (license date), Pickaway Co.

1811 May 30   Miller, William and Ena Town (license date), Pickaway Co.

1814 Mar 17   Miller, Wm. and Margaret Forseman by Wm. Jones, JP, Pickaway Co.

1826 Mar 30   Miller, Woodford and Mary Evans by Geo. Jefferies, MG, Franklin Co.

1816 Dec 8   Millerd, Joseph P. and Betsy Pritchard by John Russell, JP, Washington
               Co.

1879 May 15   Milligan, James B. of Lancaster, O., and Amelia Guille of Putnam by
               Rev. George F. Moore, Putnam Presbyterian Church, Muskingum Co.

1805 Dec 19   Millikan, John and Mary Wyatt by James S. Webster, Ross Co.

1813 Mar 22   Millington, Caroline M. and George Hill by Daniel Brink, JP, Franklin
               Co.

1827 Jul 12   Millington, Marcus and Jane Justice by Tracy Willcox, JP, Franklin Co.

1819 3 mo 4   Mills, Anna and Elisha Mills, Miami Monthly Meeting, Warren Co.

1803 May 4   Mills, Caroline and John Shaw by Joseph Buel, JP, Washington Co.

1826 Jan 25   Mills, Caroline and John Farrir by James Hoge, Franklin Co.

1795 Mar 29   Mills, Charles and Sally Nyswonger by R.J. Meigs, Washington Co.

1807 4 mo 15   Mills, Daniel and Elizabeth Carr, Miami Monthly Meeting, Warren Co.

1819 3 mo 4   Mills, Elisha and Anna Mills, Miami Monthly Meeting, Warren Co.

1819 5 mo 5   Mills, Elizabeth and David Sayre, Miami Monthly Meeting, Warren Co.

1819 2 mo 3   Mills, Hugh and Lydia Haskett, Miami Monthly Meeting, Warren Co.

1807 11mo 18   Mills, Isaac and Catharine Richards, Miami Monthly Meeting, Warren Co.

1813 12 mo 1   Mills, James and Elizabeth Brown, Miami Monthly Meeting, Warren Co.

1814 Jul 10   Mills, Jane and Stephen Gates by John Brough, Esq., Washington Co.

1812 3 mo 4   Mills, John and Prudence Thomas, Miami Monthly Meeting, Warren Co.

1812 12 mo 13 Mills, Mary and Ruel Ragin, Miami Monthly Meeting, Warren Co.

1825 Sep 1   Mills, Mary and James Johnson by A. Allison, JP, Franklin Co.

1826 3 mo 2   Mills, Patience N. and Joseph Furnas, Miami Monthly Meeting, Warren Co.

1813 Sep 12   Mills, Sally and Jonathan Guitteau by Rev. S.P. Robbins, Washington Co.

1806 Dec 11   Mills, Sarah and Jabez True by Sam'l P. Robbins, Washington Co.

1812 1 mo 1   Mills, Sarah and Andrew Hamton, Miami Monthly Meeting, Warren Co.

1813 Jun 29   Mills, Sarah and David Cline by Anthony Sheets, JP, Washington Co.

1820 May 16   Mills, Sarah and Nathaniel Mather by James Hoge, Franklin Co.

1810 Dec 6   Mills, Thompson of Knox County and Sally Brown by James Scott,
               Licking Co.

1821 Jul 18   Mills, William and Polly Showers by Jacob Smith, JP, Franklin Co.

1817 Dec 25   Milton, Jack and Metilda German by George Hays, Franklin Co.

1826 Dec 14   Milvin, Joseph and Elizabeth Gardiner by John Tipton, JP, Franklin Co

1801 May 12   Minair, Peter and Elizabeth Picket by Alvan Bingham, JP, Washington C

1818 Sep 10   Miner, Betsey and Nathan Stephens by Wm. Rand, Washington Co.

1815 Jul 26   Miner, Mathew and Catharine Taylor by Rev. S.P. Robbins, Washington C

1810 Feb 22   Miner, Richard and Ann Marie Corner by Stephen Lindsly, Washington Co

1813 Dec 29   Miner, Richard and Esther Wilson by Thomas Seely, JP, Washington Co.

1818 Jul 2   Miner, Worrin and Jsaphina Wollon by Wm. Swayze, JP, Franklin Co.

1828 Jun 5   Minor, Griffin R. and Caroline A. Weston by James Hoge, Franklin Co.

1803 Mar 24   Minor, Philip and Elizabeth Richard by James Dunlap, JP, Ross Co.

1819 Mar 12   Minter, Jeremiah A. and Sarah McDowell by James Hoge, Franklin Co.

1807 Apr 12   Minter, Polly and Jeremiah Armstrong by James Marshall, JP, Franklin
               Co.

1815 May 4   Minton, Joseph and Rebecca Rardon by Joseph Palmer, Washington Co.

1814 May 4   Minton, Rebecca and Moses Rardon by Joseph Palmer, JP, Washington Co.

1818 Sep 9   Misavey, Marton and Hannah Bryant by John C. Smith, JP, Licking Co.

1814 Dec 28   Misner, Sally and John Allen by Stephen Guthrie, JP, Washington Co.

1806 Nov 26   Mitchel, Betsy and Samuel Amlin by Stephen Lindsly, Washington Co.

1820 Jun 8   Mitchel, Harriet and David Smith by Joseph Gorton, Franklin Co.

1817 Jan 2   Mitchel, Jane and John Robinson by Alex Bassett, Franklin Co.

1817 Jul 20   Mitchel, Mary and Joseph Hunter by James Hoge, Franklin Co.

1826 Aug 10   Mitchel (or Michel), Moses and Jemima Courtwright by Tracy Willcox,
               Franklin Co.

1806 Feb 23   Mitchel, Robert and Rohdy Handycock by Wm. Davis, JP, Ross Co.

1869 Nov 25   Mitchell, Anna and James Jackson by Rev. John Boyd, St. Luke's Church
               Marietta, Washington Co.

1817 Apr 1   Mitchell, David and Nancy Hunter by Michael Potter, JP, Franklin Co.

1810 Aug 2   Mitchell, Edward and Jane Hill by Stephen Lindsly, Washington Co.

1815 Jan 3   Mitchell, Elizabeth and Henry Coldson by Chas. Cade, JP, Pickaway Co.

1805 Oct 24   Mitchell, Frederick and Lucy Lad by Wm. Creighton, Ross Co.

1818 Nov 12   Mitchell, James and Rachel O. Blennis by Rev. Saml P. Robbins,
               Washington Co.

1806 Jun 25   Mitchell, John and Ann Plumer by Stephen Lindsly, Washington Co.

1813 May 10   Mitchell, Jos. and Jane Regalo by Isaac Fisher, Franklin Co.

1810 Aug 14   Mitchell, Mary and John Woolcutt by James Marshall, Franklin Co.

1808 Feb 24   Mitchell, Moses and Jinney Taylor by David Mitchell, Franklin Co.

1820 Jan 2   Mitchell, Nancy and James Rayner by Saml. Dye, JP, Washington Co.

1821 Jan 7   Mitchell, Nathaniel and Phebe Jackson by Dudley Davis, Washington Co.

1817 Apr 1   Mitchell, Patsey and William Fulton by John Hunter, JP, Franklin Co.

1821 Dec 27   Mitchell, Phebe and William Afflick by Sam'l Dye, JP, Washington Co.

1811 Jan 17   Mitchell, Sally and Silas Cook by Stephen Lindsly, Washington Co.

1826 Oct 26   Mitchell, William and Poly Courson by Reuben Golliday, JP, Franklin Co.

1871 Dec 7   Mitchell, William B. and Emily Whittlesey by Rev. John Boyd, St. Luke's
               Church, Marietta, Washington Co.

1815 Jan 11   Mitten, George and Sarah Rush by James Jackson, JP, Pickaway Co.

1808 Dec 22   Mixer, Sally and David Gilmore by Sam'l P. Robbins, Washington Co.

1821 Apr 9   Mixer, Sally and George Burley by Daniel H. Buell, JP, Washington Co.

1829 May 10   Mock, Margaret and Peter Voris by Leroy Swormsted, Franklin Co.

1814 Aug 25   Mock, Polly and John Crevisto by John Emmett, JP, Pickaway Co.

1870 Sep 14   Moffett, Elizabeth and Joseph H. Robinson by Rev. John Boyd, St.
               Luke's Church, Marietta, Washington Co.

1870 Dec 22   Moffett, Jane and Daniel Morey by Rev. John Boyd, St. Luke's Church,
               Marietta, Washington Co.

1805 Aug 1   Moffett, Nathan and Charrety Cox by J. Gardner, JP, Ross Co.

1805 Feb 5   Moffett, Solomon and Rebecah Cox by J. Gardner, JP, Ross Co.

1816 Dec 25   Mogrudge, Sally and Ebenezer Cunningham by John Patterson, Washington
               Co.

1810 Sep 7   Moin, George and Jenny McDole by A. Winegarner, JP, Licking Co.

1811 Feb 19   Molen, Keshe and Jane Little by Thos. Ferguson, JP, Washington Co.

1816 Sep 26   Moler, Rollin and Susanna Ransburg by James Hoge, Franklin Co.

1810 Jan 20   Mollahan, Molley Molla and Scarlott Owings by Wm. D. Hendren, Franklin
               Co.

1811 Apr 15   Mollehon, Lidia and John Pitcher by Massey Clymer, Franklin Co.

1817 Mar 27   Moller, Rollin and Susannah Ransburgh by James Hoge, Franklin Co.

1819 Mar 7   Mollery, Ira and Mary Green by Noah Fidler, Licking Co.

1802 Jul 10   Molton, Lydia and Wm. B. Leonard by Griffin Greene, JCCCP, Washington
               Co.

1805 Apr 29   Momson, John and Grace Kingam by Arthur Chinworth, JP, Ross Co.

1817 Jul 2   Monckton, Isaac and Rebecca Haskell by Danl H. Buell, JP, Washington
               Co.

1806 Jul 31   Monroe, Deborah and Charles Clarke by Josiah McKinnie, Franklin Co.

1819 Jan 14   Monroe, Moses and Elizabeth Johnston by N.W. Andrews, JP, Jackson Co.

1825 Oct 9   Monroe, Smith and Sally Davidson by J. Gander, Franklin Co.

1820 Aug 1   Montanya, Catherine and Samuel Woodrough by J.A. Cunningham, VDM,
               Licking Co.

1812 Nov 15   Montgomery, Betsy and John E. Morgan (license date), Pickaway Co.

1806 Feb 5   Montgomery, Elizabeth and Joseph Flint by Abraham Miller, Ross Co.

1800 Aug 28   Montgomery, John and Elizabeth Johnston by Josiah Munro, Washington Co.

1812 Apr 9   Montgomery, John and Prady Channell by Noah Fidler, Licking Co.

1811 Nov 6   Montgomery, Sally and Abraham Youngkin by Stephen Lindsly, Washington
               Co.

1804 Jan 17   Montgomery, William and Mary Crouch by Abm. Miller, Ross Co.

1822 Mar 26   Mooberry, Alexander and Margaret Williams by James Hoge, Franklin Co.

'823 Feb 13   Mooberry, David and Margret Stumbaugh by James Hoge, Franklin Co.

1825? Jan 25   Mooberry, John and Lydia Merrian by James Hoge, Franklin Co.

1818 Apr 2   Moodey, Elizabeth and Jonathan Taggart by Noah Fidler, Licking Co.

1827 12 mo 5   Moon, Dinah and Jesse Beals, Miami Monthly Meeting, Warren Co.

1818 4 mo 2   Moon, Jane and David D. Hampton, Miami Monthly Meeting, Warren Co.

1826 2 mo 23   Moon, John and Judith Moon, Miami Monthly Meeting, Warren Co.

1826 2 mo 23   Moon, Judith and John Moon, Miami Monthly Meeting, Warren Co.

1804 Jun 14   Mooney, Fanny and Robert Miller by Abm Miller, Ross Co.

1825 Apr 15   Moor, Martha and Hugh McCracken (license date), Marion Co.

1810 Nov 4   Moore, Anne and Bryan McNamir (license date), Pickaway Co.

1818 Sep 18   Moore, David and Sarah Wilson by T.D. Baird, Licking Co.

1819 Nov 4   Moore, David and Hannah Kirkpatrick by James Cunningham, MD, Licking
               Co.

1818 Nov 26   Moore, Eleanor and Jarvis W. Pike by James Hoge, Franklin Co.

1813 Nov 29   Moore, Elijah and Sally Mathews by John Green, JP, Licking Co.

1819 Apr 1   Moore, Eliza and Robert Patterson by James Cunningham, JP, Licking Co.

1819 Dec 22   Moore, Elizabeth and Joseph Moore by James Cunningham, Licking Co.

1811 Aug 29   Moore, Isaac and Ruth Evans (license date), Pickaway Co.

1801 Dec 16   Moore, James of Youngstown and Hetteble Thoil of Pennsylvania by
               Caleb Baldwin, JP, Trumbull Co.

1808 Mar 6   Moore, James of Ross County and Elizabeth Vanhorn by David Marks,
               Franklin Co.

1810 Nov 8   Moore, James and Precilla Dunhoe (license date), Pickaway Co.

1812 Apr 12   Moore, John and Nancy Parkinson by -----, Licking Co.

1813 Mar 14   Moore, Jonas and Patience Guitteau by Rev. S.P. Robbins, Washington Co.

1819 Dec 22   Moore, Joseph and Elizabeth Moore by James Cunningham, Licking Co.

1816 Apr 21   Moore, Katharine and Isaac Pike by Joseph Gorton, Franklin Co.

1809 Nov 28   Moore, Moses and Mange Blackburn by Rev. George Vanaman, Licking Co.

1806 Jun 30   Moore, Nancy and John S. Burns by L. Barber, JP, Washington Co.

1813 Dec 26   Moore, Nancy and William Groom (license date), Pickaway Co.

1814 Feb 14   Moore, Nelly and Jesse Outan by Rev. Geo. Alkire, Ross Co.

1813 Dec 21   Moore, Nubal and Elizabeth Stump (license date), Pickaway Co.

1825 Mar 24   Moore, Phebe and Lumen A. Sharp by G.W. Hart, JP, Franklin Co.

1820 Nov 12   Moore, Philip B. and Lyda Patterson by John Green, ECC, Licking Co.

1816 Oct 10   Moore, Robert and Sally Gavit by J. Cunningham, JPNAT, Licking Co.

1801 Mar 5   Moore, Rossana and James Irving Caldwell at Youngstown by William
               Wick, VDM, Trumbull Co.

1819 Jan 6   Moore, Samuel and Elizabeth Cunningham by T.D. Bierd, Licking Co.

1819 Dec 27   Moore, Sarah and Samuel Scott by James Cunningham, Licking Co.

1812 Feb 3   Moore, Simeon Jr. and Laura Meachum by Simeon Moore, Franklin Co.

1839 Mar 8   Moore, Sophia and Moses K. Wilkinson by Rev. A. Helfenstine, St.
               John's Church, Worthington, Franklin Co.

1820 Mar 28   Moore, William and Ann Elliott by T.D. Baird, VDM, Licking Co.

1820 May 17   Moore, William and Elizabeth King by J. Cunningham, VDM, Licking Co.

1826 Oct 1   Moore, William L. and Sally Gillmore by P. Adams, Franklin Co.

1822 Jul 3   Moore, Zopher T. and Flora Tuller by A. Buttles, Franklin Co.

1888 Mar 21   Moorehead, John R. of Rix Mills, O., and Lizzie McCormac of Chandlers-
               ville, O., by Rev. George F. Moore, Putnam Presbyterian Church,
               Muskingum Co.

1827 Sep 7   Moorehead, Maria and Isaac Holmes by James Hoge, Franklin Co.

1815 Mar 16   Moorehead, Rachael and John M. White by Joseph Gorton, Franklin Co.

1823 Feb 13   Moorehead, Sarah and Alexander White by Jacob Grubb, JP, Franklin Co.

1806 Dec 25   Moorhead, Forggy and Jane Williams by Arthur O'Harra, JP, Franklin Co.

1824 Jul 8   Moorhead, Jain and John Denison by Robert W. Riley, Franklin Co.

1819 Feb 25   Moot, Aaron and Polly McDaniel by Samuel McDowell, Jackson Co.

1809 Dec 17   Moots, Jacob and Sarah Henthorn by Nathan Conrad, JP, Licking Co.

1811 Nov 26   Moots, Mary and William Parler by Nathan Connard, Licking Co.

1820 Sep 9   Mootz, John and Ann Polin by James Porter, JP, Licking Co.

1801 May 3   More, Azuba and Cyrus Ames by I. Peine, Washington Co.

1825 Oct 26   More, Ebelina and Asahel Benedict by Aristarchus Walker, Franklin Co.

1804 Jun 24   More, John and Elizabeth Dowall by John Brough, JP, Washington Co.

1813 Sep 19   More, Isabella and William S. Prichard by Rev. T. Harris, Licking Co.

1815 Dec 13   More, Jacob and Mary Dixon by J. Green, Licking Co.

1819 Jan 21   Moredock, Eliza and James Shields by Patrick Shearer, JP, Jackson Co.

1825 Sep 29   Morelands, ----- and Geo. Lock by Abner Bent, JP, Marion Co.

1815 Nov 23	Morey, Daniel and Harret Reynolds by Rev. Timothy Harris, Licking Co.
1870 Dec 22	Morey, Daniel and Jane Moffett by Rev. John Boyd, St. Luke's Church, Marietta, Washington Co.
1821 Feb 27	Morey, Elizabeth and Alexander McCoy by Ami Lawrence, Washington Co.
1818 Oct 19	Morey, Polly and Elias Tracy by Alex Holden, JP, Licking Co.
1822 Jan 6	Morfet, John and Isabelle Bell by John True, Washington Co.
1814 9 mo 8	Morgan, David and Rebecca Brown, Miami Monthly Meeting, Warren Co.
1821 Jul 12	Morgan, James and Jane Henderson by Robert W. Riley, Franklin Co.
1812 Nov 15	Morgan, John E. and Betsy Montgomery (license date), Pickaway Co.
1805 Mar 6	Morgan, William and Polly Wolf by Samuel Smith, Ross Co.
1817 Jan 1	Morgaridge, John and Sally Cunningham by Jos. Chapman, JP, Washington Co.
1819 Mar 11	Morison, Anna and John Calb by Jno Trois, Franklin Co.
1818 Aug 31	Morison, Catharine and James Conner by Robert Elliott, Franklin Co.
1825 Feb 17	Morley, Charlotte and Geo. Waldear by Timothy Radcliffe, JP, Jackson Co.
1810 May 15	Morrell, Jesse and Mary Hanold (license date), Pickaway Co.
1816 Feb 1	Morrie (or Morris), Joseph and Rhody Crassen by James Marshall, Franklin Co.
1818 Jan 1	Morris, Amos and Burch Gratia by Amos Wilson, JP, Washington Co.
1811 Feb 24	Morris, Anna and Jabez Spinks by Dudley Davis, JP, Washington Co.
1813 May 4	Morris, Benedict and Lydia Morris (license date), Pickaway Co.
1812 Dec 3	Morris, Elizabeth and Samuel Andrews by Rev. Stephen Lindley, Washington Co.
1813 Sep 27	Morris, Elizabeth and John Whitmire by John Green, JP, Licking Co.
1817 Jan 25	Morris (or Harris), Elizabeth and Daniel Melphrey by John Green, Licking Co.
1809 Nov 16	Morris, Henretta and Jesse Cheadle by Stephen Lindsly, Washington Co.
1811 Mar 28	Morris, Henry and Charity Selby (license date), Pickaway Co.
1820 Nov 2	Morris, Hetty and Michael Story by Rev. Saml. P. Robbins, Washington Co.
1828 Sep 9	Morris, Huldah and James Evans by John F. Solomon, Franklin Co.
1827 Mar 29	Morris, Isaac and Margaret Chambers by W.T. Martin, Franklin Co.
1815 Apr 16	Morris, Jacob and Catherine Strouse by James Jackson, JP, Pickaway Co.
1826 Nov 9	Morris, Jane and Jeremiah Clark by James Hoge, Franklin Co.
1826 Feb 26	Morris, Joab and Rebecca Martin by Thomas Vaughn, Jackson Co.
1816 May 2	Morris, John and Sally Ellison by Amos Wilson, JP, Washington Co.
1818 May 14	Morris, John C.A. and Elizabeth Vanclief by Titian Kimball, JP, Washington Co.

1811 Sep 10   Morris, Joseph and Peggy DeWitt (license date), Pickaway Co.

1813 Sep 3   Morris, Joseph and Eliza McCullum by Thomas White, JP, Washington Co.

1816 Feb 1   Morris (or Morrie), Joseph and Rhody Crassen by James Marshall,
               Franklin Co.

1870 Jul 12   Morris, Lucy C. and Daniel C. Sheppard by Rev. John Boyd, St. Luke's
               Church, Marietta, Washington Co.

1813 May 4   Morris, Lydia and Benedict Morris (license date), Pickaway Co.

1816 Apr 18   Morris, Mary and Gideon Lawrence by Thomas White, Washington Co.

1812 Jul 5   Morris, Nancy and George Medskel (license date), Pickaway Co.

1813 Oct 12   Morris, Nancy and James Robinson (license date), Pickaway Co.

1814 Jul 5   Morris, Paterson and Christine Borrer by Nicholas Gaicthies,
               Franklin Co.

1803 Oct 14   Morris, Rachel and Elisha Pratt by Daniel Story, Clerk, Washington Co.

1819 Sep 23   Morris, Sarah and John Dolin by Titan Kimble, JP, Washington Co.

1814 Mar 24   Morris, Thomas and Nancy Wolverton by Henry Davis, JP, Pickaway Co.

1821 Sep 1   Morris, Thomas and Sarah Reid by James Hoge, Franklin Co.

1809 Dec 1   Morris, William and Hannah Newell by James Quinn, Washington Co.

1819 Apr 7   Morris, William and Betsey Mason by Amos Wilson, JP, Washington Co.

1806 Jul 4   Morrison, Alexander Jr. and Sally Buttles by James Kilbourn, JP,
               Franklin Co.

1813 Jul 1   Morrison, Henry and Julia Lewis by Ezra Griswold, Franklin Co.

1817 Feb 13   Morrison, Orrel and Charles Thompson by Isaac Case, Franklin Co.

1893 Oct 22   Morrison, Oscar J. of Wheeling, W.Va., and Julia M. Sauck of Zanes-
               ville, by Rev. George F. Moore, Putnam Presbyterian Church,
               Muskingum Co.

1804 Feb 8   Morrison, Polly and Abner Putnim Pinny by Zachariah Stephen, JP,
               Franklin Co.

1811 Nov 24   Morrison, Prescilla and Joseph Anderson (license date), Pickaway Co.

1802 Jun 24   Morrison, Samuel and Nancy Burrill by Seth Cashart, Washington Co.

1811 Aug 4   Morrow, Eleanor and Robert Flemming (license date), Pickaway Co.

1826 May 29   Morrow, Elizabeth and Plina Commans by Joseph Baker, MG, Jackson Co.

1836 May 12   Morrow, Dr. T.V. and Isabella Greer by Rev. E. Burr, St. John's
               Church, Worthington, Franklin Co.

1809 Sep 10   Morse, Justice and Margaret Hart by Wm. Gray, JP, Washington Co.

1818 Sep 9   Morton, Isaac Jr. and Elmy Warden by Rev. Timothy Harris, Licking Co.

1815 Sep 28   Morton (or Marton), John and Hanna Miller by Percival Adams, Franklin
               Co.

1881 Nov 16   Morton, Llewellyn and Sarah M. Skinner by Rev. John Boyd, St. Luke's
               Church, Marietta, Washington Co.

1817 Sep 4   Moses, Jacob and Elizabeth Moyer by Andrew Hinkle, MG, Licking Co.

1816 Feb 29   Moses, Phebe and John Stetton by Daniel Poppleston, Licking Co.

1825 Mar 10   Moss, Bethany and Paul Shreck by Vincent Southard, JP, Jackson Co.

1824 Apr 19   Moss, Bythama and Phillips Waldren by Geo. Claypoole, JP, Jackson Co.

1821 Jan 1   Moss, Diantha and Otis Wheeler by Rev. Saml. P. Robbins, Washington Co

1881 Jun 21   Moss, Edward and Mrs. Mary Ann Pyper by Rev. John Boyd, St. Luke's
               Church, Marietta, Washington Co.

1801 Oct 28   Moss, Joseph and Polly Clark at Burton by Turhand Kirtland, Justice
               of Court of Common Pleas, Trumbull Co.

1805 Apr 16   Moss, Nancy and John Eamins by John Davidson, Ross Co.

1807 1 mo 13   Mote, Jonathan and Susana Hollingsworth, Miami Monthly Meeting, Warren
               Co.

1820 May 18   Motes, Abraham and Barbary Nicholas by John Stinson, JP, Jackson Co.

1813 Jun 30   Motes, David and Elizabeth Brown by S. Dunnavan, JP, Licking Co.

1816 Mar 16   Motherspaw,Daniel and Lena Freazel by Uriah Hull, JP, Licking Co.

1813 Jun 15   Mothersaw,John and Mary Spencer by S. Dunnavan, JP, Licking Co.

1821 Apr 1   Mott, Silas and Mercy Hopkins by Thos. Scott, JP, Licking Co.

1816 Oct 11   Motz, John and Elizabeth Crow by David Mitchell, JP, Jackson Co.

1797 Dec 28   Moulton, Anna and Josiah Hart by Josiah Munro, Washington Co.

1804 Jul 19   Mount, Elornor and Thomas Grimes both of Pe Pe Tp. by John Johnson,
               Ross Co.

1804 Aug 28   Mountain, James and Rebecca Campbell of New Market Tp. by John David-
               son, Ross Co.

1882 Aug 1   Mowery, Rhoda and Thomas H. Cole by Rev. John Boyd, St. Luke's Church,
               Marietta, Washington Co.

1813 Apr 1   Moyer, Abraham and Priscilla Angles (license date), Pickaway Co.

1811 Nov 2   Moyer, Barbara and George List (license date), Pickaway Co.

1811 Jun 16   Moyer, Dorothy and George Pontius (license date), Pickaway Co.

1878 Oct 7   Moyer, Mrs. Eliza (nee Emery) of Putnam and Edward Richards of
               Cleveland by Rev. George F. Moore, Putnam Presbyterian Church,
               Muskingum Co.

1817 Sep 4   Moyer, Elizabeth and Jacob Moses by Andrew Hinkle, MG, Licking Co.

1868 Feb 4   Moyer, John and Lida Emery by Rev. A. Kingsbury, Putnam Presbyterian
               Church, Muskingum Co.

1817 Nov 5   Mulakin, Nancy and Stephen Short by Ebenezer Washburn, Franklin Co.

1800 May 8   Mulford, Daniel and Mary Jolly by Alvin Bingham, Washington Co.

1828 Sep 7   Mullen, Elizabeth and Johnathan Lee by J. Gander, JP, Franklin Co.

1820 Mar 15   Mullen, Jacob and Mary Havens by George Smith, JP, Washington Co.

1820 Jul 13   Mullen, James and Sarah Rowland by Rev. Saml. P. Robbins,
               Washington Co.

1812 Mar 10   Mullen, Jane and Henry Raredon by Cornelius Hougland, Washington Co.

1817 Jun 18	Mullen, John and Polly Woodruff by Salmon N. Cook, JP, Washington Co.
1812 Mar 11	Mullen, Mary and James Ray by Joseph Palmer, JP, Washington Co.
1827 Sep 13	Mullen, Rhoda and Zebulon See by I. Gander, JP, Franklin Co.
1819 Mar 18	Mullin, Charlott and David Williams by Elihu Bigelow, JP, Licking Co.
1875 Sep 23	Munch, Isabel and William S. Bell by Rev. A. Kingsbury, Putnam Presbyterian Church, Muskingum Co.
1814 Jan 10	Munkton, Isaac and Lucy Colly by Isaac Baker, Esq., Washington Co.
1811 Feb 12	Munley, Theodocia and John Powers (license date), Pickaway Co.
1800 Apr 3	Munro, Sally and Daniel Converse by D. Loring, Washington Co.
1801 Feb 9	Munro, Susanna and James Kirkpatrick by Josiah Munro, Washington Co.
1818 Dec 17	Munsel, Elysia and Anthony Phillips by Samuel Bancroft, JP, Licking Co.
1819 Oct 25	Munsel, Harriet and John Gaffield by Knowls Linnel, JP, Licking Co.
1789 Dec 14	Munsell, Levi and Lucretia Oliver by Ben Tupper, Washington Co.
1821 Jan 11	Munsell, Solomon and Roberts Edwards by Knowles Lennel, JP, Licking Co.
1812 May 28	Munson, Augustine and Polly Mead by Rev. T. Harris, Licking Co.
1872 Jun 6	Munson, Gilbert D. and Lulu S. Potwin by Rev. A. Kingsbury, Putnam Presbyterian Church, Muskingum Co.
1816 Mar 8	Munture, Nancy and Jacob Leaf by Percival Adams, Franklin Co.
1815 Feb 7	Murdick, Daniel and Elizabeth Thompson by Noah Fidler, Licking Co.
1818 Dec 24	Murdock, Joseph and Nancy South by D. Mitchell, JP, Jackson Co.
1826 Apr 22	Murdock, Patrick and Mary McDougal by John Potter, JP, Jackson Co.
1819 Jan 19	Murphey, Thomas and Elizabeth May by Michael Patton, Franklin Co.
1825 Apr 1	Murphy, Elizabeth and Samuel Crabtree by David W. Walton, JP, Jackson Co.
1813 Dec 19	Murphy, Joseph and Praise ----- by Wm. O'Bannon, Licking Co.
1819 Dec 9	Muprhy, Mary and Peter Wagoner by Simeon Overturf, JP, Licking Co.
1819 Nov 4	Murphy, Nancy and James Sheredian by John Russell, JP, Washington Co.
1805 Oct 17	Murphy, Sarah and David Downs by Wm. Creighton, Ross Co.
1820 Jul 10	Murphy, Sarah and James Sproll by W. O'Bannon, JP, Licking Co.
1804 Aug 24	Murphy, Wm. and Debary Flouron by Geo. Vinsanhaler, Ross Co.
1819 Jan 3	Murphy, William and Nancy Rogers by John McMahan, Licking Co.
1818 Jan 15	Murrey, William and Polly Tison by David Stephens, JP, Washington Co.
1816 Jun 7	Murris, Stanton and Elizabeth Piper by Alexander Bassett, Franklin Co.
1813 Aug 26	Murz, Caty and Asa Robinson by S. Harris, JP, Franklin Co.
1813 Mar 26	Muskings, John and Nancy Coleston (license date), Pickaway Co.
1805 Oct 6	Mussellman, Daniel and Christeena Weider by Abraham Miller, Ross Co.
1826 Oct 5	Mussey, Jephthea and Lucy Corn by John Shumate, JP, Jackson Co.

1826 Nov 2   Mussey, Rebecca and Peter Corn by John Shumate, JP, Jackson Co.

1800 Dec 27   Mustard, Mary and Aaron Camp by John Struthers, JP, Trumbull Co.

1825 Feb 29   Mutchler, Mary and Jacob Butt by Abner Bent, JP, Marion Co.

1821 May 13   Myers, Andrew and Jane Smith by A. Goff, CP, Licking Co.

1804 Oct 11   Myers, Catharine and John McCullough by John G. McCan, Ross Co.

1824 Apr 13   Myers, Eliza and Phillip Berkstresser by N. Goetschius, Franklin Co.

1814 Nov 10   Myers, Jacob and Amelia Farmer by G. Callanhan, EMEC, Licking Co.

1828 Jan 15   Myers, Joseph and Elizabeth Blakely by I. Gander, JP, Franklin Co.

1815 Sep 26   Myers, Lewis and Jane Winn by J. Hoskinson, Licking Co.

1820 Sep 19   Myers, Margaret and Samuel Coulter by Noah Fidler, MG, Licking Co.

1818 Nov 28   Myers, Mary and Joshua Gosnell by M. Thorp, JP, Licking Co.

1822 Feb 21   Myers, Patty and John Ellis by Asa Cheadle, JP, Washington Co.

1822 Dec 31   Myers, Polly and Nicholas Foos by N. Goetschies, Franklin Co.

1801 Dec 25   Myers, Roesey and Thomas Dixon by Henry Smith, JP, Washington Co.

1824 Sep 12   Myers (Maire), Sally and Christian Horlocker by John Davis, JP,
               see note under Christian Horlocker, Franklin Co.

1823 Jul 30   Myers, Samuel and Eleanor Ragar by Nicholas Goetschius, Franklin Co.

1815 Jan 13   Myers, Solomon and Dolly Bates by Wm. Taylor, Licking Co.

1820 Mar 1   Myers, Susanna and Christopher Fulk by Thomas Cunningham, JP, Licking
               Co.

1820 Oct 11   Myers, Teney and John Long by Nicholas Goetschius, JP, Franklin Co.

1828 May 12   Mytinger, John and Betsy Sells by Wm. Long, Franklin Co.

1818 Dec 11   Nally, Catharine and Joseph Eubanks by Thomas Scott, JP, Jackson Co.

1826 May 16   Nally, Milly and Joshua E. Stephenson by Thos. Daugherty, JP,
               Jackson Co.

1809 May 16   Napier, Elizabeth and William Jenkins by Sam'l P. Robbins, Washington
               Co.

1815 Jan 23   Nash, Chester and Lucy Henderson by Stephen Guthrie, Washington Co.

1805 Jan 4   Nash, David and Nancy Putnam by Thos. Stanley, Washington Co.

1806 Apr 3   Nash, Elizabeth and Resolved Fuller by Thos. Stanley, JP, Washington
               Co.

1818 Dec 10   Nash, Elizabeth and Robert Aikens, Jr., by Rev. Thos. A. Morris,
               Washington Co.

1849 Sep 18   Nash, Rev. Rodney S. and Sarah G. Thrall by W.C. French, St. Luke's
               Church, Granville, Licking Co.

1811 Nov 5   Nash, Uriah and Matilda Pewthers by Stephen Lindsly, Washington Co.

1828 Jun 28   Naydenbush, M.J. and Ignatius Wheeler by Wm. Lush, JP, Franklin Co.

1798 Feb 1   Neal, Abigail and Joseph Seamans by Josiah Munro, Washington Co.

1824 Nov 2   Neal, Elizabeth and David Baughman by Alex Kinnear, MG, Marion Co.

1819 Sep 2   Neal, James and Anna Dougal by J. Cunningham, JP, Licking Co.

1848 Oct 31   Neal, Josephine C. of Parkersburg, Va., and William Rolb of Wheeling
                by Rev. D.W. Tolford, St. Luke's Church, Marietta, Washington Co.

1819 Apr 4   Neale, Mary O. and Hezekiah Peck by Rev. James McAboy, Washington Co.

1842 Oct 30   Neas, Israel and Mary Anne Heaton by Rev. R.S. Elder, St. John's
                Church, Worthington, Franklin Co.

1822 Dec 5   Needles, Alexander and Elizabeth Cubbage by Charles Waddell,
                Franklin Co.

1812 May 1   Needles, Andrew and Sarah Needles by Wm. D. Hendren, Franklin Co.

1828 Jul 15   Needles, Anna and Littleton Gray by Nathan Emery, Elder in the
                Methodist E. Church, Franklin Co.

1823 Apr 20   Needles, Archibald C. and Nancy Kile by Richard Courtright, Franklin
                Co.

1829 Mar 10   Needles, Mary and Jesse Hutson by John F. Solomon, Franklin Co.

1827 Oct 18   Needles, Rachel and Thomas Needles by John F. Solomon, Franklin Co.

1812 May 1   Needles, Sarah and Andrew Needles by Wm. D. Hendren, Franklin Co.

1822 Oct 21   Needles, Sarah and James Conway by Richard Courtright, Franklin Co.

1827 Oct 18   Needles, Thomas and Rachel Needles by John F. Solomon, Franklin Co.

1821 Apr 10   Needles, William and Mary Collins by Richard Courtright, JP, Franklin
                Co.

1824 Jul 7   Needly, Thos. and Mary Lusk by H. Matthews, Franklin Co.

1817 Sep 9   Neff, Anna and George Slerogin by Joseph Gorton, JP, Franklin Co.

1806 Mar 31   Neff, Cornelius and Catharine Cox by J. Gardner, JP, Ross Co.

1816 Apr 23   Neff, George and Barbara Dispennet by Isaiah Hoskinson, JP, Licking
                Co.

1817 May 8   Neff, Margaret and William Taylor by Isaiah Hoskinson, JP, Licking Co.

1820 Dec 6   Neher, John and Sarah Davis by John Waggonner, JP, Licking Co.

1817 Jan 30   Neibarger, Elizabeth and Mathias Kleiver by J.D. Baird, Licking Co.

1819 Sep 2   Neibarger, Rebecca and William Ryan by Wm. O'Bannon, JP, Licking Co.

1819 Dec 20   Neiber, Joseph and Sarah Crock by M. Trout, JP, Licking Co.

1818 Jan 22   Neighbarger, John M. and Hulda Denman by John Jonston, JP, Licking Co.

1816 Dec 5   Neighbarger, Polly and William Denman by Wm. O'Bannon, JP, Licking Co.

1815 Jul 27   Neighbarger, Sarah and Andrew Hite by Wm. O'Bannon, Licking Co.

1824 Dec 30   Neiswender, Frederick and Mary Turney by C. Henkel, Franklin Co.

1824 Nov 30   Nelson, David and Mary Taylor by James Hoge, Franklin Co.

1819 Jan --   Nelson, Elizabeth and Samuel Bunn by D. Mitchell, JP, Jackson Co.

1824 Jan 8   Nelson, Farnee and Henry Strausse (son of John) by Sam'l Carrick, JP, Jackson Co.

1820 Oct 5   Nelson, Jane and John Walles by Vincent Southard, JP, Jackson Co.

1871 Feb 4   Nelson, John and Ellen Dornan by Rev. John Boyd, St. Luke's Church, Marietta, Washington Co.

1878 Sep 5   Nelson, John T. and Lucy A. Bennett by Rev. John Boyd, St. Luke's Church, Marietta, Washington Co.

1807 Mar 17   Nelson, Martha and Edward Livingston by Robert I. Wilson, Min., Franklin Co.

1809 May 2   Nelson, Mary and James Shannon by Arthur O'Harra, Franklin Co.

1811 Aug 24   Nelson, Nancy and John Barr by James Hoge, Franklin Co.

1825 Sep 18   Nelson, Nancy and Isaac Strausse by J.B. Gilliland, JP, Jackson Co.

1826 Sep 28   Nelson, Nancy and David Taylor by James Hoge, Franklin Co.

1817 Nov 27   Nesmith, Nancy and Irdediah Fuller by Rev. Saml. P. Robbins, Washington Co.

1810 Sep 3   Nevill, Mary and Joseph Hedges (license date), Pickaway Co.

1808 Jun 6   Newbury, Joseph and Sally Withington by Rev. Sam'l P. Robbins, Washington Co.

1822 Feb 12   Newcomb, George and Elizabeth Sifers by Amos Wilson, Washington Co.

1813 Jun 31   Newcomer, Christopher and Susan Sells by Daniel Brink, Franklin Co.

1818 Dec 24   Newel, Mathias and Peggy Carl by Samuel Stewart, Licking Co.

1809 Dec 1   Newell, Hannah and William Morris by James Quinn, Washington Co.

1813 May 6   Newell, Matilda and Abram Jones by Simon Cochran, JP, Franklin Co.

1822 Apr 11   Newell, Meham and Lydia Sloper by Aristorchus Walker, Franklin Co.

1817 Feb 6   Newell, Prudence and Thomas Hartley by Daniel Harrel, JP, Jackson Co.

1792 Dec 23   Newell, William and Patty Seamans by J. Gilman, Washington Co.

1814 Feb 22   Newhorter, John and Rebecca Wildhan by Sam'l Lybrand, Pickaway Co.

1810 Oct 2   Newhouse, Mary and Hugh Stall (license date), Pickaway Co.

1823 Aug 24   Newhouse, Matilda and John Hays by Uriah Clark, JP, Franklin Co.

1817 Dec 26   Newland, Jacob and Sarah Tew by Nathan Pan, JP, Washington Co.

1808 2 mo 17 Newlin, John and Esther Stubbs, Miami Monthly Meeting, Warren Co.

1822 11 mo 6   Newman, Elizabeth and William Edwards, Miami Monthly Meeting, Warren Co.

1823 3 mo 12 Newman, Mary Earl and Ellis Ward, Miami Monthly Meeting, Warren Co.

1820 Nov 13   Newman, Wesley and Lucy Cook by Eli C. King, Franklin Co.

1827 Feb 4   Newswender, M.M. and Matias Redenor by C. Henkel, Franklin Co.

1806 Dec 26   Newton, Abie and George Castle by L. Barber, Washington Co.

1804 Dec 18   Newton, Betsey and Philip Cubbage by John Brough, JP, Washington Co.

1810 Jan 1   Newton, Betsey and T. Wolbridge by Stephen Lindsly, Washington Co.

1818 Apr 21	Newton, Harriet and John Eveland by Asa Cheadle, JP, Washington Co.
1812 Nov 11	Newton, John and Fanny Rose by Jeremiah Dare, JP, Washington Co.
1814 Sep 25	Newton, John and Lydia Rose by Samuel Dye, JP, Washington Co.
1814 Aug 30	Newton, Nathan and Catharine Keath by Thos. Seely, Esq., Washington Co.
1810 Mar 13	Newton, Oren and Almira Fuller by Thos. Stanley, JP, Washington Co.
1824 May 30	Newton, Purlina and John Snook by David Culbertson, MG, Jackson Co.
1815 Jun 29	Newton, Sally and Peter Vanelief by Richard Cheadle, Washington Co.
1791 Sep 1	Newton, Sarah and Benjamin Baker by Benj. Tupper, ICCCP, Washington Co.
1804 Jan 25	Niblack, Wm. and Sidney Clark by Wm. Creighton, Ross Co.
1819 --- --	Nichels, John and Catherine Aubent? by -----, Licking Co.
1822 Jan 3	Nicherson, Betsey and Washington McLane by Nicholas Goetschius, Franklin Co.
1867 Feb 14	Nichol, Alf. M. and Fanny T. Fosdick by Wm. Bower, St. Luke's Church, Granville, Licking Co.
1820 May 18	Nicholas, Barbary and Abraham Motes by John Stinson, JP, Jackson Co.
1881 Mar 30	Nicholas, Dora and Levi C. Miller by Rev. John Boyd, St. Luke's Church, Marietta, Washington Co.
1878 Mar 26	Nicholas, George H. and Josephine M. Hart by Rev. John Boyd, St. Luke's Church, Marietta, Washington Co.
1827 Dec 14	Nicholes, Mary and John S. Gilmore by S. Hamilton, Franklin Co.
1811 Nov 14	Nicholls, Elizabeth and Henry Hill by Thos. Ferguson, JP, Washington Co.
1811 Jan 7	Nicholls, James and Elizabeth Bailey by James Sharp, Washington Co.
1821 Jan 2	Nicholls, Joanna and William Guthridge by Thomas Cummins, JP, Licking Co.
1820 Apr 9	Nicholls, Nancy and Joseph Merry by Osgood McFarland, JP, Washington Co.
1806 Jan 31	Nichols, Balace and Melinda Gibbs by James Quinn, Ross Co.
1818 Mar 18	Nichols, Elizabeth and Samuel Everett by Joseph Grate, Franklin Co.
1818 Apr 9	Nichols, Hannah and Eneas Beuher by Rev. T. Harris, Licking Co.
1818 Aug 6	Nichols, James and Christianna Benson by Wm. Dana, JP, Washington Co.
1818 Aug 16	Nichols, Sally and Peter Lagor by James M. Booth, JP, Washington Co.
1819 May 27	Nichols, Thomas and Judith Parrish by R. Golliday, Franklin Co.
1819 May 4	Nichols, Townsend and Mary McCoy by James Hoge, Franklin Co.
1826 Jul 28	Nicholson, Benjamin and Juliana Dixon by Joseph Baker, MG, Jackson Co.
1818 Dec 30	Nicholson, James and Mary Ann Pickle by Wm. How, JP, Jackson Co.
1819 Dec 23	Nicholson, Pheby and Sayrs Holstead by Joseph Gorton, Franklin Co.

1815 Feb 9   Nicholson, Polly and Jacob McVay by Thos. Ferguson, Esq., Washington Co.

1812 Dec 31   Nicholson, Uzziah and Hannah Johnson by Wm. D. Hendren, Franklin Co.

1825 Mar 30   Nickels, Rebecca and Gasper Boyord by Daniel Clark, JP, Jackson Co.

1818 Sep 20   Nickerson, Lesta and Zebulon Lee by Billingslea Bull, JP, Franklin Co.

1821 Jul 10   Nickins, Archabald and Caty Jackson by W.T. Martin, Franklin Co.

1803 Dec 22   Nickins, Eva and Henry Hile by J. Gardner, Ross Co.

1804 Aug 14   Nickins, Sally and James Cambridge by J. Gardner, JP, Ross Co.

1827 Dec --   Nickens, Moses and Betsy Griffin by Geo. Jefferies, Franklin Co.

1822 Jan 3   Nickerson, Betsey and Washington McLane by Nicholas Goetschius, Franklin Co.

1819 Sep 19   Nickison, Joseph and Margaret Coble by Richard Courtright, JP, Franklin Co.

1821 Aug 3   Nickleson, Phebe and Darias Bennet by Richard Courtright, Franklin Co.

1825 Dec 3   Nickols, Affa and Peter Schoonover by Wm. Godman, Franklin Co.

1820 May 6   Nicoll, Edward and Patty Nicoll by Rev. T. Harris, Licking Co.

1820 May 6   Nicoll, Patty and Edward Nicoll by Rev. T. Harris, Licking Co.

1817 Apr 23   Nicosan, Sarah and Samuel Cady (or Cody), by Emmor Cox, Franklin Co.

1809 Aug 27   Niel, Patience and Hugh Allison by Rev. N. Davis, Washington Co.

1836 --- --   Nielssen, Ollef and Elizabeth Bohl by Rev. J.T. Wheat, St. Luke's Church, Marietta, Washington Co.

1809 Aug 10   Nighswinges, Hamilton and Nancy Vandervender by Sol Langdon, Washington Co.

1794 Feb 18   Nime, Louise and Francois Marian by J.G. Petitt, Washington Co.

1816 1 mo 3   Ninde, Benjamin and Jane Whitacre, Miami Monthly Meeting, Warren Co.

1797 Nov 19   Niswanger, John and Peggy Coleman by Josiah Munro, Washington Co.

1819 May 13   Nixon, Betsey and Salvanus Olney by Thos. White, JP, Washington Co.

1813 Feb 25   Nixon, John and Samany Blackmorx by Thomas White, JP, Washington Co.

1817 Jul 23   Nixon, Margaret and Presley Petty by Saml. P. Robbins, MCC, Washington Co.

1810 Dec 23   Nixon, William and Eliza Jennings by Stephen Lindsly, Washington Co.

1811 Dec 25   Nixson, George and Margaret Jennings by Stephen Lindsly, Washington Co

1808 Jun 10   Nobill, Betsey and James Philips by James Marshall, Franklin Co.

1805 Oct 31   Noble, Nancy and William Williams by Thos. Hicks, Ross Co.

1817 May 31   Noble, Rachel and James Reed by Dan'l H. Buell, JP, Washington Co.

1806 Dec 3   Noble, Reverend Seth and the widow Margaret Riddle by James Kilbourn, JP, Franklin Co.

1822 Apr 11   Noe, Abram and Elizabeth Rose by John Davis, Franklin Co.

1800 Aug 12   Nogle, Isaac and Nancy Patten by J. Munro, Washington Co.

1806 Feb 13	Nopp, John and Rachel Richie by John Johnston, JP, Ross Co.
1825 5 mo 5	Nordyke, Abram and Henrietta P. Anthony, Miami Monthly Meeting, Warren Co.
1824 May 13	Noris, Benjamin and Lutisha Griffith by Jacob Gundy, Franklin Co.
1804 Feb 21	Norman, Cleranda and John Graham by James Graham, JP, Washington Co.
1809 Oct 20	Norman, Grandison and Ann Combs by John Brough, JP, Washington Co.
1817 Dec 25	Norman, James and Harriet Stephens by Solomon N. Cook, JP, Washington Co.
1816 Feb 4	Norris, Jemimah and William McMahan by Alex Basset, JP, Franklin Co.
1866 Sep 12	Norris, Josephine and Dr. J.M. Christian by N.C.N. Dudley, St. Paul's Church, Marion, Marion Co.
1824?Mar 30	Norris, Phebe, widow, and Sanford Babbet, widower, by Aristarchus Walker, Franklin Co.
1856 Apr 2	Norris, Thomas B. and Mrs. Sally Ann Dodge by Rev. John Boyd, St. Luke's Church, Marietta, Washington Co.
1874 Aug 26	North, Ellen L. and Albert A. Martin by Rev. John Boyd, St. Luke's Church, Marietta, Washington Co.
1802 May 27	Northup, Henry and Susannah Painter by Seth Cashart, JP, Washington Co.
1802 May 27	Northup, Jane and James McCall by Seth Cashart, JP, Washington Co.
1816 Feb 29	Northup, Thurston and Huldah Johnson by Sam'l Dye, Washington Co.
1818 Oct 18	Norton, Gideon and Frances Ellenwood by Jonathan Dunham, JP, Washington Co.
1804 Feb 12	Norton, Moses and Polly White Cotton by John Johnston, JP Pope Tp., Ross Co.
1859 Jul 25	Norton, Sarah M. of Harmar and George T. McMurray of California by Rev. John Boyd, St. Luke's Church, Marietta, Washington Co.
1819 Mar 29	Norwood, Jane and Edmund C. Gold by Jacob Smith, JP, Franklin Co.
1804 Aug 30	Noteman, Andrew and Betsay McCune by W. Robinson, Ross Co.
1826 Aug 3	Notin, William and Polly Holton by Wooley Conrad, JP, Franklin Co.
1797 Jan 2	Nott, Elisabeth and Russell Isham by -----, Washington Co.
1814 Mar 1	Nott, George and Cynthia Hoyt by Thomas Seely, Washington Co.
1817 Jan 1	Nott, Graven R. and Rhoda Lane by P. White, JP, Washington Co.
1803 Aug 13	Nott, James and Phebe Richmond by Robert Oliver, JP, Washington Co.
1802 Aug 2	Nott, Mary and Daniel Coleman by Robert Oliver, JP, Washington Co.
1819 Dec 2	Nott, Rhoda and William Benjamin by John D. Chamberlain, JP, Washington Co.
1804 Jul 15	Nott, Samuel and Emme Van Clief by Jacob Lindly, Washington Co.
1821 May 31	Nott, Simeon P. and Sally Kent by Thomas White, JP, Washington Co.
1804 Feb 8	Nott, Thomas and Jane Bentley by Jacob Lindly, Washington Co.

1825 Jan 13 Null, Isaac and Jane Snotgrass by John Anglin, JP, Jackson Co.

1815 Oct 1 Null, Samuel and Anna Ames by Artemas Knapp, JP, Washington Co.

1806 Mar 18 Nulton, George and Ann Corner by Robert Oliver, JP, Washington Co.

1807 Apr 16 Nulton, Katherine and Edward Miller by Robert Oliver, Washington Co.

1807 Dec 27 Nulton, Nancy and Israel Linscott by Robert Oliver, JP, Washington Co.

1813 Dec 30 Nulton, Susanna and Thomas Dennis by George Miller, JP, Washington Co.

1815 Aug 29 Nurce, Isabel and Nathan Benton by Recompence Stansbery, Franklin Co.

1819 Mar 22 Nute, Jonathan and Nancy D. Walker by Dudley Davis, JP, Washington Co.

1802 Nov 21 Nye, Ebenezer and Silence Gardner by Nehemiah Davis, MG, Washington Co.

1873 Oct 7 Nye, Fanny S. of Putnam and John M. Jolly of Mansfield, O., by Rev. A. Kingsbury, Putnam Presbyterian Church, Muskingum Co.

1850 May 14 Nye, Frances R. and Shelton Sturgess of Duncan's Falls by Rev. D.W. Tolford, St. Luke's Church, Marietta, Washington Co.

1808 Dec 20 Nye, George and Lydia Gardner by J. Wright, Washington Co.

1811 Jun 18 Nye, George and Sarah Paschal (license date), Pickaway Co.

1856 Dec 18 Nye, Harriet and Henry A. Towne by Rev. John Boyd, St. Luke's Church, Marietta, Washington Co.

1860 Feb 13 Mye, Mary Francis and Thomas Potts by Rev. A. Kingsbury, Putnam Presbyterian Church, Muskingum Co.

1813 Mar 21 Nye, Nathan and Rhoda E. Barker by S. Stone, JP, Washington Co.

1807 Jan 29 Nye, Panthea and Rothens Haywood by Sam'l P. Robbins, Washington Co.

1822 Feb 4 Nye, Rowena and Wm. Pitt Putnam by Rev. Sam'l P. Robbins, Washington Co.

1797 May 4 Nye, Sarah and Azariah Pratt by Josiah Munro, Washington Co.

1814 Mar 13 Nye, Theodrus and Rebecca Warnum by Sardine Stone, Washington Co.

1793 Jan 10 Nyghswonger, Suekey and Hamilton Kerr by J. Gilman, Washington Co.

1810 Dec 11 Nyswanner, John and Barbara Young by Wm. D. Hendren, Franklin Co.

1795 Mar 29 Nyswonger, Sally and Charles Mills by R.J. Meigs, Washington Co.

1820 Sep 21 Oakley, Lydia and Jacob Cooper by John D. Chamberlain, JP, Washington Co.

1804 Jan 22 Obrian, John and Polly Foster by Wm. Davis, JP, Ross Co.

1822 Apr 25 O'Brien, Suson and Milton Smith by Jacob Young, Washington Co.

1820 Mar 22 Ockerman, William and Milly Judd by John Russell, Washington Co.

1825 Apr 28 Odell, Eli and Asenath Parcher (license date), Marion Co.

1816 Mar 14 Oden, Matilda and Jessie Chilson by Michael Patton, Franklin Co.

1806 Feb 5   Odle, Elizabeth and Elisha Carpenter by John Odle, JP, Ross Co.

1805 Sep 1   Odle, Mary and Martin Boots by J. Gardner, JP, Ross Co.

1822 Jan 27   Offerall, John and Nicy Brown by Jacob Grundy, Franklin Co.

1825 May 26   Ogden, Aaron and Mary Hawken by John Hawken, JP, Franklin Co.

1821 Jan 4   Ogden, Abegal and Joseph Edger by Thos. B. Patterson, JP, Franklin Co.

1880 Jun 22   Ogden, Duncan C. and Elizabeth W. Scott at Chillicothe by Rev. John
              Boyd, St. Luke's Church, Marietta, Washington Co.

1816 Jun 15   Ogden, Elias and Huldah C. Whitehead by Joseph Gorton, Franklin Co.

1816 Feb 4   Ogden, Elizabeth and Danl Smith by Thos. B. Patterson, Franklin Co.

1878 Nov 5   Ogden, George of Abilene, Kan. and A. Lillian Haver of Putnam by Rev.
              George F. Moore, Putnam Presbyterian Church, Muskingum Co.

1814 Jan 30   Ogden, Lewis and Jane Edgar by Jacob Thompson, Franklin Co.

1822 May 16   Ogden, Lydia and Michael Stagg by Jacob Smith, Franklin Co.

1826 May 4   Ogden, Sally and James Canfield by D.W. Deshler, Acting JP, Franklin
              Co.

1808 Feb 8   Ogle, Ann and Benjamin Witham by Thos. Stanley, Washington Co.

1814 Apr 26   Ogle, Elias and Mary Walker by Wm. Miller, Esq., Washington Co.

1813 Apr 8   Ogle, George and Polly Shirley by Simeon Tuttle, JP, Washington Co.

1809 Feb 14   Ogle, James and Margaret Walker by Amos Porter, Washington Co.

1817 Mar 20   Ogle, James and Jane Dixon by John True, JP, Washington Co.

1820 Aug 1   Ogle, Margaret and John Hupp by Dudley Davis, JP, Washington Co.

1808 Sep 22   Ogle, Polly and Parley Chapman by Amos Porter, JP, Washington Co.

1812 May 28   Ogle, William and Betsy Perkins by Amos Porter, JP, Washington Co.

1827 May 6   O'Hail, Thomas and Elenor Harris by Geo. Jefferies, Franklin Co.

1811 Aug 6   O'Hara, Elizabeth and Samuel Vize (license date), Pickaway Co.

1805 Feb 19   O'Harra, Arthur and Henrietta Jamison by Zachariah Stephen, JP,
              Franklin Co.

1826 Oct 11   O'Harra, Arthur and Maximilion Fisher by James Hoge, Franklin Co.

1822 Oct 17   O'Harra, Arthur Jr. and Matilda McElvain by Eli C. King, Franklin Co.

1825 Jun 23   O'Harra, Charles and Mariah Flemming by Reuben Golliday, JP, Franklin
              Co.

1824 Nov 11   O'Harra, Daniel and Sally Foley, dau of John Foley, by Henry Matthews,
              Minister of the Methodist E. Church, Franklin Co.

1809 Oct 3   O'Harra, Elizabeth and Elias N. DLashmutt by James Marshall,
              Franklin Co.

1826 Jul 25   O'Harra, John and Polly Smith by H. Mathews, Minister of the M.E.
              Church, Franklin Co.

1825 Apr 28   O'Harra, Joseph and Mary Ann Wynkoop by Henry Mathews, Minister of
              the M.E. Church, Franklin Co.

1810 Aug 26	O'Harra, Nancy and Samuel Pursel by Wm. Brundridge, Franklin Co.
1828 Dec 4	O'Harra, Thomas and Lucinda Legg by George Jefferies, MG, Franklin Co.
1827 Jul 8	Olinger, Daniel and Louisa Rose by M.M. Hencle, VDM, Franklin Co.
1806 Nov 22	Oliver, Alexander and Patsy Graham by S. Lindsly, Washington Co.
1789 Aug 27	Oliver, Christian and Wm. Burnham by Ben Tupper, Washington Co.
1819 Apr 21	Oliver, Drusilla and Hiram Snodgrass by Joseph Dickerson, JP, Washington Co.
1795 Apr 28	Oliver, Elanor and Thomas Lord by Robert Oliver, JP, Washington Co.
1825 Sep 1	Oliver, Elizabeth and Volantine Acord by John Anglin, JP, Jackson Co.
1800 Oct 28	Oliver, Isabella and James Brown by Robert Oliver, JP, Washington Co.
1801 Apr 9	Oliver, John and Catharine Mathews by Daniel Story, Washington Co.
1817 Oct 9	Oliver, Lancelot and Elizabeth Akins by Pelatiah White, JP, Washington Co.
1795 Mar 19	Oliver, Liza and William Oliver by Thomas Lord, JP, Washington Co.
1799 Mar 31	Oliver, Lucinda and George Putnam by Joseph Barker, JP, Washington Co.
1789 Dec 14	Oliver, Lucretia and Levi Munsell by Ben Tupper, Washington Co.
1805 Jan 1	Oliver, Mahala and Calvin Shepard by Enoch Wing, JP, Washington Co.
1818 Sep 3	Oliver, Nelly and David Tice by Wm. Dana, JP, Washington Co.
1790 Jul 3	Oliver, Peggy and Robert Potts by Benj Tupper, Washington Co.
1795 Mar 19	Oliver, William and Liza Oliver by Thomas Lord, JP, Washington Co.
1818 Aug 6	Oliver, Wm. and Nancy Smith by John Horton, JP, Jackson Co.
1824 Feb 13	Olmstead, Elijah and Juliann Bloget by Nathan Emery, E. in M.E.C., Franklin Co.
1819 Mar 18	Olmstead, Thomas N. and Betsey Peirce by Matthew Taylor, Franklin Co.
1813 Mar 25	Olmsted, Cloe and Ahan Palmer by E. Griswold, Franklin Co.
1821 Apr 14	Olney, Anna and Lyman Lawrence by Thomas White, JP, Washington Co.
1816 Nov 3	Olney, Cogswell and Matilda P. Smith by Rev. Nehemiah Davis, Washington Co.
1801 Apr 23	Olney, Discovery and Sarah Slack by Nehemiah Davis, Washington Co.
1795 Jan 7	Olney, Drusilla and Daniel Davis by R.J. Meigs, JP, Washington Co.
1809 Jan 26	Olney, Elizabeth and Asa Emerson, Jr. by Thos. Seely, Washington Co.
1813 Apr 14	Olney, Gilbert and Abigail Sprague by Sardine Stone, JP, Washington Co.
1804 Dec 28	Olney, Huldah and Wm. Sherman by Enoch Wing, JP, Washington Co.
1802 Mar 25	Olney, Joanna and Asa Davis by Nehemiah Davis, Washington Co.
1795 Oct 18	Olney, Lois and James Converse by Robert Oliver, Washington Co.
1820 Jul 30	Olney, Mary and Andrew Cole by John Green, JP, Washington Co.
1815 Mar 12	Olney, Nathaniel and Mary Smith by Sardine Stone, JP, Washington Co.
1817 Mar 21	Olney, Oran and Tryphena Cheadle by Asa Cheadle, JP, Washington Co.

1796 Jul 18   Olney, Patience and Phinehas Cobern by Robert Oliver, JP,
               Washington Co.

1809 Jan 26   Olney, Rachel and John Vincent by Thos. Seely, Washington Co.

1799 Feb 14   Olney, Sally and Daniel Davis by Robert Oliver, Washington Co.

1819 May 13   Olney, Salvanus and Betsey Nixon by Thos. White, JP, Washington Co.

1806 Oct 8   Olney, Sarah and Ephraim Foster by Nehemiah Davis, Washington Co.

1818 Aug 13   Olney, Sylvanus and Tryphena Cheadle by Wm. Davis, Washington Co.

1799 May 15   Olney, Thomas and Anna Stack by Phillip Whitten, JP, Washington Co.

1815 Dec 31   Olney, Washington and Cynthia Sprague by Jno Green, Washington Co.

1818 Aug 27   Olney, Washington and Apphia Cable by John Green, JP, Washington Co.

1805 Aug 11   O'Neal, Ann and Zadock Dorsen by James Quinn, Elder, Ross Co.

1813 8 mo 4   O'Neall, Rebecca and Micajah Johnson, Miami Monthly Meeting, Warren Co.

1820 12 mo 6   O'Neall, Rhoda and James B. Johnson, Miami Monthly Meeting, Warren Co.

1805 7 mo 24   O'Neall, Sarah and Thomas Perkins, Miami Monthly Meeting, Warren Co.

1819 Dec 21   O'Neil, Elenòr and Vincent Southard by Nathl W. Andrews, JP, Jackson
               Co.

1818 Feb 11   Oray, Francis and Franky Hughbanks by Thomas Scott, JP, Jackson Co.

1806 Jan 30   Orders, Jones and Sarah Ford by Zachariah Stephen, JP, Franklin Co.

1812 Feb 9   Orison, Mary and Jacob Gossett by Nathaniel Hamilton, JP, Washington
               Co.

1804 Jan 7   Orison, Sarah and John Biggins by Jacob Lindly, Washington Co.

1809 Sep 17   Orpat, Polly and John Losh by Holden, JP, Licking Co.

1827 Apr 12   Orr, Eliza and Almir Brellsford by Amaziah Hutchinson, Franklin Co.

1818 Apr 20   Orr, Hanna and James S. Roberts by John Shields, MNY, Franklin Co.

1822 Sep 16   Orr, James and Eliza Kilpatrick by Reuben Golliday, Franklin Co.

1819 Mar 25   Orr, Joseph and Harriet Tracy by Alex Holden, JP, Licking Co.

1810 Sep --   Orr, Peter and Ann Albany by Wm. Taylor, JP, Licking Co.

1817 Jul 3   Orr, Susanna and B. Emery by John W. Patterson, JP, Licking Co.

1818 Sep 26   Osbond?, Rymard and Catherine Meeker by Benj Beem, JP, Licking Co.

1818 Jul 18   Osborn, John and Susannah Meeker by Benj Beem, JP, Licking Co.

1813 Apr 26   Osborn, Ralph and Catherine Renick (license date), Pickaway Co.

1821 Apr 19   Otis, Lavina and Henry Wright by Rev. A. Robinson, Washington Co.

1829 Jul 5   Otstot, John and Ellen Van Voorhis by Leroy Swormstead, Franklin Co.

1841 Nov 21   Otstott, John T. and Balsara L. Bacon by Rev. R.S. Elder, St. John's
               Church, Worthington, Franklin Co.

1879 Jan 1   Ottinger, Ella E. of Putnam and Erwin C. Chapman of Zanesville by Rev.
               George F. Moore, Putnam Presbyterian Church, Muskingum Co.

1814 Feb 14   Outan, Jesse and Nelly Moore by Rev. Geo. Alkire, Ross Co.

1814 Feb 14   Outan, Jesse and Nelly Moore by Rev. Geo. Alkire, Ross Co.

1804 Apr 10   Ovens, Daniel and Hannah Allison by Jacob Lindly, Washington Co.

1806 Sep 11   Overdear, Jacob and Susan Grubb by James Marshall, JP, Franklin Co.

1803 Aug 15   Overdear, John and Martha Brown by Ezekiel Brown, JP, Franklin Co.

1816 Apr 1   Overdear, Martha and Stewart Bailey by James Hoge, Franklin Co.

1805 May 9   Overfield, Moses and Sally Whitecotten by David W. Davis, JP, Ross Co.

1805 Feb 14   Overman, Sarah and Benjamin Blumer by Samuel Evans, JP, Ross Co.

1813 Jun 15   Overturf, Elizabeth and John Payne by Samuel Dunnavan, JP, Licking Co.

1816 Feb 15   Owen, Charles and Peggy McFarlin by Jno Green, Washington Co.

1864 Jun 14   Owen, Frances H. and Wm. Wright by Wm. Bower, St. Luke's Church,
               Granville, Licking Co.

1820 Mar 28   Owen, Herman and Sally Woodruff by Benj Been, JP, Licking Co.

1816 Feb 11   Owen, Susan and Jonathan Sprague by Jno Green, JP, Washington Co.

1800 Apr 27   Owen, James and Ajucah Brown by Nehemiah Davis, Pastor Baptist
               Church, Washington Co.

1819 Jan 7   Owens, Alney and William Farley by Zach Carlisle, JP, Licking Co.

1821 Aug 27   Owens, Eliza Ann and David Bell by Noah Fidler, Licking Co.

1814 Dec 24   Owens, Mary and Amos Farmer by Rev. T. Harris, Licking Co.

1815 Jan 1   Owens, Nancy and Michael Bauch by Wm. Jones, JP, Pickaway Co.

1820 Mar 1   Owens, Owen and Phebe James by John C. Smith, JP, Licking Co.

1821 Mar 21   Owens, Susanna and James McAllister by James M. Booth, JP, Washington
               Co.

1810 May 21   Owens, Thomas and Rachel Phelps by John W. Patterson, JP, Licking Co.

1810 Aug 25   Owings, Ann and Ezra Dorraned by Rev. T. Harris, Licking Co.

1810 Jan 20   Owings, Scarlott and Molley Molla Mollahan by Wm. D. Hendren, Franklin
               Co.

1819 Jan 22   Owings, Wilfred and Eliza Coulter by Noah Fidler, Licking Co.

1814 Nov 20   Oxford, Abel and Rachael Callahan by Wm. Florence, JP, Pickaway Co.

1814 Mar 14   Oxford, Nancy and James Harvey by Rev. Jas. McHenry, Pickaway Co.

1824 Jul 13   Packard, Absalom and Nancy Fickle by J.B. Packard, JP, Marion Co.

1825 May 1   Packard, Phineas and Elizabeth Fickle by Alex Perry, JP, Marion Co.

1807 Feb 18   Paden, Obediah and Christina Cline by Philip Witten, Washington Co.

1854 Dec 4   Page, Edward Postlethwayte and Margaret Jane Carter by Rev. John
               Boyd, St. Luke's Church, Marietta, Washington Co.

1816 Oct 30   Page, Eliza and George Avery by Rev. T. Harris, Licking Co.

1804 Jul 19   Page, John and Margrett Emmery by Isaac Cook, JP, Ross Co.

1810 Oct 1   Page, Stephen and Nancy Collins by Wm. Brundridge, Franklin Co.

1820 Sep 21   Pain, Charles and Jane Gregg by Wm. Woodford, JP, Washington Co.

1819 Feb 28   Pain, Lydia and Bunas Krewson by Wm. Woodford, JP, Washington Co.

1811 Mar 17   Paine, John and Sarah Lawrence (license date), Pickaway Co.

1821 Jun 12   Paine, Matthias S. and Lucinda Hutchinson by John Curtis, JP,
               Washington Co.

1812 Sep 12   Paine, William and Eleanor Kelso by Peter Pence, JP, Licking Co.

1823 Nov 16   Painter, Nathaniel and Polly Anderson by Joseph Smith, JP, Franklin
               Co.

1828 Jul 24   Painter, Nathaniel and Martha McEntire by Hugh Liams, JP, Franklin Co.

1826 Mar 19   Painter, Sarah and John Martin by Joseph Carper, Franklin Co.

1802 May 27   Painter, Susannah and Henry Northup by Seth Cashart, JP, Washington
               Co.

1806 Jan 14   Pairl, John and Hannah Bradley by J. Brough, JP, Washington Co.

1821 Jul 3   Palmer, Achsah and Erastus Guthrie by James Whitney, JP, Washington
               Co.

1813 Mar 25   Palmer, Ahan and Cloe Olmsted by E. Griswold, Franklin Co.

1867 Jan 30   Palmer, Anna E. and Joseph R. Larzelere, M.D., by Rev. A. Kingsbury,
               Putnam Presbyterian Church, Muskingum Co.

1817 Nov 27   Palmer, Benjamin F. and Margaret Houghland by Salmon N. Cook, JP,
               Washington Co.

1855 Jan 14   Palmer, Caroline and Elias Eveleigh, Jr. by Rev. John Boyd, St.
               Luke's Church, Marietta, Washington Co.

1818 Sep 22   Palmer, Chloe L. and John Russel by Ebenezer Washburn, S Dell,
               Franklin Co.

1881 May 4   Palmer, Franklin C. and Nancy E. Corner by Rev. John Boyd, St. Luke's
               Church, Marietta, Washington Co.

1814 Mar 31   Palmer, Jerusha and Caleb Greene by Cornelius Horyland, JP,
               Washington Co.

1866 Sep 19   Palmer, Major Jewett Jr. and Sadie Scott by Rev. John Boyd, St.
               Luke's Church, Marietta, Washington Co.

1884 May 8   Palmer, John N. Jr. of Zanesville and Mattie A. Josselyn of Putnam,
               by Rev. George F. Moore, Putnam Presbyterian Church, Muskingum Co.

1834 Jul 10   Palmer, Julia Ann and Elijah Short by Rev. J.T. Wheat, St. Luke's
               Church, Marietta, Washington Co.

1819 Jan 14   Palmer, Layton and Catherine Whetzel by Jacob Delay, MG, Jackson Co.

1820 May 4   Palmer, Mary and Samuel Porter by Dudley Davis, Washington Co.

1801 Sep 20   Palmer, Minerva and Titus Brockway at Vernon by Martin Smith, JP,
               Trumbull Co.

1817 Mar 13   Palmer, Thomas and Polly Philbrook by Rev. Timothy Harris, Licking Co.

1822 Feb 28   Pancake, Catharine and John Whitsell by Nicholas Goetschius, Franklin
               Co.

1829 Feb 15   Pancake, David and Elizabeth Bishop by Leroy Swornstead, Franklin Co.

1812 Jun 11   Pancake, Doratha and Thomas Jones by Arthur O'Harra, Franklin Co.

1824 Feb 26   Pancake, Eleanor and Andrew Jamison by Jacob Grubb, Franklin Co.

1823 Dec 31   Pancake, Jesse and Elizabeth Keller by Jacob Grubb, Franklin Co.

1822 Feb 28   Pancake, John and Polly Bennet by Nicholas Goetschius, JP, Franklin Co

1804 Mar 22   Pancake, Susanna and Wm. McConnell by Geo. Williams, Ross Co.

1805 Apr 4   Pancake, Valentine and Polly G. Rooks by David W. Davis, Ross Co.

1805 Aug 15   Pancason, Senon and Elizabeth Reed by Charles Cade, JP, Ross Co.

1814 Mar 27   Pane, Zachariah and Sally Thompson by Wm. Creighton, JP, Pickaway Co.

1816 Sep 13   Pangbourn, Polly and Titus Brown by Simion Overturf, Licking Co.

1816 Jul 28   Pankake, Sally and William Crossley by Joseph Grate, Franklin Co.

1821 Aug 19   Pantenny, Sarah and Abram Williams by John Davis, Franklin Co.

1825 May 3   Parcel, William D. and Harriett Humphrey by Alex Perry, JP, Marion Co.

1825 Apr 28   Parcher, Asenath and Eli Odell (license date), Marion Co.

1824 Jul 13   Parcle, John and Mercey Manley by J.B. Packard, JP, Marion Co.

1803 Oct 18   Parcuson, George and Rebecca Ross by James Evans, Ross Co.

1823 Oct 21   Parish, Clarissa and George Anthony by Charles Waddell, Franklin Co.

1814 Dec 29   Parish, Ira Wingfield and Ruth Chenoweth by John Turner, Franklin Co.

1818 Nov 16   Parish, John R. and Mary Phillips by James Hoge, Franklin Co.

1805 Aug 1   Parish, Jolly and Elizabeth Smith by Thos. Hicks, Ross Co.

1814 Dec 22   Parish, Meredith and Sarah Galbreath by Wm. Jones, JP, Pickaway Co.

1825 Apr 12   Parish, Merideth Sr. (widower) and Servier Swift (widow) by Jacob
               Gundy, JP, Franklin Co.

1827 Jan 31   Park, Almeda and David B. Barker by J.W. Ladd, JP, Franklin Co.

1827 Sep 20   Park, Arthur and Edney Perrin by Reuben Golliday, Franklin Co.

1816 Feb 15   Park, Hannah and Henry Hilbrant by Geo. Callanhan, EMEC, Licking Co.

1817 Mar 27   Park, Jane and Robert Culbertson by James Hoge, Franklin Co.

1824 Nov 18   Park, Kesia and Archabald Badger by Joseph Badger, JP, Franklin Co.

1802 Feb 18   Park, Mary and Adam Whiting by John Struthers, JP, Trumbull Co.

1820 Mar 22   Park, Nancy and Robert Badger by James Hoge, Franklin Co.

1814 Oct 23   Park, Rachel and Amos Lee by George Callanhan, EMEC, Licking Co.

1820 May 31   Park, Robert and Margret Mannan by Jacob Keller, Franklin Co.

1802 Feb 18   Park, William and Margaret Whiting by Jonthan Struthers, JP, Trumbull
               Co.

1817 Jul 20   Parker, Charity and John Erwin by Pelatiah White, JP, Washington Co.

1803 May 5   Parker, Clark and Peggy Jurdon by Jesse Phelps, JP, Trumbull Co.

1826 Dec 10   Parker, Cyrus and Livinia Gridley by James Hoge, Franklin Co.

1818 Jan 15   Parker, Elinda and John Ridesy by Rev. T. Harris, Licking Co.

1807 Apr 30   Parker, Fanny and John Fordyce by Stephen Lindsly, Washington Co.

1818 Aug 15   Parker, Hannah and John Cannon by Danl H. Buell, JP, Washington Co.

1819 Dec 19   Parker, Hannah and Carlton Lockwood by Spencer Wright, JP, Licking Co.

1825 Apr 12   Parker, Jane and Joel Lee (license date), Marion Co.

1807 May 2   Parker, John and Lucy Coton by Stephen Lindsly, Washington Co.

1819 Jul 1   Parker, Margaret and Oliver A. Thrall by Spencer Wright, JP, Licking Co.

1813 Feb 15   Parker, Mary and James Johnston by ----- Phillips, JP, Licking Co.

1816 Aug 19   Parker, Nathan and Sally Conner by John Johnston, JP, Licking Co.

1812 Jan 14   Parker, Rebecca and Uriah Shadwick by Rev. G. Vanaman, Licking Co.

1803 Feb 12   Parker, Reuben and Sarah Walker both of Hudson by David Hudson, JP, Trumbull Co.

1813 Apr 20   Parker, Robert and Hannah Conner by Jacob Hahn, JP, Licking Co.

1813 Oct 24   Parker, Sam'l and Susanna Hanson by Sardine Stone, JP, Washington Co.

1813 Mar 8   Parker, Sarah and Abner Suber by Isaac Baker, Washington Co.

1821 Jun 21   Parker, Sarah and Norman Chapman by Samuel Bancroft, JP, Licking Co.

1828 Sep 13   Parker, Selah and Catharine Sulsor by Geo. Jefferies, Franklin Co.

1819 Apr 29   Parker, Thomas and Mary Thrall by Thomas Carr, ME Ch, Licking Co.

1803 Aug 2   Parker, William and Elizabeth Davis by Wm. Davis, JP, Ross Co.

1812 Apr 12   Parkinson, Nancy and John Moore by -----, Licking Co.

1815 May 9   Parkinson, Sally and Thomas Strawn by J.H. Patterson, JP, Licking Co.

1819 Oct 13   Parks, Elizabeth and Michael Barnhart by John McMahan, Licking Co.

1821 Jan 10   Parks, Rebecca and John Hilbrant by Noah Fidler, Licking Co.

1820 Apr 25   Parks, Ruth and Jacob Edington by Uriah Hull, JP, Licking Co.

1811 Nov 26   Parlar, William and Mary Moots by Nathan Connard, Licking Co.

1873 Nov 17   Parlow, Mrs. Mary Angeline and Elias Gill by Rev. John Boyd, St. Luke's Church, Marietta, Washington Co.

1797 Apr 27   Parmonteir, Jean and Joseph W.D. Vacht by Robert Safford, Washington Co.

1807 3 m 18   Parnell, Sarah and David Horner, Miami Monthly Meeting, Warren Co.

1810 Aug 3   Parr, Hannah and John McEnlarf by A. Holden, JP, Licking Co.

1815 Feb 2   Parr, John and Rachel Debolt by J.W. Patterson, JP, Licking Co.

1818 Jan 8   Parr, John and Sarah Patterson by John W. Patterson, MG, Licking Co.

1817 Jul 17   Parr, Judith and Lewis Holden by J.W. Patterson, JP, Licking Co.

1818 Jul 9   Parr, Mary and Jacob White by Alex Holden, JP, Licking Co.

1813 Oct 14   Parr, Richard and Elizabeth Patterson by J.W. Patterson, JP, Licking Co.

1817 Jan 5   Parr, Richard and Polly Miller by John Cunningham, JP, Licking Co.

1815 Mar 28   Parr, Samuel and Elizabeth Harris by Wm. Taylor, Licking Co.

1817 Oct 12   Parr, Samuel and Amelia Earnest by John W. Patterson, JP, Licking Co.

1819 Oct 24   Parr, Samuel and Grace Holden by Moses Williamson, JP, Licking Co.

1818 Feb 12   Parr, Samy and Candia Cooly by Alex Holden, JP, Licking Co.

1817 Nov 16   Parr, Stephen and Nancy Dailey by Rev. David Smithers, Washington Co.

1819 May 27   Parrish, Judith and Thomas Nichols by R. Golliday, Franklin Co.

1821 Dec 23   Parrish, Lucy and Elexander Grant by Jacob Grundy, JP, Franklin Co.

1829 Jul 16   Parrish, Micajah and Nancy Duff by Geo. Jefferies, Franklin Co.

1890 Dec 2   Parshall, Goodcil B. and Carrie Snits both of Zanesville by Rev.
               George F. Moore, Putnam Presbyterian Church, Muskingum Co.

1882 Jun 12   Parsons, Henry M. and Florence M. Hallsman both of Zanesville by Rev.
               George F. Moore, Putnam Presbyterian Church, Muskingum Co.

1873 Apr 10   Parsons, Robert J. and Ruth H. Emery by Rev. A. Kingsbury, Putnam
               Presbyterian Church, Muskingum Co.

1817 Mar 27   Parsons (or Persans), Samuel and Jane McClealland (or McClellan) by
               James Hoge [see note on Samuel Persans], Franklin Co.

1811 Jun 18   Paschal, Sarah and George Nye, Pickaway Co.

1802 Mar 25   Paterson, Patty and Benjamin Tupper by Daniel Story, Clerk, Washington
               Co.

1826 Jan 12   Patrick, Permilia and Samuel Higgins by James Boyd, Franklin Co.

1843 Nov 20   Patrick, Dr. Spicer of Charleston, Va., and Mrs. Ellen J. Steele, by
               Rev. Edward Winthrop, St. Luke's Church, Marietta, Washington Co.

1819 Oct 7   Patrick, Thomas and Polly Seymor by William Jones, Franklin Co.

1825 Dec 8   Patrick, William and Polly Clarke by Wm. Godman, Franklin Co.

1806 Oct 21   Patten, Harriet and John Randall by L. Barber, JP, Washington Co.

1800 Aug 12   Patten, Nancy and Isaac Nogle by J. Munro, Washington Co.

1806 Apr 6   Patten, Rebeckah and John Chinenton by L. Barber, Washington Co.

1805 Jul 20   Patten, Richard and Sally Wier by John Brough, JP, Washington Co.

1806 Mar 20   Patten, Ruth and Thomas Humphrey by John Brough, JP, Washington Co.

1800 Jun 7   Patten, Wm. and Mary Harden by J. Munro, Washington Co.

1810 Jul 29   Patterson, Abigal and Amos Pratt by J.W. Patterson, JP, Licking Co.

1824 Sep 14   Patterson, Abigail and Simeon McKinney by R.W. Coles, JP, Franklin Co.

1819 Jun 2   Patterson, Able and Margaret Smith by B. Black, JP, Licking Co.

1820 Jan 24   Patterson, Adam and Ann Crow by John Green, MG, Licking Co.

1804 May 27   Patterson, Betsy and Preserved Seamans by Enoch Wing, Washington Co.

1822 Jan 22   Patterson, David and Lucy Goodrich by A. Buttles, Franklin Co.

1813 Oct 14   Patterson, Elizabeth and Richard Parr by J.A. Patterson, JP, Licking
               Co.

1818 Dec 5   Patterson, Esther and Walter Hall by Amos Wilson, JP, Washington Co.

1818 Nov 26   Patterson, James and Betsey Landsdown by Eli C. King, Franklin Co.

1810 Jun 12   Patterson, Jane and William Arnhart (license date), Pickaway Co.

1821 Mar 15   Patterson, Jesse and Fanny Drake by Sanford Converse, JP, Licking Co.

1825 Mar 8   Patterson, John and Mary Stephenson by Joseph Carper, Franklin Co.

1818 Jan 29   Patterson, Lydia and John Hoskinson by John W. Patterson, Licking Co.

1820 Nov 12   Patterson, Lyda and Philip B. Moore by John Green, ECC, Licking Co.

1801 Feb 4   Patterson, Peggy and Thomas Wells by Nehemiah Davis, Washington Co.

1820 Nov 20   Patterson, Rebecca and Matthew Rose by James Hoge, Franklin Co.

1819 Apr 1   Patterson, Robert and Eliza Moore by James Cunningham, JP, Licking Co.

1870 Mar 10   Patterson, Robert H. and Kate M. Safford by Rev. John Boyd, St. Luke's
               Church, Marietta, Washington Co.

1818 Jan 8   Patterson, Sarah and John Parr by John W. Patterson, MG, Licking Co.

1809 Oct 26   Patterson, Thomas and Jenny Kilgore by Michael Dickey, Franklin Co.

1804 Jun 14   Patterson, Wm. and Mary Herrod by Enoch Wing, Washington Co.

1820 Jan 27   Pattin, Eleanor and Samuel Royal Smith by Philip Cole, JP, Washington
               Co.

1814 Jul 13   Pattin, Thomas and Nancy Cole by Isaac Humphreys, Esq., Washington Co.

1816 Jun 6   Patton, Alexander and Nancy Green by James Marshall, Franklin Co.

1814 Apr 10   Patton, Alexander and Elizabeth Carns (or Cann) by Daniel Hess,
               Franklin Co.

1819 May 17   Patton, Michael and Catharine Martin by Eli C. King, Franklin Co.

1819 Jun 21   Patton, Robert and Elizabeth Bartholemew by J.W. Patterson, MG,
               Licking Co.

1810 Jan 11   Pauch, John and Mary Turner by James Hoge, Franklin Co.

1818 Sep 7   Pavrish?, Abraham and Elizabeth Warner by Isaiah Hoskinson, JP,
               Licking Co.

1806 10 mo 15 Paxson, Jacob and Sitnah Richards, Miami Monthly Meeting, Warren Co.

1827? Jan 23   Paxton, Nancy and Preserved Leonard by Lynes L. Lattimore, Franklin Co.

1823 Sep 11   Paxton, Samuel and Anny Wilcox by Robert Boyd, Franklin Co.

1814 Apr 7   Payne, Abraham and Philomela Pixley by Rev. Stephen Lindsley, Washing-
               ton Co.

1820 Mar 17   Payne, Anna and Henry Winsor by Wm. Woodford, JP, Washington Co.

1820 Jan 2   Payne, Austin and Lucinda Lyon by Jno Trois, Franklin Co.

1813 Jun 15   Payne, John and Elizabeth Overturf by Saml Dunnavan, JP, Licking Co.

1814 Dec 1   Payne, Nancy and Francis R. Stanley by Joseph Chapman, JP, Washington
               Co.

1818 Aug 13   Payne, Norman and Lydia Hussey by Daniel G. Stanley, Washington Co.

1819 Apr 16   Payne, Rachel and Samuel Hannah by John Spencer, JP, Licking Co.

1814 Oct 5   Payne, Rufus and Mary Perkins by Rev. Thos. Moore, Washington Co.

1813 Apr 7   Payne, Sarah and Henry Kelso by P. Pence, JP, Licking Co.

1813 Sep 8   Payne, William and Ellen Kelso by P. Pence, JP, Licking Co.

1872 Mar 25   Peaker, William and Sarah Draper by Rev. John Boyd, St. Luke's Church, Marietta, Washington Co.

1791 Jun 4   Peaksley, Elijah and Thamur Sherwood by Benj. Tupper, Washington Co.

1816 Jun 4   Pear, Polly and John Kinsale (or Kinsal or Kinsel) by Percival Adams, Franklin Co.

1819 Mar 7   Pearsons, Anna and John Gibson by James M. Booth, JP, Washington Co.

1820 Dec 11   Pease, Lovey and Hiram Twining by Rev. L. Harris, Licking Co.

1814 Jun 22   Peck, Elizabeth and Gideon Herr by Rob't Bradshaw, JP, Pickaway Co.

1819 Apr 4   Peck, Hezekiah and Mary O. Nealee by Rev. James McAboy, Washington Co.

1797 Dec 14   Peck, Lavina and Simeon Blake by Josiah Munro, JP, Washington Co.

1803 Jul 14   Peck, Rachael and Gilbert Devol by Nehemiah Davis, Pastor, Washington Co.

1821 Oct 18   Peck, Zachariah and Matilda Gossett by Wm. Woodford, JP, Washington Co.

1818 Mar 19   Peddicord, Isabel and John J. Jackson by Noah Fidler, Licking Co.

1807 3 m 18   Peddrick, Ann and John Comton, Miami Monthly Meeting, Warren Co.

1813 10 m 6   Pedrick, Hannah and Thomas Evans, Miami Monthly Meeting, Warren Co.

1808 1 m 20   Pedrick, Lydia and Joseph Canby, Miami Monthly Meeting, Warren Co.

1822 11 m 6   Pedrick, Richard and Mary Evans, Miami Monthly Meeting, Warren Co.

1804 Aug 21   Peerce, Thomas and Betsy Francis by J. Gardner, JP, Ross Co.

1811 Jun 19   Peese, Eliza and John S. Clark by Stephen Lindsly, Washington Co.

1821 Jul 26   Pegg, Ezekiel and Polly Hays by Jacob Keller, Franklin Co.

1823 Oct 9   Pegg, Margaret and Ephraim Fisher by John McCan, JP, Franklin Co.

1804 Dec 30   Peik, Samuel and Charity Younge by Wm. Harper, Washington Co.

1810 Oct 21   Peir, Ira W. and Sally Bradford by Sam'l P. Robbins, Washington Co.

1819 Mar 18   Peirce, Betsey and Thomas N. Olmstead by Matthew Taylor, Franklin Co.

1869 Oct 8   Peker, John P. and Phelista Dutton by Rev. John Boyd, St. Luke's Church, Marietta, Washington Co.

1806 Nov 13   Pell, Mahitable and John Taylor by Simeon Pell, Washington Co.

1819 Aug 19   Pemelton, Richard and Jemima Hill by Vincent Southard, JP, Jackson Co.

1818 May 13   Pemitton, Nancy and John Higganbotham by David Mitchell, JP, Jackson Co.

1812 Jun 25   Pen, Mary and Joshua Barry by John Green, JP, Licking Co.

1806 May 7   Penace, Edward and Sally Ball by James Marshall, JP, Licking Co.

1819 May 10   Pence, Abraham and Susannah Woods by Simeon Overturf, JP, Licking Co.

1820 Jan 17   Pence, Margaret and Wm. Carpenter by Simeon Overtruf, JP, Licking Co.

1820 Aug 5   Pence, Patsey and Joseph Lemmon by John Spencer, JP, Licking Co.

1814 Jul 7   Penee, Sarah and David Hughes by John Cunningham, Licking Co.

1824 Jan 4   Penix, Edward and Sally Furguson by Reuben Golliday, Franklin Co.

1827 Sep 13   Penix, Nancy and W. Risley by P. Adams, Franklin Co.

1813 May 5   Penn, Peggy and Elijah Ryan by John Green, Licking Co.

1813 Jun 22   Pennell, Sarah and Samuel Barr by Nath Cushing, JP, Washington Co.

1810 Nov 27   Pennington, Nancy and John Guffy by Billingslea Bull, JP, Franklin Co.

1816 Oct 6   Penny, Catharine and Daniel McDaniel by Jos. Chapman, JP, Washington
              Co.

1816 Sep 24   Penny, Daniel and Sally Taylor by B.W. Talbot, JP, Washington Co.

1817 Jul 31   Penny, Sally and Lara Briggs by Sardine Stone, JP, Washington Co.

1818 Nov 20   Penrode?, Samuel and Elizabeth Starts? by Alex Holden, JP, Licking Co.

1814 Aug 4   Peppers, Albert and Margaret Launes by Wm. Jones, JP, Pickaway Co.

1825 Apr 12   Perday (or Purday), George W. and Barbara Shults by John Long,
              Franklin Co.

1818 12m 2   Perdue, Gershom and Elizabeth Dukeminer, Miami Monthly Meeting,
              Warren Co.

1817 Apr 13   Perfect, Thomas and Joanna Cook by Geo. Hoover, JP, Licking Co.

1827 Nov 1   Perffers, Swain and Mary Raney by Sam'l Hamilton, Elder, Franklin Co.

1801 Nov 5   Perking, Stephen and Mrs. Ruth Bishop both of Hudson by David Hudson,
              JP, Trumbull Co.

1818 Jul 2   Perkins, Ann and Milton Pixley by Ira Hill, JP, Washington Co.

1809 Feb 22   Perkins, Asa and Jemima Twigs by Stephen Lindsly, Washington Co.

1819 Jul 8   Perkins, Asenath and Thomas Fowler by Dudley Davis, JP, Washington Co.

1812 May 28   Perkins, Betsy and William Ogle by Amos Porter, JP, Washington Co.

1808 Jun 1   Perkins, Cynthia and Joseph Stacy by Stephen Lindsly, Washington Co.

1819 Oct 21   Perkins, Cynthia and Willey Fowler by Dudley Davis, JP, Washington Co.

1818 Sep 24   Perkins, Edward and Cynthia Pixley by Dudley Davis, JP, Washington Co.

1802 Mar 24   Perkins, Eliphaz and Catharine Green by Griffin Green, JP, Washington
              Co.

1808 Oct 6   Perkins, Elizabeth and Elisha Allen by Stephen Lindsly, Washington Co.

1813 Feb 9   Perkins, John and Sarah Hatfield by Wm. Moody, JP, Licking Co.

1821 Oct 2   Perkins, John and Miriam Fowler by John True, JP, Washington Co.

1814 Oct 5   Perkins, Mary and Rufus Payne by Rev. Thos. Moore, Washington Co.

1820 Apr 11   Perkins, Nancy and Andrew Worly by Michael Trout, JP, Licking Co.

1805 May 7   Perkins, Sally and Isaac Chapman by Stephen Lindly, Washington Co.

1805 7m 24   Perkins, Thomas and Sarah O'Neall, Miami Monthly Meeting, Warren Co.

1811 Aug 27   Perkins, Thomas and Margaret Churchan by -----, Licking Co.

1827 Sep 20   Perrin, Edney and Arthur Park by Reuben Golliday, Franklin Co.

1827 Feb 15   Perrin, Elizabeth and John McCracken by John Long, JP, Franklin Co.

1827 Mar 28   Perrin, John and Sarah Hopper by Rheuben Golliday, Franklin Co.

1817 Nov 27   Perrin, Mary and Samuel Sandusky by Joseph Grate, Franklin Co.

1825 Jan 27   Perrin, Rachel and Thomas Chinoweth by Robert W. Riley, JP, Franklin
               Co.

1818 Jan 29   Perrin, William and Betsy Hopper by Joseph Grate, Franklin Co.

1809 Jan 24   Perrish, Robert and Salley Davis by James Marshall, Franklin Co.

1825 Apr 25   Perry, Alanson and Sally Beal by Thomas Barcus, JP, Franklin Co.

1813 Nov 29   Perry, Edmund and Levi Prudence Mellor by David Young, MG, Washington
               Co.

1816 Dec 5   Perry, Edmund and Anna Taylor by P. White, Washington Co.

1848 Jul 9   Perry, Elizabeth H. and George C. Hutchinson by Rev. D.W. Tolford,
               St. Luke's Church, Marietta, Washington Co.

1813 Jan 14   Perry, Ellery and Olive Lawrence by Joseph Frye, JP, Washington Co.

1818 May 12   Perry, James and Nancy Crawford by James Hoge, Franklin Co.

1803 Mar 17   Perry, John and Delilah Stevens by Wm. Burnham, Washington Co.

1818 Jan 29   Perry, Nancy and Robert Welch by B.W. Talbot, JP, Washington Co.

1811 Jun 6   Perry, Susanna and Benjamin Greene by Thomas Stanley, JP, Washington
               Co.

1817 Mar 27   Persans (or Parsons), Samuel and Jane McClealland (or McClellan) by
               James Hoge. In deeds and other court records Samuel Persans and
               Samuel Parsons are interchangeable. Early residents of Franklin-
               ton and Columbus, to whom he was the beloved physician, called
               him Dr. Persans as often as Dr. Parsons. His will is signed
               Samuel Parsons. It is Samuel Parsons and Jane McClellan upon
               the family monument. Franklin Co.

1824 Jan 10   Peterbook, John and Sarah Alebrion by Robert W. Riley, Franklin Co.

1810 Nov 19   Peters, Elizabeth and Jacob Sharen by Rev. G. Vanaman, Licking Co.

1823 Mar 7   Peters, Lidia and Samuel Godner by Richard Courtright, JP, Franklin Co

1815 Sep 7   Peters, Peter and Susanna Beaty by John Turner, Franklin Co.

1810 Sep 23   Peters, Rachel and James Vanderwort (license date), Pickaway Co.

1811 Feb 28   Peters, Tunis and Mary E. Glaze (license date), Pickaway Co.

1820 Oct 22   Peterson, James and Mary F. Carow by Alex Anderson, JP, Jackson Co.

1807 Jun 23   Peterson, Rhoda and Richard Stevenson by Massay Clymer, Franklin Co.

1820 Aug 10   Peterson, Ruth and John Clemmons, Jr. by Sam'l W. McDowell, JP,
               Jackson Co.

1795 Apr 20   Petit, John G. and Lucy Woodbridge by Thomas Lord, Washington Co.

1812 Jan 14   Pettee, Hira and Jane Cunningham by Rev. G. Vanaman, Licking Co.

1826 Sep 14   Petters, Absalom and Fanny Swisher by James Petters, MG, Franklin Co.

1822 Dec 19   Pettet, Charles and Betsey Kilgore by James Hoge, Franklin Co.

1814 Dec 1   Petty, Absolom and Luzen Baley by Henry Davis, JP, Pickaway Co.

1812 Nov 30   Petty, Ebeneezer and Susana Slagel (license date), Pickaway Co.

1812 Feb 4   Petty (or Pitty), John and Tene Seymore by Wm. Haines, JP, Licking Co.

1814 Mar 13   Petty, Lydia and Patrick Archer by Dan'l H. Buell, JP, Washington Co.

1817 Jul 23   Petty, Presley and Margaret Nixon by Saml P. Robbins, MCC, Washington Co.

1815 Jan 11   Petty, Susana and Obed. Hedges by Henry Coonrod, JP, Pickaway Co.

1811 Nov 5   Pewthers, Matilda and Uriah Nash by Stephen Lindsly, Washington Co.

1820 May 25   Peyton, Christiana and John Tice by Joseph Dickerson, Washington Co.

1894 Nov 18   Pfaff, Charles and Lizzie Pyle both of Zanesville by Rev. George F. Moore, Putnam Presbyterian Church, Muskingum Co.

1877 Jun 4   Pfeiffer, George and Fannie J. Shawan by Rev. John Boyd, St. Luke's Church, Marietta, Washington Co.

1804 Nov 28   Phebus, Nancy and John Riddon by John Hoddy, Ross Co.

1811 Feb 17   Phebus, Polly and John Hibbs (license date), Pickaway Co.

1821 Apr 20   Phelin, James and Catharin Wiseman by Jacob Keller, JP, Franklin Co.

1817 Nov 1   Phelps, Chloe and Moses Gillaspie by Ebenezer Washburn, Franklin Co.

1817 Jun 26   Phelps, Edward and Betsy Jamisan by Ebenezer Washburn, VDM, Franklin Co.

1819 Feb 8   Phelps, Elizabeth and James Eaging by J. Evans, JP, Licking Co.

1818 Jul 20   Phelps, James M. and Patty Wickizer by Eli C. King, Franklin Co.

1806 Aug 23   Phelps, John and Sarah Blake by Edwin Putnam, Washington Co.

1817 Jul 10   Phelps, Lucinda and William Williams by Ebenezer Washbourn, JP, Franklin Co.

1838 Nov --   Phelps, Lucy and Jeremiah Armstrong by Rev. A. Helfenstine, St. John's Church, Worthington, Franklin Co.

1817 Feb 8   Phelps, Martha and Silas Mead by Rev. Harris, Licking Co.

1810 May 21   Phelps, Rachel and Thomas Owens by John W. Patterson, JP, Licking Co.

1813 Dec 26   Phelps, Sally and John Straight by Eli Steadman, Washington Co.

1820 Mar 23   Phelps, Thomas and Mary Alden by Thomas White, JP, Washington Co.

1824 Aug 21   Phelps, William and Jane Watt by T. Lee, JP, Franklin Co.

1819 Nov 30   Philbrook, Cyrus and Anna C. Martin by Samuel Bancroft, JP, Licking Co.

1817 Mar 13   Philbrook, Lydia and Eli Buttle by Rev. Timothy Harris, Licking Co.

1817 Mar 13   Philbrook, Polly and Thomas Palmer by Rev. Timothy Harris, Licking Co.

1818 Apr 2   Philbrook, Seth and Peggy Ward by Samuel Bancroft, JP, Licking Co.

1810 Aug 27   Philip, Mary and John Brown by Dudley Davis, JP, Washington Co.

1803 Nov 17   Philips, James and Mary Harr by Thomas Scott, JP Scioto Tp., Ross Co.

1808 Jun 10   Philips, James and Betsey Nobill by James Marshall, Franklin Co.

1821 Jun 14   Philips, Jesse and Sally Devees by Richard Taylor, JP, Washington Co.

1816 Dec 12   Philips, Mary and Stephen Maynard by R. Stansbury, Franklin Co.

1823 Aug 6   Philips, Mary and Jebide Gillunon by John F. Solomon, MG, Franklin Co

1812 Jun 11   Philips, Peggy and John Hays by Henry Jolly, JP, Washington Co.

1796 Jun 20   Phillipean, Anthony and Editha Flagg by J. Gilman, Washington Co.

1818 Dec 17   Phillips, Anthony and Elysia Munsel by Samuel Bancroft, JP, Licking
               Co.

1814 Dec 8   Phillips, Chancy and Mary Chidwick by Rev. T. Harris, Licking Co.

1816 Nov 3   Phillips, Daniel and Cynthia Devol by Sardine Stone, JP, Washington C

1803 Apr 27   Phillips, Elizabeth and James McGee by Sam'l Williamson, JP, Washing-
               ton Co.

1815 Dec 14   Phillips, Eva and Sampson Violet by Elihu Bigelow, Licking Co.

1797 Oct 12   Phillips, Ezra and Polly Scott by J. Munro, Washington Co.

1826 Apr 6   Phillips, Garshum and Lydia Stroud by Wm. Ayers, JP, Jackson Co.

1806 Mar 21   Phillips, James and Margaret Woodfield by John Johnston, JP, Ross Co.

1820 Aug 20   Phillips, Jenkin and Elizabeth Funston by David Culbertson, DD,
               Jackson Co.

1818 Nov 16   Phillips, Mary and John R. Parish by James Hoge, Franklin Co.

1820 Feb 17   Phinney, Jonathan and Sally Wilson by John Smith, JP, Franklin Co.

1825 May 19   Phinney, Joseph P. and Elisa McCloud by Nathan Emery, MG, Franklin Co

1814 Jan 19   Phipps, Jacob and Betsey Wyatt by Wm. Droddy, JP, Franklin Co.

1811 Aug 11   Phips, Maria and William Phips by Arthur O'Harra, Franklin Co.

1811 Aug 11   Phips, William and Maria Phips by Arthur O'Harra, Franklin Co.

1813 Mar 28   Phoebus, Polly and Jacob Adkins (license date), Pickaway Co.

1813 Feb 24   Phoebus, Samuel and Polly Crable (license date), Pickaway Co.

1805 Mar 25   Pickens, John and Nancy Carlisle by Wm. Creighton, Ross Co.

1819 Jan 10   Picket, Charles Hull and Ann Lyman by Rev. T. Harris, Licking Co.

1801 May 12   Picket, Elizabeth and Peter Minair by Alvan Bingham, JP, Washington
               Co.

1801 Jan 27   Picket, Nancy and Aaron Young by Alvan Bingham, Washington Co.

1808 Aug 7   Pickiron, Deborah and Jonathan Richards by Alexander Holden, JP,
               Licking Co.

1828 Feb 25   Pickle, Margaret and William Avery by Lyndes L. Latimer, JP, Franklin
               Co.

1818 Dec 30   Pickle, Mary Ann and James Nicholson by Wm. How, JP, Jackson Co.

1817 8 mo 14   Pidgeon, Sarah and Abraham Hollingsworth, Miami Monthly Meeting,
               Warren Co.

1839 Mar --   Pierce, L.A. and Laura K. Greer by Rev. A. Helfenstine, St. John's Church, Worthington, Franklin Co.

1802 Jul 20   Pierce, Lois and James Ryther by Griffin Greene, Washington Co.

1819 Dec 2   Pierce, Robert and Susan Dye by Rev. Saml P. Robbins, Washington Co.

1812 Oct 1   Pierce, Stephen and Hannah R. Plummer by Rev. S.P. Robbins, Washington Co.

1828 Oct 16   Piercy, James and Sally Coble by Wm. Long, JP, Franklin Co.

1821 Apr 19   Pierson, Phebe and Harvey Jones by James Cunningham, Licking Co.

1820 Mar 13   Pike, Caty and James White by Joseph Gorton, JP, Franklin Co.

1816 Apr 21   Pike, Isaac T. and Katharine Moore by Joseph Gorton, Franklin Co.

1818 Nov 26   Pike, Jarvis W. and Eleanor Moore by James Hoge, Franklin Co.

1826 Apr 9   Piles, Ruhaney and John Woshon by John Horton, JP, Jackson Co.

1820 Feb 28   Pilgrim, Mariah and Robert Gilmore by James Hoge, Franklin Co.

1891 Jan 28   Pinkerton, Sherwood Mortley and Julia Buckingham both of Zanesville by Rev. George F. Moore, Putnam Presbyterian Church, Muskingum Co.

1813 Aug 30   Pinkring, Prisilla and Henry Johnston by W. Taylor, Licking Co.

1810 Jul 15   Pinney, Chester and Lucretia Thompson by Ezra Griswold, Franklin Co.

1825 Apr --   Pinney, Chester and Cintha Barker by P. Chase, Franklin Co.

1828 Mar 27   Pinney, Darias and Caleb R. Jewett by Aristarchus Walker, Franklin Co.

1843 Nov 6   Pinney, Eli and Marilla Sells of Dublin by Rev. R.S. Elder, St. John's Church, Worthington, Franklin Co.

1833 Dec 11   Pinney, Lois and Richard Catley by Rev. E. Burr, St. John's Church, Worthington, Franklin Co.

1819 Nov 25   Pinney, Patty alias Martha and William Spooner by Stephen Maynard, JP, Franklin Co.

1804 Feb 8   Pinny, Abner Putnim and Polly Morrison by Zachariah Stephe, JP, Franklin Co.

1814 Nov 25   Pinny, Darcey and Stephen Maynard by Ezra Griswold, Franklin Co.

1804 Feb 8   Pinny, Levi and Chalotte Beach by Zachariah Stephen, JP, Franklin Co.

1824 Feb 26   Piper, Anne and William Hays by Uriah Clark, Franklin Co.

1828 Sep 27   Piper, Daniel and Elizabeth Jones by I.N. Walter, ECC, Franklin Co.

1816 Jun 7   Piper, Elizabeth and Stanton Murris by Alexander Bassett, Franklin Co.

1828 Mar 17   Piper, George R. and Ann Williams by M.T.C. Wing, Deacon, Franklin Co.

1816 Jul 28   Piper, Nancy and Uriah Clark by Alexander Bassett, JP, Franklin Co.

1805 Feb 1   Piper, Philip and Betsy Maneer by Samuel Smith, Ross Co.

1814 Jul 17   Pitcher, Elizabeth and Phillip Searfaus by Jesse Morral, JP, Pickaway Co.

1811 Apr 15   Pitcher, John and Lidia Mollehon by Massey Clymer, Franklin Co.

1812 Feb 4   Pitty (or Petty), John and Tene Seymore by Wm. Haines, JP, Licking Co

1821 Apr 15   Pitzer, Benjamin and Sarah Callanhan by A. Goff, MG, Licking Co.

1816 Mar 30   Pitzer, Elizabeth and Daniel Green by Noah Fidler, Licking Co.

1821 Jan 17   Pitzer, John and Elizabeth Debott by J.W. Patterson, MG, Licking Co.

1817 Nov 27   Pitzer, Nash L. and Jane Gilmore by James Hoge, Franklin Co.

1821 Mar 8   Pitzer, Sarah and William Green by Geo. Callanhan, EMEC, Licking Co.

1818 Sep 24   Pixley, Cynthia and Edward Perkins by Dudley Davis, JP, Washington Co

1868 Apr 5   Pixley, Martha and William Strachan by Rev. John Boyd, St. Luke's
              Church, Marietta, Washington Co.

1818 Jul 2   Pixley, Milton and Ann Perkins by Ira Hill, JP, Washington Co.

1814 Apr 7   Pixley, Philomela and Abraham Payne by Rev. Stephen Lindsly,
              Washington Co.

1821 Dec 20   Place, Lucy and Wm. Root by Asa Morey, JP, Washington Co.

1818 Dec 13   Place, Nathaniel and Martha Allard by Stephen Guthrie, Washington Co

1828 Mar 30   Platt, Benjamin and Lucy Jewett by Jason Bull, Franklin Co.

1825 Oct 30   Platt, Maria and Erastus Luce by W.T. Martin, JP, Franklin Co.

1822 Apr 2   Platt, Parmelia and David Gregory by James Hoge, Franklin Co.

1810 Feb 8   Ploucher, Jacob and Jane Hill by Jonathan Mintchell, Franklin Co.

1810 Feb 15   Plow, Nancy and John Dilly by E.B. Dana, Washington Co.

1815 Jun 4   Plum, Susan and Sam'l Riley by Percival Adams, JP, Franklin Co.

1838 Dec --   Plumb, Mary and John Loofborrough in Berkshire by Rev. A. Helfenstin
              St. John's Church, Worthington, Franklin Co.

1806 Jun 25   Plumer, Ann and John Mitchell by Stephen Lindsly, Washington Co.

1805 Aug 12   Plumer, Catherine and Stephen Shepard by Stephen Lindsly, Washington
              Co.

1812 Feb 5   Plummer, Clarissa and Timothy Buell by Stephen Lindsly, Washington C

1818 Jun 4   Plummer, Esther N. and Bun Bradley by Jacob Lindley, VDM, Washington
              Co.

1812 Oct 1   Plummer, Hannah R. and Stephen Pierce by Rev. S.P. Robbins, Washing-
              ton Co.

1820 Feb 7   Plummer, Hetty and Cornelius Tinkham by Rev. Saml. P. Robbins,
              Washington Co.

1819 Jan 5   Plummer, Joshua and Nancy Gladden by Samuel Stover, JP, Licking Co.

1820 May 24   Plummer, Nancy B. and Jeremiah Dale by Rev. Saml. P. Robbins,
              Washington Co.

1814 Mar 1   Plummer, Sarah and John S. Preston by Rev. Stephen Lindsley,
              Washington Co.

1810 --- --   Pogue, Margret and John Brooks by -----, Licking Co.

1815 Mar 28   Pogue, Samuel and Sarah Farmer by Z. Carlisle, JP, Licking Co.

1811 Feb 28   Poland, Jane and George Messick (license date), Pickaway Co.

1820 Sep 9   Polin, Ann and John Mootz by James Porter, JP, Licking Co.

1816 Sep 17   Pollock, Robert and Caty Saurs by Michael Patton, Franklin Co.

1818 Jan --   Polsan, William and Nancy Turner by Reuben Golliday, JP, Franklin Co.

1812 Dec 10   Pond, Louis and Robert Bradford by Rev. John Green, Washington Co.

1808 Nov 29   Ponshing, Philip and Cotain Reary by Massey Clymer, Franklin Co.

1814 Mar 22   Pontious, Daniel and Polly Metger by Jacob Leist, JP, Pickaway Co.

1811 Jun 3   Pontius, Caty and Adam Martin (license date), Pickaway Co.

1811 Jun 16   Pontius, George and Dorothy Moyer (license date), Pickaway Co.

1813 Jan 19   Pontius, Margaret and Hector Curtis (license date), Pickaway Co.

1811 Jun 30   Pontius, Samuel and Mary Evans (license date), Pickaway Co.

1812 May 10   Pool, Charlotte and James Hutchinson by Henry Jolly, Washington Co.

1824 Oct 5   Pool, Chloe, widower of Pool deacest, and Elisha Hays, widower, by
              Brice Hays, JP (license date, return filed 10 Dec), Franklin Co.

1814 Jan 23   Pool, Dennis and Elizabeth Ellis by Anth'y Sheets, Washington Co.

1814 Jul 3   Pool, Elizabeth and Adam Hayes by Anth'y Sheets, Washington Co.

1819 Apr 22   Pool, Livinia and David Roberts of Delaware County by Ezra Griswold,
              Franklin Co.

1814 May 18   Pool, Moriah and Josiah Higgins, Sr. by Ezra Griswold, Franklin Co.

1804 Jul 20   Pool, Nancy and John Bell by John Brough, JP, Washington Co.

1810 Oct 5   Pool, Polly and James B. Gardiner by Jeremiah Dare, JP, Washington Co.

1816 Mar 14   Pool, Sally and Jonathan Thompson by Recompence Stanbery, Franklin Co.

1829 Mar 5   Pool, Simeon and Maria McCloud by Leroy Swornstead, Franklin Co.

1807 3m 19   Pope, Betsy and Thomas Sanders, Miami Monthly Meeting, Warren Co.

1816 Oct 11   Pope, Catharine and James Bensley by P. White, Washington Co.

1821 Feb 25   Pope, Elizabeth and Isaac Childs by Rev. Elnathan Raymond, Washington
              Co.

1818 Jan 4   Pope, John and Intenda Van Valey by John Patterson, Washington Co.

1805 4m 17   Pope, William and Grace Lupton, Miami Monthly Meeting, Warren Co.

1812 Oct 18   Poor, John and Phebe Willson by John Turner, Franklin Co.

1818 Sep --   Poor, Sarah and Christopher Hanna by Nath'l W. Andrews, JP, Jackson
              Co.

1812 Dec 10   Porter, Amos and Sally Sutton by Wm. Miller, JP, Washington Co.

1815 Mar 3   Porter, Cummings, Eleanor Johnston by Stephen Guthrie, JP, Washington
              Co.

1815 Feb 23   Porter, Jane and James Kilpatrick by Alex Rowen, JP, Pickaway Co.

1814 Jul 17   Porter, John R. and Joanna Stump by Thos. White, Esq., Washington Co.

1870 Aug 14   Porter, Laura J. and Samuel Wilson by Rev. John Boyd, St. Luke's
              Church, Marietta, Washington Co.

1811 Nov 16   Porter, Mary and Amos Knowles by Dan'l Goodno, JP, Washington Co.

1821 Mar 13   Porter, Mathew and Sarah Carroll by John Spencer, JP, Licking Co.

1806 Sep 25   Porter, Nancy and Jacob Aulcram by Stephen Lindsly, Washington Co.

1829 Jul 12   Porter, Nancy and Franklin B. Chester by Geo. Jefferies, Franklin Co.

1797 Dec 19   Porter, Prissilla and James Smith by Peregrine Foster, JCCCP,
               Washington Co.

1802 Apr 28   Porter, Rebecca and David White by Peregrine Foster, JCCCP,
               Washington Co.

1820 May 4   Porter, Samuel and Mary Palmer by Dudley Davis, Washington Co.

1804 Sep 27   Porter, Simon and Elizabeth Still by Dudley Davis, Washington Co.

1821 Nov 15   Porter, Thomas and Rhoda Sutton by John True, JP, Washington Co.

1818 Nov 22   Porter, William and Mary Sutton by Dudley Davis, Washington Co.

1819 Jul 23   Porters, William and Fanny Seely by Joseph Gorton, Franklin Co.

1811 Mar 24   Posey, Frances and William Alcock by Stephen Lindsly, Washington Co.

1809 Nov 2   Posey, Marian and Wm. M. Case by Stephen Lindsly, Washington Co.

1815 Jun 13   Posey, Nancy and John Henry by Sam'l Dye, JP, Washington Co.

1820 Jan 26   Posey, Sally and William Alcock by Danl H. Buell, JP, Washington Co.

1820 Nov 14   Postle, Gabriel and Rebecca Young by Jacob Grubb, JP, Franklin Co.

1819 Jan 7   Postle, Polly and Samuel Cooper by Joseph Grate, Franklin Co.

1826 Mar 16   Postles, Ann and James Boyd by John McCan, JP, Franklin Co.

1825 Sep 13   Postles, Gabriel and Polly Grant by Wm. C. Duff, Franklin Co.

1818 Dec 18   Potten, Susannah and Hyatt Willison by Geo. Hoover, JP, Licking Co.

1824 Nov 18   Potter, Catharine and Joel Beard by W.T. Martin, JP, Franklin Co.

1811 Aug 19   Potter, George and Polly Hyatt (license date), Pickaway Co.

1817 Jan 1   Potter, Peleg and Nancy Cutwright by Joseph Armstrong, JP, Jackson Co.

1814 Jun 2   Potts, Anthony and Cloe Smith by Rev. Thos W. Suruney, Pickaway Co.

1886? Feb --   Potts, David and Mrs. Mary R. Galbraith both of Zanesville by Rev.
               George F. Moore, Putnam Presbyterian Church, Muskingum Co.

1818 Apr 7   Potts, Elizabeth and Jacob Doneker by Pelatiah White, Washington Co.

1818 May 31   Potts, Hannah and Walter Hart by Pelatiah White, JP, Washington Co.

1804 Jan 12   Potts, Margaret and John Waterman by Robert Oliver, JP, Washington Co.

1808 Apr 21   Potts, Polly and Wm. Quigley by Rob't Oliver, JP, Washington Co.

1790 Jul 3   Potts, Robert and Peggy Oliver by Benj Tupper, Washington Co.

1860 Feb 13   Potts, Thomas and Mary Francis Nye by Rev. A. Kingsbury, Putnam
               Presbyterian Church, Muskingum Co.

1876 Sep 6   Potwin, Cora of Putnam and Charles F. Ellis of St. Louis, Mo., by Rev.
               A. Kingsbury, Putnam Presbyterian Church, Muskingum Co.

1847 Mar 23   Potwin, Carolina A. and William Sturges by Rev. A. Kingsbury, Putnam
               Presbyterian Church, Muskingum Co.

1890 Nov 19   Potwin, Charles Albert and Adelaid Wheeler Stevens both of Zanesville,
               by Rev. George F. Moore, Putnam Presbyterian Church, Muskingum Co.

1848 Aug 8   Potwin, Charles W. and Sarah Sturges by Rev. A. Kingsbury, Putnam
               Presbyterian Church, Muskingum Co.

1873 Sep 25   Potwin, Julia H. of Putnam and John R. Holmes of St. Louis, Mo., by
               Rev. A. Kingsbury, Putnam Presbyterian Church, Muskingum Co.

1885 Oct 22   Potwin, Kate B. of Zanesville and Fred Malcolm of New York by Rev.
               George B. Moore, Putnam Presbyterian Church, Muskingum Co.

1872 Jun 6   Potwin, Lulu S. and Gilbert D. Munson by Rev. A. Kingsbury, Putnam
               Presbyterian Church, Muskingum Co.

1845 Nov 4   Potwin, Martha E. and Benjamin H. Buckingham by Rev. A. Kingsbury,
               Putnam Presbyterian Church, Muskingum Co.

1852 May 25   Potwin, Mary E. of Putnam and William C. Van Allen of New York City by
               Rev. A. Kingsbury, Putnam Presbyterian Church, Muskingum Co.

1813 Feb 11   Poulsen, Elisha and Nancy Thompson (license date), Pickaway Co.

1829 Mar 5   Pountious, Christiana and Abraham Rainear by J.F.S., Franklin Co.

1815 Dec 6   Powel, William and Mary Dukes by John Stipp, Franklin Co.

1826 Dec 30   Powell, Elisabeth and David McCollin by John Long, Franklin Co.

1814 Mar 3   Powell, George and Malinda Genn by John Stevenson, Franklin Co.

1888 Oct 23   Powell, George C. of Zanesville and Ida C. Slack of Powell's Mills, O.,
               by Rev. George F. Moore, Putnam Presbyterian Church, Muskingum Co.

1815 Jan 19   Powell, Mary and George Stevenson by Richd Suddick, JP, Franklin Co.

1827 Aug 27   Powell, Rachel and David McCracken by Wm. Patterson, JP, Franklin Co.

1810 Jan 15   Powell, Samuel and Elizabeth Allkire by John Smith (another entry on
               27 Feb 1810), Franklin Co.

1897 Mar 29   Powell, Mrs. Sare E. and Howard H. Smith both of Zanesville by Rev.
               George F. Moore, Putnam Presbyterian Church, Muskingum Co.

1811 Jan 31   Power, Luther and Elizabeth Lysle by James Hoge, Franklin Co.

1867 Jun 8   Powers, Alex. C. and Mrs. Cornelia J. Hicks by Rev. A. Kingsbury,
               Putnam Presbyterian Church, Muskingum Co.

1814 Jun 26   Powers, Catherine C. and Jones Fry by Wm. Taylor, Licking Co.

1826 Oct 15   Powers, Dolly and John Jones by Henry Matthews, Minister of the M.E.
               Church, Franklin Co.

1802 May 24   Powers, Hanford and Charlotte Devol by Wm. Burnham, JP, Washington Co.

1819 Oct 28   Powers, Hickman and Harriet Dauthet by John Horton, Jackson Co.

1802 Feb 9   Powers, Isaac and Leah Frazee by Jonthan Struthers, JP, Trumbull Co.

1823 May 13   Powers, Jane and Elias Baldwin by Nathan Emery, JP, Franklin Co.

1811 Feb 12   Powers, John and Theodocia Munley (license date), Pickaway Co.

1812 Oct 26   Powers, Theophilus H. and Mary Story by E. Cogswell, JP, Washington Co.

1818 Mar 26   Powers, William J. and Nancy Butterfield by Ezra Griswold, JP,
               Franklin Co.

1811 Jul 25   Powlson, William and Elizabeth England (license date), Pickaway Co.

1818 May 20   Praither, John and Deborah Colemans by David Mitchell, JP, Jackson Co.

1819 Jan 31   Pratt, Aaron and Anna Granger by Rev. Timothy Harris, Licking Co.

1810 Jul 29   Pratt, Amos and Abigal Patterson by J.W. Patterson, JP, Licking Co.

1797 May 4   Pratt, Azariah and Sarah Nye by Josiah Munro, Washington Co.

1820 Apr 19   Pratt, Calvin and Elizabeth Scott by James Cunningham, Licking Co.

1803 Oct 14   Pratt, Elisha and Rachel Morris by Daniel Story, Clerk, Washington Co.

1825 Sep 14   Pratt, Horace and Esther Bucklin by Benj Davis, JP, Marion Co.

1806 Nov 4   Pratt, Mahepsa and Joseph Slary by Stephen Lindley, Washington Co.

1820 Jun 20   Pratt, Philip and Susan Beaver by Benj. Cloves (his mark) Baptist
               minister, Licking Co.

1821 Mar 25   Pratt, Polly F. and Nathan Brooks by S. Bancroft, JP, Licking Co.

1827 May 27   Pratton, C.N. and Alon Bowers by A. Miller, Franklin Co.

1821 Jan 5   Prause, David and Elizabeth Sprouse by Andrew Donnelly, JP, Jackson Co

1821 Jan 11   Predmore, Benjamin and Masey Evans by Zach Carlisle, JP, Licking Co.

1847 Feb 15   Prentiss, Mary M. and Thomas M. Williams of Parkersburg, Va. by
               Edward Winthrop, St. Luke's Church, Marietta, Washington Co.

1820 Oct 21   Preston, Artimacy and Thomas Whitney by Wm. Rand, JP, Washington Co.

1873 Dec 25   Preston, Francis M. and Mary Wiseman by Rev. John Boyd, St. Luke's
               Church, Marietta, Washington Co.

1814 Mar 1   Preston, John S. and Sarah Plummer by Rev. Stephen Lindsley, Washing-
               ton Co.

1820 Dec 7   Prevolt, John and Comfort Johnson by Peter Clover, JP, Franklin Co.

1811 Jul 4   Prewitt, Rachel and Thomas Hinkley by Joseph Palmer, JP, Washington Co

1821 Sep 3   Price, Anna and John Lovet by John Green, JP, Licking Co.

1873 Mar 31   Price, Anna L. of Putnam and J. Munro Brown of New York City by Rev.
               A. Kingsbury, Putnam Presbyterian Church, Muskingum Co.

1816 Aug 8   Price (or Rice), Caleb and Mary Fulton by John Hunter, JP, Franklin Co

1809 Apr 1   Price, Christopher and Nancy Hatfield by W. Haines, JP, Licking Co.

1818 Feb 19   Price, Christopher and Catherine Ward by Noah Fidler, Licking Co.

1812 Jul 5   Price, Elizabeth and Thomas Hatfield by James McMillen, JP, Licking Co

1807 Dec 3   Price, Hannah and Abraham Lyon by Jos. Eaton, Franklin Co.

1817 Aug 21   Price, Mary and John Davis by Eli C. King, Franklin Co.

1820 Oct 12   Price, Nancy and Joseph Harris by David Davis, JP, Washington Co.

1824 Dec 30   Price, Rob't and Eliza Ann Caldwell by Mathias Markley, JP, Marion Co.

1819 Sep 20   Prichard, A.H. and Fhidelia Gilman by Samuel Bancroft, JP, Licking Co.

1855 Jun 14   Prichard, Caroline E. and John J. Metzgar by T. Corlett, St. Luke's
               Church, Granville, Licking Co.

1841 --- --   Prichard, Mary F. and Henry D. Wright, St. Luke's Church, Granville,
              Licking Co.

1813 Sep 19   Prichard, William S. and Isabella More by Rev. T. Harris, Licking Co.

1857 Oct 1   Priest, Izora M. and Frederick P. Leffner by Rev. Geo. B. Sturges,
              St. Paul's Church, Marion, Marion Co.

1866 Oct 3   Prince, Ellen D. and Boyd Kennedy by Rev. John Boyd, St. Luke's
              Church, Marietta, Washington Co.

1825 Jan 16   Prince, Joseph and Mary Cary by Conrad Roth, JP, Marion Co.

1820 Aug 19   Pringle, Samuel and Mary Wolf by Joel Tuttle, Jr., JP, Washington Co.

1858 Dec 30   Prior, Evany and George Rogers by Rev. John Boyd, St. Luke's Church,
              Marietta, Washington Co.

1801 Apr 12   Prior, Sally and John Galbraith by Robt Safford, Washington Co.

1803 Apr 17   Prior, Sally and Joseph Darrow both of Hudson by David Hudson, JP,
              Trumbull Co.

1824 Jun 10   Priscott, Martha and Joseph Davidson by Jacob Grubb, Franklin Co.

1820 Aug 9   Pritchard, Betsey and Samuel Hensly by Wm. Hull, JP, Licking Co.

1816 Dec 8   Pritchard, Betsy and Joseph P. Millerd by John Russell, JP, Washington
              Co.

1818 Aug 29   Pritchard, David and Jane Cuddington by Sardine Stone, JP, Washington
              Co.

1818 Mar 15   Pritchard, Mary and Solomon Churchill by Sardine Stone, JP, Washington
              Co.

1821 Nov 21   Pritchett, Sally and Peter Drumm by Edward Hursey, JP, Licking Co.

1802 Apr 17   Prizel, Sarah and James Harding by Griffin Greene, JCCCP, Washington
              Co.

1797 Jan 5   Procter, Jacob and Elisabeth Wells by Robert Oliver, Washington Co.

1817 Aug 28   Procter, Levina and Mathew Henry by Cornelius Houghland, JP, Washing-
              ton Co.

1818 Jan 8   Procter, Phebe and John Henry by Cornelius Hougland, JP, Washington Co.

1805 Oct 21   Proctor, Sally and Ezra Greene by Jacob Lindly, Washington Co.

1821 Jan 25   Prosser, Joseph and Eliza Kinner by Eli C. King, Franklin Co.

1866 Oct 23   Prossor, Sarah and Leopold Burckhart by N.C.N. Dudley, St. Paul's
              Church, Marion, Marion Co.

1814 Oct 30   Protsman, Catharine and Reuben Cartwright by Dan'l H. Buell, Esq.,
              Washington Co.

1817 Jan 30   Protzman, Ann and Lewis Soyes by Dan'l H. Buell, JP, Washington Co.

1819 Feb 16   Protzman, Royall and Lincoln C. Shaw by Rev. Saml Hamilton, Washington
              Co.

1811 Aug 9   Prouds, Anna and James Bliss by Thomas Morris, Franklin Co.

1819 Feb 7   Prouty, Rachel and Jeffery Buchanan by John Russell, JP, Washington Co.

1821 Apr 15   Prouty, Simon and Lyda Bassett by Spencer Wright, JPGT, Licking Co.

1805 May 15   Provatt, Elizabeth and Josiah Wilson by John Johnston, Ross Co.

1806 lm 15   Pugh, Bathsheba and Samuel Jay, Miami Monthly Meeting, Warren Co.

1814 Sep 28   Pugh, Evan and Sarah Clute by Peter Pence, JP, Licking Co.

1814 7m 7   Pugh, Lot and Rachel Anthony, Miami Monthly Meeting, Warren Co.

1819 Jan 30   Pugh, Mary and Henry Corns by Salmon N. Cook, JP, Washington Co.

1802 Apr 4   Pugsley, Joseph and Olive Pugsley by A. Bingham, JP, Washington Co.

1804 Feb 13   Pugsley, Mary and Elisha Tuttle by Samuel Brown, Washington Co.

1802 Apr 4   Pugsley, Olive and Joseph Pugsley by A. Bingham, JP, Washington Co.

1822 Apr 20   Puntney, Matilda and Isaac Huff by Thos. B. Patterson, Franklin Co.

1813? -----   Purce, Maria and Enoch Henry (license date), Pickaway Cq.

1825 Apr 12   Purday (or Perday), George W. and Barbora Shults by John Long,
               Franklin Co.

1817 Apr 9   Purdey, William and Elizabeth Sworden by James Taylor, Franklin Co.

1820 Feb 25   Purdy, Elizabeth and Anthony Bitzer by Lemuel Lain, Franklin Co.

1818 Mar 19   Purdy, Matilda and Peter Yarnell by Richd. Suddick, Franklin Co.

1810 Feb 27   Purgett, Polly and Jacob Foster by John Smith, Franklin Co.

1809 Jun 20   Purket, Abner and Sary Somtion by John Smith, Franklin Co.

1822 Nov 16   Purse, Zedina and Loice Abbott by Eli C. King, JP, Franklin Co.

1814 Dec 27   Pursel, Isaiah and Abigal Vance by Emmor Cox, JP, Franklin Co.

1810 Aug 26   Pursel, Samuel and Nancy O'Harra by Wm. Brundridge, Franklin Co.

1805 Jul 4   Pursell, Hanah and Samuel Miller by Wm. Robinson, Ross Co.

1791 Jun 23   Putnam, Aaron Waldo and Charlotte Loring by Rufus Putnam, ITNWRO,
               Washington Co.

1791 Apr 10   Putnam, Abigail and Wm. Browning by Rufus Putnam, Washington Co.

1821 Aug 14   Putnam, Benjamin P. and Mary Dana by Jacob Lindley, VDM, Washington Co.

1804 May 3   Putnam, Bethia and Edward W. Tupper by Enoch Shepard, Washington Co.

1797 Dec 7   Putnam, Betsy and Joel Craigg by Peregrine Foster, JCCCP, Washington
               Co.

1803 Oct 13   Putnam, Catherine and John Thomas by J. Gardner, JP, Ross Co.

1805 Nov 27   Putnam, Catherine and Ebenezer Buckingham by Stephen Lindsly (parents
               of Gen. Catharinus Putnam Buckingham), Washington Co.

1844 May 16   Putnam, Douglas of Marietta and Mrs. Eliza W. Tucker of Putnam by Rev.
               A. Kingsbury, Putnam Presbyterian Church, Muskingum Co.

1840 Sep 10   Putnam, Elizabeth A. and William B. Clark both of Union by Rev. James
               Bonnar, St. Luke's Church, Marietta, Washington Co.

1882 Oct 10   Putnam, Elizabeth P. and Samuel Doubt by Rev. John Boyd, St. Luke's
               Church, Marietta, Washington Co.

1799 Mar 31   Putnam, George and Lucinda Oliver by Joseph Barker, JP, Washington Co.

1816 Feb 6   Putnam, Harriet and Hugh Jackson by Joseph Chapman, JP, Washington Co.

1821 Aug 24 Putnam, Israel and Elizabeth Wiser by Philander Chase, Bishop E. Ch.,
             St. Luke's Church, Marietta, Washington Co.

1805 Jan 4 Putnam, Nancy and David Nash by Thos. Stanley, Washington Co.

1798 May 2 Putnam, Persis and Pearly Howe by Josiah Munro, Washington Co.

1816 Apr 1 Putnam, Peter and Susan Eagler by Rev. James Hoge, Franklin Co.

1798 Oct 21 Putnam, Polly and Daniel Mayo by Peregrine Foster, JCCCP, Washington
             Co.

1807 Dec 17 Putnam, Rosella and Daniel G. Stanley by S. Lindsly, Washington Co.

1796 Nov 2 Putnam, Sarah and Sam'l Thornly by J. Munro, JP, Washington Co.

1822 Feb 4 Putnam, Wm. Pitt and Rowena Nye by Rev. Sam'l P. Robbins, Washington
             Co.

1802 Feb 7 Putnam, William R. and Jerusha Gitteau by Daniel Story, Washington Co.

1894 Nov 18 Pyle, Lizzie and Charles Pfaff both of Zanesville by Rev. George F.
             Moore, Putnam Presbyterian Church, Muskingum Co.

1826 May 6 Pyle, Phebe and Isaac Wooshan by J.B. Gilleland, JP, Jackson Co.

1881 Jun 21 Pyper, Mrs. Mary Ann and Edward Moss by Rev. John Boyd, St. Luke's
             Church, Marietta, Washington Co.

1865 Nov 7 Quackenbush, Alpheus B. and Augusta Cadwallader by Rev. John Boyd,
             St. Luke's Church, Marietta, Washington Co.

1818 Jan 19 Queen, Hannah and Edward Daugherty by Wm. Brawn, Franklin Co.

1820 Mar 26 Quick, George and Sally Avery by Osgood McFarland, JP, Washington Co.

1815 Apr 16 Quick, James and Susan McConell by Henry Davis, JP, Pickaway Co.

1808 Nov 27 Quigley, Mary and Jeremiah Reeve by Rob't Oliver, JP, Washington Co.

1808 Apr 21 Quigley, Wm. and Polly Potts by Rob't Oliver, JP, Washington Co.

1879 Aug 21 Quimby, William and Mrs. Martha Jones by Rev. John Boyd, St. Luke's
             Church, Marietta, Washington Co.

1816 Jan 1 Rabourn, James and Catherine McQune by James Marshall, JP, Franklin Co.

1853 Dec 19 Rachly, C.F. and May M. Gilson by Rev. Geo. B. Sturges, St. Paul's
             Church, Marion, Marion Co.

1825 Jul 28 Radabaugh, Henry and Lydia Henson by John Horton, JP, Jackson Co.

1825 Mar 3 Radabaugh, John and Mary Elliott by Samuel Carrick, JP, Jackson Co.

1823 Nov 27 Radabaugh, Margaret and James Jenkins by John Horton, JP, Jackson Co.

1815 Jul 7 Radcliff, Deborah and John Evans by Z. Carlisle, JP, Licking Co.

1817 Jul 9 Radcliff, Elizabeth and John Evans by Zach Carlisle, JP, Licking Co.

1811 Mar 24 Radcliff, Mary and Wm. Evans by Zachariah Carlisle, JPHT, Licking Co.

1813 Feb 2   Radcliffe, Isaac and Polly McKinney (license date), Pickaway Co.

1826 Feb 11   Radcliffe, Sarah and John Faught by J.B. Gilliland, Jackson Co.

1817 Feb 14   Radebaugh, Catherine and Benjamin Arthur by John Horton, JP, Jackson Co.

1821 Dec 28   Rader, Philip and Mary Sahl by C. Henkel, Franklin Co.

1805 Dec 21   Raderick, Catharine and John Long by John Guthree, Ross Co.

1823 Jul 30   Ragar, Eleanor and Samuel Myers by Nicholas Goetschius, Franklin Co.

1820 Sep 8   Ragart, Jorge and Rebecah Armitage by Robert Elliott, JP, Franklin Co.

1829 Jun 11   Rager, Mary and Andrew Whitsell by Abram Shoemaker, JP, Franklin Co.

1812 12m 13   Ragin, Ruel and Mary Mills, Miami Monthly Meeting, Warren Co.

1802 May 17   Ragon, Jacob and Jean McClimane by Henry Smith, JP, Washington Co.

1824 Feb 19   Raimer, Daniel and Huldy Lanning by Charles Waddell, Franklin Co.

1829 Mar 5   Rainear, Abraham and Christiana Pountious by J.F.S., Franklin Co.

1808 May 11   Rairy, John and Effy Hickman by Arthur O'Harra, Franklin Co.

1861 Dec 7   Rake, Rebecca J. and Charles H. Rumbolds by Rev. John Boyd, St. Luke's Church, Marietta, Washington Co.

1819 Jan 28   Rambaugh, Wm. and Anna Aldridge by Jacob Delay, MG, Jackson Co.

1829 Jun 11   Ramsey, Amos W. and Eleaner Riley by Geo. Jefferies, Franklin Co.

1819 Jun 30   Ramsey, Elizabeth and Thomas Wood by Richard Courtright, Franklin Co.

1823 Apr 8   Ramsey, Elizabeth and William McComb by James Hoge, Franklin Co.

1826 Jan 18   Ramsey, James and Susan Brown by Percival Adams, JP, Franklin Co.

1817 Apr 17   Ramsey, John and Ann Cox by George Hays, Franklin Co.

1826 Oct 15   Ramsey, John and Mary Cox by John F. Solomon, Franklin Co.

1817 Jan 23   Ramsey, William and Hanna Cox by George Hays, JP, Franklin Co.

1818 Feb 18   Ramsey, William and Mary Dunn by James Hoge, Franklin Co.

1826 Jan 17   Ramsey, William and Elizabeth Boman by Percivel Adams, Franklin Co.

1817 Nov 1   Randal, Nehimiah and Charlette Thrall by Rev. T. Harris, Licking Co.

1825 Mar 4   Randall, Abigal and Robert Loveland by Wm. Long, JP, Franklin Co.

1806 Oct 21   Randall, John and Harriet Patten by L. Barber, JP, Washington Co.

1810 Dec 13   Randaver, Martin B. and Maria Goremly by Isaac Case, Franklin Co.

1827 Nov 22   Randol, Ebenezer and Betsy Griffin by Jacob Gundy, Franklin Co.

1802 May 2   Randols, Elizabeth and Jacob Lerne by Sam'l Williamson, Washington Co.

1815 Mar 26   Rnadom, Maria and Isaac Whiten by Isaac Case, Franklin Co.

1826 May 18   Raney, Eliza and John Turney by C. Hinkel, Franklin Co.

1826 Oct 29   Raney, Mary and Ezekiel Gooderich by John Davis, JP, Franklin Co.

1827 Nov 1   Raney, Mary and Swain Perffers by Sam'l Hamilton, Elder, Franklin Co.

1870 May 15   Rankin, Hellen A. of White Cottage and Harry Fracker of Zanesville, O., by Rev. A. Kingsbury, Putnam Presbyterian Church, Muskingum Co.

1872 Jan 10   Rankin, Lillie N. of White Cottage and John D. Wheeler of Zanesville
               by Rev. A. Kingsbury, Putnam Presbyterian Church, Muskingum Co.

1856 Dec 23   Rankin, Margaret M. of Putnam and George W. Duvall of Baltimore, Md.,
               by Rev. A. Kingsbury, Putnam Presbyterian Church, Muskingum Co.

1865 Jun 28   Rankin, Martha A. of Putnam and Charles Duvall of Baltimore, Md., by
               Rev. A. Kingsbury, Putnam Presbyterian Church, Muskingum Co.

1818 Oct 8   Rankins, James and Elizabeth Campbell by Rev. Noah Fidler, Licking Co.

1801 Apr 1   Rankins, Rachael and William Hill by Robt Safford, Washington Co.

1825? Feb 10   Ransburgh, Sarah and Thomas Carper by James Hoge, Franklin Co.

1816 Sep 26   Ransburgh, Susanna and Rollin Moler by James Hoge (another entry on
               27 Mar 1817), Franklin Co.

1822 Jan 11   Ransom, Theophilus and Sarah Sheppard by John Russell, JP, Washington
               Co.

1817 Apr 10   Ransom, Truman and Temperance Lord by John Green, Washington Co.

1807 Nov 15   Rarden, William and Jane Vandeventer by Joseph Palmer, JP, Washington
               Co.

1818 Apr 2   Rardin, William and Elizabeth Andrews by Salmon N. Cook, Washington Co.

1810 Jan 22   Rardon, David and Margaret DeWitt by Joseph Palmer, JP, Washington Co.

1806 Sep 16   Rardon, Mary and Amos Bartlett by Rob't Oliver, Washington Co.

1814 May 4   Rardon, Moses and Rebecca Minton by Joseph Palmer, JP, Washington Co.

1815 May 4   Rardon, Rebecca and Joseph Minton by Joseph Palmer, JP, Washington Co.

1826 Mar 30   Raredon, George and Sarah Downs by Henry Matthews, Franklin Co.

1812 Mar 10   Raredon, Henry and Jane Mullen by Cornelius Hougland, Washington Co.

1817 May 21   Raredon, Samuel and Charity Harrington by S.N. Cook, JP, Washington Co.

1800 Aug 18   Raridin, Jane and Thomas Coleman by D. Loring, JCCCP, Washington Co.

1800 Dec 24   Rarredon, Thomas and Polly Ray by Alvan Bingham, JP, Washington Co.

1819 Jul 27   Rary, Christine and John Solomon by Michl. Ellis, Franklin Co.

1805 Mar 28   Rasor, Benjamin and Susanna ----- by John Greene, Washington Co.

1802 Jan 28   Rasor, Dennis and Mary Holden by Saml Williamson, JP, Washington Co.

1800 Nov 11   Rasor, Elizabeth and Aaron Strait by Samuel Williamson, Washington Co.

1808 Jun 8   Rathbone, Electa and Isaac French by Edmund B. Dana, JP, Washington Co.

1822 May 22   Rathbone, Elizabeth and Amon Jenkins by Russell Bigelow, Franklin Co.

1812 Nov 14   Rathbone, Gideon and Ann Ditzel by Wm. Moody, JP, Licking Co.

1804 Jul 21   Rathbone, Louise and Stephen Taylor by Enoch Shepard, Washington Co.

1817 Dec 17   Rathborn, Cynthia and James Delzal by -----, Licking Co.

1817 May 18   Rathburn, Ebenezer and Martha Hall by Cyrus Ames, Washington Co.

1821 Jul 24   Rathburn, John W. and Roanna James by Jacob Delay, MG, Jackson Co.

1808 Oct 1   Rathbun, Elisha and Prudy Richardson by D. Loring, JP, Washington Co.

1819 Dec 9   Rathbun, Mercy and John Ingles by Cyrus Ames, Washington Co.

1816 Mar 21   Rathbun, Parr and Ruth White by J.W. Patterson, JP, Licking Co.

1822 6m 12   Ratliff, Cornelius and Mary Kindley, Miami Monthly Meeting, Warren Co

1809 Apr 14   Ratliff, Rachiel and Abraham Vanmetre by John Turner, Franklin Co.

1892 Sep 14   Ravennaugh, Electa of High Hill, O., and James W. Lyons of South
               Zanesville by Rev. George F. Moore, Putnam Presbyterian Church,
               Muskingum Co.

1819 Dec 23   Raver, William and Barbara Bower by Charles Bradford, JP of Bowling
               Green Tp., Licking Co.

1819 Dec 28   Rawles, David and Mrs. Margaret Johnston by Jeremiah Brown, JP,
               Jackson Co.

1806 Dec --   Rawlings, Letticia and John Denny by Wm. Bennett, JP, Franklin Co.

1807 Jan 4   Rawlings, Moses and Sally McCandlis by Nathan Rawlings, JP, Franklin
               Co.

1811 Sep 10   Rawlins, David and Jane Martin (license date), Pickaway Co.

1820 Apr 13   Ray, Frances and John Dixon by Thos. Cox, JP, Jackson Co.

1812 Mar 11   Ray, James and Mary Mullen by Joseph Palmer, JP, Washington Co.

1824 Jun 13   Ray, John and Dinah Dixon by Geo. Claypoole, JP, Jackson Co.

1886 Jun 16   Ray, Mary and John J. Williams both of Zanesville by Rev. George F.
               Moore, Putnam Presbyterian Church, Muskingum Co.

1800 Dec 24   Ray, Polly and Thomas Rarredon by Alvan Bingham, JP, Washington Co.

1820 Jan 2   Rayner, James and Nancy Mitchell by Saml Dye, JP, Washington Co.

1890 Jul 30   Rayse, Julia M. and Harry E. Griems both of Zanesville by Rev. George
               F. Moore, Putnam Presbyterian Church, Muskingum Co.

1811 9m 5   Rea, Rebekah and Joel Stratton, Miami Monthly Meeting, Warren Co.

1816 Feb 18   Reab, Jacob and Milly Mays by Joseph Gorton, Franklin Co.

1826 Feb 2   Read, Adam and Keziah Climer by J. Gander, Franklin Co.

1824 Dec 2   Read, Catharine and Thomas Hamilton by James Hoge, Franklin Co.

1825 Dec 28   Read, Elizabeth and Samuel Robbins (or Robins) by Abm Williams, JP,
               Franklin Co.

1826 Nov 28   Read, John and Elizabeth Sharp by Wm. Patterson, Franklin Co.

1827 Mar 18   Read, Nancy and S.V. Johnston by P. Adams, Franklin Co.

1817 Feb 2   Read, Polly and Ezekiel Wells by Wm. O'Bannon, JP, Licking Co.

1827 Mar 20   Read, Thomas P. and Adaline Eliza Wiswell by A. Walker, JP, Franklin
               Co.

1822 Oct 1   Read, William and Margret Keller by Jacob Grubb, Franklin Co.

1817 Feb 1   Reading, Pricilla and Walter Devon by T.D. Baird, Licking Co.

1810 Jul 26   Reads, John and Elizabeth Vicars (license date), Pickaway Co.

1824 Dec 30   Reams, Lovina and Thomas McCloud by John Goodrich, Jr., JP, Franklin
               Co.

1825 Apr 14   Reamy, James and Sally Vezey by Rob't Hopkins, JP, Marion Co.

1819 Jun 15   Reans, Leah and William Whettimore by John Smith, Franklin Co.

1808 Nov 29   Reary, Cotain and Philip Ponshing by Massey Clymer, Franklin Co.

1812 Apr 7   Reary, Elizabeth and Thomas Hannan by Massey Clymer, Franklin Co.

1813 Jan 16   Reason, Samuel and Phoebe Howard (license date), Pickaway Co.

1800 Jan 23   Reburn, William and Jenny Daniel by Robert Safford, Washington Co.

1799 Apr 12   Recharts, Sarah and Charles Fornark by Henry Smith, JP, Washington Co.

1845 Feb 27   Reckard, Lucy W. and George A. Richards by Rev. Edward Winthrop, St.
               Luke's Church, Marietta, Washington Co.

1809 Dec 7   Reckord, Oliver and Hannah Clark by E.B. Dana, Washington Co.

1809 Jan 1   Record, Calvin and Rhoda Westgate by Dan'l Dunfee, Washington Co.

1813 Oct 13   Record, Huldah and Samuel Fuller by John H. White, JP, Washington Co.

1816 Mar 1   Record, Joseph and Delilah Jennings by Rev. Stephen Lindsley, Washing-
               ton Co.

1820 May 31   Record, Margaret and Joseph Thompson by James Whitney, PP, Washington
               Co.

1809 Feb 9   Record, Mary and Stephen Fuller by Thos. Stanley, Washington Co.

1811 Apr 21   Rector, Pency and David Alexander (license date), Pickaway Co.

1814 Apr 25   Reddin, Elizabeth and Frederick Blue by Rev. Geo. Alkire, Pickaway Co.

1814 Nov 22   Reddin, Nancy and Thos. Van Hook by Chas. Cade, JP, Pickaway Co.

1803 Sep 12   Redding, Elizabeth and Andrew Chovey by John Hoddy, JP, Ross Co.

1827 Feb 4   Redenor, Matias and M.M. Newswender by C. Henkel, Franklin Co.

1803 Apr 14   Reding, Patty and Benjamin Davis by Wm. Robinson, JP, Ross Co.

1819 Apr 29   Redman, Bailis and Sarah W. Crawn? by Joseph Thorp, MG, Licking Co.

1828 Jun 24   Reece, Jane and James C. Smith by James Hoge, Franklin Co.

1805 Jun 14   Reed, Alexander and Phebe Cary by Hiram Merick Curry, Franklin Co.

1864 Sep 28   Reed, Almira and John R. McIntire by Rev. John Boyd, St. Luke's
               Church, Marietta, Washington Co.

1816 Oct 11   Reed, Anna and David McGarry by Jos. Chapman, Washington Co.

1820 May 25   Reed, Civilla and Frederick Cook by Noah Fidler, Licking Co.

1805 Aug 15   Reed, Elizabeth and Senon Pancason by Charles Cade, JP, Ross Co.

1838 Nov 7   Reed, Eveline and Timothy Abbot Smith, St. Luke's Church, Granville,
               Licking Co.

1819 Feb 25   Reed, Hugh and Nancy Edwards by Noah Fidlet, Licking Co.

1813 Apr 20   Reed, James and Hannah Kelley (license date), Pickaway Co.

1817 May 31   Reed, James and Rachel Noble by Dan'l H. Buell, JP, Washington Co.

1819 Feb 23   Reed, Jeremiah R. and Sarah Smith by James Stephenson, JP, Jackson Co.

1814 Sep 22   Reed, John and Delilah Harvey by Thomas Mace, JP, Pickaway Co.

1818 Jul 2   Reed, Joseph and Jane Jackson by Dudley Davis, Washington Co.

1815 Feb 9   Reed, Joshua and Margaret Bilsland by Jno. Scott, JP, Pickaway Co.

1825 Nov 24   Reed, Lucinda and William Camble by A. Allison, Franklin Co.

1814 Oct 15   Reed, Major and Sylvina Barstow by Rev. Marcus Lindsey, Washington Co.

1814 Nov 23   Reed, Margaret and John Fleeharty by Jno. Ludwing, JP, Pickaway Co.

1818 Jan 1   Reed, Margaret and Joshua Edwards by Noah Fidler, Licking Co.

1811 Sep 26   Reed, Margarite and John Lamb (license date), Pickaway Co.

1816 Mar 16   Reed, Mary and Isaiah Cramer by Wm. O'Bannon, Licking Co.

1806 Feb 25   Reed, Nancy and Benjamin Duvall by Wm. Bennett, JP, Franklin Co.

1820 Jan 17   Reed, Peggy and Jacob Bowers by Achiel Hussey, Minister of the
              Christian Church, Jackson Co.

1818 Jun 25   Reed, Polly and Preserved Seameans by Dudley Davis, JP, Washington Co.

1818 Jun 1   Reed, Sally and Russell Fearing by John Patterson, JP, Washington Co.

1805 Apr 16   Reed, Thomas and Nancy Hustone by Wm. Craighton, Ross Co.

1828 Jun 5   Reeder, Catherine and Jacob Hoover by J. Davis, JP, Franklin Co.

1867 Oct 11   Reeder, Eura and Festus Oden Sams by Rev. John Boyd, St. Luke's
              Church, Marietta, Washington Co.

1811 Oct 29   Reeder, Polly and David Heter (license date), Pickaway Co.

1815 Jan 26   Reeder, Sarah and Anthony Bowsher by Jas. Jackson, JP, Pickaway Co.

1816 Apr 1   Rees, Alexr. and Jane Henderson by James Hoge, Franklin Co.

1881 Dec 14   Reese, Hiram V. and Olive N. Hart by Rev. John Boyd, St. Luke's Church
              Marietta, Washington Co.

1826 Sep 3   Reese, Matilda and Hiram Sensabaugh by A. Allison, JP, Franklin Co.

1808 Nov 27   Reeve, Jeremiah and Mary Quigly by Rob't Oliver, JP, Washington Co.

1811 May 30   Reeves, Elizabeth and James Berbrige (license date), Pickaway Co.

1819 Jun 15   Reeves, Isabella and Jacob Hoffman by John Smith, Franklin Co.

1813 May 10   Regalo, Jane and Jos. Mitchell by Isaac Fisher, Franklin Co.

1821 Dec 27   Regnier, Alfred and Mary Ann Rowland by Judah M. Chamberlain,
              Washington Co.

1860 Jun 21   Renier, Austin B. of Harmar and Eunice E. Anderson by Rev. John Boyd,
              St. Luke's Church, Marietta, Washington Co.

1820 Dec 21   Regnier, Hannah and Wm. W. McIntosh by Judah M. Chamberlain, JP,
              Washington Co.

1835 Sep 23   Regnirs, Felix and Eliza Barber by Rev. J.T. Wheat, St. Luke's
              Church, Marietta, Washington Co.

1818 Jun 25   Reighter, John and Mary Drake by Benj. Beem, JP, Licking Co.

1814 Apr 5   Reichelderfer, Susana and Daniel Fetherolf by Jacob Leist, JP,
              Pickaway Co.

1810 Aug 9   Reid, Amelia and Robert Gibson (license date), Pickaway Co.

1821 Sep 1   Reid, Sarah and Thomas Morris by James Hoge, Franklin Co.

1821 Mar 22   Reim, John and Nancy Simmons by Wm. Richardson, Franklin Co.

1813 Nov 16   Reiter, Henry and Mary Shuck (license date), Pickaway Co.

1813 Apr 26   Renick, Catherine and Ralph Osborn (license date), Pickaway Co.

1813 Mar 22   Renick, Jonathan and Lucinda Suddith (license date), Pickaway Co.

1805 Mar 25   Renick, Rachel and Joseph Vanmeter by Peter Jackson, JP, Ross Co.

1825 Apr 21   Rennick, Rebecca and Noah E. Wadham by C. Henkle, Franklin Co.

1824 Jul 1   Renny, John and Elizabeth Salmon by Robert Hopkins, JP, Marion Co.

1807 Nov 29   Renolds, Margaret and Jacob Seavere by Thos. Stanley, Washington Co.

1827 Nov 15   Reose, Phebe and Jacob Beam by J. Davis, JP, Franklin Co.

1867 Oct 22   Reppert, Anna and Joseph S. Cone by Rev. John Boyd, St. Luke's
               Church, Marietta, Washington Co.

1868 Dec 1   Reppert, George L. of Pittsburg and A. Grace Fell by Rev. John Boyd,
               St. Luke's Church, Marietta, Washington Co.

1826 Dec 19   Rettinhouse, Livey and Hannah Cinnett by James Hoge, Franklin Co.

1812 Aug 13   Reuby, Reuben and Sally Meeker by James Marshall, Franklin Co.

1803 Apr 7   Reves, Stephen and Mary Baeggs by Henry Smith, JP, Washington Co.

1825 Oct 27   Reynolds, Hanah and George Shoemaker by Persinal Adams, JP, Franklin
               Co.

1815 Nov 23   Reynolds, Harret and Daniel Morey by Rev. Timothy Harris, Licking Co.

1815 Oct 5   Reynolds, John and Margaret Severs by Joel Tuttle, JP, Washington Co.

1819 Mar 28   Reynolds, Luke and Isabella Barr by Cyrus Ames, JP, Washington Co.

1818 Jan 8   Reynolds, Samuel and Lucinda Gardner by John Russell, JP, Washington
               Co.

1819 Apr 23   Reynolds, Samuel H. and Palmela Green by Rev. Abel Robinson, Washing-
               ton Co.

1820 Nov 9   Reynolds, Melcha and James Beaty by Reuben Golliday, JP, Franklin Co.

1821 Nov 4   Reynolds, Thomas and Nancy Carnahan by Reuben Golliday, JP, Franklin
               Co.

1790 Sep 14   Rhea, Rebecca and Noah Feering by Benj. Tupper, Washington Co.

1816 May 16   Rhew, Sally and Jesse Lenard by James Marshall, Franklin Co.

1828 Dec 4   Rhoades, Phillip and Eleanor Colwell by Geo. Beals, JP, Franklin Co.

1818 Jul 23   Rhoads, Catherine and William Beam by Geo. Callahan, MG, Licking Co.

1816 Sep 26   Rhoads, Elizabeth and Thomas Allbery by Noah Fidler, Licking Co.

1825 Sep 25   Rhoads, Levi and Catherine Cramer by Abm. Williams, JP, Franklin Co.

1820 Apr 22   Rhoads, Rachel and Michael Beem by Rev. Geo. Callanhan, Licking Co.

1805 Feb 19   Rhodes, Abraham and Magaret McCarty by John Hoddy, Ross Co.

1846 Nov 12   Rhodes, Charles R. of St. Louis, Mo., and Mary Elizabeth Ward by Rev.
               Edward Winthrop, St. Luke's Church, Marietta, Washington Co.

1875 Jun 1   Rhodes, Rev. Dudley Ward and Laura Wiggins at St. Louis, Mo., by Rev.
              John Boyd, St. Luke's Church, Marietta, Washington Co.

1877 Jan 11   Rhodes, Harriet D. and William W. Harris by Rev. John Boyd, St.
              Luke's Church, Marietta, Washington Co.

1871 Jun 1   Rhodes, Kate R. and Romein Bunn by Rev. John Boyd, St. Luke's
              Church, Marietta, Washington Co.

1878 Oct 3   Rhodes, Mary E. and Frank R. Ellis by Rev. Dudley W. Rhodes, St.
              Luke's Church, Marietta, Washington Co.

1817 Jan 2   Ricaback, Reuben and Mary Martin by Jacob Delay, Licensed Deacon of
              the Methodist Church, Jackson Co.

1821 Nov 25   Rice, Adam and Eliza B. Jett by Rev. James McAboy, Elder, Washington
              Co.

1816 Aug 8   Rice (or Price), Caleb and Mary Fulton by John Hunter, JP, Franklin Co.

1817 Jan 25   Rice, Electy and Robert Boyd by Daniel Brunk, JP, Franklin Co.

1809 Aug 28   Rice, Elizabeth and Samuel Stacy by Rev. Neh. Davis, Washington Co.

1820 Feb 3   Rice, Elizabeth and John Bell by Eli C. King, JP, Franklin Co.

1800 Apr 1   Rice, Ezekiel and Elizabeth Miller by Robert Safford, Washington Co.

1814 Jul 14   Rice, Ezekiel and Lucinea Havens by Joseph Grate, JP, Franklin Co.

1816 Dec 25   Rice, Isaac and Lucy Devol by D.H. Buell, JP, Washington Co.

1824 Mar 30   Rice, Margaret and Silas S. Gohagan by Charles Waddell, Franklin Co.

1803 Jun 26   Rice, Polly and Benajah Seamans by Enoch Wing, JP, Washington Co.

1810 Mar 17   Rice, Polly and Cyrus Aymes by Daniel Goodno, Washington Co.

1828 Mar 30   Rice, Reuben and Lydia Early by Samuel Hamilton, Franklin Co.

1814 Apr 24   Rice, Zilpha and Elias Witham by Sardine Stone, JP, Washington Co.

1803 Mar 24   Richard, Elizabeth and Philip Minor by James Dunlap, JP, Ross Co.

1895 Mar 14   Richards, Alex. C. and Ella A. Abell both of Zanesville by Rev.
              George F. Moore, Putnam Presbyterian Church, Muskingum Co.

1807 11m 18   Richards, Catharine and Isaac Mills, Miami Monthly Meeting, Warren Co.

1878 Oct 7   Richards, Edward of Cleveland and Mrs. Eliza Moyer (nee Emery) of
              Putnam by Rev. George F. Moore, Putnam Presbyterian Church,
              Muskingum Co.

1880 Oct 28   Richards, Ella E. of Putnam and David S. Hurlbut of Hazelhurst, Mich.,
              by Rev. George F.Moore, Putnam Presbyterian Church, Muskingum Co.

1824 Feb 8   Richards, Esther and Clemthy Smith by Robert Boyd, Franklin Co.

1845 Feb 27   Richards, George H. and Lucy W. Reckard by Rev. Edward Winthrop, St.
              Luke's Church, Marietta, Washington Co.

1842 May 1   Richards, Henry L. and Cynthia Cowles by Rev. R.S. Elder, St. John's
              Church, Worthington, Franklin Co.

1808 Aug 7   Richards, Jonathan and Deborah Pickiron by Alex. Holden, JP, Licking
              Co.

1824 Mar 16   Richards, Jos. and Martha Gillespy by Thos. Daugherty, JP, Jackson Co.

1876 Jul 26   Richards, Mary F. of Putnam and Asa M. Brigham of Beverly, O., by
               Rev. A. Kingsbury, Putnam Presbyterian Church, Muskingum Co.

1855 Jan 3   Richards, Peter and Mary L. Daniel by T. Corlett, St. Luke's Church,
               Granville, Licking Co.

1808 6m 15   Richards, Sarah and Judah Foulke, Miami Monthly Meeting, Warren Co.

1869 Sep 30   Richards, Mrs. Sarah Jane and Major N. Brooker, of Lowell by Rev.
               John Boyd, St. Luke's Church, Marietta, Washington Co.

1806 10m 15   Richards, Sitnah and Jacob Paxson, Miami Monthly Meeting, Warren Co.

1851 Sep 7   Richards, Timothy and Sarah Cave by Rev. John Boyd, St. Luke's Church,
               Marietta, Washington Co.

1816 Apr 4   Richards, Wm. and Sarah Wilson by Simon Merwin, Washington Co.

1804 Jan 25   Richardson, Elizabeth and James McCafferty by Samuel Smith, Ross Co.

1818 Apr 5   Richardson, Nathaniel and Nancy Bodkin by John Russell, Washington Co.

1808 Oct 1   Richardson, Prudy and Elisha Rathbun by D. Loring, JP, Washington Co.

1814 Jun 19   Richardson, Sally see Sally Kenion

1803 Jun 2   Richardson, Samuel and Mary Comer by Jos. Gardner, JP, Ross Co.

1815 Jul 2   Richardson, Wm. and Polly Saurs by James Marshall, JP, Franklin Co.

1805 Jan 1   Richee, William and Betsey Galbreth by David Shelby, Ross Co.

1826 Feb 9   Richey, Cinthia and Wyatt Johnson by Joseph Carper, Franklin Co.

1806 Feb 13   Richie, Rachel and John Nopp by John Johnston, JP, Ross Co.

1818 Jun 18   Richmond, Harvey and Eliza Cobborly by L. Randall, JP, Licking Co.

1803 Aug 13   Richmond, Phebe and James Nott by Robert Oliver, JP, Washington Co.

1816 Aug 9   Rickabaugh, Elizabeth and Henry Dixson, Jr. by Francis Holland, JP
               Scioto Tp., Jackson Co.

1825 Jul 28   Rickets, Nancy and John W. Bull by Wm. D. Henderson, JP, Franklin Co.

1820 7m 5   Rickitt, Mary and George Mather, Miami Monthly Meeting, Warren Co.

1820 Apr 6   Riddell, Betsy and Matthias Swain by Michael Patton, JP, Franklin Co.

1806 Dec 3   Riddle, widow Margaret and Reverend Seth Nobel by James Kilbourn, JP,
               Franklin Co.

1804 Feb 8   Riddle, Nancy and Robert Hunter by Zachariah Stephen, JP, Franklin Co.

1812 Mar 7   Riddle, Peggy and John M. Strain by James Hoge, Franklin Co.

1810 Apr 11   Riddle, Rebecca and Wm. McIlvaine by James Hoge, Franklin Co.

1804 Nov 28   Riddon, John and Nancy Phebus by John Hoddy, Ross Co.

1825 Apr 28   Ridenauer, Catherine and Philip Borman by C. Hinkle, Franklin Co.

1811 Nov 26   Ridenour, David and Elizabeth Boughman by Simeon Moore, JP, Franklin
               Co.

1823 Jan 21   Ridenour, George and Mary Sterrit by C. Henkel, Franklin Co.

1816 Feb 8   Ridenower, Catharine and John Scott, Jr. by Thos. B. Patterson, JP,
               Franklin Co.

1816 Oct -- Rider, Mathew and Nancy Rolins by David Mitchell, JP, Jackson Co.

1818 Jan 15 Ridesy, John and Elinda Parker by Rev. T. Harris, Licking Co.

1825 Jan 19 Ridgely, Andrew and Rebecca Hatton (license date), Marion Co.

1825 Dec 19 Ridgley, Lillian and John Walters (license date), Marion Co.

1818 Jan 15 Ridley, Sally and Roswell Graves by T. Harris, Licking Co.

1812 Apr 9 Ridgway, Mary Ann and Enoch Dye by Henry Jolly, Washington Co.

1811 Dec 8 Ridgway, Priscilla and John Dye by Henry Jolly, JP, Washington Co.

1871 Feb 2 Riggs, George and Mrs. Rebecca Youch by Rev. John Boyd, St. Luke's
             Church, Marietta, Washington Co.

1805 Sep 7 Riggs, Jane and Moses Williamson by Philip Whitten, Washington Co.

1800 Feb 13 Riggs, Jeremiah and Rachel Keller by Josiah Munro, JP, Washington Co.

1802 Jul 7 Riggs, John and Sarah Wilson by Sam'l Williamson, JP, Washington Co.

1810 Sep 18 Riggs, Samuel and Elizabeth Henthorn Ross by Henry Jolly, Washington
             Co.

1806 Apr 3 Right, John and Catharine Dildine by Wm. Bennett, JP, Franklin Co.

1817 Nov -- Right, Sally and Abraham Mettle by John Hunter, Franklin Co.

1811 May 17 Riler, Nancy and John Kimble (license date), Pickaway Co.

1829 Jun 11 Riley, Eleaner and Amos W. Ramsey by Geo. Jefferies, Franklin Co.

1817 May 14 Riley, George and Patty Burchett by Nathl. Hamilton, JP, Washington
             Co.

1825 Mar 20 Riley, Hugh and Peggy Devore by J.B. Gilliland, JP, Jackson Co.

1827 Sep 20 Riley, I.N. and John Skidmore by Reuben Golliday, JP, Franklin Co.

1818 Oct 11 Riley, Jane and Alexander Brown by Simeon Pool, JP, Washington Co.

1813 Sep 29 Riley, John and Nancy Waterman (license date), Pickaway Co.

1810 Jul 26 Riley, Mary and Abraham Anderson (license date), Pickaway Co.

1819 Apr 1 Riley, Mary and Uz Foster by James M. Booth, Washington Co.

1815 Jun 4 Riley, Sam'l and Susan Plum by Percival Adams, JP, Franklin Co.

1811 Dec 5 Riley, Sarah and Joseph Waddle (license date), Pickaway Co.

1813 Jan 28 Riley, Sarah and Silas Warner (license date), Pickaway Co.

1814 Sep 10 Riley, Susan and Daniel Gossett by Danl. H. Buell, JP, Washington Co.

1813 Jul 15 Riley, William and Margaret Gossett by Nath. Hamilton, Washington Co.

1806 May 3 Rily, Betsy and Robert Kenion by L. Barber, Washington Co.

1801 Nov 8 Rimely, Michael and Maria Catharine Barrowy by Lewis Hubener, MG,
             Washington Co.

1829 Jan 25 Rimer, Sarah and Jacob Clevenger by John F. Solomon, Franklin Co.

1827 Sep 3 Rine, Nancy and John Helsel by I. Gander, Franklin Co.

1826 Feb 9 Rine, Sarah and Washington Elder by J. Gander, Franklin Co.

1815 Nov 5 Rion, Margaret and Ephraim Woods by F. Ferguson, JP, Washington Co.

1820 Feb 29   Risley, Caroline and Jacob Losey by Philip Cole, JP, Washington Co.

1820 May 25   Risley, Levonia and Purdy McElvain by Eli C. King, Franklin Co.

1823 Dec 9   Risley, Lewis and Mary Ball by Charles Waddle, LM, Franklin Co.

1827 Sep 13   Risley, W. and Nancy Penix by P. Adams, Franklin Co.

1812 Nov 24   Ritchee, Jeptha and Sarah Browning by Rev. S.P. Robbins, Washington Co.

1807 Nov 18   Ritchey, Patty and John Hill by Stephen Lindsly, Washington Co.

1806 Oct 14   Ritter, Frederick and Mary Blair by James Marshall, JP, Franklin Co.

1820 Feb 16   Ritter, Polly and Thomas Robbins by James Hoge, Franklin Co.

1808 Jan 2   Rnard, Lucy and Anselm Wood by Thos. Stanley, Washington Co.

1817 Feb 19   Roach, Daniel and Sally Stephens by John Green, JP, Washington Co.

1813 Oct 10   Roach, John and Pamela Mason by John Green, JP, Washington Co.

1821 Feb 15   Roach, Polly and Barney McCurdy by Amos Wilson, JP, Washington Co.

1816 Feb 26   Roach, William and Lucinda Sprague by John Green, JP, Washington Co.

1812 Aug 30   Roads, Catherine and John Sockrider (license date), Pickaway Co.

1810 Sep 11   Roads, Manda and Jacob Martin (license date), Pickaway Co.

1810 Jun 12   Roads, Marah and John Briner (license date), Pickaway Co.

1823 Jun 24   Roads, Margaret and Paul Johnston by Isaac Painter, Franklin Co.

1816 May 7   Roads, Mary and John Ruffner by J.W. Patterson, JP, Licking Co.

1807 11m 26   Robarts, Rebekah and Nathan Hawkins, Miami Monthly Meeting, Warren Co.

1823 Mar 18   Robb, Hamilton and Sarah Smith by Charles Waddell, LM, Franklin Co.

1817 Dec 7   Robbins, Abigail and John Wayson by Cyrus Ames, Washington Co.

1814 Apr 10   Robbins, Matthias and Catherine McConnelly by Thos. Mace, JP, Pickaway Co.

1815 Mar 14   Robbins, Nancy and Jeremiah Shoppel by Benj. Kepner, JP, Pickaway Co.

1825 Dec 28   Robbins (or Robins), Samuel and Elizabeth Read by Abm. Williams, JP, Franklin Co.

1810 Sep 5   Robbins, Rev. Sam'l P. and Patty Burlingame by Timothy Harris, Washington Co.

1824 Feb 26   Robbins, Susannah and John Kizler by Abraham Williams, JP, Franklin Co.

1820 Feb 16   Robbins, Thomas and Polly Ritter by James Hoge, Franklin Co.

1804 Apr 10   Robenet, Sarah and Charles French by Sam'l Williamson, JP, Washington Co.

1807 Apr 12   Robenette, Susanna and Bazel Evens by James Riggs, JP, Washington Co.

1807 Aug 4   Robenson, Samuel, a black man, and Dyner a free black gril by Arthur O'Harra, Franklin Co.

1828 Feb 5   Roberts, Andrew and Madleen Smith by George Jefferies, Franklin Co.

1819 Feb 11   Roberts, Catherine and Danie Benner by John Spencer, JP, Licking Co.

1819 Dec 16	Roberts, Charles and Rebecca Booker by -----, Licking Co.
1804 Mar 16	Roberts, Daniel and Rebecca Hinton by Abm. Miller, Ross Co.
1819 Apr 22	Roberts, David of Delaware County and Livinia Pool by Ezra Griswold, Franklin Co.
1812 Feb 14	Roberts, Elizabeth and Zachariah Davis by James McMillen, JP, Licking Co.
1818 Nov --	Roberts, Ezekiel W. and Elizabeth Cozad by David Mitchell, JP, Jackson Co.
1797 Jun 19	Roberts, Grace and Ebenezar Griffing by D. Loring, Jus. Com. Pleas, Washington Co.
1809 Aug 4	Roberts, Isaac and Sary West by Nehemiah Gates, Franklin Co.
1813 Dec 23	Roberts, Jacob and Rachael McDolle by John B. Johnston, Franklin Co.
1822 May 23	Roberts, James and Margann Grifith by Jacob Gundy, Franklin Co.
1818 Apr 20	Roberts, James S. and Hanna Orr by John Shields, M NY, Franklin Co.
1827 Dec 27	Roberts, John and Martha Dyer by John Tipton, JP, Franklin Co.
1821 May 19	Roberts, Joseph and Mime Floyd by James Hoge, Franklin Co.
1817 Aug 28	Roberts, Kaziah and Isaac Kidd by Simon Merwin, Washington Co.
1812 Feb 27	Roberts, Margaret and Robert Eliot by -----, Licking Co.
1885 Jun 18	Roberts, Thomas E. and Carrie E. Atkinson both of Zanesville by Rev. George F. Moore, Putnam Presbyterian Church, Muskingum Co.
1866 Apr 26	Roberts, William and Mary E. Smith by Rev. John Boyd, St. Luke's Church, Marietta, Washington Co.
1798 Apr 19	Robertson, Elizabeth and Samuel Lucas by Josiah Munro, JP, Washington Co.
1813 Feb 14	Robertson, Hannah and John Johnson by John Green, Washington Co.
1808 Apr 28	Robin, Elizabeth B. and Jesse Harris by John Emmet, Licking Co.
1806 --- --	Robins, Daniel and Mary Harper by John Robins, Ross Co.
1825 Dec 28	Robins (or Robbins), Samuel and Elizabeth Read by Abm Williams, JP, Franklin Co.
1813 Aug 26	Robinson, Asa and Caty Murz by S. Harris, JP, Franklin Co.
1871 Sep 14	Robinson, Charles F. and Irene Dornan by Rev. John Boyd, St. Luke's Church, Marietta, Washington Co.
1826 Oct 23	Robinson, Elanor and Cornelius Lynch by Benj. Britton, Franklin Co.
1812 Dec 8	Robinson, Elizabeth and Frederick Ford by James Marshall, Franklin Co
1813 Sep 23	Robinson, Elizabeth and Amons Willey (license date), Pickaway Co.
1824 Aug 19	Robinson, Gorge and Betsey Marble by Jacob Gundy, JP, Franklin Co.
1807 Aug 25	Robinson, James and Molly Johnston by Rob't Oliver, JP, Washington Co
1813 Oct 12	Robinson, James and Nancy Morris (license date), Pickaway Co.
1815 Apr 27	Robinson, James and Margaret Wilson by J.W. Patterson, JP, Licking Co

1817 Jan 2   Robinson, John and Jane Mitchel by Alex Bassett, Franklin Co.

1870 Sep 14   Robinson, Joseph H. and Elizabeth Moffett by Rev. John Boyd, St.
               Luke's Church, Marietta, Washington Co.

1825 Sep 4   Robinson, Lucy Ann and Hiram Hays by C. Hinkel, Franklin Co.

1819 May 13   Robinson, Margaret and Richard Willet by T.D. Baird, VDM, Licking Co.

1794 Feb 14   Robinson, Margaret Letite and John Gardner by J.G. Petitt, Washington
               Co.

1816 Dec 2   Robinson, Martin and Christina Hass by John Green, Licking Co.

1815 Jan 3   Robinson, Mary and Hanson Stephens by Stephen Guthrie, Washington Co.

1816 Jan 8   Robinson, Patrick and Elizabeth Wheeler by J. Cunningham, Licking Co.

1819 Jan 7   Robinson, Phoebe and James Haguman by John Patterson, Washington Co.

1824 Jun 1   Robinson, Robert and Mary Miller by James Hoge, Franklin Co.

1806 Jun 26   Robinson, Samuel and Matty Hunter by Zachariah Stephen, JP, Franklin
               Co.

1819 Jul 8   Robinson, Sidney and Adam Hass by T.S. Beard, VDM, Licking Co.

1826 Oct 29   Robinson, Stephen and Polly Kerr by H. Matthes, Franklin Co.

1818 Oct 22   Robinson, Sylvia and Moses Hewitt by Jonathan Dunham, JP, Washington
               Co.

1865 Jul 26   Robinson, William and Mary Ann McCollough by Rev. John Boyd, St.
               Luke's Church, Marietta, Washington Co.

1812 Feb 13   Robison, Nancy and Abraham Hoover by James Marshall, Franklin Co.

1815 Apr 19   Roby, Sally and Wm. Taylor by James Hoge, Franklin Co.

1806 Feb 18   Roche, Mary and John Scott by N. Davis, Washington Co.

1879 Oct 9   Rock, Flora E. of Zanesville, O., and Walter J. Manley of Shawnee,O.,
               by Rev. George F. Moore, Putnam Presbyterian Church,Muskingum Co.

1823 Oct 26   Rode, Adam and Sally Shaffer by Wm. Godman, Franklin Co.

1810 Aug 30   Rodgers, John and Mary Skidmore by James Marshall, Franklin Co.

1813 Aug 29   Rodgers, Matilda and John John and J. Marshall, Franklin Co.

1825 Mar 9   Rodgers, Rachel and Anthony Comines by Joseph Clara, JP, Marion Co.

1816 Nov 21   Rodgers, Welthy and Aristhenes Walker by Tracy Wilcox, Franklin Co.

1804 Feb 2   Rody, Jean and William Tinlow by Sam'l Edwards, JP, Ross Co.

1828 Jun 19   Roe, Archabald and Elizabeth Loy by Jason Bull, Franklin Co.

1834 Nov 20   Roe, Rosanna and Joseph Ely Hall by Rev. J.T. Wheat, St. Luke's
               Church, Marietta, Washington Co.

1846 Apr 22   Roe, Sarah D. and Dr. E.D. Safford of Parkersburg, Va., by Rev.
               Edward Winthrop, St. Luke's Church, Marietta, Washington Co.

1804 May 5   Roger, John and Catharine Valentine by Sam'l Edwards, Ross Co.

1819 Oct 19   Rogers, Altha and Ezekel Brown by Stephen Maynard, Franklin Co.

1817 May 22   Rogers, Anna and Samuel Hunter by Joseph Grate, Franklin Co.

1825 May 12   Rogers, Betsey and Lester Tuller by Aristarcus Walker, Franklin Co.

1821 Jul 26   Rogers, David and Ann Meed by Chandler Rogers, Franklin Co.

1858 Dec 30   Rogers, George and Evany Prior by Rev. John Boyd, St. Luke's Church, Marietta, Washington Co.

1789 Jul 9   Rogers, John and Marianne Capron by Ben Tupper, Washington Co.

1816 4m 3   Rogers, Josiah and Abigal Cleaver, Miami Monthly Meeting, Warren Co.

1814 Apr 14   Rogers, Michael W. and Polly Cole by J.W. Patterson, Licking Co.

1819 Jan 3   Rogers, Nancy and William Murphy by John McMahan, Licking Co.

1810 Nov 1   Rogers, Rachel and Dayton Whiticor by Geo. Wells, JP, Licking Co.

1818 Jan 4   Rogers, Savina and Wm. Henry Buell by Rev. Saml. P. Robbins, Washington Co.

1817 Mar 4   Rogers, William and Sophia Wiggins by Edward Hursey, JP, Licking Co.

1826 Feb 11   Rogers, William and Sarah Michael by Wm. Godman, Franklin Co.

1820 Feb 12   Roice, Daniel and Amanda Taylor by A. Buttles, JP, Franklin Co.

1848 Oct 31   Rolb, William of Wheeling and Josephine C. Neal of Parkersburg, Va., by Rev. D.W. Tolford, St. Luke's Church, Marietta, Washington Co

1816 Nov 9   Rold, Lara and Joshua Smith by Rev. T. Harris, Licking Co.

1816 Oct --   Rolins, Nancy and Mathew Rider by David Mitchell, JP, Jackson Co.

1801 Sep 14   Rolland, Joseph and Mary Doyl by Wm. Harper, JP, Washington Co.

1806 Feb 18   Rollings, Janny and Joseph Bogart by Wm. Bennett, JP, Franklin Co.

1873 Oct 1   Rolston, Alice L. and Cambridge C. Clarke by Rev. John Boyd, St. Luke's Church, Marietta, Washington Co.

1871 Sep 14   Rolston, Sarah V. and Edward R. Dale by Rev. John Boyd, St. Luke's Church, Marietta, Washington Co.

1824 Jul 1   Romine, David and Naomah Vansciver by Jacob Gundy, Franklin Co.

1817 Feb 2   Rood, Charity and Aaron Fall by Obadiah Scott, Washington Co.

1817 Mar 20   Rood, Ira and Lydia Fall by Obadiah Scott, Washington Co.

1805 Apr 4   Rooks, Polly G. and Valentine Pancake by David W. Davis, Ross Co.

1816 May 31   Root, Charles and Mary Jackson by Noah Fidler, Licking Co.

1821 Feb 22   Root, Noble and Harriet Bushnell by Rev. T. Harris, Licking Co.

1807 Oct 25   Root, Parthena and Noah Spalding by Thomas Brown, Franklin Co.

1821 Dec 20   Root, Wm. and Lucy Place by Asa Morey, JP, Washington Co.

1884 Mar 22   Roper, Edward F. and Esther R. Weaver both of Putnam by Rev. George F Moore, Putnam Presbyterian Church, Muskingum Co.

1802 Apr 18   Roring, Abraham and Johanna Barrowy by Lewis Hubener, Washington Co.

1821 May 13   Rose, Abraham and Sally Rose by Simeon Avery, MG, Franklin Co.

1819 Jul 15   Rose, Alcey C. and Daniel Humphrey by Samuel Bancroft, JP, Licking Co

1826 Dec 28   Rose, Ann and Robert S. Kelso by A. Allison, JP, Franklin Co.

1818 Feb 10   Rose, Cathrin and Iray Bennet by Tho. B. Patterson, Franklin Co.

1808 Nov 22   Rose, Cornelias and Elisybeth Beaty by Wm. Shaw, Franklin Co.

1812 Nov 7   Rose, E. and C. Graves by Rev. T. Harris, Licking Co.

1811 Nov 7   Rose, Electa and Cladious Graves by Rev. T. Harris, Licking Co.

1811 Mar 12   Rose, Elisha and Zeppora Fuller by Stephen Lindsly, Washington Co.

1817 Apr 27   Rose, Elisha and Rebecca Cook by Samuel Dye, JP, Washington Co.

1822 Apr 11   Rose, Elizabeth and Abram Noe by John Davis, Franklin Co.

1812 Nov 11   Rose, Fanny and John Newton by Jeremiah Dare, JP, Washington Co.

1812 Mar 3   Rose, Hannah and Anthony Birnett by Jacob Tharp, JP, Franklin Co.

1815 Apr 19   Rose, Haseon and Emily Woolcut by James Hoge, Franklin Co.

1818 Mar 17   Rose, Hiram P. and Chloe Harris by Samuel Bancroft, JP, Licking Co.

1803 Nov 3   Rose, Jane and George Squires by Jacob Earhart, JP, Washington Co.

1828 Mar 15   Rose, Jonathan and Margaret Kalb by I. Gander, Franklin Co.

1815 Mar 1   Rose, Lemuel and Adah Howe by Rev. T. Harris, Licking Co.

1812 Nov 27   Rose, Louisa and Oliver C. Dickenson by -----, Licking Co.

1827 Jul 8   Rose, Louisa and Daniel Olinger by M.M. Hencle, VDM, Franklin Co.

1825 Sep 28   Rose, Lucinda and Michael Bum by Jacob Smith, JP, Franklin Co.

1814 Sep 25   Rose, Lydia and John Newton by Samuel Dye, JP, Washington Co.

1814 Nov 11   Rose, Lydia and William Clemmans by Rev. T. Harris, Licking Co.

1819 Jul 2   Rose, Lydia and Oliver Dickerson by Rev. Timothy Harris, Licking Co.

1819 Jan 15   Rose, Matilda and Giles Hickox by Rev. T. Harris, Licking Co.

1820 Nov 20   Rose, Matthew and Rebecca Patterson by James Hoge, Franklin Co.

1814 Dec 4   Rose, Mima and Matthias Dagg (or Dague) by Jacob Tharp, JP, Franklin Co.

1809 Nov 15   Rose, Miriam and Elkanah Linnell by Rev. Timothy Harris, Licking Co.

1819 Mar 14   Rose, Nancy and Thomas W. Leach by Jacob Delay, MG, Jackson Co.

1812 Nov 29   Rose, Ruth and Thomas Andrews by Jacob Tharp, Franklin Co.

1816 Feb 6   Rose, Ruth and Hezekiah Lewis by Sam'l Dye, JP, Washington Co.

1817 Aug 1   Rose, Sabre and Revel Everitt by Samuel Bancroft, JP, Licking Co.

1821 May 13   Rose, Sally and Abraham Rose by Simeon Avery, MG, Franklin Co.

1810 Dec 20   Rose, Samantha and William Stedman by Rev. T. Harris, Licking Co.

1812 Apr 16   Rose, Simeon and Susanna Groves by Philip Cole, JP, Washington Co.

1810 Feb 27   Rose, Susannah and Amos Carpenter by Rev. T. Harris, Licking Co.

1819 Nov 17   Rose, Timothy M. and Matildah Mead by Samuel Bancroft, JP, Licking Co.

1809 Sep 5   Rosebury, Polly and Abraham Johnston by M. Dickey, JP, Franklin Co.

1823 Apr 1   Ross, Alexander and Nancy Dean by James Hoge, Franklin Co.

1828 May 27   Ross, Ann and Daniel Hedges by James Hoge, Franklin Co.

1817 Jan 29   Ross, Charles and Dolly Burnham by Simon Merwin, Washington Co.

1819 Nov 18   Ross, Charlotte and Wm. Burris by Rob't G. Hanna, Jackson Co.

1814 Jul 18   Ross, Deborah and Thomas Towers by David Kinnear, JP, Pickaway Co.

1821 Mar 27   Ross, Dorcas and Giles Edgerton by Moses Williamson, JP, Washington Co

1810 Sep 18   Ross, Elizabeth Henthorn and Samuel Riggs by Henry Jolly, Washington Co.

1865 Sep 28   Ross, Hannah M. and James Mendenhall by Rev. John Boyd, St. Luke's Church, Marietta, Washington Co.

1818 Oct 3   Ross, Hugh M. and Nancy Crosset by Matthew Taylor, Franklin Co.

1820 Dec 14   Ross, Isaac Jr. and Phebe Swift by Thomas White, JP, Washington Co.

1805 Oct 17   Ross, James and Levy Williams by Samuel Edwards, Ross Co.

1816 Apr 1   Ross, James and Mary Brackenrige by James Hoge, Franklin Co.

1805 Feb 19   Ross, Jenny and George Carder by John Hoddy, Ross Co.

1809 Jun 30   Ross, John and Betsey Logan by Nehemiah Gates, Franklin Co.

1811 Feb 10   Ross, John and Jemimah Burchett by Rev. John Green, Washington Co.

1852 Sep 2   Ross, John S. and Emma Humphrey by Rev. A. Kingsbury, Putnam Presbyterian Church, Muskingum Co.

1805 Nov 16   Ross, Letitia and John Cook by Samuel Edwards, Ross Co.

1824 Apr 18   Ross, Lydia and Robert Ross by H. Robb, DMEC, Franklin Co.

1819 Apr 15   Ross, Margarette and David Taylor by Matthew Taylor, Franklin Co.

1874 Jun 3   Ross, Mary Hildreth and James Watson Edgerton by Rev. John Boyd, St. Luke's Church, Marietta, Washington Co.

1819 Jun 15   Ross, Peggy and David Taylor by Mathew Taylor, JP, Franklin Co.

1813 Jun 12   Ross, Rachel and Richard Hobbs (license date), Pickaway Co.

1803 Oct 18   Ross, Rebecca and George Parcuson by James Evans, Ross Co.

1820 Apr 6   Ross, Richard and Mary Corey by Thomas White, JP, Washington Co.

1824 Apr 18   Ross, Robert and Lydia Ross by H. Robb, DMEC, Franklin Co.

1804 Aug 2   Ross, Sarah and Martin Bobo by J. Graham, JP, Washington Co.

1813 Jun 12   Ross, Thomas and Nancy Baker (license date), Pickaway Co.

1896 Feb 29   Rosser, Cora B. of McLuney, O., and Williard F. Ater of Zanesville by Rev. George F. Moore, Putnam Presbyterian Church, Muskingum Co.

1813 Jan 21   Roth, Peter and Catharine Huffman by Jas. Marshall, Franklin Co.

1803 Nov 11   Roult, James and Abigail Willet by Thomas Scott, JP Scioto Tp., Ross Co.

1803 Feb 15   Roun, Betsey and Levi Barber by Daniel Story, Clerk, Washington Co.

1799 Jan 4   Rouse, Catherine and Peter Lalance by Josiah Munro, Washington Co.

1795 Nov 28   Rouse, Cynthia and Paul Fearing by J. Gilman, Washington Co.

1814 Jul 31   Rouse, Stephen and Maria Theresie McClare by Obadiah Scott, JP, Washington Co.

1818 May 7   Rowe, Margaret and David Beers by John Smith, JP, Franklin Co.

1816 Jul 6   Rowland, James and Jane Jamison by Samuel Rogue, JP, Licking Co.

1821 Dec 27   Rowland, Mary Ann and Alfred Regnier by Judah M. Chamberlain, Washington Co.

1820 Jul 13   Rowland, Sarah and James Mullen by Rev. Saml. P. Robbins, Washington Co.

1879 Dec 3   Rowlands, Francis L. and Jessie E. Cowles by Rev. John Boyd, St. Luke's Church, Marietta, Washington Co.

1825 Feb 22   Rowles, Elizabeth and Conrad Deal by Hugh S. Smith, JP, Marion Co.

1818 Sep 8   Roy, William and Barbary Ery by Amisiah Hutchinson, JP, Franklin Co.

1817 Aug 10   Ruark, Shadreck and Sarah Hall by Joseph Thrap, MG, Licking Co.

1820 Apr 10   Ruble, Rebecca and Michael Crossmock by M. Black, JP, Licking Co.

1803 Apr 7   Rudie, William and Rachel Cox by Felix Renick, Ross Co.

1816 May 7   Ruffner, John and Mary Roads by J.W. Patterson, JP, Licking Co.

1819 Nov 9   Rugg, Elizabeth and James Meade by Spencer Wright, JP, Licking Co.

1814 Apr 12   Rugg, Moses and Lydia McCalip by Noah Fidler, Licking Co.

1815 Jun 17   Rugg, Moses and Rebecca Ward by John Green, Licking Co.

1813 May 16   Ruly, Rosannah and Daniel Ganda by Peter Pence, Licking Co.

1861 Dec 7   Rumbolds, Charles H. and Rebecca J. Rake by Rev. John Boyd, St. Luke's Church, Marietta, Washington Co.

1818 Dec 6   Rumford, John and Nabby Bigelow by Noah Fider, MG, Licking Co.

1804 Jan 12   Rumson, Sarah and Cornelius Westfall by John Odle, JP, Ross Co.

1817 Apr --   Runkle, George and Patsy McGranahan by John Hunter, Franklin Co.

1816 Aug 25   Runkle, Jacob and Kitty McGranahan by John Hunter, Franklin Co.

1812 May 28   Runnells, Joseph and Sally Bysor by Dudley Davis, JP, Washington Co.

1851 Aug 14   Runyan, Noah M. and Harriet E. Wilson by Rev. Geo. B. Sturges, St. Paul's Church, Marion, Marion Co.

1827 Dec 1   Runyon, John S. and Sally Brown by James Hoge, Franklin Co.

1825 Nov 24   Ruse, Jacob and Sarah Chaney by W.T. Martin, JP, Franklin Co.

1818 Oct 15   Rusel, John and Catherine Kisow by Michael Trout, JP, Licking Co.

1804 Jan 29   Rush, Henry and Rachel Creviston by Samuel Smith, Ross Co.

1813 Mar 25   Rush, Jacob and Amelia Davis (license date), Pickaway Co.

1804 Mar 20   Rush, James and Polly Creviston by Samuel Smith, Ross Co.

1814 Sep 24   Rush, Moses and Margaret Eaker by James Emmett, JP, Pickaway Co.

1811 Aug 22   Rush, Peter and Peggy Creviston (license date), Pickaway Co.

1800 Nov 3   Rush, Rebecca and Stephen Baldwin both of Youngstown by William Wick, V.D.M., Trumbull Co.

1815 Jan 11   Rush, Sarah and George Mitten by James Jackson, JP, Pickaway Co.

1804 Jan 24   Rush, William and Nelly Graves by Samuel Smith, Ross Co.

1819 Jan 20   Russel, James and Jane Conard by John Green, MG, Licking Co.

1818 Sep 22   Russel, John and Chloe L. Palmer by Ebenezer Washburn, S Dell, Franklin Co.

1805 Aug 9   Russele, John and Elizabeth Humphreys by J. Gardner, JP, Ross Co.

1820 Jun 9   Russell, Betsey and Tillinghast Cook by Sardine Stone, JP, Washington Co.

1868 Dec 22   Russell, Mrs. Clarinda Jane and E.S. McIntosh of Beverly by Rev. John Boyd, St. Luke's Church, Marietta, Washington Co.

1822 Jun 17   Russell, Isaac K. and Rachel McDonald by W.T. Martin, Franklin Co.

1794 Apr 2   Russell, John and Betsy Smith by R.J. Meigs, JP, Washington Co.

1861 Nov 5   Russell, Julia M. and Robert M. Applegate of Zanesville by Rev. John Boyd, St. Luke's Church, Marietta, Washington Co.

1821 Oct 18   Russell, Mary Ann and Samuel Dennis by Rev. Wm. Davis, Washington Co.

1819 Mar 1   Russell, Polly and Pardon Cook by Sardine Stone, JP, Washington Co.

1810 Jan 16   Russell, Robert and Polly Kain by James Hoge, Franklin Co.

1867 Jan 10   Russell, Romulus S.T. and Mattie E. Cockrell by Rev. A. Kingsbury, Putnam Presbyterian Church, Muskingum Co.

1822 Oct 1   Russell, Samuel and Hannah Greenwood by Samuel Gillet, JP, Franklin Co.

1890 Dec 18   Russi, John J. and Maggie S. Deselm both of Zanesville by Rev. George F. Moore, Putnam Presbyterian Church, Muskingum Co.

1803 Jul 4   Ryan, Ebenezer and Sarah Barker by Henry Smith, JP, Washington Co.

1813 May 5   Ryan, Elijah and Peggy Penn by John Green, Licking Co.

1816 Mar 17   Ryan, John and Polly Slosson by Alexander Bassett, Franklin Co.

1884 Dec 31   Ryan, Maggie and Charles Baum both of Zanesville by Rev. George F. Moore, Putnam Presbyterian Church, Muskingum Co.

1819 Sep 2   Ryan, William and Rebecca Neibarger by Wm. O'Bannon, JP, Washington C

1816 Jun 27   Rynard, Sarah and James Elder by Nathan Tarr, JP, Washington Co.

1811 Feb 7   Rynear, Susana and Joshua Cole (license date), Pickaway Co.

1817 Aug 12   Rynolds, Thomas and Margaret Browning by Samuel Dyer, Franklin Co.

1802 Jul 20   Ryther, James and Lois Pierce by Griffin Greene, Washington Co.

1820 Oct 26   Sabin, Josiah and Chloe Calkins by Rev. Philander Chase, Franklin Co.

1826 Feb 6   Sable, Hannah and Philip Bumgartner by Wm. C. Duff, Franklin Co.

1824 Jun 24   Sackett, Elijah and Martha McCormick by B. Bull, JP, Franklin Co.

1822 Dec 31   Sackett, William and Rachel Lisle by James Hoge, Franklin Co.

1846 Apr 22   Safford, Dr. E.D. of Parkersburg, Va., and Sarah D. Roe by Rev. Edward Winthrop, St. Luke's Church, Marietta, Washington Co.

1854 Oct 9   Safford, Edwin P. of Chillicothe and Romaine M Vinton of Putnam by Rev. A. Kingsbury, Putnam Presbyterian Church, Muskingum Co.

1856 Aug 11   Safford, Hannah M. of Putnam and D.L. Triplett of Coshocton by Rev. A. Kingsbury, Putnam Presbyterian Church, Muskingum Co.

1870 Mar 10   Safford, Kate M. and Robert H. Patterson by Rev. John Boyd, St. Luke's Church, Marietta, Washington Co.

1801 Jul 15   Safford, Robt and Catherine Cameron by E. Cutler, Washington Co.

1808 Apr 14   Sage, Mira and George Case, Jr. by James Kilbourn, Franklin Co.

1807 Nov 18   Sage, Philamela and Cahuncy Barker by James Kilbourn, Franklin Co.

1824 Mar 30   Sahl, Leonard, widower, and Polly Alderfer, widow, by C. Henkel, Franklin Co.

1821 Dec 28   Sahl, Mary and Philip Rader by C. Henkel, Franklin Co.

1824 Jul 1   Salmon, Elizabeth and John Renny by Robert Hopkins, JP, Marion Co.

1818 Sep 21   Salmon, John and Anna Breck by Daniel G. Stanley, Washington Co.

1816 Jan 16   Salret, William and Elizabeth Wingit by Jacob Keller, Franklin Co.

1806 May 1   Saltonstall, Nancy and Stephen Lindsly by Jacob Lindsly, Washington Co.

1851 Jul 4   Sam, Sarah and Alvah Dick Sanford by E.A. Strong, St. Luke's Church, Granville, Licking Co.

1805 Feb 3   Samard, Sarah and William Gibson by Wm. Creighton, Ross Co.

1804 Apr 3   Sammas, Elizabeth and Samuel Ligen by Samuel Stage, Ross Co.

1817 Dec 16   Sampha, William and Ruth Ward by Geo. Callanhan, EMEC, Licking Co.

1867 Oct 11   Sams, Festus Oden and Eura Reeder by Rev. John Boyd, St. Luke's Church, Marietta, Washington Co.

1824 Oct 24   Sanborn, Jean and Daniel Brinkley by George Jefferies, MG, Franklin Co.

1810 Feb 1   Sandburn, Polly and Philip Abbot by Rev. S.P. Robbins, Washington Co.

1817 Jan 18   Sanders, Isaac and Susanna Silvins by John Patterson, Washington Co.

1807 3m 18   Sanders, Jonathan and Lydia Lupton, Miami Monthly Meeting, Warren Co.

1807 3m 19   Sanders, Thomas and Betsy Pope, Miami Monthly Meeting, Warren Co.

1816 Jan 13   Sandusky, Polly and John Dier by Jacob Keller, JP, Franklin Co.

1817 Nov 27   Sandusky, Samuel and Mary Perrin by Joseph Grate, Franklin Co.

1851 Jul 4   Sanford, Alvah Dick and Sarah Sam by E.A. Strong, St. Luke's Church, Granville, Licking Co.

1827 Apr 27   Sanford, D.A. and George McDermot by James Hoge, Franklin Co.

1790 Jul 3   Sanford, Huldah and Joel Tuttle by Benj. Tuttle, Washington Co.

1844 Feb 7   Sanford, John Percival and Celinda Corner by Rev. Edward Wintrhop, St. Luke's Church, Marietta, Washington Co.

1848 Apr 25   Sanford, Margaret and Henry Tudor Fay by W.C. French, St. Luke's Church, Granville, Licking Co.

1848 Jul 3   Sanford, Solomon N. and Mary L. Huggins by W.C. French, St. Luke's Church, Granville, Licking Co.

1803 Nov 27   Sanford, Thomas and Esther Lavens by Daniel Story, Clerk, Washington
               Co.

1828 Nov 20   Sarber, Abraham and Louisa Henderen by Geo. Jefferies, Franklin Co.

1797 Feb 18   Sarot, Mary Catterine Avedine and Andrew Lecroix by Robert Safford,
               Washington Co.

1812 Apr 29   Satha, Francis and Elizabeth Hasght by Wm. Haines, JP, Licking Co.

1824 11m 3   Satterthwaite, Abigail and Moses Kelly, Miami Monthly Meeting,.Warren
               Co.

1822 10m 3   Satterthwaite, Benjamin L. and Ruth Evans, Miami Monthly Meeting,
               Warren Co.

1823 3m 5   Satterthwaite, Mary and Benjamin Lukens, Miami Monthly Meeting, Warren
               Co.

1893 Oct 22   Sauck, Julia M. of Zanesville and Oscar J. Morrison of Wheeling, W.
               Va. by Rev. George F. Moore, Putnam Presbyterian Church, Muskingum
               Co.

1827 Mar 27   Saul, Joseph and Christeanna Hone by A. Allison, Franklin Co.

1825 Jun 18   Sault, Jonathan and Eve Yockhover by Thos. Rodgers, JP, Marion Co.

1819 May 27   Saunders, Irandus and Ann Kelso by Simoen Overturf, JP, Licking Co.

1819 Jun 22   Saunder, Jesse and Julia Campt by R. Stansberry, Franklin Co.

1816 Sep 17   Saurs, Caty and Robert Pollock by Michael Patton, Franklin Co.

1815 Jul 2   Saurs, Polly and Wm. Richardson by James Marshall, JP, Franklin Co.

1806 Dec 28   Sawyer, Andrew and Sarah Bishop by Asa Shinn, MG, Franklin Co.

1804 Oct 21   Sawyer, Dorcas and Frederick Tubbs by Enoch Shepard, Washington Co.

1802 Mar 14   Sawyer, Lydia and John Walker by I. Peine, Washington Co.

1811 Feb 5   Sayler, Mary and John H. Lutz (license date), Pickaway Co.

1819 5m 5   Sayre, David and Elizabeth Mills, Miami Monthly Meeting, Warren Co.

1860 Dec 27   Scarvell, Lewellen and Amelia Gussinger by Rev. A. Kingsbury, Putnam
               Presbyterian Church, Muskingum Co.

1820 Jan 18   Schellenger, Eliza and Silas Lake by Vincent Southard, JP, Jackson Co.

1882 Jul 11   Schleiermacher, Charles L. and Lydia Mercer by Rev. John Boyd, St.
               Luke's Church, Marietta, Washington Co.

1870 Oct 1   Schofield, Joseph C. and Alice Athey by Rev. John Boyd, St. Luke's
               Church, Marietta, Washington Co.

1807 Mar 12   Schonoover, Mary and Wm. Scoby by Mossey Clymer, Franklin Co.

1822 May 21   Schonover, Abraham and Margret Baker by Richard Courtright, JP,
               Franklin Co.

1818 Feb 8   Schonover, Temperance and John Fulsome by Stephen Guthrie, Washington
               Co.

1812 Jun 21   Schoonover, John and Sally Mallahon by Elijah Austin, JP, Franklin Co.

1825 Dec 3   Schoonover, Peter and Affa Nickols by Wm. Godman, Franklin Co.

1822 Dec 24   Schoonover, Rebecca and Isaac Baker by C. Waddell, LM, Franklin Co.

1838 Jun 22   Schwartz, John George to Bessy Denker by Rev. C.L.F. Haensel, St.
               Luek's Church, Marietta, Washington Co.

1822 Mar 24   Sciscoe, Sarah and Abraham Smith by Russel Bigelow, MG, Franklin Co.

1823 Jul 3   Scisson, Peleg and Mary Buttles by C. Henkel, Franklin Co.

1807 Mar 12   Scoby, Wm. and Mary Schonoover by Mossey Clymer, Franklin Co.

1823 Feb 26   Scooner, Joseph and Margaret L. Hughes by Charles Waddell, LM,
               Franklin Co.

1821 Jun 14   Scoonover, Elizabeth and Solomon Lee by Russel Bigelow, MI, Franklin
               Co.

1820 Feb 1   Scoppe, John A. and Elizabeth Stone by -----, Licking Co.

1805 Oct 10   Scote, Lavina and Andrew Willoughby by Wm. Creighton, Ross Co.

1828 Mar 4   Scotharn, Elaza and Jacob Swisher by John Long, JP, Franklin Co.

1814 Oct 20   Scothorn, Mary and John Carr by Jesse Morral, JP, Pickaway Co.

1820 Jun 22   Scothorn, Samuel and Mary Smith by B. Bull, JP, Franklin Co.

1820 Feb 3   Scott, Almira and Samuel Cushing by Wm. Rand, Washington Co.

1813 Jan 13   Scott, Andrew and Sarah State by Jacob Tharp, Franklin Co.

1887 Mar 23   Scott, Carrie E. and John C. Dickson both of Zanesville by Rev.
               George F. Moore, Putnam Presbyterian Church, Muskingum Co.

1817 Dec 4   Scott, Eliza and Samuel Jamison by Rev. James Scott, Licking Co.

1824 Dec 27   Scott, Catharene and Reuben Floyd by Wm. T. Martin, Franklin Co.

1817 Aug 3   Scott, Celestina and Nathaniel Fuller by Pelatiah White, Washington Co.

1827 Jul 12   Scott, Charles and Nancy Allison by H. Mathews, M MEC, Franklin Co.

1806 Apr 10   Scott, Cynthia and Nathaniel Eveland by Robt Oliver, Washington Co.

1811 Jul 28   Scott, Eleanor and John Bowen by Philip Whitten, JP, Washington Co.

1805 Oct 3   Scott, Elenor and Isaac Bradley by Thos. Hicks, Ross Co.

1810 Dec 41[sic]Scott, Eliza and Samuel West (license date), Pickaway Co.

1820 Apr 19   Scott, Elizabeth and Calvin Pratt by James Cunningham, Licking Co.

1880 Jun 22   Scott, Elizabeth W. and Duncan C. Ogden at Chillicothe by Rev. John

1876 Sep 14   Scott, Ernest M. and Clara J. Wait by Rev. A. Kingsbury, Putnam
               Presbyterian Church, Muskingum Co.

1807 Aug 17   Scott, Esther and Sam'l Fairlamb by S. Lindsly, Washington Co.

1860 Mar 20   Scott, Henry M. and Elizabeth Wiseman by Rev. John Boyd, St. Luke's
               Church, Marietta, Washington Co.

1818 Nov --   Scott, Hugh and Susana McCune by -----, Jackson Co.

1815 Apr 18   Scott, Isabella and William Smith by Nathan Cunningham, Licking Co.

1810 Jul 16   Scott, Rev. James and Jane Wilson by Rev. Geo. Varnaman, Licking Co.

1819 Feb 17   Scott, James and Nancy Walker by George Hays, Franklin Co.

1825 Jan 16   Scott, James and Nancy White by Samuel McDowell, JP, Jackson Co.

1824 Dec 14   Scott, Jane and David Anderson by Samuel McDowell, JP, Jackson Co.

1816 Jan 1   Scott, Jesse and Anna Sherman by Obadiah Scott, JP, Washington Co.

1806 Feb 18   Scott, John and Mary Roche by N. Davis, Washington Co.

1810 Jun 28   Scott, John and Mary Beard by Thomas Seely, JP, Washington Co.

1816 Feb 8   Scott, John Jr. and Catharine Ridenower by Thos. B. Patterson, JP,
               Franklin Co.

1805 Jan 31   Scott, Joseph and Martha Finley by Wm. Creighton, Ross Co.

1827 Mar 13   Scott, Joseph and Keziah Everret by G.W. Hart, Franklin Co.

1805 Feb 15   Scott, Josiah and Anna Dickson by John Brough, JP, Washington Co.

1814 Feb 17   Scott, Mallisa and Dickson Henst by Anth'y Sheets, JP, Washington Co.

1814 Feb 13   Scott, Margaret and James Witten by Anth'y Sheets, JP, Washington Co.

1817 Oct 9   Scott, Mary and John Watts by John Crow, Licking Co.

1821 Nov 21   Scott, Nancy and John Lynch, Jr. by Isaac Painter, Franklin Co.

1818 Dec 31   Scott, Nath'l and Amy McDowell by Alex Anderson, JP, Jackson Co.

1812 Sep 7   Scott, Peggy and Hiram Bennett by Jacob Tharp, Franklin Co.

1797 Oct 12   Scott, Polly and Ezra Phillips by J. Munro, Washington Co.

1813 Sep 21   Scott, Rachel and Daniel Johnston by Rev. James Scott, Licking Co.

1866 Sep 19   Scott, Sadie and Major Jewett Palmer, Jr. by Rev. John Boyd, St.
               Luke's Church, Marietta, Washington Co.

1819 Dec 27   Scott, Samuel and Sarah Moore by James Cunningham, Licking Co.

1801 May 28   Scott, Sarah and Falander B. Stewart by Philip Witten, JP, Washington
               Co.

1820 Feb 10   Scott, Sylvester and Hannah Johnson by Wm. Rand, Washington Co.

1799 Sep 24   Scott, Thomas and Betsey Keller by J. Munro, Washington Co.

1883 Jan 3   Scott, Thomas and Alice E. Thorniley by Rev. John Boyd, St. Luke's
               Church, Marietta, Washington Co.

1823 Jan 2   Scott, William and Patsy Golliday by Jacob Gundy, JP, Franklin Co.

1809 Apr 20   Scripton, William and Sarah Bowen by Philip Witten, JP, Washington Co.

1802 Aug 3   Scritchfield, Catharine and George McCullock by Seth Cashart,
               Washington Co.

1825 May 26   Scurlock, Geo. and Elizabeth Hanna by John Stephenson, JP, Jackson Co.

1819 Jan 28   Scurlock, James and Margaret Jenkins by Rob't G. Hanna, JP, Jackson
               Co.

1822 Jun 10   Scurlock, Joseph and Elenor Stephenson by Samuel Carrick, JP,
               Jackson Co.

1819 Jul 29   Scurlock, Joshua and Martha Lang by Rob't G. Hanna, JP, Jackson Co.

1827 Nov 2   Seals, Joseph and Keziah Cady by William Long, Franklin Co.

1801 Jan 20   Seaman, Polly and Reuben Atchinson by Josiah Munro, Washington Co.

1803 Jun 26   Seamans, Benajah and Polly Rice by Enoch Wing, JP, Washington Co.

1797 May 18   Seamans, Gilbert and Anna Hammon by Robert Oliver, JP, Washington Co.

1798 Feb 1   Seamans, Joseph and Abigail Neal by Josiah Munro, Washington Co.

1792 Dec 23   Seamans, Patty and William Newell by J. Gilman, Washington Co.

1804 May 27   Seamans, Preserved and Betsy Patterson by Enoch Wing, Washington Co.

1792 Sep 18   Seamans, Sabra and Jonathan Sprague by J. Gilman, Washington Co.

1797 Nov 28   Seamans, Samuel and Sarah Law by Robert Oliver, JP, Washington Co.

1818 Jun 25   Seameans, Preserved and Polly Reed by Dudley Davis, JP, Washington Co.

1814 Jul 17   Searfaus, Phillip and Elizabeth Pitcher by Jesse Morral, JP, Pickaway
               Co.

1821 Feb 3   Searl, Polly and Joseph Carpenter by Sanford, Converse, JP, Licking Co.

1820 Dec 7   Searl, Sophia and Benjamin Carpenter by Sanford Converse, JP, Licking
               Co.

1820 Oct 19   Searls, Selvester and Lavinna Ayers by T. Lee, Franklin Co.

1807 8m 19   Sears, John and Penelope Johnson, Miami Monthly Meeting, Warren Co.

1820 Nov 6   Sears, Mary and Thomas Broadhurst by Stephen Lindsley, VDM, Washington
               Co.

1807 Nov 29   Seavere, Jacob and Margaret Renolds by Thos. Stanley, Washington Co.

1817 Aug 21   Seavers, John and Nancy Devol by Simon Merwin, Washington Co.

1817 Apr 19   Seber, William and Maria Gowns by -----, Licking Co.

1825 Oct 12   Sebring, Roelinda and John Smothers by G.W. Hart, JP, Franklin Co.

1825 Nov 11   Sebring, William of Genoa Township, Delaware County and Abler (Abber)
               Vantapell by G.W. Hart, Franklin Co.

1817 Jul 20   Seddick, James and Christena Tupper by James Hoge, Franklin Co.

1813 Sep 29   Seddick, Rebecca and William Long by Ja. Hauge, Franklin Co.

1827 Sep 13   See, Zebulon and Rhoda Mullen by I. Gander, JP, Franklin Co.

1822 Aug 1   Seeds, Aaron and Mary Ann Miller by Woolry Conrad, Franklin Co.

1829 Aug 14   Seeds, John and Asenith Britton by Geo. H. Patterson, ECC, Franklin
               Co.

1818 May 21   Seeds, Mary and Archibald Badger by Wm. Brown, JP, Franklin Co.

1811 Sep 4   Seeds, Robert and Catharine Hornbacker by David Spangler, Franklin Co.

1819 Apr 4   Seeley, John B. and Martha McLaughlin by Stephen Maynard, Franklin Co.

1818 Feb 2   Seeley, Reuby and Edward W. Bentan by Stephen Maynard, JP, Franklin
               Co.

1818 Apr 16   Seely, Abigail and Jane McMillen by Wm. Rand, Washington Co.

1816 Nov 26   Seely, Elizabeth and Enoch S. McIntosh by John Green, JP, Washington
               Co.

1819 Jul 23   Seely, Fanny and William Porters by Joseph Gorton, Franklin Co.

1812 Feb 6   Seely, Sarah and Nathan Dearborn by Jer. Greenman, JP, Washington Co.

1825 Jan 19   Seemors, Thomas and Margaret Hoffman by Samuel Reed, JP, Jackson Co.

1811 Mar 28   Selby, Charity and Henry Morris (license date), Pickaway Co.

1819 Jun 11   Seley, Mathew and Lawra Geer by Rev. Philander Chase, Franklin Co.

1826 Oct 4   Sells, Abraham and Louisa Brown by Charles Sells, JP, Franklin Co.

1828 May 12   Sells, Betsy and John Mytinger by William Long, Franklin Co.

1824 Oct 20   Sells, Catharine and Stephen Grace by Benjamin Briton, Franklin Co.

1822 Mar 7   Sells, Charles and Amanda Hutchesson by Alex. Bassett, JP, Franklin Co

1820 Aug 20   Sells, Eliot and Polly Sells by Chandler Rodgers, JP, Franklin Co.

1827 Apr 5   Sells, J. and Samuel Black by Samuel S. Davis, JP, Franklin Co.

1823 Jan 12   Sells, John Jr. and Merenia Hutchinson by Wm. Kilbourn, JP, Franklin
                Co.

1808 May 18   Sells, Margaret and Henry Coffman by Arthur O'Harra, Franklin Co.

1843 Nov 6   Sells, Marilla of Dublin and Eli Pinney by Rev. R.S. Elder, St.
                John's Church, Worthington, Franklin Co.

1822 Oct 31   Sells, Matilda and William Kilbourn by Nathan Emery, Franklin Co.

1807 Sep 3   Sells, Peter and Salley Casey by James Marshall, Franklin Co.

1820 Aug 20   Sells, Polly and Eliot Sells by Chandler Rodgers, JP, Franklin Co.

1828 May 15   Sells, Rachael and John McCoy by Sam'l Hamilton, Elder in the M.E.
                Church, Franklin Co.

1807 Apr 22   Sells, Saml and Elizabeth Woolcutt by Arthur O'Harra, JP, Franklin Co

1806 Jul 31   Sells, Suffiah and John Ashbaugh by James Marshall, JP, Franklin Co.

1813 Jun 31   Sells, Susan and Christopher Newcomer by Daniel Brink, Franklin Co.

1882 Jan 26   Semon, Emma L. and George W. Miller by Rev. John Boyd, St. Luke's
                Church, Marietta, Washington Co.

1809 Mar 30   Sennett, Wm. and Polly Kile (or Hile) by Arthur O'Harra, Franklin Co.

1819 Nov 25   Sennit, Elizabeth and Warren Harris by A. Goff, MG, Licking Co.

1826 Sep 3   Sensabaugh, Hiram and Matilda Reese by A. Allison, JP, Franklin Co.

1818 May 24   Sentiff, Julia and Luther Dearborn by Asa Cheadle, Washington Co.

1806 Feb 20   Sergent, Elizabeth and James Barnes by Wm. Talbott, Ross Co.

1882 Sep 6   Severance, Mrs. Addie and William R. Cassell by Rev. John Boyd, St.
                Luke's Church, Marietta, Washington Co.

1815 Oct 5   Severs, Margaret and John Reynolds by Joel Tuttle, JP, Washington Co.

1810 May 31   Seward, James and Hannah Beward by Robert Clark, MMC, Licking Co.

1820 Aug --   Sewel, James and Polly Beaty by Reuben Golliday, JP, Franklin Co.

1854 Jan 24   Sexton, David B. of Cleveland and Caroline E. Hale of Putnam by Rev.
                A. Kingsbury, Putnam Presbyterian Church, Muskingum Co.

1819 Oct 7   Seymor, Polly and Thomas Patrick by Wm. Jones, Franklin Co.

1817 May 20   Seymore, Christina and John Manning by Zach Carlisle, JP, Licking Co.

1820 Dec 14   Seymore, Jane and Andrew Dildine by Wm. Jones, Franklin Co.

1809 Feb 16   Seymore, Mary and Aquella Smith by Wm. Haines, JP, Licking Co.

1812 Feb 4   Seymore, Tene and John Pitty (Petty) by Wm. Haines, JP, LIcking Co.

1821 Apr 12   Seymore, William and Mary Dildine by John F. Solomon, Franklin Co.

1819 Apr 29   Seymaur, Jesse and Mary Welton by John B. Whittlessy, MG Lancaster,
              Ohio, Franklin Co.

1883 Aug 6   Seymour, Robert B. of Alliance, O., and Mollie L. Griffith of Putnam,
              by Rev. George F. Moore, Putnam Presbyterian Church, Muskingum
              Co.

1825 Sep 4   Seymour, William and Elezabeth Dildine by Wm. Godman, Franklin Co.

1821 Feb 4   Shad, Rachel and John Miller by Eli C. King, Franklin Co.

1819 Mar 20   Shadley, William and Rebecca Frances by J. Johnston, JP, Licking Co.

1820 Jul 18   Shadly, Amelia and Samuel Frances by J. Johnson, JP, Licking Co.

1812 Jan 14   Shadwick, Uriah and Rebecca Parker by Rev. G. Vanaman, Licking Co.

1822 Jan 6   Shafe (or Shofe), Rachael and Daniel Stimell by John F. Solomon,
              Franklin Co.

1820 Mar 1   Shafer, Abraham and Farlana House by Bial Stedman, JP, Washington Co.

1825 Apr 14   Shafer, Jacob and Mary Ann Smith by Alex Kinnear, JP, Marion Co.

1814 Jul 28   Shafer, Mary and Caleb Crath by Jno Scott, Pickaway Co.

1895 Dec 25   Shaffer, Charles F. of Pittsburg, Pa., and Grace A. Lybarger of Zanes-
              ville by Rev. George F. Moore, Putnam Presbyterian Church, Mus-
              kingum Co.

1823 Oct 26   Shaffer, Sally and Adam Rode by Wm. Godman, Franklin Co.

1818 Jun 6   Shaklee, William H. and Margaret Wilson by Wm. Rand, JP, Washington Co.

1819 Jun 7   Shakley, Sally and William Mason by Amos Wilson, JP, Washington Co.

1819 Nov 18   Shan, Boylston and Eliza Hamlin by Wm. Rand, Washington Co.

1867 Jul 10   Shank, George W. and Mary C. Thompson by Rev. A. Kingsbury, Putnam
              Presbyterian Church, Muskingum Co.

1811 May 14   Shanklen, Catharine and John Shirley by Thomas Seely, JP, Washington
              Co.

1817 Jan 2   Shannon, Elizabeth and John McLaughlin by John Drips, JP, Licking Co.

1809 May 2   Shannon, James and Mary Nelson by Arthur O'Harra, Franklin Co.

1804 Dec 27   Shannon, Jane and Abner Connal by Wm. Harper, JP, Washington Co.

1826 Apr 11   Shannon, John and Mary Stumbaugh by James Hoge, Franklin Co.

1821 Jan 1   Shannon, Margaret and Wm. Tarvey by James Cunningham, VD, Licking Co.

1817 Dec 22   Shannon, William and Mary Culbertson by James Hoge, Franklin Co.

1819 Jul 14   Shannon, William and Polly Carga by Josias Ewing, JP, Licking Co.

1810 Nov 19   Sharen, Jacob and Elizabeth Peters by Rev. G. Vanaman, Licking Co.

1811 Aug 8   Sha(r)er, David and Nancy Grove by J.W. Patterson, Licking Co.

1820 Feb 12   Sharp, Abigail and William Waterman by James M. Booth, Washington Co.

1826 Nov 28   Sharp, Elizabeth and John Read by Wm. Patterson, Franklin Co.

1825 Aug 25   Sharp, John and Mary Jones by Robert Ward, JP, Jackson Co.

1827 Dec 12   Sharp, Joseph and Sopena Sharp by G.W. Hart, Franklin Co.

1825 Mar 24   Sharp, Lumen A. and Phebe Moore by G.W. Hart, JP, Franklin Co.

1828 Jun 5   Sharp, Matthias and Sarah Sone by Aristaches Walker, JP, Franklin Co.

1822 Dec 5   Sharp, Nancy and Adam Andrews by Wm. C. Duff, JP, Franklin Co.

1827 Dec 12   Sharp, Sopena and Joseph Sharp by G.W. Hart, Franklin Co.

1801 Mar 24   Sharp, Thomas and Unity Merril by Wm. Harper, JP, Washington Co.

1890 May 14   Sharpe, Harvey Alfred and Lula Cassel Ingalls both of Zanesville by
                 Rev. George F. Moore, Putnam Presbyterian Church, Muskingum Co.

1819 Oct 16   Shattock, Simon and Sarah Simpson by Wm. Long, Franklin Co.

1827 Jul 29   Shatts, Jacob and Rachel Coons by John Hanover, Franklin Co.

1880 Apr 19   Shaver, Cyrus and Mrs. Laurinda L. Vaughn by Rev. John Boyd, St.
                 Luke's Church, Marietta, Washington Co.

1819 Dec 7   Shaver, Sarah and John Groves by John W. Patterson, MG, Licking Co.

1817 Jan 26   Shaw, Betsey and Randolph Fearing by John Patterson, Washington Co.

1815 Feb 2   Shaw, Catherine and Enoch Whipple by Moses Foster, JP, Licking Co.

1821 Dec 27   Shaw, Daniel and Mary Harvie by Rev. Sam'l P. Robbins, Washington Co.

1821 Aug 10   Shaw, James and Susan Hale by -----, Licking Co.

1801 Mar 24   Shaw, John and Anna (or Ann) Stevens by Jonthan Struthers, JP,
                 Trumbull Co.

1803 May 4   Shaw, John and Caroline Mills by Joseph Buel, JP, Washington Co.

1814 4m 7   Shaw, John and Elizabeth Wright, Miami Monthly Meeting, Warren Co.

1806 Dec 16   Shaw, Jonathan and Ruth Welch by Josiah McKenny, Franklin Co.

1819 Feb 16   Shaw, Lincoln C. and Royall Protzman by Rev. Saml. Hamilton,
                 Washington Co.

1813 Jul 18   Shaw, Lucinda and Asa Weaver by Ezra Griswold, Franklin Co.

1886 Oct 28   Shaw, Lulu and G.A. Wlty both of Zanesville by Rev. George F. Moore,
                 Putnam Presbyterian Church, Muskingum Co.

1810 Apr 10   Shaw, Margaret and Wm. Long by James Hoge, Franklin Co.

1820 Oct 26   Shaw, Margaret and Jason Humiston by James Whitney, JP, Washington Co

1807 Jan 29   Shaw, Mary and Isaac Welsh by Josiah McKinney, JP, Franklin Co.

1798 Apr 17   Shaw, Sally and Benjamin Dana by Robert Oliver, JP, Washington Co.

1810 Feb 5   Shaw, Wm. and Abe. Hunter by James Hoge, Franklin Co.

1877 Jun 4   Shawan, Fannie J. and George Pfeiffer by Rev. John Boyd, St. Luke's
                 Church, Marietta, Washington Co.

1839 Apr 1   Shawhan, Rezin K. and Elvira Tuller by Rev. A. Helfenstine, St.
                 John's Church, Worthington, Franklin Co.

1818 Dec 21   Shead, J. and Mary H. McGown by James Hoge, Franklin Co.

1805 Mar 22   Sheagley, Nancy and David Harr by Thomas Scott, JP, Ross Co.

1824 Dec 2   Shearer, Louisa and Joseph McKinnis by Robert Ward, JP, Jackson Co.

1826 May 7   Sheehea, John and Hannah Mason by Wm. Ayers, JP, Jackson Co.

1803 Nov 1   Sheets, Martin and Sarah Collans by Samuel Williamson, JP, Washington Co.

1821 Jun 7   Sheets, Mary and John Kyger by David Smithers, MMEC, Washington Co.

1821 Oct 6   Sheets, Oliver and Rachel Devol by Rev. John McMahon, Washington Co.

1821 Oct 16   Sheets, Sally and John Harris by Jacob Keller, Franklin Co.

1790 Jul 29   Sheffield, Hannah and Wm. Stacy by Benj. Tupper, Washington Co.

1806 Feb 17   Sheilds, Mary and William Smith by Thomas Hicks, Ross Co.

1804 Feb 7   Shekley, Mary and Joath Hammond by Enoch Wing, JP, Washington Co.

1811 Jun 28   Shelby, Joseph and Sarah Steeley (license date), Pickaway Co.

1801 Jul 9   Shelden, Abiah and Ruth Wood by Edwin McGinnis, Washington Co.

1801 Nov 21   Sheldon, Mrs. Huldah and Amzi Atwater of Hudson by Ebenezer Sheldon, JP, Trumbull Co.

1810 Jul 30   Sheoman, William and Rebeckah Delong by Thomas Seely, Washington Co.

1805 Jan 1   Shepard, Calvin and Mahala Oliver by Enoch Wing, JP, Washington Co.

1821 Oct 11   Shepard, Henry and Huldah Shepard by Judah M. Chamberlain, JP, Washington Co.

1821 Oct 11   Shepard, Huldah and Henry Shepard by Judah M. Chamberlain, JP, Washington Co.

1817 Oct 31   Shepard, John and Lucy Beech by Danl. H. Buell, Washington Co.

1798 Oct 19   Shepard, Lorena and John Clark by Josiah Munro, JP, Washington Co.

1803 Mar 29   Shepard, Rachael and Henry Castle by J. Graham, JP, Washington Co.

1792 Jun 21   Shepard, Rhoda and Nathan McIntosh by J. Gilman, Washington Co.

1805 Aug 12   Shepard, Stephen and Catherine Plumer by Stephen Lindsly, Washington Co.

1821 Aug 30   Sheperd, Mary and William Domigan by Eli C. King, Franklin Co.

1803 Mar 7   Shephard, Isaiah and Sarah Wadkins by J. 'Graham, Washington Co.

1804 Dec 2   Shephard, James and Francis Daily by John Hoddy, JP, Ross Co.

1803 Jul 19   Shepherd, David and Elizabeth Betz (or Botz) by John G. McCan, Ross Co.

1815 Oct 31   Shepherd, Simons and Rachael Colvin by Recompence Stanbery, Franklin Co.

1870 Jul 12   Sheppard, Daniel C. and Lucy C. Morris by Rev. John Boyd, St. Luke's Church, Marietta, Washington Co.

1862 Oct 28   Sheppard, Julia and Rodney N. Stimson by Rev. John Boyd, St. Luke's Church, Marietta, Washington Co.

1822 Jan 11   Sheppard, Susan and Theophilus Ransom by John Russell, JP, Washington Co.

1804 Jan 15   Sheppart, Nelly and John Douglass by Jacob Earhart,JP, Washington Co.

1819 Nov 4   Sheredian, James and Nancy Murphy by John Russel, JP, Washington Co.

1795 Sep 3   Shereman, Lucy and John Conrad Shoeman by Robert Oliver,Washington Co.

1885 Sep 23   Sherlock, William W. and Annie C. Mace both of Zanesville by Rev.
               George F. Moore, Putnam Presbyterian Church, Muskingum Co.

1819 Nov 17   Sherman, Abel and Louisa Wells by Sardine Stone, JP, Washington Co.

1820 Jun 1   Sherman, Abel and Margaret Brown by John Patterson, Washington Co.

1816 Jan 1   Sherman, Anna and Jesse Scott by Obadiah Scott, JP, Washington Co.

1829 Feb 14   Sherman, Betsey and Joseph Spangler by Leroy Swornstead, Franklin Co.

1794 Nov 11   Sherman, Clarissa and Jonathan Devol by Robert Oliver, Washington Co.

1815 Jan 1   Sherman, Curtis and Lydia Cuddington by Thomas Seely, Washington Co.

1804 Oct 27   Sherman, Eli and Margaret Findlay by Jacob Lindly, Washington Co.

1820 May 4   Sherman, Heman and Catharine Vaughan by John Patterson, JP,
               Washington Co.

1818 May 17   Sherman, Jonithan and Betsy Coe by Ezra Griswold, Franklin Co.

1798 Apr 30   Sherman, Josiah and Polly Brown by Robert Oliver, Washington Co.

1821 Jan 29   Sherman, Parmina and Bernard Merchant by Samuel Bancroft, JP,
               Licking Co.

1804 Dec 28   Sherman, Wm. and Huldah Olney by Enoch Wing, JP, Washington Co.

1801 Jun 2   Shermon, Lucy and Casper Hollenbuk by Nehemiah Davis, MG,
               Washington Co.

1815 Jul 10   Sherr, Sally and David Howel by Josiah Hoskinson, JP, Licking Co.

1819 Mar 3   Sheward, Nathan and Martha E. Boggs by Adriel Hussey, Elder in the
               Christian Church, Jackson Co.

1791 Jun 4   Sherwood, Thamur and Elijah Peaksley by Benj Tupper, Washington Co.

1800 Nov 24   Shevenin, Nicholas and Hannah Mior Malden by Robert Safford,
               Washington Co.

1815 Nov 2   Shewey, Martin and Anna Dunbar by Jno Russell, Washington Co.

1804 Mar 15   Shickley, Michael and Sally Sollers by Isaac Cook, JP, Ross Co.

1803 Jun 21   Shidler, Jacob and Letty Bobo by Wm. Harper, JP, Washington Co.

1819 Jan 21   Shields, James and Eliza Moredock by Patrick Shearer, JP, Jackson Co.

1888 Dec 6   Shilling, Clarence F. of Morgan Co. and Sarah Gray of Zanesville by
               Rev. George F. Moore, Putnam Presbyterian Church, Muskingum Co.

1815 Apr 27   Shind, Sophia and Robert Canon (or Carson) by Joseph Gorton,
               Franklin Co.

1828 Oct 19   Shinn, Elizabeth and Samuel T. Shinn by P. Adams, JP, Franklin Co.

1828 Oct 19   Shinn, Samuel T. and Elizabeth Shinn by P. Adams, JP, Franklin Co.

1811 Nov 12   Shipman, Charles and Frances Dana by Stephen Lindsly, Washington Co.

1866 Jan 18   Shipman, Sarah E. and J. Addison Kingsbury by Rev. A. Kingsbury,
               Putnam Presbyterian Church, Muskingum Co.

1821 Feb 15   Shipman, William H. and Mary Ann Edgerton by Rev. Saml P. Robbins, Washington Co.

1820 Nov 20   Ships, Betsey Ann and James Irwin by Abner Goff, MEC, Licking Co.

1815 Aug 8   Shirley, Elizabeth and Adam Keith by Obadiah Scott, JP, Washington Co.

1811 May 14   Shirley, John and Catharine Shanklen by Thomas Seely, JP, Washington Co.

1814 Dec 6   Shirley, Joseph and Elizabeth Keath by Thomas Seely, Washington Co.

1813 Apr 8   Shirley, Polly and George Ogle by Simeon Tuttle, JP, Washington Co.

1812 Jun 10   Shirtz, Henry and Jane Eliot by -----, Licking Co.

1811 Jul 21   Shoap, Thomas and Sarah Martin (license date), Pickaway Co.

1818 Jul 2   Shockley, Betsey and Peter Keith by Wm. Rand, Washington Co.

1826 Sep 21   Shoemaker, Abraham and Margaret Wilson by John F. Solomon, MEGC, Franklin Co.

1825 Oct 27   Shoemaker, George and Hanah Reynolds by Persinal Adams, JP, Franklin Co.

1828 Nov 20   Shoemaker, Henry and Susan Tillbery by J. Gander, JP, Franklin Co.

1825 Mar 22   Shoemaker, John and Mary Burnside by J.B. Gilliland, JP, Jackson Co.

1795 Sep 3   Shoeman, John Conrad and Lucy Shereman by Robert Oliver, Washington Co.

1824 Jan 29   Shofe, Abraham and Mary Ann Stimmel by C. Henkel, Franklin Co.

1822 Jul 20   Shofe, Catharine and David Cole by John F. Solomon, Franklin Co.

1822 Jan 6   Shofe (or Shafe), Rachael and Daniel Stimell by John F. Solomon, Franklin Co.

1826 Mar 30   Shoof, Jacob and Elisha Gray by P. Adams, Franklin Co.

1815 Apr 13   Shook, Margaret and Jacob Teegardin by Shad. Cole, JP, Pickaway Co.

1815 Mar 14   Shoppel, Jeremiah and Nancy Robbins by Benj Kepner, JP, Pickaway Co.

1834 Jul 10   Short, Elijah and Julia Ann Palmer by Rev. J.T. Wheat, St. Luke's Church, Marietta, Washington Co.

1853 Dec 29   Short, Margaret E. and Jacob R. Harshberger by Rev. Geo. B. Sturges, St. Paul's Church, Marion, Marion Co.

1853 Apr 23   Short, Martha A. and John Cuningham by Rev. Geo. B. Sturges, St. Paul's Church, Marion, Marion Co.

1803 Oct 27   Short, Stephen and Jane Bennett by Wm. Bennett, JP, Franklin Co.

1817 Nov 5   Short, Stephen and Nancy Mulakin by Ebenezer Washburn, Franklin Co.

1818 Nov 11   Shout, Henry and Betsy Smith by John Sells, JP, Franklin Co.

1821 Jul 18   Showers, Polly and William Mills by Jacob Smith, JP, Franklin Co.

1824 Jul 23   Showers, Susannah and John McGowen by J.B. Packard, JP, Marion Co.

1825 Mar 10   Shreck, Paul and Bethany Moss by Vincent Southard, JP, Jackson Co.

1810 May 8   Shreve, Israel and Mary Whead by Adam Winegarner, JP, Licking Co.

1825 Oct 6   Shrom, Joseph and Mary Gordon by Jacob Grubb, JP, Franklin Co.

1828 Sep 8   Shrum, Mary and John Miller by Adam Miller, Franklin Co.

1813 Nov 16   Shuck, Mary and Henry Reiter (license date), Pickaway Co.

1825 Apr 12   Shults, Barbora and George W. Perday (or Purday) by John Long,
               Franklin Co.

1825 May 26   Shumate, Mary and John S. Stephenson by John Stephenson, JP, Jackson
               Co.

1810 Aug 23   Shuttlesworth, Joshua and Nancy Fleharty by Joseph Palmer, JP,
               Washington Co.

1802 Oct 31   Sibley, Solomon and Sally Sproat by Daniel Story, Clerk, Washington Co

1824 Oct 18   Sidner, George and Polly Delly by Alex Perry, JP, Marion Co.

1824 Mar 2   Sidney, Susan and John Stumbaugh by James Hoge, Franklin Co.

1822 Feb 12   Sifers, Elizabeth and George Newcomb by Amos Wilson, Washington Co.

1821 May 21   Siffers, Jacob and Sarah Willis by Amos Wilson, JP, Washington Co.

1817 Feb 13   Silais, Elizabeth and Joseph Harris by T.D. Baird, Licking Co.

1815 Jun 1   Siler, Jacob and Nancy Hutchinson by Uriah Hull, Licking Co.

1815 Apr 9   Siler, Phillip and Lavinia Channell by Noah Fidler, Licking Co.

1802 Feb 3   Silliman, Willis and Deborah W. Cass by Seth Coshart, JP, Washington
               Co.

1810 Jan 27   Sills, Sarah and John Cheadle by Asa Cheadle, JP, Washington Co.

1820 Jun 1   Silva, Elizabeth and John Dickson by Amos Wilson, Washington Co.

1808 6m 22   Silver, Anna and Noah Haines, Miami Monthly Meeting, Warren Co.

1806 1m 2   Silver, Lettitia and David Linton, Miami Monthly Meeting, Warren Co.

1822 Oct 10   Silvester, Matilda and Benjamin Carpenter by Jacob Smith, Franklin Co.

1853 Apr 7   Silvey, James of Chillicothe and Esther S. Guthrie of Putnam by Rev.
               A. Kingsbury, Putnam Presbyterian Church, Muskingum Co.

1820 Feb 24   Silvey, Sarah and William Devol by John Patterson, JP, Washington Co.

1817 Jan 18   Silvins, Susanna and Isaac Sanders by John Patterson, Washington Co.

1816 Aug 22   Simmon, Tilman and Catherine Dickey by John Green, MG, Licking Co.

1805 Jan 5   Simmons, Betsy and John McVay by John Greene, Washington Co.

1826 Aug 2   Simmons, Edward and Rebecca Swing (or Young) by Jacob Delay, LM,
               Jackson Co.

1802 Apr 1   Simmons, John and Rebecka Woods by Sam'l Williamson, JP, Washington Co

1806 Sep 18   Simmons, Mary and David Jones by James Marshall, JP, Franklin Co.

1821 Mar 22   Simmons, Nancy and John Reim by Wm. Richardson, Franklin Co.

1790 Apr 4   Simmons, Samuel and Lydia Tillson by Benj Tupper, Washington Co.

1815 Mar 15   Simmons, Van and Sarah Beecher by J. Green, Licking Co.

1818 Jun 18   Simons, Anna and Caleb Furby by Joseph Grate, Franklin Co.

1820 Sep 7   Simons, Faulkner and Sally Chandler by Amos Wilson, Washington Co.

| 1809 May 4 | Simpson, Mary and James Williams by John Hollister, JPHT, Licking Co. |

1809 May 4   Simpson, Mary and James Williams by John Hollister, JPHT, Licking Co.

1819 Oct 16   Simpson, Sarah and Simon Shattock by Wm. Long, Franklin Co.

1820 Mar 13   Simpson, Thomas and Agnes Holmes by Joseph Thrap, MG, Licking Co.

1825 Nov 17   Sims, Abraham and Susanna Bair by Benj Davis, JP, Marion Co.

1849 --- --   Sims, D. Ross of Greenupsburg, Ky., and Catharine W. Gabandan by Rev.
               D.W. Tolford, St. Luke's Church, Marietta, Washington Co.

1860 Dec 31   Sims, Josephine and Milton H. Chapman by Rev. A. Kingsbury, Putnam
               Presbyterian Church, Muskingum Co.

1881 Feb 16   Sims, Philander and Nellie Summerville by Rev. John Boyd, St. Luke's
               Church, Marietta, Washington Co.

1822 Apr 4   Sinclair, Nancy and Andrew Allison by John Green, JP, Washington Co.

1810 Mar 21   Sinclair, Wm. and Nancy Bailey by John Brough,JP, Washington Co.

1820 Mar 4   Sinkey, James and Mary Twigg by Simeon Aver, MG, Licking Co.

1818 May 28   Sinnet, Ishu? and Leuine? Gardner by Rev. T. Harris, Licking Co.

1813 Sep 16   Sinnet, Peggam and Titus Knox by Rev. T. Harris, Licking Co.

1891 Sep 12   Singleton, David A. and Charlotte Williamson both of Zanesville by
               Rev. George F. Moore, Putnam Presbyterian Church, Muskingum Co.

1826 Mar 29   Sisco, Margret and Samuel Devenport by Abms Williams, JP, Franklin Co.

1824 Jun 2   Skeels, Almeda and James Brown by A. Walker, JP, Franklin Co.

1821 Oct 24   Skeels, Harvey and Betsey Andrews by Nathl Little, Franklin Co.

1825 Aug 23   Skeels, Harvey and Huldah Vining by Nathan Emery, MG, Franklin Co.

1821 Dec 7   Skeels, Polly and James H. Wilson by Aristarchus Walker, Franklin Co.

1821 Oct 18   Skeels, Roxina and Russell Town by Nathl Little, Franklin Co.

1820 Mar 9   Skeels, Susanna and Silas Lanson by Stephen Maynard, Franklin Co.

1827 Apr 19   Skeels, Truman and Betsy B. Wiswell by A. Walker, Franklin Co.

1807 May 26   Skidmore, John and Mary Hopper by James Marshall, JP, Franklin Co.

1827 Sep 20   Skidmore, John and I.N. Riley by Reuben Golliday, JP, Franklin Co.

1810 Aug 30   Skidmore, Joshua and Nelly Hopper by James Marshall, Franklin Co.

1810 Aug 30   Skidmore, Mary and John Rodgers by James Marshall, Franklin Co.

1818 Jan 22   Skinner, James and Cendian McMillin by Joseph Grate, Franklin Co.

1817 Oct 20   Skinner, Sarah and Nahum Ward by Rev. Saml. P. Robbins, Washington Co.

1881 Nov 16   Skinner, Sarah M. and Llewellyn Morton by Rev. John Boyd, St. Luke's
               Church, Marietta, Washington Co.

1806 Jun 9   Slack, Elizabeth and Orlando Barker by Ezekiel Brown, JP, Franklin Co.

1888 Oct 23   Slack, Ida C. of Powell's Mills, O., and George C. Powell of Zanesville
               by Rev. George F. Moore,Putnam Presbyterian Church,Muskingum Co.

1808 Jan 18   Slack, Miley and Seth Billington by Jos. Eaton, Franklin Co.

1801 Apr 23   Slack, Sarah and Discovery Olney by Nehemiah Davis, Washington Co.

1812 Nov 30   Slagel, Susana and Ebeneezer Petty (license date), Pickaway Co.

1814 Mar 3   Slane, Jane and Abraham Agney by Noah Fidler, Licking Co.

1806 Nov 4   Slary, Joseph and Mahepsa Ptratt by Stephen Lindley, Washington Co.

1819 Apr 15   Slaughter, Desdemonia and Samuel B. Jones by Daniel H. Buell, JP,
               Washington Co.

1817 Sep 9   Slerogin, George and Anna Neff by Joseph Gorton, JP, Franklin Co.

1821 Aug 16   Sligh, Henry and Mrs. Mary Higgins by Robert W. Riley, Franklin Co.

1826 Sep 14   Sloan, David and Sarah Lantis by C. Henkel, Franklin Co.

1860 Nov 3   Sloan, Thomas M. of Zanesville and Charlotte E. Eveleigh by Rev.
               John Boyd, St. Luke's Church, Marietta, Washington Co.

1874 Jun 15   Slocum, Ida M. and George C. Butts by Rev. John Boyd, St. Luke's
               Church, Marietta, Washington Co.

1819 Aug 26   Sloper, Charles and Lydia Matthes by Wm. Long, JP, Franklin Co.

1805 Dec 13   Sloper, Eunice and Adam Hosack by Ezekiel Brown, JP, Franklin Co.

1822 Apr 11   Sloper, Lydia and Neham Newell by Aristarchus Walker, Franklin Co.

1805 May 6   Sloper, Mary and Ruben Lamb by Ezekiel Brown, JP, Franklin Co.

1812 Jan 3   Sloper, Samuel and Lydia Maynard by. Isaac Fisher, MG, Franklin Co.

1807 Sep 13   Sloper, Scynthia and Reuben Lamb by Thomas Brown, JP, Franklin Co.

1821 Jul 3   Slosser, Daniel and Sally Woodring by George Weizz, MG, Franklin Co.

1816 Mar 17   Slosson, Polly and John Ryan by Alex. Bassett, Franklin Co.

1824 Jun 6   Slusher, Gatright and Isaac Hall by Michael J. Stick, MG, Franklin Co.

1818 May 17   Slusser, Solome and Myers Bennit by Michael J. Steck, MG, Franklin Co.

1823 Feb 6   Sly, Henry and Susan Hopper by Joseph Badger, JP, Franklin Co.

1890 Oct 14   Smaill, Chyde M. and Frank S. Burns both of Zensville by Rev.
               George F. Moore, Putnam Presbyterian Church, Muskingum Co.

1828 Dec 11   Smallman, John and Lydia Wagoner by Jacob Smith, JP, Franklin Co.

1812 Sep 1   Smart, Isaac and Margaret Smith by A. O'Harra, Franklin Co.

1817 Jul 13   Smedley, William and Mrs. Lucy Bancroft by Samuel Bancroft, JP,
               Licking Co.

1817 Jan 2   Smith, Abraham and Ruth Vance by J.W. Patterson, JW, Licking Co.

1818 Feb 2   Smith, Abraham and Elizabeth Straight by Jacob Smith, JP, Franklin Co.

1822 Mar 24   Smith, Abraham and Sarah Sciscoe by Russel Bigelow, MG, Franklin Co.

1828 Jun 24   Smith, Abram and Sally Ann Spain by J. David, JP, Franklin Co.

1815 Nov 9   Smith, Adam and Nancy Hungerford by D.H. Buell, JP, Washington Co.

1815 Jul 13   Smith, Alla and John Gavit by J. Cunningham, Licking Co.

1827?--- --   Smith, Ann M. and Elias Chester, Jr. by George Jefferies, MG,
               Franklin Co.

1819 Nov 5   Smith, Anson and Trifena Smith by James Hoge, Franklin Co.

1809 Feb 16   Smith, Aquella and Mary Seymore by Wm. Haines, JP, Licking Co.

1804 Aug 21   Smith, Arra and Rebecca Crouch by Abm Miller, Ross Co.

1819 Aug 23   Smith, Asa and Nancy McClintick by James Whitney, JP, Washington Co.

1797 Oct 5   Smith, Benjamin and Almy Barker by Peregrine Foster, JCCCP, Washington Co.

1805 Mar 21   Smith, Betsey and Isaac Ater by Peter Jackson, JP, Ross Co.

1794 Apr 2   Smith, Betsy and John Russell by R.J. Meigs, JP, Washington Co.

1818 Jan 24   Smith, Betsey and David Emerson by Thomas White, JP, Washington Co.

1818 Nov 11   Smith, Betsy and Henry Shout by John Sells, JP, Franklin Co.

1822 Oct 29   Smith, Betsy and Robert Jamison by E. Washburn, VDM, Franklin Co.

1871 Sep 5   Smith, Carrie C. and Homer Cammel by Rev. John Boyd, St. Luke's Church, Marietta, Washington Co.

1802 Nov 27   Smith, Catharine and Samuel Folsom by John Robinson, JP, Washington Co.

1821 Apr 23   Smith, Catherine and Samuel Wheeler by Michael Trout, JP, Licking Co.

1824 Apr 8   Smith, Catharine and G.B. Smith by Henry Matthews, Minister of the M.E. Church, Franklin Co.

1825 Nov 17   Smith, Catharine and John Thompson by Abm Williams, Franklin Co.

1826 Dec 21   Smith, Charles and Melvina Devenport by Abraham Williams, Franklin Co.

1816 Jun 16   Smith, Charlotte and Burfot Goldsmith by Simon Merwin, JP, Washington Co.

1824 Feb 8   Smith, Clemthy and Esther Richards by Robert Boyd, Franklin Co.

1814 Jun 2   Smith, Cloe and Anthony Potts by Rev. Thos. W. Suruney, Pickaway Co.

1816 Feb 4   Smith, Danl and Elizabeth Ogden by Thos. B. Patterson, Franklin Co.

1820 Jun 8   Smith, David and Harriet Mitchel by Joseph Gorton, Franklin Co.

1806 Sep 26   Smith, David G. and Sally Bradley by Seth Washburn, Washington Co.

1808 May 25   Smith, Dolly and John Lathby by Henry Smith, JP, Licking Co.

1854 Sep 16   Smith, E.W. of Mansfield and Sarah G. Metcalf of Putnam by Rev. A. Kingsbury, Putnam Presbyterian Church, Muskingum Co.

1806 Feb 9   Smith, Easten and Freeman King by Peter Jackson, JP, Ross Co.

1819 Jan 21   Smith, Edward and Sarah Brown by Eli C. King, Franklin Co.

1817 Oct 5   Smith, Elihue and Naomi Withington by Cyrus Ames, Washington Co.

1814 Jan 12   Smith, Eliza and Enoch Soper by Timothy M. Gates, JP, Washington Co.

1828 Aug 7   Smith, Eliza and Joseph Thompson by Chandlor Rodgers, JP, Franklin Co.

1805 Mar 10   Smith, Elizabeth and Michael Crider by Abraham Miller, Ross Co.

1805 Aug 1   Smith, Elizabeth and Jolly Parish by Thos Hicks, Ross Co.

1815 Sep 1   Smith, Elizabeth and Robert Wills by Z. Carlisle, Licking Co.

1819 Dec 20   Smith, Elizabeth and John Sparks by Geo. Callanhan, JP, Licking Co.

1826 Jun 8   Smith, Elizabeth and David Martin by Geo. Jefferies, Franklin Co.

1828 Dec 11   Smith, Elizabeth and David F. Squires by John Davis, Franklin Co.

1853 Sep 6   Smith, Elizabeth and Lewis Hyar by Rev. John Boyd, St. Luke's
               Church, Marietta, Washington Co.

1818 Nov 6   Smith, Esther and John Walbridge by Stephen Guthrie, Washington Co.

1825 9m 7   Smith, Fanny and Moorman Butterworth, Miami Monthly Meeting, Warren Co

1803 Aug 11   Smith, Feby and William Buck by Wm. Bennett, JP, Franklin Co.

1824 Apr 8   Smith, G.B. and Catharine Smith by Henry Matthews, Minister of the
               M.E. Church, Franklin Co.

1809 Mar 22   Smith, George and Elizabeth Fraize by Wm. Haines, JP, Licking Co.

1820 Mar 4   Smith, George and Sarah Smith by Thos. B. Patterson, JP, Franklin Co.

1816 Jun 25   Smith, Gilbert and Nely Courtright by Joseph Grate, Franklin Co.

1818 May 10   Smith, Hannah and Philip Woolf by James McLish, JP, Franklin Co.

1818 Jun 23   Smith, Hannah and Nathaniel Blackman by John Vance, JP, Licking Co.

1820 Nov 1   Smith, Henry and Anny Lisses by John Davis, JP, Franklin Co.

1802 Jun 7   Smith, Hezekiah and Susan Goodale by J. Pierce, Washington Co.

1897 Mar 29   Smith, Howard H. and Mrs. Sare E. Powell both of Zanesville by Rev.
               George F. Moore, Putnam Presbyterian Church, Muskingum Co.

1827 Aug 4   Smith, I.M. and Mary Loffland by Wm. Long, JP, Franklin Co.

1825 Feb 16   Smith, Israel Jr. and Louise Bears by Alex Kinnear, MG, Marion Co.

1820 Apr 22   Smith, Jacob and Susan Havins by Thos. B. Patterson, Franklin Co.

1797 Dec 19   Smith, James and Prissilla Porter by Peregrine Foster, JCCCP,
               Washington Co.

1800 Jun 12   Smith, James and Mary Beel by Philip Whitten, Washington Co.

1824 1m 7   Smith, James and Mary C. Brown, Miami Monthly Meeting, Warren Co.

1825 Mar 24   Smith, James and Catharine Evans by Joseph Carper, Franklin Co.

1828 Jun 24   Smith, James C. and Jane Reece by James Hoge, Franklin Co.

1821 May 13   Smith, Jane and Andrew Myers by A. Goff, CP, Licking Co.

1819 Aug 8   Smith, Jemima and William Talbot by James M. Booth, JP, Washington Co.

1814 Feb 24   Smith, Jeremiah and Rhoda Hedges, Pickaway Co.

1804 Sep 5   Smith, John and Omy Buck by James Marshall, JP, Franklin Co.

1807 Jul 21   Smith, John and Charlott Welch by Arthur O'Harra, Franklin Co.

1813 Apr 4   Smith, John and Olive Willson by Jos. S. Hughes, QDP, Franklin Co.

1813 May 19   Smith, John and Jane Tupper by Richd Seddick, JP, Franklin Co.

1816 Apr 14   Smith, John and Sally Courtright by Daniel Brunk, Franklin Co.

1817 Dec 14   Smith, John and Catherine Dispennet by John W. Patterson, MG, Licking
               Co.

1818 Jul 24   Smith, John and Philena Thomas by Geo. Templeton, JP, Washington Co.

1816 Jan 4   Smith, John R? and Sophiah Bond by James Marshall, Franklin Co.

1810 Apr 22   Smith, Joseph and Nancy Stump by J. Greenman, JP, Washington Co.

1818 Sep 29   Smith, Joseph and Hannah Hull by Wm. Hull, JP, Licking Co.

1814 Jan 25   Smith, Joseph T. and Lucy Mider by Samuel Dye, JP, Washington Co.

1816 Nov 9   Smith, Joshua and Lara Rold by Rev. T. Harris, Licking Co.

1817 Nov 2   Smith, Julia Ann and Ebenezer Colburn by Danl H. Buell, JP, Washington Co.

1821 Aug 14   Smith, Keziah and William Latham by James Hoge, Franklin Co.

1828 Jan 24   Smith, M.A. and Thomas Stagg by S. Hamilton, Franklin Co.

1828 Feb 5   Smith, Madleen and Andrew Roberts by George Jefferies, Franklin Co.

1812 Sep 1   Smith, Margaret and Isaac Smart by A. O'Harra, Franklin Co.

1819 Jun 2   Smith, Margaret and Able Patterson by B. Black, JP, Licking Co.

1829 Jun 17   Smith, Margaret and Alonso Williams by Geo. Jefferies, Franklin Co.

1804 Jan 22   Smith, Martha and Daniel Whetzell by Abm. Miller, Ross Co.

1809 3m 16   Smith, Mary and Mercer Brown, Miami Monthly Meeting, Warren Co.

1811 Apr 25   Smith, Mary and Mark Hashman by Thomas Morris, Franklin Co.

1812 May 12   Smith, Mary and William Thomas by Thomas Morris, Franklin Co.

1815 Mar 12   Smith, Mary and Nathaniel Olney by Sardine Stone, JP, Washington Co.

1820 Jun 22   Smith, Mary and Samuel Scothorn by B. Bull, JP, Franklin Co.

1825 Apr 14   Smith, Mary Ann and Jacob Shafer by Alex Kinnear, JP, Marion Co.

1866 Apr 26   Smith, Mary E. and William Roberts by Rev. John Boyd, St. Luke's Church, Marietta, Washington Co.

1815 Jan 17   Smith, Math and Sarah Sutherland by Rev. Sam'l Wilson, Pickaway Co.

1816 Nov 3   Smith, Matilda P. and Cogswell Olney by Rev. Nehemiah Davis, Washington Co.

1813 Mar 26   Smith, Mersy and Abner Bell (license date), Pickaway Co.

1822 Apr 25   Smith, Milton and Suson O. Brien by Jacob Young, Washington Co.

1805 Nov 14   Smith, Nancy and James Benny by Thomas Hicks, Ross Co.

1806 Mar 20   Smith, Nancy and Edward Crabb by Peter Jackson, JP, Ross Co.

1818 Aug 6   Smith, Nancy and Wm. Oliver by John Horton, JP, Jackson Co.

1824 Dec 25   Smith, Nancy and James Wait by Tracy Willcox, JP, Franklin Co.

1825 Jan 13   Smith, Nancy and John Denoon by George Jefferies, ordained and licensed Minister, Franklin Co.

1828 May 29   Smith, Nancy and Jacob Stuls by J. Davis, JP, Franklin Co.

1814 Feb 13   Smith, Nathaniel and Jemima Broom by Dan'l H. Buell, JP, Washington Co.

1819 Dec 21   Smith, Nathaniel W. and Rebecca Culbertson by James Hoge, Franklin Co

1820 Dec 14   Smith, Phebe and Daniel Demerest by Nicholas Goetschius, Franklin Co.

1825 Mar 31   Smith, Pheby and Joseph Winslow by Hugh M. Smith, JP, Marion Co.

1812 Dec 27   Smith, Phillip and Polly Strouse (license date), Pickaway Co.

1796 Dec 6   Smith, Polly and Sardine Stone by D. Loring, Jus.C.P., Washington Co.

1814 Mar 20   Smith, Polly and Marvel Starlin by Isaac Baker, Esq., Washington Co.

1817 Aug 3   Smith, Polly and James Barr by Cyrus Ames, Washington Co.

1826 Jul 25   Smith, Polly and O'Harra by H. Mathews, MG in M.E. Church, Franklin Co

1806 12m 31   Smith, Rachel and Nathan Linton, Miami Monthly Meeting, Warren Co.

1807 12m 16   Smith, Rosannah and James Townsend, Miami Monthly Meeting, Warren Co.

1819 Jul 1   Smith, Sally and Nicholas Demorest by Joseph Gorton, Franklin Co.

1813 Jul 9   Smith, Salmon and Catharine Mays by John Brough, JP, Washington Co.

1804 Jul 19   Smith, Samuel and Isabella McDaniels by J. Graham, JP, Washington Co.

1820 Jan 27   Smith, Samuel Royal and Eleanor Pattin by Philip Cole, JP, Washington
               Co.

1825 Jan --   Smith, Samuel and Louis Gleason by Thomas Rodgers, JP, Marion Co.

1825 Jul 21   Smith, Samuel and Betsey Casey by J. Gander, JP, Franklin Co.

1816 May 7   Smith, Sarah and Elijah Drew by Nathan Cunningham, Licking Co.

1819 Feb 23   Smith, Sarah and Jeremiah R. Reed by James Stephenson, JP, Jackson Co.

1820 Mar 4   Smith, Sarah and George Smith by Thos. B. Patterson, JP, Franklin Co.

1820 May 16   Smith, Sarah and Joseph Feris by Chandler Rogers, JP, Franklin Co.

1821 Jun 3   Smith, Sarah see Sarah Archer

1822 May 20   Smith, Sarah and Levin Culver by John F. Solomon, Franklin Co.

1823 Mar 18   Smith, Sarah and Hamilton Robb by Charles Waddell, LM, Franklin Co.

1873 Dec 2   Smith, Sarah E. and Ason McNeal by Rev. John Boyd, St. Luke's Church,
               Marietta, Washington Co.

1817 May 15   Smith, Silas and Polly Jones by Wm. Brown, Franklin Co.

1825 Mar 5   Smith, Susan and Benj Meeker by Alex Kinnear, MG, Marion Co.

1819 Dec 8   Smith, Thomas and Catherine Gray by T.D. Bierd, Licking Co.

1838 Nov 7   Smith, Timothy Abbot and Eoeline Reed, St. Luke's Church, Granville,
               Licking Co.

1819 Nov 5   Smith, Trifena and Anson Smith by James Hoge, Franklin Co.

1822 Feb 19   Smith, Vincent and Eleanor Hougland by Rev. Cornelius Springer,
               Washington Co.

1806 Feb 17   Smith, William and Mary Sheilds by Thomas Hicks, Ross Co.

1815 Apr 18   Smith, William and Isabella Scott by Nathan Cunningham, Licking Co.

1819 Aug 8   Smithson, Mary Ann and John T. Jewell by Rev. Levi Jewell, Washington
               Co.

1867 Dec 3   Smitley, George W. of White Cottage and Frank B. Hall[sic] by Rev. A.
               Kingsbury, Putnam Presbyterian Church, Muskingum Co.

1821 Apr 29   Smothers, Hannah and John Adams by Russel Bigelow, Franklin Co.

1825 Oct 12   Smothers, John and Roelinda Sebring by G.W. Hart, JP, Franklin Co.

1816 Dec 20   Smothers, Mabel and Elijay Bennet by Thomas B. Patterson, JP,
               Franklin Co.

1815 Aug 7   Sneas, Peggy and Samuel Gobin by Thomas White, JP, Washington Co.

1890 Dec 2   Snits, Carrie and Goodcil B. Parshall both of Zanesville by Rev.
               George F. Moore, Putnam Presbyterian Church, Muskingum Co.

1819 Apr 21   Snodgrass, Hiram and Drusilla Oliver by Joseph Dickerson, JP,
               Washington Co.

1858 Apr 5   Snodgrass, John W. of Parkersburg, Va. to Eunice F. Hall by Rev.
               John Boyd, St. Luke's Church, Marietta, Washington Co.

1820 Nov 2   Snodgrass, Margaret and John Bardmass by David Davis, Washington Co.

1825 Aug 14   Snook, Anna and Wm. Winters by John Potter, JP, Jackson Co.

1821 Jan 28   Snook, Henry and Susanah Cune by David Culbertson, DD, Jackson Co.

1824 May 30   Snook, John and Purlina Newton by David Culbertson,MG, Jackson Co.

1820 Oct 9   Snook, Mathias and Sarah Craige by David Culbertson, DD, Jackson Co.

1825 Jan 13   Snotgrass, Jane and Isaac Null by John Anglin, JP, Jackson Co.

1871 Nov 22   Snyder, Anna B. and Isaac Springer by Rev. A. Kingsbury, Putnam
               Presbyterian Church, Muskingum Co.

1870 Nov 17   Snyder, Mary E. and James Cusac by Rev. A. Kingsbury, Putnam
               Presbyterian Church, Muskingum Co.

1864 Nov 17   Snyder, Mary M. and William M. Merritt by Rev. John Boyd, St. Luke's
               Church, Marietta, Washington Co.

1818 Nov 15   Snyder, Sarah and Samuel Williams by James Holmes, Licking Co.

1800 Apr 14   Soates, Joseph and Margery Daugherty by Seth Cashart, Washington Co.

1810 Aug 17   Sobdate, Julia and Gideon Cornwell by J.W. Patterson, Licking Co.

1818 Feb 13   Sobditt, Matilda and Joseph Johnson by Stephen Guthrie, JP,
               Washington Co.

1812 Aug 30   Sockrider, John and Catherine Roads (license date), Pickaway Co.

1818 Apr 30   Sole, Prissilla and Sollimon Malbone by Wm. Swayze, Itenrant minister
               in the Methodist Episcopal Church, Franklin Co.

1806 Jan 5   Sollars, Anna and John Brown by Peter Jackson, JP, Ross Co.

1804 Apr 13   Sollers, Nancy and Jacob Eator by John Hoddy, JP, Ross Co.

1804 Mar 15   Sollers, Sally and Michael Shickley by Isaac Cook, JP, Ross Co.

1819 Jul 27   Solomon, John and Christine Rary by Michl Ellis, Franklin Co.

1809 Jun 20   Somtion, Sary and Abner Purket by John Smith, Franklin Co.

1828 Jun 5   Sone, Sarah and Matthias Sharp by Aristaches Walker, JP, Franklin Co.

1810 Jun 26   Soo, Samuel and Sabra Case by Rev. T. Harris, Licking Co.

1814 Jan 12   Soper, Enoch and Eliza Smith by Timtohy M. Gates, JP, Washington Co.

1826 Mar 24   Sorden (or Sordon), Margaret and Daniel Gibbs by Percival Adams,
               Franklin Co.

1819 Mar 25   Soul, Almond Jr. and Dolly Kimble McClure by Dudley Davis, Washington
               Co.

1824? Mar 25   Soule, Mary and David Colvin by Aristarchus Walker, Franklin Co.

1818 Dec 24   South, Nancy and Joseph Murdock by D. Mitchell, JP, Jackson Co.

1814 Sep 1   Southard, Betsey and John Kinney by Chas. Cade, JP, Pickaway Co.

1819 Dec 21   Southard, Vincent and Elenor O'Neil by Nath'l W. Andrews, JP, Jackson
               Co.

1817 Jan 30   Soyes, Lewis and Ann Protzman by Dan'l H. Buell, JP, Washington Co.

1859 Oct 27   Soyez, Isabelle C. and William Loomis DeBeck by Rev. John Boyd, St.
               Luke's Church, Marietta, Washington Co.

1805 Apr 4   Spacht, Polly and Jacob Humphry by D. Loring, Washington Co.

1811 Aug 10   Spade, Caty and Jacob Hartle (license date), Pickaway Co.

1801 May 14   Spafford, Anna and John Cram both of Cleveland by James Kingsbury,
               Judge of Court of Common Pleas, Trumbull Co.

1828 Jun 24   Spain, Sally Ann and Abram Smith by J. Davis, JP, Franklin Co.

1826 Oct 22   Spake, Frederick and Stacy Baker by C. Henkel, Franklin Co.

1895 Dec 25   Spalding, John A. and Annie Campbell both of Marietta, O., by Rev.
               George F. Moore, Putnam Presbyterian Church, Muskingum Co.

1807 Oct 25   Spalding, Noah and Parthena Root by Thomas Brown, Franklin Co.

1810 Aug 28   Spangler, Catherine and Isaac Harnden (license date), Pickaway Co.

1810 Dec 9   Spangler, Catherine and John Zehring (license date), Pickaway Co.

1822 Mar 12   Spangler, Eli and Mary Barbee by James Hoge, Franklin Co.

1828 Dec 13   Spangler, Frederick and Rebeca Lambert by John F. Solomon, Franklin Co.

1824 Feb 10   Spangler, Joseph and Cumfort Williams by James Hoge, Franklin Co.

1826 Mar 19   Spangler, Joseph and Polly McCloud by C. Hinckel, Franklin Co.

1829 Feb 14   Spangler, Joseph and Betsey Sherman by Leroy Swornstead, Franklin Co.

1814 Aug 6   Spangler, Polly and Solomon Glick by Jacob Leist, JP, Pickaway Co.

1819 Jun 17   Spark, George and Mary Lyons by Billingslea Bull, Franklin Co.

1819 Dec 20   Sparks, John and Elizabeth Smith by Geo. Callanhan, JP, Licking Co.

1813 Dec 9   Sparks, Patty and John Wells by G. Callanhan, EMEC, Licking Co.

1821 May 19   Sparks, Polly and Nicholas Best by Nicholas Goetschius, Franklin Co.

1816 Oct 6   Sparling, John and Joanna Collins by Cyrus Ames, Washington Co.

1827 Feb 13   Sparrow, William and Francis G. Ingraham by Amos G. Baldwin, Minister
               of the Pr Ep Ch'h, Franklin Co.

1819 Jan 26   Spears, Susanna and Gideon Kidder by Dudley Davis, JP, Washington Co.

1803 Jun 2   Speed, Nancy and James Lackey by J. Graham, Washington Co.

1812 Sep 22   Spelman, Betsy and David Harris by Rev. G. Vanaman, Licking Co.

1813 Feb 11   Spelman, Elizabeth and Timothy Case by Rev. Timothy Harris, Licking Co.

1813 Jul 4   Spelman, Hannah and Ralph Granger by J. Tulloss, JP, Licking Co.

1808 Aug 11   Spelman, Spencer and Ruth Gilman by Rev. Timothy Harris, Licking Co.

1821 Nov 4   Spelman, Sylvester and Emily Boardman by Samuel Bancroft, JP,
               Licking Co.

1810 Feb 27   Spelman, Thomas and M. Clark by Rev. T. Harris, Licking Co.

1881 Aug 6   Spencer, Annie and John Thomas by Rev. John Boyd, St. Luke's Church, Marietta, Washington Co.

1818 Feb 24   Spencer, Isaac and Mary Ann Wagner by Wm. Rand, JP, Washington Co.

1813 Jun 15   Spencer, Mary and John Mothersaw by S. Dunnavan, JP, Licking Co.

1820 Nov 12   Spencer, Mary and Gilis C. Harrington by Rev. T. Harris, Licking Co.

1817 May 1   Spencer, Polly and Phineas Coburn by John Patterson, JP, Washington Co.

1812 Jan 9   Spencer, Shelden and Polly Waterman by Jer. Greenman, JP, Washington Co.

1821 Jan 25   Spencer, Wills and Nancy Eairs by Thos. B. Patterson, Franklin Co.

1810 Aug 23   Spiker, Henry and Elizabeth Todd (license date), Pickaway Co.

1811 Feb 24   Spinks, Jabez and Anna Morris by Dudley Davis, JP, Washington Co.

1812 Jun 25   Spohn, Henry and Barbary Fry by A. Winegarner, JP, Licking Co.

1817 Apr 23   Spooner, Cyrus and Mary Wing by Rev. S.P. Robbin, Washington Co.

1819 Nov 25   Spooner, William and Patty (alias Martha) Pinney by Stephen Maynard, JP, Franklin Co.

1828 Apr 2   Spooner, William and Edey Gray by Adam Miller, Franklin Co.

1813 Apr 14   Sprague, Abigail and Gilbert Olney by Sardine Stone, JP, Washington Co.

1806 Nov 11   Sprague, Anson and Susanna Sprague by Nehemiah Davis, Washington Co.

1815 Dec 31   Sprague, Cynthia and Washington Olney by Jno Green, Washington Co.

1813 Aug 2   Sprague, George and Jane Mason by John Green, JP, Washington Co.

1792 Sep 18   Sprague, Jonathan and Sabra Seamans by J. Gilman, Washington Co.

1816 Feb 11   Sprague, Jonathan and Susan Owen by Jno Green, JP, Washington Co.

1817 Jan 2   Sprague, Joshua and Phebe G. Brown by John Green, JP, Washington Co.

1816 Feb 26   Sprague, Lucinda and William Roach by John Green, JP, Washington Co.

1818 Apr 22   Sprague, Lucy and William Mason by Wm. Rand, Washington Co.

1810 Dec 11   Sprague, Nancy and David Emerson by Thomas Seely, JP, Washington Co.

1815 Nov 11   Sprague, Polly and John Starlin by Wm. Oliver, JP, Washington Co.

1821 Jan 10   Sprague, Ruby and Simeon Devol by John Green, JP, Washington Co.

1816 May 12   Sprague, Sally and Joseph Mason by John Green, JP, Washington Co.

1795 May 15   Sprague, Samuel and Hannah Delong by Robert Oliver, Washington Co.

1807 Dec 17   Sprague, Sarah and Charles Thomas by N. Davis, Washington Co.

1806 Nov 11   Sprague, Susanna and Anson Sprague by Nehemiah Davis, Washington Co.

1796 Aug 18   Sprague, Wilber and Gratry Holleraff by Robert Oliver, Washington Co.

1811 Mar 5   Sprague, Wm. and Arta Emerson by Dudley Davis, Washington Co.

1815 Dec 4   Sprague, Wayne and Lucinda Devol by John Green, JP, Washington Co.

1819 Jul 9   Spranklin, John and Lydia Goss by Rev. A. Robinson, Washington Co

1891 Jul 4   Spratt, Viola and David E. McGregar both of High Hill, O., by Rev.
               George F. Moore, Putnam Presbyterian Church, Muskingum Co.

1805 11m 27   Spray, Dinah and John Cook, Miami Monthly Meeting, Warren Co.

1820 Jun 24   Springer, Abigail and Joshua Bickford, Jr. by Cyrus Ames, JP,
               Washington Co.

1806 Oct 22   Springer, Benjamin and Elizabeth Biles by Nehemiah Gates, Franklin Co.

1816 Jan 11   Springer, Clark N. and Polly Wilson by Isaac Baker, JP, Washington Co.

1888 Jan 21   Springer, Hattie B. and Samuel A. Thomas both of Zanesville by Rev.
               George F. Moore, Putnam Presbyterian Church, Muskingum Co.

1871 Nov 22   Springer, Isaac and Anna B. Snyder by Rev. A. Kingsbury, Putnam
               Presbyterian Church, Muskingum Co.

1886 Mar 30   Springer, Kate and Charles V. Terry both of Zanesville by Rev.
               George F. Moore, Putnam Presbyterian Church, Muskingum Co.

1816 Jan 7   Springer, Lucy and Whiting Hudson by J. Greenman, Washington Co.

1791 Feb 17   Springer, Peleg and Sally Welles by Benj Tupper, Washington Co.

1809 --- 19   Springer, Silas and Margaret Kilgore by Michael Dickey (signed by
               justice on 1 Nov., record 27 Feb. 1810), Franklin Co.

1807 May 10   Springer, Thomas and Rhue McGill by David Mitchel, JP, Franklin Co.

1802 Oct 31   Sproat, Sally and Solomon Sibley by Daniel Story, Clerk, Washington Co.

1820 Jul 10   Sproll, James and Sarah Murphy by W. O'Bannon, JP, Licking Co.

1820 Jul 20   Sproull?, Margaret and Wm. Davies? by W. O'Bannon, JP, Licking Co.

1821 Jan 5   Sprouse, Elizabeth and David Prause by Andrew Donnelly, JP, Jackson Co.

1824 May 13   Spurgeon, Moses R. and Martha Coe by Henry Matthews, Franklin Co.

1825 Nov 6   Spurgeon, Zilla and Sam'l Hartel by J.B. Finley, JP, Marion Co.

1828 Dec 11   Squires, David F. and Elizabeth Smith by John Davis, Franklin Co.

1803 Nov 3   Squires, George and Jane Rose by Jacob Earhart, JP, Washington Co.

1818 Nov 9   Squires, Maria and Edward Wolcott by Samuel Bancroft, JP, Licking Co.

1798 Dec 23   Staats, Abraham and Elizabeth Hughs by D. Loring, JCCCP, Washington Co.

1799 Mar 10   Staats, Rebecca and Dudley Langford by D. Loring, Washington Co.

1808 Aug 16   Stacey, Abigail and James McClaer by N. Davis, Minister, Washington Co.

1799 May 15   Stack, Anna and Thomas Olney by Phillip Whitten, JP, Washington Co.

1804 Oct 11   Stacker, Abey and James Hall by John G. McCan, Ross Co.

1804 Sep 8   Stackhouse, Elizabeth and Jacob Hubbard by Thos. Scott, Ross Co.

1817 Jan 30   Stackhouse, Susanna and Hazle Butt by Elihu Bigelow, Licking Co.

1821 Jan 24   Stacy, Beulah and Jonas Mason by John Green, JP, Washington Co.

1808 Jun 1   Stacy, Joseph and Cynthia Perkins by Stephen Lindsly, Washington Co.

1812 Dec 29   Stacy, Joseph and Frances Williams by Rev. Stephen Lindley, Washington
               Co.

1819 Jun 8   Stacy, Mary and Elijah Boyce by Rev. Saml. P. Robbins, Washington Co.

1821 Aug 1   Stacy, Oliver and Orra Matoon by Russel Bigelow, MG, Franklin Co.

1809 Aug 28   Stacy, Samuel and Elizabeth Rice by Neh. Davis, MG, Washington Co.

1796 Apr 13   Stacy, Susanna and Joseph Fuller by Josiah Munro, Washington Co.

1790 Jul 29   Stacy, Wm. and Hannah Sheffield by Benj Tupper, Washington Co.

1816 Mar 21   Stadden, Margaret and Stephan Giffin by T.D. Baird, UDM, Licking Co.

1819 Jan 13   Stadden, Mary and Anson R. Thrall by T.D. Bierd, Licking Co.

1801 Jan 5   Staden, John and Elizabeth Green by Henry Smith, JP, Washington Co.

1811 Aug 27   Stage, Richard and Eliza Glaze (license date), Pickaway Co.

1820 Mar 7   Stagg, Anne and James Edgar by James Hoge, Franklin Co.

1820 Oct 26   Stagg, Harriet and John D. Windel by James Hoge, Franklin Co.

1828 Nov 27   Stagg, Jonah and Mariah Baldwin by Wm. Long, JP, Franklin Co.

1813 Apr 4   Stagg, Michael Jr. and Eunis Thadley by Jacob Tharp, Franklin Co.

1822 May 16   Stagg, Michael and Lydia Ogden by Jacob Smith, Franklin Co.

1828 Jan 24   Stagg, Thomas and M.A. Smith by S. Hamilton, Franklin Co.

1804 Apr 5   Staggs, Wm. and Betsy Clawson by Wm. Robinson, Ross Co.

1814 Oct 20   Stairwalt, Frederick and Rachael Ford by James Marshall, Franklin Co.

1824 Dec 23   Staley, Elizabeth and Martin Dickens by John Stealy, JP, Marion Co.

1810 Oct 2   Stall, Hugh and Mary Newhouse (license date), Pickaway Co.

1883 Mar 17   Stallman, Savannah and Wornick Bibee by Rev. John Boyd, St. Luke's
               Church, Marietta, Washington Co.

1808 Mar 12   Staltz, Daniel and Catherine Miers by John Hollister, JPHT, Licking Co.

1816 Jan 25   Stanbery, Phebe and R.R. Chapman by Recompence Stanbery, Franklin Co.

1825 Jul 6   Stancliff, Anna and Geo. Grant by Robert Ward, JP, Jackson Co.

1820 Jul 25   Stanley, Abigail and Ezekiel Deming by Danl. H. Buell, JP, Washington
               Co.

1870 Jun 26   Stanley, Clarence and Eliza Collins by Wm. Bower, St. Luke's Church,
               Granville, Licking Co.

1807 Dec 17   Stanley, Daniel G. and Rosella Putnam by S. Lindsly, Washington Co.

1820 Dec 28   Stanley, Elizabeth and Seldon Chapman by Joel Tuttle, Jr., JP,
               Washington Co.

1814 Dec 1   Stanley, Francis R. and Nancy Payne by Joseph Chapman, JP, Washington
               Co.

1813 Mar 25   Stanley, James and Urania Hill by Rev. Jas. Cunningham, Washington Co.

1813 Apr 4   Stanley, Lucy and Benjamin Blake by Rev. James Cunningham, Washington
               Co.

1810 May 15   Stanley, Nancy and John Brick by Stephen Lindsly, Washington Co.

1814 Mar 27   Stanley, Robert and Betsey Center by Wm. Creighton, JP, Pickaway Co.

1821 Apr 15   Stanley, Thirza and Lucius Cross by Rev. Saml. P. Robbins,
               Washington Co.

1816 Oct 31   Stanley, Thomas F. and Angelania Goldsmith by Rev. S.P. Robbins,
               Washington Co.

1818 Feb 19   Stanton, Emily and Hiram Fairchild by Pelatiah White, JP, Washington
               Co.

1810 11m 7   Stanton, Frederick and Hannah Suffrins, Miami Monthly Meeting, Warren
               Co.

1824 Nov 11   Stanton, George and Celia Butcher by Henry Matthews, Franklin Co.

1828 Apr 5   Stanton, Samuel and Sricky Thomas by Wm. T. Martin, Franklin Co.

1813 May 5   Stapleton, Eve and John Goodman (license date), Pickaway Co.

1820 Dec 25   Star, John and Mary Weas by Vincent Southard, JP, Jackson Co.

1818 Nov 5   Starks, David and Susanna Cannon by Cyrus Ames, Washington Co.

1820 Apr 13   Starlin, Betsey and Lynde Humiston by Rev. Abraham Lippet, Washington
               Co.

1812 Oct 9   Starlin, Deborah and John P. Deming by Nath'l Hamilton, JP, Washington
               Co.

1810 Oct 4   Starlin, John and Rachel Mason by Ephraim Matthews, JP, Washington Co.

1815 Nov 11   Starlin, John and Polly Sprague by Wm. Oliver, JP, Washington Co.

1814 Mar 20   Starlin, Marvel and Polly Smith by Isaac Baker, Esq., Washington Co.

1813 Apr 25   Starlin, Polly and Ilyna Danielson by Nath Hamilton, JP, Washington Co.

1805 Nov 24   Starlin, Samuel and Rebekah Woodard by Ephraim Mathews, Washington Co.

1822 Mar 10   Starling, Daniel and Eliza Grubb by Eli C. King, JP, Franklin Co.

1824 Jun 24   Starns, Elizabeth and Joseph Littlejohn by Jacob Gundy, JP, Franklin
               Co.

1822 Dec 10   Starr, Betsey and Aaron C. Humphrey by James Hoge, Franklin Co.

1821 Feb 22   Starr, Emely and Harvey Crosby by Jacob Drake, NDM, Franklin Co.

1814 Aug 18   Starr, Eunice and Joseph Hunter by James Hoge, Franklin Co.

1827 Sep 26   Starr, James M. and Mira Talley by James Hoge, Franklin Co.

1825? Feb 17   Starr, Jane and James Dean by James Hoge, Franklin Co.

1867 Sep 18   Starr, Mary E. and James W. Williams by Rev. John Boyd, St. Luke's
               Church, Marietta, Washington Co.

1813 Nov 7   Starten, William and Margaret Collins by N. Hamilton, Washington Co.

1818 Nov 20   Starts?, Elizabeth and Samuel Penrode? by Alex Holden, JP, Licking Co.

1813 Jan 13   State, Sarah and Andrew Scott by Jacob Tharp, Franklin Co.

1817 May 1   Statler, Peggy and Select Hoyt by John Johnson, JP, Licking Co.

1815 Jan 15   Statten, George and Harriet Daval by Z. Carlisle, Licking Co.

1816 Dec 19   Statz, Reuben and Catherine Kissingar by Percival Adams, JP, Franklin
               Co.

1895 Apr 25   St. Clair, Cora M. and Elmer J. West both of Cumberland, O., by Rev.
               George F. Moore, Putnam Presbyterian Church, Muskingum Co.

1805 May 22   Steadman, Alexander and Comfort Crepin by Joseph Strickland, Washing-
               ton Co.

1826 Aug 15   Steadman, Amelia and Jacob Bevelhymer by Absm Williams, JP, Franklin
               Co.

1808 Jan 4   Steadman, Bial and Mary Prescot Miles by S.P. Robbins, Washington Co.

1828 Aug 24   Steadman, Louisa and Mathias Teeg by J. Davis, JP, Franklin Co.

1825 Sep 21   Stealey, Catharine and Sam'l C. Straw (license date), Marion Co.

1805 11m 27   Steddom, Christiana and Joseph Comton, Miami Monthly Meeting, Warren
               Co.

1807 12m 3   Steddom, Mary and John Jay, Miami Monthly Meeting, Warren Co.

1815 11m 8   Steddom, Samuel and Susanna Teague, Miami Monthly Meeting, Warren Co.

1875 Jul --   Stedman, ----- and Mary Bryan by Mr. Nash, St. Luke's Church,
               Granville, Licking Co.

1809 Jan 1   Stedman, Nabby and Samuel Stone by D. Loring, Washington Co.

1810 Dec 20   Stedman, William and Samantha Rose by Rev. T. Harris, Licking Co.

1805 May 23   Steel, Robert and Mary Williamson by David Shelby, JP, Ross Co.

1821 Nov 7   Steel, Wm. and Margaret Lebody by Rev. Cornelius Springer, Washington
               Co.

1843 Nov 20   Steele, Mrs. Ellen J. and Dr. Spicer Patrick of Charleston, Va., by
               Rev. Edward Winthrop, St. Luke's Church, Marietta, Washington Co.

1813 Dec 30   Steeley, Elizabeth and Benjamin Davis (license date), Pickaway Co.

1811 Jun 28   Steeley, Sarah and Joseph Shelby (license date), Pickaway Co.

1824 Jul 13   Steen, Elizabeth and James Stewart (license date), Marion Co.

1824 Sep 7   Steen, Jane and Joseph Stewart (license date), Marion Co.

1818 Nov 3   Stennit, Elizabeth and Joshua Stokesbery by Geo. Callanhan, MG,
               Licking Co.

1826 Jan 10   Stephen, Calista and James Carson by John F. Solomon, Franklin Co.

1808 Apr 14   Stephens, Amirila and Nathaniel Chapman by Thos. Stanley, JP, Washing-
               ton Co.

1823 Jun 4   Stephens, Epraim and Rebeckah Cox by W.T. Martin, JP, Franklin Co.

1815 Jan 3   Stephens, Hanson and Mary Robinson by Stephen Guthrie, Washington Co.

1817 Dec 25   Stephens, Harriet and James Norman by Solomon N. Cook, JP, Washington
               Co.

1810 Oct 26   Stephens, Josephus and Amelia (belonging to Isaac Williams) by John
               Brough, JP, Washington Co.

1811 Dec 25   Stephens, Justus and Jane Carpenter by Rev. T. Harris, Licking Co.

1879 Sep 17   Stephens, Mary and William M. Goodloe by Rev. John Boyd, St. Luke's
               Church, Marietta, Washington Co.

1818 Sep 10   Stephens, Nathan and Betsey Miner by Wm. Rand, Washington Co.

1820 Jun 8   Stephens, Peter and Hannah Stephenson by John Tevis, Franklin Co.

1817 Oct 13   Stephens, Polly and John Edwards by Abner Goff, MG, Licking Co.

1805 Jun 27   Stephens, Pricilla and Robert Donough by Wm. Creighton, Ross Co.

1806 Jul 14   Stephens, Sally and Joseph Williams by Jacob Lindly, Washington Co.

1817 Feb 19   Stephens, Sally and Daniel Roach by John Green, JP, Washington Co.

1818 Jul 26   Stephenson, Alexander and Nancy Jenkins by Isaac Baker, JP, Jackson Co.

1819 Apr 13   Stephenson, Alex. and Rhoda Hale by James Stephenson, JP, Jackson Co.

1822 Jun 10   Stephenson, Elenor and Joseph Scurlock by Samuel Carrick, JP, Jackson
               Co.

1820 Jun 8   Stephenson, Hannah and Peter Stephens by John Tevis, Franklin Co.

1826 Jan 12   Stephenson, Jame and Arthur McClure by John Shumate, JP, Jackson Co.

1825 May 26   Stephenson, John S. and Mary Shumate by John Stephenson, JP, Jackson
               Co.

1818 Aug --   Stephenson, Joseph and Elizabeth Bowen by D. Mitchell, JP, Jackson Co.

1826 May 16   Stephenson, Joshua E. and Milly Nally by Thos. Daugherty, JP, Jackson
               Co.

1825 Mar 8   Stephenson, Mary and John Patterson by Joseph Carper, Franklin Co.

1813 Feb 4   Stephenson, Rachael and Philip Hooper by John Stephenson, JP, Franklin
               Co.

1824 Jan 15   Stephenson, Samuel and Martha McClure by John Shumate, JP, Jackson Co.

1826 Mar 30   Stephenson, Smith and Mary Varyann by J.B. Gilliland, JP, Jackson Co.

1825 Feb 8   Stephenson, Wm. and Milley Hale by Jacob Miller, JP, Jackson Co.

1823 Jan 21   Sterrit, Mary and George Ridenour by C. Henkel, Franklin Co.

1816 Feb 29   Stetton, John and Phebe Moses by Daniel Poppleston, Licking Co.

1801 May 2   Stevart, Samuel S. and Jane Coldwell by Philip Witten, Washington Co.

1890 Nov 19   Stevens, Adelaid Wheeler and Charles Albert Potwin both of Zanesville
               by Rev. George F.Moore, Putnam Presbyterian Church, Muskingum Co.

1801 Mar 24   Stevens, Ann and John Shaw by Jno. Struthers, JP, Trumbull Co.

1803 Mar 17   Stevens, David and Elenor Bentley by Wm. Burnham, JP, Washington Co.

1803 Mar 17   Stevens, Delilah and John Perry by Wm. Burnham, JP, Washington Co.

1811 Jan 17   Stevens, Ebenezer and Sally Grooms by Massey Clymer, Franklin Co.

1814 Mar 17   Stevens, Hanry and Alois Maynard by Daniel Hess, Franklin Co.

1814 Mar 20   Stevens, Nancy and James Davis by Simeon Deming, JP, Washington Co.

1815 Jan 19   Stevenson, George and Mary Powell by Richd. Suddick,JP, Franklin Co.

1815 Jan 18   Stevenson, John and Barbara Ballard by Wm. Florence, JP, Pickaway Co.

1826 Nov 20   Stevenson, Joshua and Rebecca Hooper by Wm. Patterson, Franklin Co.

1829 Jan 15   Stevenson, Joshua and Mrs. Ann Hopkins by Leroy Swornstead, Franklin
               Co.

1815 Feb 2   Stevenson, Polly and James Knight by Henry Coonrod, JP, Pickaway Co.

1823 Jun 27   Stevenson, Rebecca and George W. Colb by Richard Courtright, Franklin
               Co.

1807 Jun 23   Stevenson, Richard and Rhoda Peterson by Massay Clymer, Franklin Co.

1821 2m 7   Stevenson, Samuel and Hepsabah Evans, Miami Monthly Meeting, Warren Co.

1812 Jul 27   Stevenson, Zachariah and Polly Glaze (license date), Pickaway Co.

1812 Apr 3   Stewalt, William and Susan Hickman by James Marshall, Franklin Co.

1816 Jan 4   Steward, Mary and Peter Beman by Noah Fidler, Licking Co.

1867 Feb 26   Stewart, Andrew and Sarah Emery by Rev. A. Kingsbury, Putnam Presby-
               terian Church, Muskingum Co.

1817 Dec 26   Stewart, Colbert and Elizabeth Early by Townsend Nichols, JP, Franklin
               Co.

1801 May 28   Stewart, Falander B. and Sarah Scott by Philip Witten, JP, Washington
               Co.

1824 Jul 13   Stewart, James and Elizabeth Steen (license date), Marion Co.

1818 Dec 30   Stewart, John and Margaret Stewart by T.D. Baird, Licking Co.

1805 May 23   Stewart, Jno. and Elizabeth Kinkead by Wm. Davis, JP, Ross Co.

1824 Sep 7   Stewart, Joseph and Jane Steen (license date), Marion Co.

1815 Oct 14   Stewart, Lydia and Joseph Jamison by James Hoge, LDM, Franklin Co.

1812 Aug 18   Stewart, Margaret and Moses Brown (license date), Pickaway Co.

1818 Dec 30   Stewart, Margaret and John Stewart by T.D. Baird, Licking Co.

1819 Apr 21   Stewart, Mary and Robert C. Henderson by James Hoge, Franklin Co.

1816 May 30   Stewart, Rebecka and Archibald Benfield by Joseph L. Hughs, Franklin
               Co.

1811 Mar 12   Stewart, William and Elizabeth Fisher by James Hoge, Franklin Co.

1824 Apr 1   Stiarwalt, Rachel and David Dearduff by Jacob Grubb, Franklin Co.

1820 Aug 28   Stickley, Elizabeth and David Hite by Noah Fidler, Licking Co.

1876 May 11   Stickney, Irene of Cincinnati and George Haver of Putnam by Rev. A.
               Kingsbury, Putnam Presbyterian Church, Muskingum Co.

1837 Oct 25   Stiles, S.C. and Cicero Comstock by Rev. E. Burr, St. John's Church,
               Worthington, Franklin Co.

1800 Feb 6   Still, Ebenezer and Mary Still by Robert Oliver, JP, Washington Co.

1804 Sep 27   Still, Elizabeth and Simon Porter by Dudley Davis, Washington Co.

1800 Feb 6   Still, Mary and Ebenezer Still by Robert Oliver, JP, Washington Co.

1806 Jun 9   Still, Olivel and Axey Cowgill by Ezekiel Brown, JP, Franklin Co.

1828 Feb 17   Still, Oliver and Ann Baker by Wm. Dalzell, Franklin Co.

1819 Oct 19   Stillson, Cynthia and Zedekiah Crandol by James M. Booth, JP, Washing-
               ton Co.

1822 Jan 6   Stimell, Daniel and Rachael Shafe (or Shofe) by John F. Solomon,
               Franklin Co.

1811 Apr 15   Stimets, Nelly and Edward Hatfield by W. Haines, JP, Licking Co.

1826 Aug 31   Stimmel, Daniel and Polly Lantis by C. Henkel, Franklin Co.

1817 Jun 24   Stimmel, Jacob and Mary Lantis by Percival Adams, Franklin Co.

1824 Jan 29   Stimmel, Mary Ann and Abraham Shofe by C. Henkel, Franklin Co.

1817 Apr 3   Stimmel, Peter and Elizabeth Landis by Percival Adams, Franklin Co.

1862 Oct 28   Stimson, Rodney M. and Julia Sheppard by Rev. John Boyd, St. Luke's
               Church, Marietta, Washington Co.

1825 Feb 6   Stinor, Margaret and Wm. Bowen by J.B. Gilliland, JP, Jackson Co.

1805 Jan 8   Stinson, Elizabeth and William Graves by Robert Adams, Ross Co.

1855 Jan 25   Stitt, Martha and Henry Bate by Rev. John Boyd, St. Luke's Church,
               Marietta, Washington Co.

1803 Jun 2   Stockey, Abraham and Eva Bush by Jos. Gardner, JP, Ross Co.

1816 Jan 17   Stockham, Anne and John Bennett by D. Mitchell, JP Lick Tp, Jackson Co.

1857 Oct 8   Stockton, Wm. K. and Mary Jane Miller by Rev. Geo. B. Sturges, St.
               Paul's Church, Marion, Marion Co.

1799 Jul 3   Stokely, David and Abigal Hulbert by Robert Oliver, Washington Co.

1806 Jun 21   Stokes, Habsebas and Daniel Garwood by David Mitchell, Franklin Co.

1810 Jun 13   Stokes, Nithie and Thomas Wollington (license date), Pickaway Co.

1804 Apr 5   Stokes, Susannah and John Brickel by James Marshall, JP, Franklin Co.

1818 Nov 3   Stokesbery, Joshua and Elizabeth Stennit by Geo. Callanhan, MG,
               Licking Co.

1813 Feb 21   Stone, Benjamin F. and Hannah Cartwright by Rev. S.P. Robbins,
               Washington Co.

1810 Mar 1   Stone, Benj J. and Rosanna Devol by Stephen Lindsly, Washington Co.

1820 Feb 9   Stone, Eliz and Jeremiah Channel by Rev. Noah Fidler, Licking Co.

1796 Jul 21   Stone, Elizabeth and Freeman Guthrie by J. Gilman, Washington Co.

1820 Feb 1   Stone, Elizabeth and John A. Scoppe by -----, Licking Co.

1821 May 1   Stone, George and Prudence Channel by Noah Fidler, Licking Co.

1799 Mar 17   Stone, Grace and Luther Dana by Peregrine Foster, JCCCP, Washington Co..

1796 Aug 20   Stone, Israel and Mary Corner by J. Gilman, Washington Co.

1802 Oct 4   Stone, James and Ruth Ashcraft by Wm. Burnham, JP, Washington Co.

1810 Jan 14   Stone, James and Mary Ashcroft by Wm. Nixon, JP, Washington Co.

1826 Mar 26   Stone, James and Ruth Cunningham by Geo. Callanhan, EMEC, Licking Co.

1801 Oct 11   Stone, Jasper and Polly Lucens by Nehemiah Davis, Washington Co.

1819 Sep 26   Stone, John and Charlotte P. Loring by Cyrus Ames, JP, Washington Co.

1868 Jul 30   Stone, Julia A. and John Hudson by I.B. Britton, St. Paul's Church,
               Marion, Marion Co.

1803 Dec 4   Stone, Lydia and Ezra Hoyt by Stephen Lindley, Washington Co.

1865 Aug 10   Stone, Margaret and Harry J. Campbell by Rev. John Boyd, St. Luke's
               Church, Marietta, Washington Co.

1817 May 11   Stone, Melissa W. and Joseph Backer, Jr. by Rev. S.P. Robbins,
               Washington Co.

1801 Apr 13   Stone, Noyes and Peggy Hanson by Daniel Story, Washington Co.

1814 Jan 2   Stone, Rufus P. and Eliza Barker by Peter Howe, JP, Washington Co.

1809 Jan 1   Stone, Samuel and Nabby Stedman by D. Loring, Washington Co.

1796 Dec 6   Stone, Sardine and Polly Smith by D. Loring, Jus. CP, Washington Co.

1821 Sep 2   Stone, Susan and Jarvis Burroughs by Rev. Saml. P. Robbins, Washing-
               ton Co.

1815 Sep 23   Stonemia, Sally and Pompey King by J. Cunningham, Licking Co.

1813 Jan 14   Stonerock, George and Margaret Lewis (license date), Pickaway Co.

1805 Mar 1   Stonerock, William and Rebecca Jones by Samuel Smith, Ross Co.

1812 Oct 26   Story, Mary and Theophilus H. Powers by E. Cogswell, JP, Washington
               Co.

1820 Nov 2   Story, Michael and Hetty Morris by Rev. Saml. P. Robbins, Washington
               Co.

1818 Apr 22   Stotts, Abraham and Polly Hoffman by Joseph Grate, Franklin Co.

1814 Sep 4   Stotts, Catherine and Jacob Comb by Wm. Taylor, Licking Co.

1814 Apr 12   Stotts, Daniel and Mary Hunter by Wm. Taylor, Licking Co.

1813 Jul 9   Stotts, Jacob and Elizabeth Hunter by W. Taylor, Licking Co.

1826 Sep 7   Stotts, Malinda and Nocholas Kisner by C. Hinkel, Franklin Co.

1826 Feb 23   Stotts, Margaret and John Lowery by C. Hinkel, Franklin Co.

1851 Jul 29   Stout, Martha P. and Edward T. Hull by Rev. Geo. B. Sturges, St.
               Paul's Church, Marion, Marion Co.

1819 Mar 21   Stover, Barbara and Abraham B----? by Noah Fidler, Licking Co.

1819 Jul 1   Stover, Elizabeth and Jacob Wilkins by Noah Fidler, Licking Co.

1820 Jul 29   Stover, Polly and Joseph Grove by Noah Fidler, Licking Co.

1868 Apr 5   Strachan, William and Martha Pixley by Rev. John Boyd, St. Luke's
               Church, Marietta, Washington Co.

1818 Nov 29   Strader, Elizabeth and Lewis Johnston by James Hoge, Franklin Co.

1822 Feb 21   Straight, Ambresy C. and Sarah Devenport by Jacob Smith, Franklin Co.

1818 Feb 2   Straight, Elizabeth and Abraham Smith by Jacob Smith, JP, Franklin Co.

1813 Dec 26   Straight, John and Sally Phelps by Eli Steadman, Washington Co.

1816 Mar 31   Straight, Sally and Richard Hill by Rev. Saml P. Robbins, Washington
               Co.

1824 Apr 29   Strain, Angelina and Benjamin Merriss by Uriah Clark, Franklin Co.

1812 Mar 7   Strain, John M. and Peggy Riddle by James Hoge, Franklin Co.

1821 Mar 10   Strain, John M. and Elizabeth Bessey by James Hoge, Franklin Co.

1854 Sep 2   Strain, Rachel and John Wagh of Newport by Rev. John Boyd, St. Luke's
               Church, Marietta, Washington Co.

1805 Feb 7   Strain, Sarah and John J. Finley by John Davidson, Ross Co.

1800 Nov 11   Strait, Aaron and Elizabeth Rasor by Samuel Williamson, Washington Co.

1881 Dec 29   Strait, Jacob N. and Carrie J. Worstall both of Zanesville by Rev.
               George F. Moore, Putnam Presbyterian Church, Muskingum Co.

1897 Jul 18   Straley, James of Lancaster, O., and Mrs. Solo. O. Dilles of Zanes-
               ville by Rev. George F. Moore, Putnam Presbyterian Church,
               Muskingum Co.

1825 Jul 20   Stranahan, Isabella and Joseph Barker by W.C. Duff, JP, Franklin Co.

1819 Dec 23   Stranahan, William and Margaret Brown by James Hoge, Franklin Co.

1826 Mar 1   Strand, Wm. and Christina Long by Zeph Brown, JP, Jackson Co.

1812 Apr 30   Strate, Mrs. Jemime and John Dague by Jacob Tharp, Franklin Co.

1811 9m 5   Stratton, Joel and Rebekah Rea, Miami Monthly Meeting, Warren Co.

1825 Mar 3   Straub, Andrew and Pricella Crawford by Thos. Rodgers, JP, Marion Co.

1815 Aug 1   Strause, Adam and Nancy Beach by Michael Patton, JP, Franklin Co.

1824 Jan 8   Strausse, Henry (son of John) and Farnee Nelson by Sam'l Carrick, JP,
               Jackson Co.

1825 Sep 18   Strausse, Isaac and Nancy Nelson by J.B. Gilliland, JP, Jackson Co.

1825 Jun 24   Straw, Ann and William McFarland (or McParland) by Brice Hays, JP,
               Franklin Co.

1822 Mar 18   Straw, Daniel and Patsey Bennett by Reuben Carpenter, Franklin Co.

1818 Jul 23   Straw, George and Sally Floyd by Michael Patton, Franklin Co.

1825 Oct 25   Straw, Sally and Samuel Logue by R.W. Cowles, JP, Franklin Co.

1825 Sep 21   Straw, Sam'l C. and Catharine Stealey (license date), Marion Co.

1805 11m 21   Strawn, Anna and Henry Milhouse, Miami Monthly Meeting, Warren Co.

1815 May 9   Strawn, Thomas and Sally Parkinson by J.H. Patterson, JP, Licking Co.

1803 Dec 13   Streng, Barbery and Daniel Grubb by John G. McCan, Ross Co.

1806 Feb 20   Strevy, Petery and Tibitha Thomas by Theorge Vinsonhalen, Ross Co.

1828 Jan 27   Strickland, Moses and Nancy Blodgett by Wm. Dalzell, JP, Franklin Co.

1824 Aug 29   Strickland, Moses H. and Lovisa Manning by John Hawkens, JP, Franklin
               Co.

1826 Aug --   Strickley, William and Elizabeth Cornett by I. Gander, Franklin Co.

---- --- --   Strong, Aurelia and John Stump by Rev. Wm. Preston, St. John's Church,
               Worthington, Franklin Co.

1865 Sep 13   Strong, Edward P. and Mary C. Guthrie by Rev. A. Kingsbury, Putnam
               Presbyterian Church, Muskingum Co.

1827 Dec 23   Strong, L.C. and Mahala Andress by H. Hubbert, PC, Franklin Co.

1823 Apr 17   Strong, Maria and Benjamin F. Willey by Nathan Emery, JP, Franklin Co.

1816 Dec 19   Strong, Rachel Ann and Charles Hoover by J.W. Patterson, JW, Licking
               Co.

1826 Apr 6   Stroud, Lydia and Garshum Phillips by Wm. Ayers, JP, Jackson Co.

1798 Aug 14   Stroud, Rebecca and Francis Whitmore by D. Loring, Jus.Com Pleas,
               Washington Co.

1798 Feb 6   Stroud, William and Mary Lindsey by Peregrine Foster, Washington Co.

1815 Apr 16   Strouse, Catherine and Jacob Morris by James Jackson, Pickaway Co.

1813 Sep 2   Strouse, Phillip and Deborea Grun (license date), Pickaway Co.

1812 Dec 27   Strouse, Polly and Phillip Smith (license date), Pickaway Co.

1810 Nov 12   Strouser, Christina and Anthony Bauder (license date), Pickaway Co.

1803 Mar 31   Strouss, Mich'l and Mary Walker by Oliver Ross, Ross Co.

1808 2m 17   Stubbs, Esther and John Newlin, Miami Monthly Meeting, Warren Co.

1822 7m 4   Stubbs, Hannah and Jacob Doan, Miami Monthly Meeting, Warren Co.

1812 Jun 24   Stubbs, Hester and Charles Allison by John Greene, JP, Washington Co.

1816 Aug 18   Stull, Anna and Marvel Davis by Obadiah Scott, JP, Washington Co.

1820 May 18   Stull, Catharine and Seneca Clark by John Patterson, Washington Co.

1828 May 29   Stuls, Jacob and Nancy Smith by J. Davis, JP, Franklin Co.

1828 Aug 28   Stults, Elizabeth and James Hudson by John Long, JP, Franklin Co.

1814 Jul 25   Stultz, Henry and Rachael Hanshaw by Abm Christ, JP, Pickaway Co.

1817 Mar 18   Stultz, Polly and William Watson by Wm. O'Bannon, JP, Licking Co.

1824 Mar 2   Stumbaugh, John and Susan Sidney by James Hoge, Franklin Co.

1823 Feb 13   Stumbaugh, Margret and David Mooberry by James Hoge, Franklin Co.

1826 Apr 11   Stumbaugh, Mary and John Shannon by James Hoge, Franklin Co.

1819 Feb 14   Stump, Cassandra and Daniel Dennis by Thos. White, Washington Co.

1811 Mar 31   Stump, David and Susanah Adi by Z. Carlisle, JPHT, Licking Co.

1813 Dec 21   Stump, Elizabeth and Nubal Moore (license date), Pickaway Co.

1814 Jul 17   Stump, Joanna and John R. Porter by Thos. White, Esq., Washington Co.

---- --- --   Stump, John and Aurelia Strong by Rev. Wm. Preston, St. John's Church,
               Worthington, Franklin Co.

1816 Apr 9   Stump, Mary and John Lawson by Thomas White, JP, Washington Co.

1810 Apr 22   Stump, Nancy and Joseph Smith by J. Greenman, JP, Washington Co.

1815 Apr 14   Stump, Sarah and Christian Mathews by Joseph Thrap, JP, Licking Co.

1854 Jun 5   Sturges, Amanda B. and John H. Bond by Rev. A. Kingsbury, Putnam
               Presbyterian Church, Muskingum Co.

1862 Oct 16   Sturges, George of Chicago, Ill., and Mary Delafield of Duncan Falls,
               O., by Rev. A. Kingsbury, Putnam Presbyterian Church, Muskingum
               Co.

1854 Jun 6   Sturges, Hezekiah and Amelia Belknap by Rev. A. Kingsbury, Putnam
               Presbyterian Church, Muskingum Co.

1853 May 5   Sturges, Lucy H. and Ebenezer Buckingham by Rev. A. Kingsbury, Putnam
               Presbyterian Church, Muskingum Co.

1844 Jun 20   Sturges, Mary of Putnam and Chester Wells of Hanover by Rev. A.
               Kingsbury, Putnam Presbyterian Church, Muskingum Co.

1848 Aug 8   Sturges, Sarah and Charles W. Potwin by Rev. A. Kingsbury, Putnam
               Presbyterian Church, Muskingum Co.

1847 Mar 23   Sturges, William and Caroline A. Potwin by Rev. A. Kingsbury, Putnam
               Presbyterian Church, Muskingum Co.

1853 Oct 4   Sturgess, James D. of Duncan's Falls and Rebecca N. Cram by Rev. John
               Boyd, St. Luke's Church, Marietta, Washington Co.

1850 May 14   Sturgess, Shelton of Duncan's Falls and Frances R. Nye by Rev. D.W.
               Tolford, St. Luke's Church, Marietta, Washington Co.

1805 Jul 18   Stuthard, Betsey and Phielden Hubbard by Thos. Hicks, Ross Co.

1813 Mar 8   Suber, Abner and Sarah Parker by Isaac Baker, Washington Co.

1813 Mar 22   Suddith, Lucinda and Jonathan Renick (license date), Pickaway Co.

1810 11m 7   Suffrins, Hannah and Frederick Stanton, Miami Monthly Meeting,
               Warren Co.

1820 Mar 26   Suiter, William and H. Watsbaugh by Noah Fidler, Licking Co.

1817 Mar 2   Suitor, Jane and William Thompson by Francis Holland, JP Scioto Tp,
               Jackson Co.

1817 Mar 7   Suitor, Sarah and Joseph Thompson by Francis Holland, JP Scioto Tp,
               Jackson Co.

1804 Feb 13   Sull, Thomas and Nancy Abel by Samuel Smith, Ross Co.

1812 Sep 8   Sullivan, Charles and Clarissa Devol by Jeremiah Greenman, JP,
               Washington Co.

1840 Jul 23   Sullivan, Emma and Wyllys Hall by Rev. James Bonnar, St. Luke's
               Church, Marietta, Washington Co.

1855 May 15   Sullivan, Eveline A. and D.G. Mathews by Rev. John Boyd, St. Luke's
               Church, Marietta, Washington Co.

1879 Jan 4   Sullivan, Theodore G. of Providence, R.I. and Lizzie M. Cox of Zanes-
               ville by Rev. George F. Moore, Putnam Presbyterian Church,
               Muskingum Co.

1824 Apr 7   Sullivant, William S. and Jane Marshall by Jacob Grubb, Franklin Co.

1828 Sep 13   Sulsor, Catharine and Selah Parker by Geo. Jefferies, Franklin Co.

1819 May 13   Summers, Elizabeth and Thomas Groves by Andrew Dill, JP, Franklin Co.

1881 Feb 16   Summerville, Nellie and Philander Sims by Rev. John Boyd, St. Luke's
               Church, Marietta, Washington Co.

1819 Nov 16   Sunard, Abiah and Mathew Wistervilt by Reuben Carpenter, JP,
               Franklin Co.

1814 Apr 7   Surgart, John and Eliza White by Henry Coonrod, JP, Pickaway Co.

1815 Feb 15   Sustemme, Catherine and Elisha Banham by Isaiah Wilkinson, Licking Co.

1818 Jul 21   Sutherd, Eliza and Levi Chapman by John Johnston, JP, Licking Co.

1817 Sep 3   Sutherds, John and Hannah Lyons by Townsend Nichols, Franklin Co.

1815 Jan 17   Sutherland, Sarah and Math. Smith by Rev. Sam'l Wilson, Pickaway Co.

1885 May 13   Sutphen, John A. and Campsiadell H. Inskeep both of Zanesville by Rev.
              George F. Moore, Putnam Presbyterian Church, Muskingum Co.

1828 Sep 11   Suttle, William and Annah Groom by Wm. Stirewalt, JP, Franklin Co.

1817 Oct 19   Sutton, Amaniah and Drusilla Hughes by Amos Wilson, Washington Co.

1812 Jan 2   Sutton, Betsey and James Evens by Amos Porter, JP, Washington Co.

1814 Oct 27   Sutton, Mary and George Clarke by Wm. Taylor, Licking Co.

1818 Nov 22   Sutton, Mary and William Porter by Dudley Davis, Washington Co.

1814 Jan 27   Sutton, Moses and Sarah Chenoweth by J.W. Patterson, JP, Licking Co.

1811 Feb 11   Sutton, Rachel and Thomas Harris by Wm. Taylor, JP, Licking Co.

1821 Nov 15   Sutton, Rhoda and Thomas Porter by John True, JP, Washington Co.

1796 Dec 29   Sutton, Robert and Elisabeth Cline by J. Munro, Washington Co.

1812 Dec 10   Sutton, Sally and Amos Porter by Wm. Miller, JP, Washington Co.

1818 Nov 26   Sutton, William and Statua Hartshorn by Dudley Davis, Washington Co.

1871 Jul 24   Swadley, Thomas and Joanna Linnett by Rev. John Boyd, St. Luke's
              Church, Marietta, Washington Co.

1822 Jan 9   Swain, John and Marthy Marsh by Uriah Clark, Franklin Co.

1820 Apr 6   Swain, Matthias and Betsy Riddell by Michael Patton, JP, Franklin Co.

1819 Oct 14   Swan, Gustavus and Amelia Weston by James Hoge, Franklin Co.

1838 Sep 25   Swan, Lewis and Magdalen Adams, St. Luke's Church, Granville, Licking
              Co.

1823 Dec 16   Swan, Martha and John Beard by Charles Waddle, Franklin Co.

1838 Jul 26   Swan, Samuel and Alvina Jones, St. Luke's Church, Granville, Licking
              Co.

1812 Jun 28   Swank, Isaac and Sarah Madden (license date), Pickaway Co.

1802 Nov 11   Swank, Pamelia and Edward Bethel by Robert Oliver, JP, Washington Co.

1811 Aug 29   Swank, Peter and Nancy McMahon (license date), Pickaway Co.

1813 Apr 26   Swank, Rachel and Vetchel Howard (license date), Pickaway Co.

1813 May 5   Swank, Richard and Mary Frickle (license date), Pickaway Co.

1814 Jan 12   Swank, William and Polly Lloyd by Wm. Florence, JP, Pickaway Co.

1815 May 11   Swardon, Sarah and William Swardon by James Taylor, Franklin Co.

1815 May 11   Swardon, William and Sarah Swardon by James Taylor, Franklin Co.

1806 Dec 14   Swearingame, Phoebe and William French by Luther Dana, Washington Co.

1827 Dec 23   Sweet, Sullivant and Rhoda Harris by Sam'l Hamilton, Elder in the
              M.E. Church, Franklin Co.

1797 Mar 23   Swett, Keziah and Daniel Dunham by Josiah Munro, Washington Co.

1827 Nov 12   Swickard, John and Elizabeth Baughman by A. Allison, JP, Franklin Co.

1824 Jan 1   Swickard, Jonathan and Sally Baughman by C. Henkel, Franklin Co.

1822 Jun 11   Swickerd, Andrew and Sally Dage by John Davis, Franklin Co.

1820 Dec 14   Swift, Phebe and Isaac Ross, Jr. by Thomas White, JP, Washington Co.

1825 Apr 12   Swift, Servier (widow) and Merideth Parish, Sr. (widower) by Jacob
               Gundy, JP, Franklin Co.

1806 Jul 31   Swinerton, James and Lucinda Carpenter by Josiah McKinnie, Franklin
               Co.

1826 Aug 2   Swing (or Young), Rebecca and Edward Simmons by Jacob Delay, LM,
               Jackson Co.

1818 Oct 13   Swisgood, John and Ann Hoover by Jacob Keller, Franklin Co.

1826 Sep 14   Swisher, Fanny and Absalom Petters by James Petters, MG, Franklin Co.

1814 Jul 28   Swisher, Hannah and Alexander Frazer by Rev. Phillip Clurry, Pickaway
               Co.

1828 Mar 4   Swisher, Jacob and Elaza Scotharn by John Long, JP, Franklin Co.

1828 Jan 13   Swisher, Sarah and John Beam by Abraham Williams, JP, Franklin Co.

1813 May 26   Switzer, Metehany and John Tesler by Samuel Pogue, Licking Co.

1817 Apr 9   Sworden, Elizabeth and William Purdey by James Taylor, Franklin Co.

1820 Mar 26   Sylvester, Charles and Rhoda Bodwell by James M. Booth, JP, Washington
               Co.

1827 Dec 18   Sylvester, W.B. and Irona Carr by Hugh Liams, Franklin Co.

1818 Apr 2   Taggart, Jonathan and Elizabeth Moodey by Noah Fidler, Licking Co.

1815 Jan 1   Talbot, Michel and Benjamin James by Anth'y Sheets, JP, Washington Co.

1819 Aug 8   Talbot, William and Jemima Smith by James M. Booth, JP, Washington Co.

1821 Oct 2   Tall, William and Sarah Ann Decker by John Shields, MG, Franklin Co.

1795 Apr 23   Tallage, Jean Baptiste Nicholas and Catherine Worth by J. Gilman,
               Washington Co.

1827 Sep 26   Talley, Mira and James M. Starr by James Hoge, Franklin Co.

1794 Feb 1   Talliur, John Baptiste C. and Marie Francois-Charlotte Le Roi by
               J.G. Petitt, Washington Co.

1811 Mar 2   Tanner, Elizabeth and John Henry by Z. Carlisle, JPHT, Licking Co.

1823 Jun 9   Tappan, Benjamin and Betsey Frazer by James Hoge, Franklin Co.

1821 Jan 1   Tarvey, Wm. and Margaret Shannon by James Cunningham, VD, Licking Co.

1806 --- --   Tate, Robert and Jane Harper by John Robins, Ross Co.

1818 Nov 9   Taylor, Abiathar N. and Margaret Cowden by James Hoge, Franklin Co.

1820 Feb 12   Taylor, Amanda and Daniel Roice by A. Buttles, JP, Franklin Co.

1821 Mar 8   Taylor, Amanda M. and Thos. J.Y. Hart by T. Lee, Franklin Co.

1816 Dec 5   Taylor, Anna and Edmund Perry by P. White, Washington Co.

1877 Mar 8   Taylor, Mrs. Augusta A. and Edward A. Farquhar, M.D., by Rev. A.
              Kingsbury, Putnam Presbyterian Church, Muskingum Co.

1815 Jul 26   Taylor, Catharine and Mathew Miner by Rev. S.P. Robbins, Washington Co.

1816 Oct 16   Taylor, Christina and Tracy Wilcox by E. Griswold, Franklin Co.

1817 Nov 13   Taylor, Cynthia and James Gill by Noah Fidler, Licking Co.

1819 Apr 15   Taylor, David and Margarette (or Peggy) Ross by Mathew Taylor
              (another entry 15 June 1819), Franklin Co.

1826 Sep 28   Taylor, David and Nancy Nelson by James Hoge, Franklin Co.

1821 Nov 25   Taylor, Ebenezer S. and Phebe Tuttle by Joel Tuttle, Jr., JP,
              Washington Co.

---- --- --   Taylor, Elizabeth and John Falkner by James Hoge, Franklin Co.

1817 Apr 9   Taylor, Elizabeth and Charles Wood by James Taylor, Franklin Co.

1817 Jul 20   Taylor, Elizabeth M. and Edward M. Elsey by James Hoge, Franklin Co.

1820 Feb 23   Taylor, Ellin and John Flowers by Wm. Woodford, Washington Co.

1819 Nov 14   Taylor, Frances and Orlands Fuller by James Hoge, Franklin Co.

1805 Jul 25   Taylor, George and Mary Thomas by Peter Jackson, JP, Ross Co.

1809 Sep 6   Taylor, Jacob and Tena Mathan (Mathew) by David Mitchell, Franklin Co.

1806 Jan 23   Taylor, James and Susannah Cating by John Odle, JP, Ross Co.

1810 Feb 22   Taylor, James and Margaret Black by Rev. Geo. Vanaman, Licking Co.

1813 Sep 29   Taylor, James and Margaret Breckenridge by Jas. Hauge, Franklin Co.

1815 Jul 11   Taylor, James and Rebecca Cully by Nathan Cunningham, Licking Co.

1816 Feb 25   Taylor, James and Elizabeth Gibbs by David Stevens, Washington Co.

1824 Apr 29   Taylor, James W. and Martha Graham by John Donaldson, Franklin Co.

1808 May 12   Taylor, Jane and John Miller by Stephen Lindly, Washington Co.

1820 Jan 15   Taylor, Jane and Samuel Crossett by Matthew Taylor, Franklin Co.

1822 Aug 13   Taylor, Jane and Milton Thompson by Rev. James Hoge, Franklin Co.

1813 Jun 1   Taylor, Jasper and Elizabeth Hill by Rev. Stephen Lindsley, Washington
              Co.

1808 Feb 24   Taylor, Jinney and Moses Mitchell by David Mitchell, Franklin Co.

1805 Jul 25   Taylor, John and Elizabeth McCullough by David Mitchell, JP,
              Franklin Co.

1806 May 10   Taylor, John and Mary Harrison by J. Brough, JP, Washington Co.

1806 Nov 13   Taylor, John and Mahitabel Pell by Simeon Pool, Washington Co.

1819 Mar 25   Taylor, John and Mary Kipple by Dudley Davis, Washington Co.

1822 Mar 19   Taylor, John and Maryan Derrick by B. Bull, Franklin Co.

1818 Jun 10   Taylor, Joseph and Prudence Hull by Alex Holden, JP, Licking Co.

1816 Oct 24   Taylor, Lidia and Mathew Taylor by Richard Suddick, JP, Franklin Co.

1806 Oct 25   Taylor, Lois and George Miller by Rob't Oliver, JP, Washington Co.

1814 Jun 22   Taylor, Margaret and Mathew Long by James Hoge, Franklin Co.

1807 Apr 16   Taylor, Maria and Benjamin Gitteau by Samuel P. Robbins, Washington Co.

1817 Sep 30   Taylor, Mary and James Mahollum by Noah Fidler, Licking Co.

1824 4m 8   Taylor, Mary and Ezekiel L. Cleaver, Miami Monthly Meeting, Warren Co.

1824 Nov 30   Taylor, Mary and David Nelson by James Hoge, Franklin Co.

1811 Sep 19   Taylor, Mary B. and James Gates by Jeremiah Dare, Washington Co.

1816 Oct 24   Taylor, Mathew and Lidia Taylor by Richard Suddick, JP, Franklin Co.

1811 Apr 22   Taylor, Matthew and Lydia Wilson (license date), Pickaway Co.

1824 Oct 9   Taylor, Mirandor and Benjamin Bell by T. Lee, JP, Franklin Co.

1809 Nov 15   Taylor, Nancy and Matthew Black by Rev. Timothy Harris, Licking Co.

1815 Sep 6   Taylor, Peter and Margaret Ashcroft by Stephen Lindsley, MG, Washington Co.

1804 Mar 29   Taylor, Rebecca and Robert Dunlap by Noble Crawford, Ross Co.

1820 Jan 13   Taylor, Rudalphus and Rebecca Fethengale by Richard Courtright, Franklin Co.

1816 Sep 24   Taylor, Sally and Daniel Penny by B.W. Talbot, JP, Washington Co.

1815 Mar 30   Taylor, Sarah and Christopher Gramer by Frederick Peterson, JP, Franklin Co.

1820 Aug 2   Taylor, Sophronia D. and Elisha Gilman by Rev. T. Harris, Licking Co.

1804 Jul 21   Taylor, Stephen and Louise Rathbone by Enoch Shepard, Washington Co.

1812 Nov 11   Taylor, Susannah and Luther Case by E. Griswold, Franklin Co.

1815 Oct 27   Taylor, Thomas and Nancy Jackson by John True, Washington Co.

1816 Feb 8   Taylor, Thomas and Laura Wells by T.D. Baird, Licking Co.

1816 Jun 27   Taylor, Townley and Polly Jones by Cyrus Ames, JP, Washington Co.

1809 Jan 12   Taylor, William and Eliza Casto by David Mitchell, Franklin Co.

1815 Apr 19   Taylor, Wm. and Sally Roby by James Hoge, Franklin Co.

1815 Nov 23   Taylor, William (son of Judge James Taylor and was himself Associate Judge) and Sarah McDougla by T.S. Baird, Licking Co.

1817 May 8   Taylor, William and Margaret Neff by Isaiah Hoskinson, JP, Licking Co.

1813 Apr 15   Taylor, Zelpha and Peter Barker by Ezra Griswold, Franklin Co.

1816 Jul 4   Taylor, Zilpha and Thomas Warren by Recompence Stansbury, JP, Franklin Co.

1810 Jul 10   Teague, George and Polly Boughman by Wm. Shaw, Franklin Co.

1815 11m 8   Teague, Susanna and Samuel Steddom, Miami Monthly Meeting, Warren Co.

1816 --- --   Tedrick, John and Naomi Mesmore by Alex Holden, Licking Co.

1828 Aug 24   Teeg, Mathias and Louisa Steadman by J. Davis, JP, Franklin Co.

1815 Apr 13   Teegardin, Jacob and Margaret Shook by Shad Cole, JP, Pickaway Co.

1812 Jul 30   Teeters, Sarah and Jesse Justice (license date), Pickaway Co.

1803 May 8   Templin, Salmon and Agnes Wilson by Wm. Robinson, JP, Ross Co.

1828 Dec 25   Temple, Margaret and William Britton by Wm. Delzell, Franklin Co.

1869 Dec 9   Templeton, Jacob and Elizabeth Creighton by Rev. John Boyd, St.
               Luke's Church, Marietta, Washington Co.

1816 Feb 22   Terey, Mary and Samuel Barr by Cornelius Hougland, Esq., Washington
               Co.

1826 Apr 11   Terner, William and Rebeccah McComb by Rev. James Hoge, Franklin Co.

1825 May 26   Terney, Catherine and Jesse Baughman by C. Henkel, Franklin Co.

1884 Oct 15   Terrell, Jeremiah of Roney Point, W.Va., and Mary Ann Gammel of
               Putnam by Rev. George F. Moore, Putnam Presbyterian Church,
               Muskingum Co.

1821 May 24   Terrill, Elizabeth and William Young by John True, JP, Washington Co.

1821 Jun 9   Terrill, Laura Ann and Averill Harris by Philip Cole, JP, Washington
               Co.

1886 Mar 30   Terry, Charles V. and Kate Springer both of Zanesville by Rev.
               George F. Moore, Putnam Presbyterian Church, Muskingum Co.

1812 Jun 28   Terry, Mary and James Vaughn by Wm. D. Hendren, Franklin Co.

1813 May 26   Tesler, John and Metehany Switzer by Samuel Pogue, Licking Co.

1826 Feb 16   Teters, Margaret and John Brown by Peter Clover, JP, Franklin Co.

1821 Jul 21   Tevenderf, Betsey and John T. Auten by Robert W. Riley, JP, Franklin
               Co.

1817 Dec 26   Tew, Sarah and Jacob Newland by Nathan Pan, JP, Washington Co.

1812 Aug 6   Tewel, Daniel and Polly Main by Henry Jolly, JP, Washington Co.

1811 Apr 7   Tewel, Polly and Reuben F. Dye by Henry Jolly, JP, Washington Co.

1813 Apr 4   Thadley, Eunis and Michael Stagg, Jr. by Jacob Tharp, Franklin Co.

1804 Sep 20   Tharp, Anna and Benjamin Hinson by Wm. Bennett, JP, Franklin Co.

1858 Dec 16   Tharp, Jane and Jacob R. Harshberger by Rev. H. Hollis (in presence
               of F.P. Seffner and others), St. Paul's Church, Marion, Marion Co.

1826 Jan 19   Thavely, Samuel D. and Elizabeth Wiley by John F. Solomon, Franklin Co.

1815 May 25   Thierry, Francis and Fanny Blake by D.H. Buell, JP, Washington Co.

1804 Nov 27   Thiller, Elizabeth and Samuel ArrowSmith by Abraham Miller, Ross Co.

1801 Dec 16   Thoil, Hetteble of Pennsylvania and James Moore of Yountgstown by
               Caleb Baldwin, JP, Trumbull Co.

1821 Mar 8   Thomas, Catherine and Joshua Jermon by John F. Solomon, Franklin Co.

1818 6m 4   Thomas, Charity and Nicholas Tucker, Miami Monthly Meeting, Warren Co.

1807 Dec 17   Thomas, Charles and Sarah Sprague by N. Davis, Washington Co.

1825 Oct 20   Thomas, Christiana and James Kesller by Percival Adams, JP, Franklin
               Co.

1817 12m 4   Thomas, Elijah and Naomi Cadwalader, Miami Monthly Meeting, Warren Co.

1811 Jun 10   Thomas, Elizabeth and John Gilleland by Rev. Simon Cokrane, Franklin
              Co.

1820 Dec 20   Thomas, Elizabeth and Thomas Jones by Geo. Evans, MG, Licking Co.

1800 Aug 14   Thomas, Francis and Nancy Anerum by Philip Witten, JP, Washington Co.

1817 Mar 27   Thomas, Hannah and Wm. Brown by James Hoge, Franklin Co.

1816 Dec 19   Thomas, Hanson and Sarah Armstrong by J.W. Patterson, JP, Licking Co.

1809 1m 16   Thomas, Isaac and Lidia Hufman, Miami Monthly Meeting, Warren Co.

1803 Oct 13   Thomas, John and Catherine Putnam by J. Gardner, JP, Ross Co.

1809 Jul 26   Thomas, John and Polly Mickey by Benj'n Sells, JP, Franklin Co.

1881 Aug 6   Thomas, John and Annie Spencer by Rev. John Boyd, St. Luke's Church,
              Marietta, Washington Co.

1815 Feb 16   Thomas, M.A. and John Hornback by Joseph Hays, JP, Pickaway Co.

1805 Jul 25   Thomas, Mary and George Taylor by Peter Jackson, JP, Ross Co.

1819 Aug 3   Thomas, Mary and Cook Devol by Wm. Rand, JP, Washington Co.

1816 Jun 27   Thomas, Muhlan and Lidia Woolcutt by Michael Patton, JP, Franklin Co.

1804 Oct 11   Thomas, Nancy and Isaac Johnson by John Sharp, Washington Co.

1812 Apr 14   Thomas, Nancy and Benj'n Ford by Arthur O'Harra, Franklin Co.

1823 Aug 14   Thomas, Nancy and Samuel Graham by Wm. Duff, Franklin Co.

1818 Jul 24   Thomas, Philena and John Smith by Geo. Templeton, JP, Washington Co.

1812 3m 4   Thomas, Prudence and John Mills, Miami Monthly Meeting, Warren Co.

1820 12m 7   Thomas, Rachel and Hiram Bailey, Miami Monthly Meeting, Warren Co.

1881 Dec 28   Thomas, Roscoe E. of Darke Co., O., and Gertrude Garges of Putnam by
              Rev. George F. Moore, Putnam Presbyterian Church, Muskingum Co.

1888 Jan 21   Thomas, Samuel A. and Hattie B. Springer both of Zanesville by Rev.
              George F. Moore, Putnam Presbyterian Church, Muskingum Co.

1818 Oct 15   Thomas, Sarah and Wm. Hedrick by Percival Adams, JP, Franklin Co.

1826 11m 1   Thomas, Seth and Dinah Kindley, Miami Monthly Meeting, Warren Co.

1828 Apr 5   Thomas, Sricky and Samuel Stanton by Wm. T. Martin, Franklin Co.

1807 Sep 10   Thomas, Stephen and Hannah Kile by Arthur O'Harra, Franklin Co.

1806 Jun 12   Thomas, Thomas and ----- McCoy by Zachariah Stephen, JP, Franklin Co.

1806 Feb 20   Thomas, Tibitha and Peter Strevy by George Vinsonhalen, Ross Co.

1818 6m 4   Thomas, Vashti and Thomas Cadwalader, Miami Monthly Meeting, Warren Co.

1820 Apr 20   Thomas, Weston and Maria McFarland by Rev. Saml P. Robbins,
              Washington Co.

1812 May 12   Thomas, William and Mary Smith by Thomas Morris, Franklin Co.

1803 Oct 20   Thompson, Amos and Jennie McBane by Jacob Earhart, JP, Washington Co.

1820 May 21   Thompson, Bethena and Moses Wilkinson by Rev. Philander Chase,
              Franklin Co.

1816 Apr 23   Thompson, Betsey and Richard Decker by Frederick Peterson, Franklin Co.

1817 Feb 13   Thompson, Charles and Orrel Morrison by Isaac Case, Franklin Co.

1865 Mar 14   Thompson, Chas. C. and Matilda Messenger by Rev. H.H. Messenger (in presence of Mr. & Mrs. Turney and others at Turney's house), St. Paul's Church, Marion, Marion Co.

1816 Oct 22   Thompson, Eli and Maria Barslow by Stephen Guthrie, Washington Co.

1811 Jun 6   Thompson, Elias and Nancy Lewis by Rev. G. Vanaman, Licking Co.

1809 Feb 20   Thompson, Elizabeth and Joseph Higgins by Stephen Lindsly, Washington Co.

1815 Feb 7   Thompson, Elizabeth and Daniel Murdick by Noah Fidler, Licking Co.

1801 May 16   Thompson, Enos and Elizabeth Higgins by Wm. Harper, Washington Co.

1826 Jul 16   Thompson, Hannah and Samuel Everett by Amaziah Hutchinson, JP, Franklin Co.

1809 Apr 12   Thompson, Harriett and Nathaniel W. Little by Alex'r Morrison, Jr., Franklin Co.

1821 Jul 8   Thompson, Henry and Dolly Cole by Walter Curtis, JP, Washington Co.

1816 Jul 26   Thompson, Hugh and Emily Middleswart by Geo. Templeton, Esq., Washington Co.

1812 Sep 17   Thompson, John and Elizabeth Foster by John Turner, Franklin Co.

1816 Jul 23   Thompson, John and Elizabeth Elsey by James Taylor, Franklin Co.

1825 Nov 17   Thompson, John and Catharine Smith by Abm Williams, Franklin Co.

1816 Mar 14   Thompson, Jonathan and Sally Pool by Recompence Stanbery, Franklin Co.

1817 Mar 7   Thompson, Joseph and Sarah Suitor by Francis Holland, JP Scioto Tp., Jackson Co.

1820 May 31   Thompson, Joseph and Margaret Record by James Whitney, JP, Washington Co.

1828 Aug 7   Thompson, Joseph and Eliza Smith by Chandlor Rodgers, Franklin Co.

1819 Dec 11   Thompson, Joseph C. and Mary Guy by Rev. Philander Chase, Franklin Co.

1815 Mar 20   Thompson, Kiziah and John Hilands by Abner Christ, JP, Pickaway Co.

1810 Jul 15   Thompson, Lucretia and Chester Pinney by Ezra Griswold, Franklin Co.

1821 1m 4   Thompson, Mary and Clark Williams, Miami Monthly Meeting, Warren Co.

1867 Jul 10   Thompson, Mary C. and George W. Shank by Rev. A. Kingsbury, Putnam Presbyterian Church, Muskingum Co.

1820 May 21   Thompson, Mila and George Harlow Griswold by Rev. Philander Chase, Franklin Co.

1822 Aug 13   Thompson, Milton and Jane Taylor by Rev. James Hoge, Franklin Co.

1811 Jan 30   Thompson, Nancy and Stephan Lee by Rev. G. Vanaman, Licking Co.

1813 Feb 11   Thompson, Nancy and Elisha Poulsen (license date), Pickaway Co.

1813 Sep 29   Thompson, Peggy and Elias Hinckle by Jas. Hauge, Franklin Co.

1808 Jul 30   Thompson, Polly and Daniel McFain by Henry Smith, JPHT, Licking Co.

1819 Dec 27   Thompson, Rosey and Royal Carpenter by Samuel Lain, Franklin Co.

1819 Jun 15   Thompson, Ruhema and John Armstrong by James Hoge, Franklin Co.

1804 Feb 29   Thompson, Ruth and Lake Freeland by John Hoddy, JP, Ross Co.

1814 Mar 27   Thompson, Sally and Zachariah Pane by Wm. Creighton, JP, Pickaway Co.

1812 Nov 30   Thompson, Samuel and Ann James by Jeremiah Dare, JP, Washington Co.

1826 Apr 2   Thompson, Samuel and Sarah Ann Crum by Henry Matthews, Franklin Co.

1826 Apr 11   Thompson, Samuel and Martha Wilson by James Hoge, Franklin Co.

1818 Dec 21   Thompson, Sarah and Robert Armstrong by James Hoge, Franklin Co.

1816 Jul 18   Thompson, William and Margaret Billingsley by Wm. O'Bannon, JP,
               Licking Co.

1817 Jan 2   Thompson, Wm. and Hozanna Baldwin by Jos. S. Hughes, JP, Franklin Co.

1817 Mar 2   Thompson, William and Jane Suitor by Francis Holland, JP Scioto Tp.,
               Jackson Co.

1824 Dec 13   Thompson, William and Susanna Bosset by Uriah Clark, JP, Franklin Co.

1825 Apr 6   Thomson, Elezebeth and Peter Titler by Wm. Godman, JP, Franklin Co.

1819 May 16   Thomston, Rody and Samuel Ballinger by Samuel Dyer, JP, Franklin Co.

1817 Apr 12   Thorla, Richard and Cammilla McAllister by Dan'l H. Buell, JP,
               Washington Co.

1806 Jul 3   Thorn, Martin and Polly Williams by J. Brough, JP, Washington Co.

1817 Feb 13   Thorn, Mary and Zadoh Dickerson by Dan'l H. Buell, JP, Washington Co.

1825 May 31   Thorn, Sally and John Kline (license date), Marion Co.

1807 9m 16   Thornburgh, Mary and Jacob Beals, Miami Monthly Meeting, Warren Co.

1807 Jun 9   Thornelly, Harriet and Joshua Armitage by Sam'l P. Robbins, Washing-
               ton Co.

1883 Jan 3   Thorniley, Alice E. and Thomas C. Scott by Rev. John Boyd, St. Luke's
               Church, Marietta, Washington Co.

1808 Dec 31   Thornley, Mary and Benj Corp by Stephen Lindsly, Washington Co.

1796 Nov 2   Thornly, Sam'l and Sarah Putnam by J. Munro, JP, Washington Co.

1799 Jul 23   Thornton, Nancy and Nathaniel White by Robert Safford, Washington Co.

1827 Oct 16   Thrailkill, William and Hannah Carver by G.W. Hart, Franklin Co.

1819 Nov 29   Thrall, Alexander and Rosanna Atwood by George Evans, MG, Licking Co.

1819 Jan 13   Thrall, Anson R. and Mary Stadden by T.D. Bierd, Licking Co.

1819 Aug 19   Thrall, Caroline and Samuel Cooper by Spencer Wright, JP, Licking Co.

1817 Nov 1   Thrall, Charlette and Nehimiah Randal by Rev. T. Harris, Licking Co.

1816 Aug 2   Thrall, Cotton Mather and Sally Jones by Samuel Bancroft, JP, Licking
               Co.

1819 Apr 29   Thrall, Mary and Thomas Parker by Thomas Carr ME Ch, Licking Co.

1819 Jul 1   Thrall, Oliver A. and Margaret Parker by Spencer Wright, JP, Licking
               Co.

1809 Sep 14	Thrall, Sally and Jacob Goodrich by Rev. Timothy Harris, Licking Co.
1816 Nov 9	Thrall, Samuel and Mahala Mead by Rev. T. Harris, Licking Co.
1849 Sep 18	Thrall, Sarah G. and Rev. Rodney S. Nash by W.C. French, St. Luke's Church, Granville, Licking Co.
1825 May 12	Thrall, Wm. and Margret Barnett by Henry Mathews, Franklin Co.
1816 Nov 6	Thrap, Moses and Sarah Gosnel by John Spencer, JP, Licking Co.
1819 Nov 23	Throckmorton, Alsay and James Crabtree by Sam'l McDowell, Jackson Co.
1805 Dec 2	Throup, Wm. and Catharine Long by John Guthree, Ross Co.
1820 Nov 16	Thrum, Geo. and Mary Farding by Edw. Cating, JP, Jackson Co.
1812 Dec 22	Thudy, Simon and Caty Fouglar (license date), Pickaway Co.
1813 Nov 24	Thurlo, Ruth and Robert McKee by Joel Tuttle, JP, Washington Co.
1807 May 7	Tibbott, Mary and John Watkins by Josiah McKinney, Franklin Co.
1807 Dec 20	Tibbott, Richard and Sarah Dixon by David Marks, JP, Franklin Co.
1818 Sep 3	Tice, David and Nelly Oliver by Wm. Dana, JP, Washington Co.
1820 May 25	Tice, John and Christiana Peyton by Joseph Dickerson, Washington Co.
1809 May 16	Tice, Solomon and Rosannah Cline by James Riggs, JP, Washington Co.
1811 Apr 18	Tice, William and Jane Matheney by Ephraim Matthews, JP, Washington Co.
1814 Mar 3	Tiffin, John and Sarah Maddox (license date), Pickaway Co.
1803 Oct 20	Tiffin, Joseph and Nancy Wood by J. Gardner, JP, Ross Co.
1814 May 24	Tiffin, Phoebe and Matthew Earl by Charles Cade, JP, Pickaway Co.
1822 Jul 11	Tilberry, Henry and Hannah Miller by N. Goetschius, Franklin Co.
1828 Nov 20	Tillbery, Susan and Henry Shoemaker by J. Gander, JP, Franklin Co.
1810 Aug 19	Tillbury, Elenor and Conrad Decker by Ebenezer Richards, Franklin Co.
1790 Apr 4	Tillson, Lydia and Samuel Simmons by Benj Tupper, Washington Co.
1797 Aug 21	Tilton, Joseph and Bathsheba Dunham by J. Pierce, Washington Co.
1825 Jul 28	Timberman, Hannah and Phillip Anthony by Rob't Ward, JP, Jackson Co.
1825 Jan 23	Timberman, Paul and Mary Anthony by Robert Ward, JP, Jackson Co.
1804 Sep 20	Timmons, Elinor and James Johnston by Abraham Miller, Ross Co.
1820 Feb 7	Tinkham, Cornelius and Hetty Plummer by Rev. Saml P. Robbins, Washington Co.
1819 Feb 8	Tinkham, Huldah and John W. Carpenter by Reuben Carpetner, JP, Franklin Co.
1827 Jun 28	Tinkham, Isaac and Sarah Mapes by Jason Bull, JP, Franklin Co.
1819 May 26	Tinkham, Mary and Ezekel Fuller by Reuben Carpenter, Franklin Co.
1804 Feb 2	Tinlow, William and Jean Rody by Sam'l Edwards, JP, Ross Co.
1819 Jun 15	Tinsley, Margaret and Samuel Manby by James N. Booth, JP, Washington Co.

1825 Jun 9   Tiper, George and Laura Gleason by J.B. Finley, MG, Marion Co.

1805 Jan 31   Tippy,Uriah and Susanna Chadwick by Wm. Harper, Washington Co.

1825 Nov 29   Tipton, David and Sally Kent, Marion Co.

1825 Mar 25   Tipton, Eliza and Isaac Fickle (license date), Marion Co.

1811 Jun 27   Tipton, Nancy and Samuel W. Manning by W. Haines, JP, Licking Co.

1817 Feb --   Tipton, Sarah and Richard Heth by Ruben Goliday, JP, Franklin Co.

1813 Dec 26   Tipton, Thomas and Elizabeth Tomlinson by Asa Sheppard (another entry
              26 Feb 1814), Pickaway Co.

1828 Oct 1   Tipton, Thomas and Elizabeth Zinn by W.T. Martin, Franklin Co.

1815 Oct 23   Tison, Ida and Joseph Ames by Jno. Russell, JP, Washington Co.

1818 Jan 15   Tison, Polly and William Murrey by David Stephens, JP, Washington Co.

1825 Apr 6   Titler, Peter and Elezebeth Thomson by Wm. Godman, JP, Franklin Co.

1824 Mar 22   Tittler, George and Effy Decker by N. Goetschius, Franklin Co.

1810 Aug 23   Todd, Elizabeth and Henry Spiker (license date), Pickaway Co.

1806 Mar 18   Todd, John and Sally Todd by Jacob Lindly, Washington Co.

1810 Aug 23   Todd, Jonah and Amanda Williams (license date), Pickaway Co.

1823 Apr 20   Todd, Joseph and Catharine Lee by B. Bull, JP, Franklin Co.

1805 Jun 14   Todd, Robert and Martha Williams by Jacob Lindly, Washington Co.

1806 Mar 18   Todd, Sally and John Todd by Jacob Lindly, Washington Co.

1817 Nov 23   Toleman, Chester and Betsey Fowler by Solomon Goss, MMEC, Washington
              Co.

1811 Oct 7   Toleman, Jerusia and John True by Amos Porter, JP, Washington Co.

1820 Feb 7   Toll, Alpheus and Hannah McGowen by Samuel Lain, Franklin Co.

1796 Nov 8   Tolman, Mary and Linus Tuttle by J. Munro, Washington Co.

1804 Dec 6   Tomlin, Catharine and Richard Tomlin by Wm. Davis, Esq., Ross Co.

1804 Dec 4   Tomlin, Mary and Elisha Webb by Wm. Davis, Esq., Ross Co.

1804 Aug 7   Tomlin, Nancy and John Heath by Wm. Davis, JP, Ross Co.

1804 Dec 6   Tomlin, Richard and Catharine Tomlin by Wm. Davis, Esq., Ross Co.

1813 Dec 26   Tomlinson, Elizabeth and Thomas Tipton by Asa Sheppard (another entry
              on 26 Feb 1814), Pickaway Co.

1821 Jul 8   Tompkins, Abel and Elizabeth Heindel by Charles Henkel, Franklin Co.

1825 Sep 13   Tompkins, Elizabeth B. and Wm. M. Baker by Wm. Cochran, JP, Marion Co.

1805 Dec 30   Toops, Henry and Sally Hall by Wm. Creighton, Ross Co.

1825 Mar 27   Toosinge, Susan and Isaac Davis by Wm. Henden, JP, Franklin Co.

1817 May 3   Toothaker, Nathaniel and Catherine Campbell by -----, Licking Co.

1813 Apr 10   Tootle, John and Polly Armstrong (license date), Pickaway Co.

1840 Aug --   Toppin, Eunice G. and William C. Andros by Rev. A. Helfenstine, St.
              John's Church, Worthington, Franklin Co.

1824 Aug 11   Topping, Dayton and Margret Douglass by R.W. Cowls, Franklin Co.

1826 Oct 25   Topping, Edwin H. and Delia Caulkins by John W. Ladd, JP, Franklin Co.

1808 Mar 3   Topping, John and Elizabeth Lucas by Alex'r Morrison, Jr., Franklin
               Co.

1796 Oct 30   Torry, Sally and Nath'l Hinckley by Robert Oliver, Washington Co.

1825 May 7   Tower (Towers), Mathaniel and Sally Garrison by George Jefferies,
               Ordained Minister of the Gospel, Franklin Co.

1814 Jul 18   Towers, Thomas and Deborah Ross by David Kinnear, JP, Pickaway Co.

1811 May 30   Town, Ena and William Miller (license date), Pickaway Co.

1821 Oct 18   Town, Russell and Roxina Skeels by Nathl. Little, Franklin Co.

1856 Dec 18   Towne, Henry A. and Harriet Nye by Rev. John Boyd, St. Luke's Church,
               Marietta, Washington Co.

1821 Mar 15   Townsend, Betsey and Peter Grubb by John D. Chamberlain, JP,
               Washington Co.

1807 12m 16   Townsend, James and Rosannah Smith, Miami Monthly Meeting, Warren Co.

1807 12m 10   Townsend, Martha and James Coldwell, Miami Monthly Meeting, Warren Co.

1854 Oct 17   Townsend, Norton S. of Elyria and Margaret A. Bailey of Putnam by
               Rev. A. Kingsbury, Putnam Presbyterian Church, Muskingum Co.

1807 11m 18   Townsend, Rachel and William Harvey, Miami Monthly Meeting, Warren Co.

1814 Apr 3   Trachey, Mary and Joseph Decker by Shadrach Cole, JP, Pickaway Co.

1879 Oct 2   Tracy, Charles F. and Mollie A. Turner by Rev. John Boyd, St. Luke's
               Church, Marietta, Washington Co.

1818 Oct 19   Tracy, Elias and Polly Morey? by Alex Holden, JP, Licking Co.

1819 Mar 25   Tracy, Harriet and Joseph Orr by Alex Holden, JP, Licking Co.

1809 Oct 26   Trakes (or Frakes), Rachiel and Enoch Hanyman by Michael Dickey,
               Franklin Co.

1816 Nov 12   Traves, Enoch and Lucy Clark by Rev. T. Harris, Licking Co.

1823 Mar 5   Travis, Sherman and Julian Courtright by Robert Boyd, JP, Franklin Co.

1826 Mar 30   Traxler, Catharine and Moses Faught by J.B. Gilliland, JP, Jackson Co.

1826 Apr 23   Traxler, David and Sarah Crabtree by J.B. Gilliland, JP, Jackson Co.

1814 Jun 19   Treat, Amariah and Sally Kenion alias Sally Richardson by Jos.
               Gordon, JP, Franklin Co.

1860 Mar 8   Trevor, Eliza H. and Joseph E. Hall, Jr. by Rev. John Boyd, St. Luke's
               Church, Marietta, Washington Co.

1835 Dec 24   Trevor, Hugh and Maria Holden by Rev. J.T. Wheat, St. Luke's Church,
               Marietta, Washington Co.

1815 Jun 17   Trig, Samuel and Ruth Low by John Green, Licking Co.

1814 Apr 12   Trimble, Abner and Mary Maythorn by John Turner, Franklin Co.

1846 Jun 4   Trimble, William H. of Hillsboro and Martha H. Buckingham of Putnam by
               Rev. A. Kingsbury, Putnam Presbyterian Church, Muskingum Co.

1801 Aug 13   Trindle, Nancy and John Blackburn at Youngstown by Turhand Kirtland,
Judge of Court of Common Pleas, Trumbull Co.

1819 Nov 2   Trindle, Sarah and James Young by T.D. Bierd, VDM, Licking Co.

1821 Jun 3   Triplet, Daniel and Sarah Archer alias Sarah Smith by John Davis, JP,
Franklin Co.

1856 Aug 11   Triplett, D.L. of Coshocton and Hannah M. Safford of Putnam by Rev. A.
Kingsbury, Putnam Presbyterian Church, Muskingum Co.

1867 Mar 8   Triplett, John B. and Susan V. Cox by Rev. John Boyd, St. Luke's
Church, Marietta, Washington Co.

1828 Mar 27   Tripp, Stephen and Anna Bacon by Jason Bull, Franklin Co.

1815 Sep 2   Trobridge, Philo and Martha Blake by John Russell, JP, Washington Co.

1851 Sep 25   Trot, Zebedee and Phebe Ann Carl by Rev. Geo. B. Sturges, St. Paul's
Church, Marion, Marion Co.

1800 Dec 16   Trotter, William and Polly Cooper by Robt Safford, JP, Washington Co.

1819 Feb 4   Trout, Michael and Sarah Baker by Thomas Scott, JP, Licking Co.

1813 Mar 7   Trowbridge, David and Sophronia Howe by Peter Howe, JP, Washington Co.

1819 Jun 3   Trowbridge, Eliphalet and Polly Mantanney by James Cunningham, Licking
Co.

1808 Mar 16   True, Ephm and Elizabeth Amlin by Thos Stanley, Washington Co.

1806 Dec 11   True, Jabez and Sarah Mills by Sam'l P. Robbins, Washington Co.

1811 Oct 7   True, John and Jerusia Toleman by Amos Porter, JP, Washington Co.

1805 --- --   True, Josiah and Almira Tuttle by E. Cyrus Paulk, Washington Co.

1826 Apr 6   Truil, Gorge P. and Mary King by John F. Solomon, Franklin Co.

1813 Apr 19   Trullinger, Jacob and Polly Gordy (license date), Pickaway Co.

1818 Mar 5   Trumbo, Mathias and Rebecca Groves by Alex. Holden, JP, Licking Co.

1804 Dec 20   Trusam, Catharine and Frederick Lenes by Peter Jackson, JP, Ross Co.

1804 Oct 21   Tubbs, Frederick and Dorcas Sawyer by Enoch Shepard, Washington Co.

1844 May 16   Tucker, Mrs. Eliza W. of Putnam and Douglas Putnam of Marietta by
Rev. A. Kingsbury, Putnam Presbyterian Church, Muskingum Co.

1814 Feb 4   Tucker, Frances and Artemas Knapp by John Green, JP, Washington Co.

1813 Aug 22   Tucker, Lydia and William White by Stephen Lindsley, Washington Co.

1816 Apr 7   Tucker, Mary and Benjamin Lamb by John Russell, JP, Washington Co.

1819 Mar 4   Tucker, Nancy and Isaac Johnston by Eli C. King, Franklin Co.

1818 6m 4   Tucker, Nicholas and Charity Thomas, Miami Monthly Meeting, Warren Co.

1825 Feb 23   Tuller, Carmi and Polly Bidwell by Aristarcrus Walker, JP, Franklin
Co.

1839 Apr 1   Tuller, Elvira and Rezin K. Shawhan by Rev. A. Helfenstine, St. John's
Church, Worthington, Franklin Co.

1822 Jul 3   Tuller, Flora and Zopher T. Moore by A. Buttles, Franklin Co.

1825 May 12   Tuller, Lester and Betsey Rogers by Aristarcrus Walker, JP,
               Franklin Co.

1825 Apr 3   Tuller, Mrs. Lydia and Dr. Benjamin Stewart Pitt Dodge, by
               Aristarcrus Walker, Franklin Co.

1814 Sep 11   Tullinger, Abraham and Margaret Tullinger by Henry Davis, Pickaway Co.

1814 Sep 11   Tullinger, Margaret and Abraham Tullinger by Henry Davis, Pickaway Co.

1814 Oct 20   Tullinger, Phillip and Caty West by Henry Daus, Pickaway Co.

1827 Apr 3   Tully, W.A. and Elizabeth Bailey by Samuel Hamilton, Elder in the
               MEC, Franklin Co.

1821 Jan 15   Tunis?, James and Christena Gale by Shadrick Ruark?, MG, Licking Co.

1802 Mar 25   Tupper, Benjamin and Patty Paterson by Daniel Story, Clerk, Washing-
               ton Co.

1817 Jul 20   Tupper, Christena and James Seddick by James Hoge, Franklin Co.

1804 May 3   Tupper, Edward W. and Bethia Putnam by Enoch Shepard, Washington Co.

1871 Oct 11   Tupper, Elizabeth and Martin L. Lacey of West Auburn, Pa., by Rev. A.
               Kingsbury, Putnam Presbyterian Church, Muskingum Co.

1813 May 19   Tupper, Jane and John Smith by Richd Seddick, JP, Franklin Co.

1802 Apr 10   Tupper, Reuben and Hila Hubbard by Caleb Baldwin, JP, Trumbull Co.

1821 Jun 5   Turner, Adam and Martha McComb by James Hoge, Franklin Co.

1816 Sep 26   Turner, Caleb and Sylvy Bradley by Joseph Armstrong, JP, Jackson Co.

1867 Jul 4   Turner, David and Mrs. Janette Waters by Rev. John Boyd, St. Luke's
               Church, Marietta, Washington Co.

1821 Nov 6   Turner, Elizabeth and Samuel McComb by James Hoge, Franklin Co.

1817 Oct 28   Turner, George and Frances Lincoln by Rev. Saml P. Robbins,
               Washington Co.

1840 Apr 8   Turner, John A. and Harriet Mahan, St. Luke's Church, Granville,
               Licking Co.

1820 Aug 29   Turner, John L. and Margaret McComb by James Hoge, Franklin Co.

1811 Feb 4   Turner, Margaret and Otho Johnston by James Hoge, Franklin Co.

1810 Jan 11   Turner, Mary and John Pauch by James Hoge, Franklin Co.

1826 Apr 30   Turner, Mary and Daniel Boman by MEC John F. Solomon, Franklin Co.

1879 Oct 2   Turner, Mollie A. and Charles F. Tracy by Rev. John Boyd, St. Luke's
               Church, Marietta, Washington Co.

1818 Jan --   Turner, Nancy and William Polsan by Reuben Golliday, JP, Franklin Co.

1828 Mar 2   Turner, Sara Ann and Barnabus Harris by George Jefferies, Franklin Co.

1823 Jun 16   Turner, Wesley and Claressa McCaron (or McCormac) by C. Waddell, JP,
               Franklin Co.

1825 Apr 7   Turner, William and Mary Dixon by Timothy Ratcliff, JP, Jackson Co.

1810 Apr 26   Turness, Dullene and George Kinser (license date), Pickaway Co.

1858 Sep 7   Turney, Gertrude Jane and Rev. H.H. Messenger by Rev. Hollis, St.
               Paul's Church, Marion, Marion Co.

1826 May 18   Turney, John and Eliza Raney by C. Hinkel, Franklin Co.

1849 Sep 5   Turney, Leah and John Merrill by Rev. Geo. Thompson, St. Paul's
               Church, Marion, Marion Co.

1824 Dec 30   Turney, Mary and Frederick Neiswender by C. Henkel, Franklin Co.

1815 Apr 18   Tusing, Nicholas and Fany Clepper by Frederick Peterson, Franklin Co.

1805 --- --   Tuttle, Almira and Josiah True by E. Cyrus Paulk, Washington Co.

1804 Feb 13   Tuttle, Elisha and Mary Pugsley by Samuel Brown, Washington Co.

1805 Dec 4   Tuttle, James and Elizabeth Greenlee by Noble Crawford, JP, Ross Co.

1790 Jul 3   Tuttle, Joel and Huldah Sanford by Benj. Tupper, Washington Co.

1796 Nov 8   Tuttle, Linus and Mary Tolman by J. Munro, Washington Co.

1821 Nov 25   Tuttle, Phebe and Ebenezer S. Taylor by Joel Tuttle, Jr., JP,
               Washington Co.

1882 Sep 18   Tweed, Jennie and Harry Wertheimer by Rev. John Boyd, St. Luke's
               Church, Marietta, Washington Co.

1820 Mar 4   Twigg, Mary and James Sinkey by Simeon Avery, MG, Licking Co.

1809 Feb 23   Twiggs, Sarah and William Hill by Thos. Stanley, JP, Washington Co.

1809 Feb 22   Twigs, Jemima and Asa Perkins by Stephen Lindsly, Washington Co.

1820 Dec 11   Twining, Hiram and Lovey Pease by Rev. L. Harris, Licking Co.

1820 Jul 27   Tyhurst, William and Mary Boger by J. Cunningham, JP, Licking Co.

1806 Dec 2   Tyson, Esther and John Fouch by Luther Dana, Washington Co.

1811 May 6   Tyson, John and Sarah Fortner by Jeremiah Dare, JP, Washington Co.

1815 Aug 22   Ulen, John and Harriet Fraiser by Rev. S.P. Robbins, Washington Co.

1816 Sep 26   Unckles (or Uncles), James and Betsey Kiswell by James Hoge (another
               entry 27 Mar 1817), Franklin Co.

1822 Aug 27   Updegraft, John and Mary Booker by Jacob Sharp, Franklin Co.

1817 Mar 4   Usher, Thomas and Catharine Bird by Danl G. Stanley, JP, Washington Co

1797 Apr 27   Vacht, Joseph W.D. and Jean Parmonteir by Robert Safford, Washington
               Co.

1815 Apr 26   Valentine, Betsey and Phillip Zinmer by Thomas Mace, JP, Pickaway Co.

1804 May 5   Valentine, Catharine and John Roger by Sam'l Edwards, Ross Co.

1814 Apr 10   Valentine, Mary and Wm. Edwards by Thos. Mace, JP, Pickaway Co.

1814 Aug 14   Valentine, Sophia and John Foltz by Jacob Leist, JP, Pickaway Co.

1815 Dec 28   Valey, Mary Van and Dugal Walker by Obadiah Scott, Washington Co

1798 Sep 18   Valodin, Francis and Maria Gabriel LaForge by Robert Safford,
               Washington Co.

1857 Nov 30   Van Allen, Mrs. Hannah and John R. Butler by Rev. John Boyd, St.
               Luke's Church, Marietta, Washington Co.

1852 May 25   Van Allen, William C. of New York City and Mary E. Potwin of Putnam
               by Rev. A. Kingsbury, Putnam Presbyterian Church, Muskingum Co.

1814 Dec 27   Vance, Abigal and Isaiah Pursel by Emmor Cox, JP, Franklin Co.

1816 Aug 8   Vance, Alice and George Armstrong by Alex Holden, Licking Co.

1813 Apr 8   Vance, Elisha and Anne Gardy (license date), Pickaway Co.

1818 Jul 6   Vance, Jacob and Rachel Godfrey by James Campbell, JP, Licking Co.

1805 Oct 3   Vance, Joseph and Cyntha Hart by Zachariah Stephen, JP, Franklin Co.

1818 Sep 13   Vance, Nancy and Samuel Barker by Rev. Philander Chase, Franklin Co.

1817 Jan 2   Vance, Ruth and Abraham Smith by J.W. Patterson, JW, Licking Co.

1817 Jul 20   Vance, Thomas and Elizabeth Decker by James Hoge, Franklin Co.

1804 Mar 22   Vance, Wm. of Belmont Co. and Mary Kirk of Scioto Tp. by Wm.
               Creighton, Ross Co.

1819 Sep 19   Vance, William and Maria Holden by John Petterson, MG, Licking Co.

1808 Feb 14   Van Clief, Abigail and Cyrus Cheadle by Asa Cheadle, JP, Washington Co.

1818 May 14   Vanclief, Elizabeth and John C.A. Morris by Titian Kimball, JP,
               Washington Co.

1804 Jul 15   Van Clief, Emme and Samuel Nott by Jacob Lindly, Washington Co.

1818 Sep 10   Vandbarch, Margaret and George Grove by Abner Goff, Licking Co.

1829 Aug 6   Vanderburgh, James and Ann W. House by Leroy Swormstead, MG, Franklin
               Co.

1809 Aug 10   Vandervender, Nancy and Hamilton Nighswinger by Sol Langdon,
               Washington Co.

1807 Nov 15   Vandeventer, Jane and William Rarden by Joseph Palmer, JP, Washington
               Co.

1819 Jan 7   Vandevender, Philip and Elizabeth Evans by John Green, JP, Licking Co.

1810 Sep 23   Vanderwort, James and Rachel Peters (license date), Pickaway Co.

1821 Jun 7   Vandimark, Mary and Jesse Blair by Nicholas Goetschius, Franklin Co.

1811 May 2   Vandoran, William and Mollie Gay (license date), Pickaway Co.

1804 Jan 5   Vandurn, Calrew? and Richard Harbert by Sam'l Edwards, JP, Ross Co.

1815 Apr 6   Vanduyn, Rachel B. and Robert C. Barton by Rev. Stephen Lindsley,
               Washington Co.

1815 Jun 29   Vanelief, Peter and Sally Newton by Richard Cheadle, Washington Co.

1814 Nov 22   Van Hook, Thos. and Nancy Reddin by Chas. Cade, JP, Pickaway Co.

1808 Mar 6   Vanhorn, Elizabeth and James Moore of Ross Co., by David Marks,
               Franklin Co.

1810 Nov 25   Van Horn, Walter and Hope White (license date), Pickaway Co.

1818 Feb 15   Vankirk, John and Mary Benjamin by James Holmes, JP, Licking Co.

1805 Mar 25   Vanmeter, Joseph and Rachel Renick by Peter Jackson, JP, Ross Co.

1810 Jul 31   Van Meter, Susana and John Kyle (license date), Pickaway Co.

1809 Apr 14   Vanmetre, Abraham and Rachiel Ratliff by John Turner, Franklin Co.

1813 May 17   Van Metre, Rebecca and James Hulse (license date), Pickaway Co.

1823 May 29   Vansciver, Hesther and Roland Gary by Wm. C. Duff, JP, Franklin Co.

1824 Jul 1   Vansciver, Naomah and David Romine by Jacob Gundy, Franklin Co.

1804 Sep 27   Vansickle, Nancy and Richard Glaze by Geo. Williams, JP, Ross Co.

1818 Mar 15   Vanskay, Pheabe and Peter Borer by Daniel Harrel, JP, Jackson Co.

1825 Nov 11   Vantapell, Abler (Abber?) and William Sebring of Genoa Township,
               Delaware Co., by G.W. Hart, Franklin Co.

1820 Jul 25   Vanvaley, Hannah M. and William Cowee by John Patterson, JP,
               Washington Co.

1818 Jan 4   Van Valey, Intenda and John Pope by John Patterson, Washington Co.

1810 Oct 14   Vanvaley, Phebe and Seth Baker by Wm. Gray, JP, Washington Co.

1829 Jul 5   Van Voorhis, Ellen and John Otstot by Leroy Swormstead, Franklin Co.

1825 Nov 20   Vanvorst, John, widower, and Catharine Jackson, widow, by Joseph
               Carper, Franklin Co.

1812 Jul 27   Van Wickel, Daniel and Christiana Holt (license date), Pickaway Co.

1866 Jun 20   Van Zandt, Clara M. and D. Perkins Bosworth, Jr. by Rev. John Boyd,
               St. Luke's Church, Marietta, Washington Co.

1825 Feb 24   Varian, Elizabeth and Jefferson Livisay by John Shumate, JP, Jackson
               Co.

1820 Apr 27   Varner, Samuel and Margaret Lake by Rev. Abraham Lippet, Washington Co.

1813 Aug 22   Varnum, Mary and Daniel Barker by Sardine Stone, JP, Washington Co.

1826 Mar 30   Varyann, Mary and Smith Stephenson by J.B. Gilliland, JP, Jackson Co.

1820 May 4   Vaughan, Catharine and Heman Sherman by John Patterson, JP,
               Washington Co.

1821 Feb 15   Vaughan, Patty and Dan Lawrence by Thomas White, JP, Washington Co.

1806 Aug 5   Vaughn, Alexander and Jane McMillan by Jacob Lindly, Washington Co.

1812 Jun 28   Vaughn, James and Mary Terry by Wm. D. Hendren, Franklin Co.

1880 Apr 19   Vaughn, Mrs. Laurinda L. and Cyrus Shaver by Rev. John Boyd, St.
               Luke's Church, Marietta, Washington Co.

1815 Apr 17   Vaux, Lidia D. and George Berely (or Beverly) by John Stipp, Franklin
               Co.

1811 Sep 24   Veil, Jacob and Margaret Graham (license date), Pickaway Co.

1819 11m 4   Venable, Mariah and Evan Benbow, Miami Monthly Meeting, Warren Co.

1881 Sep 28   Vergne (de la Vergne), Estelle and James R. Hall by Rev. John Boyd,
               St. Luke's Church, Marietta, Washington Co.

1816 Jul 25   Vernam, Elisha and Elizabeth Kinnison by John Brown, MG, Jackson Co.

1825 Dec 1   Vernem, Mary and Wm. Ware by John Stephenson, JP, Jackson Co.

1821 Jul 26   Vernon, Wm. and Jane Martin by Jeremiah Brown, JP, Jackson Co.

1825 Apr 14   Vezey, Sally and James Reamy by Rob't Hopkins, JP, Marion Co.

1820 Mar 6   Viall, Daniel and Mary Hilderbrand by Rev. Saml P. Robbins,
               Washington Co.

1810 Jul 26   Vicars, Elizabeth and John Reade (license date), Pickaway Co.

1799 Jan 23   Vincent, Anthony Claudius and Florence Bathilot by Josiah Munroe,
               Washington Co.

1863 Sep 22   Vincent, Don and Mary A. Hendrick by Rev. John Boyd, St. Luke's Church,
               Marietta, Washington Co.

1809 Jan 26   Vincent, John and Rachel Olney by Thos. Seely, Washington Co.

1812 Apr 5   Vincent, Mary and William H. Coley by Edwin Putnam, JP, Washington Co.

1809 Sep 3   Vinhirk, Nancy and James Marks by Arthur O'Harra, Franklin Co.

1816 Jul 25   Vining, Almira and Warren Wilcox by Isaac Case, JP, Franklin Co.

1807 Aug 6   Vining, Elkana and Catharine White by Wm. Shaw, JP, Franklin Co.

1825 Aug 23   Vining, Huldah and Harvey Skeels by Nathan Emery, MG, Franklin Co.

1814 Oct 2   Vining, Luther and Libbel Webster by Obadiah Scott, Washington Co.

1818 Dec 6   Vining, Persy M. and Lyman Andrews by Vinol Stewart, Franklin Co.

1825 Aug 18   Vinson, Malachi and Catharine Brown by John Brown, MG, Jackson Co.

1805 Mar 28   Vinson, William and Sarah Willoughby by Wm. Creighton, Ross Co.

1854 Oct 9   Vinton, Romaine M. of Putnam and Edwin P. Safford of Chillicothe by
               Rev. A. Kingsbury, Putnam Presbyterian Church, Muskingum Co.

1799 Mar 22   Violet, Margeret and Peter Ferrard by Robert Safford, Washington Co.

1815 Dec 14   Violet, Sampson and Eva Phillips by Elihu Bigelow, Licking Co.

1793 May 30   Visinier, Charles Nicholas and Sophia Carteron by J.G. Petitt,
               Washington Co.

1811 Aug 6   Vize, Samuel and Elizabeth O'Hara (license date), Pickaway Co.

1829 May 10   Voris, Peter and Margaret Mock by Leroy Swormsted, Franklin Co.

1812 Jun 25   Voshell, Peter and Jane Wayson by Rev. Stephen Lindley, Washington Co.

1817 1m 2   Votaw, Jonathan and Elizabeth Hampton, Miami Monthly Meeting, Warren
               Co.

1798 Nov 17   Vovers, William and Peggy Bradley by Josiah Munro, Washington Co.

1811 Oct 12   Waddle, James and Barbara Freese (license date), Pickaway Co.

1811 Dec 5   Waddle, Joseph and Sarah Riley (license date), Pickaway Co.

1824 May 24   Wade, Susannah and Joshua Bearss by J.P. Packard, JP, Marion Co.

1825 Apr 21   Wadham, Noah E. and Rebecca Rennick by C. Henkle, Franklin Co.

1803 Mar 7   Wadkins, Sarah and Isaiah Shephard by J. Graham, Washington Co.

1816 Oct 29   Wagener, Catharine and John Decker by Jacob Smith, Franklin Co.

1821 Aug 4   Wagener, July and Richard Henry by Jacob Smith, Franklin Co.

1827 May 21   Wagganer, Susan and Lewis Devenport by A. Allison, Franklin Co.

1816 Aug 8   Waggoner, Abraham and Hannah Cady by Emmor Cox (or Cady), JP,
               Franklin Co.

1813 Jul 16   Waggoner, David and Susan Fry by S. Pogue, JP, Licking Co.

1825 Jun 16   Waggoner, George and Mary Ceasy by John F. Solomon, Franklin Co.

1824 Dec 30   Waggoner, Martin and Elizabeth Havens by A. Allison, Franklin Co.

1854 Sep 2   Wagh, John of Newport and Rachel Strain by Rev. John Boyd, St. Luke's
               Church, Marietta, Washington Co.

1818 Feb 24   Wagner, Mary Ann and Isaac Spencer by Wm. Rand, JP, Washington Co.

1828 Dec 11   Wagoner, Lydia and John Smallman by Jacob Smith, JP, Franklin Co.

1826 Oct 24   Wagoner, Martin and Sally Emley by Jacob Smith, JP, Franklin Co.

1819 Dec 9   Wagoner, Peter and Mary Murphy by Simeon Overturf, JP, Licking Co.

1876 Sep 14   Wait, Clara J. and Ernest M. Scott by Rev. A. Kingsbury, Putnam
               Presbyterian Church, Muskingum Co.

1818 Jan 1   Wait, Henry and Sophia Wells by Simon Merwin, Washington Co.

1824 Dec 25   Wait, James and Nancy Smith by Tracy Willcox, JP, Franklin Co.

1821 Dec 1   Wait, Lois and Matthew Barnwell by Danl. H. Buell, JP, Washington Co.

1810 Aug 11   Wait, Lucy and Wm. Armistead by Benjamin Lakin, GM, Franklin Co.

1814 Oct 13   Wait, Nancy and John Goetcheus by James Marshall, Franklin Co.

1868 Oct 12   Waite, Christopher C. of Toledo and Lillian P. Guthrie by Rev. A.
               Kingsbury, Putnam Presbyterian Church, Muskingum Co.

1818 Nov 6   Waits, William and Jane White by James Hoge, Franklin Co.

1819 Dec 16   Wakefield, Hiram and Irene Cutler by T. Lee, Franklin Co.

1818 Nov 6   Walbridge, John and Esther Smith by Stephen Guthrie, Washington Co.

1825 Feb 17   Waldear, Geo. and Charlotte Morley by Timothy Radcliffe, JP, Jackson
               Co.

1810 Mar 1   Waldo, John and Polly Goldsbrough by D. Loring, JP, Washington Co.

1824 Mar 25   Waldren, Elizabeth and William Graves by Geo. Claypoole, JP, Jackson
               Co.

1824 Apr 19   Waldren, Phillips and Bythama Moss by Geo. Claypoole, JP, Jackson Co.

1824 Aug 26   Waldren, Solomon and Susanna Cassill by Geo. Claypoole, JP, Jackson Co.

1812 Oct 4   Waldron, Elizabeth and Benjamin Cu(s)terline by Wm. Moody, JP, Licking
               Co.

1818 Nov 8   Wales, Ruby and George Lincoln by Rev. T. Harris, Licking Co.

1817 Sep 18   Walker, Abigail and James Hootan by Wm. Badger, JP, Franklin Co.

1816 Nov 21   Walker, Aristhenes and Welthy Rodgers by Tracy Wilcox, Franklin Co.

1812 May 16   Walker, Dougal and Elizabeth Wells by Edwin Putnam, Washington Co.

1815 Dec 28   Walker, Dugal and Mary Van Valey by Obadiah Scott, Washington Co.

1814 Feb 10   Walker, Eleanor and William Goldsmith by Rev. S.P. Robbins, Washington
                Co.

1819 Feb 4   Walker, Elizabeth and Moses Lawrence by Pelatiah White, Washington Co.

1813 Jan 14   Walker, James and Nancy Bird by Wm. Miller, Washington Co.

1802 Mar 14   Walker, John and Lydia Sawyer by I. Peine, Washington Co.

1805 Jan 20   Walker, John and Polly Waterman by Stephen Lindly, Washington Co.

1812 Sep 9   Walker, John and Rachel Martin (license date), Pickaway Co.

1815 Jan 10   Walker, Lewis and Phebe Hughes by Thomas Seely, Washington Co.

1820 Sep 14   Walker, Lucy and Daniel Hinkley by Thomas White, JP, Washington Co.

1809 Feb 14   Walker, Margaret and James Ogle by Amos Porter, Washington Co.

1803 Mar 31   Walker, Mary and Mich'l Strouss by Oliver Ross, Ross Co.

1814 Apr 26 or 20 Walker, Mary and Elias Ogle (or Ayles) by Wm. Miller, Esq.,
                Washington Co.

1805 Oct 18   Walker, Nancy and Mathew Hungerford by John Brough, JP, Washington Co.

1819 Feb 17   Walker, Nancy and James Scott by George Hays, Franklin Co.

1825 Mar 3   Walker, Nancy and George Garrett by J.B. Finley, MG, Marion Co.

1819 Mar 22   Walker, Nancy D. and Jonathan Nute by Dudley Davis, JP, Washington Co.

1805 Jun 6   Walker, Obadiah and Cassandra Halsay by D. Loring, Washington Co.

1819 Feb 17   Walker, Peggy and John Brackinridge by George Hays, Franklin Co.

1809 Nov 4   Walker, Polly and Elizur Carver by J. Dare, JP, Washington Co.

1820 Apr 2   Walker, Polly and Flavius Waterman by Wm. Woodford, JP, Washington Co.

1803 Feb 12   Walker, Sarah and Reuben Parker both of Hudson by David Hudson, JP,
                Trumbull Co.

1824 Dec 23   Walker, Sidney and Samuel Clover by Henderson Crabb, Deacon MEC,
                Franklin Co.

1802 Jun 29   Wallace, George and Harriet Menough both of Trumbull Co. by Wm. Wick,
                VDM, Trumbull Co.

1817 Apr 17   Wallace, John and Betsy Andrews by Ezra Griswold, Franklin Co.

1821 Jul 26   Wallace, Salmon and Abigal Gale by Chandler Rogers, JP, Franklin Co.

1817 Sep 18   Waller, Catharine and Moses Grandstaff by John Patterson, Washington
                Co.

1817 Sep 18   Waller, Eleanor and Ephraim Hanson by John Patterson, Washington Co.

1820 Oct 5   Walles, John and Jane Nelson by Vincent Southard, JP, Jackson Co.

1803 Jul 27   Walls, Malander and John Edington by Seth Cashart, JP, Washington Co.

1814 Mar 10   Walston, Rose and Abraham Champ by Rev. Geo. Alkire, Pickaway Co.

1826 Jan 6   Walter, Burinde and Joseph Compona by Eigah Smurgan, Franklin Co.

1825 Dec 19   Walters, John and Ridgley Lillian (license date), Marion Co.

1824 Dec 7   Walters, Phatima and Andrew Decker by Wm. Godman, JP, Franklin Co.

1811 May 23   Wanamacher, Susana and David Grim (license date), Pickaway Co.

1809 Aug 20   Ward, Aaron and Nancy Evans by Zachariah Carlisle, Esq., Licking Co.

1809 May 8   Ward, Ann and Jacob Humphreys by Wm. Haines, JP, Licking Co.

1818 Feb 19   Ward, Catherine and Christopher Price by Noah Fidler, Licking Co.

1823 3m 12   Ward, Ellis and Mary Earl Newman, Miami Monthly Meeting, Warren Co.

1821 10m 3   Ward, Evan and Catharine Jeffers, Miami Monthly Meeting, Warren Co.

1851 Nov 27   Ward, Harriet C. and Goodrich H. Barbour of Madison, Ind., by Rev.
               John Boyd, St. Luke's Church, Marietta, Washington Co.

1852 Dec 8   Ward, Henrietta D. and Ezra G. Leonard of Madison, Ind., by Rev.
               John Boyd, St. Luke's Church, Marietta, Washington Co.

1800 Apr 2   Ward, Israel and Rhoda Barker by Alvin Bingham, Washington Co.

1820 6m 7   Ward, John and Hannah Ann Evans, Miami Monthly Meeting, Warren Co.

1828 Apr 10   Ward, Mary and Uriah Jones by Wooley Conrad, Franklin Co.

1846 Nov 12   Ward, Mary Elizabeth and Charles R. Rhodes of St. Louis, Mo. by Rev.
               Edward Winthrop, St. Luke's Church, Marietta, Washington Co.

1803 Aug 18   Ward, Mima and George Carvel by Robert Oliver, JP, Washington Co.

1817 Oct 20   Ward, Nahum and Sarah Skinner by Rev. Saml P. Robbins, Washington Co.

1818 Apr 2   Ward, Peggy and Seth Philbrook by Samuel Bancroft, JP, Licking Co.

1813 Apr 18   Ward, Phoebe and Dan'l H. Buell by Rev. Stephen Lindley, Washington Co.

1815 Jun 17   Ward, Rebecca and Moses Rugg by John Green, Licking Co.

1817 Dec 16   Ward, Ruth and William Sampha by Geo. Callanhan, EMEC, Licking Co.

1829 Jan 15   Ward, Sarah and William Cox by George Jefferies, Franklin Co.

1821 Jan 6   Ward, Steward and Ann McKinley by Benj Coves, MG, Licking Co.

1825 Jan 13   Ward, Susan and Samuel R. Johnson by J.G. Billiland, JP, Jackson Co.

1872 Mar 7   Ward, Thos. O. and Helen Case by Wm. Bower, St. Luke's Church,
               Granville, Licking Co.

1816 Jan 4   Ward, William and Pheby Beam by Geo. Callanhan, EMEC, Licking Co.

1818 Sep 9   Warden, Elmy and Isaac Morton, Jr. by Rev. Timothy Harris, Licking Co.

1825 Dec 1   Ware, Wm. and Mary Vernem by John Stephenson, JP, Jackson Co.

1820 Apr 6   Warner, Christopher and Maria Loge by Osgood McFarland, JP, Washington
               Co.

1814 Dec 24   Warner, Drucy and Samuel H. Everitt by Rev. T. Harris, Licking Co.

1818 Sep 7   Warner, Elizabeth and Abraham Pavrish? by Isaiah Hoskinson, JP,
               Licking Co.

1823 Oct 22   Warner, John and Maryann Hunterman by D.W. Deshler, JP, Franklin Co.

1805 Apr 10   Warner, Levi and Massie Winder by Peter Jackson, JP, Ross Co.

1820 Mar 20   Warner, Rev. Peter and Elizabeth Williams by John F. Solomon,
               Franklin Co.

1827 Sep 13   Warner, Polly and James Wood by James Hoge, Franklin Co.

1813 Jan 28   Warner, Silas and Sarah Riley (license date), Pickaway Co.

1814 Mar 13   Warnum, Rebecca and Theodorus Nye by Sardine Stone, Washington Co.

1823 Mar 30   Warren, Deloss and Sylvia Griswold by A. Buttles, JP, Franklin Co.

1793 Dec 8   Warren, Elijah and Patty Davenport by R.J. Meigs, JP, Washington Co.

1820 Dec 24   Warren, Fanny and Oliver R. Loring by Rev. Saml P. Robbins, Washington
               Co.

1813 May 18   Warren, Lavina and John Bratton by Percival Adams, JP, Franklin Co.

1820 Apr 2   Warren, Lucretia and Lewis Johnson by John Russell, JP, Washington Co.

1819 Oct 31   Warren, Nancy and Thomas Hutcheson by Orgillous Doan, JP, Washington
               Co.

1816 Jul 4   Warren, Thomas and Zilpha Taylor by Recompence Stansbury, JP, Franklin
               Co.

1827 Dec 30   Warson, Annah and I.F. Miller by A. Hutchinson, JP, Franklin Co.

1828 Oct 2   Warson, Rosey Ann and James C. Miller by Daniel Beard, Franklin Co.

1793 Aug 29   Warth, Catherine and Joseph Fletcher by J. Gilman, Washington Co.

1795 Apr 23   Warth, Catherine and Jean Baptiste Nicholas Tallage, by J. Gilman,
               Washington Co.

1794 Jan 31   Warth, Robert and Katherine LaLance by J. Gilman, Washington Co.

1814 Apr 11   Warts, Christian and Caty Whistler by Thomas Mace, JP, Pickaway Co.

1810 Aug 16   Wash, Barbara and Simeon Herder (license date), Pickaway Co.

1825 Nov 6   Washburn, Elizabeth and E.H. Crosby by Conrad Roth, JP, Marion Co.

1803 Jul 20   Washburn, James and Elizabeth Countriman by Wm. Davis, JP, Ross Co.

1805 Nov 22   Washburn, James and Nancy Cutright by Charles Cade, Ross Co.

1823 Jun 20   Washington, Rachel and Cyrus Baker by Wm. Gilmer, JP, Franklin Co.

1828 Dec 14   Wasson, Sally and David Croy by Amaziah Hutchinson, Franklin Co.

1820 Apr 2   Waterman, Flavius and Polly Walker by Wm. Woodford, JP, Washington Co.

1819 Oct 18   Waterman, Horace and Lydia Wilson by Wm. Woodford, JP, Washington Co.

1805 Jun 16   Waterman, Ignatius and Nelly Crawford by James Quinn, Elder,
               Washington Co.

1804 Jan 12   Waterman, John and Margaret Potts by Robert Oliver, JP, Washington Co.

1814 Jan 9   Waterman, Levi and Patty Adams by Isaac Baker, Esq., Washington Co.

1820 Nov 28   Waterman, Levi L. and Mary Ann Cutler by Rev. Saml P. Robbins,
               Washington Co.

1820 Mar 3   Waterman, Lydia and Levi Brewster by Wm. Woodford, Washington Co.

1813 Sep 29   Waterman, Nancy and John Riley (license date), Pickaway Co.

1805 Jan 20   Waterman, Polly and John Walker by Stephen Lindly, Washington Co.

1812 Jan 9   Waterman, Polly and Shelden Spencer by Jer. Greenman, JP, Washington
               Co.

1812 Nov 6   Waterman, Rhoda and Ephraim White by Eli Cogswell, JP, Washington Co.

1822 Mar 18   Waterman, Sherman and Nancy Wilson by Seth Baker, JP, Washington Co.

1820 Feb 12   Waterman, William and Abigail Sharp by James M. Booth, Washington Co.

1867 Jul 4   Waters, Mrs. Janette and David Turner by Rev. John Boyd, St. Luke's
               Church, Marietta, Washington Co.

1793 Oct 30   Waters, Sally and Selah Heart by R.J. Meigs, Washington Co.

1803 Jul 20   Watkins, David and Margaret Chad by Griffin Greene, JP, Washington Co.

1807 May 7   Watkins, John and Mary Tibbott by Josiah McKinney, Franklin Co.

1826 Oct 10   Watkins, Sarah and Mathias Kensel by C. Henkel, Franklin Co.

1814 Jun 12   Watrous, William and Priscilla Bodwell by Dan'l H. Buell, JP,
               Washington Co.

1820 Mar 26   Watsbaugh, H. and William Suiter by Noah Fidler, Licking Co.

1807 Jul 30   Watson, David and Mary Helpinstine by Nehemiah Gates, JP, Franklin Co.

1864 Mar 21   Watson, Frank F. of Vincennes, Ind., and Jane M. Medlicott by Rev.
               John Boyd, St. Luke's Church, Marietta, Washington Co.

1815 Mar 13   Watson, James and Rebecca Cunningham by Rev. T. Harris, Licking Co.

1806 Jul 17   Watson, William and Sally White by Alexander Morrison, Jr., JP,
               Franklin Co.

1817 Mar 18   Watson, William and Polly Stultz by Wm. O'Bannon, JP, Licking Co.

1824 Aug 21   Watt, Jane and William Phelps by T. Lee, JP, Franklin Co.

1816 Jan 28   Watts, Ann and John Foster by Joseph Gorton, Franklin Co.

1817 Oct 9   Watts, John and Mary Scott by John Crow, Licking Co.

1828 Dec 4   Watts, Maria and Otho Godman by Leroy Swornstead, Franklin Co.

1828 Apr 15   Watts, Nicholas and May Ann Claybaugh by Sam'l Hamilton, Franklin Co.

1821 Aug 2   Watts, Polly and Asa Wilcox by A. Allen, Franklin Co.

1809 Feb 11   Watts, Salley and Wm. Merrian by James Hoge, Franklin Co.

1827 Aug 9   Watts, Trifenia and Peter Willicox by Geo. Jefferies, Ordained
               Minister, Franklin Co.

1812 Jun 25   Wayson, Jane and Peter Voshell by Rev. Stephen Lindley, Washington Co.

1817 Dec 7   Wayson, John and Abigail Robbins by Cyrus Ames, Washington Co.

1820 Apr 22   Waytes, John and Eliza Massie by Moses Williamson, JP, Washington Co.

1829 Jan 25   Weaks, Sarah Ann and William M. Bills by Isaac Fisher, Elder CC,
               Franklin Co.

1820 Dec 25   Weas, Mary and John Star by Vincent Southard, JP, Jackson Co.

1817 Apr 30   Weatherbee, Deborah and James McLaughlin by Stephen Guthrie, JP,
               Washington Co.

1814 Nov 9   Weatherby, Lydia and Job Coggshall by Stephen Guthrie, Esq.,
               Washington Co.

1814 Jun 3   Weatherington, Wm. and Sarry Hellzel by Percival Adams, Franklin Co.

1813 Jul 18   Weaver, Asa and Lucinda Shaw by Ezra Griswold, Franklin Co.

1825 Jul 17   Weaver, David and Amanda Andrews by Aristarchus Walker, Franklin Co.

1884 Mar 22   Weaver, Esther R. and Edward F. Roper both of Putnam by Rev. George F.
               Moore, Putnam Presbyterian Church, Muskingum Co.

1842 Oct 25   Weaver, Lydia Ann and Timothy Griffith by Rev. R.S. Elder, St. John's
               Church, Worthington, Franklin Co.

1810 Oct 1   Weaver, Mary and Enoch Williams (license date), Pickaway Co.

1851 Aug 19   Weaver, William and Templeton Gammel by Rev. A. Kingsbury, Putnam
               Presbyterian Church, Muskingum Co.

1887 Oct 20   Weaver, William A. and Anna M. Deacon both of Zanesville by Rev.
               George F. Moore, Putnam Presbyterian Church, Muskingum Co.

1804 Dec 4   Webb, Elisha and Mary Tomlin by Wm. Davis, Esq., Ross Co.

1820 Apr 4   Webb, Martha W. and Benjamin Graves, Jr. by A. Buttles, JP, Franklin
               Co.

1814 Oct 14   Webb, Nellie and Benjamin Freeman by Rev. Geo. Alkire, Pickaway Co.

1813 Jan 29   Webb, Robert and Nancy Fitzgerald (license date), Pickaway Co.

1820 Nov 14   Webb, Susan and John Adams by Sanford Converse, JP, Licking Co.

1814 Nov 17   Webster, Adelphia and Mary Coburn by Thos. White, JP, Washington Co.

1794 Apr 3   Webster, Andrew and Sally Brown by R.J. Meigs, Washington Co.

1817 Oct 15   Webster, Elihu and Nancy Anderson by Eli C. King, Franklin Co.

1804 Jan 24   Webster, James Brice and Millia Dawson by Abm Miller, Ross Co.

1805 May 2   Webster, John and Elizabeth Winder by Peter Jackson, JP, Ross Co.

1821 Jan 14   Webster, John L. and Mary Burris by John Patterson, JP, Washington Co.

1814 Oct 2   Webster, Libbel and Luther Vining by Obadiah Scott, Washington Co.

1819 Jul 2   Webster, Lucinda and Oliver H. Halcamb by Ezra Griswold, Franklin Co.

1815 Jun 7   Webster, William Jr. and Emily Case by Ezra Griswold, Franklin Co.

1805 Feb 14   Weeder, Catharine and Henry Frederick by Isaac Damson, Ross Co.

1819 Feb 11   Weedman, Jacob and Catherine Byshop by Charles Waddell, MG, Licking Co.

1807 Nov 29   Weeks, Daniel Jr. and Elizabeth Fisher by James Kilbourne, Franklin Co.

1803 Feb 11   Weethn, Daniel and Lucy Wilkins by Alvan Bingham, JP, Washington Co.

1819 Jul 11   Weid, Mehitable and John Jones by J. Thrap, Licking Co.

1805 Oct 6   Weider, Christeena and Daniel Mussellman by Abraham Miller, Ross Co.

1801 May 21   Welch, Abigail and Francis Battle by Rufus Putnam, JP, Washington Co.

1807 Jul 21   Welch, Charlott and John Smith by Arthur O'Harra, Franklin Co.

1808 Jan 8   Welch, Fodilla and Isaac Lewis by Nathaniel Wyatt, Franklin Co.

1870 Jun 15   Welch, Johnson M. of Athens, O., and Ellen Cadwallader by Rev. John
               Boyd, St. Luke's Church, Marietta, Washington Co.

1816 Mar 25   Welch, Joseph and Polly Cutler by Ezra Griswold, Franklin Co.

1818 Jan 29   Welch, Robert and Nancy Perry by B.W. Talbot, JP, Washington Co.

1806 Dec 16   Welch, Ruth and Ellis James by Josiah McKenny, Franklin Co.

1792 Dec 25   Welch, Sally and Thomas Hutchinson by Robert Oliver, Judge,
               Washington Co.

1805 Feb 7   Welch, Sally and Solomon Dickey by J. Brough, JP, Washington Co.

1791 Apr 17   Welles, David and Polly Corey by Benj Tupper, Washington Co.

1791 Feb 17   Welles, Nancy and Thomas Corey by Benj Tupper, Washington Co.

1791 Feb 17   Welles, Sally and Peleg Springer by Benj Tupper, Washington Co.

1791 Feb 24   Welles, Susanna and Pelatiah White by Benj Tupper, Washington Co.

1825 Oct 20   Wellman, James and Peggy Wetsel by Wm. McClintic, JP, Jackson Co.

1820 Apr 16   Wells, Candace and Caleb R. Harris by Joel Tuttle, Jr., JP,
               Washington Co.

1811 Feb 5   Wells, Chester and Polly Case by Rev. T. Harris, Licking Co.

1844 Jun 20   Wells, Chester of Hanover and Mary Sturges of Putnam by Rev. A. Kings-
               bury, Putnam Presbyterian Church, Muskingum Co.

1797 Jan 5   Wells, Elisabeth and Jacob Procter by Robert Oliver, Washington Co.

1812 May 16   Wells, Elizabeth and Dougal Walker by Edwin Putnam, Washington Co.

1817 Feb 2   Wells, Ezekiel and Polly Read by Wm. O'Bannon, JP, Licking Co.

1869 Oct 5   Wells, Jane E.P. and Arthur F. Ludlow both of England by Rev. John
               Boyd, St. Luke's Church, Marietta, Washington Co.

1818 Mar 22   Wells, Joel and Mila Ingham by Samuel Bancroft, JP, Licking Co.

1813 Dec 9   Wells, John and Patty Sparks by G. Callanahan, EMEC, Licking Co.

1819 Jun 27   Wells, Joseph C. and Amanda Fall by Amos Wilson, JP, Washington Co.

1816 Feb 8   Wells, Laura and Thomas Taylor by T.D. Baird, Licking Co.

1819 Nov 17   Wells, Louisa and Abel Sherman by Sardine Stone, JP, Washington Co.

1849 Sep 5   Wells, M.P. and Harriet M. Butler by Rev. D.W. Tolford, St. Luke's
               Church, Marietta, Washington Co.

1880 May 31   Wells, Maggie and Quincey Wilson by Rev. John Boyd, St. Luke's
               Church, Marietta, Washington Co.

1819 Jan 12   Wells, Marinda and Henry Mathews by Charles Waddle, PE, Licking Co.

1826 Apr 4   Wells, Martha and William Cozad by Solomon Redfern, JP, Jackson Co.

1810 Jan 9   Wells, Nichalas and Rachel Witten by Henry Jolly, JP, Washington Co.

1805 Nov 7   Wells, Narnum G. and Sarah Davis by N. Davis, Washington Co.

1814 Dec 22   Wells, Robert and Hannah Case by Rev. S.P. Robbins, Washington Co.

1813 May 1   Wells, Sally and Thomas Alcock by Rev. Stephen Lindsley, Washington Co.

1799 May 9   Wells, Sarah and Joseph Johnson by Daniel Story, Clerk, Washington Co.

1801 Sep 8   Wells, Sarah and Joseph Archer by Philip Witten, Washington Co.

1818 Jan 1   Wells, Sophia and Henry Wait by Simon Merwin, Washington Co.

1801 Feb 4   Wells, Thomas and Peggy Patterson by Nehemiah Davis, Washington Co.

1819 Dec 4   Wells, Truman and Patience Babcock by Elijah Dunlap, Licking Co.

1807 Jan 29   Welsh, Isaac and Mary Shaw by Josiah McKinney, Franklin Co.

1808 Dec 12   Welson, John and Nansey Whitaker by Joseph Badger, Franklin Co.

1821 Aug 30   Welton, Amnis and Thomas Elder by Wm. Jones, Franklin Co.

1819 Apr 29   Welton, Mary and Jesse Seymaur by John B. Whittlessy, MG Lancaster,
              Ohio, Franklin Co.

1886 Oct 28   Welty, G.A. and Lulu Shaw both of Zanesville by Rev. George F. Moore,
              Putnam Presbyterian Church, Muskingum Co.

1880 Jan 22   Wendell, John K. and Jennie Black both of Putnam by Rev. George F.
              Moore, Putnam Presbyterian Church, Muskingum Co.

1882 Sep 18   Wertheimer, Harry and Jennie Tweed by Rev. John Boyd, St. Luke's
              Church, Marietta, Washington Co.

1874 Mar 23   Wertsberger, Sebastin and Susan Giffens by Rev. John Boyd, St. Luke's
              Church, Marietta, Washington Co.

1819 Apr 26   Wesson, Joseph and Abigail Wilson by John Patterson, JP, Washington Co.

1814 Jul 3   West, Barbara and William Hall by Wm. Florence, JP, Pickaway Co.

1824 Apr 15   West, Benjamin and Anne Avry by Uriah Clark, Franklin Co.

1814 Jun 28   West, Catherine and James Abrahams by J. Crow, JP, Licking Co.

1814 Oct 20   West, Caty and Phillip Tullinger by Henry Daus, Pickaway Co.

1805 Dec 22   West, Elisabeth and James Blue by Wm. Bennett, JP, Franklin Co.

1895 Apr 25   West, Elmer J. and Cora M. St. Clair both of Cumberland, O., by Rev.
              George F. Moore, Putnam Presbyterian Church, Muskingum Co.

1819 Nov 10   West, Mary and Benjamin Mesewey by John C. Smith, JP, Licking Co.

1813 Feb 14   West, Nancy and Tulman Martin (license date), Pickaway Co.

1798 Jan 1   West, Phebe and Daniel Louvat by Peregrine Foster, JCCCP, Washington
              Co.

1810 Dec 41[sic] West, Samuel and Eliza Scott (license date), Pickaway Co.

1806 May 22   West, Sarah and Jacob Barthley by Wm. Bennett, JP, Franklin Co.

1809 Aug 4   West, Sary and Isaac Roberts by Nehemiah Gates, Franklin Co.

1827 Jun 24   West, Thomas and Polly Justice by Geo. Jefferies, Ordained MG,
              Franklin Co.

1819 Aug 26   Westbrook, Solomon and Rebecca Hide by Elihu Bigelow, Licking Co.

1821 Jan 1   Westcott, Samuel A. and Sarah L. Edgerton by Rev. Saml P. Robbins,
              Washington Co.

1804 Jan 12   Westfall, Cornelius and Sarah Rumson by John Odle, JP, Ross Co.

1818 --- --   Westfall, Eli and Ruth Jones by Jacob Delay, MG, Jackson Co.

1814 Mar 14   Westfall, Newton E. and Annaliza Frazer by Rev. Stephen Lindsley,
               Washington Co.

1818 Sep 10   Westfall, Tabitha and Ambrose Leach by Jacob Delay, Licensed Minister
               of the Gospel, Jackson Co.

1808 Sep 4   Westgate, Paty and Elezer Calkings by Daniel Dunfee, Washington Co.

1809 Jan 1   Westgate, Rhoda and Calvin Record by Dan'l Dunfee, Washington Co.

1819 Oct 14   Weston, Amelia and Gustavus Swan by James Hoge, Franklin Co.

1828 Jun 5   Weston, Caroline A. and Griffin R. Minor by James Hoge, Franklin Co.

1820 Feb 2   Westorn, Abner and Edna Mast by Emmor Cox, JP, Franklin Co.

1823 Feb 13   Westover, Alexander and Electa Beal by Joseph Badger, JP, Franklin Co.

1843 Nov 6   Weters, Warren and Eunice Lewis by Rev. R.S. Elder near Mt. Vernon,
               St. John's Church, Worthington, Franklin Co.

1825 Oct 20   Wetsel, Peggy and James Wellman by Wm. McClintic, JP, Jackson Co.

1819 May 19   Whaley, Mary and Hiram Maddox by Samuel McDowell, JP, Jackson Co.

1820 Apr 19   Wharf, William and Deborah Clay by Dudley Davis, JP, Washington Co.

1827 12m 5   Wharton, Hannah and Richard Hopkins, Miami Monthly Meeting, Warren Co.

1810 May 8   Whead, Mary and Israel Shreve by Adam Winegarner, JP, Licking Co.

1825 Apr 21   Wheatley, Rosan and Archibald Leach by Robert Ward, JP, Jackson Co.

1896 Feb 19   Wheeler, Annie and John A. McLean both of Zanesville by Rev. George
               F. Moore, Putnam Presbyterian Church, Muskingum Co.

1806 Oct 19   Wheeler, Betsy and John Miller by Sam'l P. Robbins, Washington Co.

1820 Sep 28   Wheeler, David A. and Elzada McGonnigal by Amos Wilson, Washington Co.

1816 Jan 8   Wheeler, Elizabeth and Patrick Robinson by J. Cunningham, Licking Co.

1860 Oct 1   Wheeler, Frances and William B. Loomis by Rev. John Boyd, St. Luke's
               Church, Marietta, Washington Co.

1828 Jun 28   Wheeler, Ignatius and M.J. Naydenbush by Wm. Lush, JP, Franklin Co.

1819 Jan 14   Wheeler, James and James Hughes by Geo. Callanhan, EMEC, Licking Co.

1872 Jan 10   Wheeler, John D. of Zanesville and Lillie N. Rankin of White Cottage,
               by Rev. A. Kingsbury, Putnam Presbyterian Church, Muskingum Co.

1872 Dec 25   Wheeler, Julia and J. Dallas Cadwallader by Rev. John Boyd, St.
               Luke's Church, Marietta, Washington Co.

1814 Apr 28   Wheeler, Margaret and Joseph Cunningham by ----- Licking Co.

1817 Aug 28   Wheeler, Maria and Levi Bils by Rev. Saml P. Robbins, Washington Co.

1821 Jan 1   Wheeler, Otis and Diantha Moss by Rev. Saml P. Robbins, Washington Co.

1808 Apr 21   Wheeler, Rebekah and Robert Harrison by J. Brough, JP, Washington Co.

1821 Apr 23   Wheeler, Samuel and Catherine Smith by Michael Trout, JP, Licking Co.

1819 Nov 10   Wheeler, Solomon and Lillian Chissman by Noah Fidler, Licking Co.

1816 Sep 26   Wherry, Jane and John Wherry by James Hoge (another entry 27 Mar 1817),
               Franklin Co.

1816 Sep 26   Wherry, John and Jane Wherry by James Hoge (another entry 27 Mar 1817), Franklin Co.

1818 Mar 24   Wherry, Martha and William White by James Hoge, Franklin Co.

1803 May 17   Whetstone, Catherine and Josias Devore by Jos. Gardner, JP, Ross Co.

1819 Jun 15   Whettemore, William and Leah Reans by John Smith, Franklin Co.

1819 Jan 14   Whetzel, Catherine and Lyaton Palmer by Jacob Delay, MG, Jackson Co.

1825 Dec 29   Whetzel, John and Massee Braley by Zephaniah Brown, JP, Jackson Co.

1819 Dec 16   Whetzel, Margary and Wm. Howard by Jacob Delay, MG, Jackson Co.

1804 Jan 22   Whetzell, Daniel and Martha Smith by Abm Miller, Ross Co.

1876 Sep 13   Whiffing, Mary P. and Willis H. Johnson by Rev. John Boyd, St. Luke's Church, Marietta, Washington Co.

1815 Feb 2   Whipple, Enoch and Catherine Shaw by Moses Foster, JP, Licking Co.

1863 Sep 16   Whips, Wm. D. and Frances Adeliade Koons by Rev. H.H. Messenger (see wedding guests under bride entry), St. Paul's Church, Marion, Marion Co.

1814 Apr 11   Whistler, Caty and Christian Warts by Thomas Mace, JP, Pickaway Co.

1814 6m 1   Whitacre, Andrew and Mary Kelly, Miami Monthly Meeting, Warren Co.

1816 1m 3   Whitacre, Jane and Benjamin Ninde, Miami Monthly Meeting, Warren Co.

1813 12m 1   Whitacre, Priscilla and Jonah Cadwalader, Miami Monthly Meeting, Warren Co.

1820 12m 7   Whitacre, Rhoda and Joseph Hollingsworth, Miami Monthly Meeting, Warren Co.

1808 Dec 12   Whitaker, Nansey and John Welson by Joseph Badger, Franklin Co.

1852 Jan 14   Whitcomb, Abigail B. and Jas. P. Lyddane by Rev. Geo. B. Sturges, St. Paul's Church, Marion, Marion Co.

1823 Feb 13   White, Alexander and Sarah Moorehead by Jacob Grubb, JP, Franklin Co.

1813 Apr 18   White, Anna and Charles S. Cory by Thomas White, JP, Washington Co.

1807 Aug 6   White, Catharine and Elkana Vining by Wm. Shaw, JP, Franklin Co.

1813 Apr 12   White, Charles and Polly Hinton (license date), Pickaway Co.

1811 Jan 31   White, Christopher L. and Ann Caldwell by James Marshall, Franklin Co.

1815 Feb 19   White, Cynthia and James Grubb by Isaac Baker, Esq., Washington Co.

1802 Apr 28   White, David and Rebecca Porter by Peregrine Foster, JCCCP, Washington Co.

1809 Jan 22   White, David and Catharine Briggs by Sam'l P. Robbins, Washington Co.

1814 Apr 7   White, Eliza and John Surgart by Henry Coonrod, JP, Pickaway Co.

1812 Nov 6   White, Ephraim and Rhoda Waterman by Eli Cogswell, JP, Washington Co.

1810 Oct 31   White, Fanny and Enos Glaspy by Isaac Case, JP, Franklin Co.

1821 Feb 6   White, George and Mary Kilgore by James Hoge, Franklin Co.

1880 Jun 9   White, Gideon and Julia Maria Jones by Rev. John Boyd, St. Luke's Church, Marietta, Washington Co.

1829 Jan 22   White, Hannah and Thomas Martin by George Jefferies, Franklin Co.

1810 Nov 25   White, Hope and Walter Van Horn (license date), Pickaway Co.

1818 Jul 9   White, Jacob and Mary Parr by Alex Holden, JP, Licking Co.

1820 Mar 13   White, James and Caty Pike by Joseph Gorton, JP, Franklin Co.

1825 Nov 25   White, James and Nancy Masters by Wm. McClintic, JP, Jackson Co.

1817 Feb 27   White, James H. and Selinda Biglaw by Isaac Griswold, JP, Franklin Co.

1814 Jan 2   White, Jane and Josiah Fisher by Glass Cochran, JP, Franklin Co.

1818 Nov 6   White, Jane and William Waits by James Hoge, Franklin Co.

1803 Mar 24   White, Jaremiah and Sarah Burton by Wm. Bennett, JP, Franklin Co.

1789 Oct 11   White, John and Presilla Devoll by Ben Tupper, JCCCP, Washington Co.

1818 Oct 8   White, John and Elizabeth Clark by Wm. How, JP, Jackson Co.

1815 Mar 16   White, John M. and Rachael Moorehead by Joseph Gorton, Franklin Co.

1816 Feb 14   White, John S. and Sarah R. Bondinct by Rev. Stephen Lindsley,
               Washington Co.

1815? -- --   White, Lydia and Joab Jones by Jeremiah Greenman, JP, Washington Co.

1821 Jun 7   White, Mary and Thomas Bolton by Nathl. Little, Franklin Co.

1825 Jan 16   White, Nancy and James Scott by Samuel McDowell, JP, Jackson Co.

1799 Jul 23   White, Nathaniel and Nancy Thornton by Robert Safford, Washington Co.

1791 Feb 24   White, Pelatiah and Susanna Welles by Benj Tupper, Washington Co.

1806 Oct 16   White, Polly and Amos Miller by Sam'l P. Robbins, Washington Co.

1820 Dec 22   White, Polly and Jermiah Kindal by Wm. Hull, JP, Licking Co.

1826 Feb 9   White, Polly and Lewis Harmon by John White, Jackson Co.

1819 Nov 24   White, Rebecca and Jacob Hoffman by Jacob Keller, Franklin Co.

1821 Jan 4   White, Rebecca and Rufus Lawrence by John D. Chamberlain, JP,
               Washington Co.

1816 Mar 21   White, Ruth and Parr Rathbun by J.W. Patterson, JP, Licking Co.

1806 Jul 17   White, Sally and William Watson by Alexander Morrison, Jr., JP,
               Franklin Co.

1812 Jul 7   White, Samuel and Nancy Ballinger by James Hoge, Franklin Co.

1819 Aug 4   White, Samuel M. and Fanny Ceask by Jacob Keller, Franklin Co.

1810 Jan 11   White, Sophia and Ebenezer Blackstone by Stephen Lindsly, Washington
               Co.

1817 Jun 20   White, Sophia and James Baker by Titan Kimball, JP, Washington Co.

1809 Apr 9   White, Stewart and Elizabeth Hamilton by James Marshall, Franklin Co.

1821 Mar 28   White, Thomas Hatfield and Joana Wood by Wm. Woodford, JP, Washington
               Co.

1820 Jun 1   White, Wells and Sally Evans by Thomas White, JP, Washington Co.

1813 Aug 22   White, William and Lydia Tucker by Stephen Lindsley, Washington Co.

1818 Mar 24   White, William and Martha Wherry by James Hoge, Franklin Co.

1820 Dec 16   White, Willis and Betsey Berry by Wm. Hull, JP, Licking Co.

1818 Oct 19   Whitebery, Jonathan and Rebecca Cafrey by Alex Holden, JP, Licking Co.

1805 May 9   Whitecotten, Sally and Moses Overfield by David W. Davis, JP, Ross Co.

1818 Jun 29   Whitehead, Elizabeth and George Calahan by James Holmes, JP, Licking
               Co.

1816 Jun 15   Whitehead, Huldah C. and Elias Ogden by Joseph Gorton, Franklin Co.

1818 Nov 19   Whitehead, Onessimas and Pyrine Case by R. Stansbery, Franklin Co.

1802 Sep 7   Whitehouse, Mary and George Howe by Griffin Greene, JP, Washington Co.

1815 Mar 26   Whiten, Isaac and Maria Random by Isaac Case, Franklin Co.

1814 Sep 18   Whitesel, Margaret and George Cremer by Emmor C. Cox, JP, Franklin Co.

1813 Jun 25   Whiteside, Mary and James Casler (license date), Pickaway Co.

1797 Oct 5   Whitham, Mehitabel and Simeon Wright by Josiah Munro, Washington Co.

1825 Apr 14   Whitherd, Joseph and Clarinda Beadle by Conrad Roth, JP, Marion Co.

1810 Nov 1   Whiticor, Dayton and Rachel Rogers by Geo. Wells, JP, Licking Co.

1802 Feb 18   Whiting, Adam and Mary Park by John Struthers, JP, Trumbull Co.

1802 Feb 18   Whiting, Margaret and William Park by Jonthan Struthers, JP, Trumbull
               Co.

1810 Jun 26   Whitman, George and Rebecca Heath (license date), Pickaway Co.

1813 Sep 27   Whitmire, John and Elizabeth Morris by John Green, JP, Licking Co.

1826 Jun 3   Whitmore, Elizabeth and William Elder by I. Gander, JP, Franklin Co.

1798 Aug 14   Whitmore, Francis and Rebecca Stroud by D. Loring, Jus Com Pleas,
               Washington Co.

1826 Dec 17   Whitmore, George and Hannah Fairchilde by Lysides L. Latimore, JP,
               Franklin Co.

1812 Apr 13   Whitmore, John and Polly Hornbacon by Thomas Morris, Franklin Co.

1807 Nov 14   Whitney, James and Ruth Greene by S.P. Robbins, Washington Co.

1821 Mar 1   Whitney, John and Sarah Chapman by Saml Beach, JP, Washington Co.

1804 Jul 12   Whitney, Thomas and Marea Emmery by Isaac Cook, JP, Ross Co.

1820 Oct 21   Whitney, Thomas and Artimacy Preston by Wm. Rand, JP, Washington Co.

1829 Jun 11   Whitsell, Andrew and Mary Rager by Abram Shoemaker, JP, Franklin Co.

1829 Jul 9   Whitsell, Frederick and Polly Hews by Abram Shoemaker, JP, Franklin
               Co.

1822 Feb 28   Whitsell, John and Catharine Pancake by Nicholas Goetschius,
               Franklin Co.

1827 Jan 31   Whitsill, Samuel and Caroline Fraley by Wm. Patterson, Franklin Co.

1806 12m 18   Whitson, Willis and Rebekah Comton, Miami Monthly Meeting, Warren Co.

1807 Jan 20   Whitten, Peter and Rachel Bowen by James Riggs, Washington Co.

1871 Dec 7   Whittlesey, Emily and William B. Mitchell by Rev. John Boyd, St.
              Luke's Church, Marietta, Washington Co.

1828 Nov 16   Whitzel, Sally and John Bishop by J. Gander, JP, Franklin Co.

1814 Apr 3   Wickingham, Joseph and Fanny Miller by Rev. Isaac Quinn, Washington
              Co.

1818 Jul 20   Wickizer, Patty and James M. Phelps by Eli C. King, Franklin Co.

1816 Jun 2   Widders, Daniel and Sylvia Little by J. Cunningham, JPNAT, Licking Co.

1805 Jul 20   Wier, Sally ad Richard Patten by John Brough, JP, Washington Co.

1809 Sep 30   Wigdon, Wm. and Jane Young by James Marshall, Franklin Co.

1820 Dec 31   Wiggins, Joseph and Sarah Foster by Reuben Golliday, Franklin Co.

1875 Jun 1   Wiggins, Laura and Rev. Dudley Ward Rhodes at St. Louise, Mo., by
              Rev. John Boyd, St. Luke's Church, Marietta, Washington Co.

1814 Apr 3   Wiggins, Ruth and Chales Medford by Wm. D. Hendren, Franklin Co.

1817 Mar 4   Wiggins, Sophia and William Rogers by Edward Hursey, JP, Licking Co.

1854 Sep 25   Wightman, A.J. and Jane Wood by T. Corlett, St. Luke's Church,
              Granville, Licking Co.

1815 Nov 5   Wightman, George and Elizabeth Hinald by Percival Adams, Franklin Co.

1823 Oct 9   Wilber, Olive and James Downs by Robert W. Riley, JP, Franklin Co.

1823 Sep 11   Wilcox, Anny and Samuel Paxton by Robert Boyd, Franklin Co.

1821 Aug 2   Wilcox, Asa and Polly Watts by A. Allen, Franklin Co.

1806 Jul 16   Wilcox, Azenith and Truman Case by Arthur O'Harra, JP, Franklin Co.

1817 Jan 9   Wilcox, Dorcus and John Cary by R. Stansbury, Franklin Co.

1820 Jul 4   Wilcox, Emily and Opolos Maymard by A. Buttles, Franklin Co.

1826 Jan 19   Wilcox, George and Rebecca Kain by Henry Matthews, Franklin Co.

1825 Apr 20   Wilcox, Harriet and John B. Benard by Aristarcrus Walker, Franklin Co.

1826 Aug 31   Wilcox, Isreal S. and Sarah D. Messenger by R.W. Cowls, JP, Franklin
              Co.

1826 Jan 19   Wilcox, John and Betsy Delay by Zeph Brown, JP, Jackson Co.

1812 Oct 15   Wilcox, Rebecca and Amaziah Bray by Rev. S.P. Robbins, Washington Co.

1824 May 27   Wilcox, Thomas and Mary Hopper by Joseph Badger, Franklin Co.

1812 Oct 16   Wilcox, Tracy and Christina Taylor by E. Griswold, Franklin Co.

1816 Jul 25   Wilcox, Warren and Almira Vining by Isaac Case, JP, Franklin Co.

1814 Feb 22   Wildhan, Rebecca and John Newhorter by Sam'l Lybrand, Pickaway Co.

1824 Sep 25   Wiles, Mariah and George H. Anderson by Isaac Fisher, Franklin Co.

1819 Feb 8   Wiles, Polly and Henry Casel by D. Mitchell, JP, Jackson Co.

1826 Jan 19   Wiley, Elizabeth and Samuel D. Thavely by John F. Solomon, Franklin Co.

1827 Oct 4   Wiley, Levy and Elizabeth Legg by Geo. Jefferies, MBC, Franklin Co.

1825 Oct 20   Wiley, Margret and James Haward by John F. Solomon, Franklin Co.

1870 Jun 1   Wiley, William W. of Orange, N.J., and Joanna R. Clark of Putnam by
              Rev. A. Kingsbury, Putnam Presbyterian Church, Muskingum Co.

1804 Jul 19   Wilfong, David and Susan Chaply by Abm Miller, Ross Co.

1861 Sep 11   Wilgus, Catherine and Samul Lightfritz by Rev. John Boyd, St. Luke's
              Church, Marietta, Washington Co.

1815 Dec 20   Wilk, Martha and Charles Howard by Z. Carlisle, Licking Co.

1817 Apr 22   Wilkins, Catherine and John P. Baker by J.W. Patterson, JP, Licking
              Co.

1813 Mar 10   Wilkins, Daniel and Rebecca Barnes by J.W. Patterson, Licking Co.

1813 May 6   Wilkins, Elizabeth and William Horn by -----, Licking Co.

1805 Jan 3   Wilkins, Godfry and Catharine Lance by John Davidson, Ross Co.

1819 Jul 1   Wilkins, Jacob and Elizabeth Stover by Noah Fidler, Licking Co.

1803 Feb 11   Wilkins, Lucy and Daniel Weethn by Alvan Bingham, JP, Washington Co.

1897 Aug 31   Wilkins, S. Emerson of Mt. Perry and Florence McGee of Meadow Farm,
              O., by Rev. George F. Moore, Putnam Presbyterian Church,
              Muskingum Co.

1820 Sep 14   Wilkins, Sarah and James Hall by Alex. Anderson, JP, Jackson Co.

1825 Oct 23   Wilkins, Sam'l and Mary McIntire by Abner Bent, JP, Marion Co.

1820 May 21   Wilkinson, Moses and Bethena Thompson by Rev. Philander Chase,
              Franklin Co.

1839 Mar 8   Wilkinson, Moses K. and Sophia Moore by Rev. A. Helfenstine, St.
              John's Church, Worthington, Franklin Co.

1819 Feb 4   Wilkinson, Rachel and Joseph Dixon by Jesse Rudrick, JP, Jackson Co.

1816 Jun 13   Willard, Samuel and Sophrona Williams by Ezra Griswold, Franklin Co.

1812 Mar 8   Willard, Windsor and Lovice Manning by Reuben Carpenter, JP, Franklin
              Co.

1816 Jul 14   Willcox, Asa and Mary Carter by Robert Elliott, JP, Franklin Co.

1817 Jan 30   Willcox, Roswell and Ann Faulkner by R. Stansbury, JP, Franklin Co.

1823 Jan 7   Willcox, Tracy and Prescilla Malbone by Aristochus Walker, Franklin
              Co.

1814 Feb 3   Willcox, Violet and Elam Barber by Ezra Griswold, Franklin Co.

1803 Nov 11   Willet, Abigail and James Roult by Thomas Scott, JP Scioto Tp., Ross
              Co.

1819 May 13   Willet, Richard and Margaret Robinson by T.D. Baird, VDM, Licking Co.

1814 Oct 13   Willets, Susan and Robert Fields by Samuel Lybrand, JP, Pickaway Co.

1813 Sep 23   Willey, Amons and Elizabeth Robinson(license date), Pickaway Co.

1823 Apr 17   Willey, Benjamin F. and Maria Strong by Nathan Emery, JP, Franklin Co.

1821 Aug 19   Williams, Abram and Sarah Pantenny by John Davis, Franklin Co.

1829 Jun 17   Williams, Alonso and Margaret Smith by Geo. Jefferies, Franklin Co.

1810 Aug 23   Williams, Amanda and Jonah Todd (license date), Pickaway Co.

1828 Mar 17   Williams, Ann and George R. Piper by M.T.C. Wing, Deacon, Franklin Co.

1896 Dec 9   Williams, Arthur O. and Rosa E. Gibson both of Roseville, O., by Rev.
               George F. Moore, Putnam Presbyterian Church, Muskingum Co.

1816 Nov 21   Williams, Charlotte and John Collins by Ezra Griswold, JP, Franklin Co.

1821 1m 4   Williams, Clark and Mary Thompson, Miami Monthly Meeting, Warren Co.

1824 Feb 10   Williams, Cumfort and Joseph Spangler by James Hoge, Franklin Co.

1813 Dec 9   Williams, David and Sarah McKenzie (license date), Pickaway Co.

1819 Mar 18   Williams, David and Charlott Mullin by Elihu Bigelow, JP, Licking Co.

1802 Jul 26   Williams, Eleanor and Silas Durgee by Daniel Story, Clerk, Washington
               Co.

1804 Sep 26   Williams, Elias and Chrislar Countriman by Wm. Davis, JP, Ross Co.

1802 Jan 18   Williams, Eliza and Abner Bent by Daniel Story, Clerk, Washington Co.

1808 Apr 7   Williams, Elizabeth and Thomas Baker by J. Brough, Washington Co.

1820 Mar 20   Williams, Elizabeth and Rev. Peter Warner by John F. Solomon,
               Franklin Co.

1810 Oct 1   Williams, Enoch and Mary Weaver (license date), Pickaway Co.

1812 Dec 29   Williams, Frances and Joseph Stacy by Rev. Stephen Lindley, Washington
               Co.

1804 Nov 16   Williams, George and Sarah Cavender by Samuel Edwards, Ross Co.

1810 Aug 13   Williams, Hannah and Asa Goodwin by Stephen Lindsly, Washington Co.

1816 Feb 15   Williams, Henry and Lydia Abbott by Obadiah Scott, Washington Co.

1813 Jun 20   Williams, Isaiah and Comfort Worthington by P. Adams, JP, Franklin Co.

1809 May 4   Williams, James and Mary Simpson by John Hollister, JPHT, Licking Co.

1824 May 6   Williams, James and Catharin Bats by Andrew Allison, JP, Franklin Co.

1853 Feb 21   Williams, James W. and Martha Graham by Rev. Geo. B. Sturges, St.
               Paul's Church, Marion, Marion Co.

1867 Sep 18   Williams, James W. and Mary E. Starr by Rev. John Boyd, St. Luke's
               Church, Marietta, Washington Co.

1806 Dec 25   Williams, Jane and Forggy Williams by Arthur O'Harra, JP, Franklin Co.

1819 Feb 4   Williams, Jane and Joseph Willson by Percival Adams, Franklin Co.

1821 Feb 25   Williams, Jeremiah and Lovine Carpenter by Reuben Carpenter, Franklin
               Co.

1807 Jun 7   Williams, John and Peggy Worthington by James Marshall, JP, Franklin
               Co.

1811 Sep 21   Williams, John and Hannah Johnson (license date), Pickaway Co.

1864 Nov 3   Williams, John J. and Ellen Rush Jones by Rt. Rev. G.T. Bedell, St.
               Paul's Church, Marion, Marion Co.

1886 Jun 16   Williams, John J. and Mary Ray both of Zanesville by Rev. George F.
               Moore, Putnam Presbyterian Church, Muskingum Co.

1806 Jul 14   Williams, Joseph and Sally Stephens by Jacob Lindly, Washington Co.

1824 Sep 16   Williams, Joseph and Sarah Brintlinger by Robert W. Riley, JP,
               Franklin Co.

1805 Oct 17   Williams, Levy and James Ross by Samuel Edwards, Ross Co.

1812 Jul 6   Williams, Lydia and James Carpenter by Rev. T. Harris, Licking Co.

1817 Oct 14   Williams, Margaret and John Bordinot by John Patterson, Washington Co.

1822 Mar 26   Williams, Margaret and Alexander Mooberry by James Hoge, Franklin Co.

1855 Apr 12   Williams, Margaret P. and George P. Cross by T. Corlett, St. Luke's
               Church, Granville, Licking Co.

1820 Mar 1   Williams, Maria and John Haughton by James Whitney, JP, Washington Co.

1805 Jun 14   Williams, Martha and Robert Todd by Jacob Lindly, Washington Co.

1801 Feb 17   Williams, Nancy and George Kelly by Robert Safford, Washington Co.

1804 May 22   Williams, Nathaniel and Anna Hoyt by Asahel Cooley, Washington Co.

1816 Aug 15   Williams, Nathaniel and Jane Harris by Simion Overturf, Licking Co.

1804 Feb 26   Williams, Othniel and Temperance Lord by Daniel Story, Clerk,
               Washington Co.

1806 Jul 3   Williams, Polly and Martin Thorn by J. Brough, JP, Washington Co.

1817 Aug 5   Williams, Robert and Mary Meacham by Danl H. Buell, JP, Washington Co.

1855 Jun 6   Williams, Robert of Beverly and Grace Devol of Dowell by Rev. John
               Boyd, St. Luke's Church, Marietta, Washington Co.

1818 Nov 15   Williams, Samuel and Sarah Snyder by James Holmes, Licking Co.

1859 Mar 7   Williams, Samuel G. and Sarah E. Bestwick by Rev. John Boyd, St.
               Luke's Church, Marietta, Washington Co.

1825 Apr 5   Williams, Sarah and Hugh McElhaney by James Hoge, FCCC, Franklin Co.

1816 Jun 13   Williams, Sophrona and Samuel Willard by Ezra Griswold, Franklin Co.

1811 Nov 25   Williams, Temperance and Thomas Bacchus by James Marshall, Franklin Co.

1847 Feb 15   Williams, Thomas M. of Parkersburg, Va., and Mary M. Prentiss by Rev.
               Edward Winthrop, St. Luke's Church, Marietta, Washington Co.

1805 Oct 31   Williams, William and Nancy Noble by Thos. Hicks, Ross Co.

1817 Jul 10   Williams, William and Lurinda Phelps by Ebenezer Washbourn, UDM,
               Franklin Co.

1894 Jul 4   Williamson, Alexander of Findlay, O., and Cora A. Emery of Zanesville
               by Rev. George F. Moore, Putnam Presbyterian Church, Muskingum Co.

1891 Sep 12   Williamson, Charlotte and David A. Singleton both of Zanesville by
               Rev. George F. Moore, Putnam Presbyterian Church, Muskingum Co.

1806 May 31   Williamson, Christina and Henry Jolly by P. Whitten, Washington Co.

1811 Apr 14   Williamson, Deborah and Zepheniah Dison by Philip Witten, JP,
               Washington Co.

1810 Sep 16   Williamson, Drucilla and Ishabelle Camble (license date), Pickaway Co.

1810 Nov 10   Williamson, Jane and Bazel Meeks by Henry Jolly, JP, Washington Co.

1805 May 23   Williamson, Mary and Robert Steel by David Shelby, JP, Ross Co.

1801 Mar 31   Williamson, Moses and Hannah Linn by Samuel Williamson, JP,
              Washington Co.

1805 Sep 7   Williamson, Moses and Jane Riggs by Philip Whitten, Washington Co.

1800 Jun 10   Williamson, Samuel and Deborah Dickerson by Philip Whitten, JP,
              Washington Co.

1826 Aug 3   Williard, Cara and Asaph Allin by Samuel Abbott, JP, Franklin Co.

1827 Aug 9   Willicox, Peter and Trifenia Watts by Geo. Jefferies, Ordained
              Minister, Franklin Co.

1816 Jun 16   Willis, George and Betsy Dohn by Thomas White, JP, Washington Co.

1821 May 21   Willis, Sarah and Jacob Siffers by Amos Wilson, JP, Washington Co.

1818 Dec 18   Willison, Hyatt and Susannah Potten by Geo. Hoover, JP, Licking Co.

1820 Oct 26   Willison, Polly and Thomas Green by Clement D. Wolf, JP, Licking Co.

1805 Oct 10   Willoughby, Andrew and Lavina Scote by Wm. Creighton, Ross Co.

1805 Mar 28   Willoughby, Sarah and William Vinson by Wm. Creighton, Ross Co.

1801 Mar 20   Wills, Daniel and Elizabeth Anerum by Philip Witten, JP, Washington Co.

1818 Oct 12   Wills, Isabel and William Brown by Wm. Hull, JP, Licking Co.

1815 Sep 1   Wills, Robert and Elizabeth Smith by Z. Carlisle, Licking Co.

1815 Aug 10   Wills, Sarah and Samuel Farmer by Z. Carlisle, JP, Licking Co.

1820 Dec 31   Wills, Saphrona and William Crawford by Dudley Davis, Washington Co.

1820 Sep 18   Wills, William and Jane Dunlap by Wm. Hull, JP, Licking Co.

1827 Jun 30   Willson, Betsey and Alvin Fuller by Hiland Hulberd, PC, Franklin Co.

1791 Sep 26   Willson, David and Easter Convis by Benj Tupper, Washington Co.

1816 Jan 11   Willson, Jane and Benjamin Witham by Salmon N. Cook, JP, Washington Co.

1823 Feb 20   Willson, Jane and Azed Gordner by St. M. Cott, JP, Franklin Co.

1821 Feb 1   Willson, Jeremiah and Mary McKindley by Samuel Beach, JP, Washington
              Co.

1819 Feb 4   Willson, Joseph and Jane Williams by Percival Adams, Franklin Co.

1791 Sep 26   Willson, Mary and Nathan Kenne by Benj Tupper, Washington Co.

1813 Apr 4   Willson, Olive and John Smith by Jos. S. Hughes, QDP, Franklin Co.

1812 Oct 18   Willson, Phebe and John Poor by John Turner, Franklin Co.

1828 Jan 10   Willson, Sam'l and C. Butcher by Geo. Jefferies, Franklin Co.

1850 Sep 15   Wilner, Marcus W. and Susan Adams by E.A. Strong, St. Luke's Church,
              Granville, Licking Co.

1818 Nov --   Wils, Elizabeth and John Cahill by David Mitchell, JP, Jackson Co.

1819 Apr 26   Wilson, Abigail and Joseph Wesson by John Patterson, JP, Washington Co.

1803 May 8   Wilson, Agnes and Salmon Templin by Wm. Robinson, JP, Ross Co.

1817 May 20   Wilson, Alexander and Dorothy Hogg by J.W. Patterson, JP, Licking Co.

1821 Dec 12   Wilson, Almedia and William Brown by Joseph Palmer, JP, Washington Co.

1821 Jul 27	Wilson, Andrew and Betsey Hagans by Dudley Davis, JP, Washington Co.
1820 Sep 23	Wilson, Betsey and Charles Bosworth by Rev. Saml P. Robbins, Washington Co.
1821 Jun 27	Wilson, Cynthia and Elijah Wilson by Wm. Woodford, JP, Washington Co.
1814 Feb 23	Wilson, Daniel and Sally Gordy by John Ludwig, JP, Pickaway Co.
1895 Sep 14	Wilson, David M. of Lancaster, O., and Mrs. Sarah E. Gibbons of Zanesville by Rev. George F.Moore,Putnam Presbyterian Ch., Muskingum Co.
1825 Apr 19	Wilson, Eleanor and William E. Holloway, widower, by John F. Solomon, MG, Franklin Co.
1821 Jun 27	Wilson, Elijah and Cynthia Wilson by Wm. Woodford, JP, Washington Co.
1813 Dec 23	Wilson, Elizabeth and Louis Gravis (license date), Pickaway Co.
1814 Dec 15	Wilson, Elizabeth and Andrew McMillen by Nathan Cunningham, Licking Co.
1820 Jul 5	Wilson, Elizabeth and John Grubb by John D. Chamberlain, JP, Washington Co.
1897 Sep 22	Wilson, Elizabeth and Edgar V. Cherry both of White Cottage, O., by Rev. George F. Moore; Putnam Presbyterian Church, Muskingum Co.
1813 Dec 29	Wilson, Esther and Richard Miner by Thomas Seely, JP, Washington Co.
1820 Jan 26	Wilson, Fidelia and Thompson Bull by John Smith, Franklin Co.
1851 Aug 14	Wilson, Harriet E. and Noah M. Runyan by Rev. Geo. B. Sturges, St. Paul's Church, Marion, Marion Co.
1810 May 2	Wilson, Isaac and Fedelia Darlington by John W. Patterson, JP, Licking Co.
1814 Jun 11	Wilson, James and Dolly McDill, widow, both black persons by Arthur O'Harra, Franklin Co.
1825 Jul 6	Wilson, James and Michal Gilem by David W. Walton, JP, Jackson Co.
1827 May 17	Wilson, James and Mary Fisher by A. Allison, Franklin Co.
1821 Aug 26	Wilson, James C. and Catharine Gridley by James Hoge, Franklin Co.
1821 Dec 7	Wilson, James H. and Polly Skeels by Aristarchus Walker, Franklin Co.
1810 Jul 16	Wilson, Jane and Rev. James Scott by Rev. Geo. Varnaman, Licking Co.
1820 Feb 10	Wilson, Joseph and Jane Hanna by Geo. Burris, MG, Jackson Co.
1805 May 15	Wilson, Josiah and Elizabeth Provatt by John Johnston, Ross Co.
1811 Apr 22	Wilson, Lydia and Matthew Taylor (license date), Pickaway Co.
1819 Oct 18	Wilson, Lydia and Horace Waterman by Wm. Woodford, JP, Washington Co.
1815 Apr 27	Wilson, Margaret and James Robinson by J.W. Patterson, JP, Licking Co.
1818 Jun 6	Wilson, Margaret and William H. Shaklee by Wm. Rand, JP, Washington Co.
1826 Sep 21	Wilson, Margaret and Abraham Shoemaker by John F. Solomon, MEGC, Franklin Co.
1822 Aug 27	Wilson, Margret and Ira B. Henderson by James Hoge, Franklin Co.
1818 Dec 23	Wilson, Mariah and Isaac Grist by James Holmes, Licking Co.

1823 Sep 16   Wilson, Martha and Christian Heath by Joseph Baker, Minister of the
               Christian Church, Jackson Co.

1826 Apr 11   Wilson, Martha and Samuel Thompson by James Hoge, Franklin Co.

1865 Apr 29   Wilson, Martin and Lucinda Gossett by Rev. John Boyd, St. Luke's
               Church, Marietta, Washington Co.

1822 Mar 18   Wilson, Nancy and Sherman Waterman by Seth Baker, JP, Washington Co.

1811 Dec 20   Wilson, Nelly and Isaac Freeman (license date), Pickaway Co.

1816 Jan 11   Wilson, Polly and Clark N. Springer by Isaac Baker, JP, Washington Co.

1880 May 31   Wilson, Quincey and Maggie Wells by Rev. John Boyd, St. Luke's Church,
               Marietta, Washington Co.

1815 Mar 11   Wilson, Rebecca and Stephen Devol by Rev. Thomas Moore, Washington Co.

1815 10m 4   Wilson, Rebekah and Henry Coate, Miami Monthly Meeting, Warren Co.

1806 Jan 30   Wilson, Robert and Rebecca Henderson by Zachariah Stephen, JP,
               Franklin Co.

1820 Feb 17   Wilson, Sally and Jonathan Phinney by John Smith, JP, Franklin Co.

1870 Aug 14   Wilson, Samuel and Laura J. Porter by Rev. John Boyd, St. Luke's
               Church, Marietta, Washington Co.

1802 Jul 7   Wilson, Sarah and John Riggs by Sam'l Williamson, JP, Washington Co.

1816 Apr 4   Wilson, Sarah and Wm. Richards by Simon Merwin, Washington Co.

1818 Sep 18   Wilson, Sarah and David Moore by T.D. Baird, Licking Co.

1827 Sep 3   Wilton, Elizabeth and Frederick Fruchey by I. Gander, Franklin Co.

1821 Aug 7   Winchell, William and Deborah Coffman by Seth Baker, JP, Washington Co.

1820 Oct 26   Windel, John D. and Harriet Stagg by James Hoge, Franklin Co.

1805 May 2   Winder, Elizabeth and John Webster by Peter Jackson, JP, Ross Co.

1805 Apr 10   Winder, Massie and Levi Warner by Peter Jackson, JP, Ross Co.

1824 Dec 6   Wine, Susanna and Henry Hinkle by John Stealy, JP, Marion Co.

1813 Apr 22   Wing, Docia and Oliver Dodge, Jr. by Sardine Stone, Washington Co.

1817 Apr 23   Wing, Mary and Cyrus Spooner by Rev. S.P. Robbins, Washington Co.

1808 Mar 28   Winget, Luther and the widow Ingram by Nehemiah Gates, Franklin Co.

1816 Jan 16   Wingit, Elizabeth and William Salret by Jacob Keller, Franklin Co.

1815 Sep 26   Winn, Jane and Lewis Myers by J. Hoskinson, Licking Co.

1826 Jan 5   Winser, John and Polly Kimmons by Jacob Gundy, JP, Franklin Co.

1808 Aug 29   Winset, John and Catharine Harruff by Wm. Shaw, Franklin Co.

1825 Jul 21   Winslow, John and Elizabeth Longwell (license date), Marion Co.

1825 Mar 31   Winslow, Joseph and Pheby Smith by Hugh M. Smith, JP, Marion Co.

1824 Dec 29   Winslow, Sarah and Isaac Longwell by Rob't Hopkins, JP, Marion Co.

1819 Apr 2   Winson, Archelaus and Catharine Eagler by James Hoge, Franklin Co.

1802 Oct 3   Winson, Jacob and Cintia Flarnenan by Sam'l Williamson, JP, Washington
               Co.

1820 Mar 17   Winsor, Henry and Anna Payne by Wm. Woodford, JP, Washington Co.

1825 Aug 14   Winters, Wm. and Anna Snook by John Potter, JP, Jackson Co.

1827 Jul 30   Winterstein, S.A. and I.A. Kile by John Long, Franklin Co.

1815 Apr 23   Wise, Catherine and Henry Metzgar by Thomas Mace, JP, Pickaway Co.

1826 Sep 3   Wise, John and Roxaann Lamphair by John H. Power, MG in Methodist E.
               Church, Franklin Co.

1821 Apr 20   Wiseman, Catharin and James Phelin by Jacob Keller, JP, Franklin Co.

1860 Mar 20   Wiseman, Elizabeth and Henry M. Scott by Rev. John Boyd, St. Luke's
               Church, Marietta, Washington Co.

1873 Dec 25   Wiseman, Mary and Francis M. Preston by Rev. John Boyd, St. Luke's
               Church, Marietta, Washington Co.

1864 Mar 24   Wiseman, Thomas and Lottie Geren by Rev. John Boyd, St. Luke's
               Church, Marietta, Washington Co.

1821 Aug 24   Wiser, Elizabeth and Israel Putnam by Bishop Chase, St. Luke's
               Church, Marietta, Washington Co.

1819 Jun 18   Wiser, John and Hannah Briggs by James Whitney, JP, Washington Co.

1821 Aug 24   Wiser, Elizabeth and Israel Putnam by Philander Chase, Bishop E. Ch.,
               Washington Co.

1820 Oct 28   Wisham, Rachel and Wm. Fuller by Alex. Anderson, JP, Jackson Co.

1819 Nov 16   Wistervilt, Mathew and Abiah Sunard by Reuben Carpenter, JP, Franklin
               Co.

1827 Mar 20   Wiswell, Adaline Eliza and Thomas P. Read by A. Walker, JP, Franklin
               Co.

1825 Mar 31   Wiswell, Amase Jr. and Rebecca Lockwood by Aristarcrus Walker,
               Franklin Co.

1827 Apr 19   Wiswell, Betsy B. and Truman Skeels by A. Walker, Franklin Co..

1808 Feb 8   Witham, Benjamin and Ann Ogle by Thos. Stanley, Washington Co.

1816 Jan 11   Witham, Benjamin and Jane Willson by Salmon N. Cook, JP, Washington Co.

1814 Apr 24   Witham, Elias and Zilpha Rice by Sardine Stone, JP, Washington Co.

1816 Jan 21   Witham, Maria and Newman Matthews by J. Russell, JP, Washington Co.

1811 May 15   Withee, James and Deborah Cole by Philip Cole, Washington Co.

1813 Sep 19   Withington, Betsy and Richard Bodkin by Rev. S.P. Robbins, Washington
               Co.

1817 Oct 5   Withington, Naomi and Elihue Smith by Cyrus Ames, Washington Co.

1808 Jun 6   Withington, Sally and Joseph Newbury by Rev. Sam'l P. Robbins,
               Washington Co.

1808 Aug 20   Witighin, Hannah and Archabald Dancey by Joseph Palmer, JP, Washington
               Co.

1814 Apr 12   Witmer, Betsey and Martin Cassner by Jacob Leist, JP, Pickaway Co.

1814 Feb 13   Witten, James and Margaret Scott by Anth'y Sheets, Washington Co.

1810 Jan 9   Witten, Rachel and Nichalas Wells by Henry Jolly, JP, Washington Co.

1813 Dec 30   Wittits, Josiah and Henrietta Allison (license date), Pickaway Co.

1810 Jan 1   Wolbridge, T. and Betsey Newton by Stephen Lindsly, Washington Co.

1818 Nov 9   Wolcott, Edward and Maria Squires by Samuel Bancroft, JP, Licking Co.

1817 Mar 27   Wolcott, J.M. and Maril Brodrick by James Hoge, Franklin Co.

1804 Mar 20   Wolf, Christopher and Rhoda Dorr by Samuel Brown, Washington Co.

1824 Dec 16   Wolf, Magdelina and Henry Miller by John Stealy, JP, Marion Co.

1806 May 27   Wolf, Mary and Samuel Bishop by Wm. Bennett, JP, Franklin Co.

1820 Aug 19   Wolf, Mary and Samuel Pringle by Joel Tuttle, Jr., JP, Washington Co.

1805 Mar 6   Wolf, Polly and William Morgan by Samuel Smith, Ross Co.

1810 Jun 13   Wollington, Thomas and Nithie Stokes (license date), Pickaway Co.

1818 Jul 2   Wollon, Jsaphina and Worrin Miner by Wm. Swayze, JP, Franklin Co.

1814 Mar 24   Wolverton, Nancy and Thomas Morris by Henry Davis, JP, Pickaway Co.

1828 Nov 20   Wood, Abraham and Elizabeth Gundy by John Tipton, Franklin Co.

1808 Jan 2   Wood, Anselm and Lucy Rnard by Thos. Stanley, Washington Co.

1820 Dec 26   Wood, Benjamin and Isabella Grant by Reuben Golliday, JP, Franklin Co.

1821 Apr 15   Wood, Caius M. and Sophia Hall by Sardine Stone, JP, Washington Co.

1817 Apr 9   Wood, Charles and Elizabeth Taylor by James Taylor, Franklin Co.

1813 Jun 9   Wood, Drusella and Richard Clark by John Turner, Franklin Co.

1846 Apr 6   Wood, Hannah and John A. Linnel by W.C. French, St. Luke's Church,
               Granville, Licking Co.

1827 Sep 13   Wood, James and Polly Warner by James Hoge, Franklin Co.

1854 Sep 25   Wood, Jane and A.J. Wightman by T. Corlett, St. Luke's Church,
               Granville, Licking Co.

1816 Nov 18   Wood, Jesse and Ladotia Blake by Rev. Jacob Young, Washington Co.

1827 Oct 4   Wood, Jesse and Rachel Chenoweth by John Rathbone, JP, Franklin Co.

1821 Mar 28   Wood, Joana and Thomas Hatfield White by Wm. Woodford, JP, Washington
               Co.

1872 Mar 20   Wood, Joseph and Susan Wood by Rev. John Boyd, St. Luke's Church,
               Marietta, Washington Co.

1850 Sep 25   Wood, Mary F. and Christopher Green both of Newport, Ky., by Rev. D.W.
               Tolford, St. Luke's Church, Marietta, Washington Co.

1803 Oct 20   Wood, Nancy and Joseph Tiffin by J. Gardner, JP, Ross Co.

1821 Feb 7   Wood, Rasellus and Keziah Bartlett by John D. Chamberlain, JP,
               Washington Co.

1801 Jul 9   Wood, Ruth and Abiah Shelden by Edwin McGinnis, Washington Co.

1872 Mar 20   Wood, Susan and Joseph Wood by Rev. John Boyd, St. Luke's Church,
               Marietta, Washington Co.

1819 Jun 30   Wood, Thomas and Elizabeth Ramsey by Richard Courtright, Franklin Co.

1806 Jun 18   Woodard, Molly and Abel Mathews by Ephm. Mathews, Washington Co.

1805 Nov 24   Woodard, Rebekah and Samuel Starlin by Ephraim Mathews, Washington Co.

1807 Nov 28   Woodbridge, Dudley and Jane Robbins Gilman by S.P. Robbins, Washington
               Co.

1826 Jul 13   Woodbridge, James Ely and Lyia Tuller by Samuel Abbott, Franklin Co.

1877 Apr 4   Woodbridge, Laura H. and John A. Gallaher by Rev. John Boyd, St.
               Luke's Church, Marietta, Washington Co.

1795 Apr 20   Woodbridge, Lucy and John G. Petit by Thomas Lord, Washington Co.

1803 May 29   Woodbridge, Sally and John Mathews by Daniel Story, Washington Co.

1815 May 12   Woodcock, William and Elizabeth Davison by James Taylor, JP, Franklin
               Co.

1861 May 30   Woodcock, Wm. and Anna Jane Day by Rev. Henry Payne, St. Paul's
               Church, Marion (in presence of Geo. Smith, Mr. Woodcock, Sr.,
               and others), Marion Co.

1820 Oct 18   Wooder, Samuel and Hathander Hughes by J.B. Gilliland, JP, Jackson Co.

1806 Mar 21   Woodfield, Margaret and James Phillips by John Johnston, JP, Ross Co.

1799 Oct 13   Woodford, William and Dianna Ford by Thos. Stanley, JP, Washington Co.

1821 Jul 3   Woodring, Sally and Daniel Slosser by George Weizz, MG, Franklin Co.

1829 Jan 29   Woodring, Solomon and Catherine Dildin by J.F.S., Franklin Co.

1811 Jan 13   Woodrough, Isaac and Margaret Green by John Green, MG, Washington Co.

1820 Aug 1   Woodrough, Samuel and Catherine Montanya by J.A. Cunningham, VDM,
               Licking Co.

1820 Feb 21   Woodruff, Betsey and Thaddeus Goodno by Rev. I. Hooper, Washington Co.

1817 Aug 18   Woodruff, Elias and Eleanor McGuire by Jacob Young, MG, Washington Co.

1817 Aug 25   Woodruff, Hulda and Edwin Washington Coit by John Cunningham, JP,
               Licking Co.

1819 Nov 20   Woodruff, Leuman and Ann Butler by Samuel Bancroft, JP, Licking Co.

1817 Sep 4   Woodruff, Moses and Mary Herrington by Salmon N. Cook, Washington Co.

1804 Apr 15   Woodruff, Polly and John Curtiss by Simeon Deming, Washington Co.

1817 Jun 18   Woodruff, Polly and John Mullen by Salmon N. Cook, JP, Washington Co.

1820 Mar 28   Woodruff, Sally and Herman Owen by Benj. Been, JP, Licking Co.

1815 Nov 5   Woods, Ephraim and Margaret Rion by F. Ferguson, JP, Washington Co.

1811 Apr 9   Woods, Isaac and Elizabeth Martle (or Mantel) by Rev. Simon Cokrane,
               Franklin Co.

1825 Feb 10   Woods, Isaac and Hannah Baker by Rob't Hopkins, JP, Marion Co.

1802 Apr 1   Woods, Rebecka and John Simmons by Sam'l Williamson, JP, Washington Co.

1817 Aug 28   Woods, Rebecca and John Hughs by John Spencer, JP, Licking Co.

1819 May 10   Woods, Susannah and Abraham Pence by Simeon Overturf, JP, Licking Co.

1805 May 9   Woods, Zachariah and Mary Bruff by Thomas Scott, JP, Ross Co.

1814 Mar 13   Woodward, Eleanor and Philo Matthews by Sardine Stone, JP, Washington
               Co.

1816 Jan 26   Woodward, Oliver and Mary McGrath by Rev. Stephen Lindsley, Washing-
               ton Co.

1820 Aug 10   Woodword, Highly C. and Marcus D. Briggs by Sardine Stone, JP,
               Washington Co.

1817 Jun 12   Woolard (or Woollard), John and Sally Frederick by Eli C. King,
               Franklin Co.

1818 Nov 3   Woolard, Peggy and G. Griffith by Noah Fidler, Licking Co.

1804 Jun 28   Woolcox, Ira and Lois Bristol by James Marshall, JP, Franklin Co.

1816 Sep 28   Woolcut, Elizabeth and William Droddy by Michael Patton (or Hatton),
               JP, (another entry 28 Nov 1816), Franklin Co.

1815 Apr 19   Woolcut, Emily and Haseon Rose by James Hoge, Franklin Co.

1815 Jan 12   Woolcut, Sally and Abram Kepler (no JP), Franklin Co.

1810 Feb 5   Woolcutt, Christean and Enes Dewalt by James Marshall, Franklin Co.

1807 Apr 22   Woolcutt, Elizabeth and Saml Sells by Arthur O'Harra, JP, Franklin Co.

1810 Aug 14   Woolcutt, John and Mary Mitchell by James Marshall, Franklin Co.

1810 Oct 3   Woolcutt, Johnston and Betsey Ewing by James Marshall, Franklin Co.

1816 Jun 27   Woolcutt, Lidia and Muhlan Thomas by Michael Patton, JP, Franklin Co.

1811 May 11   Wooley, Sarah and David Bowen (license date), Pickaway Co.

1818 May 10   Woolf, Philip and Hannah Smith by James McLish, JP, Franklin Co.

1817 Jun 12   Woollard (or Woolard), John and Sally Frederick by Eli C. King,
               Franklin Co.

1818 Mar 26   Woollard, John and Polly Hottsbury by Alex Holden, Licking Co.

1826 May 6   Wooshan, Isaac and Phebe Pyle by J.B. Gilliland, JP, Jackson Co.

1811 Jan 3   Word, George and Mary Heckerthorn (license date), Pickaway Co.

1820 Apr 11   Worly, Andrew and Nancy Perkins by Michael Trout, JP, Licking Co.

1881 Dec 29   Worstall, Carrie J. and Jacob N. Strait both of Zanesville by Rev.
               George F. Moore, Putnam Presbyterian Church, Muskingum Co.

1822 Mar 24   Worstell, Mary Ann and Simeon P. Cowan by Dan'l H. Buell, Washington
               Co.

1791 Jul 21   Worth, Polly and Picket Marvin by -----, Washington Co.

1813 Jun 20   Worthington, Comfort and Isaiah Williams by P. Adams, JP, Franklin Co.

1861 Jul 11   Worthington, Edward of Sterling, Ill., and Caroline Haver of Putnam by
               Rev. A. Kingsbury, Putnam Presbyterian Church, Muskingum Co.

1816 Nov 7   Worthington, Isaac and Sarah Bacon by P. White, Washington Co.

1828 Jan 10   Worthington, Margared and Jacob Hindle by Geo. Jefferies, Franklin Co.

1807 Jun 7   Worthington, Peggy and John Williams by James Marshall, JP, Franklin
               Co.

1811 Jul 30   Worthington, Thomas and Sally Dye by Stephen Lindsly, Washington Co.

1826 Apr 9   Woshon, John and Ruhaney Piles by John Horton, JP, Jackson Co.

1826 Aug 31   Woten, Nathan and Elizabeth Beatty by John Horton, JP, Jackson Co.

1812 Jun 4   Wright, Abraham and Jane Hughes by Peter Pence, Licking Co.

1819 Jan 14   Wright, Catharine and Joseph Dunneick by Richard Courtright, JP,
               Franklin Co.

1819 Apr 25   Wright, Danl and Margaret Chesters by Jeremiah Converse, MG, Franklin
               Co.

1806 5m 14   Wright, Elijah and Susannah Hoover, Miami Monthly Meeting, Warren Co.

1814 4m 7   Wright, Elizabeth and John Shaw, Miami Monthly Meeting, Warren Co.

1814 Oct 27   Wright, George and Catharine Cochran by Jos. Gorton, Franklin Co.

1821 Apr 19   Wright, Henry and Lavina Otis by Rev. A. Robinson, Washington Co.

1841 --- --   Wright, Henry D. and Mary F. Prichard, St. Luke's Church, Granville,
               Licking Co.

1798 May 16   Wright, Huldah and Samuel Lackey by Josiah Munro, Washington Co.

1828 Nov 10   Wright, Jennett and Horace Loomis by Gideon W. Hunt (or Hart), JP,
               Franklin Co.

1817 1m 2   Wright, Joel and Ann Bateman (Miami Monthly Meeting), Warren Co.

1826 Nov 6   Wright, Mary and James S. Freeman by Henry Matthes, Franklin Co.

1818 Jan 8   Wright, Naomi and Adam Croan (or Cone) by Abner Goff, MG, Licking Co.

1819 Jun 6   Wright, Potter and Larra Maynard by R. Stanberry, Franklin Co.

1826 Apr 13   Wright, Sarah and James Corbit by John Stephenson, JP, Jackson Co.

1791 Jul 24   Wright, Simeon and Ruth Dunham by Benj Tupper, Washington Co.

1797 Oct 5   Wright, Simeon and Mehitable Whitham by Josiah Munro, Washington Co.

1864 Jun 14   Wright, Wm. and Frances H. Owen by Wm. Bower, St. Luke's Church,
               Granville, Licking Co.

1815 Nov 5   Wrightman, George and Elizabeth Hinald by Percival Adams, Franklin Co.

1814 Jan 19   Wyatt, Betsey and Jacob Phipps by Wm. Droddy, JP, Franklin Co.

1805 Dec 19   Wyatt, Mary and John Millikan by James S. Webster, Ross Co.

1808 Jan 9   Wyatt, Wm. and Elizabeth Hannaman by Wm. Brundridge, Franklin Co.

1821 Nov 29   Wyley, Charles and Lucy Lewis by Nathl. Little, Franklin Co.

1821 Nov 29   Wyley, Isaac and Eliza Lewis by Nathl. Little, Franklin Co.

1821 Nov 27   Wyley, Martha and Elias Lewis by Nathl. Little, Franklin Co.

1820 Jan 23   Wyman, John and Nancy Johnson by Adriel Hussey, MG, Jackson Co.

1825 Apr 28   Wynkoop, Mary Ann and Joseph O'Harra by Henry Mathews, Minister of the
               ME Church, Franklin Co.

1818 Mar 19   Yarnell, Peter and Matilda Purdy (or Pursdy) by Richd Suddick, JP,
               Franklin Co.

1799 Jun 10   Yates, Samuel and Phebe Brion by Robert Safford,JP, Washington Co.

1875 Sep 2   Yeoman, J.A.O. and Mary M. Boyd at Hillsboro by Rev. John Boyd, St.
              Luke's Church, Marietta, Washington Co.

1825 Jun 18   Yockhover, Eve and Jonathan Sault by Thos. Rodgers, JP, Marion Co.

1871 Feb 2   Youch, Mrs. Rebecca and George Riggs by Rev. John Boyd, St. Luke's
              Church, Marietta, Washington Co.

1801 Jan 27   Young, Aaron and Nancy Picket by Alvan Bingham, Washington Co.

1813 Jun 1   Young, Abraham and Mary Young by Nathan Connard, JP, Licking Co.

1883 Aug 8   Young, Alice and Joseph P. Emery both of Zanesville by Rev. George
              F. Moore, Putnam Presbyterian Church, Muskingum Co.

1810 Dec 11   Young, Barbara and John Nyswanner by Wm. D. Hendren, Franklin Co.

1811 May 19   Young, Catharine and Daniel Herrington by James Marshall, Franklin Co.

1821 Jan 25   Young, Elanor and Benjamin Hayens by Wm. Richardson, JP, Franklin Co.

1817 Sep 25   Young, Hannah and Thomas Larimore by James Campbell, Licking Co.

1809 Oct 26   Young, Henry and Nancy Davis by James Riggs, JP, Washington Co.

1819 Nov 2   Young, James and Sarah Trindle by T.D. Bierd, VDM, Licking Co.

1822 Nov 7   Young, James and Rachel Line by Richard Courtright, Franklin Co.

1808 Aug 8   Young, Jane and Townsen Hickmon by James Marshall, Franklin Co.

1809 Sep 30   Young, Jane and Wm. Wigdon by James Marshall, Franklin Co.

1824 Jun 15   Young, John and Mary Ann Hodgskins by C. Waddell, Franklin Co.

1819 Oct 19   Young, Joseph and Rebeccah Lisle by Wm. Long, Franklin Co.

1817 Aug 31   Young, Margaret and Samuel Mellor by John Patterson, JP, Washington Co.

1813 Jun 1   Young, Mary and Abraham Young by Nathan Connard, JP, Licking Co.

1813 Apr 22   Young, Nancy and Daniel Justice by Arthur O'Harra, Franklin Co.

1825 Dec 1   Young, Nancy and Isaac H. Fickle by Conrad Roth, JP, Marion Co.

1820 Nov 14   Young, Rebecca and Gabriel Postle by Jacob Grubb, JP, Franklin Co.

1826 Aug 2   Young (or Swing), Rebecca and Edward Simmons by Jacob Delay, LM,
              Jackson Co.

1812 Feb 15   Young, William and Polly Coffman by -----, Licking Co.

1819 Nov 18   Young, William and Eliza Cammel by Jacob Keller, Franklin Co.

1821 May 24   Young, William and Elizabeth Terrill by John True, JP, Washington Co.

1804 Dec 30   Younge, Charity and Samuel Peik by Wm. Harper, Washington Co.

1811 Nov 6   Youngkin, Abraham and Sally Montgomery by Stephen Lindsly, Washington
              Co.

1810 Dec 9   Zehring, John and Catherine Spangler (license date), Pickaway Co.

1815 Apr 26   Zinmer, Phillip and Betsey Valentine by Thomas Mace, JP, Pickaway Co.

1828 Oct 1   Zinn, Elizabeth and Thomas Tipton by W.T. Martin, Franklin Co.

1825 Jul 19   Zinn, Henry and Sarah Agler by C. Henkel, Franklin Co.